With Essays by

Jessie Bernard
Pennsylvania State University

Alfred C. Clarke
The Ohio State University

Ronald G. Corwin
The Ohio State University

Ronald G. Gallimore
University of Hawaii

Joel E. Gerstl
Temple University

Donald A. Hansen
*University of California
Berkeley*

Marvin K. Opler
*State University of New York
at Buffalo*

Robert Perrucci
Purdue University

David F. Ricks
Columbia University

Jim L. Turner
University of Missouri

Don H. Zimmerman
*University of California
Santa Barbara*

George K. Zollschan

Explorations in Sociology and Counseling

---

edited by

DONALD A. HANSEN

University of California
Berkeley

HOUGHTON MIFFLIN COMPANY · BOSTON

New York

Atlanta

Geneva, Illinois

Dallas

Palo Alto

To the Memory of "Bish"
Gary Robert Anderson
1933–1965

Foreword

Counseling is a curious paradox. It is the child of both fact and sentiment, of science and humanism. While claiming to be a profession based upon a science (this is to ensure respectability) counseling can be an arrant dictatorship or a warm relationship. It quarrels with terms: psychotherapy, psychoanalysis, behavior conditioning, guidance; yet it is all of these. A lusty growth has added to its confusion. People believe in it, expect too much of it. Counselors with role concepts of twenty years ago work side by side with new entrants who may be existentialists, behavior conditioners, or computer devotees. Counseling is a function claimed by many: ministers, physicians, social workers, teachers, even lawyers. Those who are "counselors" — engaging in various kinds of personal helping relationships as their major responsibility — look askance at those who counsel as only part of their task. Counseling is — well, what *is* counseling? It needs examination both by those who are "counselors" and by those who are on the outside looking in.

This book is a major attempt to permit a group of scholars, mostly sociologists, to examine counseling within broad social contexts. The academic preparation of most people who consider themselves full-time counselors in any setting is focused in psychology or education. Few counselors, except those in social work, have had much exposure to sociology. So it is fitting that sociology, as a discipline concerned with all social functions, should examine counseling and that counselors should become familiar with sociological concepts and criteria as they apply to counseling.

This book is a "first" and is appropriately entitled *Explorations.* Some of the chapters — the first and the last — attempt a survey of the total field of counseling and its possible future. From the point of view of a psychologist-editor I might have included different things in the introductory chapter, for example. I probably would not have designated social work as "the largest of the counseling professions" but would have named secondary school counseling. In 1966 this profession numbered 23,500 full-time persons and 18,500 part-time (the full-time figure represents a 140 percent increase since 1960). I might also have included counseling psychologists in college and university counseling centers (perhaps 2,500 in number), elementary school counselors (2,000), vocational rehabilitation counselors (5,000), employment service counselors (3,000), and counseling psychologists in hospitals and business. And I might not have interpreted the future of "counseling" entirely in terms of psychotherapy and mental health as was done in the last chapter.

These very differences, however, are what make this book valuable to counselors who are not oriented in sociology. It is of vital significance that we see how thoughtful scholars from this broadly oriented field think of counselors. The book includes some remarkably cogent theories of interpersonal and intrapersonal relations that are fresh and pertinent to the counseling field: motivation in terms of sociological concepts, language coding and social relations, faith as a therapeutic variable, consensus, influence, and compliance in a theory of coordination. Several chapters are devoted to an analysis of institutional and organizational influences upon the conduct of the counseling function — chapters that probably only sociologists could have written. They even comfort the counselor a bit by making clear that some of his frustrations are not due to personal inefficiency but are inherent in the social order in which he operates.

The theme of the book, as I see it, is that relations between individuals are influenced fully as much by the social context within which interaction takes place (sociology's concern) as by the intra-individual characteristics of the participants (more basically the concern of psychology). One gets the feeling that counseling could be more fully perceived if *both* these domains were given full credit for their respective influences, as this book attempts to do.

Such a major project of exploration in both counseling and sociology could perhaps have been undertaken only by a person with the distinctive qualifications of its chief author and editor, Donald A. Hansen. With earned doctorates in both sociology (University of Minnesota) and counseling (Northwestern University), he has for some years been developing the organization of this book and securing his coauthors. I first corresponded with him in 1962, when he was a visiting professor at the University of Otago in New Zealand. The folder containing the correspondence between us in the intervening period is over an inch thick!

The book has been carefully conceived, written and rewritten, organized and reorganized. I commend its use to at least four groups of professionals: (1) sociologists who wish to understand better the increasing prominence in our society of the psychologically helping professions coming under the rubrics of counseling and of psychotherapy; (2) counselors and counseling psychologists whose orientation finds them weak in sociological understandings; (3) social workers who are often expected to carry out the counseling function but who have very little specific preparation in this area; and (4) members of several professions who are expected to know something of counseling and psychotherapy but who often do not: physicians, ministers, lawyers, etc. This book is designed to stimulate all thoughtful students of the psychological and social scene to see that no one group is alone in its mission nor does any one group have exclusive rights.

C. Gilbert Wrenn

Preface

"Therapists are dangerous! They twist a
man's guts; they claim they're curing, but
their only cures are those old barnyard games
that turn stroppy young bulls into steers...."

So began a scruffy manuscript that I found in my mailbox some months ago. The manuscript, which was not signed, is similar to those of a variety of critics who in recent decades have approached counseling and therapy with jaundiced eye and acid tongue. True, the author of my mailbox polemic was uncommonly offensive in style ("... and counselors, Christ! Those con-jobs are right at the front of a grand march to some Brave New World, some chrome-plated Eden where there won't even be any apples hanging around, where we won't even be able to tell what temptation *is,* for Christsake!"). Beyond such overly energetic imagery, however, he offered little that was new, trudging heavy-footed along well-worn paths of criticism, laboring over the oft-charted routes of those who worry about freedom and identity, massification and cultural debilitation, power elites and the manipulation of atomized nonelites, and then—just when labor and care were needed—skipping lightly around the thorny questions about the human meanings of counseling and therapy.

Those questions, which focus on the relationship of the human arts to the rest of contemporary life, are important, and (just as the polemicist insisted) today remain very much unresolved. The greatest failing of the critic, it seems, was not that he approached the wrong questions but that he approached them ineffectually, answering them from a base of prejudiced ignorance without seeking evidence, without developing and weighing alternatives. His was a view from without, but it was an incomplete, irresponsible view.

What is offered in the fifteen chapters of this volume are other views from without, views, however, that are intended to be objective, restrained, and systematic. By design the essays are not definitive but suggestive, they are written to stimulate thought and to identify arguments and constructs that are potentially helpful to one in understanding counseling and psychotherapy. Their character is best described by the term objective critiques. At times the critiques may well be unfair or inaccurate in the degree that objectivity from without suffers from lack of intimate knowledge of a subject; but this failing goes hand in hand with their strength: namely, the insights and perspectives they provide, insights that often can be gained only by those who have distance from a subject. The view from within does not sensitize in these ways, and to restrict oneself to that intimate perspective is to encourage a partial awareness grounded in relative ignorance. It is common knowledge that most married persons, however closely they are able to describe some features of their spouses, are totally blind to other features. It is not unfair to suggest that the counselor or psychotherapist, or any professional, experiences similar sensitivities and blindnesses to his profession and its practices and that the degree both of senstivity and of blindness is directly related to the degree of his professional involvement.

On another side of reality, a second analogy is instructive: that of the investigator who attempts to find out "what it's really like" in a culture to which he is a stranger. Some things cannot be known, except through the eyes of those involved. The investigator—as he asks questions, say, in a Negro ghetto or riot area—legitimately might be told, "If you've got to ask, you'll never know." It may well be that in their view from without, sociologists miss certain essentials, are insensitive to the tacit knowledges of the profession, to those "things that we know but cannot tell," as Michael Polanyi put it.

What is required is a continuing exchange, a symbiotic independence, between those who view from within and those who view from without. It would not be enough for the two to converge on a single perspective, for each enjoys possibilities the other does not. Yet each must attempt to benefit from the views of the other, neither rejecting too quickly nor accepting uncritically but, rather, attending, attempting to understand, evaluating and testing the view of the other, and modifying his own when this is required.

These essays cover four general areas of concern to counseling and psychotherapy. As a sociologist, my impulse was to present first that area which is most general and provides the context for the others, that is, to start with the societal and cultural overview and work downward toward the more elemental—moving from societal contexts of counseling and psychotherapy to organizational contexts, then to a focus on the psychotherapist and client in a dyad or group relationship, and finally to the individual, social human. By its nature, however, the subject matter seemed to argue that acting on this sociological prejudice would unnecessarily obscure and exaggerate the distance between the view from without and the view from within.

In an introductory essay, Gerstl discusses role diversity and specialization, identifying the breadth of meaning accepted in this volume for the terms "counseling" and "psychotherapy." In subsequent chapters, each author focuses on some few or many of these specialized roles. Little effort has been made to establish a unity of focus or even to identify carefully which statements in a specified discussion—say of educational counseling—may be appropriate to other specialities in counseling and psychotherapy. Again, the intent is to suggest, and the reader is invited to participate in the process by identifying such appropriateness.

In the first of the four sections, three essays discuss facets of the socius as they relate to counseling and psychotherapy. In the first essay of that section (Chapter 1), Zollschan and I, arguing that extant theories of motivation are inadequate to social realities, present a theory that moves toward constructs capable of describing and explaining the relation of individual behavior to social organization and change. Chapters 2 and 3, the latter by Gallimore and Turner, take up closely related discussions: the interplay of language capabilities and expectancies with the individual's capacities for effective experiences in psychotherapy and counseling. The authors view each of these subjects as closely interlinked with individual motivation, yet as inextricable from social and cultural processes.

In the second section the focus is widened as interpersonal relationships are viewed more closely. In Chapter 4, I present a preliminary theory of coordination in counseling and psychotherapy. My aim is not to describe specific processes but rather to identify *forms* of process relationship in a way that will stimulate exploratory research and bring practical insight. In Chapter 5, the theory is applied to a discussion of compliance and of the "therapist's dilemma." Perrucci's focus in Chapter 6 is somewhat broader as he discusses the decision-making processes that can be identified in the interactions of patients and the various members of a psychiatric staff.

In the third section the focus is widened to the organizational level. Corwin and Clarke, in Chapter 7, examine the processes and consequences of bureaucratization and professionalization, attending to the variables of both organization and profession as they converge in the role of the counselor. Zimmerman's essay, perhaps more than any other one in this collection, avoids the problems of viewing from without as he seeks to identify the ways in which workers in a public welfare agency choose between alternative approaches to the management of their daily work tasks. His discussion is heavy with implications for the study of routines in counseling and psychotherapy. In Chapter 9, Perrucci applies anomie theory in an inquiry into the ways that belief systems and ideologies are related to the development of general dissatisfaction and collective disturbances in a psychiatric ward.

The final section presents the broadest perspective, viewing counseling and therapy as social movements within societal and cultural contexts.

Corwin and Clarke, in Chapter 10, argue that the counseling movement has not always adapted to the changes in American society over the past decades and that when it has adapted, its basic goals and character have been transformed. The development and certain value foundations of social psychiatry are discussed by Opler in Chapter 11. Bernard, in Chapter 12, identifies some differing functions of counseling and psychotherapy and the various limitations of each as factors in individual and institutional change. In Chapter 13, she continues the discussion, relating counseling and psychotherapy to efforts to alleviate social and societal problems.

In the final chapter, Ricks, a counseling psychologist, undertakes the difficult job of looking to the future, attempting to forecast developments in counseling and psychotherapy. His is a view from within looking without. Not surprisingly, his forecasts differ—but not entirely—from those found in the wild manuscript mentioned above.

The book moves, then, from the elemental to the organizational to the societal. The underlying assumption, however, is that neither man, dyad relationship, organizational process, nor social movement can be adequately understood, or even adequately viewed, unless all are understood; that there is, to put it in simplest terms, an interpenetration of socialized man and society. The essays in this book represent the individual efforts of a dozen persons to deal with certain aspects of that interpenetrant reality. The picture is far from complete; many areas have not been covered, and the links between the chapters are at times tenuous. For the tentativeness, incompleteness, and disjunctions, no excuse is needed, however, for the areas the authors have attempted to chart have been but rarely explored.

———————————

Far too many years have passed since the idea for this symposium first took form. In those years, many persons have encouraged and assisted me in the varied and at times frustrating tasks involved in developing a coherent volume from the work of many minds. From the inception of the book, C. Gilbert Wrenn has offered invaluable advice and support, both as a consulting editor and as a colleague. Most credit necessarily goes to the authors of the chapters herein; without their competent efforts, patience, and reasonable cooperation this book would have remained unrealized. On editorial matters, Joan Parsons and Gloria Peyrat labored long and well, and Laurie Newberg effectively coordinated the never ending secretarial work. To all these persons, my sincere thanks.

I must also attempt to acknowledge my debt to Gary Robert Anderson, in part because "Bish" was the first to encourage the idea for this symposium when it took misty form some eight years ago. In a less direct way, however, his contribution is more profound. For Bish demonstrated the potentials of counseling, offered an example of the ideal therapist, the human being who helps others by living his own life with integrity and energy. That Bish chose to enter counseling is incidental: the professional recognition only endorsed the fact that his life was good for others and it was good for him. This book is dedicated to his memory.

Donald A. Hansen
Berkeley

Contents

Contents

PART THREE

PART FOUR

Explorations in Sociology and Counseling

Introduction

COUNSELING AND PSYCHOTHERAPY
TODAY: Role Specialization and Diversity

Joel E. Gerstl / Temple University

Today, "counselors" and "psychotherapists" seem to be everywhere — in colleges and universities, in clinics and hospitals, in high schools, grade schools and business organizations, and in employment agencies, community centers and diverse other settings, including many of those created in federal moves toward a "Great Society." So ubiquitous are counselors and psychotherapists that an important fact is easily neglected: the field is not limited to the practice of "professional" counselors and psychotherapists. Rather, counseling roles are frequently played by policemen, teachers, physicians, lawyers and ministers, and countless others in less formal positions.

The importance of this fact is suggested by the sociological observation that the activities, programs, and goals of social actors are in part determined by the occupational institutions within which they are acting. For instance, the teacher-counselor may differ from the physician-counselor in part simply because of their differing vocational roles. The purpose of this chapter is to consider some aspects of these occupational influences on counseling and psychotherapy in contemporary society, thereby setting the stage for discussion by the other authors in this book of the relation of cultural and social contexts to counseling and psychotherapy.

An Institutional Overview

Consider the simplest definition of counseling: the giving of information, advice, and aid. Defined in this way, the practice has, of course, gone on since the beginning of social time. Even in the simplest societies it frequently took the form of a specialization, whether involving merely the prerogative of the elders of the tribe or resembling the psycho-

1

therapeutic relationship approximated by some witch doctors (*Kiev, 1964*).

The modern proliferation of "helping-professions" is, however, a relatively recent phenomenon stemming from advanced industrialization. It is part of the growth of tertiary service occupational functions and the development of expertise. More specifically, "The growth in scale and complexity of social organizations . . . [has created] a demand for liaison and contact men of all kinds. We need guides, so to speak, through a new kind of civilized jungle" (*Wilensky and Lebeaux, 1958*, p. 286). Furthermore, "now that sustained governmental policies and elaborate administrative organizations are busy taking care of the stereotyped and classifiable material ills, the counsellor can throw himself fully into the study of personal and intimate miseries" (*Halmos, 1965*, p. 28). The growth of counseling, in other words, reflects both the complexities of contemporary society and the approval of personal service in its midst.

In an indirect way, modern man is perennially and involuntarily surrounded by "guides" who need to be distinguished from those filling counseling roles. They differ in that the aim of their "advice" is to persuade or sell, and not to give solace. They are the mass persuaders, represented most obviously by Madison Avenue, but also by opinion moulders in the mass media and political life. They not only influence consumer behavior and political decisions, but strongly contribute to the shaping of a wide range of individual values and goals. They are the stuff of the "civilized jungle." It is in juxtaposition to such impersonal mass influences that counseling — which ideally involves intimate, personal relations — must be seen.

Between the extremes of mass persuaders and personal counseling lies a significant source of advice concerning the gamut of human problems. This is advice in its written form, directed at a mass market. The most obvious example of this category is the newspaper advice column, whether dealing with matters of health, sex, or flower arrangement. Even more important in terms of social consequences are such things as baby manuals, with some fifty million copies of Spock and *Infant Care* currently in circulation. The range of topics dealt with in books, manuals, and articles giving advice is as diverse as is the competence of the authors. Indeed, it is partly due to the swell in the literature that counseling experts are needed. For the volume of writing represents not only the publication explosion but more specifically the growth of specialized knowledge. On both counts the layman needs guidance, at least to direct him to appropriate sources of guidance.

An additional type of counseling at a considerable distance from the intimate relationship which is the essence of personal counseling is that of consultancy. To the extent that the consultant is frequently dealing with a large organization as his client, the relationship is highly impersonal. The increasing prevalence of consultancy in various settings is explainable by the same factors that account for the growth of written forms of advice and for personal counseling, namely increasing specialization and the concomitant need for expertise.

But even when one turns to a narrower view of counseling, defined in terms of personal guidance, the areas for which specialist advice-givers have developed are still extensive and the scope of issues they work with highly variable. At the one extreme are those attempting to cope with a wide range of problems individuals face — for example the psychoanalyst dealing with the total adjustment of the individual to his social milieu, in all roles and social relationships. A great deal of counseling work, however, tends to be functionally specific, centering, for example, upon occupational or marital problems. But the great dilemma in these areas is the extent to which solutions to specific problems can be attempted without invoking broader contexts of personality and social development.

Above all else, counseling serves to aid in periods of transition. Seen in terms of the major stages of the life cycle, it is most important in the bridge from childhood to adult life, along the various stages of the educational ladder and above all in connection with the step from the status of student to that of member of an occupation. Similarly, the work of marriage counselors, like that of vocational counselors, involves decisions faced during a period of transition — whether into, through, or out of marriage. In addition to such major but typical periods of transition, counseling is also important in the stages between deviant and normal life patterns, for example in overcoming mental illness, physical incapacitation, or criminality.

While few fields of counseling could be conceived of as entirely limited to one social institution, institutional boundaries, frequently corresponding to work settings, suggest the types of emphases involved. A school counselor, for ready example, needs to be primarily concerned with educational problems growing out of the educational setting. An institutional overview aids in specifying the range of functions and contexts of counseling.

To begin with the family, we encounter the one institution which has, since the origins of human society, incorporated advice-giving within its own boundaries, counsel passing from one generation to the next. The frequent turning to outsiders for help is as modern a phenomenon as is our form of the nuclear family, explainable in part by the family *being* nuclear, and confronted by the vicissitudes of a changing urban industrial society.

3

The two major types of problems faced by families are those involving the marital relationship and child-rearing. For the former, there has developed a specific counseling occupation — that of the marriage counselor. Advice in matters of child-rearing, beyond the baby manuals, comes increasingly from pediatricians rather than family doctors. Child psychiatrists are still few in number. In addition, social workers are often involved with family problems, whether with "problem families" as such or in the context of youth work.

The most frequent form of guidance dealing with problems of children is, significantly, not contained within familial institutions. It is instead to be found in the educational setting. The school is *the* major locus of counseling as far as current usage of the word is concerned. Why this is the case indicates a great deal about the essential function of counseling. For the school is an institution of socialization and transition, not only teaching but also sorting and placing, and dealing with educational and career decisions which have a decisive impact upon entire life patterns. Guidance is most essential for the making of such decisions which occur at an age when comprehension of "the civilized jungle" is bound to be superficial, at best.

Religious counseling, although stemming from a separate institutional sphere, tends more often to deal with personal problems, including those of family life, than it does with matters of the soul. In this case, the pastoral context suggests the type of orientation that is likely to be taken more than it does the nature or scope of problems dealt with.

The changes that have occurred in economic institutions are almost synonymous with the division of labor and the increasing complexity of contemporary life. Their impact is most fundamentally reflected in an aspect of counseling to a large extent connected with educational institutions. Vocational counseling and guidance attempts to interpret the nature of occupational information, a most necessary task in a society whose *Dictionary of Occupational Titles* yields over 25,000 alternatives. Another aspect of counseling connected with the world of work is that of vocational rehabilitation. Apart from the growth of consultancy, however, little resembling counseling has developed in the context of industry itself. The Hawthorne experiment with personnel counseling, for example, which largely served the function of increasing management's control, has not spread (*Wilensky and Wilensky, 1951*).

Another major counseling role intimately connected with economic institutions is that of welfare work, the most common concern of social workers. Thus, counseling in economic life enters upon the process of getting work, rehabilitation for new types of work, and getting and dispensing welfare for those without work. It seldom deals with the end products of economic activity. Advisory functions in the form of consumer societies and investment counseling have little if any resemblance to the model of personal guidance. Another aspect of economic life that is likely to become more problematic and perhaps in need of specialized counselors in the future is that of time left over from work. As the working week diminishes and as longevity increases, leisure and retirement counseling may become as important as vocational counseling.

In the context of social control, in connection with political and legal institutions, a variety of counseling roles exist. The linkage is readily illustrated by the British usage of the term "counsellor" for an advising barrister. In the legal situation the layman is dramatically confronted by the intricacies of an overwhelmingly complex social mechanism in which the specialized knowledge of the expert is crucial. Counsel in this realm is not limited to guidance through legal mazes (which in any case may well be far removed from intimate solace). Frequently it may involve keeping the client away from the sanctions that the court may impose if he does not heed advice. The probation officer's role may also be conceived in this manner, as may that of judges of family and juvenile courts. The policeman too is often looked upon as "philosopher, guide and friend" (*Cumming, Cumming, and Edell, 1965*).

Finally, to complete the institutional outline, there is the realm of health. Subsumed under this category there is the one occupational role closest to the intrinsic function of counseling — that of the psychotherapist. But the ordinary physician whose work with physical health involves a considerable amount of advice-giving also has a most extensive counseling role. He ranks with the clergyman as the prime source of advice outside the kinship and family circle, and like the clergyman he is frequently confronted with diverse problems not necessarily because of his expertise, but because of his accessibility and prestige.

Counseling Specializations

The wide range of counseling roles is vividly indicated by their pervasiveness in all the basic social institutions — the family, education, religion, economics and welfare, politics and law, and health. Clearly it would not be feasible to analyze all of the occupational variants in each of these contexts. Rather, this chapter will attempt to consider only the major counseling professions which represent these institutional spheres. We shall briefly mention the situation of the doctor, lawyer, and minister, who represent counseling by "outsiders," to the extent that although they are major sources of counsel, it is more often than not extrinsic to their professional roles. Our major focus will be upon four occupations in which counseling is a core function — marriage counselors, school counselors, social workers, and psychiatrists.

Counseling by "Outsiders"

Since one of the essential earmarks of a profession is a specialized body of knowledge, all professionals, as experts, will tend to be purveyors of advice to those seeking out their services. In most cases, the nature of the advice will be functionally specific. For example, the architect may go beyond house design to advise on aesthetics, but this still remains within his area of special competence.

The prestige that professionals hold in society tends, however, to give them the aura of "wise-men," and they are consequently also subject to advise on matters outside — or marginal to — their specialities. The pattern is most strongly developed with physicians. In addition to being highly visible in any community, a necessary professional contact at various points in an individual's life, and the one profession with the very highest prestige, the work of the doctor — in dealing with life and death — has the quality of sacredness and magic. For all of these reasons he is likely to be turned to for counsel of all sorts.

To the extent that the subject matter in question is totally divorced from professional knowledge, the physician is in no worse a position than anyone else, except in being more likely to be sought out. He may give his opinion as a layman, and still acting as a layman — hopefully an intelligent one — he may suggest an appropriate source where expert knowledge may be obtained. But the issue is more complex in those areas where there *appears* to be a relationship to professional competence.

The greatest problem in this connection is the relationship between physiological and psychological knowledge. While there is, no doubt, variability in the performance of physicians *qua* physicians, an adequate level of minimal performance is assured by professional institutions. No comparable minimal level of knowledge can be assumed with respect to human psychology. The field of sexual behavior is probably the best case in point. As a report of a recent population conference stated: "Judging by bullish Ben Casey and dreamboat Dr. Kildare, the modern American doctor is as knowledgeable about sex as Kinsey and as proficient in dealing with aberrations as Freud. But in real life, it appears, the new interns are about as sexually wise as Mary Poppins" (*Newsweek*, 1964, p. 101). Although the medical student is taught about the physical process of pregnancy and childbirth, apparently he remains embarrassed to talk about the sexual aspects of a patient's life. For the link between medical knowledge and psychological implications is by no means automatic. Not only does the medical student share middle-class sexual anxieties, he also tends to be unusually inhibited — an "overcontrolled" personality type (*Lief, 1964*). Similar inconsistencies arise in other areas in which the physician is called upon not merely to heal but to counsel. Knowledge of children's diseases, for example, does not by any means invariably subsume knowledge of child development.

The doctor's dilemma is that he is looked upon as a counselor in spite of himself. Given his societal status and the limited development of professional counseling, this would appear inevitable. The dilemma is more that of the declining breed of the family doctor than it is of the modern specialist. The latter, whatever his prejudices against the psychological aspects of health and behavior, is more likely to incorporate them in the course of his practice. Even if not specifically oriented or trained in these realms, he has the advantage of experience in particular specialities. But in any event, cultural lag is involved: "in the past the clergy and the doctors did all the counselling, today they have become laymen who occasionally dabble in a technique in which they have received no training and hold no qualification" (*Halmos, 1965,* p. 36).

The counseling function is in numerous ways even more problematic for the clergyman than it is for the physician. Like the physician he is highly accessible, and implicit in his occupational role is the ability to understand human problems and offer guidance. Not only does the clergyman, like the physician, frequently lack the knowledge or ability to act as a counselor, but in addition, there are structural aspects of his role specifically detrimental to effective counseling.

The clergyman, at the same time that he aims to be a confidant in the counseling role is also an authority of the appropriate point of view for his flock. He is not anonymous, but a public figure with an organized clientele, his congregation. His client is a soul, not a case. "Given these considerations, it would follow that counselling is nowadays easily considered an appropriate part of the minister's role while at the same time there are various reasons why it cannot become preeminent unless his role is fairly radically reconstituted in several respects" (*Naegele, 1956,* p. 50). One solution to the tensions between the various roles of the minister which has been followed in some of the most "successful" Protestant churches has been the appointment of separate ministers for the separate roles — a preacher, a social group leader, and a pastoral counselor (*Hagstrom, 1957*). The need for this type of division of labor indicates the severity of role conflict and the incompatability of counseling and other clerical duties.

In spite of the strains in the counseling role of the clergy, the growing importance of pastoral counseling is hard to ignore, and conclusions such as this appear unfair: "It seems likely that the really serious work of rehabilitation of deviants and the indoctrination of moral values will be performed by secular practitioners, and the functions left to the clergy will be those of professional sentimentalists in an unsentimental age" (*Hagstrom, 1957,* p. 65). It is true that the clergyman is unlikely to attempt to rehabilitate extreme cases of deviant behavior. But his accessibility forces him into at least functioning as a major source of referral and even this is strongly influenced by role conflicts (*Cumming and Harrington, 1963*). The simple fact that many clergymen spend a major portion of their time in counseling activities alone suggests the necessity of greater attention to both their success and their difficulties.

A third established profession, law, differs greatly from medicine and the clergy in counseling activities. The lawyer is much less likely to be looked to for help concerning the types of problems which are — appropriately or not — brought to doctors and ministers. The counsel that the lawyer gives tends to be more narrowly defined. In spite of the "enormous range of things done by lawyers for clients . . . a private attorney's job is to advise his client in relation to a *concrete* situation" (*Parsons, 1954*, p. 379).

Reference to the activity of the lawyer suggests strong contrasts with the doctor and minister. The physician's task — to heal — is fairly specific, but the line between sickness and health is not clearly definitive, nor is that between physical and mental health. The minister's task, on the other hand, is clearly diffuse. It is for this reason that the counseling function has been assumed to be part of his obligation, even when it stands in conflict with other aims. The lawyer's counseling is most specific of all, being defined by the highly routinized procedures of legal practice. He is also important as an agent of referral, but less so than the doctor or pastor.

In each of these three cases, the occupational institutions in question and the position of the occupation in society explain the type of counseling that has been incorporated as part of the professional's work. Many of the complex interrelations between the orientations of those in the established professions and counseling functions are illustrated in marriage counseling, where practitioners in fact tend to be members of other professions.

Marriage Counseling

Like other counseling professions, marriage counseling is a new specialization. It is one of the newest, so much so that a recent overview of the field (*Leslie, 1964*) suggests that because of its youth its character has not yet been fully developed.

Its scope, focusing upon the marital relationship, would appear circumscribed. Yet there is considerable heterogeneity due to the diverse orientations and occupational affiliations of practitioners. This is true even if one excludes what is the most typical form of help concerning marital problems — that of unskilled members of the community, from the bartender, to the hairdresser, to the woman who provides the understanding that the wife does not. Since only some ten percent of marriage counseling in the United States today is done by professional marriage counselors, it is most often undertaken as an incidental activity by those primarily involved in other professions *(AAMC, 1964)*.

Consequently, the separate perspectives of the professions involved inhibit the development of a consistent frame of reference. The lack of agreement concerning both procedures and aims of marriage counseling is well documented by the responses of members of various professions to a query as to who is best equipped to be a marriage counselor. Clergymen, physicians, social workers, and attorneys all felt *their own* profession would be the ideal one — more capable than full-time marriage counselors themselves *(Kerckhoff, 1953)*. Clergymen tend to define marriage counseling as religious work stressing the sacredness of marriage, just as doctors emphasize the physiological aspects and attorneys the legal ones. These alternative perspectives involve not only the types of problems approached, but also the manner in which they are dealt with.

The mainstream in marriage counseling however, does not consist of an indiscriminate blending of various professional perspectives. While the usual process in the development of professional specialization has involved a fractioning of segments of an established profession *(Bucher and Strauss, 1961)*, in this case a coalition of segments of distinct professions is being drawn together.

Major influences may be seen in considering the evolution of the field. Its origins some forty years ago stem from both marriage education courses in colleges and universities and from marriage consultation centers *(Stone, 1949)*. Both of these provided needed but incomplete undertakings which highlighted the desirability of additional services in the form of personal counseling. Thus counseling as a *technique,* using the process of interpersonal guidance, has been basic from the beginning. The model has been that of psychotherapy, even if short-range and usually involving only limited transference. "Marriage counseling has emerged — because of the need for a field of counseling intermediate to educational guidance and intensive psychotherapy" *(Vincent, 1957, p. 1)*.

In spite of the difficulties inherent in the interdisciplinary nature of marriage counseling, it is becoming professionalized. The American Association of Marriage Counselors, "an inter-professional organization dedicated to the task of establishing and maintaining standards in the newly developing field" *(AAMC, 1964, p. 3)* came into being in 1942. Since then it has grown slowly, remaining a small association, at present with fewer than 500 members. Because many members are qualified in more than one discipline, a breakdown of affiliations is difficult to determine. Excluding these, 1964 figures show the largest proportion of AAMC members to be trained in social work, followed by psychology, religion, medicine, sociology, education, and law last of all.

9

An important aspect of professionalization has been instigated by forces outside the AAMC, in the recent emergence of state regulations. Largely in reaction to the publicity given the growing number of marriage counseling quacks in California (America's most fertile breeding-ground for both quacks and for marital problems), that state adopted a bill regulating practice, and other states have begun to follow suit. The 1963 California bill licensing marriage counselors has been found deficient in a number of respects (*AAMC, 1964*), but is most curious in exempting doctors, lawyers, and clergymen, regardless of their counseling qualifications, merely on the basis of the sacredness of their professional status.

The long range effect of such legislation is highly problematic. For although levels of standards and training facilities are crucial touchstones for a profession, those that have been set and proposed by state legislation are lower than those of the AAMC. Indeed, it is likely that the assessment and maintenance of high standards by the professional body has been strengthened by the lesser standards specified in legislation.

Licensing and certification by themselves are not, of course, automatic indicators of the attainment of professional standing. But to the extent that marriage counseling involves a specialized area of technical competence, adherence to a service ideal, and supporting norms of professional conduct, it is becoming professionalized. It will become increasingly so with further development of training schools in which marriage counseling as such is the focus. At present, the dual identities of marriage counselor and pastor, doctor, or social worker limit the extent to which distinct professional identity might develop.

Educational Counseling

The work of most professionals, including that of many types of counselors, involves a routinization of what for their clients is a crisis — for example in dealing with illness, marital conflict, or mental breakdown (*Hughes, 1958*). In this respect, the work of the school counselor (like that of the teacher) is unique. For, however his function may be defined, he is increasingly part of the "normal" educational system. His influence thus extends more widely than that of any other counseling occupation to the extent that its potential scope includes every child in society.

Unlike marriage counseling, where the function performed tends to be specific in spite of the heterogeneity of procedures and practitioners, school counselors' actual duties are diffuse and their aims frequently disputed. In light of the history of the field, stemming from concerns of social reformers with problems of vocational guidance (see, for example, *Brewer, 1942; Borow, 1964; Miller, 1964*), the world of work and occupational placement would appear to be crucial frames of reference. But today such circumscribed emphasis more accurately describes counseling in community agencies than in schools. As guidance moved increasingly into the educational system during the past half century, as the dominant label changed from "vocational counselor" to "school counselor," the school setting itself was among the factors that influenced the occupational role and the scope of the activities involved.

The growth of both counseling functions and personnel in American schools is an important point of departure. While neither counselor-student ratios nor absolute numbers explicitly reveal what has taken place due to the variety of tasks subsumed under the rubric "counseling" and the extreme variability by size of school and region of country, a pattern of expansion and general acceptance is unmistakable. Expectations of future development are even greater (*Hitchcock, 1966; Wrenn, 1962; Goals for Guidance, 1960*). Even the lowest projected national average of one counselor per school — which gives undue weight to the smaller school and is accordingly unrepresentative of likely future trends — is impressive.

Thus we begin with the fact that the counselor is part of the organization of the present-day educational system. But his role, partly due to its novelty, is highly ambiguous. Whether one considers the ideologies expounded by counseling educators, the perspectives of the counselors themselves, or the expectations of teaching colleagues or students, lack of agreement is a predominant theme. While there is little question raised that the counseling function is an essential (or at least useful) one in the educational system, consensus concerning both its scope and procedures is small.

An occupational specialization concerned with counseling in schools is one involving duties previously assumed by teachers. Among the teacher's various roles (*Waller, 1932*) some form of personal guidance is frequently involved, for the teacher is the most accessible adult for the child outside the home. (It is not accidental that a large part of the script of Mr. Novak showed him involved with non-academic student problems.) The feasibility of counselors fulfilling a general advisory role is lessened by their necessarily limited contact with students. Such structural constraints partially explain why, although a majority of high school students would on occasion like to talk over personal problems with a sympathetic adult, few think of the counselor in this capacity. Reflecting the viewpoints of their teachers, students tend to feel counselors are mainly appropriate for specifically academic and vocational problems, the counselors' broader definitions of their own work notwithstanding (*Grant, 1954; Dipboye, 1959*).

Ambiguities in the school counselor's role may also be seen to be both a result of and a buffer against various role conflicts in the school

11

situation. In spite of the teacher's greater contact with students, she is likely to fear that the satisfying task of guidance will be usurped by the counselor. In addition the authority of the teacher is diminished as evaluations of students and such things as course assignments are taken out of her hands — authority both in terms of students and administration. The smaller teaching assignment of the counselor, which defies the basic educationist ideology of the virtue of classroom exposure, is another source of antagonism (*Cicourel and Kitsuse, 1963*). For all of these reasons, the aims of the counselors, even if explicit at the start, are likely to be subverted. In a bureaucratized setting however, counseling goals have been shown to be more readily accommodated (*ibid.*).

Relations with administration are, of course, crucial in explaining the counselor's situation. A basic conflict of interest is that between professional counseling criteria and organizational allegiances to the school. Because counseling posts tend to be defined as being on the administrative hierarchy, and since they frequently do lead to a principal-ship or even higher, professional identity is likely to suffer. Being a counselor will be seen not as a career, but a step (*Super, 1964; Dipboye, 1959*). Finally, in the context of role relationships in school, mention must be made of what would appear to be a considerable over-lap between counselors, psychologists, and social workers. A study which considered the relationship of the three found less conflict or competition than expected, perhaps because all are insecure and groping for role clarification. The direction of potential conflict is nonetheless suggested in that while testing and educational and vocational guidance may readily be assigned to psychologists and counselors, "deep-emotional" problems are more problematic. Rather than refer them to social workers and psychologists, the counselors might keep such juicy cases for themselves be redefining them as "surface" problems (*Cicourel and Kitsuse, 1963*).

Most important of all, however, counselors themselves are not clear about what they should be doing. What they actually spend most of their time on is counseling in connection with high school programs and college entrance, with testing and teaching taking almost as much of their time. Much further down the list are counseling for "developing potential" and "inadequate achievement," with vocational counseling far behind in priority (*Wrenn, 1962*). Yet, curiously, as many as 30 to 40 percent of counselors in another study felt it was not their job to assist failing students or counsel with their parents, interpret test results to teachers, assist pupils in course planning, assist pupils with occupational plans, or consult with teachers about pupils' problems (*Hitchcock, 1953*). There would appear to be more agreement about what counselors should not do than there is about their appropriate task. The frequent emphasis upon the onus of administrative work ignores the universality of this complaint in all white-collar occupations (especially educational ones). But concern with the degrading nature of such assignments as lavatory supervision does suggest that the professional skills of counselors might not be fully utilized. Attempting to enhance professional status by stressing the amount of inappropriate work forced upon counselors indicates a negative approach which requires balancing attention to occupational goals in order to be fruitful.

The mixed parentage of counseling greatly contributes to dissension about aims. Voices from education, sociology, and economics pull in various directions. While the influence of psychology predominates, it subsumes the most serious conflict of orientations of all — that of psychotherapeutic, client-centered counseling as contrast with the viewpoint of the testing technician, or, counseling psychology as opposed to guidance. Although by no means universal, the psychotherapeutic model tends to predominate as a professional ideology. Yet, in practice, it is seldom relevant or feasible as evidenced by the actual work done by counselors in schools. The result is that school counselors tend to fall between two stools: "Seeing themselves as psychotherapists in being or becoming, they have rejected the functions of vocational guidance . . . [but] better a competent, accepted and self-accepting sharer of occupational information than an ill-trained, self-appointed, and unaccepted psychotherapist. Better still a counselor who understands adolescent and adult development and is inclined to further it through the media which counselors know best, education and work" (*Super, 1964,* p. 580). This plea summarizes the considerable hiatus between occupational ideology and actual practice in school counseling. In referring to work, presumably Super does not mean that counselors should work harder, but that they should pay more attention to vocational problems.

Education not only represents an area that counselors know about and work in, it is also something they are short of themselves. The limited advanced training of many in the area of counseling (*Wrenn, 1962*) is an even greater obstacle to the professionalization of the field than is the multiplicity of aims. As in marriage counseling, not certification, but training and the maintenance of standards will be the source of future professional development.

Social Work

"Social work" is probably the most amorphous occupational label among the helping professions, since it subsumes such diverse tasks as: "budgeting for relief applicants, a study of a couple desiring to adopt a child, supportive psychotherapy, initiation of court action against parents neglecting their children, community organization to pressure the city council into action to improve a neighborhood, informal education through relationships and play with a group of chronically ill children

13

in a hospital, or helping adolescents to feel socially at ease in the teen-age canteen of a neighborhood settlement house. . . . (In sum) social workers were found to be doing almost everything that aimed at helping people with social, economic, psychological, and educational problems. They were engaged in 145 different vocational functions (*Hollis and Taylor, 1951*, pp. 60–63), but with no exclusive jurisdiction over any of them" (*Eaton, 1956*, p. 11).

Given the broad concern with "helping people," social work would appear co-terminous with counseling — referring to a social function rather than an occupational boundary, still less to an area of professional specialization. While it has been suggested that "social workers have gained a profession by forfeiting a mission" (*Saunders, 1957*, p. 57; *Corwin*, in this volume), it is not clear to what extent social work has, in fact, gained full professional standing. Greenwood (*1957*) has stated that social work *is* a profession because it is not otherwise classifiable. But clearly the professional label does not equally apply to all those concerned with charity and community service, nor even to all those classified as "social workers" by the labor bureau. The specific pattern of professionalization in social work requires consideration if current trends are to be assessed.

The road to professionalization is being trod by many occupations today, as appears inevitable in an advanced industrial society. But the steps to professional status, which seem to differ for many occupational groups involved in the journey, are difficult ones, as the history of social work reveals. No other occupation has been so explicitly concerned with the canons of the professions for so long with such limited success. A half century ago, social workers were first confronted with the question: "Is Social Work a Profession?" (*Flexner, 1915*). Efforts to institutionalize procedures that would allow an affirmative response were slow and obstacles (when known and remediable) were many. Today, although segments of the occupation measure up to the majority of identifiable professional criteria, the bulk of practitioners still do not warrant an unqualified "yea."

A major part of the explanation lies in that, "there are a number of social welfare occupations, diverse not only in skill and job content, but also in degree of identification with and preparation for social work as professionally conceived" (*Wilensky and Lebeaux, 1958*, p. 291). Organizationally, this is demonstrated by the separate associations for psychiatric, medical, school, group, community, and research social workers, which were not merged into the National Association of Social Workers until 1955 (*Cohen, 1955*). These specialities all, however, shared a professional orientation. Sharper cleavages derive from the settings in which social workers are employed, whether government bureaucracies or private agencies, some of which are overtly antagonistic to the ideology identified with professional social work (e.g., "tender-minded"), and even to the necessity of the high educational requirements specified by the NASW.

The major indicator of segmentation, and indeed the greatest obstacle to professionalization, is the variability of specialized training requirements and attainments. The largest single group — about a third of the 100,000 estimated employed in social work in 1960 — were in the area of public assistance. Only some 4 percent of these had graduate training in social work. In fact, only a fifth of all "social workers" had two or more years of graduate study in a school of social work (*U.S. Dept. of Labor, 1961; U.S. Dept. of H.E.W., 1965*).

Whatever else professional standing involves, its attainment is rewarded by societal prestige. The limited prestige accorded to social workers reveals the extent to which professional claims have not been realized, and at the same time suggests some of the unique features of the social work field. For, cultural values, the occupational structure itself, and the characteristics of incumbents are the basic determinants of prestige judgments.

The diverse tasks pursued by social workers result in a blurred occupational image. What stereotype does exist is likely to be somewhat negative in terms of our cultural values: social workers tend to be seen as meddlers in the lives of others or as perpetrators of bureaucratic obstacles. The functional importance of social work is neither clear nor, when ascertained, is it highly rated. In this, social work stands in bold contrast not only to the established professions, but also to such low prestige professions as teaching.

Many aspects of the occupational structure of social work itself detract from its prestige value. The previously mentioned factor of low entrance requirements, the vast majority of practitioners being without advanced training, is most important. Increasingly, however, advanced training is becoming more typical. Other facets of the occupational structure are less readily alterable. These include: a subject-matter lacking in *mystique,* clients who are the least prestigeful members of the community, an occupational label of "worker," limited autonomy in terms of supervision practices or being in an ancillary position to other professionals, and low salary standards (*Kadushin, 1958*).

The characteristics of social workers themselves also have a negative influence upon their prestige. While the proportion of men in the field is increasing, social work tends to be thought of as a female — and therefore low prestige — profession. In 1950 almost 60 percent of social workers in the U.S. were women (*U.S. Dept. of Labor, 1961*). Those who pursue graduate training in social work rank quite low in academic performance *(Davis, 1964)*. In terms of their values they are exceptional and almost culturally deviant in emphasizing working with people, political liberalism, unconventional opinions and values, and lack of concern with making money *(ibid.)*. In addition, while it is not clear that the social origins of social workers are more lowly than are those of members of other professions *(ibid.; Pins, 1963)*, "social work recruits a large proportion of its personnel from minority groups, such as women and Negroes . . . persons most likely to be satisfied with the middle range status of the profession" *(Eaton, 1956, p. 20)*.

Reflecting the self-conscious concerns with prestige, professionalization, and standards, many changes and advances have taken place in social work in the past decades. The organizational coalition which the NASW represents and the related specification of entrance requirements, together with the development of a distinctive route of training *(Eaton, 1956)* have been major steps. But the diversity of activities subsumed by the vague label "social work" persists as a major source of ambiguity. The basic contrast, between group work and case work and the alternative knowledge base of each *(Kadushin, 1959)*, is especially crucial. The fruitfulness of attention to questions of occupational development is indicated by Meyer's *(1959, p. 340)* conclusion: ". . . social work is sure to struggle with the concomitants of professionalization for a long time. Such a struggle is characteristic of a vigorous profession."

Psychiatry

Psychiatry would appear to have more distinct boundaries than other counseling professions. It is, first of all, a medical specialty, but one that subsumes numerous schools and an even greater number of roles. A basic polarity is between "talking" and "shocking" psychiatrists, but while only one in ten of the profession are qualified psychoanalysts,[1] a somatotherapeutic orientation was found predominant among less than a fourth of the psychiatrists investigated in a recent study *(Strauss et al., 1964)*. Similarly, Menninger has indicated that, "while perhaps as many as ten thousand patients are being treated in the United States today with psychoanalysis, it is probable that over a hundred thousand patients are being treated with other forms of psychotherapy, many of which depend ultimately upon the scientific principles for furthering recovery through psychological means established by Sigmund Freud" *(1963,*

[1] Reports of the numbers of psychiatrists and psychoanalysts are not entirely consistent. Halmos *(1965)* estimates that in 1960 there were 11,637 psychiatrists and 1,540 psychotherapists — the latter based on the Roster of Members of American Psychoanalytic Societies. Schofield *(1964)* reports that in 1962 there were 7,100 diplomates in psychiatry of the American Board of Psychiatry and Neurology, 9,450 active members and fellows of the American Psychiatric Association, and slightly over 1,000 members of the American Psychoanalytic Association. Journalistic reports have given the number of psychiatrists as high as 17,000 *(National Observer, 1965)*.

p. 337). There can be little question that psychotherapy is the most influential model.[2]

But a misleading stereotype is common, both among laymen and other counseling professionals. The image tends to be that of the dyadic couched relationship between patient and analyst, representing the epitome of counseling ideology in involving the luxury of depth of treatment over extended periods of time. Yet, most psychiatry is still administered in hospitals, though the state hospital, where the profession was born a century ago, is now but one of the multitudinous settings of psychiatric work.

> In terms of the range of roles and settings: The psychoanalytic psychiatrist today is called upon in every organized attempt at the rectification of social difficulties. He is asked to work with children's courts, criminal courts, domestic relations courts, prisons and reformatories, and to consult with social agencies, churches and educational institutions of every level from nursery school to graduate school. He is increasingly asked by industry for help with personnel problems and the allocation of men to appropriate tasks and work loads. Sometimes his aid is sought on larger issues of national and international import, and he participates today in many federal organizations. This list does not yet touch on his prime function as a physician and part of the medical profession. He shares work on medical and surgical wards and the speciality services with adults and children in every outpatient clinic, and especially in institutions devoted to chronic disabling impairments. Not yet mentoned are his important duties as a teacher and administrator in medical schools and general hospitals. And last, but far from least, are the needs for his services in the psychiatric hospitals, in the psychiatric outpatient departments, the psychoanalytic institutes, in the supervision and training of psychiatric residents, and in the actual clinic practice of psychiatry (*Zinberg, 1963*, p. 820).

Although the social functions of the psychiatrist are more diverse than those of any of the other counseling professions, and in fact, subsume all of the concerns of other types of counselors, the essence of their influential theory derives from the process of talking-out, from the psychotherapeutic relationship. The prime point to be noted is that psychoanalysis represents the vanguard of counseling, the head of the helping procession. In a similar vein, Berger (*1965*) states, "surrounding the institutional core of psychoanalysis there is a ring of satellite organizations and activities that may be called, loosely, the counseling and testing complex" (p. 27).

As we have indicated, the growth of counseling, especially in the United States (which, for example, has some three and a half times as

[2] By psychotherapy or psychoanalytic thought, reference is being made to a cultural configuration rather than to any specific psychoanalytic theory or school (cf. *Berger, 1965*).

many professional counselors as Britain; *Halmos, 1965,* p. 47), represents a response to the complexities of contemporary society. But the forms, techniques, and orientations involved tend to mirror the acceptance and diffusion of psychoanalytic thinking, which again has occurred in the United States to a much greater extent than in Europe.

Zinberg *(1963),* in discussing the reasons for the extraordinary absorption of psychoanalytic thought in America points to the role of key individuals who accepted Freudian thinking — interestingly, more in medicine than in psychology — and to receptive features in American culture. The latter include the appeal of new ideas that seem to offer definite answers, the salience of an identity search in a mobile society and, consistent with American materialism, the notion of "knowledge of one's self as a possession . . . (which) can be conspicuously displayed" (p. 814). In addition, Zinberg refers to the dissatisfaction with neurological psychiatry in American medicine. Yet, he also indicates, a good deal of the value system of psychoanalysis conflicts with values prized in American culture: for example, moral relativism, emphasis upon the instinctual life, and the belief that insight is good.

It is partly to counter such value conflicts that the analyst has so frequently assumed teaching responsibilities. This, in turn, has enhanced receptivity to psychoanalytic ways of thought, especially among fellow counselors. For, those in other counseling professions have shared values with the analyst, more closely than has the medical community. The conflicts between medicine and psychoanalysis have seldom been visible to those not involved. Counselors look up to the psychoanalyst because of his access to the unquestionable prestige of the medical profession — both on the grounds of science and mystique — while sharing a knowledge base with the social sciences and the humanities. The shared knowledge base, however, serves to make the psychoanalyst an "outsider" in medicine — with ways of thinking and procedures not merely foreign but at times obverse to those employed by other doctors. It would appear that ". . . psychiatry, the medical *outsider,* plays the powerful role of *medical* speciality in confronting non-medical groups" (*Smith, 1955,* p. 315; *Binger, 1964*).

Conclusion

In all fields of counseling, the youth of the area of specialization explains a great deal of its current situation. Problems of definition — of aims, roles, and boundaries — loom large. Even the most prestigeful and established of the counseling occupations, psychiatry, shares such dilemmas in its relation to medicine, as well as in its relation to other counselors and the social sciences. The president of the American Psychiatric Association, at a recent convention, urged that psychiatrists "abandon the 'invidious' conviction that they alone can understand and control the vagaries of human behavior" (*New York Times, 1966,* p. 27). The psychiatrist does not even have a unique license and mandate for the technique of psychotherapy. Indeed, in his provocatively entitled *Psychotherapy: The Purchase of Friendship,* Schofield (*1964*) has argued:

> As the definition of neurosis has been gradually broadened so as to encompass symptoms ranging from actual failure of performance to lack of basic zest for living, and as the optimal treatment of such disorders has increasingly assigned a critical role to the therapeutic conversation, it becomes less and less clear that there is any one group of experts in our culture whose background and professional training uniquely equips them to function in the role of psychotherapist — as emotional tutor, as intimate counselor, as master philosopher, or as guide in the quest for self-realization (p. 144).

Schofield's thesis is that the psychiatrist, psychologist, and social worker alike possess specialized skills, but "psychotherapy is neither the primary nor unique skill of any one of these professions" (*ibid.,* p. 121). Other studies have also brought out the curious mixtures of responsibilities between mental health professions, the division of labor emerging from a process of negotiation rather than *a priori* specialization (*Strauss et al., 1964; Zander et al., 1957; Rushing, 1964*). The intersection of occupational and organizational systems in these instances frequently produces results unanticipated by either. Increasingly research is taking cognizance of the mental health *team,* whose viability varies not only in terms of the professional identities, orientation, and relationships of those involved, but also from one setting to another.

All fields of counseling involve the complexities of professions in process. In those areas where several specialists work together, the most immediate question will be that of the division of labor. This is, in turn, a reflection of a knowledge base which is not as clearly esoteric or compartmentalized as is that of the established professions. Because the knowledge base for counseling is of an interdisciplinary nature — including social sciences which are themselves in a formative stage — the traditional pattern of carving out an area of professional expertise cannot be easily followed.

As our society becomes increasingly professionalized and as service occupations assume an ever-increasing significance, it may well be that the counseling specializations will reveal novel emergent patterns of professionalization. To the extent that they attempt to emulate previous pathways to professional standing, perhaps they are worshiping at the wrong shrines.

The functions of professional groups include maintaining or enhancing their status. Aspiring professionals are only human in seeking recognition; like their clients, they wish to be loved. But they may be working against their own interests if they stress their quest at the expense of their unique contribution, either in terms of an area of knowledge or service. The danger is of means becoming ends. It is not entirely paradoxical that the rewards of recognition and prestige will more likely come about if they are less explicitly sought. Attention to professional canons will aid in the clarification of occupational goals and standards, which in turn will bring recompense. The dynamics will, however, differ in light of the unique enigmas in the various counseling fields.

In marriage counseling the major problem is that of dual identities and the vested interests of those in other professions who practice in the area. The school counselor also faces conflicts of jurisdiction within the school, but the most serious quandary here is the definition of occupational goals. For both fields, current steps being undertaken regarding routes of professional training and specification of standards will tend to alleviate many present ambiguities.

The largest of the counseling professions, social work, suffers from the concomitants of its size. In light of a number of criteria, it is clear that not all sharing the label "social worker" are involved in work of a professional caliber. Here, the routinization of training and up-grading of standards will differentiate professional social workers from a very necessary but quite distinct category of technical sub-professionals. The counterpart of this process may also be seen in other branches of counseling work (see *Hansen, 1965*). Given this development, the muddled clamour for professional status visible in so many new areas of specialization will be allowed to develop on a more rational basis. Similarly, the development of new professions — perhaps including that of a psychotherapist who is neither psychiatrist, psychologist, nor social worker, as Schofield (*1964*) advocates — may be desirable.

There can be little question that the existing variety of counseling specializations has become defined as a necessity of our society. Every indication suggests that they will continue to grow in numbers, specializations, and importance. With increasing recognition of functional importance, the likelihood of claims to professional standing being met will be increased. But at the same time, it is also clear that the present stage of development of the counseling professions leaves many unsolved problems. The counselors have emerged from a variety of occupational contexts. While struggling with their yet to be articulated social roles and responsibilities, they have been encumbered with detracting lineages and precedents. Even when these roots are recognized as distracting, they are not easily disposable. Despite their occasionally excessive status-striving, the self-conscious attention of counselors to questions of their routes, roles, and goals has been largely generated by the critical stance of the social sciences which they share. The emulation of psychothera-peutic perspectives also common among counselors has further enhanced the degree of introspection. It is this aspect of their present situation which augurs well for future struggles and development.

References

American Association of Marriage Counselors (1964). *The State Regulation of Marriage Counselors,* Report of Conference held in New York (June 5–6).

Berger, Peter L. (1965). "Toward a Sociological Understanding of Psycho-analysis," *Social Research,* 32 (Spring), 26–41.

Binger, Carl (1964). "The Psychiatrist in the Looking Glass," *Harpers,* 228 (June), 62–67.

Borow, Henry (ed.) (1964). *Man in a World at Work,* Houghton Mifflin.

Brewer, J. M. (1942). *History of Vocational Guidance,* Harper & Brothers.

Bucher, Rue, and Anselm Strauss (1961). "Professions in Process," *AJS,* 66 (January), 325–334.

Cicourel, Aaron V., and John I. Kitsuse (1963). *The Educational Decision Makers,* Bobbs-Merrill.

Cohen, Nathan E. (1955). "Professional Social Work Faces the Future," *Social Work Journal,* XXXVI, 79–86.

Cumming, Elaine, Ian Cumming and Laura Edell (1965). "Policeman as Philosopher, Guide & Friend," *Social Problems,* 12 (Winter), 276–286.

Cumming, Elaine, and Charles Harrington (1963). "Clergyman as Counselor," *AJS,* 69 (November), 234–243.

Davis, James A. (1964). *Great Aspirations,* Aldine Publishing Company.

Dipboye, Wilbert J. (1959). "The Professional Self-Concept of the Counselor," in *New Frontiers in Guidance-Personnel Work,* M. E. Hilton (ed.), Syracuse University Press.

Eaton, Joseph W. (1956). "Whence and Whither Social Work? A Sociological Analysis," *Social Work,* 1 (January), 11–26.

Flexner, Abraham (1915). "Is Social Work a Profession?" *Proceedings of National Conference of Social Work 1915,* 576–590.

"Goals for Guidance" (1960). *(1960) White House Conference on Children and Youth,* U.S. Government Printing Office.

Grant, C. W. (1954). "The Counselor's Role," *Personnel and Guidance Journal* 33, 74–77.

Greenwood, Ernest (1957). "Attributes of a Profession," *Social Work* 2 (July), 45–55.

Hagstrom, Warren (1957). "The Protestant Clergy as a Profession: Status and Prospects," *Berkeley Publication in Society & Institution,* 3 (Spring), 54–69.

Halmos, Paul (1965). *The Faith of the Counsellors,* Constable & Company.

Hansen, Donald A. (1965). "Functions and Effects of 'Sub-professional' Personnel in Counseling," in *Counselor Development in American Society,* John McGowan (ed.), U.S. Government Printing Office.

Hitchcock, Arthur A. (1966). "Counselors: Supply, Demand, Need," in *Counselor Development in American Society,* John McGowan (ed.), U.S. Government Printing Office.

Hitchcock, W. L. (1953). "Counselors Feel They Should," *Personnel and Guidance Journal,* 32, 72–74.

Hollis, Ernest V., and Alice L. Taylor (1951). *Social Work Education in the U.S.,* Columbia University Press.

Hughes, Everett C. (1958). *Men and Their Work,* The Free Press.

Kadushin, Alfred (1958). "Prestige of Social Work—Facts and Factors," *Social Work,* 3 (April), 37–43.

——— (1959). "The Knowledge Base of Social Work," in *Issues in American Social Work,* Alfred J. Kahn (ed.), Columbia University Press.

Kerckhoff, Richard K. (1953). "The Profession of Marriage Counselor as Viewed by Members of Four Allied Professions: A Study in the Sociology of Occupations," *Marriage and Family Living,* XV (November), 340–344.

Kiev, Ari (ed.) (1964). *Magic, Faith and Healing,* The Free Press.

Leslie, Gerald R. (1964). "The Field of Marriage Counseling," in *Handbook of Marriage and the Family,* Harold Christensen (ed.), Rand-McNally.

Lief, Harold I. (1964). "What Your Doctor Probably Doesn't Know About Sex," *Harpers,* 229 (December), 92–96.

Menninger, Karl (1963). *The Vital Balance,* The Viking Press.

Meyer, Henry J. (1959). "Professionalization and Social Work," in *Issues in American Social Work,* Alfred J. Kahn (ed.), Columbia University Press.

Miller, Carroll H. (1964). "Vocational Guidance in the Perspective of Cultural Change," in *Man in a World of Work,* H. Borow (ed.), Houghton Mifflin.

Naegele, Kasper D. (1956). "Clergymen, Teachers, and Psychiatrists: A Study in Roles and Socialization," *Canadian Journal of Economics and Political Science,* 22, 46–62.

National Observer (1965). "The Psychiatrist and His Changing Mission," (January 11), 22.

N.Y. Times (1966). "Psychiatrists Are Told to Admit Others Can Help Mentally Ill" (May 10), 27.

Newsweek (1964). "Sex and the Doctors" (November 23), 101.

Parsons, Talcott (1954). "A Sociologist Looks at the Legal Profession," in his *Essays in Sociological Theory,* The Free Press.

Pins, Arnold M. (1963). *Who Chooses Social Work, When and Why,* Council on Social Work Education.

Rushing, William A. (1964). *The Psychiatric Professions,* University of North Carolina Press.

Sanders, Marion K. (1957). "Social Work: A Profession Chasing Its Tail," *Harpers,* 214 (March), 56–62.

Schofield, William (1964). *Psychotherapy: The Purchase of Friendship,* Prentice-Hall.

Smith, Harvey L. (1955). "Psychiatry: A Social Institution in Process," *Social Forces,* 33 (May), 310–316.

Stone, Abraham (1949). "Marriage Education and Marriage Counseling in the U.S.," *Marriage and Family Living,* XI (May), 38–40.

Strauss, Anselm, *et al.* (1964). *Psychiatric Ideologies and Institutions,* The Free Press.

Super, Donald E. (1964). "The Professional Status and Affiliations of Vocational Counselors," in *Man in a World of Work,* H. Borow (ed.), Houghton Mifflin.

U.S. Dept. of Labor (1961). *Occupational Outlook Handbook,* Bureau of Labor Statistics.

U.S. Dept. of H.E.W. (1965). *Closing the Gap in Social Work Manpower* (November).

Vincent, Clark E. (1957). *Readings in Marriage Counseling,* Thomas Y. Crowell.

Waller, Willard (1932). *The Sociology of Teaching,* John Wiley.

Wilensky, Harold L., and Charles N. Lebeaux (1958). *Industrial Society and Social Welfare,* Russell Sage Foundation.

Wilensky, Jeanne L., and Harold L. Wilensky (1951). "Personnel Counseling: The Hawthorne Case," *American Journal of Sociology,* 57 (November), 265–280.

Wrenn, C. Gilbert (1962). *The Counselor in a Changing World,* American Personnel and Guidance Association, Commission on Guidance in American Schools.

Zander, Alvin, *et al.* (1957). *Role Relations in the Mental Health Professions,* Institute for Social Research.

Zinberg, Norman E. (1963). "Psychiatry: A Professional Dilemma," *Daedalus,* 92 (Fall), 808–823.

PART ONE

Motivation, Language and Expectancy:

Some Perspectives on the Individual

To be adequate, a sociological perspective on counseling and therapy must bring into focus a diversity of subjects, including some of those traditionally considered "psychological." As yet, however, sociology is not fully prepared to offer such perspective; indeed, one of the major benefits of increased attentions to counseling and therapy might be the expansion of traditional sociological foci on societal, group and interpersonal phenomena to more fully include the intrapersonal.

Motivation and "Interpenetrant Reality"

Sociological theory, no less than theories of counseling and therapy, today requires attention to intraindividual development and processes as psychosocial forms; "man alone," in all of his uniqueness and for all of his integumentations, is but one part of interpenetrant human reality. In basic form, statements such as this have become clichés in sociology. It is generally accepted that, as the individual's capacities for cognitive awareness emerge, they are increasingly structured by his experiences, which, however unique, are in overwhelming part interpersonal and social. In this process the individual alters and continues the experiences, restructuring them in socially relevant fashion as he fits them into arrangements of symbolic representations. These representations, which are shared with other human beings, enable the person to recognize himself not only as a member of a group or society, but also as a distinct being; they in some way permit him to release and regrasp experiences and hence to mold his own world and self; they link him to others in intricate and often tacitly assumed arrays of expectations that constrain, impel and lure him toward or from some possible acts, some styles of life and self-presentation, rather than others.

Arguments such as this, which emphasize the importance of social influences on "personality," "self" and "motivation," often picture an individual who, however closely interlinked to others, engages in behavior that to him is "meaningful," "goal directed" or in some way "situationally appropriate." These theories, popularly endorsed by sociologists, remain in large part unelaborated, in the basic forms suggested decades ago by Weber, Dewey, Thomas and Mead. The endurance of these forms may not be entirely due to their fundamental validity; rather, it may be due in large part to the general indifference of sociologists to those questions of motivation not immediately and clearly related to the study of interpersonal cohesion, change and dynamics. Sociologists, that is, with concern for the institutional, organizational and interpersonal, have themselves failed to carefully attend to the sociological importance of the intrapersonal. In recent years, however, interest appears to have increased, as some few efforts to cope with the intra-individual as a sociological–psychological phenomena have appeared.

The first two of the three chapters of this section are concerned with the general neglect of the social character of the intraindividual. In Chapter 1 Zollschan and Hansen attempt to develop foundations for a sociological theory of motivation that not only will afford the capability of attending to intrapersonal dynamics and to individual differences in motivation, but also will offer an adequate base for a sociological theory of social structure, cohesion and change. Zollschan and Hansen suggest that goal-directedness is the distinguishing quality of "meaningful" action, as distinct from the "merely reactive" behavior that is implicit in most theories in both psychology and sociology. In the discussion, Freudian themes blend with the basic theories of Weber and Mead, and a picture begins to emerge of the individual as capable to some degree of volition, of establishing and moving toward socially relevant goals and, in so doing, of participating in, responding to and influencing social forms and processes. Intrapersonal motivation, then, is here presented as social phenomena; human activity is identified as more than a simple stream of reactions to biological, psychological and social pressures, needs and drives. It is also — at least at some times in some situations — meaningful, striving, the subject of actual choice. Thus, the

26

intrapersonal is interlinked with the interpersonal and institutional.

If the intraindividual is, indeed, so closely a function of social experiences and relationships, and of socially relevant phenomenal representations, it can readily be argued that social patterns may be related to the character of intraindividual development. Of the many inquiries suggested by this statement, one of the more central might seek to identify the relation of symbolic representations to social and sociological patterns.

Language, Expectation and Social Forms

Once again, precedents in theory and research for such an inquiry have begun to appear only recently. In the long history of linguistic inquiry sociological variables have played but small parts; linguists have conscientiously studied structural properties of language, seeking uniformities to aid in linguistic description. More recently, they have begun to turn their linguistic theories to the study of society, but in the main the exercise is distinctly different from that required either for sociological theory or for the understanding of relations in counseling and psychotherapy. Most simply, the problem is that in their search for descriptive properties of language, linguists have continued to emphasize uniformities, seeking universals, in essence separating linguistic forms from the varieties of social contexts in which they might appear. Not all linguistic theory is of this sort, yet even recently one of the most prominent of theorists has suggested that:

> Linguistic theory is concerned primarily with an ideal speaker-listener, in a completely homogenous speech-community, who knows its language perfectly, and is unaffected by such grammatically irrelevant conditions as memory limitations, distractions, shifts of attention and interest, and errors (random or characteristic) in applying his knowledge of the language in actual performance. This seems to me to have been the position of the founders of modern general linguistics, and no cogent reason for modifying it has been offered. (*Chomsky, 1965,* pp. 3–4.)

Trends both more compatible with sociological perspectives and more appropriate to the study of counseling and therapy are apparent in some recent works, however, representing a convergence of interest in linguistic structures with interest in the variable functions of social forms. Most significantly, in these works emphasis is on functions of language structures, which are seen as inextricable from social contexts. Close attention to variation and diversity is, thereby, required; varieties of speech and coding procedures, traditionally postulated or assumed to be peripheral in the search for uniform structures, are now being accepted as problematic and the proper subjects for investigation. (See, for example, *Hymes, 1962; Bernstein, 1965; Cicourel,* forthcoming.)

The work of Basil Bernstein, in present form, is especially receptive to a discussion of counseling and therapy. In Chapter 2, his discussions of linguistic codes and their relation to certain social capacities and contexts are summarized and discussed. The discussion turns on the concepts of elaborated and restricted language codes which the individual might use to organize his speech. Every mature adult possesses some range of speech codes and may alternate between them; indeed, the ability to switch codes controls the ability to switch roles. That is to say, as experience is transformed into linguistically relevant forms, intellectual, evaluative and emotional organization is elaborated and altered; new possibilities of individual choice emerge and others may be rendered unavailable. Thus, despite similar potentials, children reared in different social structures develop different social and intellectual procedures, and differing capacities for linguistic coding.

The implications of these differences for counseling and therapy are profound. Not only do they suggest socially relevant differences in perception and even in the form of "identity"; they also suggest that counseling and therapy relationships can by their very nature virtually assure failure with some clients, as they require kinds of coding capacities that may not be available to all persons. This in itself is interesting sociologically, but Bernstein's theories also suggest questions fundamental to the most basic of concerns about social structures and process, and about intraindividual development and functioning. Some few of these are speculated on in Chapter 2, suggesting the potential developments of this line of sociolinguistic inquiry.

The concept of "expectation" is more central in traditional sociological inquiry; indeed, it is one of the basic building blocks of much sociological theory, identifying elemental links between interacting persons, basic qualities of social cohesion and on-going order, and suggesting the fundamental dynamics of the processes of forming social identity. In Chapter 3, Gallimore and Turner, writing as psychologists, relate this familiar sociological concept to "faith" and "placebo effects" in psychotherapy. Their discussion is immediately suggestive for theories and practices of counseling and psychotherapy, but sociologists may also find the discussion illustrative, as a specification of a pervasive social theory.

Overall, then, in these three essays may be found suggestions for a few of the many possible lines of development relevant to counseling and therapy that might emerge as the sociological perspective is focused on the intraindividual.

References

Bernstein, Basil (1965). "A Socio-linguistic Approach to Social Learning," in *Social Science Survey,* J. Gould (ed.), Pelican.

Chomsky, Noam (1965). *Aspects of the Theory of Syntax,* M.I.T. Press.

Cicourel, Aaron V. (forthcoming). "The Acquisition of Social Structure: Towards a Development Sociology of Language and Meaning," in *Contributions in Ethnomethodology*, H. Garfinkle and H. Sacks (ed.), Indiana University Press.

Hymes, Dell (1966). "Anthropological Linguistics and Congeners," *American Anthropoligist*, 68, 143–153.

1 | ON MOTIVATION:

Toward Socially Pertinent Foundations

George K. Zollschan
Donald A. Hansen / University of California, Berkeley

Questions about the causes of human action have so long exercised man's imagination that their origins are lost in antiquity. Answers also are long in ancestry. When we tacitly assume that acts obey some still unknown "laws" of motion similar to laws of physics, for example, we echo Hume's suggestion of over two centuries ago that "the conjunction between motives and voluntary action is as uniform as that between cause and effect in any part of nature" (*1955*, p. 98).

Hume's list of "passions" — "ambition, avarice, self-love, vanity, friendship, generosity, public spirit" (*1955*, pp. 92–93) — was but one in a continuing history of attempts to traverse the long roads toward understanding man's actions. Today those roads are strewn with skeletons of exhausted arguments, testifying to the difficulty of the quest and offering tribute to its intrigue. Few paths have carried such heavy intellectual traffic.

In recent decades — years in which counseling and psychotherapy have emerged as distinct practices — the quest for an adequate theory of motivation has been continued primarily by psychologists and psychiatric theorists, with some contributions from the ranks of sociology and anthropology. Disparate strains of theory have developed and, with varying energy, vied for attention. But, it will be argued in this essay, none of the strains most active and popular today offers a unified and adequate

Revision of part of Office of Education Report S — 148: Donald A. Hansen and George K. Zollschan, "A Sociological Framework for the Study of Education: The Case of Motivation," mimeographed, Summer 1964. The authors are grateful to Walter Buckley and Thomas J. Scheff for comments on an earlier version of this essay.

base for understanding the processes of counseling and psychotherapy. For, whatever their individual strengths and inadequacies, theories of human behavior share this general problem: None is capable of treating a full range of individual human experience and at the same time accounting for the involvement of individuals in cultural patterns of shared meanings and values and in social intercourse with others.

It is the intent of this chapter to comment on these general inadequacies, concentrating mainly on theories of motivation associated with a number of sociological viewpoints, and to offer suggestions for the development of a theoretical orientation more adequate for the understanding of motivation in all its aspects — biological, psychological, and social.

Inadequacies of Current Perspectives

In general, counseling and psychotherapy require the ability to identify the social relevance of a client's actions; they require an ability to recognize his capacities for change and to identify those possible changes which might be most "psychotherapeutic"; and they require an ability to relate these changes to the social contexts in which the individual lives, has lived, and is likely to live in the future. These are sweeping requirements, and all turn on the nature of the human predicament in a very broad sense of the term. Counselors and psychotherapists, that is, need a perspective which fosters (or, at least, allows) understanding of individual life in its intimate linkages with community structures and with changes in these social structures.

In practice, such perspective is available in common-sense knowledge and understanding. Such common-sense perspectives undoubtedly have served well in counseling and psychotherapy, as they have in jurisprudence, in legislation, in social work, and in diverse other practices concerned with the understanding and regulation of human behavior. But common-sense knowledge is notoriously defective; common-sense wisdom is closely tied to norms and expectations extant at a particular time and, in the face of rapid social change, quickly grows vague and inappropriate. Though counseling and psychotherapy, as any human arts, necessarily involve the exercise of common-sense, if today's practices are to improve, common-sense and its allies — empathy and intuition — must be supplemented by more powerful and sensitive orientations toward motivational phenomena.

In turn, "applied" theories of counseling and psychotherapy require more sensitive and powerful "pure" theories of man in society. In seeking to escape the limitations of common-sense, counselors and psychotherapists have embraced various psychological theories of human behavior, such as Freudian theories, Learning theories, Existential theories, and others related and unrelated to these general types. But even these theories require of the practitioner large exercises of common-sense. None has offered the sweep of perspective required in actual practice. Some, including those as disparate as behaviorist learning theories and psychoanalytic theories, have developed special sensitivities to intrapersonal development and dynamics. Through these perspectives intraindividual variables are viewed as dependent variables while interpersonal and community relations assume secondary importance as peripheral factors. The psychotherapist who bases his practices only on such theoretical foundations is forced to rely heavily on common-sense when dealing with his client's social realities.

Other theories, conversely, especially those developed by sociologists and anthropologists, have developed suggestive sensitivities to interpersonal relations, to group processes and to community and societal structures. Of these, the social-behavior theories of George Herbert Mead and his followers are especially promising. But Meadian theories — like others based on sociological, as distinct from individualistic perspectives — pay too little attention to intrapersonal dynamics and to individual differences in motivation. Attending closely to the "motivating" influences of interpersonal, cultural, and societal relationships, and to the relation of these to phenomenal constructs (such as "identification" and "self") these theorists give only passing attention to linkages with the levels of behavior approached in psychological and biological research. Again, the counselor who limits himself to such theoretical bases must rely heavily on common-sense.

It is possible, of course, for a contemporary counselor or psychotherapist to embrace theories of both types. Intuitively he might recognize, for example, that there is no basic incompatibility between symbolic interactionist (Meadian) theories and behavioral learning theories. In his practice, the therapist might alternate with some facility between the two types of theory. But in his alternations — however successful his practice might be — the therapist is jumping troublesome gaps between the theories. Though common-sense bridges over such gaps have to suffice for today's practitioner, they are both theoretically and practically inadequate for the attempted task. In the nature of their work therapists and counselors — to use Sorokin's vigorous words — cannot view "the total personality . . . as a dumping field of congeries of psychological odds and ends" (*Sorokin, 1966,* p. 150). Instead, they require an orientation which can help them to integrate the variety of human experience and of motivational manifestations.

With respect to such an integrated view of human motivation, current theories evidence critical deficiencies which thwart understanding of both social and individual change, and hence of counseling and therapy. The sweep of individual human experience has yet to be confronted. Allport

(1960, pp. 304–305) imaginatively discussed this general deficiency by appealing to Hindu wisdom:

> Most men, the Hindus say, have four central desires. To some extent, though only roughly, they correspond to the developmental stages of life. The first desire is for pleasure — a condition fully and extensively recognized in our Western theories of tension reduction, reinforcement, libido, and needs. The second desire is for success — likewise fully recognized and studied in our investigation of power, status, leadership, masculinity, and need-achievement. Now the third desire is to do one's duty and to discharge one's responsibilities . . . Here our Western work begins to fade out. Excepting for some pale investigations of parental punishment, in relation to the development of childhood conscience, we have little to offer on the "duty" motive . . . Finally, the Hindus tell us that in many people all of these three motives pall, and they then seek intensely for greater understanding — for a philosophical or religious meaning — that will liberate them from pleasure, success, and duty.

It can well be claimed that this "wisdom" also falls far short of the goal of adequate explanation of motivation. Yet the illustration is valid: much individual action and development are neglected in contemporary theories of motivation, and these deficiencies are compounded when societal phenomena are considered. Even a superficial consideration of sociology would reveal basic questions far beyond the scope of current theories of motivation, such as:

1. What is the relation of individual motivation and action to social order; how does the observable capacity of the individual for social participation develop? How does order develop among the collectivity?

2. What is the relation of individual motivation to social restraint? How does the observable capacity of the individual for collectivity-orientation, rather than the self-orientation, develop? How does social control develop among the collectivity?

3. What is the relation of individual motivation to social change, to institutionalization and cultural innovation? How does the observable capacity of the individual for innovation, and especially for controlled innovation develop? How and why do modification of collective patterns of behavior and relationships occur?

In short, counseling and psychotherapy require a theory of motivation in which knowledge, evaluation, and action are related in usch a way as to account for even self-transcendence and self-negation, and in which this process in one person relates to those in others in such a way that the dynamic stability of a community can result.

Not too surprisingly, perhaps, the need for such a theory of motivation has also made itself felt in the discipline of sociology — particularly where concern is with problems of social change. In a continuing effort, Zollschan and his colleagues (Zollschan, 1964; Zollschan and Gibeau, 1964; Zollschan and Perrucci, 1964) have moved in the direction of such a theory; attempting to develop constructs capable of explaining social change and institutionalization in a manner sensitive to the structuring power of social environments, yet allowing for the possibility of individual autonomy and innovation. Although initially an unintended by-product of a broader theoretical framework — developed to explain the formation of stable and recurring patterns of personal and interpersonal action, their maintenance, and their dissolution — we feel that our orientation to the problem of motivation deserves elaboration in its own right.[1]

Prior to presenting our statement of this orientation (and, in the nature of the case, it is a tentative, initial statement at present) we shall identify some especially troublesome problems in contemporary theories of motivation. For reasons to be discussed below we shall concentrate on sociological orientations toward the problem of motivation, confining our consideration of psychological theories to a few very brief remarks.

The Hiatus Between Action and Behavior

Our view — favoring an integrated orientation to the explanation of motivational phenomena in such a way that a picture emerges of individuals capable of striving and innovating, just as they are capable of vegetating and simple responsiveness — is contrary to the perspectives of some modern critics of motivation theory. If the expression "motivation" means different things to different theorists, such critics maintain, the differences are rooted not simply in divergent perspectives on the same problem. The term itself, they suggest, conjures up quite different kinds problems for investigators starting out from distinct theoretical bases. The English philosophical analyst R. S. Peters, for example, distinguishes three types of explanation involving motivation, each springing, he believes, from a different sort of question which may be asked about human behavior (*Peters, 1960,* pp. 3–11). He calls them "His Reason" explanations, "The Reason" explanations, and "Causal" explanations. The first two types of explanations are distinguished only by their source; the first being a subjective account of the purpose of an action presented by the actor himself, while the second would be a possibly different account presented by an observer. Both involve what Peters calls the "purposive rule-following" model of action. The third type of explanation is used

---

1 Though we see the theory of motivation as part of a larger effort to develop a theory of institutionalization, the reader might prefer to view it as suggestive for other purposes. System theorists, in particular, may see in the construct possibilities for explaining *why* the system works. We would encourage such explanatory efforts, for systems theory is a useful tool which can supplement other theories of many types. (*See Hansen and Hill, 1964,* pp. 787–792; *Buckley, 1967,* especially Chapter 6.)

when a kind of behavior appears to "happen to a man" rather than being determined by him. The last type of explanation is used — in Peters' view — when there is a deviation from the rule-following model with respect to an efficiency norm or norms of appropriateness and legitimacy.

There is nothing particularly new or original in these distinctions (as will become abundantly clear in our discussion below of various socio-logical approaches to motivation) except that Peters proceeds to claim that they demonstrate that an integrated theory of motivation is *logically* (!) impossible. He then proclaims in great glee that "the role of the Galileo of psychology must be forever unoccupied" (p. 156).[2] We do not intend to enter into competition with Peters in the role of prophets whose purpose is to foresee the advent (or failure to appear) of future Galileos in fields concerned with the explanation of human be-havior. Instead, we see what may be called the "hiatus between action and behavior" as a bothersome obstacle to integrated conceptions of psychotherapy and counseling; it is not an original and conclusive dis-covery of linguistic philosophy requiring the abandonment of attempts to establish integrated conceptions.

Consider the most elementary of models, the now outdated Stimulus-Response (S-R), which posited some sort of "hollow men, filled with straw" or perhaps not filled at all. Such an image is a luxury to be enjoyed only for limited purposes. Eliot used it, fleetingly, as a poetic metaphor of the moral poverty of a generation; in the research laboratory it has served effectively to simplify descriptive relations between stimuli and behavior. To anyone interested in human action in society, how-ever, it fails as a model of man, representing him akin to a robot, as an empty, though mobile stage for the reflexive interplay of stimulus and response.[3] As implied above, this "empty organism" approach has gen-

---

2 It would be curious to speculate about how Galileo himself might have fared at the hands of linguistic philosophers. Might not the idea of "frictionless inclines," for instance, have been dismissed by them as a "misuse of language," much as some of them dismiss motivational concepts such as "unconscious purpose"?

3 Most research advances in the area have been made with the help of this "Reflex Model" until recently. Indeed, so much of an article of faith did this model — originally developed by physiologists — become that Miller, Galanter and Pribram (*1960*, p. 22) recently were moved to write: "You might as well deny the small intestine or the medulla oblongata as to doubt the reflex arc." These critics have the temerity to proceed to do precisely that, and replace a cybernetic concept — the feedback loop or test-operate-test-exit (TOTE) unit — for the reflex arc. Their criticism of traditional motivational concepts in experimental psychology is all the more persuasive for emanating from the same general intellectual tradition as the one in which the concepts they are criticizing were bred. A part of their lengthy quotation of Noam Chomsky's critical review of a book which uncompromisingly upholds a version of the old behaviorist view is worth reproducing:

The notions of "stimulus," "response," "reinforcement" are relatively well defined with respect to the bar-pressing experiments and others similarly restricted. Before

erally been replaced by various research conceptions of man as an intricate complex of afferent and efferent nerves and assemblies through which organismic connections are made between stimulus and response. Such mechanico-chemical models, no matter how complex and no matter what their promise, also miss many of the essentials of human social life. They do, however, emphasize one of the most urgent questions in contemporary theories of human behavior: How does the *connection* take place between afferent impulse and efferent impulse or, to use a mechanistic metaphor, how is the gap bridged between input and output?

This question can be asked on other than the neurological level; on the cognitive level it has led some investigators in both psychology and sociology to consider the importance of *meaning* in human behavior. Such perspectives have moved towards a motivation theory adequate to either the counselor's needs, or to a full study of society or individual behavior. As yet, however, they have not moved far enough. Cognitive theories of behavior bridge the input-output gap only half-way, for at a crucial point they accept, however unintentionally, the assumption that action automatically follows cognition. It is one thing, however, to say that a man recognizes the action potentials of a situation and even that he decides a certain action is called for; it is quite another thing to explain why he then acts — if, indeed, he does. To know is not necessarily to do; something else is required to complete a bridge over the gap. Without a bridge, we have little hope of developing an adequate theory of motivation, of more adequately identifying the nature of the relation of man to society, or indeed of establishing causal connections between social phenomena.

Nor is it enough to bridge that gap. Indeed, the bridging constructs which we suggest in the latter part of this essay actually derive from a tentative resolution of another problem in current motivational theory, a problem which involves age-old ontological differences in conceptions of human and social reality. The differences, readily apparent in current social and psychological theories, turn on the question: Are all human actions and thoughts necessarily determined by conditions (including physical states) in some sense extraneous to the personality of the actor? That is, what is the role of the "subjective" in determining behavior?

---

we can extend them to real-life behavior, however, certain difficulties must be faced. We must decide, first of all, whether any physical event to which the organism is capable of reacting is to be called a stimulus on a given occasion, or only one to which the organism in fact reacts; and correspondingly, we must decide whether any part of behavior is to be called a response, or only one connected with stimuli in lawful ways. Questions of this sort pose something of a dilemma for the experimental psychologist. If he accepts the broad definitions, characterizing any physical event impinging on the organism as a stimulus and any part of the organism's behavior as a response, he must conclude that behavior has not been demonstrated to be lawful (*Chomsky, 1959*, p. 30).

Indeed, on this very question rests the hiatus between the laboratory theories of motivation and those required by the psychotherapist and the social theorist — the hiatus between behavior and action. Is man such a being that his activity is determined solely by "forces" or causes external to man's subjectivity, and beyond his control? Or is man capable of purposive action, of actually choosing and seeking goals at least in some part independently? Is he, in other words, merely a reactor or is he also capable of pro-action?[4] This distinction will be discussed further below — for now it is adequate to be aware of the question and the terms: behavior refers to "the merely reactive," action refers to the purposive or meaningful. (In the following discussion we use the term "activity" generally; "behavior" and "action," then, are both sub-types of "acting.")

The sociologist, at any rate, assumes that purposive action rather than reflex or reactive behavior is the content of the drama whose explanation is his concern. He sees the social actor as a highly selective sieve of raw stimuli occurring in the environment. More often than not, the social actor transforms such stimuli into symbolic representations before taking some kind of action, and the symbolic representations seem to follow laws of their own. What is more, the social actor lives in an elaborate secondary environment itself largely constituted of such symbols — symbols which assume the characteristics of "stimuli" in the sense, at least, that they elicit behavioral responses. Thus, quite beyond the question of how acceptable it is to speak of stimuli and responses at all in explaining organismic behavior, social action appears to require explanation by concepts such as *meaning* and *rationale*.[5]

---

[4] To some readers, this point may be expressed through a distinction proposed by the poet W. H. Auden, and discussed by Erick Erikson (*1964*, p. 162) — that between "deeds" and "behavior": a deed is an action that in some sense "makes a difference" as against the stereotypically enacted "behavior." The difference which is made, however, is subjective — if the individual is actively involved in *choice*, the subsequent action in meaningful — i.e., is a deed, indeed. Some deeds, then are to the objective observer irrational; similarly some behavior which is subjectively void of meaning might appear meaningful.

[5] Perhaps a few words are necessary to elaborate and refine the intuitive sense conveyed by the terms "meaning" and "rationale." In its cognitive usage, the term "meaning" suggests denotation or connotation; some sort of linkage, in other words, between an expression and what is expressed by it. An expression which has no meaning would be a totally random one — "signifying nothing" as it were. In much the same way, the connotative or "action" usage of "meaning" is also concerned with a linkage, one between means and ends. An act becomes meaningful when it is not random or aimless but directed towards ends. Meaning, therefore, is a relationship between an expression and its *denotanium*, or between an action and its *agendum* (if we may be allowed to coin a word) or what is to be achieved by it. More generally it may be interpreted as any relationship between means and ends. The relationship between an act or a description and what it is to achieve or describe suggests *directed purpose*. The concept, therefore, is both subjective or phenomenological and goal-directed.

Weber introduced the concept of "meaning" in connection with a particular meth-

The sociologist Max Weber, who is responsible for introducing the expression "meaning" into sociology as a motivational concept (*1947,* pp. 86 f.), expressed his analysis of it in the form of a typology including two types of rational action (*Zweckrational* and *Wertrational*), traditional action, and affective action. All of these Weber contrasted with "merely reactive behavior," though Weber felt that the latter two types bordered on the line between meaningful action and reactive behavior.

Weber's typology is of considerable interest for sociological analysis, but need not concern us here in any detail. For our purposes in this discussion, the importance of Max Weber's contribution lies in his emphasis on action as rational or meaningful when ends are attained by the employment of more or less appropriate means — for the real issue of rationality has to do with the achievability of ends and the existence of real alternatives, independently of whether or not emotion ("affect") or custom ("tradition") are involved. Meaningful action implies the possibility of *directed purpose,* and this is what lends the concept importance for motivation theory.

We may add that not all meaningful goals are achievable — some are, and are destined to remain, in the realm of phantasy. What is more, man often is placed in a position in which he reacts to "external" demands — of his community, other men, or even his own body — even while he tells himself that he is acting to achieve his own ends. Is such action irrational? Clearly not, yet neither is it simply reactive. To denote such action, in which the individual's goals may be unachievable because of competing or conflicting goals of higher priority or are by nature unachievable, Zollschan and Gibeau (*1964,* pp. 159–160; 163–167) employed the term *rationale.* This term refers to action not technically rational — that is, not directed toward achievable ends — but which is nevertheless meaningful to the actor and relevant in explaining his motives.

Given the illuminating start made by Max Weber toward developing concepts capable of satisfying at least some of the requirements we have set for an adequate theory of motivation, it seems appropriate to devote some time to an examination of how sociologists have handled problems of motivation. Such an examination becomes the more appropriate when it is considered that a psychiatrist, Thomas S. Szasz, has proclaimed that psychiatrists, viewed as theorists, are indistinguishable from sociologists. Szasz (*1961,* p. 292) is greatly influenced by the work of R. S. Peters to which we have referred above, particularly by the idea of the rule-

---

odological approach to the social sciences — that of *verstehen.* The methodological issue of explanation by intuitive understanding (verstehen) versus explanation by descriptive conceptualization (*begreifen*) has been largely left behind in current discussion. The concept itself, however, independently of the reason for its introduction, has been retained in sociology as a criterion of demarcation between social action and reactive behavior.

following model of behavior which he, like Peters, recognizes as being essentially a sociological model.

The Neglect of Motivation in the Analysis of Social Action

In discussing the hiatus between action and behavior we have suggested that meaningful action as much as reactive behavior must be explicable in terms of a theory of motivation adequate for the needs of counselors and psychotherapists. Our examination of the treatment of motivation in some major sociological theories, however, will reveal serious neglect by sociologists. In attempting to explain this neglect, the following distinction by Martindale (*1965*, pp. 150–151) of two ways in which social reality is conceptualized will be of aid. Martindale distinguishes between what he calls "holist" and "elementist" (or individualistic) approaches to the nature of social reality. A holist view, he suggests:

> . . . is the view that the basic social reality consists of inter-related wholes which are superior to the individual and his acts. One may, to be sure, analyze the place of the individual and his actions in the whole, but one cannot reduce the whole to the actions of the individual. Such wholes must be explained in their own terms. One cannot, of course, have a whole without parts, but the whole is prior to the parts in the sense that its operations are irreducible to these parts and their properties.

An elementist view, by contrast:

> . . . is the view that the basic social reality is constituted by individuals and their acts. Social events consist solely in their interaction. Any notion that interaction possesses new or emergent properties such that some sort of whole with irreducible properties of its own arises is a pure product of reification. In most charitable construction, it is a distorted estimation of the mutual modification of behavior that occurs in the course of the interaction of a plurality of individuals.

Thus, discussion of current theories of motivation involves two critical polarities, reflected in these questions:

1. Is all human behavior simply reactive, or is it possible that subjective goals can determine or influence action?
2. What is the basic social reality, the real social context in which action takes place?

This essay is hardly the place to become entangled in these exhausting distinctions, yet it is useful to recognize that differing stances on these basic problems, which lurk just beneath the surface of current motivation theories, find roots deep in the tradition of Western thought.[6]

6 The emphasis in experimental psychology on the "merely reactive," for example, can be traced to nineteenth century mechanistic metaphysics. In this ideology, ob-

The distinctions, however, should emphasize our point that the weakness of behaviorist learning theory has been its bias in favor of reactive behavior. The neglect of motivation in sociology, we shall see, is attributable to the holistic bias harbored by most sociologists.

1

Even in ideal (and rather gross) type, holistic theory has certain utility and immediate appeal, tending toward teleological conceptions in which individual behavior is determined by the whole — the individual is "driven" (as in Freudian theories) by his organism, or required to act by his personality system or a societal system or its subsystems. Sociological functionalists are aware of the problems such commitments could entail, and, goaded on by their critics, have attempted to avoid them — indeed, it might be said that the functionalist school in sociology has established a main theme in the skirting of motivational issues (cf. *Buckley, 1967*).

The accounts of sociological functionalism between Horace Kallen's (*1931*) and Kingsley Davis' (*1959*) have been varied and confusing, yielding little by way of a consistent definition of functionalism as a distinct orientation. At least one common theme may be detected, however: an emphasis on the *consequences* rather than *causes* of action. Action, within this general orientation, is either in conformity with, or deviant from, cultural norms, or standards and role expectations. Thus it becomes possible to circumscribe the complex issues presented by the problem of motivation through the use of two rather simple questions. The

---

jectivity was a supreme goal, and was interpreted in such a way as to exclude all subjective states. Further, teleology of any kind was considered quite inadmissible as a scientific principle: All behavior had to be explained by reference to antecedent causes (stimuli). Purposive action was excoriated as a kind of teleological fiction. In some respects this view was reminiscent of the Cartesian conception of the motion of physical bodies occurring by *push*, which had held dogmatic supremacy in physics a century earlier — so much so, in fact, that Newton had exhibited a certain amount of embarrassment in introducing the conception of attraction or "pull," and particularly of "action at a distance" (see *Popper, 1962*, pp. 196–197).

Similar ideologies helped shape theories in both anthropology and sociology, although in dealing with order in social and historical change, it more quickly proved difficult to sidestep *both* subjectivism and teleological assumption. Even the theories of the earliest of sociologists developed an organismic teleology (that is, again to be simplistic, they implied or assumed that the "social organism" determined the actions of its component parts — i.e., that society is the prior determinant of individual behavior).

Reaction developed to the early ontological commitments. In psychology, cognitive behaviorists such as Tolman developed objective schemes of subjective variables, which did not much disturb the commitment to either elementism or mechanistic determination of behavior. Gestaltists, however, offered holistic and subjective alternatives, and other phenomenologists (especially the existentialists) offered strikingly different conceptions of subjective determinants. In sociology, Max Weber early introduced "meaning" as a motivational concept (*1947*, pp. 86 f.), emphasizing both the subjective and elementistic; similar conceptions were developed by W. I. Thomas and George Herbert Mead.

first is, "Why do people conform?" and the rather uncritical standard answer is, "because of socialization and the operation of social sanction." The second question, "Why do some people deviate?" is less easily circumvented. The simplest answer, which merely requires some variant of the assumption that the socialization of deviants was inadequate or inappropriate, failed in some respects to carry explanatory conviction. A somewhat more complicated answer was provided by Merton (*1957*, esp. 131–160), who saw disjunctions between institutional means and cultural goals as the cause of deviant conduct. In his view, it is the social structure itself that exerts pressures upon individuals engaged in deviant conduct. Motives, whether to conformity or to deviation, are thus provided by cultural prescriptions and societal structures.

Quite apart from the impoverishment of sociological theory that occurs when it is limited to categories of conformity and deviance, such a limitation of theoretical perspective also begs the question regarding the sources of motivation in socialization. Motives, in this view, appear not to come from the individual but from some abstracted "social order." Merton refers at the beginning of the same paper to a tendency for previous theorists (the ones, we may assume, that antedate modern functionalism) to set biological impulses against the society which is seen as ". . . essentially an apparatus for the management of impulses, for the social processing of tensions . . ." (p 131). Instead, Merton sees society in itself as the very source of human impulse. The culture gives man the goals for which he strives, the social structure provides the normative means for their achievement. Where the normative means do not lead unproblematically to cultural goals, deviance occurs. In other words, there are no satisfactions besides those upheld by the society.[7]

Whether a person (acting within culture, to be sure, or at least within the overlap of several cultures) develops goals and strives toward them is not Merton's question. Merton contends, instead, that the goals or values are given — lodged in the culture itself — and assimilated, perhaps at different rates by various members of the society (though he stresses that these rates themselves are socially patterned — see *1959*, p. 178). The argument is brilliant and useful, and deserves the attention it has received from other sociologists. On the problem of motivation, it offers little, however, for it avoids the basic questions as it divorces motives from actions and locates them instead in some "socio-cultural system."

It should not be thought that such deficiencies are to be found only in

---

[7] Analysis of social structures in relation to conformity and deviance presumes a prior knowledge of limited and specifiable sets of norms, expectations, and values which are postulated to exist in the society. This presupposes not only a very high degree of consensus regarding such norms, but also a high degree of normative stability over time. An exclusive perspective of conformity and deviance, thus, is necessarily ahistorical.

functional or other holistic theories, for the constructs of Gerth and Mills are basically similar in argument, though they are markedly elementist.

2

Gerth and Mills (*1953*) handle the hiatus between behaviorist and actionist perspectives on motivation by distinguishing levels, each of which is governed by its own laws. The levels are those of the *organism,* the *psyche,* and the *person.* In their view each level is characterized by a different equilibrium; that for the organism being "health," that for the psyche being "pleasure," while personal equilibrium consists of a "balance of self-image with the appraisals of others" (p. 112).

Motives on the level of meaning are determined by the direction of action, and are not seen as reservoirs of energy. Rather than being "springs of action" they are "terms which persons typically use in their interpersonal relations." This may sound suspiciously like the substitution of what Freud calls "rationalizations" for motives proper; and the sound is not altogether deceptive. What Gerth and Mills suggest in fact, is that motives on the level of the person are nothing more than ". . . social justifications for one's own conduct and . . . a means of persuading others to accept and further one's own conduct" (p. 129).

It cannot be denied that the desires to manipulate and to be accepted by others act as determinants of the direction of action for many persons — even if for no other reason than the fact that interpersonal cooperation is often required for reaching personal goals. Acceptability to others may even be a goal in its own right for some persons in certain cultures (it is a prominent goal for many persons in America, for example). Yet it surely cannot be denied that there are some persons who are not particularly concerned with the use of terminologies of motives for their effect on their fellows. One wonders whether in the view of Gerth and Mills such persons would have to be considered totally unmotivated on the personal-social level.

The reduction of social motivation to the adoption of certain prevalent vocabularies — to linguistic conventions — fails to convey a sense of striving. Even if one accepts motivation as a directional principle solely on the social-personal level, and even if one accepts the argument that language capabilities are related in some ways to role performances, one is bound to wonder whether *all* of a person's actions can change direction as readily as one vocabulary can be discarded in favor of another one.

Finally, since the "springs of action" are, presumably, to be found in the organic or psychic levels, one would be inclined to look for mechanisms of energy transmission from one level to another. One looks in vain for anything like an adequate discussion of such mechanisms in *Character and Social Structure.* It would seem that the design of their argument corresponds to the analysis they present: it seems to make an intellectual hiatus with which they were stuck acceptable to the scholarly community.

3

It is difficult to characterize the many-tentacled motivation theory impacted in the convolutions of Talcott Parsons' general system. To many persons, it is a functional theory, *par excellence* — but closer examination suggests that such a categorization ignores the *potentials* of the theory (as are hinted at in the work of Olds). Parsons' theory holds that motivation is intimately bound with the characteristics of three types of action systems: cultural, social, and personal. Such systems share four functional problems: adaptation to their larger environments, goal attainment, internal integration, and finally, the general problem of keeping going ("pattern maintenance" and "tension management"). (See *Parsons, 1959*, pp. 13–16.)

Besides identifying functional problems, these four categories also identify phases of action process in each of the action systems. That is, each functional problem holds primary importance in the system at some time, and they do so in specifiable sequence. For example, adaptation to any kind of new external event or integration (presumably in face of some disorganizing "internal" event) is followed by goal attainment activity. This is then "absorbed" by the system as an achievement to be in some sense incorporated and maintained in the face of new events which again precipitate the cycle. (*See Parsons, Bales, and Shils, 1953*.)

Nowhere does Parsons clearly inform his reader whether motivation refers only to the personality systems, or whether it is a generic term for describing the cyclical movements of any action system from primacy of one functional problem to the next. Neither does he attempt to specify the goals to be achieved. In some respects his insistence upon maintaining a view of the whole is reminiscent of Parmenides' full world. Parmenides, as once every schoolboy knew, insisted that "what is not, cannot be" and consequently no empty space was left in the world of the mind. It remained for Leucippus and Democritus, with their conception of "atoms and the void" to relieve congestion and make motion theoretically possible as well as actually observed!

There is something inert in the clockwork motions of Parsons' all-encompassing interpenetrating systems, as Max Black notes in asking whether Parsons' actor ever "acts" (*Black, 1961*, pp. 274–277). Similarly one may well wonder whether the ponderous motions of systems from one functional emphasis to another is not too abstracted from the battle-ground of the "passions" to partake in any directly meaningful sense of what is commonly understood as "Motivation."

Were it not for a remarkable book by James Olds (*1956*), which actually attempts to bridge the gap between S R theory and a version of the Parsonian view, one would be hard put to formulate an adequate re-action to the latter within the set of problems we have posed in our chapter. As it happens, Olds presents a simultaneous clarification and extension of the Parsonian treatment of motivation which makes in-formed criticism of it both possible and relevant to our argument.

4

Olds has joined motivational concepts at a variety of explanatory levels ranging from neurology to the Parsonian theory of action systems. For him, a *stimulus* corresponds to any sense datum and a *response* to any operation (p. 86). For each stimulus with which the organism has "repeated commerce" (p. 118) there develops an *idea* ("call assembly") and for each response which the organism has in its repertoire there develops a *want* ("response control unit"). Ideas and wants have fluctuat-ing amounts of both positive and negative motive force attached to them, *intrinsic* motive force being relatively fixed (though it declines during "firing") and "added *instrumental* motive force" which varies with the presence or absence of other ideas or wants to whose achievement the original ideas and wants serve as means.

Ideas and wants are thus likened to a sort of neurological systems with two thresholds, one of "reverberation" or activation of the hitherto latent idea or want, and one of overflow (or firing) in which the object is actually perceived (idea) or enjoyed (want). After firing, Olds speaks of a "refractory" stage of satiation or boredom in which motive force is greatly lowered. The difference between ideas and wants seems to lie in the amount of intrinsic motive force. When this is high the activation threshold appears as a want, where it is low it appears as an idea (p. 113).

A basic assumption of the theory is that "every assembly is a motivator" (p. 123), in other words, that every latent idea or want has some intrinsic motive force. Motivation is not something that has to be introduced from some external source, but is inherent in the structure itself, that is, in the latent idea or want. When an assembly is first formed, its intrinsic motive force depends upon the time interval between the threshold of activation and that of firing ("delay") (p. 132).

In uniting this view with the Parsonian action system model, Olds introduces what he calls "concepts," corresponding to "means" represent-ing stimuli and responses. These are *object concepts* and *action concepts*. "Thus one can speak of the 'idea of an object' on the one hand, and the 'idea of an action or an operation' on the other" (p. 147). The ele-mentary action system Sa-R-Sb is formed by the associational relation going from object concept Sa through action concept R to object concept Sb. The associational relationship forms the three into an action system.

Each concept has other "roles" in other action systems; these are defined by other associational relations.[8]

Where there exists what Olds calls a "motive differential" between Sa and Sb favoring the latter (p. 157) the following roles come to be played respectively by these concepts: concept Sa plays the *integrative-adaptive* role in the system, concept R the *instrumental-adaptive* role, and concept Sb the *gratificatory* role. Gratification drains the system of motive force. Latency allows the motive force in the system to reach its "proper" level again.

Thus Olds procedes to discuss the traditional reinforcement sequence of learning psychology as an elementary action system, with phases corresponding to Parsons' phase-cycle. Instead of the order of adaptation, gratification, integration, latency (or perhaps, integration, gratification, adaptation, etc.) Olds proposes an orbit of integrative-adaptive, instrumental-adaptive, gratificatory, and latent phases.

In developing his analysis of less elementary action systems than the one to which we have referred, Olds makes a distinction between two kinds of motivation provided, on the one hand, by *curiosity* and, on the other hand, by *goals* (pp. 197–198). Clearly, object concept Sb in his previous discussion may be viewed as the goal of the action system under consideration. The curiosity motive, apparently, expresses itself by the emission of an action ("response") where such an object concept of a goal is not present. Mercifully, Olds thus leaves the door open for the organism of its own accord to enter into "commerce" with objects, actively sought in the "environment" or "object realm."

[8] It is not entirely clear how the earlier terminology of "ideas" and "wants"— which is abandoned in the book in making the theoretical transition to "action"— fits into the action system described. "Concepts" as Olds discusses them are clearly *ideas* about actions as well as objects. This gap in his theory is remarkable in that all action seems to become frozen in mere contemplation as soon as Olds comes directly under the influence of Parsons' ideas — so pervasive appears to be the influence of inactivity inherent in Parsons' "theory of action." To close this gap it might be proposed that the quantum of the motive differential between Sa and Sb ought to determine whether concept R remains merely an idea or whether the response R is, indeed, enacted.

Other criticisms may be made of the points so far presented. One is bound to question the meaning of Olds' phrase "repeated commerce" with a stimulus or sense datum. In saying that this is a condition for the formation of an idea or concept one is bound to wonder whether Olds means to imply that it is the only condition. Does repeated bombardment by a stimulus necessarily lead to an object concept, and how many exposures to the stimulus are necessary before the idea is formed? Cannot an idea about a sense datum be formed upon one exposure to the stimulus and without "repeated commerce"? And, conversely, do all object concepts (even "elementary" ones) necessarily refer to sense data? The latter view would be strongly reminiscent of Wittgenstein's (*1918*) conception of distinct elementary symbols (Sachverhalte) corresponding to "atomic facts" in some object realm (*1918*) and subject to the same criticisms (see *Popper, 1959*, pp. 36–37). Of course, it is not symbols but neurological cell assemblies to which Olds makes reference, but his epistemological assumptions and Wittgenstein's are similar and equally questionable.

In his attempt to build analogues of Parsons' system orbits at differing levels of complexity, Olds makes a genuine contribution in showing how elementary systems build into more complex ones. But the difficulty of this conceptualization in terms of "wheels within wheels" is concentrated in the most elementary system of Sa-R-Sb upon which the whole structure is built. This unit action concept goes back to Parsons' original suggestions of "unit acts" as the proper "atoms" of sociology. Interestingly enough, after suggesting that social action is built up of such unit acts (*Parsons, 1937*) Parsons forsook the unit act concept for investigation of the properties of macroscopic structural-functional systems. Olds' motivational theory of elementary reinforcement sequences thus brings Parsons' microscopic and macroscopic conceptions together in the attractive model of phase orbits.

While Olds can be severely criticized for his ambitious efforts, they do in our view, more than any other behaviorist work, escape from the confinements of the pigeon coop and the odor of the doghouse. Indeed, by leaving the door open for a "curiosity motive" he took by implication a position quite near to Miller, Galanter, and Pribram's conception of the TOTE unit to which we have made reference above.

Yet Olds' picture of motivation conveys the sense of behavior more than that of action.[9] His model of phase orbits in reinforced response systems evokes an image of learned routine behaviors. The parallel is striking between his creature emitting learned responses and the smiling and conforming actor of functional sociology. If one were compelled to answer the rather natural question "Can people really be like that?" in the affirmative, one would surely have to balk at the idea that all people are like that all of the time. The picture conveyed in Olds' remarkable theory is not only of activity that certainly will not make much of a difference, but which is entirely devoid of any sense of those "passions" which arouse clinical interest in motivation. A theory of motivation depicting motivated persons as passionless conformists preparing for stereotyped action simply loses sight of the desperate struggle for goals out of which life is fashioned. It fails to explain convincingly those of our motives of which we become most agonizingly aware.

In the following section, we suggest a resolution of this hiatus, and indicate a possible bridge to the gap between input and output. Before

[9] In describing a sequence of "motivated" behavior, Olds employs the following imagery:

> On a warm summer afternoon the subject is resting on the porch and not thinking about much of anything . . . a picnic is mentioned and the subject wants to have a picnic at the beach. (*1956*, p. 104).

Of course this excerpt does not complete the sequence Olds wishes to portray, but the very choice of the picture of a man on his front porch lazily deciding that he wants to go to a picnic conveys perhaps more than any criticism we are able to formulate the underlying feeling-tone of Olds' theory.

turning to our arguments, however, let us emphasize the essentials of our discussion in this section.

The requirements for explanatory theory in both clinical and social theory differ from those more delimited needs of the experimentalist. Holistic perspectives, evident in both psychological and sociological theories in this century, have been of some use in developing clinical techniques, yet they have little to offer for the development of explanatory clinical theory. Elemental theories which are potentially capable of such explanation differ markedly in emphases on behavior vs. action. Contrary to popular perceptions of their nature, psychologically-oriented theories have depicted man as at best a modifier of the behavior demanded by physical systems. The elementists — heavily repreesnted in sociology, as well as in existential types of psychology — represent man as less determined, as (in best form) capable of originating action. Yet, whatever its promise for the increased understanding of human social life and of counseling and psychotherapy, this latter type of theory remains poorly conceptualized.

The perspectives on motivated action presented in the next section differ markedly from any of those few discussed here, suggesting foundations for a theory of human life which are more socially adequate — and which, thereby, may prove more adequate to the development of theories in counseling and psychotherapy. We do not pretend that our construction can match the completeness even of Olds' incomplete formulations, but we have tried to avoid the criticism we have leveled against his and others' work. We urge the reader to judge our success sharply — for extant theories of motivation evidence that without the falsification offered by others, a developing theory will develop but inadequately.

A Partial Theory of Motivation

The critic often falls victim to the diseases he discerns in others. To this academic vulnerability we unblushingly confess, as we follow our cavalier criticism of extent theories of motivation with a suggested redirection of theory. If taken as offered, as a partial and preliminary conception of a theory which may offer foundations less inadequate to individual and social activity, perhaps the effort will appear worthy of growth-inducing criticism.

Exigency, Articulation and Need

Analogues from physics — of impulsions and attractions, inertia and tensions — are common in the literature of motivation, and offer many conventions useful for communicating theoretical ideas. As with any analogues, care must be taken to remember that they rarely can be more than illuminating or sensitizing; demonstration of the dangers of uncritically attributing properties of the analogue to the subject are unfortunately common. Yet we feel the advantages of the analogues outweigh such dangers and we shall offer as rather undefined terms analogues such as "inertia" and "equilibrium." Above all, the use of such conventions saves the reader from the encumbrance of "new" conceptualizations of established and accepted ideas that (however basic and important) are but preliminary to the innovations we have to offer.

1

As a point of departure, we take Rapaport's expansion of Freud's distinction between primary and secondary process. Rapaport (*1959*) suggests the primal objective of the organism is some sort of inertia, or freedom from excitations. On the physiological-neural level of primary process, the active organism through more-or-less random activity is seeking *"gratification,"* or the removal of all excitations.

This conception, which we follow, is markedly different from those which focus most closely on stimuli, *per se*. If stimulus refers to an event having the potential of eliciting a response from an organism (or a class of organisms), *"excitation"* refers to a *relationship* between stimulus and organism: it is the actual triggering by an event (stimulus) or activity in the organism. By treating excitations rather than stimuli as our basic units of analysis, we avoid begging questions concerning the classes of events which stimulate activity and the circumstances under which they are effective in eliciting responses.

That the distinction between excitations and stimuli is no quibble is demonstrated in the contrast of Olds' and Rapaport's views of the formation of ideas. For Olds, a number of encounters with an event creates an idea of it. Distinct from this conception of a realm of pre-packaged sense data which the organism apprehends by "repeated commerce" with it, Rapaport suggests that an idea is formed when activity fails to lead directly to gratification — a delay becomes "structuralized" and conceptions of objects are formed. Object realms, thus, are created and elaborated from contacts with obstacles in the way of the primal objective (inertia).[10]

Delay in gratification thus gives rise to secondary process (and, in more general and popular terms, to "personality" with its mechanisms of defense and established routes for the detour of immediately gratifying behavior). A *"tension"* is created when an excitation cannot be immediately

---

10 These two perspectives also relate to quite different conceptions of the formation of generalizations. Olds' view conforms to the traditional epistemology of inductivism, suggesting that generalizations are the result of repeated observations. By contrast, we would emphasize organismic dispositions (risking misunderstanding for the sake of communication, we suggest these might be considered as archaic "protogeneralizations") which when not gratified or satisfied lead to modification and elaboration of existing subjectively approached object realms.

removed. Gratification gives way to *"satisfaction,"* in which activity consists of more or less organized attempts to establish an *"equilibrium of tensions"* — hence the tensions become bound in the experiential realm itself. As the experiential realm is increasingly ramified, a number of diverse and competing tensions accumulate.

Though Rapaport's conception of primary process activity presents a "deficit" model of behavior in which activity occurs only when there is excitation, the conception of secondary process (with its implicit conception of an equilibrium of tensions) does not require "deficit" assumptions: At the level of secondary process, a given stimulation may lead to either aversive or appetitive reactions according to the effect of the stimulation on the equilibrium of tensions: a favorable re-equilibration is related to appetitive responses, disequilibration to aversive.

It is important to note that the distinction between primary and secondary process does not parallel the distinction between "behavior" and "action" (as we defined these terms on pages 34–38). Though "primary process" implies "behavior," not all secondary process activity is action. An undisturbed equilibrium of tensions would be characterized by routine, repetitive, automatic behavior — from the point of view of a theory of meaningful action an equilibrium of tensions may also be regarded as some sort of inertia, and the closer the organism to such equilibrium, the less likely is meaningful action. As our intent in this paper is to move toward a theory of motivation on the level of meaningful action, we shall not cope further with primary process (except in one or two special cases) or with secondary process "inertia." It must be restated that this preference does not reflect on the importance of such activity; rather, given limited time we shall attend to other levels of activity, taking care only to not contradict the most viable "behavior" theory extant.

2

Our concern, then, is with processes whereby are established goals toward which actions are directed. These processes we propose are initiated by special kinds of excitation, which we term *"exigencies"* and provisionally define as disturbances in tension equilibrium. Exigencies do not give rise to meaningful action directly. It is common, for instance, that a person is "upset" without really being aware of it ("I didn't recognize it at the time, but I was so unhappy"). In such a condition, tension-reducing activity may appear as more or less compulsive behavior which in dramatic forms has been dubbed "acting-out."

The essential point here is this: meaningful action is possible only if the exigency is *"articulated"* by the actor as a *"need,"* which has associated *"goals"* toward which action can be directed in efforts to mitigate the need (note, not the exigency).

Leaving aside issues connected with the choice goals where a need is associated with alternative ones we may briefly describe locomotion toward goals. In the simplest instance one can conceive of a situation where a goal can be reached by a single act. Such instances are but one step removed from S-R Models of behavior, and different from such models only in that the action is not directly touched off by the exigency but mediated by articulation. Such single need-alleviating act we may call a *"goal-jump."* Other goals (most of the sociologically and clinically interesting ones) cannot be attained by such short-lived activity; they require prolonged and complex activity in the direction of the goal. Such prolonged goal-directed activity has been called a *"pathway"* by Zollschan (*1964*, pp. 191–192; *Zollschan and Gibeau, 1964*, p. 169).[11] An activity may continue along the same pathway either if the need is enduring (i.e., when there is continuing exigency), or if the pathway leads to unanticipated goals other than the originating one. A given pathway, in effect, can come to be the road leading to many and varied goals.

Even if a given pathway is conceived of as leading to one final goal, we can subdivide it in terms of "stopping places" or stations. Thus, if a man's goal is to publish a book on some subject, the first station might consist of obtaining a publishing contract, a subsequent to complete the manuscript he decided was worth publishing, yet another to get the proofs and index completed. These stations can be conceived of as goals in their own right, though, to be sure, for the man wanting to publish the book they would not be stations at which an indefinite stop would be welcome. But when the book is finally published, new articulations may well extend the pathway beyond this goal and lead to activities dedicated to promoting the already published book. Thus we appear to have a chain of goals along the pathway, to which the original goal of publishing constitutes only one link. For a person on a pathway, the "goal" toward which he is acting may thus appear to be the immediate next stopping place, or a station further along the line, or, perhaps, just to keep going along the route.

There is another (though closely related) sense in which a pathway may be seen as leading to more than one goal. Once a given pathway is established it may be used by the actor as a route along which action passes in order to achieve new and additional goals. A new exigency will tend, where possible, to be articulated in terms of needs which can be satisfied along the pathways that the actor has already established. (Freud termed this tendency "over-determination" of action; in line with our emphasis on the attraction of action *toward* goals, the term *"conservation of action"* is more appropriate.)

11 Miller, Galanter and Pribram (*1960*) mean something very similar when they speak of a *plan.*

We shall have more to say in this essay on goals and their formation. The central concern at the moment is with another point, implicit in the distinction between exigencies on the one hand, and needs and goals on the other: some concept such as articulation is critical to a theory of motivation adequate to social action, for it refers to the mediation from organic behavior to meaningful action.

But articulation is no simple process, nor is an exigency as simple as we have so far suggested. In order to be articulated as a need, an exigency must have certain properties: Affectively, it must be salient; cognitively, it must be specifiable; evaluatively, it must be justifiable (or at least not "counter-justified"). That is, we may speak crudely of salience, specifiability and justifiability as pre-requisites for the articulation of a need.[12] These terms should be recognized as co-ordinates, implying that, for example, even an exigency of relatively high salience may not be articulated as a need if specifiability is lacking (that is, if there are no cognitive elements available to the actor in terms of which a need would be identified and categorized). Behavior elicited by such an exigency would occur on an organismic level, rather than on the level of meaning. Similarly, if an exigency is highly salient and specifiable, but if the specification is not justifiable the exigency will either fail to reach articulation (and also give rise to the merely organismic reactions) or it will be falsely articulated in a manner which *is* justifiable. (It should be clear that when there is false articulation — that is, when a need is articulated which does not reflect the exigency — action will be directed to the goals related to this falsely articulated need and not toward resolution of the exigency.)

These coordinate variables — salience, specifiability and justifiability — imply that our view of motivation is bound up with conceptions of psychic structure. They also reflect our use of physical analogues, especially those of "energy," even in discussions of secondary process motivation. It is time to identify less imprecisely the nature of the structures and their relation to "energy."

Energy and Structure

Most simply, we see secondary processes as a function of three analytically distinct structures: an equilibrium of tensions (characterized by degrees of salience); a horizon of justifications (characterized by degrees of justifiability); a horizon of expectations (characterized by degrees of specifiability). We have already suggested that the condition of these structures influences articulation. Further (once again using physics

[12] Salience, specifiability and justifiability are functions respectively, of the equilibrium of affective-physical tensions, the horizon of expectations and the horizon of evaluations. These conceptions will be discussed briefly below, and are more fully identified in Zollschan (*1964*).

analogues) much as there is a tendency toward equilibrium of tensions, the two horizons may be said to strain toward constancy; hence disturbance of any one (disequilibrium or contradiction) may be considered an exigency. But how do these structures develop, and how do they relate to "energy?"

We have suggested that delay in gratification gives rise not only to tensions, but also to conceptions of objects. Initially, such conceptions are archaic, conceptually diffuse and fluid. We assume that the earliest phenomenological world of the infant reflects the tensions which he experiences; indeed, that the continually and perfectly gratified infant (if such could ever exist) would remain in organismic inertia and develop no conception of objects (nor, of course, an equilibrium of tensions). Fortunately, the world is not so overly-kind. The infant is forced to forsake inertia, simple excitations denied gratification give way to tensions and to vague conceptions of objects (obstacles to gratification), and gradually a primitive equilibrium of tensions is established. Though such equilibrium is certainly imperfect, it seems likely that some degree of "quietness" must be experienced at least periodically by any infant if it is to develop psychically (and perhaps even survive). The primitive equilibrium, then, requires some degree of constancy; similarly, terms like "pattern" and "order" might be applied to the primitive object realm even in early phases of development.

Zollschan has argued (*1964*, pp. 189–190) that a tendency toward constancy is the structural matrix of the "horizon of justifications." The archaic evaluative object conceptions in the horizon of justifications may, then, be said to "borrow" some of the energy in the equilibrium of tensions and thereby become a relatively autonomous repository of latent energy. After the initial establishment of an equilibrium of tensions and the formation of "preferred" behavior sequences and patternings in the primitive horizon of justifications, the developmental process is increasingly one of differentiation and clarification of objects and goals. This emerging object realm constitutes the infant actor's cognitive world; it is, in other words, a primitive horizon of expectations.

In early states of development, objects perceived as blocking satisfactions become conceived of as "bad" (that is, they are laden with negative affect — see the discussion of cathexis in the next section), while those related to successful satisfaction become "good" objects. Such objects, either good or bad, initially are attached to the relatively undifferentiated horizons of justifications and expectations. They have the effect of specifying the subjective (i.e., affect-laden) equilibrium of tensions and system of justifications.

As the cognitive and evaluative horizons develop, potential exigencies multiply. The likelihood of evaluative discrepancies and, eventually, of cognitive discrepancies increases apace with the development of the horizons — hence widening varieties of experiences are received psychically, and may take the form of exigency. Under increasing bombardment by exigencies, cognitive (as well as evaluative) representations are constantly modified. This continual modification has the effect of loosening emerging cognitive forms from the energy-invested equilibrium of tensions and the horizon of justification (allowing the development of cognitions which are affectively neutral, i.e., "objectified," rather than subjectively bound). To give rise to exigencies, cognitions, of course, also require energy. We will discuss the emergence of cognitive energy later; suffice it for now to say that the affect-free cognitions may be joined by energy that is borrowed from the other structures and stored, relatively autonomously, in the horizon of expectations.

The horizon of expectations has the weakest fund of autonomous energy and a cognitive discrepancy will not arouse much affect or result in the articulation of *valent* (roughly, "highly desired") goals unless the disturbed expectation also carries a loading of justification and plays some sort of role in maintaining the equilibrium of tensions. As the phenomenological world of the actor becomes well stocked with highly variegated cognitions it becomes possible for him to utilize energy from the horizon of expectations to construct object representations relatively free of affect, and even some cognitively elaborated justification ("evaluations") become relatively affect-free. Thus a fairly pure cognitive discrepancy can result in the terminal articulation of new expectations without leading to action (even purely cognitive action) or release of affect. Exigencies whose articulation results in valent goals, as already indicated, must draw their energy from one or both of the more primitive psychic structures.

The attentive reader may recognize that our conceptions of psychic structures are in some ways similar to those of Freud. To give a full account of similarities and differences (as well as a detailed justification) would be beyond the scope of this chapter, but one major difference does require elaboration. *Libido,* which Freud sees as the primary motivant of action through all of his progressive conceptualizations of psychic structure, does not receive much stress in our discussion. This is not because we wish to deny the importance of libidinal excitations (though we do leave the door open for excitations of a not strictly libidinal character becoming bound in the equilibrium of tensions). Rather it is that we are operating at a somewhat higher level of abstraction than did Freud in his metapsychological contributions. For us *libido* has to be conceptualized as a stress of specifiable excitations from within the organism. Whether these excitations outweigh all others in importance is an empirical question which we are happy to leave for others to battle over.

Freud's early conception of the *dream censor* and his later one of the *superego* are rather similar to our views of the horizon of justifications. Our description of the origin of this structure builds upon that of his follower David Rapaport. There are differences however. We would suggest, for example, this approach to *primal repression:* Some new activity stimulated by excitation may come into conflict with already established structures in the horizon of justifications. Broadly speaking, two outcomes are possible in such a situation; either the horizon of justifications (or relevent parts of it) is reabsorbed by the equilibrium of tensions and has to develop again in different form, or the new activity is repressed. (Of course, after an autonomous horizon of expectations is established, repression takes a different form.) This strikes us as somewhat more promising approach to primal repression than Rapaport's "counter-cathexis" model, which he described with the metaphor of "a river which where it is slowed down builds sand bars to slow it further" *(1951,* p. 695).

Our model of the horizon of expectations has some similarities to Freud's early conceptions of conscious and pre-conscious systems, though it also contains cognitions and expectations that have undergone repression proper ("after-expulsion"). As already indicated, the horizon of expectations is the seat of what Freud calls "hypercathexes" and Rapaport "attention cathexes." Before we proceed with our discussion of this important structure, some words concerning the concepts of "object" and "cathexis" are in order.

Objects, Cathexis and Goals

We have suggested that the inarticulate objects of primary process are heavily invested with affect — their existence for the organism depends upon their relationship to energy discharges from the equilibrium of tensions and the horizon of justifications. As the horizon of expectations forms, these primitive objects are transformed into cognitive objects, which may be accompanied by some affective energy liberated from the equilibrium of tensions and horizon of justifications.

Not all objects are equally inverted with affective energy, however. Some remain virtually without vitality, others are so heavily charged with affect that they may influence cognitive activity and play a central role in the actor's selection of activity. They are, in short, heavily cathected. We reserve the term *"cathexis"* for the attachment of energy and its accompanying affect to articulated objects; the detachment of such energy and affect may then be termed decathexis. *Cathexis* may be termed "positive" or "negative" depending on whether the object invested is a goal facilitator or goal barrier. (Although we shall not pursue the intriguing and important problem of the object which is a facilitator for one goal and a barrier to another, the direction such discussion might take is implied in the use of the modifier, "ambivalence." Ambivalent

cathexis would refer to a mix of positive and negative affective investment.) Articulated objects, then, become cathected when they are ap-
prehended as facilitating or blocking goals (or, more primitively, helping
to attain or denying "satisfaction"). But negatively or positively cathected
objects acquire the characteristics of potential second order goals. The
preservation of positively cathected objects and the avoidance or destruction of negatively cathected ones is a diffuse latent goal for every actor.
Consequently, it is a particularly significant aspect of cathexis from the
point of view of motivation theory that cathected objects have the property of being antennae for the receipt of exigencies. Once objects are
cathected, the actor, as it were, "spreads a net" for the receipt of exigencies. Viewed in another way, the distribution of cathexes to objects
at any point in time reflects the actor's equilibrium of tensions and its
objectification in horizons of justifications and expectations. It is often
through threats to positively cathexed objects or through losses of such
objects that new exigencies are manifested.

The subject of second order exigencies — new exigencies that arise in
the actual pursuit of goals — should also be mentioned in connection
with the generation of exigencies for individuals. Perhaps the most
significant set of such exigencies has been discussed by Zollschan and
Gibeau *(1964)* in connection with questions of irrational conduct and
alienation. Alienative exigencies arise when goals are *inelastic* (that is
to say, in cases where a given articulated goal cannot be substituted by
other goals) and are unachievable or present some problem in their
achievement. Besides unachievability, generic problems connected with
the attainment of goals are unpredictability, and with respect to an
individual's conception of the wider society, illegitimacy and non-shared-
ness. The generalized second order exigencies presented by these problems may be called respectively, frustration, anxiety, guilt (or fear of
punishment) and shame.[13]

It is with respect to unachievable or otherwise problematic goals that
concepts such as *fixation* and regression acquire importance in our view.
Fixation involves the incapacity of an individual to develop new pathways and objects in relation to problematic goals. Regression involves
an actual retreat from the problematic goal and reversion to earlier pathways and objects. It is, of course, well known by counselors and psycho-

---

[13] It may be of interest for counselors and therapists to consider a distinction made
by Zollschan and Gibeau concerning the question of whether a condition of alienation
is objectively "real" or not. Clearly, the exigencies of frustration, anxiety, guilt, and
shame arise in relation to situations subjectively defined by the actor. Some assumed
all-knowing (that is, perfectly objective) observer might not always agree with such
subjective definitions. Conditions such as inhibition or infantile omnipotence can be
quite rigorously defined in terms of the disagreement between subjective and "objective" definitions of whether a given goal is problematic or not. (See *Zollschan and
Gibeau, 1964,* pp. 163–164.)

therapists that construction of the most original and daring new pathways often occurs after initial regression.

It is clear that our use of the term "object" is not far removed from that of the Freudians, though some of the latter have a tendency to reserve it (albeit systematically) for *persons* within the cognitive field of the actor, including the actor's representations of "self" and "ideal self." We systematically extend the definition of the terms to include inanimate objects, social groups, and cultural symbols, and even symbolic abstractions (such as "God"). We use it also to refer to body images or partial body images. Thus an adolescent girl may hate her ugly face (the face being a negatively cathected object in this case), or a young boy may have a positive cathexis for his bulging biceps.

A particularly important variety of object within our extended meaning of the term is comprised of learned skills which enable rapid and accurate travel along the pathways to goals. Although they consist of no more than particular systematic sequences of action, it is undeniable that they become representationally objectified both in phenomenology and common linguistic usage. Use of language itself, indeed, provides an example of what we mean by a skill, and we may add tools and instruments, at least in as far as they are conceived of as extensions of skill and not merely as "things." The stage actor's attachment to his language or the workman's to his tools may be as cathic in character as is a man's to his wife. The objectification of skills is not difficult to describe. Initially, at least, they present themselves to the actor as external objects to be mastered and, as it were, "incorporated." To be able to use language and say "I want milk" under most circumstances has clear and considerable technical advantages over the mere emission of a howl (the latter, after all, is capable of erroneous interpretation by the all-powerful dispenser of milk), yet the linguistic expression is a skill that must be acquired by learning and of whose lack the young actor may be painfully aware.

In speaking above of the loosening of cathectic investment from pre-articulate objects in the course of their articulation we did not mean to imply the existence of a generalized trend toward decathexis as objects become differentiated, solidified, and articulated. Evaluative discrepancies and cognitive falsifications result in the decathexis of particular individual objects as the actor's object realm undergoes progressive reorganization. We have seen that this only means that cathexes become increasingly mobile and not necessarily that cathexis in general is reduced. Indeed, the valence of a goal is the measure of its cathexis, and the novel articulation of any valent goal is tantamount to positively cathecting both the goal (viewed as an object) and facilitating objects along the pathway toward the goal. In addition to loosening affect and energy from archaic objects discrepancies and falsifications have the effect of loosening cognitions from particular objects and actions, thus giving rise to *generalized* expectations and justifications (i.e., moral and aesthetic norms). Such cognitive and evaluative generalizations become utilized for the articulation of new needs and the breaking of new pathways.

The particularity or generality of expectations and justifications is largely independent of their strength of cathectic investment. Indeed, instances where generalizations acquire a very high level of valency deserve particular attention. What we have in mind are instances of intellectual innovation — and it is well known that this process is typically accompanied by strong affective states of euphoria and despondency. Intellectuals and, in particular, intellectual innovators make the consistency and high elaboration of the horizon of expectations (or, rather, a substantial segment of it) their major concern. What is more, a great deal of their activity as well as thought (activity such as reading and writing, for example) is directed toward goals which are primarily cognitive or conceptual in nature. Since the autonomous energy of the horizon of expectations is relatively weak, we must assume that in these cases the relevant sector of the horizon of expectations itself takes on the characteristics of a positively cathected object. This contention is not as far-fetched as it might appear at first glance. If our argument above that skills become cathected objects for actors is acceptable, then it is but one step to the assertion that the horizon of expectations is an actor's repository of generalized skills. And while many intellectual innovators earn their bread (and thus ward off the occurence of the salient excitations of hunger!) in the "officially designated" workshops of the horizon of expectations, this in no way adds to the valency of their purely intellectual goals.

The cathexis of a part of the horizon of expectations does not, of course, mean that there is a reversion of the cognitions that stock it to pre-cognitive "things of action." On the contrary, "things of abstraction" although unambiguously located within the horizon of expectations, are invested with energy from the more archaic structures for their intrinsic "interest" to the actor. Theories, as it were, become prized "objects" and refutations take on the aspect of salient exigencies becoming articulated as needs for new theory construction (or needs for explanation) and this — as we have suggested — can take place quite independently of any extrinsic rewards there might exist for developing knowledge. Indeed, in contrasting the distinctly intellectual goals of the scientific innovator with the extrinsic element of "making a living" we have touched upon the rather fundamental distinction between intrinsic goals and objects (objects *an sich*) and merely instrumental ones. If we may be allowed to go back to our image of a pathway as a chain of goals, some of these goals are valent in their own right while other stations along the pathway derive their valency indirectly from the intrinsically valent ones by an "act of will." Such acts of will obey syllogisms of the following character: "only if I complete the index can my book be published (at least, in the form in which I want it to appear). Therefore — I *will* to complete the index.

Indeed, it is entirely possible that locomotion toward some instrumental goals may be intrinsically punishing (negatively cathected), but if the intrinsic goal or goals further along the pathway outweigh in their positive valence the negative valence of the instrumental goals, the punishment inherent in reaching the latter cannot be avoided. Of course, where the unattractiveness of the instrumental goal is greater than the attractiveness of the intrinsic one, action will not take place along the pathway in question. The amount of confidence in being able to reach distant intrinsic goals as well as their positive cathexis is a factor affecting their relative valency. An examination of the various conditions of confidence in reaching goals (and consequently "tolerance" for delayed satisfaction), however, is beyond the scope of this chapter. Situations of conflict between instrumental and intrinsic goals have concerned one of the authors on a previous occasion (*Zollschan and Gibeau, 1964*).

The mobility of cathexis implies that an instrumental goal may become directly invested with cathexis and thereby become transformed into an intrinsic goal. Indeed, our account of the development of psychic structure suggests that early goals have their genesis as stopping places on pathways to the primal objective of inertia; in other words, that they begin as instrumental goals.

But that does not imply that all instrumental goals necessarily become, as it were, "cathectically autonomous." To revert to our publishing example: for some prolific writers the construction of indices may become an intrinsic sub-goal, cathected and "satisfying" in its own right. For others it remains an instrumental stopping place on their action pathways, unavoidable perhaps but entirely devoid of intrinsic attraction.

The analysis of negatively cathected objects is somewhat more intricate. It leads us to considerations of the actor's level of frustrations. We have seen that all tensions originate in a delay of gratification, and the transmutation of gratification into satisfaction is accompanied by the formation of conceptions of reality in which temporary delays do not come to be felt as frustrations. Indeed, infantile gratification in returning to organismic inertia is largely replaced by satisfaction in reaching articulated goals, and any particular tension as such is not perceived as "painful." We have seen, on the contrary, that an equilibrium or balance of such tensions may be viewed as the fundamental psychic structure. But certain goals (or, satisfactions) are not reached, or the actor is unable to replace certain gratifications by structural goals susceptible of attainment of satisfaction. Under these circumstances we may speak of painful tensions or frustrations, which find their objectification in negatively cathected "bad" objects.

It is interesting to note that what we have called "counter-justifications" to the articulation of needs and goals are closely related to reactions to, or avoidance of contact with, negatively cathected objects. Insofar as negatively cathected objects mirror the level of frustration in the equilibrium of tensions at any given time, their destruction or disappearance corresponds to a lowering of the level of frustration (accompanied, presumably, by the opening of previously blocked pathways or the articulation of new pathways). Occasionally, however, a negatively cathected object represents a falsely articulated or archaic and currently inoperative blockage in a pathway. In such instances satisfaction at attaining the goal of destroying the bad object may be experienced by the actor without the actual level of frustration in his equilibrium of tensions being diminished. It is, of course, the kind of instance which furnishes material for descriptions of "aggressive instincts" and the like. But the crucially distinctive element in such aggressive actions stems from the fact that the bad object is not an eikonic of "true" objectification of the level of frustration, or the "real" obstacle in the way of satisfaction along a pathway it ostensibly blocks. Nonetheless, a bad object is an objectification even if it is a false one, and some satisfaction may be derived from its destruction. Thus, to give an example: If I represent my department chairman as a bad object standing in the way of my goal of promotion, the professional or even physical destruction of the chairman becomes a latent (or perhaps not so latent) goal in its own right — even in the absence of any necessary subjective connotation along the line, "if I destroy him, I shall be promoted."

This preliminary model of psychic structure and human phenomenology leaves us with many puzzles: To what extent (if at all) does the distribution of quanta of energy and affect to objects at any given point in time accurately reflect such objects' contributions to the maintenance of the equilibrium of tension, and what are the consequences if the reflection is inaccurate? Under what circumstances, if at all, do affectively neutral objects become cognitively presented *de novo*, or are they necessarily cognitive precipitates of the decathexis of things of action? Under what circumstances do instrumental goals become intrinsic? Puzzles there are, but hopefully our model brings them into the open clearly and sharply and thereby renders them accessible to attempted manipulation, both theoretical and (eventually, we trust) operational.

Conclusion

We have presented a kind of gravitational conception of motivation in which goals attract action along pathways. The processes whereby such goals are established, out of the articulation of exigencies acting upon hypothetical psychic structures, have also been discussed. What is more, these considerations have necessitated a lengthy speculative discussion of the psychic structures, which were termed equilibrium of tensions, horizon of justification, and horizon of expectations. The latter two of these structures, respectively, were viewed as outgrowths of the previous structure each in response to pressures to which human organisms are subject at different stages of their development. The equilibrium of tensions was depicted as incorporating bound organismic excitations which could not find immediate quietus in gratification. The horizon of justifications was seen in effect as an elaboration of the repetition compulsion, an analogue to Spinoza's *Conatus in suo esse perseverandi,* imposing order and pattern upon experience. Finally, the horizon of expectations was depicted as transforming the precognitive things of action into things of abstraction, or concepts, and making possible realistic and successful manipulation of self and environment.

All of this discussion has been in terms of the individual organism and actor, and it would be legitimate to ask how this basic conception is more adequate than others to the facts of social life. In conclusion we must turn to questions of inter-personal action, and how these relate to our model.

It is clear that among certain species, and certainly the human one, inter-organismic behavior is a biological requisite for survival. In other words, where inter-organismic behavior of some kind does not occur the species dies out. For instance, certain minimal relations between mothers and their infants ("suckling relationships") are implicit in the psysiological structure of mammals. Human infants, because of their prolonged biological dependency upon adult humans, necessarily exist and mature in environments populated by others — and consisting in large part of situations created and controlled by others. The preponderance of others in the child's experiential space (as also, of course, the fact of infantile dependency in itself) implies that early gratification and satisfaction are obtained in and through others. Thus in the case of the somatic excitation of hunger, the mother's breast becomes an early object. What is more, the utility of the mother for the infant in reaching a whole plethora of goals establishes the infant's cathexis to the mother herself as an object, as soon as she becomes represented cognitively by the infant. Similarly, out of initially diffuse bodily sensations and skills cognitive representations of "self" as an object arise.

The strongly inter-organismic character of infantile human experience implies the centrality of communication in the development of knowledge. Symbols — which have their origin in interpersonal communication — are, of course, the material out of which the major part of the horizon of expectations is fashioned. Even before the development of symbolic language, the "body language" of others as it impinges upon the infant may well be a major determinant of the horizon of justification.

But, in addition to the interpersonal matrix that must exist if human horizons of justifications and expectations are to form, there exist goals conducive to the development and maintenance of interpersonal and social patterns. The most obvious goals of this nature are those for the response of other persons. But it is characteristic of many other goals — even impersonal ones — that their achievement requires the conjoint activity of several persons. Eliciting or enforcing co-operation of others becomes a subsidiary goal in such cases. Or, for that matter, compliance to the wishes of others will occur when this facilitates the attainment of one's own goals. (In special cases it may, of course, constitute a goal or sub-goal in its own right.) Zollschan and Perrucci (*1964*, pp. 99–125) have undertaken an initial analysis of social systems built up out of actors' pursuit of goals. We cannot report that argument here, and interested readers are referred to their work. It must be sufficient, in this connection, to point out that interpersonal pathways have game-like characteristics. How these games are played and, particularly, how they can "go wrong" is a matter of obvious interest to counselors and therapists. To suggest, however, (as do those sociologists who skirt consideration of motivation, or psychiatrists like Szasz who see games as the "be all and end all" of behavior) that such games can be understood without reference to motivation strikes us as absurd. If there is no motive to play a game, it simply "is not worth the candle" for the player!

When all is said and done, the mechanisms of motivation of any actor must be located in the actor, however much the structures determining and energizing his motives may be affected by commerce with others. However useful for some purposes, attempts to locate the sources of motivation only in society or culture serve to evade the task of explaining action. But our "methodological individualism" does not render specifically sociological types of explanation questionable or minimize, in any way, their legitimacy and importance.

For all of its many gaps and shortcomings, our model suggests a bridge over the hiatus between action and behavior; it does attempt to cope with different orders of concepts ranging from "reflex" to "self actualization." From its generalization may be deduced propositions testable in the laboratory, the school, the counselor's office, the psychoanalytic couch and (in its sociological elaboration) the stage of human history. This is not achieved at the cost of static or holist assumptions, or the postulation of prematurely closed systems. On the contrary, if we err it is in the direction of playing down routine actions and ascribing more originality and thrust to our actor than perhaps he deserves — our actor's actions make a difference.

References

Allport, Gordon (1960). "The Open System in Personality Theory," *Journal of Abnormal and Social Psychology*, 61, 301–310.

Black, Max (1961). "Some Questions About Parsons' Theories," in *The Social Theories of Talcott Parsons*, Max Black (ed.), Prentice-Hall.

Buckley, Walter (1967). *Sociology and Modern Systems Theory*, Prentice-Hall.

Chomsky, Noam (1959). "Review of B. F. Skinner, Verbal Behavior," *Language*, 35, 26–58.

Davis, Kingsley (1959). "The Myth of Functional Analysis," *American Sociological Review*, 24, 757–772.

Erickson, Eric H. (1964). *Insight and Responsibility*, Norton.

Gerth, Hans, and C. Wright Mills (1953). *Character and Social Structure*, Harcourt Brace.

Hansen, Donald A., and Reuben Hill (1964). "Families Under Stress," in *Handbook of Marriage and the Family*, Harold Christiensen (ed.), Rand-McNally, 782–819.

Hume, David (1955). *An Inquiry Concerning Human Understanding*, Charles W. Hendel (ed.), Liberal Arts Press.

Kallen, Horace (1931). "Functionalism," in *Encyclopedia of the Social Sciences*, 6, Macmillan.

Martindale, Don (1965). "Limits of and Alternatives to Functionalism in Sociology," in *Functionalism in the Social Sciences*, American Academy of Political and Social Science, monograph 5, 144–162.

Merton, Robert K. (1957). *Social Theory and Social Structure*, The Free Press.

Miller, George A., Eugene Galanter, and Karl H. Pribram (1960). *Plans and the Structure of Behavior*, Holt.

Olds, James (1956). *The Growth and Structure of Motives*, The Free Press

Parsons, Talcott (1937). *The Structure of Social Action*, McGraw-Hill.

Parsons, Talcott, Robert F. Bales, and Edward Shils (1953). "Phase Movement in Relation to Motivation, Symbol Formation, and Role Structure," in *Working Papers in the Theory of Action*, The Free Press, 163–269.

Parsons, Talcott (1959). "The Role of General Theory in Sociological Analysis," *Alpha Kappa Deltan*, 29, 12–38.

Peters, R. S. (1960). *The Concept of Motivation*, Routledge & Kegan Paul (second edition).

Popper, Karl R. (1959). *The Logic of Scientific Discovery*, Basic Books.

Popper, Karl R. (1962). *Conjectures and Refutations*, Basic Books.

Rapaport, David (1951). *The Organization and Pathology of Thought*, Columbia University Press.

———— (1959). "The Structure of Psychoanalytic Theory: A Systematizing Attempt," in *Psychology: A Study of a Science*, Sigmund Koch (ed.), 3, McGraw-Hill.

Sorokin, Pitirim A. (1966). *Sociological Theories of Today*, Harper & Row.

Szasz, Thomas S. (1961). *The Myth of Mental Illness*, Hoeber-Harper.

Weber, Max (1947). *The Theory of Social and Economic Organization* (trans. A. M. Henderson and Talcott Parsons), Oxford University Press.

Wittgenstein, Ludwig (1922; original publication 1918). *Tractatus Logico-Philosophicus,* Kegan, Paul.

Zollschan, George K. (1964). "Beyond the 'Reality Principle': Problems and Perspectives leading to the Theory of Institutionalization," in *Explorations in Social Change,* George K. Zollschan and Walter Hirsch (eds.), Houghton Mifflin, 175–201.

Zollschan, George K., and Philip Gibeau (1964). "Concerning Alienation: A System of Categories for the Exploration of Rational and Irrational Behavior," in Zollschan and Hirsch, *op. cit.,* 152–174.

Zollschan, George K., and Robert Perrucci (1964). "Social Stability and Social Process: An Initial Presentation of Relevant Categories," in Zollschan and Hirsch, *op. cit.,* 99–124.

2 | LANGUAGE CODES, SOCIAL RELATIONS AND PSYCHOTHERAPY

Donald A. Hansen / University of California, Berkeley

Sociologists, concerned with the nature of order, diversity and change in the relationships of men, have traditionally considered language as one of the most fundamental of social phenomena. This is not to say that they have continually studied the phenomena, however; as in the case of motivation, attention to language has been less than rigorous. In spite of the works of influential theorists, in spite of continuing arguments about the effects of "objective rationality" on modes of thought and social structure in Western society, in spite of the popularity of theories of social change that represent ideas as causally potent, in spite of these and diverse other theories in sociology that emphasize the importance of language, little systematic attention has been given the subject by sociologists. Textbooks and theoretical constructs celebrate man's symbolic capacities, but the implications of these capacities have been energetically ignored.

Given the centrality of language to sociological and psychological theories and its relationship to individual motivation and hence to causal social analysis, it can well be said that one of the most important developments in social inquiry in the 20th century has been the convergence of natural and social sciences on the study of linguistics.

At the moment, the study of linguistics is virtually exploding. Old ideas and constructs are called into question, debunked and derided; new ideas and constructs take their place and in turn are subject to the slings and arrows of outraged insights. As one result, linguistic constructs are likely to be "outmoded" before their practical implications — for education, for counseling or psychotherapy, or even for sociological

The author is greatly indebted to Basil Bernstein, both for generously permitting access to his unpublished works and for his comments and criticisms.

research — have even been considered. This kind of knowledge gap is far from unique; but in few instances is the gap so great, are the innovations so rapid, are the implications so potentially important.

In this chapter I attempt to identify some implications for counseling and psychotherapy of but one line of development in theories of language. That line of development — the study of language codes by Basil Bernstein and his colleagues over the last decade — is perhaps a less difficult vehicle than most, for Bernstein himself has persistently linked his abstract theories to practical situations, including a discussion of speech systems and psychotherapy *(Bernstein, 1964)*.

The thread of argument is rather straightforward. The first task is to summarize and comment on Bernstein's argument that language codes are directly relevant to the capacities of the individual to enter various types of interpersonal relationships as well as individual roles. Differences in the two types of codes — elaborated and restricted — suggest that those individuals who do not possess elaborated coding capacities are unlikely to respond effectively to current types of psychotherapy. Clearly such incapacities are correlated with sociological variables, such as social class. Beyond the question of correlation, the question of what it is that leads to the development of such differences in coding capacities is approached, through focus on but one small aspect of the processes: the types of relationships and interpersonal influences to which the individual is subject. Finally, the idea is entertained that these types of relationships and influences can help identify types of family relationships that seem to be related to the development of linguistic codes and other capacities necessary for effective therapy.

The discussion rests on a few propositions about the linguistic requirements for successful psychotherapy — requirements that involve not only the client, but also the counselor or psychotherapist.

Language and Therapy

Generally in therapy the attempt is to aid the client in structuring and restructuring his discrete experiences — his horizons of knowledge and justification — in verbally significant form *(Bernstein, 1963)*. Of particular importance in the restructuring are those aspects of his horizons that are affectively salient, or catheteced. That is, in psychotherapy the identity of the patient is supposed to undergo a transformation by means of the communication between the psychotherapist and the client. Necessarily, the communications are filtered through the purposes, goals, beliefs, and emotional commitments of the patient — qualities that are closely interlinked with those individuals and structures in the client's natural groups. That is, to the counseling relationship the patient brings his own "common-sense" world organized affectively and evaluatively as well as cognitively. Through this "common-sense" world the psychotherapy relationship is filtered, and in the process it may be distorted, enhanced, or thwarted.

Two points about this filtering are critical. First, generally, to the extent that it occurs, psychotherapy is hindered. If the client continues to refer much of his psychotherapy experiences to his "common-sense" world, the probability of restructuring his cognitive and evaluative horizons is lessened. Second, generally, to the extent that psychotherapy relationships are not established with close reference to the "common-sense" world of the client, psychotherapy is impossible. For the common-sense world offers essential tools for psychotherapy, as well as subject matter to be worked with and understood. At the same time, however, it presents emotionally charged materials and distorted perspectives and commitments that interfere with effective psychotherapy.

The filtering process, and both of these critical points, are implicit in existing theories and techniques of psychotherapy. The psychotherapy relationship, then, is based on the belief that psychotherapy can be advanced in a context where authority is ambiguous and structural constraints are subtle, supple, and at least in part, constructed by the client himself. Further, psychotherapy provides situations in which the patient's social identity is held in a state of suspension or abeyance and where the referent for communication is the discrete experience of the patient himself.

To meet the requirements of this relationship, the psychotherapist undergoes years of training and critical examination by himself as well as by others. But the client does not always enjoy such preparation; he must feel his way into the relationship, learn how to deal with the requirements within the structure provided by the psychotherapy context and through the psychotherapist's communication. It is apparent that some persons learn to meet the requirements with little effort. It is equally apparent that others never quite succeed, and some fail totally.

These differences in abilities to meet the requirements of psychotherapy, it will be argued below, are not simply idiosyncratic. Rather, they appear to be related to various social categories, such as social class, ethnic grouping, and subcultural membership. Obviously, there may be great differences between the abilities of two persons in the same social class to meet the psychotherapy requirements, but comparing lower class members as a group with middle class members suggests that real differences exist between the groups *in toto*.

That is to ask: is there significant variation in capacities for effective psychotherapy not only *within* groups, but also *between* groups? The example of the lower class is perhaps most dramatic. It is generally recognized that the psychotherapist is oftentimes ill-equipped to deal adequately with the common-sense world of the lower-class client. In part the problem rests on the rational and logical orders of the theories and of the language with which the psychotherapist works. In part, the problem might rest also in the general poverty of knowledge of the social structures and constraints and pressures within which the psychotherapy process takes place. But in part, also, the problem may rest on a requirement that the psychotherapist share with the client in a wide array of common understandings that go far beyond simply sharing *knowledge about* the client's social structure and world. The inabilities of psychotherapists (and, indeed, of sociologists) to enter these common-sense worlds of lower-class persons or of others of different cultures are generally recognized, however little analyzed. Similarly recognized and similarly neglected are the incapacities of the lower-class client to participate in the psychotherapist's or counselor's world. Incapacity and inadequacy in either member can be highly destructive to effective psychotherapy.

It is argued, then, that the capacities and adequacies of both client and psychotherapist are closely dependent upon language, and that basic and pervasive differences in language patterns are reflected in the capacities of individuals to participate in effective psychotherapy. From the psychotherapist's perspective, the client may appear negative and passive or compliant, he may evidence lower levels of insight and his communications may appear inadequate, forcing the psychotherapist to take a more dominant role than he desires. From the client's perspective, the psychotherapist may appear unfair or strange in his references to sources of motivation and to his questions about the client's experience.

Bernstein's theories suggest that, at base, these difficulties may be closely related to differences not only in the *content* of the psychotherapist's and client's speech systems and value systems, but also to differences in the very *forms* of speech — of language codes — with which they are able to work. Language enables the individual to organize his world in meaningful ways and to release immediate experience and to regrasp it in new ways, to essentially abstract himself from his immediate experiences, allowing reconstruction of the continuous stream of events that characterize daily existence into coherent, integrated patterns. The grasping and regrasping is made possible through language; the *forms* of reconstruction, and indeed the very patterning of grasping and regrasping, are consequences of the language codes. The argument is not simply that the horizons of knowledge and justifications evidence different representations and values. Rather, it is suggested that the very forms of these differ from individual to individual.

Further, it is argued that different positions in the social structure tend to result in different types of language codes, which are reflected in differing capacities and modes of relating to and perceiving experience.

That is, the experiences of individuals in similar social categories (such as lower-class Northern Negroes) might lead to the development of similar language codes which are different both in content and in form from those of individuals in other social categories.

In a sense, Bernstein suggests, language codes are linguistic translations of the meanings of social structure. At base they are nothing more than verbal planning activities at the psychological level, and only at this level can they be said to exist. They are, then, closely related to this discussion of motivation in the previous chapter and can be seen as systems of organizing and rearranging experience in the cognitive and evaluative horizons, of articulating exigencies into goal-related needs, and of planning activity and phenomenally traversing pathways. Hence, they are critically relevant to the development of personality, and even to social organization and social change. More specifically, they are closely relevant to the expectations, motivations, and capacities of both psychotherapist and client and to the probability of success in effectively relating to and working with one another.

Careful identification of the nature of these codes, and of their exercise in the psychotherapy relationship promises abundant returns in the development of theory not only in sociology, but also in counseling and psychotherapy. The argument in the next two sections, then, follows Bernstein's work and relates it to the motivational theory of Chapter 1.

Language Codes

Two distinctly sociological perspectives on language might be taken in a discussion of psychotherapy. The first would seek to identify structures and forms of language found generally in a culture, or even universally. Linguistic forms thereby tend to be studied apart from the variety of social contexts in which they might appear. The sociological potentials of such a perspective are evidenced, however, in discussions of Western conceptions of "rationality" and its relation to the organization of Western thought, or more systematically in the work of Whorf and his followers. My lack of attention to such work should be recognized not as a commentary on the utility of searching for general forms of language, but rather reflects limitations imposed by time and energy.

It can be argued, however, that the perspective represented by Bernstein is more immediately relevant to a sociological study of psychiatric and counseling processes. Bernstein's approach rests on the argument that social structure is a major factor in shaping fashions of speaking or language patterns. In the context of the common culture, this focus emphasizes the importance of distinctive linguistic forms unique to individuals or shared among groupings within the general society. These differing forms induce in their speakers different ways of relating to objects and persons.

Bernstein draws a distinction between speech, which is taken to refer to messages, and language, which refers to a code, to a set of rules to which the speech complies. Differing speech codes are permitted by any particular language code; which speech code is chosen is a function of the social relations of the speaker, or of those he perceives himself to be in. Bernstein's work, then, might be simplistically characterized as essentially a study of syntax in a variety of social-cultural contexts. But it is more than that, for he is concerned as well with semantics, and with what Morris (*1938*) termed the "pragmatics" of communication, that is with the relevance of communication to human activities. (See discussion in Chapter 4, pages 139–141, of this volume.)

Every mature adult possesses some range of speech codes, and is capable of choosing among these in his communications. The social relations in which he is acting in great part regulate the choices, and the choices, in turn, affect his subsequent social relations. In talking to a child, for example, an adult uses speech forms in which both the syntax and the vocabulary are simple. The same adult will use quite a different speech pattern in speaking to his spouse when dining out, another one in his superior's office, and perhaps still another in the seclusion of a boudoir. That is, social relations may establish for the individual principles of choice, so that in any certain situation, a certain syntax and a certain lexical range may be chosen rather than another. Changes in the form of social relations affect both the speaker's choice of speech codes and the orientations and expectations of the listener. The speech system, then, is taken to be a consequence of the form of social relations, or as a quality of the social structure.

This is not to deny the influence of innate capacities, but rather to emphasize that the development of speech capabilities, as the development of any other social capability, is a process in which social, biological, and psychological forms interpenetrate. It is also to emphasize the perspective that one of the primary vehicles of social influence is linguistic communication. From another perspective, that of the motivation theory presented in Chapter 1, verbal communication is seen as one of the primary sources of socially-relevant falsifications which lead to the development and restructuring of the horizons of knowledge and justifications. Conversely, the horizons of justifications and falsification in great part determine the capacities of the individual to receive communications, and to act verbally. It should be obvious that speech itself is a major form of motivated activity.

In these terms, linguistic codes can be seen to be meta-pathways (see page 50, Chapter 1), appropriate to diverse messages and goals. If brought to consciousness it would be as if the individual were to say, "If I speak to Zoltan Karpathy using this linguistic code (meta-pathway), I shall be more likely to influence him than if I use the code that so easily downs Liza Doolittle."

The proposition that speech and language codes are major factors in the interpenetration of social, biological and psychological forms has further implications. Not only do learned codes influence perception and motivated action, but individuals also come to learn their roles in great part through processes of communication. That is, communication is a primary vehicle of cultural transmission, of role formation, of socialization. A role from this point of view is a constellation of shared learned meanings, enabling an individual to enter into persistent and recognized forms of interaction with others.

Bernstein suggests that, if the communications system most critical in defining a role behaviorally is that of speech, it would seem reasonable to distinguish critical roles in terms of the speech forms they regulate. As a person is increasingly oriented toward symbolic meanings, that is, as his horizons of expectations and justifications elaborate, new orders of relationships are made available to him. As he comes to see himself more and more in terms of social categories that are linguistically relevant, experience is given special forms, roles are constrained, and social identity develops. That is, the increasing transformation of experience into linguistically relevant forms both opens new horizons of possible activity, and renders others unavailable and even unattainable. Thus children reared in different social structures adopt different social and intellectual procedures — that is, develop intellectually, evaluatively, and even emotionally — in quite different ways despite common potentials.[1]

In this perspective, it is apparent that any specific type of relationship in psychotherapy is potentially more pertinent to some clients than to others, and may even be completely inappropriate to an individual whose language codes and horizons differ markedly from those exercised in the psychotherapy relationship. A member of the lower-working class, for instance, may be required in psychotherapy to make a radical change in his normal language activities. What psychotherapy requires to be linguistically organized may be almost the antithesis of what is usually organized by the lower-working class individual's normal coding process — a process supported, it should be remembered, by the salient common-sense world he has internalized and developed.

[1] This discussion can be seen as a specification of general sociological perspectives. In focusing on the effects of social structure on language and speech forms as thus far presented, it neither denies nor affirms the subjective-elementism that characterizes the discussion of motivation and social forms in Chapter 1. It should be recognized that the current discussion of language is compatible with that motivation theory; the question of causal primacy, however, is unessential to the current discussion and is gladly skirted.

It is pertinent, then, to ask a number of questions including especially these: What kinds of language systems are related to what kinds of social relationships? What kinds of relationships do these language systems give access to and support?

In seeking preliminary answers to these questions, the following discussion will be general, representing gross analyses and specifications.

Elaborated and Restricted Codes

Bernstein has identified two general types of codes: elaborated and restricted. On a linguistic level, he has identified them in terms of the probability of predicting for any speaker which syntactic elements will be used to organize meaning across the representative range of speech. The speaker employing an elaborated code will select from a relatively extensive range of alternatives and the probability of prediction is greatly increased. On the psychological level or motivational level, the codes may be distinguished by the extent to which they facilitate (elaborated code) or inhibit (restricted code) the tendency to verbally symbolize intent. The activities related to each of these codes will result in different modes of self-regulation, and hence in different forms of relationship.

It should be remembered that Bernstein is speaking not of content, nor of tendency to speak, nor of frequency of speech, but of forms of organizing speech. It should also be clear that Bernstein's descriptions are but beginning approximations: Though he has identified linguistic and behavioral indices which suggest the presence of such codes, considerable work and specification remains before adequate definition can be pretended. Further, it should be recognized that Bernstein's ideas could well be couched in the terms used by Zollschan and Hansen (Chapter 1) to discuss cognitive horizons.

Restricted Code. The purest form of this code would allow complete predictability for speakers and listeners of all words — and hence predictability of the structures in which they take place regardless of their degree of complexity. These pure forms are found in highly ritualistic relationships: in those regulated by protocol, in religious litany, in highly conventionalized drama and story-telling. In such relations, individual differences can be signaled only through extraverbal signals such as rhythm, stress, pitch, or through gestures, physical sets and facial modifications. Essentially, the individual is allowed, or is capable of no choice of sequence or routine:

> Consider the case of a mother telling her child stories which they both know by heart. "And little Red Riding Hood went into the wood" (ritualistic pause). "And what do you think happened?" (rhetorical question). If the mother wishes to transmit her discrete experience, her uniqueness, she is unable to do this by varying her words. She can only do it by varying the

signals transmitted through extra verbal channels; through changes in intonation, pitch, speech rhythm, facial set, gesture, or even through changes in muscular tension, if she is holding the child. The code defines the channels through which new information (i.e., learning) can be made available. The discrete intents of mother and child, interpersonal aspects of the relation, can only be transmitted extra-verbally *(Bernstein, 1965)*.

In less pure form, consider the dramatic renditions of a traditional play such as Hamlet. The extraordinary talent of Richard Burton is attested by his capacity to transmit, through extra-verbal channels, new insights and interpretations and, at the same time, to communicate the uniqueness of his perspective. The words are precisely defined, the script familiar and revered. Yet, with gestures and intonations, with quiet, sudden giddiness, with clownish posture and winsome grin, the player adds qualities to the character not suggested in the comparatively measured renditions of earlier Hamlets, which depicted more simply a man of bemused power. The words are the same, the sequences and routines entirely predictable (as attested by the proverbial story of Churchill's mutterings of Hamlet soliloquies in rough cadence with Burton's stage performance) — but suddenly through the extra-verbal channels, Hamlet is explosively volatile, flippantly, almost childishly agonized. With gestures, pacings, and sensitive intonations, Burton updates Hamlet to the age of identity and anxiety.

It may be the case that, in situations allowing only restricted codes that afford close lexical prediction, perception of nonverbal communications can become exceptionally sensitive. Consider the audience attending Burton's performance. Given the familiar sequences and verbal channels of Hamlet, the actor's genius is all the more apparent as he brings new meanings and excitement to a line grown familiar. The very verbal predictability makes the audience all the more sensitive to subtleties expressed through the nonverbal channels.

Psychiatrists are noted for their sensitivity to nonverbal signals, particularly in highly predictable situations. A client arriving for the first interview, for example, can be expected to go through one of the common sequences, all of which are fairly similar to one another. But even the familiar "How do you do — won't you sit down — isn't this a grand day" sequence can carry, even in first meetings, nonverbal signals that the sensitive observer might identify and in which he will seek information about the special individuality of the other. Likely the client, too, is especially attuned to nonverbal signals, but it is critical to recognize that client and psychotherapist are relating at that point to each other essentially through the social position or status that they occupy. Given a situation in which there is an exchange of verbal messages of maximal predictability, such as the "Hello, how are you" routine, the psychotherapist and client will have *low* predictability about one another's individual attributes. Dealing in the restricted code offers a possibility of deferred commitment to the relationship. It is possible that some relationships, even in psychotherapeutic situations, will not develop significantly beyond this initial, position-determined stage. If in these stages orientation is toward extra-verbal channels as the source of new information, it may be that the psychotherapist and client will be "out of communication" extra-verbally. Futher, if the psychotherapist too readily pushes for verbal, elaborated messages, communications may be so disrupted that the client (whether from psychological defensiveness, confusion, or incapacity) may adopt a combative or compliant stance (see Chapter 5 of this volume).

A restricted code that is so highly predictable (lexically), Bernstein suggests, is not nearly so common as one in which prediction is possible only at a *syntactic level.* Generally this sort of code emerges in a relationship based on a common, extensive set of closely shared identifications and expectations self-consciously held by the members. Restricted codes, then, can be found in the relationship of prisoners, servicemen, peer-groups of children, or husbands and wives. The social relationship is inclusive; speech is refracted through a common cultural identity that reduces the need to make intent explicit, so that the structure of speech becomes simplified and the lexicon is drawn from a narrow range. (The mere fact that a lexicon is drawn from a narrower range, however, is not sufficient to qualify the code as restricted.) How things are said and when they are said, rather than what is said, become important. Meanings are likely to be concrete, descriptive or narrative rather than analytical or abstract. In certain areas, meanings may be highly condensed. Speech is likely to be fast and fluent, articulatory cues reduced; there will be a low level of vocabulary and syntactic selection, and some meanings may become dislocated, condensed and local. Most importantly, the unique meaning of the individual is likely to be implicit — a quality that tends to inhibit the explicit articulation of individual intent and the introspective concern with motives, except on immediate and concrete bases.

In long-range psychotherapeutic relationships, some restricted codes of syntactic prediction may develop between psychotherapist and counselor, and actually contribute to the psychotherapy process. But the significance for the psychotherapeutic relationship of such restricted codes is more to be found in the common-sense worlds of the client, which may serve as continuing referents, and which offer organizing structures for the client's reception and responses to the psychotherapist's questions and comments. As will be suggested below, such restricted codes can significantly hinder psychotherapeutic processes.

Bernstein emphasizes that restricted codes are used by all members of society at some time, whether they be upper or lower-class, of below-average intelligence or the most incisive of geniuses. The major function of this sort of code is to define and reinforce the form of the social relationship by restricting the verbal signaling of individual experience.

Elaborated Codes. When intent of the other person cannot be taken for granted, there will be a tendency to expand meanings, and to raise them to higher levels of syntactic organization and lexical selection than is the case in the restricted code. The elaborated code has a major function of preparing and delivering relatively explicit meaning and is characterized by a low syntactic prediction. Bernstein (*1965*) suggests that such codes are likely to arise in social relationships that raise the tension in members to select from their linguistic resources a *verbal* arrangement that closely fits specific referents. If a restricted code facilitates a construction or exchange of conventionalized symbols, then an elaborated code facilitates the exchange of individualized or personal symbols.

It is important to note that the various codes involve differing planning activities, and may be switched with some facility, to cope with differing social relations. Bernstein (*1965*) offers the illustration of a man at a party who finds a large number of people whom he has never met before.

> He goes up to a girl. He will then use, initially, a restricted code (lexicon prediction), which will provide the basis for the social relation. He will attempt to improve upon his understanding of her specific attributes by the meaning he gives to her presence and extra-verbal transmissions. He then is likely to move toward an elaborated code (if he possesses one) so that they may both have a means for elaborating verbally their distinctive experience. The possibility of discovering common ground is in this way increased, and the man may then move into a restricted code (syntactic prediction). The quality of the relationship at this point has been shifted, and the girl may then regard this as slightly presumptious and so force the man back to an elaborated code, or, if he is very unfortunate, to a restricted code (lexicon prediction). On the other hand she may accept the change in the social relation. The important points here are that the codes are induced by the social relation, are expressing it, *and* are regulating it. *The ability to switch codes controls the ability to switch roles.*

Language Codes and Social Class: Correlates

Language codes, then, can be seen as meta-pathways, as linguistic translations of the meanings of social structure, as channels for verbal planning. They thereby affect capacities not only to receive messages from others, but also to organize responses and actions. In the restricted code, the structure of speech is simplified, the range of vocabulary choice is narrowed, the possibilities for representing the unique experience of the speaker are restricted. Speech is not used as an important means for communicating relatively explicitly unique experience, separateness and differences, and hence perceptions of self are not likely to be the objects of special analysis. Rather, the identity of the individual may be refracted to him by the concrete symbols of his groups; it is determined by status or position, rather than individually. In a sense, a person limited to a restricted code has no problem of identity because the problem is irrelevant (*Bernstein, 1963*).

By contrast, a person who, in addition to restricted codes, has learned elaborated codes becomes increasingly sensitive to and aware of orders of relationships (cognitive, evaluative and emotional), and his experiences are transformed by these relations. Language is perceived as a set of theoretical possibilities for the presentation of his own discrete experiences — thereby emphasizing his separateness, difference, uniqueness, and individual identity.

The research of Bernstein and his colleagues in England indicates that these codes are to some degree related to class. Grossly, middle-class individuals are more likely to have access to elaborated codes, lower-class individuals are more likely to be limited to restricted. Bernstein (*1962*), using small samples, found lower-class boys, compared to middle-class, were more likely to use personal pronouns referring to "you" and "they" (as contrasted with the individuating pronoun, "I"). Further, the lower-class boys were more restrictive in the use of adjectives, of uncommon adjectives and uncommon adverbs, and more simplistic in verbal forms. These findings support the thesis that the working class subjects do not so much explicate intent verbally and are less likely than the middle-class to engage in speech that individuates the speaker from the group. Further, Bernstein found a difference in the proportion of selected personal pronouns to total number of words used, suggesting that the content of lower-class speech is more likely to be descriptive and less abstract than middle-class. Similarly, Lawton (*1963, 1964a, 1964b*) found that working class boys were more likely to use egocentric sequences, especially when coding difficulty was experienced — a finding of particular significance to the discussion of the relation of the middle-class therapist to the lower-class client. Lawton's research also indicated that middle-class groups switched from descriptive to abstract codes with greater facility and frequency than the lower-class.

In another study, in attempting to identify measures that would discriminate elaborated from restricted codes in other than linguistic terms, Bernstein (*1962a*) followed Goldman-Eisler (*1954, 1961*) in analyzing hesitation phenomena. Consistent with his hypotheses, Bernstein found that the working-class subjects used longer phrase length, and spent less time pausing than did middle-class subjects, even when verbal and nonverbal intelligence were held constant. He argued that, if the speaker is oriented to an elaborated code, he might tolerate the tension associated with delay in verbal selections. Subsequently, his selection is likely to be more appropriate, and the tension more adequately reduced by the appropriateness. In restricted codes, however, raising the level of coding difficulty (complicating the problem), and thereby increasing the likelihood of delay, may lead to either a breakdown in speech or a failure to adjust to the new speech demand. Either way, the restricted code does not facilitate the toleration of tension and the reduction of tension by verbal activity. It may well be, then, in terms of the motivational theory of Chapter 1, that a restricted code is less likely to lead to the falsification and the elaboration of cognitive and evaluative horizons. In a restricted code, responses to tension tend to be channeled through somoto-motor and expressive sets. In this sense, restricted codes transform experience in such ways that the development of elaborated codes and of perceptions of unique identity are unlikely. If this nascent theory is further substantiated, it could hold demanding pertinence for the therapy process and relationship.

Other consequences of the restricted planning capacities may also prove pertinent. For instance, it is generally recognized that the number and diversity of associates are limited among the working class compared to the middle class. Although various factors contribute to this difference, it may be that a critical determinant is the verbal capacities that individuals bring to their meetings with other persons. In establishing a friendship, some sort of symbiotic relationship must be worked out, requiring a marked degree of orientation, selection, and organization of messages with close reference with those transmitted by the other. Verbal planning, then, is critical to the identification of the desires and qualities of the other. If capacities for verbalizing are restricted, the range and type of others who can be so internalized are limited. It is likely, then, that the social ties to those who are internalized may become very powerful.

If, as evidence indicates and theory argues, highly elaborated codes do not tend to develop in working-class sub-cultures, then the psychotherapist may experience real difficulty in attempting to cope with the "common-sense" world of the client. As was suggested in the opening passages of this chapter, to the extent that the communications of psychotherapist are filtered through this "common-sense" word, psychotherapy may be hindered. If this common-sense world is peopled by only a few, powerful bonds, by relationships relatively similar to one another and hence offering but few concrete alternatives for planning, then efforts to restructure self-perceptions and to bring the client to perceive himself as individuated and unique may be futile. Further, when these bonds, as well as the individual's own identity, have been little subject to critical examination, and when the client does not possess the habits or the verbal capacities to engage in such perceptive analyses, the task of psychotherapy grows from difficult to impossible.

One other consequence of restricted verbal planning may have close pertinence to the psychotherapy process: as the problem to be solved becomes more and more abstract, it is likely that inner verbal sequences will be involved that have the effect of changing the qualities of the signals responded to. When the thinker is limited to a restricted code, the verbal sequences evoked may direct perception to the more gross aspects of the environment. Thereby, his solution becomes more and more inappropriate in relation to the degree of abstraction of the problem. In some problem-solving activities, this verbal feedback may be continuously reinforced, thereby creating an even tighter bond between the thinker and the concrete and descriptive. The tighter the bond, the more difficult the psychotherapeutic enterprise.

It should be remembered that the use of these codes, and the tendency to use them may be quite independent of native ability, although the level at which a code is used undoubtedly reflects inherent capacities. It is clear, however, that the socializing and supporting capacities of social relations and of the social structure in general are critically important in determining language capabilities. Children socialized in middle-class strata can be expected to possess both elaborated and restricted codes, while children socialized in at least certain subcultures appear to be limited to restricted codes. Likely, as perception of differences in language codes become less gross, it will be useful to search for more subtle differences in language coding systems that serve to organize and constrain planning, action, and identify formation.

But soical class is only one of various social categories that appear to be related to differences in language coding capabilities. If differing socialization procedures can result in differing language and speech codes, it is apparent that differences in geographic region may be related to development and mode of content of language codes; that rural groups may contrast markedly with urban; that ethnic groupings, particularly those related to minority statuses, might evidence differences in syntactic and lexical forms. Indeed, one might expect differences in many categories of subcultures within any particular society.

It may be even more telling, however, to look at relationships that crosscut these general social categories. For instance, it is possible that various structures of positions and roles within an authority system generate, support, and activate differing codes. Similarly, it is possible that family roles and relationships of different qualities — for example, families that operate primarily via personal influences, contrasted with those which rely heavily on positional (or status) influences — would develop and support in their members differing linguistic forms that

77

pervasively influence the individual's perceptions and capacities to deal with various types of experience. In the remainder of this essay, I will speculate on this possibility.

Language Codes and Social Relations: Determinants

In the preceding pages emerged one general, overriding proposition; the more closely limited a client is to a restricted code, the less likely is effective psychotherapy. But what is it that *leads to the development* of various types of codes? Following Bernstein, I have suggested that the codes correlate in modern societies with broad social categories such as social class, ethnic grouping, and geographic regions. Quite beyond the simple question of correlations, however, the present concern is with determinants, or *causal* relations.

Developments in codes appear to be functions of the ongoing socialization of children and adults — or, in the terms of the motivational theory of Chapter 1, they are closely related to the types of falsification the individual experiences. To seek causal relationships, then, it is necessary to understand psychological relationships; from such a base, it may be possible to identify forms of social relationships that help to determine these psychological capacities. For, in theory, there is no *necessary* link between social class and type of language code. Rather, for instance, restricted codes demonstrably dominate in closed communities, or total institutions, such as prisons, hospital wards, and combat units. Similarly, they are a characteristic of the relationship between close friends, in peer groups of children and adolescents, and between husband and wife. Indeed, when the form of social relationship is based on some extensive or closely shared identifications consciously held by members, restricted codes are likely to be highly active, and unique meanings of the speaker will tend to be implicit and not verbally elaborated.

If restricted codes are generally available to all members of a community, regardless of their social categories and relationships, and, further, if it is apparent that elaborated codes are not generally available, the question becomes more direct: What experiences and types of relationships tend to restrict the individual to the development of only restricted codes? In the following discussion, I will focus on one characteristic of relationships that may be critical: the types of interpersonal influence and control to which the individual is subject.

Language Codes and Dyad Relations

Most simply stated, in seeking to influence the activity of another person, an individual relies on *personal influence* and/or on *positional influence*. This distinction arises from the proposition that in interaction, individuals tend to develop both a personal relationship, or the relation of ego to alter as individuals, and a positional relationship, or the relation of ego to alter as status or position holders in a group. That is, in a dyad or a larger group, two kinds of behavioral influence can be identified. The first is the influence members have on one another because of their personal relationships; the second, the influence they have on one another because of their position in the group structure. These relationships may be characterized either by regularities of behavior, by functional characterizations, or by the type of expectations inherent. (For a discussion of the communicational bases of these modes of influence, see Chapter 4, pages 136–141.) Although research may be most readily approached if focus is on the regularities of behavior, to define the relationship more specifically it is more useful to focus on expectations, for an essential element of the "relationship" is the members' agreement that it will probably exist largely unchanged at least in the near future. Although the following discussion, then, is couched in terms of expectations, only minor modifications would be required to identify the behavioral characteristics of the relationships.

Most generally, personal relationships develop as individuals seek solution to their own felt needs and desires and to those perceived in their alter. Because the most pressing of these needs are often not shared or even complementary, the relationship depends on concern of at least one person with the other's individual needs and desires. Positional expectations, by contrast, develop less in response to individual needs and desires than to the problems the members *share* because of conflicts and demands and requirements of members, group and community. Solutions to such problems are seen in group structures such as the authority hierarchy, the division of labor, and patterns of guidance or educative responsibility. Generally, both personal and positional relations require some predictability (for example, in situation X, Johnny will do Y), but personal also involves especially egoistic desires (for example, in situation X, I'd like Johnny to do Z no matter what people say), while positional relationships involve especially normative prescriptions (for example, in situation X, Johnny should not do P because the community expects him not to).

Elsewhere, I have advanced a number of specifying propositions about the two types of relationships (*Hansen, 1965*):

Positional	*Personal*
1. The array of expectations shared by ego and alter is generally shared by all or most other members of the group.	1. The array of shared expectations is unique to each dyad.

2. The expected behavior is primarily contractual, and is seen by ego and alter as such.

2. The expected behavior may be, in some important parts, voluntary, and may be recognized as such by the recipients.

3. Given some social stability the array prescribes actions which serve to control tension between external agents and the group.

3. The array prescribes action (or types of action) which contribute to the individual needs of ego and alter, and only indirectly to the solution of group members' shared problems, or to control of tension between external agents and the group.

4. The array may be supported by community sanction as well as by sanction of group members.

4. The array receives little or no positive sanction external to the dyad.

5. The array allows behavioral influence based on coercion or manipulation.

5. The array allows behavioral influence based only on cohesion.

6. Positional relations *tend* to be stable and rigid.

6. Personal relationships tend to be unstable and flexible.

Parallel to that inquiry, in which I related personal and positional influence modes to family vulnerability to stress, Berstein (unpublished) developed similar concepts using different terms in a discussion of family role systems and socialization. Certain of the propositions in these discussions can be combined, affording preliminary specification of the personal and positional modes of influence.

The two types of influence, then, rest on different bases of power, and imply actions that have differing consequences. Most importantly, personal influence depends on mutual assent or attraction, while positional influence can be exercised via threat or imposition of force. In short, personal influence may be characterized as "coercive." That is, coercive demands rely for their effectiveness upon the discrepancy between the relative positions, or statues, of the regulated and the regulator. The social context of control is such that the relationships are very clear-cut, the roles are un-ambiguous. The regulator is concerned primarily with the consequences of action, and focuses on manifest behaviors. Such differences in positions may be reflected in the ways a person speaks of another's reactions to him. For example, in response to the question, "How did your father feel about your being arrested," a boy may respond:

(1) "Well, he's a *father*, after all, I guess he was pretty mad because I'm his son and I let him down." (Response emphasizes positional elements of father-son relationship.)

(2) "He was really mad, and I could see that he felt hurt, and that made me feel bad too. I guess he didn't think I'd do something like that." (Response emphasizes personal elements.) (*Hansen, 1963*)[2]

Positional influences are not limited to coercion, but also allow appeals. The appeals, however, are of quite different character from those allowed in a personal relationship. Positional appeals refer the regulated to specific normative prescriptions which do not depend upon his own individual personal characteristics. In positional appeals, the special attributes of the regulated are irrelevant to the communication. As in the case of the coercive influence, focus is on manifest behaviors.

Personal appeals are very different, Bernstein (unpublished) suggests, for the regulated is referred to the *feelings* of the regulator or the *significance* of the act is related explicitly. Either way, the rule is mediated through the special characteristics of the personal relationship. In this way, the regulated has access to the regulator as a person and he has access to the significance of his own acts as they relate to him as consequences. Personal appeals tend to generate role relations in which there is a relatively wide area of discretion. The necessity of his response may result from the logic of the reasoning, or from the consequences of his actions as they relate to his own feelings or to the feelings of the regulator. Alternatives can often be worked out for transmitting a rule.

In a sense, then, in personal relations, the regulated achieves rules; in positional relationships he is assigned them. In the first case, the rule is individualized, transmitted to the regulated in a situation which is specific to him, thus serving to differentiate him from others even though they have accepted the same rules and overtly act in much the same way. In positional relationships, however, rules are transmitted in such a way that the regulated receives them in situations where the local context of the relation is less relevant. Thus, little differentiation is established between those regulated. In short, in positional relationships rules tend to be communalized, in personal, they tend to be individualized (*Bernstein, 1962*).

2 This article also suggested a number of illustrative hypotheses about such communications in the counseling situation (*Hansen, 1963*). For example, it might be hypothesized: The greater the proportion of responses through personal communication lines, the greater the affective flow between individuals.

The greater the proportion of positional responses used in references to another person, the less likely is that person to determine the behavior of the client (except by coercion or force).

The greater the proportion of responses along positional communication lines, the greater the probability the client is "playing at the role," or presenting a false image of himself.

The greater the proportion of positional responses during an interview, the lower the agreement between client and counselor about the effectiveness of the counseling.

(In this earlier discussion, the terms "group" and "structural" were used; these have here been changed to the less imprecise "personal" and "positional.")

Bernstein's (unpublished) discussion suggests a number of implications of these differences between the personal and positional influence, three of which can effectively be applied to the discussion of psychotherapy.

First, personal influence works through the explicit verbalizing of intent, whereas positional influence is directed primarily at consequences of action, in which intent is of little or no importance. This suggests that the personal influences more consistently falsify the cognative and evaluative horizons, more persistently place the individual in tension situations in which he is required to identify and verbalize not only his own intent, but also that of the person influencing him. His "I," then, is more likely to emerge, and he is more likely to develop capacities to articulate and verbalize his inner experiences. In short, he is more likely to develop those capacities required by existing modes of psychotherapy.

Second, personal influences are more likely to develop systems of inner control resting on guilt, in which the child is forced to recognize and specify the effects of his actions on persons and things. Hence, the child learns to adapt to the tensions involved in relating to persons and things mainly by being able to tolerate guilt. Positional influence, by contrast, is more likely to elicit conformity induced by shame, or as a felt experience of diminution of respect from others. Again, it might be said that guilt is individualized, shame is communalized. Once again, with the traditional modes of personal psychotherapeutic relationships, it is likely that the individual persistently limited to positional influences is less likely to develop the affective and evaluative qualities necessary for effective psychotherapy. Although the positional influence may lead to developments in which the individual is highly responsive to situational influence, although he may be able to respond to notions of wrongness and justice, feelings of guilt and personal involvement will tend to be dissociated from notions of wrongness. Affective involvement then, may be coped with by denial or projection.

Third, the lack of clarity or ambiguity in the relationship of client to counselor may pose special problems for the individual whose socialization and continued reinforcement have been dominated by positional influences. Further, because of the communalized character of the internalized social control, the individual may evidence low anxiety thresholds and an incapacity to tolerate the anxiety. He may tend to restructure communications in the psychotherapy session along lines more familiar to him in terms of his common sense world in which well-articulated structures of authority, age and sex relationships provide clear and unambiguous prescriptions for appropriate behavior. Further, because of his inability to specify his tensions with ready facility, and because of his lack of experience with successful delay and satisfactions of tensions, he is more likely to dissipate the tensions introduced intentionally in psychotherapy through more immediate, concrete channels, such as changes in muscular tensions, somato-motor sets, or in expressive behavior.

Family Relationships and Language Codes

If the argument that personal relations and positional relations have differing effects on the development of language codes is valid, it represents only the beginning of an arduous discussion. From this base, we might ask myriad questions:

Under what social conditions are various types of relationships likely to develop and dominate in an individual's experience? How wide an array of processes and structures — for example, authority structures and decision-making processes — might be associated with the development of each type of relationship? Are early relationships critically determinant of later linguistic possibilities? Does a mature individual tend to seek out structures and relationships consistent with those most satisfying in earlier conditions; does he tend to avoid those kinds most dissatisfying?

These questions are but a sketchy representation of those which might be asked, and each is capable of diverse answers. The theories presented elsewhere in this book suggest some possible answers. For instance, the motivational theory of Chapter 1 suggests that early experiences can be strongly influential of later possibilities, but that they are not as critically determinant as, say, an orthodox Freudian might hold. But we cannot speculate on such arguments here, for each of the questions requires more rigour than time or space allows.

Rather, I focus here on one question: What is the relationship of familial structures to the development of linguistic codes? This discussion turns on the above speculations on influence modes. Theoretically, families might exist without either personal or positional influence, but such pure relationships are highly improbable in real life. Rather, personal and positional expectations converge, and the actions of family members are influenced by a blend of the two. The question is, how much influence does each type of relationship have on the behavior of any member?

Bernstein (*1964,* unpublished) has employed a simple distinction, between "person-oriented" and "status-oriented" dyads and families. The distinction is useful, and organizes Bernstein's sensitive insights into the patterns and effects of influence. The construct must be recognized as an "ideal type" model, that is, as a contrast of rather polarized forms which serves to illuminate rather than accurately represent. As such, it cannot be criticized for slicing the real world up into gross dichotomies. It can, however, be criticized for failing to take into account important parts of the real world; the slicing job, that is, is incomplete, if the intent is to increase understanding of family relations. That is, Bernstein's distinction between "status oriented" and "person-oriented" does not allow attention to those families or other relationships which are *neither* status nor person oriented. Nor does the construct allow attention to those relationships which are essentially *person* oriented — for, in his model Bernstein apparently assumes that the "person-oriented" will also to some degree be status oriented; his distinction, then, is essentially between those relationships which are "person-and-status oriented" and those which are only "status-oriented."

The following discussion, whatever its own deficiencies, avoids this restriction — but it should be noted that, once again, I have benefited from Bernstein's discussions and have drawn many of the following propositions from his unpublished paper on family role systems and socialization.

It was suggested in the previous section that personal and positional influences may be legitimately treated as independent variables, rather than as a single continuum. Four ideal types of relationship may then be identified: (a) Strong in both personal and positional influences; (b) Strong in personal but weak in positional influence; (c) Strong in positional but weak in personal influence; (d) Weak in both personal and positional influence. In each ideal type, qualitative differences in relationships can speculatively be identified.

Type A. The J.B.s (strong personal and positional influence):[3] In a family of this type, intimate contact is as important to most members as are the authority and status relationships among themselves and with the community. It would tend to stability of organization, probable durability, efficiency of operation, a high degree of satisfaction felt by participants, marked conformity of members to group mores, sensitivity of individuals to the expectations of others, and marked ability of members to predict the behavior of others. Both personal and positional relationships, in times of non-stress, exert influence cohesively but, under stress, members may be effectively coerced to conformity.

In such families, decision-making processes and appeals rest on a blending of both the attributes of the individuals involved and their formal family status. Though normally, and in nonstressful situations, both appeals and decision-making may emphasize person orientation, positional differences — in terms of age, sex, strength, and/or control of material resources — may be implicit, or be introduced in stressful situations. Members may be allowed broad areas of discretion and individual

[3] From Archibald MacLeish, *J.B.* (1958). The names of these types, which refer to families depicted in popular literature in situations which highlight their mode of behavioral influence, are offered only to aid in description of the types.

choice, requiring communication of those choices and justification of intent. Hence, new meanings are facilitated, and probability is maximized not only of falsification of cognative horizons, but also of evaluative. This ideal type of family is characterized by role flexibility; though structures are strong, because of the emphasis on individual characteristics and decision-making they are also flexible. The children will *achieve* participation, but it will be participation not only in the development and continuance of personal relationships, but also of structural relationships. Differences will be displayed particularly through language, giving rise to reciprocal socialization between parents and children. As a consequence, the family as a group will be continuously reorganizing, responsively to the demands of the active members; consequently, too, individually the members will be encouraged to constantly elaborate their individual horizons, to discover new things about themselves, to develop a sense of the self as distinctive and yet collaborative. The relationship may be characterized as one of "controlled unpredictability," offering a dynamic stability. Individuals will be able to seek and expect change, yet not have to fear traumatic alterations. Hence, experiences with delay of satisfactions will tend to be profitable, and capacity for tension tolerance can be expected.

Because of this character, the legitimacy of the status structure tends not to be questioned, but rather individual members will internalize and identify with the systems of control inherent in the family processes. Because of the responsive stability of such a family, the individual is likely to experience successful tension maintenance; rather than seeking immediate gratification or satisfaction, he is likely to evidence tendencies to delay satisfaction in order to win greater satisfactions at a later date. Hence, family relations of this sort are likely to lead to future-orientation, and to strongly encourage elaboration of language codes.

This speculative discussion may be continued with those two ideal types generally considered when positional and personal relations are taken as a single continuum.[4]

Type C. The Albas (strong positional, weak personal influence):[5] Families of this sort would be typified by contractual behavior, in which services are exchanged on a profit-motive basis or are coerced; by tendency toward efficient operation; by stability as long as there is no choice of escape by members; by inflexibility. Relationships tend to be coercive; one or more individuals (for example, the patriarchal father) dominate

4 It should be recognized that the entire discussion is speculative and should be taken as a series of imprecise hypotheses. Diverse other hypotheses follow from these; specifically, it might be hypothesized that the hesitation phenomenon is more likely to appear, other things held equal, in children from type A families, and least likely to appear in children from type C and D families.

5 Federico Garcia Lorca, "The House of Bernada Alba" (1947).

the others, and force them, perhaps subtlely, to behave as the dominators desire. Internal or covert conflict may build intensely, as members fester in submissive roles. In ideal type, roles tend to be clearly differentiated, and in decision-making, status is far more important than special individual attributes. Though there may be lively conversation, there will be little mutual discussion. The norms regulating age relations will be clear-cut and unambiguous. Parents socialize children, but the latter do not socialize parents, hence, the uniqueness of each child does not play an important part in modifying relationships. As a result, the family does not tend to operate to help the individual (and especially the child) to differentiate himself as a unique person, but rather assigns him roles determined by community or familial mores and norms.

As a result, Bernstein (unpublished) has suggested, such families protect the normative order, but for persons who are socialized within them rebellion necessarily takes the form of questioning that very normative order (as distinct from Type B, The Tyrones, described immediately below, in which the parent, rather than the normative order may be questioned). Rules are assigned, and tend to be more rigid. If they are inappropriate to the individual, there is strong likelihood that he will tend to reject not only the regulator, but the entire normative order.

Because rules are assigned, there is little necessity to verbally specify the intent of the regulated, nor to justify it. Neither the dominated nor the dominator develop these tendencies and the dominated, especially, are little encouraged in differentiating the self. Appeals to conformity tend to be status-oriented. The net effect is to transmit the family norms or local culture in such a way as to increase the similarity of the socialized with others who hold a similar status. If the child rebels he is challenging *both* the demands *and* the rights of parent or regulator to make the demands, and it is this which will quickly expose the latent power in the relationship. The social context of control is such that the relationships are very clear-cut. The roles are un-ambiguous, and the regulator is concerned solely with the consequences of action. As such, high predictability and stability develop, and individuals may tend to develop a tension toleration; hence in families of this type we may expect some degree of future orientation, in which immediate satisfactions are denied in order to gain greater satisfactions at a later time.

In short, except under severe stress such families offer their members a situation of controlled predictability, in which rules are assigned, rather than achieved, in which, hence, there is little tendency to specify or justify intent on the part of either the dominated or the dominator, in which the normative order is so closely tied to the familial processes that rejection or resentment of one may require rejection of the other, in which self-differentiation is not encouraged, as rules are communalized rather than individualized, in which development of future-orientation and tension toleration is likely. Hence in this ideal type are expected no strong tendencies to elaborate language codes.

Type B. The Tyrones (strong personal, weak positional influence):[6] Families of this ideal type would tend to be unstable. Though they may be mutually satisfying, they are unable to withstand stress of many sorts, for they are based directly on the mutual satisfaction of members. Under minor stress — even, for instance, that which may result as a normally submissive person becomes under therapy more assertive and demanding — such families may be strengthened, as voluntary actions stimulate reciprocation; in this type of family decisions are made with close reference to personal attributes of the members, rather than by virtue of family positions. Status differentiations or those of age and sex are obscured by the expression of qualities unique to individuals. "Clearly if there is less role segregation, then the areas of discretion available to each member is greater with the consequence that selection from alternatives may be made on an individual basis. Inasmuch as the range of decision available to each member is relatively great then personal choices may be communicated." (*Bernstein,* unpublished.)

Because of the importance of individual choice, members tend to specify and justify their decisions; they tend to *achieve* participation. That is, there is far less tendency than in the Alba family to assign roles. Individuals are encouraged to display their differences, particularly through language. Hence, there is reciprocal socialization, and as much as the parents are responsive to the individual differences of the child, the child becomes aware of himself as distinctive and unique. Because of these reciprocal relations, and because of the importance of verbal elaboration and justification of intent, the system tends to be unstable, and gives rise to special arbitration and reconciliation procedures (Bernstein, unpublished). Conceptions of self are differentiated by continuing adjustment to the verbally differentiated intent of others — that is, there is continued falsification of horizons, including those aspects, both evaluative and cognative, most powerfully cathected. There is recognition of psychological differences and support for the child as he comes to recognize his own difference, and members learn to handle ambiguities in sex and age role relations.

In such relationships, members are less likely to question the rights of the regulator which inhere in his formal status; what may be challenged are reasons or special conditions of the regulators ("Do you always have a headache when I want to play?") — hence, it is possible that the formal rights of the regulator can be accepted, though the person might be disvalued (Bernstein, unpublished). In other words, in such relationships special or unique attributes of the regulated become verbally

6 Eugene O'Neil, *Long Day's Journey into Night* (1956).

relevant, and the discretionary element or reciprocal component enters the role relation. Taking a large number of families of this sort, it might be seen that children have achieved the same rule, but that each has received it in a context specific to him. That is, there is differentiation between children within the context of the same role (or within the same normative order).

Thus, in common with the J.B. Type, there tends in the Tyrone family to be a continuing reciprocation of members, continuing identification of intent, and hence elaboration of cognative and evaluative horizons; that is, there are likely to be tendencies toward elaboration of language codes, and differentiation of self as unique and individual. But because of the ambiguities in positional relations, many of status implications of the relationship may be missed, and social control may become problematic. The individual is less likely than in the J.B. family to have successfully maintained tension levels in order to gain greater satisfactions in the future — that is, such families may be characterized as evidencing *uncontrolled unpredictability*, and may tend to be present oriented, that is to favor the certainty of immediate satisfaction to the chances of greater satisfaction of a later time.

In short, this type of family would be characterized by uncontrolled unpredictibility, in which individuals tend to be present-oriented and lack tension tolerance, in which roles are achieved but may not be related to acceptance of general normative orders, in which, then, intent is necessarily specified and explicit, and in which, hence, there is strong tendency toward self-differentiation and elaboration of language codes.

Type D. The Boyles (weak personal and positional influence):[7] Families of this type can be hampered by instability, questionable durability and little satisfaction for members. A member who offers voluntary aid is likely to be frustrated and a member who needs help may even refuse it. Such families evidence neither cohesion nor effective coercion. Indeed, all that holds them together may be ennui or community sanctions against disorganization. What influence is available will tend to be positional and intent will not tend to be verbally specified or justified. Hence, the individual may tend to lack experience with maintaining tension in order to achieve greater satisfaction at a later time. Time orientation may tend to be present and the differentiation of self as a unique individual may be problematic.

In short, such families may be characterized as evidencing uncontrolled unpredictibility, in which individuals tend to be present-oriented and lack tension tolerance, in which there is ineffectual effort to assign rules, intent is not specified, and self differentiation is problematic. The normative order will likely be unclearly seen, and, at least in some com-

7 Sean O'Casey, *Juno and the Paycock* (1957).

munity contacts, the individual may be at once suspicious and desirous of authority.[8]

These comments refer specifically to families as if they were isolated from social contexts. Yet, indirectly, many of the propositions suggest that community contexts are critical to the family relationships, and may modify the familial influences on an individual; they also suggest that community, school and peer relations also will affect the individual's development and capacities for entering effective psychotherapy. Hence, these constructs — as the rest of our speculations in this chapter — require not only specification and elaboration, but also extension. This discussion has but begun a complex argument.

The pertinence of community contexts is also suggested by the observation that — although most readers might consider the J.B. type family most "desirable" — in some social contexts other types of families might be more appropriate. For instance, even Boyle type relationships may be highly functional in, for example, primitive tribes where community structures may substitute for familial authority. In such communities, the specification of intent and the development of self-differentiation might be explosive, tearing down community ties and subjecting individuals to anomic existence. Or, it may be that the Tyrone family type is most appropriate in a Kibbutz-type society, where community structures substitute in large part for the familial authority, and mutual satisfactions involving identification of intent and continual self-differentiation become the basis for inter-personal relationships.

It should also be apparent that this discussion of family types is related to the discussion of social class, at least in contemporary Western society. Each of the four ideal types is fairly closely approximated in all social strata, but some appear to occur more frequently in lower classes than in middle. That is, we might expect middle class families to appear commonly in all four types, but lower-class families would be overrepresented in the Alba and Boyle types (C and D). These, it should be remembered, are the families least likely to encourage the development of elaborated codes.

8 These ideal types refer to families in which all the dyad relationships of members fall within one quadrant. But many families contain isolated members: influence over one person is markedly greater or less than over others. Though many combinations are possible, even in a three person group or family, elsewhere (*Hansen, 1965*) I have suggested that two are most probable. *The Caulfields* (J. D. Salinger, *Catcher in the Rye* [1953]): parents are close and share both personal and positional influence, but little influence impinges on the child because either the child rejects and ignores the parent or the parents reject and ignore the child. *The Morels* (D. H. Lawrence, *Sons and Lovers* [1913]): The anxious parent who works alone to keep the family intact. Though these types are not discussed here, it should be recognized that they would require further elaboration of the sorts of materials we have presented.

Discussion and Summary

In short, Bernstein has argued that language codes are transformations of roles which influence not only the individual's behavior, but also his capacities for orienting, selecting and organizing communications, including those communications the individual carries on with himself. That is, language codes are directly relevant to the capacities of the individual for various types of interpersonal relationships and individual growth. They are, then, critically relevant to the psychotherapeutic process and relationship.

It was asked if any correlates could be identified with type of language codes, noting that Bernstein's research identifies social class as one correlate, with lower class persons more likely to be capable of exercising only a restricted code. If class or ethnic grouping or geographic area are, indeed, correlated with types of codes, it is then necessary to ask what it is within such groupings which give rise to differing codes; that is, what are the causal factors involved? Only one aspect of the processes and relationships which might be relevant has been discussed, suggesting that personal (contrasted with positional) influence is more likely to stimulate the development of elaborated coding. If such speculations are valid, however, myriad questions are suggested about personality organization and dynamics, and about social relationships and processes.

Focusing on but one area, the relationship of familial influence modes to the development of linguistic codes, a collection of propositions closely relevant to the psychotherapeutic process was developed. From those propositions, the following may be derived: *Families strong in both personal and positional influence (Type A) tend to encourage the elaboration of linguistic codes and self-differentiations and the development of capacities to tolerate tensions in order to increase later satisfactions. Further, such families may encourage tendencies to accept authority.*

Families which rely primarily on positional and little on personal influence (Type C) by contrast, tend little to encourage development of self-differentiation, are more restrictive in the development of linguistic codes, but may encourage development of future orientations and tensions; further, they may, more than the other types, encourage the resentment of authority structures.

Families which tend to rely principally on personal and little on positional influence (Type B), by contrast, tend to develop capacities for elaboration of codes and self-differentiation, but are less likely than either of the two above types to develop capacities for toleration of tension. Further, offering uncontrolled unpredictability, there may be a tendency to develop modes of social control which lack stability and are readily undermined.

Families which can rely on neither type of influence (Type D) tend to develop neither capacities for self-differentiation nor tendencies to elaborate language codes, and are unlikely to encourage the development of tension tolerance or to develop effective modes of social control.

These propositions suggest that successful psychotherapy can have differing effects on family relations, as the client's familial behavior changes — effects which in turn can influence the client both in psychotherapeutic sessions, and in the continuing consequences of the psychotherapeutic process even after sessions have ended.

These comments on language codes and family relationships should not be taken to suggest that some persons are incapable of entering into effective psychotherapeutic processes. They do suggest, however, that clients differ in linguistic capacities, in attitudes toward authority, in capacities to tolerate frustration, in ability to abstract themselves from their immediate situations and to introspectively analyze and discuss their experiences, relationships, and unique qualities. Further, they suggest that clients differ in their capacities to receive and respond to various types of communication involved in the psychotherapeutic processes. These capacities, it is posited here, are not simply idiosyncratic, but are closely related to the social contexts in which the individual has developed and is maintained. Both sociological correlates, and forms of relationships and processes which lead to the development of these varying capacities may be identified.

Finally, this discussion suggests that perhaps certain techniques of psychotherapy are more appropriate than others to some types of persons. If this is so, it is possible that some of the most appropriate techniques are yet to be developed. It may be that attention to linguistics, and to the sociological correlates and determinates of language and speech codes can aid in the identification and development of more appropriate and effective tools in counseling and psychotherapy.

References

Bernstein, Basil (1960). "Language and Social Class," *British Journal of Sociology*, XI.

——— (1961). "Social Class and Linguistic Development: a Theory of Social Learning," in *Economy, Education and Society*, A. H. Halsey, J. Floud, and A. Anderson (eds.).

——— (1962a). "Linguistic Codes, Hesitation Phenomena and Intelligence," *Language and Speech*, 5.

——— (1962b). "Social Class, Linguistic Codes and Grammatical Elements," *Language and Speech*, 5.

——— (1964). "Social Class, Speech Systems and Psychotherapy," *British Journal of Sociology*, 15 (March).

——— (unpublished). "Family Role Systems, Socialization and Communication," paper given at the Conference on Cross-Cultural Research into Childhood and Adolescence, University of Chicago, 1964.

———— (1965). "A Socio-linguistic Approach to Social Learning," in *Social Science Survey,* J. Gould (ed.) Pelican.

Goldman-Eisler, F. (1954). "On the Variability of the Speed of Talking and on Its Relation to the Length of Utterances in Conversations," *British Journal of Psychology,* 45.

———— (1961). "Hesitation and Information in Speech," *Information Theory, 4th London Symposium,* 162.

Hansen, Donald A. (1963). "The Indifferent Intercourse of Counseling and Sociology," *Journal of Counseling Psychology,* 10.

———— (1965). "Personal and Positional Influence in Formal Groups: Propositions and Theory for Research on Family Vulnerability to Stress," *Social Forces,* 44 (December).

Lawrence, D. H. (1913). *Sons and Lovers,* Mitchell Kinnerley.

Lawton, D. (1963). "Social Class Differences in Language Development: A Study of Some Samples of Written Work," *Language and Speech,* 6.

———— (1964a). "Social Class Language Differences in Group Discussions," *Language and Speech,* 7.

———— (1964). "Social Class Language Differences in Individual Interviews," unpublished manuscript.

Garcia Lorca, Federico (1957). *Three Tragedies,* New Directions.

Macleish, Archibald (1958). *J.B.,* Houghton Mifflin.

Morris, Charles (1938). "Foundations of the Theory of Signs," in *International Encyclopedia of Unified Science,* vol. 1, O. Neurath, R. Carnap, and C. W. Morris (eds.).

O'Casey, Sean (1957). *Three Plays,* Macmillan.

O'Neil, Eugene (1956). *Long Day's Journey Into Night,* Yale University Press.

Salinger, J. D. (1953). *Catcher in the Rye,* Little, Brown.

3 | FAITH AND PSYCHOTHERAPY:

Some Problems in Theories of Psychotherapy

Ronald G. Gallimore / University of Hawaii
Jim L. Turner / University of Missouri

Throughout history, there have been men set apart from their fellow-men to serve the function of healer. The psychotherapeutic techniques and explanations of illness successfully utilized and promoted by these healers and groups have been as diverse as the cultures which sustained them; but the representatives of these guilds typically attributed their successes to the particular medicinal skills and personal knowledge employed. It appears that in many cases their arguments were spurious; from a historical perspective one must conclude that the healers of men have been efficacious in their efforts more often because of what they were than what they knew.

Psychotherapeutic activity has been cloaked in every fad and fashion of religion and science. Amid this diversity, two factors characterize the healing relationship in all cultures and times: (1) the role and status of the healing agent and his ability to arouse and sustain faith in his ministrations and (2) the strength of the sufferer's faith in the healer's efforts. It is the significance of the latter to the efficacy of psychotherapy that this essay is addressed.

Faith as a Therapeutic Variable: A Prologue

The Importance of Faith: An Overview

The often dramatic effects obtained by practitioners or religious healing (*Frank, 1961*) and primitive psychiatry (*Kiev, 1964*) has mandated consideration of patient faith as a variable with psychotherapeutic sig-

Partially supported by a grant from the Foundation of the California State College, Long Beach, California. The helpful comments of Dr. Robert Levy are gratefully acknowledged; we thank Mrs. Phyllis Nygaard for her kind but critical editing.

93

nificance. Similarly, Twentieth century medicine has come to accept the potency of placebo effects as fundamental to the doctor-patient relationship. The patient with faith in the physician and his remedies is not only more likely to comply with instructions but is also more likely to report benefit.

The relevance of patient faith or expectancies to the practice of psychotherapy has long been recognized but seldom appreciated. For the most part, modern practitioners have viewed the patient's expectations as resistance, to be interpreted, to be ignored. Despite early recognition that "expectant faith" was of significance to psychotherapy (*Freud, 1950*, p. 250), current theories do not count faith as a central variable.

As a consequence, contemporary perspectives have suffered from cultural and social blindness. Awareness that psychotherapeutic effectiveness is not independent of the sociocultural matrix in which the relationship occurs has only recently emerged. It has become clear that much of the confusion in theories of psychotherapy stems from over-reliance on psychological explanations of behavior at the expense of sociological and cultural conceptions. As an appreciation of psychotherapy as a sociological phenomenon has grown, so has interest in patient beliefs and expectations.

In this essay we offer a brief review of the historical and scientific evidence supporting the psychotherapeutic significance of faith as a prologue to consideration of several issues confronting contemporary psychotherapy. It is our view that incorporation of faith as a variable will lead to more realistic sociological perspectives on psychological disorder and psychotherapeutic remedy. We propose a general construct to summarize the psychology of patient-sufferer responses within the sociological framework of the healing-psychotherapy relationship: this complex phenomenon, variously called faith, placebo, and expectancy, varies across individuals in likelihood of occurrence, and is elicited within socioculturally defined situations which have been reinforced by social training and experience.

Faith and Religious Healing

The healing properties of faith have been identified and commented upon by religious leaders for centuries. *The New Testament,* for example, suggests that the healing power of Christ required a condition of expectant faith on the part of the afflicted, or of his friends, or of both. Wherever there is a detailed account of a healing miracle the importance of faith is indicated. To the woman "who had had a hemorrhage for twelve years" and who is cured by touching his clothes, Christ remarked, "Your faith has cured you (Mark V)." In Nazareth, the home village of

Jesus, the people knew him as a carpenter, knew his mother and brothers as neighbors, and thus their faith in him as a healer was insufficient to effect miraculous cures (Mark VI). Although he did heal a few people suffering from diseases in his home community, Mark reports that where faith was lacking, Jesus was unable to perform "mighty deeds." To cure the blindman brought to him at Bethesda (Mark VIII) Jesus isolated him from the crowd and used simple therapeutic remedies then in favor and with which the man was undoubtedly familiar.

In each of these cases it seems apparent that the patient was immersed in an atmosphere of faith; reports of Christ's healing success were known to the crowds who surrounded the patient, his family and friends. This aura maximized the faith of the patient in the healer. The dynamics of these healing "miracles" are thus identifiable and are not inconsistent with the characteristics of therapeutic methods up to and including modern psychotherapy.

Frank (*1961*) suggests that modern religious healing occurs under conditions similar to those surrounding the healing miracles of Christ. Aside from the numerous religious sects which regularly employ faith healing rituals, and which operate within a limited social and ideological context, there are examples of faith healing which have won wide acceptance. The Shrine at Lourdes, despite its connections with the Roman Church, is visited by pilgrims from many religious faiths (*Cranston, 1957*). Whether one accepts the reported cures as genuine (fewer than one hundred have been accepted by the Roman Catholic Church as "miraculous") or prefers less dramatic explanations, it is apparently true that many sufferers find the ritual to be of great emotional benefit even though their symptoms persist. Frank (*1961*) observes that the emotionally charged atmosphere, the presence of other expectant pilgrims, the arousal of new hope in the hopeless, all contribute to a strengthening of spirit which may account for improved functioning with or without symptom relief. The reports of improvement or cure through the healing ceremonials at Lourdes share the characteristic conditions described in the New Testament. That is, the participants are emotionally aroused by the ceremony and ritual prescribed and have faith in the shrine as a healing agent.

Faith and Primitive Psychiatry

Closely paralleling the accounts of faith healing in both biblical and contemporary settings are anthropological reports of medical practices in primitive societies. Particularly illustrative is Lambo's (*1964*) report of the integration of traditional practices into a modern psychiatric setting. By keeping the treatment consistent with beliefs and expectations of the Nigerians with whom they deal, Lambo and his associates

95

have enhanced their effectiveness to a degree which they conclude could not have been matched by reliance on scientifically derived procedures alone.

Levy (*1966*) has suggested a sharp distinction, relevant to our present concern, that is observed in these studies of primitive medicine. First, some cases of patient improvement occur despite the fact that the shaman employs methods which are inert and irrelevant. For example, Levy found that success is frequently obtained by Tahitian witchdoctors through assurances to the sick, i.e. cursed, patient that a "countercurse" will be worked on his behalf. Such methods presumably rely upon patient faith alone for whatever benefit they produce.

In other instances, however, it is likely that patient benefit is a product of combining faith with a treatment possessing some degree of potency. In these cases, it is arbitrary to separate faith effects from treatment effects as they are closely intertwined within the cultural definition of disease and cure. Levy provides an excellent illustration of the difficulty of assigning relative weights to faith and treatment effects from data collected during his two year field study in Tahiti. He observed frequent use of a treatment method which capitalizes on strongly repressed, anxiety producing dependency needs fostered by the socialization practices of Tahitians. When a Tahitian exhibits anxiety, depression, or other disturbances, the witchdoctor may prescribe a week of total care by the patient's family. During this period every whim is satisfied and total license is extended to regressive-dependent behavior.

Such treatment methods clearly require faith on the part of the patient as well as those charged with his responsibility. The relative importance of faith, clearly significant in many primitive healing practices, is obscured by the apparent logic of fashioning a treatment so congruent with culturally prevalent personality traits.

At this juncture, it appears that faith influences healing in two ways: first, the faith of the patient may be the only active ingredient. Second, faith may augment or even be necessary to methods which themselves possess some degree of potency. The focus in the present analysis is on faith effects in general and for the remainder of this essay we will not generally distinguish between (1) faith as a necessary and sufficient condition and (2) faith as necessary, but not a sufficient prerequisite of successful healing. The assumption is that virtually all psychological and many physiological-organic methods currently in use are facilitated by and may even require patient faith to achieve optimal effect. The problem of unraveling the relative contribution of faith is beyond the scope of this effort: the level of analysis is ordinal and nominal, not ratio and interval.

Faith and Modern Medicine

The Western scientific-medical equivalent of the faith effect is the placebo response which is defined as relief following the administration of inert or irrelevant procedures. The patient in a modern hospital who claims benefit from sugar pills is responding no differently than the Nigerian who seeks the shaman's potion for relief. The modern importance of the placebo has been recognized and documented by numerous writers. Shapiro *(1960; 1959)* and Whitehorn *(1958)*, among others, are persuaded that the placebo effect is a principal factor in the success of modern Western medicine.

The skepticism which often greets faith or placebo results frequently obscures their value as well as their validity. To dismiss as trivial the claims of a patient that he benefited from an inert remedy suggests rejection of patient report as a criterion for all other treatments as well, scientific or otherwise. In reality, the frequency with which a treatment is employed is often dependent on patient report alone when "objective" experimental evaluations are incomplete or unavailable.

Thousands of units of vitamin B-12 are prescribed weekly by American physicians because patients claim that the shot made them feel better. Such practices capitalize upon the strongly held scientific-medical beliefs of Western societies and the faith of patients in those beliefs. Previous personal experience, reports of family and friends, and general health education reinforce the healing properties of such highly valued procedures as the intramuscular injection to such a degree that benefit is realized independent of what is administered. The active element is faith.

Faith and Psychotherapy

In recent years the obvious implications of faith and placebo phenomena for psychotherapy have received increasing attention. Much of this interest has focused on the speculation that psychotherapeutic success is, at times, not a function of specific treatment variables but rather the result of the same factors in the doctor-patient relationship which generate faith-placebo effects *(Poser, 1966; Schofield, 1964; Goldstein, 1962; Frank, 1961; Shapiro, 1960).*[1]

Goldstein (1962), in particular, has elaborated the analysis of faith-placebo effects in psychotherapy in terms of patient-psychotherapist expectancies. He concludes that the patient's attitude toward his difficulty, his beliefs about the psychotherapist and the role to be played by the psychotherapist, and his conceptions of what constitutes appropriate

[1] Poser *(1966)* calls these the "Placeboid effects"; we agree with his view but retain the term faith.

treatment add to a composite set of expectancies yielding important determinants of psychotherapeutic progress. Goldstein supports his analysis with a substantial array of empirical data which indicate that positive patient expectancies (what we call *faith*) increase psychotherapeutic effectiveness; in our view these positive expectancies are psychologically equivalent to the historical faith concept and the modern placebo.[2]

Other investigators have also reported finding a relationship between patient expectations and psychotherapeutic effectiveness (*Chance, 1959; Gliedman, et al., 1958; Heine and Trosman, 1960; Lennard and Bernstein, 1960*). Their findings and those of Goldstein strongly support the proposition that the significant ingredients in faith-placebo effects are the patient's expectancies about himself, his problem, the treatment he receives and the psychotherapist-healer-physician-shaman. The expectations or beliefs are the genesis of his faith. Faith affects outcome in psychotherapy just as it does in religious healing, primitive psychiatry, and placebo medicine.

Situational Factors in Faith Responsiveness. The arousal of positive expectations, and faith, is partially dependent on situational factors which in the individual's experience have been culturally defined and reinforced as appropriate for healing. The shaman may affect distinctive clothing in his rituals which are performed in special, holy places (*Frank, 1961*). Or as a modern example, placebo research indicates that greatest effectiveness is obtained when inert medications are administered in hospital settings by recognized medical authorities (*Roueche, 1960*). Similarly, Schofield (*1964*) has noted that the dramatic conditions surrounding the initial use of convulsive treatments with psychotics may have been responsible for the high rates of success these techniques enjoyed during the experimental phase of their evaluation. The initial effectiveness of convulsive treatments may have been spuriously inflated as the result of stimulation of patient faith and expectations by the focused attention of the experimenter. In any case, their effectiveness and acceptance have diminished considerably from the time they were first introduced (*Schofield, 1964*).

It has often been observed that the efficacy of a particular treatment procedure is significantly influenced by the degree of faith with which it is practiced. When the exhaustion theory of neuroses was popular, rest and isolation were common psychotherapeutic techniques. Thus Ross (*1938*) reports that when he first tried rest cures with patients, he obtained very satisfactory results. Later he began to have some doubt concerning the exhaustion theory and, he reports, as his doubt increased

---

[2] Transference cures, suggestion effects, and spontaneous remissions have also been presumed to be the product of nonspecific factors in the healer-patient relationship. We regard these phenomena to be faith effects; for a detailed discussion of these conceptions see Goldstein (*1962*).

his cure rate decreased, although the treatment apart from his skeptical attitude was the same. Presumably this loss of faith in rest cures was communicated to his patients, resulting in a diminution of their belief in the efficacy of the treatment, and in subsequent reductions in recovery rate.[3] Such experiences are frequently reported and illustrate clearly the impact of situational variables on expectancies and on outcome of treatment.

In psychotherapy it appears equally true that situational factors affect patient response. Hankoff, *et al. (1958)*, and Overall and Aronson *(1963)* report that low socioeconomic class patients who prematurely drop out of psychotherapy expect physicians and hospitals to be authoritative and impersonal; their expectancies do not include "warm," accepting behavior as appropriate treatment vehicles, nor, for that matter, do they perceive personal insight and introspection to be suitable means to regain health.

While this difficulty reflects the difficulty of doing psychotherapy with clients who neither understand or accept the conditions of verbal-insight psychotherapy, there are other more widely known illustrations of the significance of situational variables. For example, most psychotherapists accept as axiomatic the dictum that treatment is facilitated when the patient is required to pay a fee of sufficient magnitude to make prolonged resistance expensive. The value of fees has been frequently interpreted especially in the United States as reflecting the sociocultural assumption that efficacy and cost are directly related.

However the fee question is interpreted, it shows clearly the effect of situational variables on patient response to psychotherapy. By manipulating conditions in accordance with professionally approved procedures, the psychotherapist acts to maximize patient acceptance of the psychotherapy as appropriate. A person entering psychotherapy may carry culturally reinforced assumptions, or what Hansen (Chapter 5 of this volume) calls "institutionalized expectancies," about the nature of treatment. If the situation he enters differs markedly from these expectations, he will fail to respond much the same as the Nigerian whose physician ignores traditional methods *(Lambo, 1964)* or as the afflicted person at Lourdes who remains detached and who does not experience the uplift reported by the faithful. The relationship between faith, sociocultural factors, and psychotherapy is discussed in greater detail in the second major section of this paper.

Individual Differences in Faith Responsiveness. There are, presumably, individuals in every society who are affected more than most others by participation in culturally approved healing relationships. Our position suggests that the individual must be socialized into the expectations

---

[3] For a discussion of the transmission of psychotherapists' expectancies to clients, see Goldstein's review of verbal conditioning and differential reinforcement *(1962)*.

toward treatment methods peculiar to his culture. Further, that persons classed marginal will be less likely to share faith in the healing practices accepted by the larger social group. The study by Hankoff et al. (*1958*), of lower class patients in psychotherapy serves as an adequate example of the effect of marginality.

We further take it that there will be variability in faith responsiveness *within* the socialized group which can most adequately be explained by psychological or personality factors. This has been demonstrated in the case of placebo responders (*Goldstein, 1962*); variation in placebo responsiveness is very often attributable to individual difference variables.

Similarly, Goldstein has shown that individuals with positive expectations toward psychotherapy exhibit certain psychological characteristics: these include (1) marked subjective discomfort, (2) suggestibility, (3) strong confidence in their psychotherapist and his techniques, (4) favorable past experiences with physicians, (5) attraction to the psychotherapist, (6) other-directedness, (7) field-dependency, and (8) characteristic anxiety level. It is intuitively appealing to conclude that Goldstein has satisfactorily described the psychology of the "faith responder"; these seem very clearly the characteristics favorable to promotion of successful healing relationships.

Summary

There is considerable theoretical and empirical justification for assuming that a significant proportion of the variance observed in psychotherapeutic success is attributable to patient faith. Aside from the "psychological readiness" detailed by Goldstein (*1962*), what appears crucial for arousal of faith is not the content of medical-disease beliefs or the methods employed — although variations in sophistication are often striking — but rather congruence among the patient's expectancies, the terms of the treatment, and the behavior of the healing agent.[4]

It is not difficult to perceive a common thread running from faith in a religious figure or shaman to faith in a body of knowledge as exemplified in industrialized cultures. Faith can be psychotherapeutically efficacious whether based on a theistic hypothesis, a set of primitive beliefs, or a scientific body of data.

In the next section some major issues and controversies in contemporary theories of psychotherapy are discussed. It is our intent to demonstrate that two of the most troublesome of these issues become significantly less distressing from the perspective of faith as a psycho-

---

[4] A formulation in the language of communication and persuasion may be considered an alternative to the faith explanation. That is, the influence of the communicator (therapist) and the persuasibility of the target person (client) become the central variables. Our conception of faith effects encompasses the persuasion alternative; to reiterate, our purpose is primarily to emphasize the importance and the implications of faith and behavior change.

therapeutic variable. The purpose is speculative, not exhaustive. To preclude qualification of every point, let it be clear that the analyses offered are not intended to prove the faith hypothesis but rather to stimulate and provoke discussion.

Faith and Some Problems in Psychotherapy

Psychotherapy and the Problem of Efficacy

The paramount issue confronting psychotherapy is the question of efficacy. Controversy over the question of whether psychotherapy helps people has produced a magnificent variety of cliches, bitter exchanges, and, more recently, sophisticated research (*Goldstein, Heller, and Sechrest, 1966*). The debate began in earnest with the publication of Eysenck's (*1952*) conclusions, based on some 8,000 case studies, that psychotherapy is of doubtful value. Eysenck also suggested that certain data pointed to the possibility that a psychotherapeutic experience might be harmful to some patients independent of its value for others. The response — both positive and negative — was immediate and sustained (*Reznikoff and Toomey, 1959; Rosenzweig, 1954; DeCharms, Levy, and Wertheimer, 1954*). Criticism of Eysenck's position has ranged from penetrating to absurd. Indeed, quite aside from the validity of Eysenck's conclusions, some of the initial rebuttals from the pro-psychotherapy side (*Rosenzweig, 1954*) have provided devastating ammunition for their adversaries (*Astin, 1961*). While admitting that psychotherapeutic process was a largely unresearched mystery, those who launched the attack against Eysenck appeared to believe that good intentions were a satisfactory substitute for understanding.

Happily, in recent years a significant number of continuing research programs have been conducted by various groups and individuals; they have wisely forsaken the "one-shot" investigation strategy in favor of sustained examination of central variables. At the same time, crucial methodological and theoretical issues have been refined by a variety of authors (*Szaz, 1960; Goldstein, 1962; Frank, 1961; Bandura and Walters, 1963; London, 1964; Schofield, 1964; Goldstein, Heller, and Sechrest, 1966*). One important effect of these efforts has been to further destroy the myth of the "magic bullet," to use London's phrase, as the strategy of choice in the search for effective methods of behavioral change.

Convergent Results with Divergent Methods. Nevertheless, considerable debate continues over the value of psychotherapy in general as well as over which procedures and techniques are most efficacious. There is merit in drawing upon the religious diversity of the world as an analogue of the varieties of psychotherapies claimed to be effective. Theories and techniques abound in psychotherapy; literally dozens of sects, mutations, and hybrids can be found in the nation's clinics, counseling centers, state hospitals, and private offices, with each step of the dimension represented from "classical" to "neo-" to "influenced by." Psychotherapy has its fashions; it is seldom that any treatment procedure receives wide acceptance and none has gained convincing validation. A commonly observed cycle is for a new theory to appear, enjoy initial acceptance, and then receive little attention, save for a few converts. Typically the author of a new theory or technique is able to report results which are consistently superior, but soon negative evidence begins to accumulate and enthusiasm wanes.

From the abundance of psychotherapies, Harper (*1959*) has detailed 36 separate forms of psychotherapeutic conversation. Others could be added. If the beginnings of psychotherapy are set seventy years ago with Freud's initial work, then at a minimum, since 1895, one new theoretical model has emerged every two years. Such proliferation is not necessarily without merit since no one presumes that all disorders can be modified with a single approach. But the variety from which the psychotherapist may choose does pose the critical question of comparative evaluation.

What little comparative research there is suggests two major conclusions. First, despite wide variation in practices, some degree of success is enjoyed in all schools of psychotherapy and by most psychotherapists. Efficacy studies have consistently reported improvement rates to be about two-thirds for neurotics and one-third for psychotics regardless of the type of treatment employed. After a longterm followup, Hastings (*1958*) concluded that patients treated by a wide variety of procedures showed no significant differences in overall benefit. These and other results (*Apel, Myers, and Scheflin, 1953; Eysenck, 1952; Levitt, 1957*) have not been contradicted by any consistent body of research favoring any particular method (*Goldstein, Heller, and Sechrest, 1966; Schofield, 1964*). Each approach has its successes and its failures, its "remarkable improvements" and its "no apparent changes." The absence of differential effectiveness is particularly striking when identical problems are alleviated by psychotherapists whose personal conceptions of the behavior to be changed as well as what constitutes appropriate treatment are categorically different. In short there is no empirical foundation for the debates over whose techniques are most efficacious; the most compelling conclusion to be drawn from the efficacy studies is that many techniques and procedures apparently work equally well.

Second, other studies suggest that there is greater similarity among the actual practices of psychotherapists than their theoretical orientations would imply or than they themselves claim. The classic work by Fiedler (*1951; 1950*) indicated that age and experience distinguished practicing psychotherapists of various persuasions more than the theoretical character of their consulting room behavior. This fading of theoretical boundaries is also reflected in the casual observation that many successful psychotherapists tolerantly accept and employ concepts and techniques from a wide variety of systems, some of which in theory are mutually exclusive. A study of orthodox psychoanalysts, as an illustration, revealed little consistency in practices across a wide variety of situations even though they all considered themselves to be classical Freudians (*Glover, 1958*).

The Common Factors Hypothesis. Part of the dilemma over which form of psychotherapy ought to be employed as well as the consistency in improvement rates is thus resolved by the apparent overlap in technique. The fact that theories differ matters little if actual consulting room practices are similar. The patient does not "see" the theory as he sees the psychotherapist's behavior. Of course, it is difficult to conceive of two widely divergent personality theories with accompanying systems of psychotherapy which did not also involve some differences in practices. Part of the problem in deciding whether different schools prescribe distinguishable techniques stems from the general lack of specificity which characterizes publications concerned with procedures. Freud, for example, carefully detailed his personality theory, but was quite ambiguous about technique; a leading psychoanalyst (*Menninger, 1958*) has agreed with this analysis and bemoans the lack of interest demonstrated by his colleagues in specifying procedural details. A similar criticism can be made of the emerging forms of existential therapy (*May, 1958*) which are heavy with theory and philosophy but vague on specifics of method.

One important exception is Carl Rogers (*1942*) whose original work stimulated much interest for its explicit statements on procedures; interestingly, in the light of the history of psychoanalysis, Rogers postponed his theorizing until later (*1951*) and has been frequently criticized for doing so. However, as noted earlier, whatever differences appear to distinguish therapies, few of these appear to follow the psychotherapist into the consulting room (*Schofield, 1964*). It is therefore highly questionable to attribute the successes of various forms of psychotherapy to their distinctive features; many writers prefer the hypothesis that psychotherapeutic efficacy is the result of common factors inherent to some degree in all forms of psychotherapy. Although a number of attempts have been made to define the commonalities of psychotherapist-patient relationships, they have been for the most part descriptive rather than explanatory (*Collier, 1950; Hathaway, 1948; Ziskind, 1948*). Such concepts as catharsis, transference, insight, among others have been proposed as the features common to most methods.

More recently, however, faith (under various labels) has been advanced as an important commonality (*Goldstein, Heller, and Sechrest, 1966; Goldstein, 1962; Frank, 1961; Rosenthal and Frank, 1956*).

103

Faith as a Common Factor. Faith, as a common factor, does not imply that the psychotherapist and his techniques are necessarily irrelevant but rather that certain components of the relationship are efficacious independent of the mode treatment or the skill of the psychotherapist. *Our view, essentially, is that the importance of the healer's theory of disease and disorder must not obscure the conceptions held by the patient.*

Assuming that all psychotherapists attract patients who in some measure find their expectations met by the terms of treatment, then it is to be anticipated that success will be obtained with diverse methods. The patient finds in the psychotherapist and the relationship those characteristics with which he associates relief, hope, and expectation of change. The psychotherapist, in his culturally prescribed and reinforced role, functions in a situation and in a manner which tends to arouse the patient's faith. If the psychotherapist in fact behaves as the patient expects, then the benefits of faith will prevail regardless of the psychotherapist's theoretical orientation.

Kiev *(1964)* offers this outline of the conditions necessary for mobilization of faith and its dynamics in the psychotherapeutic relation:

> They include the initial distress of the patient, arousing of hope through dependence upon a socially sanctioned healer, a particular repetitive ritualistic relationship with the healer, a socially shared set of assumptions about illness and healing (the existence of which cannot be disproved by the sufferer's failure to respond), mobilization of guilt, heightening of self-esteem, detailed review of the patient's past life, changes in attitude, and social reinforcement of the new attitudes and behavior (*Kiev, 1964,* p. 8).

With these forces at work, the psychotherapist as the agent of the larger social group is able to achieve desired changes in the patient — faith is the catalyst of the psychotherapist's methods. What theory the psychotherapist subscribes to may be less important than whether it is one with procedural derivatives in which the patient can believe.

Thus, the consistency of improvement rates and the parallel successes of divergent methods may be partially attributable to a common element brought to the situation by the patient. Explanatory concepts and formulations which focus entirely on the psychotherapist and his theory may ignore the patient and his theory. In so doing, the contribution of faith is obscured. Theories which do not satisfactorily account for the phenomena to which they are addressed are not necessarily wrong, but they may be incomplete.

Faith, Psychotherapy and Social Class

Expectations toward treatment are set by the social group from which the patient emerges. The arousal of faith is thus determined, in large part, by the compatibility of the patient's expectations with the demands of the treatment situation. The consequences of incongruence and its implications for the practice of psychotherapy are the focus of attention in this section. For contemporary American psychotherapy these consequences find expression in the exclusion of lower class patients from treatment.

The Problem of Exclusion: A Crisis Issue. Accumulating research (*Overall and Aronson, 1963; Hollingshead and Redlich, 1958; Hankoff, et al., 1958; McMahon, 1964; Goldstein, 1963; Riessman, Cohen, and Pearl, 1964*), suggests that treatment expectations of lower class patients differ markedly from the goals of insight-oriented psychotherapy. The consequences are a significant "no return" rate after first interviews, premature termination after several fruitless sessions, and, in general, failure to benefit from psychotherapeutic intervention. Equally distressing is the demoralizing effect on public agency personnel who seek to extend psychotherapeutic aid to the disadvantaged.

Further, Brill and Storrow (*1960*) found that psychotherapists generally saw lower class patients as less amenable to therapy, less motivated, less willing to accept treatment demands, and less attractive in comparison with middle class patients. The generality of these findings is supported by Schofield's study of psychotherapist preferences.

Schofield (*1964*) has shown that psychotherapists prefer patients with middle-class characteristics and indeed appear to restrict their selection on that basis. He asked social workers, psychologists, and psychiatrists to describe both their "typical" and "ideal" patients; the results indicate that "in no instance are the paired 'typical' versus 'ideal' distributions of very marked incompatibility." Overall the three classes of psychotherapists preferred patients who presented the "Yavis" syndrome: clients who are youthful, attractive, verbal, intelligent, and successful.

Participation in psychotherapy is thus restricted by social class. It appears that psychotherapists are in agreement with their poor clients on at least one point: psychotherapy often is important with the disadvantaged.

This selectivity represents a critical issue for psychotherapists since none of the widely accepted theories of treatment necessarily specify differential effectiveness as a function of social class membership. To be sure, many writers, Freud among them, have suggested that successful individual psychotherapy requires certain patient attributes, i.e., intelligence, capacity to introspect, etc. Also, a patient with a tightly organized defensive style has been demonstrated to be a poor risk (*Strickland and Crowne, 1963*), as are certain other personality types. But in no system is socioeconomic class specifically defined as a variable limiting who can be treated.

Theoretical considerations notwithstanding, a variety of research suggests that the degree of incongruence between the treatment expectations of some persons, especially those from low income groups, and the demands of insight-oriented psychotherapy is sufficiently large to preclude a successful psychotherapeutic experience.

The Genesis of Exclusion Practices. The problem began as an historical accident. Freud and those who followed developed and elaborated psychotherapeutic theory and technique with patients drawn largely from middle and upper classes (*Hunt, 1960*). The exclusion of the poor was built into the emerging systems from the beginning; the early writers and their followers inappropriately generalized their experience from the upper two-thirds of the class structure, in part because the discipline of sociology had yet to document the compelling distinctions to be found within society.

Further complications were added by theories of psychopathology which confounded symptoms with class variations in behavior and cognitive style, e.g., the psychotic-neurotic dichotomy. Since the psychoses are most frequently observed among the lower classes (*Hollingshead and Redlich, 1958*), it was not surprising that psychotherapists long held to the dictum that psychotics were not amenable to psychotherapy.

As clinical knowledge accumulated, psychotherapeutic practices become more refined and focused on the problems of the advantaged; psychotherapists gradually developed an appreciation for certain patient characteristics. Colby's (*1951*) description of the "most suitable type of patient for psychotherapy" clearly reflects the attitudes of psychotherapists for nearly 60 years. He writes:

> He, or she, is someone between sixteen and fifty years of age and of average or above average intelligence. His intellect allows him to be articulate and imaginative in expressing himself and to be able to grasp another's almost purely verbal communications. He has shown some achievement in a competitive job or social group. He is not criminal, and his neuroses does not completely handicap him. A reasonable part of his ego permits him to step back and observe himself with some objectivity. He can see fate as mostly character and not as the "rough tyranny of circumstance." He shows courage in facing and in revealing unflattering aspects of himself. His reality situation is not overwhelming, and the secondary gains his neuroses gleans from it are small. He readily grasps the idea of participating with the therapist to form a team engaged in a joint effort. Finally he wishes (consciously, anyway) to change his attitudes or ways of life in order to help himself, and he makes sincere attempts to do so (*Colby, 1915,* p. 15).

Colby's criteria are in marked contrast to the characteristics of the poor detailed by a wide variety of writers representing many disciplines (*Hunt, 1960; McMahon, 1964; Bernstein, 1963; Deutsch, 1963; Riessman, Cohen, and Pearl, 1964; Hansen,* Chapter 2 of this volume).

As a result of the clash of expectancies and styles both patient and psychotherapist lose faith in the endeavor and terminate; the psychotherapist persuaded that it is hopeless to work with those not meeting the usual criteria and the patient reinforced in his belief that the agents of the larger social group, of which he is a disadvantaged and marginal member, are indifferent to his welfare, and indeed incapable of aiding him despite their claims to the contrary.

One remedy is clear: the basis of psychotherapeutic intervention must be broadened. Methods for increasing the congruence of patient-psychotherapist expectations within the sociocultural matrix must be devised, if necessary, at the expense of tradition. If the patient cannot believe and does not have faith, he cannot be treated — that is the lesson of history, both contemporary and ancient.

New Directions

Changing Patient Expectancies: The Traditional Approach

In one form or another the importance of congruent patient-psychotherapist expectancies has always been recognized as important by various psychotherapeutic disciplines. Consequently, strategies for modifying patient attitudes and expectations which delay and interfere with treatment progress have evolved. The most widely accepted conception of the issue is the psychoanalytic theory of resistance. When the patient's behavior departs markedly from the expectations and demands of the psychotherapist it is labelled defensive and resistant. If the resistance continues despite the therapist's efforts to interpret for the patient, then treatment may, by necessity, be discontinued or delayed.

Resistance removal is generally the first order of business in psychotherapy; this translates to changing the patient's expectations to match the expectancies of the psychotherapist. That is, the patient must learn to accept psychotherapeutic interpretations and other often unpleasant aspects of psychotherapy or forfeit any hope of benefit.

Rotter (*1954*) recognized the problem in his call for "successive restructuring." Because patient expectations are frequently and persistently at odds with the terms of psychotherapy, the psychotherapist must structure the situation repeatedly, perhaps at each session, in order to remind the patient of the rules of treatment. Overall and Aronson (*1963*) have urged "reeducation" of patients in respect to their role and their expectations of how the psychotherapist ought to behave.

Another solution involving matching patients and psychotherapists in terms of their expectancies on the basis of expectancy measures obtained prior to initiation of treatment. With the results, patients could be paired with psychotherapists whose expectancies were most similar. Goldstein's (*1962*) expectancy scales, though not intended for clinical use, represent a beginning and might be used to develop profiles of expectancies analogous to the symptom profiles of the MMPI. This solution is, however, severely limited by the attenuated range of psychotherapist expectations (*Schofield, 1964*).

Goldstein, Heller, and Sechrest (*1966*) view the reluctance of many psychotherapists to be deliberate in their manipulation of patient expectancies as the basic problem. Typically, interpretation of resistance represents the strongest measure taken to get patients to fit the "model." If resistance continues then treatment is terminated; in the case of certain patient categories, notably lower class groups, this is the model event.

In arguing for stronger methods of expectancy modification, Goldstein *et al.*, take the position that all psychotherapies are manipulative despite claims to the contrary. In their view the use of fees to commit patients to treatment is no less manipulative then their often startling extrapolations from the research literature of psychology. Anticipating criticism they offer the following defense of their position:

> Thus the "criticism" that the procedures we have to suggest — if they survive the prerequisite experimental verification and are incorporated in psychotherapeutic practice — would lead to a highly manipulative psychotherapy, whereas psychotherapy as practiced today is generally nonmanipulative, is simply an untrue comparative assertion.

> Manipulative approaches may be attacked on the grounds that they dehumanize, treat the patient as a machine or object or, more generally, that they reflect a nonhumanitarian orientation to sick or unhappy people. Our position, quite the contrary, is that *current* psychotherapeutic approaches are deficient on a humanitarianism continuum largely because they do *not* incorporate or reflect research findings regarding the most effective means of altering an individual's behavior — the raison d'etre of psychotherapy. To know that solid research dealing with attitude change, learning, and a score of other research domains offering other manipulative means of altering an individual's behavior exists, and to deny in an a priori manner the potential relevance of such research to the psychotherapy patient is to perform a disservice to both the advance of psychotherapy and to one's psychotherapy patients (*Goldstein, Heller, and Sechrest, 1966*, pp. 8–9).

As an illustration of the "stronger methods" these authors suggest, consider the following general proposition they have derived from the research literature of social psychology: ". . . by heightening the favorableness of patient attraction toward his psychotherapist, to that degree does the patient become more receptive to psychotherapist influence attempts." This proposition suggests the employment of tactics similar to those used by the shaman who seeks to increase his reputation and thereby his effectiveness through recounting of past successes (*Frank, 1961*). It is no distortion of Goldstein, Heller, and Sechrest's (*1966*) proposal to suggest that they are urging enhancement of patient faith.

To continue, the authors argue that deliberate enhancement of psychotherapist attractiveness as a means of increasing influence represents a broadening of the scope of psychotherapeutic activities and effectiveness. This suggestion is derived specifically from research on interpersonal attraction by such investigators as Schutz (*1958*). In general, it has been found that the more attractive one finds another person the more likely one is to be influenced by that person. It might be argued, then, that psychotherapists ought not to feel reluctant about employing strategies which enhance their attractiveness to patients if indeed their influence is correspondingly increased. If fees are an acceptable means of persuading patients to attend to psychotherapist influence attempts, then other methods represent an extension of current practices and not a break with tradition.

Among the possibilities suggested by Goldstein, *et al.*, is the "plant" in the waiting room who engages "the patient in conversation aimed at direct exposure of the positive value of the psychotherapist and psychotherapeutic participation." (*Goldstein et al., 1966*, p. 114). Alternatively, two accomplices might converse with each other, allowing the patient to "overhear." In either case, the information conveyed is designed to increase the likelihood of favorable patient response to the pseudo-therapist.

Also suggested is the use of overcompensation or inequitable reward. The cognitive dissonance literature (*Brehm and Cohen, 1962*) offers evidence in support of the motivating consequences of overcompensation. In brief, it appears that offering an overpayment arouses dissonance which to be reduced may require increased effort to match the overcompensation.

In applying this principle to therapy, Goldstein, *et al.* (*1966*), writes:

> In broad terms, this hypothesis proposes the arousal of cognitive dissonance in resistive patients by providing them not with "reward" for continuing to come for psychotherapy but with "overreward." This overreward may take several forms: special arrangements may be made, or purportedly be made, in the patient's behalf with regard to particularly convenient (for the patient) meeting times. The patient may be moved to the head of a waiting list, be permitted to choose his own psychotherapist from those available, or be assigned to a particularly prominent and respected psychotherapist. The psychotherapist may intervene with others of significance in the patient's life, he may ask especially low fees or, heresy of all heresies, even pay the patient for coming to psychotherapy!" (*Goldstein, et al., 1966*, pp. 123–124).

Such tactics may arouse and sustain patient faith and expectation of relief, factors central to successful healing relationships. These suggestions may be attacked on ethical grounds, but if the choice is between treatment by frankly manipulative methods and no treatment then the attack must be very persuasive to be acceptable.

Changing the Treatment to Match the Patient's Expectancies: Breaking Tradition

As the realization grows that psychotherapy in the traditional sense is closely tied to the belief systems and behavioral problems of the tightly organized and highly socialized middle and upper classes of the Western Industrialized world, greater psychotherapist role variability has emerged. It has become increasingly clear that psychotherapists are not dispensers of rigid treatment formulas analogous to medical procedures.

McMahon's (*1964*) exhortation to psychotherapists to match their methods "to the attitudes, expectations, and requests of the working class patient" illustrates the changing mood of the helping professions. The result has been an increasing willingness to "violate" traditional principles in dealing with persons who had been labelled untreatable. McMahon captures the spirit of this change with the phrase "a rather open-minded agnostic approach. . . ."

The possibilities for manipulation of treatment techniques are limited only by the variety of patient behaviors and the ingenuity of the psychotherapist. Among the possibilities offered by Goldstein, Heller, and Sechrest (*1966*) are the following three hypotheses generalized from the literature of experimental psychology to the problem of behavior change: these three propositions appear relevant to the issue of faith and patient expectancies.

"Psychotherapy with resistant patients should be oriented toward accepting and utilizing the role behaviors in which patients are already proficient" (Goldstein, Heller, and Sechrest, 1966, p. 158).

Specifically, if the patient is unprepared to deal with the psychotherapist on an equal basis and expects authoritative therapist behavior, it will be necessary, at least initially, to form a relationship on that basis. The patient may not feel sufficiently comfortable and secure to venture from the role of the passive accepting recipient of advice and guidance. The psychotherapist might, for example, actively assume the "white-coat" role if the patient expects treatment to conform to the medical model.

Also, patients who actively avoid close, intimate relationships may respond faster to impersonal situations. For example, the use of tape recorders as a "listener" reduced the frequency and severity of crimes committed by delinquents over a three-year period (*Schwitzebel, 1963*). Subjects, alone in a room, were requested to talk to a tape recorder for "research purposes"; the delinquents talked to the experimenter through the recorder as if it were the experimenter himself, and often referred to him by name. They appeared more open and expressive, and better able to accept this impersonal situation than one involving face-to-face contact.

"Resistance in psychotherapy is reduced by maximizing the opportunities for imitation learning by the patient" (Goldstein et al., 1966, p. 452).

For example, Levine (*1963*) reports regular sessions in the home by a psychotherapist who structures the situation with arts, crafts, and simple games to be particularly effective with lower class clients. The psychotherapist-social worker "takes the role of catalyst to dramatize the particular conflict, or intervenes to break into the destructive pattern of interaction, and proceeds to demonstrate on the spot ways and means of settling the dispute, with all members participating in testing out and talking about the new ways. . . ." (*Levine, 1963*.)

Considerable research (*Riessman, 1963; Deutsch, 1963; Miller and Swanson, 1960*) suggests that lower class life is dominated by the immediate, the concrete, and the overt. It is not surprising to find, as Levine did, that modelling forms of psychotherapy are effective. In work, recreation, religion, and psychopathology the forms of expression exhibited by the disadvantaged tend to be physical-motoric. The poor person is much more likely to develop hysterical conversion or catatonic symptoms (*Hollingshead and Redlich, 1958*) which appear to be extensions of his general style of life. Effective treatment methods might be similarly constructed.

"Transfer of learning from psychotherapy to extratherapy situations will be greater when the therapy stimuli are representative of extra-therapy stimuli" (Goldstein et al., 1966, p. 452).

Taking their cue from learning research, these authors argue that positive transfer of psychotherapeutic gain will be facilitated if sessions are conducted under conditions as similar to real-life as possible — as opposed to the artificial atmosphere of an office. Levine's (*1963*) in-the-home sessions are an obvious example of implementation. Spending the afternoon in the bleachers at Dodger Stadium may do more to establish rapport with a working class client than ten sessions in a carpeted office (cf. Hansen's discussion of constrained compliance, Chapter 5 of this volume). The transfer possibilities are also increased in such nonoffice settings as well. The key is to fit the context of psychotherapeutic interaction to the cognitive and verbal style of the individual.

Summary

The impact on psychotherapeutic progress of deliberate manipulation of those variables which arouse patient faith merits the interest of psychotherapists. Since Freud's introduction of the resistance concept, psychotherapists have manipulated patient expectations to increase faith in the treatment procedure. What is suggested here is not a change, but an intensification and improvement of those efforts through the application of principles generalized from basic research. With this evolution will go, hopefully, the adoption of more socially adequate conceptions of human motivation.

A sense of social revolution characterizes the contemporary literature of psychotherapy; the subtlety of class differences, in language, in perspective, in life style, and their impact on patient responsiveness have become salient discussion points for the most recent generation of psychotherapists. It is an indication that the social and behavioral sciences are approaching adolescence and that even in their adolescence they offer much of benefit to theories and practices of counseling and therapy.

References

Alexander, F. (1956). *Psychoanalysis and Psychotherapy,* Norton.

Apfelbaum, D. (1958). *Dimensions of Transference in Psychotherapy,* University of California Press.

Appel, K. E., W. T. Lhamon, J. M. Myers, and W. A. Harvey (1963). "Long Term Psychotherapy," in *Psychiatric Treatment (Research Publication 31). Association for Research in Nervous and Mental Disease,* Williams and Wilkins.

Appel, K. E., J. M. Myers, and A. E. Scheflin (1953). "Prognosis in Psychiatry: Results of Psychiatric Treatment," *Archives of Neurology and Psychiatry,* 70, 459–468.

Astin, A. W. (1961). "The Functional Autonomy of Psychotherapy," *American Psychologist,* 16, 75–78.

Ausubel, D. P. (1956). "Relationships between Psychology and Psychiatry: The Hidden Issues," *American Psychologist,* 11, 99–104.

Balint, M. (1955). "The Doctor, His Patient, and the Illness," *Lancet,* 1, 683–688.

Bandura, A., and R. H. Walters. (1963). *Social Learning and Personality Development,* Holt, Rinehart, and Winston.

Barron, F. (1953). "An Ego-Strength Scale Which Predicts Response to Psychotherapy," *Journal of Consulting Psychology,* 17, 235–241.

Beecher, H. K. (1956). "Evidence for Increased Effectiveness of Placebos with Increased Stress," *American Journal of Physiology,* 187, 163–169.

Bellak, L. (1948). *Dementia Praecox,* Grune and Stratton 1948.

——— (1952). *Manic-Depressive Psychosis and Allied Conditions,* Grune and Stratton.

Bergman, P. (1958). "The Role of Faith in Psychotherapy," *Bulletin of The Menninger Clinic,* 22, 92–103.

Bernstein, B. (1964). "Social Class, Speech Systems, and Psychotherapy," *British Journal of Sociology,* 15.

Black, J. D. (1952). "Common Factors of the Patient-Therapist Relationship in Diverse Psychotherapies," *Journal of Clinical Psychology,* 8, 302–306.

Brehm, J. W., and A. R. Cohen (1962). *Explorations In Cognitive Dissonance,* Wiley.

Brill, N. Q. and N. A. Storrow (1960). "Social Class and Psychiatric Treatment," *Archives of General Psychiatry,* 3, 340–344.

Brody, E. B., and F. C. Redlich (1952). *Psychotherapy With Schizophrenics,* International University Press.

Bromberg, W. (1959). *The Mind of Man: A History of Psychotherapy and Psychoanalysis,* Harper and Row.

Cartwright, D. S. (1955). "Effectiveness of Psychotherapy; A Critique of The Spontaneous Remission Argument," *Journal of Counseling Psychology,* 22, 290–296.

Chance, Erika (1959). *Families In Treatment,* Basic Books.

Colby, K. M. (1951). *A Primer For Psychotherapists,* Ronald Press.

Collier, R. M. (1950). "A Basis for Integration Rather than Fragmentation in Psychotherapy," *Journal of Consulting Psychology,* 14, 199–205.

Cranston, Ruth (1957). *The Miracles of Lourdes,* McGraw-Hill.

Crowne, D. P., and D. Marlowe (1964). *The Approval Motive,* Wiley.

DeCharms, R. J. Levy, and M. Werthheimer (1954). "A Note on Attempted Evaluations of Psychotherapy," *Journal of Clinical Psychology,* 10, 233–235.

Deutsch, M. P. (1963). "The Disadvantaged Child and the Learning Process," in *Education in Depressed Areas,* A. H. Passow (ed.), Teachers College, Columbia University, 163–179.

Diehl, H. S. (1933). "Medical Treatment of the Common Cold," *Journal of the American Medical Association,* 101, 2042–2054.

Eysenck, H. J. (1952). "The Effects of Psychotherapy: An Evaluation," *Journal of Consulting Psychology,* 16, 319–324.

Fenichel, O. (1945). *The Psychoanalytic Theory of Neurosis,* Norton.

Fiedler, F. (1950). "A Comparison of Therapeutic Relationships in Psychoanalytic, Nondirective, and Adlerian Therapy," *Journal of Consulting Psychology,* 4, 436–445.

———— (1951). "Factor Analyses of Psychoanalytic, Nondirective, and Adlerian Therapeutic Relationships," *Journal of Consulting Psychology* 15, 32–38.

Findley, T. (1953). "The Placebo and the Physician," *North American Clinical Medicine,* 37, 1821.

Fisher, H. K. and B. M. Dlin. (1956). "The Dynamics of Placebo Therapy: A Clinical Study," *American Journal of Medical Science,* 232, 504–512.

Frank, J. D. (1964) Foreword, in *Magic, Faith and Healing,* Ari Kiev (ed.), Free Press.

———— (1961) *Persuasion and Healing,* Johns Hopkins Press.

———— (1959). "The Dynamics of the Psychotherapeutic Relationship," *Psychiatry,* 22, 17–39.

———— *et al.* (1959). "Patient's Expectancies and Relearning as Factors Determining Improvement in Psychotherapy," *American Journal of Psychiatry,* 115, 961–968.

Freedman, N., *et al.* (1958). "Dropout from Outpatient Psychiatric Treatment," *Archives of Neurology and Psychiatry,* 80, 657–666.

Freud, S. (1950). "On Psychotherapy," *Collected Papers, Vol. I.,* Hogarth Press.

Gliedman, L. H., et al. (1958). "Reduction of Symptoms by Pharmacologically Inert Substances and by Short-Term Psychotherapy," *Archives of Neurology and Psychiatry,* 79, 345–351.

Glover, E. (1958). *The Technique of Psychoanalysis,* International University.

Goldstein, A. P. (1960). "Patient's Expectancies and Nonspecific Therapy As A Basis For (Un)-Spontaneous Remission," *Journal of Clinical Psychology,* 16, 399–403.

———— (1962). *Therapist-Patient Expectancies in Psychotherapy,* Pergamon Press.

Goldstein, A. P., K. Heller, and L. Sechrest (1966). *Psychotherapy and The Psychology of Behavior Change,* Wiley.

Haley, J. (1963). *Strategies of Psychotherapy,* Grune and Stratton.

Hankoff, L. D., N. Freedman, and D. M. Englehardt (1958). "The Prognostic Value of Placebo Response," *American Journal of Psychiatry,* 115, 549–550.

Harper, R. A. (1959). *"Psychoanalysis and Psychotherapy: 63 Systems,* Prentice-Hall.

Hastings, D. W. (1958). "Follow-up Results in Psychiatric Illness," *American Journal of Psychiatry,* 114, 1057–1066.

Hathaway, S. R. (1948). "Psychotherapy and Counseling: Summary of Discussion," *Journal of Consulting Psychology,* 12, 90–91.

Heine, R. W., and H. Trosman (1960). "Initial Expectations of the Doctor-Patient Interaction as a Factor in Continuance in Psychotherapy," *Psychiatry,* 23, 275–278.

Hollingshead, A. B., and F. S. Redlich (1958). *Social Class and Mental Illness,* Wiley.

Houston, W. R. (1928). "Doctor Himself as Therapeutic Agent," *Annals of Internal Medicine,* 11, 1416.

Hunt, M. M., *et al.* (1964). *The Talking Cure,* Harper and Row.

Hunt, R. G. (1960). "Social Class and Mental Illness: Some Implications for Clinical Theory and Practice," *American Journal of Psychiatry,* 116, 1065.

Issacs, M. L. (1959). "Personality Dimensions Associated with Positive Reaction To Placebo," Unpublished doctoral disseration, Catholic University.

Kiev, A. (ed.) (1964). *Magic, Faith, and Healing,* Free Press.

Kolb, L. C. and J. Montgomery (1958). "An Explanation for Transference Cure: Its Occurrence in Psychoanalysis and Psychotherapy," *American Journal of Psychiatry,* 115, 414–421.

Lambo, T. A. (1964). "Patterns of Psychiatric Care in Developing African Nations," in *Magic, Faith, and Healing,* A. Kiev (ed.), Free Press.

Lasagna, L., *et al.* (1954). "A Study of The Placebo Response," *American Journal of Medicine,* 16, 770–779.

Lennard, H. L., and A. Bernstein (1960). *The Anatomy of Psychotherapy,* Columbia University Press.

Levitt, E. E. (1957). "The Results of Psychotherapy with Children," *Journal of Consulting Psychology,* 21, 189–196.

Levine, Rachel A. (1964). "Treatment in the Home: An Experiment with Low Income, Multi-Problem Families," *Mental Health of the Poor,* Riessman, Cohen, and Pearl (eds.), Free Press.

London, P. (1964). *The Modes and Morals of Psychotherapy,* Holt, Rinehart, and Winston.

May, R., *et al.* (eds.), (1958). *Existence: A New Dimension in Psychiatry and Psychology,* Basic Books.

McMahon, J. T. (1964). "The Working Class Psychiatric Patient: A Clinical

View," in *Mental Health of the Poor,* Riessman, Cohen, and Pearl (eds.), Free Press.

Menninger, K. (1958). *Theory of Psychoanalytic Technique,* Basic Books.

Miller, D. R., and G. E. Swanson (1960). *Inner Conflict and Defense,* Holt, Rinehart, and Winston.

Modell, W. (1955). *The Relief of Symptoms,* W. B. Saunders.

Mowrer, O. H. (1963). "Payment or Repayment? The Problem of Private Practice," *American Psychologist,* 18, 577–580.

Noyes, A. P., and L. C. Kolb. (1958). *Modern Clinical Psychiatry,* 5th edition, W. B. Saunders.

Overall, Betty, and H. Aronson (1963). "Expectations of Psychotherapy in Patients of Lower Socioeconomic Class," *American Journal of Orthopsychiatry,* 33, 421–430.

Phillips, E. L. (1956). *Psychotherapy, A Modern Theory and Practice,* Prentice-Hall.

Poser, E. G. (1966). "The Effect of Therapists' Training On Group Therapeutic Outcome," *Journal of Consulting Psychology,* 30, 283–289.

Reznikoff, M. and Laura C. Toomey (1959). *Evaluation of Changes Associated With Psychiatric Treatment,* Charles C Thomas.

Rickles, N. K., J. J. Klein, and M. E. Bassan (1950). "Who Goes to a Psychiatrist? A Report on 100 Unselected Consecutive Cases," *American Journal of Psychiatry,* 106, 845–850.

Riessman, F. (1962). *The Culturally Deprived Child,* Harper & Row.

Riessman, F., J. Cohen, and A. Pearl (1964). *Mental Health of the Poor,* Free Press.

Rioch, D. (1951). "Theories of Psychotherapy," in *Current Trends in Psychological Theory,* W. Dennis (ed.), University of Pittsburgh Press.

Rogers, C. R. (1951). *Client-Centered Therapy,* Houghton-Mifflin.

Rosenthal, D., and J. D. Frank (1956). "Psychotherapy and the Placebo Effect," *Psychological Bulletin,* 53, 294–302.

Rosenzweig, S. (1954). "A Transvaluation of Psychotherapy — A Reply to Hans Eysenck," *Journal of Abnormal and Social Psychology,* 49, 298–204.

——— (1936). "Some Implicit Common Factors in Diverse Methods of Psychotherapy," *American Journal of Orthopsychiatry,* 6, 412–415.

Ross, T. A. (1938). *The Common Neuroses* (2nd. ed.), Wood.

Roueche, B. (1960). "Placebo," *New Yorker,* 15, 85–103.

Schofield, W. (1964). *Psychotherapy, the Purchase of Friendship,* Prentice-Hall.

Schutz, W. C. (1958). *FIRO: A Three-Dimensional Theory of Interpersonal Behavior,* Rinehart.

Schwitzgebel, R. R. (1963). "Delinquents with Tape Recorders," *New Society,* 1, 11–13.

Shapiro, A. K. (1960). "A Contribution to the History of the Placebo Effect," *Behavioral Science,* 5, 109–135.

——— (1959). "The Placebo Effect in the History of Medical Treatment: Implications For Psychiatry," *American Journal of Psychiatry,* 116, 198–304.

Shepherd, M. (1962). "Comparative Psychiatric Treatment in Different Countries," in *Aspects of Psychiatric Research,* D. Richter *et al.* (eds.), Oxford University Press.

115

Shoben, E. J., Jr. (1953). "Some Observations On Psychotherapy and the Learning Process," in *Psychotherapy: Theory and Research,* O. H. Mowrer (ed.), Ronald.

Strickland, Bonnie, and D. P. Crowne. (1963). "Need for Approval and the Premature Termination of Psychotherapy," *Journal of Consulting Psychology,* 27, 95–101.

Szasz, T. S. (1960). "The Myth of Mental Illness," *American Psychologist,* 15, 113–118.

Tibbets, R. W., and J. R. Hawkings (1956). "The Placebo Response," *Journal of Mental Science,* 102, 60–66.

Trouton, D. S. (1957). "Placebos and their Psychological Effects," *Journal of Mental Science,* 103, 344–354.

Volgyesi, F. A. (1954). "School for Patients: Hypnosis, Therapy, and Psychoprophylaxis," *British Journal of Medical Hypnosis,* 5, 10–17.

Whitehorn, J. C. (1958). "Psychiatric Implications of the Placebo Effect," *American Journal of Psychiatry,* 114, 662–664.

Wolf, S. (1950). "Effects of Suggestion and Conditioning of the Action of Chemical Agents in Human Subjects," *Journal of Clinical Investigation,* 29, 100–109.

Zilboorg, G. (1941). *A History of Medical Psychology,* Norton.

Ziskind, E. (1949). "How Specific is Psychotherapy?" *American Journal of Psychiatry,* 106, 285–291.

PART TWO

Coordination, Compliance and Evaluation:

Some Perspectives on Professional-Client Relationships

In concern with interpersonal relations, contemporary sociology is in closest affinity with contemporary counseling and psychotherapy, suggesting that, however important developments at other levels might be, the level of interpersonal relations in counseling and psychotherapy is most likely to command sociologists' attention in the next few years. This situation is not entirely disturbing, for it is apparent that many questions about interpersonal behavior are in need of answers, to provide more adequate theory in sociology and in counseling and psychotherapy. Indeed, interpersonal analysis may be particularly well suited to the development of these theories, for at this level of analysis the "interpenetration" of societal and individual reality may be most clearly revealed. The conception of "interpenetrant realities," early a tenet in the theories of W. I. Thomas and G. H. Mead, has become a basic article of faith in contemporary sociology. By it is meant that personality and society, or other observable "entities," may not in fact be strict entities, but exist only by virtue of the other's existence; to understand one, then, it is necessary to understand the other as well. The implications of this

117

sociological emphasis for counseling and psychotherapy are perhaps as profound as they are apparent.

Beyond problems of theory, however, practical reasons for interest in the interpersonal level of analysis are also close at hand; one need not be a wild-eyed alarmist nor even a serious-though-alienated critic of society, such as the late C. Wright Mills or Erich Fromm, to desire to maximize in some ways the ratio of human actuality to human potentiality. Problems of human development and freedom, whether or not they are especially serious today, likely have plagued man since he first experienced that state referred to in modern times with terms such as "free will," "choice," "volition," and "autonomy." Such problems, it is clear, are fundamental in counseling and psychotherapy, revealing these subjects as so pervasive and so burdened with overtones that the foundations of Western life ultimately become the concern of debate. In contemporary forms, such debates are likely to rest on assumptions of interpenetrant reality.

Perspectives on Autonomy

As so many debates of profound importance, however, those over autonomy and independence suffer from a lack of specification; cliches cover vagueness, as arguments fail to join in battle, save in polemics. The lack of specification is not surprising, partly because of deficiencies in knowledge of the social relevancies of human development, motivation, and behavior, as was suggested in the previous section. In illustrating this point, a speculative extension of the motivational theory of Chapter 1 might be useful in identifying some threads of discussion which unite the chapters of this book.

In the discussion of motivation (Chapter 1) is the implication that "goals," and the "pathways" the individual must follow to reach those goals, are all learned: that "falsification" (roughly, discrepancy of experience and expectation) leads to exigency (roughly, dissonance), which if articulated, is recognized as a "need" related to some goal or alternative goals and pathways (see pages 47–59). Although not developed in that theory, it is generally consistent with psychological learning theories that various saliences of exigency will have varying effects, for instance:

• Extreme exigency will lead to attempts (selection of pathways and goals) to most immediately dissolve the discrepancy, likely through escape (such as reaction formation, denial, repression);

• Moderate exigency *may* lead to efforts to reorganize horizons (including, especially, the goal arrays) in order to dissolve the discrepancy in a way most consistent with the existing horizons; the effect of this may be elaboration and refinement of horizons;

118

· Mild or no exigency (no falsification of established horizons or goals) will lead to atrophy of the horizons.

Two implications of such differences in effects are important here. First: There can be varying developments of the horizons of knowledge and of justification, and varying cathexes in these horizons, as a consequence of fairly consistent differences in the salience of exigency; that is, both the cognitive and the evaluative horizons of one person might be highly elaborated, those of another person might be comparatively undeveloped, while the cognitive horizons of a third person are highly elaborated, but the evaluative are not.

Second: The "conflict-free ego sphere" (*Hartmann, 1958,* for example) may not be appropriate to the fullest development of the individual. Optimal development, this theory implies, is attained through controlled falsification in which exigencies are neither allowed to become so intense that the individual seeks to escape nor so light that he is reduced to a conflict-free level. As a technique, however, "controlled falsification" can be used for many, often opposing ends. The present question is, how might it most effectively be used to promote autonomy? The question is difficult to answer, in part because of current confusions about the nature of "autonomy."

For example, complaints about the "homogenizing processes" of contemporary society often end with a plea for autonomy, such as this: "We've got to teach kids to think for themselves." What is usually desired is increased *cognitive independence,* or establishment of meta-pathways rather than simple pathways appropriate only to limited tasks. Some critics especially mean, in addition, the development of "creative" capacities, or of a cognitive playfulness. Usually, however, even the most avid voice for cognitive independence imposes limits, insisting that a modicum of conformity is required for social harmony, or indeed, for social coordination — that some discipline of thought must be instilled to ensure socially useful production or cooperation. All too often however, the legitimate need for some coordination is only the entree for the encouragement of habitual compliance; where autonomy of thought might flower, only energetic, conventionalized intelligence is fertilized.

To attain only cognitive independence, that is, is not to attain independence in choice of action, and it is even further short of autonomy: Free choice of action requires not only cognitive freedom, but *freedom to evaluate* possibilities from a perspective not imposed by coercion, manipulation or other control, nor imposed (as is so easily the case when evaluative horizons are underdeveloped) by primitive emotion.

Traditionally, schools in our society have intentionally ignored the development of evaluative horizons, except in subtle and not-so-subtle efforts to instill religious or national loyalties, values of hard work,

119

achievement and honesty, and other special and often instrumental values. Systematic falsification and elaboration of horizons of evaluation in the past has been the job of especially the family and church. One of the dominant critical themes of our time, however, is that these institutions no longer effectively stimulate development. If this theme is valid, it might be interpreted as in some ways favorable to development of individual autonomy in evaluation: the family and the church, it could be argued, are among the most conservative elements in our society, and to be freed from their influence and evaluation is to be freed from confining cages.

The question is, freed for what? The motivation theory suggests at least a partial answer: Ideally, freed for participation in an exchange in which the individual's unique horizons of evaluation are bombarded with moderate falsifications which, in essence, urge him to reorganize his horizons in ways ever more internally consistent, adequate to effective relations in the world of which he is a part, and consistent with his own equilibrium of deprivations (through which any "essential being" might be expressed). *"Autonomy," that is, involves far more than cognitive and evaluative independence (or independence in choice of actions); it is, in effect, "sufficient independence," involving an individual relatively free from dictation by either his organismic or social aspects, and possessing horizons of expectation and justification adequately developed and elaborated to allow him to specify and select actions which are both socially effective and consistent with his horizons and affective commitments.* Autonomy requires some sort of effective "self-reference" in selection of actions; that is, it requires horizons developed elaborately and consistently, and affective commitment to aspects of those horizons in which organismic as well as social aspects of the individual are effectively integrated. This implies that the child, and even the early adolescent, is at most capable of only degrees of independence, in which autonomy is at most foreshadowed.

Cathexis appears to be one major process in development of dependence-independence. In Chapter 1 it was stated that it is proper to speak of the individual cathecting an *object relation* (self and other in situational relationship). It is reasonable to suggest that various aspects of the object relation can be cathected. Most simply, the cathecting individual may focus on the *relationship* ("I like it; I want it to continue"), or on the *object* of the object relationship ("I want to be like Daddy"). To avoid confusion, the first type might be termed *internalization,* as it requires no cognitive identification of the object, *per se,* as the agent of satisfaction or pleasure. The second type of cathexis can be termed *identification,* and does involve cognitive specification of the object. A further distinction is useful, based on the specificity vs. the generality of the object; when the individual would "like to be like" another specific object (Daddy) *concrete identification* may be appropriate; when he would like to be like a general and/or abstract category of objects (man), the term might be *generalized identification* (taking generalization to refer also to abstraction).

It may be posited, then, that the degree of independence of a person is a direct function of the importance, in his choice of pathways, of identifications rather than internalizations; and that (holding other things constant) the more general (and/or abstract) these identifications, the more independent the individual.

Falsifications, in turn, are seen as critical in the development of independence; it is through falsifications, primarily, that the individual specifies more accurately the object of the relationship he cathects; moderate falsifications lead to the greater likelihood both of identifications and of increased generalization of the identification. This process may be illustrated by the falsifications introduced by the differences between familial and other relationships. Parsons *(1959)*, for example, suggests that, because the teacher is usually a female, the young child is confronted with a falsification of his previous conception of "women," which was based on his experiences with his mother and other women in similar roles. Further, over the years classroom roles offer constructive falsifications to the child who identifies with the teacher; because of the turnover of individuals, he is led from identification with specific individuals into a general identification. Obviously, internalization or identification with the teacher or with the teacher role can be used effectively by the teacher in encouraging or discouraging the development of autonomy.

In general, however, classrooms offer the developing individual constructive falsifications of only the cognitive horizons; excepting in early grades, when it is difficult to divorce the evaluative from the cognitive, falsifications of evaluative horizons are for the most part incidental. Harsh falsifications are the response to deviation from a vaguely defined, but relatively narrow range of values. For many children, peer-group experiences may also offer but little constructive falsification. Falsifications may be many — in contemporary society, peers are generally the most important source of evaluative falsifications after the early family-oriented years — but they may not be of a type to encourage elaboration. The intolerant cruelty of children has often been noted; even in adolescents, with the emerging capacities for empathy and tenderness, only limited deviation from the norm is permitted within one's own clique, and "outsiders" are as harshly judged as in earlier years. *In toto,* then, the developing person may be offered only inconsistent and intermittent evaluative falsifications, most of which are too harsh to encourage the development of an independent system of justifications.

121

To the extent these conditions hold, individuals will be capable of only dependent reflection of the values in their immediate situations. A few may prefer and be capable of independence, but too likely it will be an "independent atrophy" (as contrasted with "sufficient independence"). For the constructive falsifications offered by peer groups are likely inadequate to effective development, and the rest of the community offers neither a consistent system of traditional values (in which most could develop a "committed dependence" and some a "committed autonomy") nor adequate structural sources of moderate falsifications which would urge the individual to elaborate his horizons, to develop a sufficient independence based on a few key values essential to social cohesion and dynamics.

The implications for counseling and psychotherapy of such suggestions should be clear, especially if placed in the context of the mandate to maximize individual development, discussed in the introduction to section four. Indeed, it may well be that the professions of counseling and psychotherapy are among the few in a position today to potentially stimulate development of "adequate autonomy." It may also be that many activities, especially in educational and vocational counseling in fact have the opposite effect. If these speculations are at all valid, counselor and classroom teacher not only share in the failure to constructively falsify; they also actively encourage dependent reflection and offer arenas for destruction rather than elaboration of justifications.

Perspectives on the Interpersonal

Speculation, however, is far from demonstration; close investigation and research on "independence" and "autonomy" are needed. One requirement for such research is increased understanding of the intrapersonal; this, as the essays in the first section argue, cannot be understood apart from the interpersonal, or social. The essays of the present section, then, are closely related to the others in this book, and especially to those in section one. They are not intended to answer, or even to identify, the profoundly important questions of contemporary life; rather, they are presented as efforts to move toward a more accurate and less narrow understanding of interpersonal relationships, in both social and intrapersonal contexts — to suggest or develop, that is, perspectives and theories which might eventually prove useful in discussing important practical questions, such as those relating to "autonomy."

In Chapters 5 and 6, a theory of interpersonal coordination in counseling and psychotherapy is suggested. Consensus, influence modes and communication are identified as the basic elements of coordination, leading to a number of theoretical propositions which, in Chapter 5, are utilized in discussing the occurrence and problems of compliant behavior in the client — behavior which is directly related to the probability of developing independence and autonomy.

Among the basic themes in this discussion is an emphasis on the influences of the social structures within which persons interact. This theme is central also to Perrucci's discussion in Chapter 7, of the professional evaluations in the career of the mental patient. Beyond expert knowledge of a specific case, what seems to influence the staff in those decisions which are the critical switching points in the patient's career? Perrucci's discussion suggests that the illness of the patient may be a less important factor in these decisions than are a number of social and interpersonal conditions.

In this section, then, a dominant theme of this volume is repeated: Interpersonal coordination and roles, patient compliance, psychiatric decisions and illness careers, however analytically distinguishable, must be recognized as inextricable in reality not only from the intraindividual character of the individuals involved, but also from broader social contexts.

References

Hartmann, Heinz (1958). *Ego Psychology and the Problem of Adaptation,* International Universities Press.

Parsons, Talcott (1959). "The School as a Social System," *Harvard Educational Review,* 29 (Fall), 297–318.

4 | TOWARD A THEORY OF COORDINATION
IN COUNSELING AND PSYCHOTHERAPY:
Consensus, Influence and Communication

Donald A. Hansen / University of California, Berkeley

However different in functions and techniques, counseling and psychotherapy are basically similar in process: Two persons voluntarily meet periodically, with the general intent of temporarily or permanently altering the life of one in some ways, through the exchange of verbal and non-verbal messages.[1] As in any goal-oriented relationship, a range of requirements must be met if the intent is to be realized, and among the most basic is that of coordination. Client and psychotherapist, that is, must act in ways that are compatible and they must participate to some degree in a system of mutual expectations and understandings.

Coordination is a common requirement of daily interaction — passing a car being driven in the opposite direction, buying a drink in a bar, performing in a chorus line, rearing a family. Indeed, coordination is inherent in the very idea of social interaction. The *complexity* of coordination required for various activities is markedly different, however. To buy a drink is perhaps simpler than to maneuver through the traffic of modern cities, yet even this may require less complex coordination than that in an intricate choreography. More complex still is the coordination required in relationships such as those of counseling and psychotherapy, in which the regulations, directions or rules of the game are at best general, never fully explicit, and in constant flux.

But the coordination required for counseling and psychotherapy must be more than complex; it must also be to some degree durable, which implies that it must in some ways be satisfying to each participant, or at

For comments on earlier versions of this essay, the author is indebted to Walter Buckley, Aaron Cicourel, Peter M. Hall, and Thomas J. Scheff.

[1] Of course, many other characteristics distinguish counseling and psychotherapy from one another and from other relationships which share the qualities identified here. These few, however, appear to be most pertinent to the present discussion.

least hold promise of being so. This is problematic, for a number of reasons. Perhaps the most important is that the more complex the required coordination and the less well defined are the rules for interaction, the more likely is it that one or both participants will experience role conflict or confusion. Some special requirements of counseling and psychotherapy suggest that this conflict and confusion is even more likely in counseling and psychotherapy than in many other relationships requiring complex coordination.

Role conflict and confusion are observed in many relationships and are common in many professions. In part, these conditions may be due to individual concerns and incapacities, unfortunate incompatibilities of personalities and diverse other conditions special to a particular relationship. But at a more general level of analysis, it can be seen that the role conflict and confusion may derive from conditions beyond the individuals' special qualities and experiences; that they may derive from contradictions inherent in the general roles themselves. Some social positions, that is, demand incompatible behaviors of the person involved, placing him in dilemmas or binds not simply because of his individual capacities, but because of contradictions in the expectations others hold for him or which he holds for himself. Roles of the counselor and psychotherapist tend to be of this type: Role strains arise from the somewhat contradictory requirements that counseling and psychotherapy relationships be not only coordinated in complex ways, but also satisfying, durable, and expressive.

In attaining such coordination, the legitimated power of the psychotherapist can be highly useful, for it allows him to maintain social distance from the client. This has two advantages. First, it facilitates the psychotherapist's efforts to maintain an "objective" perspective. Second, it provides a base for effective sanctioning, allowing the psychotherapist, when he desires, to direct (with some subtlety if necessary) the client's activity, thereby maintaining a coordinated relationship which is consistent with both his professional commitment and his interpretation of the client's needs. That is, differences in position, with the psychotherapist in the position of power and prestige and the client in a position of dependent appellant, permit the therapist to maintain social distance, and distance promotes objectivity and effective coordination.

However useful these qualities of relationship, they pose problems in counseling and psychotherapy. In the following chapter, I discuss two of these problems: first, the inherent contradictions which are structured into the counselor's and psychotherapist's roles, which have been labeled "The Therapist's Dilemma" (*Kadushin, 1962*); second, the problems of compliance, which are likely to appear in any relationship in which one person is more powerful, and which become especially problematic in some kinds of psychotherapy. Just what is meant by "The Therapist's

Dilemma" and "Problems of Compliance" will be made clear in that chapter.

Prior to the discussion of these practical problems, however, a problem of theory must be addressed. The problem is simply this: Despite the sensitive and useful theories of interpersonal dynamics which have developed in the literature of counseling and psychotherapy, to date there is no formal and generalized theory of the ways in which two persons relate in a coordinated social relationship. This may seem a bit surprising, as there are in print many discussions of the intrapersonal dynamics of the client during therapy, and even of the psychotherapist during psychotherapy; indeed, some theorists have been acutely sensitive to dynamic interlinkings between the two. But these discussions, for one thing, have not been formalized and, for a more important thing, in focusing on exchanges between individual "systems," they have given but scant attention to the *social* "systems" in which the relationship is played — social systems which involve, for example, common background understandings, awarenesses of shared norms and conventions and of diverse ideas, perceptions, memories and affective attachments which relate each participant to other persons not present, and through which their own interpersonal relation is modified and even shaped.

In identifying this deficiency, I do not refer only to the obvious cases of learning and conditioning theories. In traditional psychoanalytic theories, for example, focus is so consistently on the intrapersonal dynamics of the individual that no systematic constructs for describing and understanding dyad behavior have developed; indeed, in psychiatric theories in general only recently have there been efforts to rigorously conceptualize relationships in dyads and larger groups. Similarly, in phenomenological theories, attention to "other persons" is usually reduced to some sort of "object relation," in which the relationship between persons in dyads or larger groups is little developed. (Indeed, this is one of the fundamental deficiencies addressed in Chapter 1, on motivation.) Even Rogerian theories are, surprisingly, lacking in this respect. In recent developments in group psychotherapies, including those of Rogers, however, increasing sophistication is apparent, and may well be reflected in the theories which might emerge from these practical innovations.

Also promising, however unsystematic, is the "games people play" perspective (*Berne, 1961;* see also *Szasz, 1961*), which might at minimum help critics and supporters identify some of the problems that have been traditionally ignored in counseling and psychotherapy. At base, many of these problems may be traced to a simple deficiency in perspective:

> The failure to see the behaviour of one person as a function of the behaviour of the other has led to some extraordinary perceptual and conceptual

aberrations that are still with us. For instance, in a sequence of moves in a social interaction between person (a) and person (b), $a_1 \longrightarrow b_1 \longrightarrow a_2 \longrightarrow b_2 \longrightarrow a_3 \longrightarrow b_3$, the sequence $a_1 \longrightarrow a_2 \longrightarrow a_3$ is *extrapolated*. Direct links are made between $a_1 \longrightarrow a_2 \longrightarrow a_3$ and this artificially derived sequence is taken as the entity or process under study. It is in turn "explained" as an *intra*personal sequence (process) due to *intra*psychic pathology. (*Laing, Phillipson, and Lee, 1966,* p. 8.)

The subject matter of this essay, then, promises to be elusive. The problem is to bring it to reasonable focus, to identify those qualities of the relationship and of the systems involved which appear most vital to complex relationships such as those of counseling and psychotherapy. In sociology the traditions of actional theories offer some perspectives, especially as brought to focus in the recent work of Scheff, which in turn draws on the discussions of Laing and Schelling. Concerned with research specification, however, these writers have developed models useful in analyzing relatively "simple" coordination, such as in game behavior. Limited though their focii, their work offers the basic frameworks from which a model of the counseling and psychotherapy relation might be developed.

Consensus and Coordination in Counseling and Therapy

I have suggested that, whatever the other requirements, counseling and psychotherapy relationships require some degree of coordination of actions between client and psychotherapist. This requires, for one thing, some degree of "consensus." By consensus, I refer to what Scheff has called "coorientation"; that is, much the same interpersonal phenomena referred to by Dewey as "interpenetration of perspectives," by Schutz as "intersubjectivity," by G. H. Mead as "successful role taking," and by Schelling as "coordinated expectations," or most simply as "a meeting of the minds." As such, consensus is enmeshed in the continuing discussion of attributions and imputations, definitions of the situation and, at base, in the problems of meaning.

Consensus, used in this way, appears to be a necessary condition of coordination: through perception (or, more accurately, attribution) of the other's intent, the individual is able to choose from his repertoire of actions those which seem most appropriate. I shall argue below that consensus is in fact not strictly necessary to coordination, but for the moment it will be most useful to follow the traditional line of argument which assumes its necessity. This is the line of argument developed by Mead and other social behaviorists who saw communication as the most important condition of consensus: though there could be consensus without communication, messages or gestures which were meaningful to the participants could alter the attributions of the other's intent; the change in consensus, in turn, affected the coordination. From this base, Scheff has developed a conception of consensus involving a theoretically infinite array of levels of attributions:

> Consensus (refers) not merely to agreement, but to a situation in which there is agreement, awareness of agreement, awareness of awareness, and so on. These higher levels of coorientation are absolutely essential to an understanding of social coordination . . . (*Scheff, 1967b*).

In coordination, then, "one is trying to guess what the other will guess one's self to guess the other to guess, and so on, infinitum" (*Schelling, 1960, p. 93*).

It should be clear that such intricacies are far from unusual in everyday life; that they might appear so is in large part due to the fact that they are rarely articulated. In this exchange from Sartre's play *Kean*, for example, the actors self-consciously identify the intents and attributions which in serious affairs they would keep to themselves:

> COUNT: Tomorrow I bow to the crowned heads of Europe; tonight I only acknowledge one queen. [*He kisses Amy's hand.*]
>
> AMY: How provoking that one can never believe you.
>
> COUNT: And why not?
>
> AMY: I know you diplomats too well — when you say yes, you mean no.
>
> COUNT: Then I shall say your dress has been cobbled together, and you have been made to look a perfect fright. [*He laughs.*]
>
> AMY: How am I to know you don't mean what you say?
>
> COUNT [*startled*]: But, dear lady . . .
>
> AMY: If I were as hideous as a scarecrow you would take advantage of my lack of confidence in diplomats and tell me the truth to make me believe you were lying. That is diplomacy of the second degree.
>
> ELENA: Yes, but supposing I were jealous and he wished to pay you compliments without arousing my suspicions? He could play on the different degrees of our belief. By telling you he thinks you ugly, he would make you believe he lied, while making me believe he was speaking the truth. That is diplomacy of the third degree.
>
> AMY: Then this is the fourth; supposing he believes you fickle, and wishes to make you jealous. He will say I am ugly to make you think he wants to make you believe he does not like me. As for the fifth . . .
>
> COUNT: Ladies, ladies, for pity's sake! I swear to you diplomacy was never so complex; if it needed so much reflection, we should have to appoint women as ambassadors.
>
> AMY: Well, Count, what do you say? Am I fair, or ugly?
>
> COUNT: Madame, I no longer know what to say. . .
>
> AMY: You have chosen the better part. I will believe in your silence. (*Sartre, 1960, 159–160.*)

In this exchange, it may seem that the Count and Amy fail to coordinate, and in some sense this is so. The Count is unable to participate in the ladies' intricate and fluid understandings and meanings. The upshot of the exchange, however, is coordinated activity: he attempts at every turn to comply and is consequently constrained. The image proves illustrative in many ways for counseling and psychotherapy.

Reciprocating Understandings in Consensus

At this point, however, what is needed is not illustration, but a clearer conception of consensus. Perfect consensus, Scheff (*1967a*) suggests, would exist if there were infinite series of reciprocating understandings; that is, in which each person was so closely attuned to the other that he would be able to say validly, "I know that you know that I know that you know that I know . . ." and so on, infinitely. Likely, such pure consensus has never existed; rather, in actual situations we may speak of various degrees of partial consensus, depending on the extensiveness achieved. Laing, Phillipson and Lee (*1966*) have derived a scheme for depicting three degrees of extensiveness in reciprocating understandings between dyads. They call the three degrees, *agreement, understanding,* and *realization.* To illustrate: A counselor might say, "You do trust me, don't you?" The client may voice agreement. Even if he does, consensus is not necessarily indicated. A researcher might question client and counselor separately, and (assuming honesty in responses) if both agreed to the statement, "Joe Smith trusts Dr. Brown," they could then be said to be in "agreement." Each of them might then be asked how the other person might answer the question. If Smith answers that Dr. Brown will agree with the statement, and in fact Brown does agree, Smith "understands" the doctor on this issue. If Smith's response does not agree with Dr. Brown's actual answer, then he "misunderstands" the doctor. At the third degree, realization, the question might be asked: "How will Dr. Brown think you have answered this question?" If Smith correctly judges how Dr. Brown thinks he's answered the question, then Smith "realizes" that he is understood by Dr. Brown. If he does not, he "fails to realize" that he is understood.

Letting A stand for agreement, D for disagreement, U for understanding, M for misunderstanding, R for realization, F for failure to realize, Laing and Phillipson developed a five letter profile, which will be useful in discussing the extensiveness of client-psychotherapist consensus. Psychotherapist — RUAUR — client indicates that the two Agree and that each Understands and Realizes he is understood. Psychotherapist — FMDMF — client indicates the psychotherapist and client Disagree and each Misunderstands and Fails to realize he is misunderstood.

These examples indicate symmetrical relationship, but it need not always be so: the psychotherapist, for instance, may clearly understand and realize he is misunderstood, while the client neither understands nor realizes he is understood: psychotherapist — RUAMF — client. Indeed, neither extensive consensus nor symmetry is necessary for the attainment of all goals, as Scheff (*1967a*) points out. Some types of relationships involve little coordination and therefore do not require extensive consensus. For example, one doesn't need to know the bartender's political opinions in order to get a drink. By contrast, the confidence man seeks a high degree of extensiveness, but it is quite asymmetrical: for obvious reasons, the two disagree, but only the confidence man understands that they disagree. This understanding is not sufficient, however: to be successful, the confidence man must also be able to realize that the victim misunderstands — that is, the confidence man must be reasonably certain that the victim mistakenly thinks they do agree: confidence man — RUDMF — victim.

This image will help suggest that the conception of coordination is not at this point adequate to the realities of counseling and psychotherapy. Let us assume that the victim, duped for some time, suddenly understands what the confidence man is up to. The confidence man usually will recognize the new awareness and, in such a case, coordination usually will break down, with the confidence man retreating in some way and the victim calling in the police or being effectively "cooled out" (see *Goffman, 1962;* see also Bernard's application to the counseling movement of the "cooling out" concept, Chapter 12 of this volume). In such situations — involving symmetrical and recognized disagreement (RUDUR) — what might usually be expected is avoidance or "contraordination." Most dramatically, the participants might fall to a fist fight or, as in the traditional movie fare, each might go hunting for the other, trying to outguess his opponent, asking himself, "What would I do in his boots?" Near the climax, the game might grow complex, as each asks himself: "Does he know I'm here?" (If not, I'll ambush him); "Does he know that I know he is here?" (If not, I'll let him think he's going to ambush me, so I can get close enough to get him before he makes his move); and "Does he know that I know that he knows that I am here?" (If not, maybe he'll try to make me think that I can ambush him — if he does, I'll pretend to fall for it, and when I get close enough, I'll make my move before he does). Though the process of role-taking is the same as in a condition of extensive consensus, the information and informed guesses are used not to increase coordination, but to thwart it; the participants are contra-oriented.

Disagreement, of course, does not necessarily lead to avoidance or contraordination. To return to the "victim" who has suddenly understood the confidence man: the fun and games really begin if he is able to keep the confidence man confident that nothing has changed. Now both understand that they disagree, but the confidence man fails to realize that the victim understands: Confidence man — FUDUA — victim. If the victim recognizes that the confidence man fails to realize, the tables may be turned; indeed, this is the basic plot repeated rather often in television shows such as "Maverick" or "The Rogues." These shows are illustrative: despite disagreement, the characters continue to coordinate their actions, often in highly complex ways. In part the coordination may be seen as a consequence of the asymmetry: each participant continues to coordinate in hopes that the asymmetry might be developed in his favor.[2] But there is more to it than that.

Lest my essential point be lost in all this drama, let me state it simply: Coordination is possible in spite of disagreement. Even more: Coordination is possible even though the disagreement is understood and realized by one or both parties. That is, though usually it is not so, *there can be coordination without consensus.* Even extensive and symmetrical dissensus does not necessarily mean that the participants will contraordinate or fail to coordinate; indeed, they may even *seek* coordination. In essence, they agree to disagree, yet succeed in coordinating their activities to a high degree; it may even be that neither tries to alter the symmetry, or otherwise gain advantage over the other. They simply cooperate, despite their basic disagreement.

This is not a derivative of a theoretical construct; rather it is an observation from daily life. The point is, the observation suggests that current conceptions of coordination must be modified if they are to be useful in understanding such complex coordination as that required in counseling and psychotherapy.

I suspect that at least part of the solution lies in two efforts: Attention to the importance of "future-orientations" in individual and social behavior and expectations, and identification of the parts played in coordination by verbal messages and by modes of interpersonal influence (that is by explicit and analogic communication). In the following paragraphs, the first of these possible modifications is discussed; in the following section, the second is considered.

"Futurity" in Consensus

The suggestion that "futurity" influences the choice of activity hardly needs to be justified: conceptions of the importance of "future-orientation" are to be found throughout sociological and psychological literature, and are central to the works of social behaviorists such as Dewey, Mead, and Allport.

Using the construct of consensus as involving a "reciprocity of perspectives," an analytic distinction can be made between those perspectives or expectations which involve imminent behavior in the relationship (what shall I do now; what does he expect me to do?) and those which involve some distant goal of the participants (what will our relationship

---

[2] For suggestive discussions of such relationships, see Schelling (*1960*) and Scheff (*1967b*).

be like next year?; what will be the outcome of my therapy?)[3] Though such perspectives would be more accurately represented with some sort of continuum, for the present discussion a simple dichotomy will again suffice: I shall refer simply to two *levels of consensus: role consensus* (involving the present or more-or-less imminent future) and *goal consensus* (involving the more-or-less distant future).[4] To illustrate: the confidence man–victim relationship might take this form:

	goals:	RUDMF	:goals	
confidence man				victim
	roles:	RUAMF	:roles	

In such a situation, though the individuals disagree on goals, the victim fails to recognize the disagreement and misunderstands the confidence man's intentions — that is, he does not recognize the difference in goals, and fails to recognize that the confidence man does. They do agree, however, on roles or methods, and it matters little for the outcome if the victim understands and realizes or misunderstands and fails to realize.

This modification, then, offers a partial answer to the question of how there can be "coordination without consensus": since "coordination" refers to overt behavior, *goal* consensus may not be necessary. Individuals who disagree markedly on basic commitments and assumptions, and whose goals are contradictory to one another might coordinate closely in daily activity, even though fully aware of their "ultimate" incompatibilities; each might see channels to future goals in the coordinated activity, or at least see no danger to goal attainment in the cooperation:

$$\text{goals:} \quad \text{RUDUR} \quad \text{:goals}$$
$$\text{roles:} \quad \text{RUAUR} \quad \text{:roles}$$

It should be clear that this model of coordinated activity is reasonably appropriate to some counseling and psychotherapy relationships, emphasizing that not all coordination implies client acceptance. More arresting is the possibility that consensus at the level of goals is asymmetrical:

[3] This distinction may be recognized as closely related to the distinction between "pathways" (and "channels"), and "goals," discussed in Chapter 1. The relationship is not accidental: though I have not identified the commonalities, the present discussion is predicated in large part on that theory of motivation.

[4] The ideas of "imminent future" and "distant future" should not be taken as simple chronological variables. Excepting at a most superficial level, relationships do not develop sequentially as a *series* of events or simple interactions, strung together on threads of time. Rather, they develop and proceed in *clusterings* of interactions, which may be markedly distant in time from one another and do not follow general conceptions of sequence. Perhaps because of the emphasis in Western thinking on cause and effect and sequential development, a chronological conception of development today dominates behavioral theory to the point of eclipsing any other perspective. That is, it may be that we are living with a pervasive cultural bias. I am hard put to think of a single sociological essay (that empirical investigation would be so couched is understandably not likely) which presents such a conception of time, but it is powerfully illustrated in Lawrence Durrell's *Alexandria Quartet* (1960).

	goals:	RUDMF	:goals	
psychotherapist	roles:	RUAUR	:roles	client

In this case, the client is, in a real sense, being manipulated (perhaps to his own benefit). Similarly, the psychotherapist may be the one who is conned:

	goals:	FMDUR	:goals	
psychotherapist	roles:	RUAUR	:goals	client

These, of course, are simple statements of logical possibility which lead directly to a normative question: How often do such relationships develop in counseling and psychotherapies? Unfortunately, such a question cannot be addressed in an essay of this character (though I suspect that few who have had contact with psychotherapy would agree that either is uncommon). It is legitimate, however, to consider in this essay the probable effects of various asymmetries. For example, contrast the confidence man with the school teacher who is concerned with developing productive and creative children. It is instructive to identify the maximal and minimal symmetry necessary for each relationship to "succeed" — that is, for at least one participant to achieve his goal. In the case of the confidence man, both goals and roles may be asymmetrical. But the asymmetry in roles is not necessary, hence *maximal symmetry* (i.e., the most symmetrical consensus that will still allow the confidence man to succeed) might be represented:

	goals:	RUDMF	:goals	
confidence man	roles:	RUAUR	:roles	victim

The minimal symmetry allowed for success in the teacher-child relationship is little different: she might succeed in effectively moving a promising child toward the development she desires, given the same symmetry which appeared minimal for the effective confidence man. But the *maximal* symmetry is quite different, for a teacher could achieve her goals, likely more efficiently, if there were complete symmetry at the level of goals, as well as roles, whereas the confidence man probably could not. Beyond a certain point, symmetry tends to thwart the confidence man or the propagandist: by contrast, it can be argued that the more symmetrical the teacher-student relationship, the more probable is attainment of the teacher's goals.

An identical argument may be made for the psychotherapy relation, but must be made a bit more carefully. In the following propositions, then, "success" is defined as attainment of the psychotherapist's goals. As a preliminary, two propositions appear reasonable: Other things equal, *if there is agreement on goals, then success is more probable given symmetrical and extensive consensus at all levels:*

psychotherapist	goals:	RUAUR	:goals	client
	roles:	RUAUR	:roles	

By contrast, if there is disagreement on goals, success is more probable given asymmetry at the level of goals, and symmetry at the level of roles.

psychotherapist	goals:	RUDMF	:goals	client
	roles:	RUAUR	:roles	

In the following chapter, it will be possible to further these propositions, by considering the varying depth of psychotherapy goals. For the moment, however, it is more important to rough out the model of coordination.

Recapitulation

In this section, it was noted that discussions of coordination emphasize the interdependent requirements of "consensus" and "communication": though there can be consensus without communication, messages or gestures that are meaningful to the participants can alter attributions of the other's intent, thereby changing consensus which in turn affects coordination. Such theories are suggestive, but not entirely adequately to a discussion of counseling and psychotherapy.

Seeking a less imprecise model, in this section I have focused on "consensus," in essence assuming communications and other variables to be constant. Consensus was taken to refer to a coorientation, involving "reciprocating understandings." Although these reciprocations might be seen as potentially infinite (e.g., I know that you know that I know that you know . . . etc.), three degrees were identified: *agreement, understanding* and *realization*.

Two individuals might agree with one another, both might understand they agree and each might realize that the other understands: psychotherapist — RUAUR — client. If only one person understands and/or realizes that they two agree or disagree, the relationship is asymmetrical: psychotherapist — RUDMF — client. This suggests that coordination is possible in spite of disagreement.

Further, it often appears to happen in actuality that there is coordination without the kind of consensus this model suggests. Some instance of such "coordination without consensus," I suggested, are artifacts: consensus may exist, though not quite as the model would permit, for it does not attend adequately to the "future-orientation" of the participants. An index of "futurity" can be added, however, by distinguishing between *levels* of consensus. Though, again, many levels might be identified, for simplicity, only two were considered: goal orientation or consensus and role orientation or consensus, each of which might be of variable extensiveness (or degree) and symmetry, as for example:

	goals:	RUDMF	:goals	
psychotherapist	roles:	RUAUR	:roles	client

Though these models are helpful, they are at this point incomplete, as is evidenced by the unanswered question: How is it that there can be "coordination without consensus"? The identification of levels of consensus only helped specify the question, allowing us to say that in some cases it only *appears* that there is no consensus — for example, that though there is disagreement on roles, there may be agreement on goals (or vice versa).

But what of the case in which there is no agreement at any level? It is not enough to say that people might participate in ignorance, that though they really disagree, neither realizes it. For in some cases, it can be that there is no agreement at any level, yet the coorientation is extensive and symmetrical:

goals:	RUDUR	:goals
roles:	RUDUR	:roles

Such a relationship of coordinated activity might most easily be seen in the compliance of the prisoner with the demands of his captor. Though such a relationship might be unusual in pure form in psychotherapy, it identifies in the model of coordination an inadequacy which is closely pertinent to counseling and psychotherapy.

The inadequacy leads to identification of the importance in coordination of the constraining powers of the structures within which counseling and psychotherapy take place. These powers, it is argued below, might be identified though attention to certain uniformities in the relationship which I call "influence modes."

Influence Modes and Coodination in Counseling and Psychotherapy

Recall the dialogue quoted in section one, from Sartre's play, *Kean*. The Count is clearly unable to fathom the lady's expectations: To the reader it is clear that she means to mock, but the clues she offers are meaningless to a vain and self-important dignitary. In their interaction, however, the two move together toward a *focal point* of agreement, which permits coordination to finally develop (albeit completely on her terms, involving an unconditional surrender by the Count). The analogue of a focal point is Schelling's; in the following passage he applies it to a bargaining situation, not unlike that of the Count and Amy, nor unlike at least some of the "games people play" in counseling and psychotherapy:

Most bargaining situations ultimately involve some range of possible out-comes within which each party would rather make a concession than fail to reach agreement at all. In such a situation any potential outcome is one from which at least one of the parties, and probably both, would have been willing to retreat for the sake of agreement, and very often the other party knows it . . . Each party's strategy is guided mainly by what he expects the other to accept or insist on; yet each knows that the other is guided by reciprocal thoughts. The final outcome must be a point from which neither expects the other to retreat; yet the main ingredient of this expectation is what one thinks the other expects the first to expect, and so on. Somehow, out of this fluid and indeterminate situation that seemingly provides no logical reason for any-body to expect anything except what he expects to be expected to expect, a decision is reached. These infinitely reflexive expectations must somehow converge on a single point, at which each expects the other not to expect to be expected to retreat.

If we then ask what it is that can bring their expectations into convergence and bring the negotiation to a close, we might propose that it is the intrinsic magnetism of particular outcomes, especially those that enjoy prominence, uniqueness, simplicity, precedent, or some rationale that makes them quali-tatively differentiable from the continuum of possible alternatives. . . . The rationale may not be strong at the arbitrary "focal point," but at least it can defend itself with the argument "If not here, where?" (*Schelling, 1960,* p. 70).

In coordination involving common interests — as is ideally the case in counseling and psychotherapy — the same searching for and seizing upon focal points can be seen: there is a sort of "mutual psychic attrac-tion" toward some expectations rather than others, stimulating the de-velopment of consensus at various levels. But "mutual psychic attrac-tion" smacks of the occult, and unnecessarily so. Why the attraction? Can we identify influences — social as well as intra-individual — that relate to the mutuality?

Two lines of attack might be made on this question. I shall not pursue the first, which would seek explanation in the similarities and interlink-ings of the participants' motivational processes. To date, little attention has been given this area: uniformly, discussions of coordination simply assume a high level of motivation on the part of participants, while dis-cussions of motivation give but scant attention to the complexities of social systems. The theory sketched in Chapter 1 of this book is an attempt to move toward correction of the latter situation; it would not be difficult, I believe, to sketch the implications of that theory for the discussion of coordination in counseling and psychotherapy. Time and space preclude such an exercise at this point, however.

Rather, I mean to take the second line of attack: to focus on the con-straining and influencing characteristics of the social situations in which the participants act — a subject that in turn might be analysed in a variety of ways, but perhaps most effectively as a condition of "communication." In this section, then, focus is reversed from the last, in essence holding consensus constant in order to better understand the relation of communication to coordination.

In the first section, it was emphasized that meaningful gestures, or communication, can alter participants' attributions of one another's intent, thereby changing the conditions of consensus, and in turn affecting coordination. "Communication," however, is a term often used ambiguously, for it can refer to at least three distinguishable qualities of human interaction: the explicit meaning or message (semantic qualities); the linguistic coding which is used to arrange the particular structure of the message (syntactical qualities; see Chapter 2) and the actions, contextual clues, cues and concomitants (the behavioral, or "pragmatic" qualities; Cf. *Watzlawick, Beavin and Jackson, 1967*).

Adding pragmatic to syntactic and semantic perspectives on communication, then, results in a conceptualization all but identical to that of "interaction."[5] A punch in the nose may be understood by both puncher and punched to mean a number of things: I don't like what you said; I don't want it to be said again; I do not so greatly respect you as you might have thought — and so on.

In Chapter 2 it was suggested that the semantic and syntactic capacities of the client and therapist are related to success in establishing an effective relationship. These capacities have to do with the ability to exchange explicit verbal messages in ways understood by both participants. Such messages might be useful to both participants in identifying compatabilities in their perceptions of role and goal orientations, and hence may serve to further coordination. It is clear, however, that exchange of explicit information may have little effect in some relationships (as is suggested in the put-downs, "if you've got to ask, you'll never know," or "if you don't know, no one can tell you."), and may in some instances even diminish coorientation, and hence reduce coordination. The idea, popular in business executive circles in recent years — that failures of coordination are due to misunderstanding and can be remedied by increased "communication" — is unfortunately fallacious, for increased information exchange may lead to an awareness of goal and role incompatibility.

5 Scheflen (*1963*), for example, suggests that "One often hears statements that some behaviors are expressive while others are communicational. Actually, whether a behavior is expressive (a reaction, response, and so forth) or communicational (a signal or message) depends upon the level from which it is viewed — organismic or social. All behaviors are both expressive and communicational. Each behavior, since it has communal meanings in a culture or group, has a communicational value, irrespective of whether or not the expressor intended it to be perceived and responded to." This perspective, however valid in itself, begs the essential question: on the *social* level can we identify regularities in communications which relate to various outcomes? That Scheflen himself recognizes this essential question is demonstrated in his suggestive discussion.

Much more than this is meant in the proposition that coordination is a function of communication, however. What purely semantic and syntactic analyses of verbal communication neglect is the level of meta-communication: cues about how an explicit message is to be taken, or about how one might be taken if it were offered. To follow Bateson's (*1951*, pp. 179–81) usage, a message not only conveys a "report" (content) it also carries a "command" (a statement about the relationship of the sender to the receiver). That is, communications not only convey information, they also serve to define relationships:

> All such relationship statements are about one or several of the following assertions: "This is how I see myself . . . this is how I see you . . . this is how I see you seeing me . . ." and so forth in theoretically infinite regress. Thus, for instance, the messages "It is important to release the clutch gradually and smoothly" and "just let the clutch go, it will ruin the transmission in no time" have approximately the same information content (report aspect) but they obviously define very different relationships.
>
> To avoid any misunderstanding about the foregoing, we want to make it clear that the relationships are only rarely defined deliberately or with full awareness. In fact, it seems that the more spontaneous and "healthy" a relationship, the more the relationship aspect of communication recedes into the background. Conversely, "sick" relationships are characterized by constant struggles about the nature of the relationship, with the content aspect of communication becoming less and less important (*Watzlawick, Beavin and Jackson, 1967*, p. 52).

It is important in an analysis of coordination to recognize qualitative differences in the content aspect ("report") and the relations aspect ("command") of communication. For, as the same authors suggest, the content aspect tends to be "digital," that is, it proceeds via words, or explicit concepts. Hence, content depends on semantic conventions, that is, on agreement on the meanings of the concept. The relational aspect, by contrast, is in greatest part inexplicit, and often can be conveyed only in "analogic" fashion. Whereas the content aspect rests on explicit agreement, the relational aspect is "self-explanatory" and eludes efforts at explicit identification.

The analogic character of relational modes of communication, then, poses difficult problems for the analysis of coordination in counseling and therapy. For, clearly, relational communication is fundamental to effective therapy; likely it is in his relations with others that the client is troubled, and it is at this extra-verbal analogic level of communication that the therapist often must reach the client if he is to be effective. Yet it is this level that we are least able to effectively conceptualize, for the conceptualization necessarily proceeds explicitly.

The importance of the analogic, relational communication in therapy is widely recognized, as in the continuing concern with "rapport." I would like to briefly consider this phenomenon, in an effort to identify some gross qualities of relational communication, as they relate to a model of coordination.

Relational Communication and Influence Modes

Though psychotherapist and client are at first strangers to one another, each recognizes with some degree of accuracy the respective roles of psychotherapist and client. To her first interview with Dr. Smith, Mary brings expectancies and fears about her relationship to a strange power-figure. Partly through his words, but perhaps more so through extra-verbal communication, the therapist may show her that he is in fact a warm and interested human who is there not to judge her but rather to help her as one human might help another. With time, the two develop a relationship which is warm and somewhat specialized; not only through explicit words, but through facial expressions, postures, body tones and other mood signs, through voice inflections, rhythms, cadences and other non-verbal cues, and from the physical surroundings of the therapist's office, its warmth, light, position of desk, comfort of chair and other contextual aspects, they define their relationship, greatly in analogic modes.

Most pertinent to the discussion of coordination, the process of establishing rapport often is seen in simplistic perspective as a movement along a continuum from a "position-oriented" relationship (therapist to supplicant) to a more "person-oriented" relationship (in a most extreme instance, "Joe" to "Mary"). Such a conception is posited on the idea of a lineal relationship between "social distance" and "rapport," in which the two are seen as poles of a single continuum, leading to the idea that to increase "rapport" is to decrease "distance," that is, to move from a relational communication characterized by a complementarity (doctor-patient) to one characterized by "symmetry" (equal-equal). Such a conception of rapport and of interpersonal relationships is inadequate to experience, however, and the inadequacy offers one clue for characterizing types of relational communication.

The clue is found in the basic sociological proposition that in interaction individuals tend to develop *both* personal and positional relations, each allowing somewhat different modes of influence. The development of each mode may be critical to effective coordination.

The interplay of personal and positional influence in psychotherapy is subtle, and may be difficult for some readers to appreciate, particularly if they endorse a client-centered, permissive, or existential perspective. Most troublesome may be the implicit argument that even the most permissive of psychotherapies relies to some degree on the constraining powers of the structures in which the counseling or psychotherapy takes place. The argument likely to be seen at least commendable by persons of such perspective may be that in such psychotherapies positional relationships are actively used by the psychotherapist in continued coordination. Indeed, even those who endorse more authoritarian modes of psychotherapy may find the argument difficult to appreciate, for the exercise of authority may be subtly camouflaged. In most psychotherapies, authority (one form of positional influence) is often intentionally kept ambiguous, ideally to allow the client to participate in the structuring of the relationship in ways that will maximize his own psychotherapeutic involvement.

However ambiguous and camouflaged, even in the most permissive of psychotherapies guideposts are offered the client around which relationships can be structured, ideally to limit the range of potential relationships to those which are most promising to psychotherapy. That is, in the psychotherapeutic relationship, cues which emphasize the positional difference of the two (in authority and other power) are given the patient, even though they may not be overtly emphasized. This point may be illustrated by the example, once again, of the confidence man and victim relationship. The relationship is particularly pertinent to the discussion of counseling and psychotherapy, for the participants — either the confidence man-victim or the counselor-client — are engaged in a voluntary, relatively durable relationship. Even more tellingly, both sets of relationship have the appearance of informality, in which each participant may actively engage in defining the terms of the relationship and roles. But neither set of relationship is, in fact, so informal. Powerful social structures are called upon by the confidence man as he manipulates, lures and allows the victim to move into a relationship which in large part was predetermined by the confidence man, and subtly structured by his professional techniques and methods. He may effectively use common background understanding, allowing the victim to surmise — incorrectly — that the two agree on certain things; even more subtly, he may encourage the client to assume not only certain specific agreements, but even to assume that they do, indeed, share membership in a particular culture or way of life, and thereby share a whole array of common understandings. "The Great Impostor" illustrates this later point nicely, as does *The Prince and the Pauper,* or indeed, the sociologist who changes his clothes and other habits to become a "participant observer" in a slum area, in a prison or even in suburbia. Unfortunately, the power of such "assumed understandings" has yet been little considered in systematic theory (see *Garfinkle, 1964,* for a suggestive discussion).

The victim does not realize that the cards are stacked against him or at least he does not know *how* they are stacked; they are so stacked, because the confidence man is able to effectively utilize not only the personal vulnerabilities of the individual, but also the sanctions, constraints and restraints of the community and more immediate social groupings. Though he effectively presents it in such a way that it is not recognized, the relationship is so structured by the confidence man that he is placed in an authority position in which (often, but not always) the victim in some important ways must be dependent upon the confidence man's decision.

That is, though it may appear otherwise, the confidence man-victim relationship is fairly formal: the relationship develops according to a script written or learned by the confidence man; control rests powerfully with him, and though it may not be verbally admitted, that control is an essential fact of the relationship. As the relationship progresses, the control is increasingly utilized, both through the use of community sanctions (a form of positional influence, which, though in great part analogic, are akin to the explicit statement, "They've got the laws loaded against us little fish who try anything big, but do like I say and you're in"), and through appeals to interpersonal qualities (personal influence, akin to the explicit statement, "You can't let me down, friend. We're partners now.").

Similarly, subtle positional cues which are given but not emphasized are important to the establishment and continuance of the psychotherapeutic relationship. If these cues are readily perceived and are familiar to the client, and especially if it is recognized that they represent a marked leniency on the part of the psychotherapist compared to other of the client's relationships, they can be highly facilitating. Though the positional relationship of psychotherapist-to-client can be deemphasized (as, for example, in recent group psychotherapies) it does not approach non-existence in any major psychotherapy, including nondirective and existential types. As personal influence affords cohesiveness and capacities to generate warmth in psychotherapeutic relationships and to recover readily from periods of interpersonal stress, positional influence is also necessary, for it affords some stability and capacities to endure the periods of stress. The psychotherapist who attempts to resort to only the cohesive influence of personal relationships (neglecting the subtle and gentle coercion available from positional differences) risks establishing a relationship which will be too volatile for most patients to endure, or too likely to disintegrate when tension and disturbance reach peak points. But in a psychotherapy relationship, the positional relation is often camouflaged and implicit in the apparent personal relationship of stronger person to weaker.

Relational Types and Coordination

It may be, useful, then, to distinguish psychotherapy and counseling relationships by the modes of relational communication and influence which are established between client and psychotherapist. I have here

141

argued that, in general, personal and positional influence modes can each contribute functional capacities to the relationship. Although it is apparent that any voluntary psychotherapy or counseling which endures for some time will involve some degree of each type of influence mode, it is also apparent that the mix of modes differs markedly from one psychotherapy relationship to another, and that various types of psychotherapy call for different mixes. In Chapter 2, it was suggested that four ideal-types can be generated by the intersection of personal relations with positional relations. The four types are: Type A, those strong in both modes; Type B, those strong in personal but weak in positional; Type C, those weak in personal, but strong in positional; Type D, those weak in both modes. (For elaboration see *Hansen, 1965,* and pages 81–91 of this book.)

The ideal types of relational influence may be differentiated with many qualities, but particularly appropriate to this discussion are: The type of sanctions — simply, "cohesive" or "coercive" — allowed or encouraged; the openness and expressiveness (i.e., the analogic loading) of explicit messages transmitted; the level of interpersonal satisfactions; the durability of the relationships; and the types of objectivity the relational modes tend to encourage or allow.

One case can be quickly dismissed. It is clear that a psychotherapeutic relationship which develops *neither positional nor personal influence (Type D)* will be at best ineffectual. If such a relationship were voluntary, likely it would quickly terminate. In coerced situations, such as in total institutions, it might continue if the client or prisoner thereby escaped punishment or alternative duties, but he would tend to neither defer to the position of the psychotherapist nor establish any warmth of personal relationship with him. Though such situations are interesting and legitimate research subjects in themselves, they bear but little relation to the present discussion. Somewhat more pertinent would be the psychotherapist-client relationship within a total institution, involving not only coerced attendance and participation, but also marked constraints on the modes of activity allowed. This, then, would approximate an extreme Type C relationship, evidenced in one of its more pure forms in the coercive persuasion developed in Chinese and Japanese rehabilitation of political and civil criminals, which when applied to American soldiers, was dramatically labelled "brainwashing." In this essay, however, I have been speaking of less unusual counseling and psychotherapy relationships, and offer these two cases as simply illustrative.

In less dramatic form, coordinated relationships which involve *strong positional and weak personal influence modes (Type C),* can be highly functional for many types of problems, and in spite of theoretical claims, it can be argued that many counseling situations, and even more psychotherapeutic situations than might be expected, involve relationships appropriately categorized in Type C. The client is held in line, that is, primarily through the positional power of the counselor or psychotherapist. The influence modes of this type allow the psychotherapist to actively apply sanctions, most likely of a coercive type resting on an authority the client implicitly invests in the psychotherapist. Nonetheless, it is possible that cohesive influences can emerge, particularly if they are supported by the institutionalized expectancies identified above, by the client's habits or by transferences. In Type C, communications may be somewhat problematic. If the cohesive influences are adequately present, communications may be open and expressive, but if they are not, restraints both in the flow and expressiveness of communications may be expected. Similarly, unless the cohesive influences resting on qualities external to the specific relationship are strong enough, client satisfaction may be problematic. Hence, the durability of the relationship may be somewhat problematic, due to the limitations discussed above, and to others related to problems in coorientation.

The Type B relationship is strong in personal, weak in positional influence. Just as I have suggested that the Type C relation may not be so desirable as is often argued, it may also be argued that the attempt to work primarily through interpersonal warmth is not so universally effective as some theories, especially some counseling theories, would have it. It has already been suggested that lack of coercive influence in such relationships might make the psychotherapeutic situation vulnerable to disintegration during crisis periods. Interestingly, it appears that many counselors attempt to develop such relationships in their daily counseling activities with students and other clients on relatively minor problems. This effort might lead not only to inefficiency, but perhaps to ineffectuality, as the relationship encourages the client to merely wander haphazardly, failing to confront the contradictions within his own life's experience which might falsify his existing cognitive and evaluative arrangements.

In this type of relationship, sanctions can, indeed, be exercised by both the psychotherapist and client. The sanctions, however, are necessarily based primarily on cohesion; the exercise of coercive sanction is possible only occasionally, unless there is a marked change in the influence modes (that is, unless the relationship moves into another of the ideal types discussed here). There is little problem with open and expressive communications in this type of relationship, and it is likely that interpersonal satisfactions and durability will not be problematic.

In the Type A relationship, involving both strong positional and personal influence, the psychotherapist and to some extent the client are able to rely on sanctions based on cohesion or coercion, and the relationship is thereby afforded the capacity to endure stressful periods (supported by the positional influence of the therapist over the client) and

143

yet to regenerate rapidly once the stress has passed. There is a tendency toward open and expressive messages, both verbal and nonverbal, and interpersonal satisfactions and durability tend not to be problematic.

Once again, it may be helpful to emphasize that these statements contain a number of variables, one of which is the depth of outcome goals. This leaves open the possibility that counseling and psychotherapy for different types of problems and toward different types of goals may optimally carry different mixes of personal and positional influence: that varying degrees of personal and positional influence can be useful for various types of psychotherapeutic tasks and goals. That is, the optimal degree of personal and positional influence depends in part on the complexity of coordination required. For example, in vocational and educational counseling in which primarily information or cognitive perspective is required, to emphasize only positional relations may be as effective and far more efficient than the attempt to emphasize personal as well. Or, for another example, in the early stages of establishing contact with exceptionally disturbed or withdrawn patients, it may be most functional to establish only the barest minimum of positional influence (in essence, establishing explicit but highly permissive boundaries to the range of behaviors permitted) and to focus efforts strongly on the development of interpersonal modes of influence. Nonetheless, as we have interwoven the variables in the above discussion, it should be recognized it is intended to apply to the situation in which outcome goals are deep leveled and in which, it is argued, coordination is necessarily complex.

One more point must be made. It will be recalled from the previous section that one of the arguments in favor of maintaining social distance from the client has to do with the exercise of the psychotherapist's objectivity. Following this line of argument, it can be argued that the Type C relationship (strong positional, weak personal influence), is most likely to allow objectivity, for only by maintaining social distance can the psychotherapist hope to maintain the required dispassion.

Critics of this view generally take positions which, without great injustice, can be categorized into Type B. These opposing lines of argument generally hold that although "dispassionate objectivity" is undoubtedly useful for certain activities, by maintaining social distance the psychotherapist often reduces the probability of establishing open and expressive communication, and thereby reduces his opportunities to gain sensitive insights. What is more desirable, such arguments often continue, is a different kind of objectivity, "an involved objectivity."

This conception of "involved objectivity" is, in turn, vulnerable to the criticism that, although it may be demonstrated to work for some psychotherapists with some clients for some time, the psychotherapist is highly vulnerable to *subjective* involvements, in which objectivity sooner or later becomes impossible. Involved objectivity, it is argued, in practical affairs is a self-contradictory term: involvement and objectivity are necessarily in tension and inherently incompatible.

Both lines of argument have face validity. But they are based on an erroneous assumption, that the only way to increase personal distance is to decrease positional distance (or, to phrase it another way, the only way to increase personal influence is to decrease positional influence). The arguments on previous pages suggest that this is not necessarily so: the forced choice between positional distance and personal closeness, at least in some cases, may be unnecessary. Relationships in which both personal and positional influences are strong may allow involvement which permits the most sensitive of perspectives, yet does not thwart objectivity.[6]

Concluding Notes

Following the section summary of pages 134–135, I suggested that discussions and theories of counseling and psychotherapy, however sensitive to interpersonal processes, often fail to identify both uniformities in relational qualities of communication and the constraining power of the structures within which the counseling or psychotherapy takes place.

With the conception of two dimensions of relational communication — positional influence modes and personal influence modes — four sensitizing types of dyad relations were identified, and discussed as pertinent to counseling and psychotherapy. The discussion, though brief, may be related to the preceding discussion of levels of consensus, allowing suggestive answers to the question posed earlier: How there can be coordination without consensus? Part of the answer to that question was found in the recognition that role consensus need not involve goal consensus (thereby recognizing that individuals may agree on what should be done at any time without agreeing on matters less imminent). Some additional part of the answer is to be found in the combination of relational influence and consensus — a model which would depict individuals able to coordinate even though they disagree on both goals and roles, as for example in the case of the prisoner who chooses to comply rather than die, or of the client who chooses to comply rather than upset the therapist.

Coordination, then, has been presented in this construct as a function of especially two factors: consensus and relational communication. The more commonly discussed aspect of communication, the transmission of explicit messages, I suspect, is not so important as is often suggested;

---

[6] What I am suggesting here is really a reflection of Goffman's (*1959*) conception of "role distance." The psychotherapist would actively participate in personal roles with the client, yet so act that both participants are continually aware that he, in addition to being humanly warm and empathic (personal closeness) also possesses special skills and perspectives which require reservations in his actions (positional distance).

rather than directly affecting coordination, its effect is a condition of qualities of interpersonal consensus and relational communication. Most generally, however, it can be suggested that, given symmetrical and extensive consensus, and efficacy of relational communications, explicit communication will contribute to the complexity of coordination.

Other propositions also appear viable. For example: The less symmetrical and extensive is consensus at any level (but especially at the level of roles) the more coordination is a function of the efficacy of relational communication — given relational efficacy, coordination will increase directly with the amount of explicit information; given lack of relational efficacy, explicit communication may diminish coordination. Or: The less efficacious the relational communication, the more coordination is a direct function of consensus and explicit communication. Or: Given disagreement on roles and goals, explicit communication will tend to diminish both efficacy and relational communication and coordination.

Clearly, a variety of propositions relating these variables could be added to the above suggestions. As clearly, the suggestions are but preliminary specifications, which both beg for and resist empirical test, for it is difficult to specify the concepts exactly enough to allow research. How does one observe influence modes, or extensiveness of consensus? The question is troublesome, but it is reasonable to expect workable answers which are at least roughly adequate. The methods used by Scheff (*1967a; 1967b*) and Laing, Phillipson and Lee (*1966* — see description on pages 129–130 of this chapter) point the way to identification of extent and symmetry of consensus. Influence modes, also, may be to some degree identifiable, despite their essentially analogic character. For example, in considering family relations, I have elsewhere (*Hansen, 1965*) suggested that the strength of the modes might be estimated by observing or asking about the frequency and topics of explicit conversation which might relate to each type of analogic communication, the frequency and subjects of conflict and techniques of resolution, and the levels of interpersonal insight and empathy. Though rather gross, such techniques both offer useful entrees for contemporary research, and suggest lines for refinement.

It should also be emphasized that in this discussion I have purposely dealt with but a few variables, ignoring others which are important to counseling and psychotherapy. Throughout, then, it is necessary to preface my propositions with the implicit qualifier: "All other things being equal. . . ."

In this discussion, it was suggested that, whatever the other requirements, counseling and psychotherapy relationships require some degree of coordination between client and psychotherapist; that is, if the relationship is to be effective the two participants must meet some basic conditions. For one, they must generally share expectations, agreeing at least somewhat on goals, methods, roles of participants, and norms of participation and recognizing the agreements — they must, in short, establish a consensus or a coorientation. For another, they must establish effective modes of analogic as well as explicit communication, which can be used by one or both individuals in their efforts to put into practice the existing consensus and/or to increase it. Complex coordination, then, is necessary to effective goal-directed interaction; in turn, three conditions — consensus, efficacious relational communication and explicit communication — in some ways contribute to coordination. The requirements appear straightforward, yet in counseling or psychotherapy situations they can become exceedingly complex and elusive.

Indeed, there is much yet to be learned about these situations, and about the processes and effects of counseling and psychotherapy practices. At best, the present discussion is but suggestive for further theory construction. Its suggestiveness, however, may not be limited to the realm of theory, as is demonstrated in the following chapter. In that essay, the theory of coordination is turned to the problems of compliance and the psychotherapist's dilemma. The result, it is hoped, is not only increased understanding of the practical problems, but further elaboration of the theory of coordination.

References

Berne, Eric (1961). *Transactional Analysis in Psychotherapy — A Systematic Individual and Social Psychiatry*, Grove Press.

Durrell, Lawrence (1960). *The Alexandria Quartet*, Dutton.

Garfinkle, Harold (1964). "Studies of the Routine Grounds of Everyday Activities," *Social Problems*, 11 (Winter), 225–250.

Goffman, Erving (1959). *The Presentation of Self in Everyday Life*, Doubleday.

Hansen, Donald A. (1965). "Personal and Positional Influence in Formal Groups: Propositions and Theory for Research on Family Vulnerability to Stress," *Social Forces*, 44 (December), 202–210.

Kadushin, Charles (1962). "Social Distance Between Client and Professional," *American Journal of Sociology*, 67 (March), 517–531.

Laing, R. D., H. Phillipson and A. R. Lee (1966). *Interpersonal Perception: A Theory and a Method of Research*, Tavistock.

Ruesch, Jurgen, and Gregory Bateson (1951). *Communications: The Social Matrix of Psychiatry*, Norton.

Sartre, J. P. (1960). *The Devil and the Good Lord*, Vintage.

Scheff, Thomas J. (1967a). "A Theory of Social Coordination Applicable to Mixed-motive Games," *Sociometry* (in press).

———— (1967b). "Toward a Sociological Model of Consensus," *American Sociological Review*, 32 (February), 32–45.

Scheflen, Albert E. (1963). "Communication and Regulation in Psychotherapy," *Psychiatry*, 26 (May), 126–136.

Schelling, Thomas C. (1960). *The Strategy of Conflict,* Harvard University Press.

Szasz, Thomas S. (1961). *The Myth of Mental Illness,* Herber.

Watzlawick, Paul, Janet H. Beavin and Don Jackson (1968). *Pragmatics of Human Communication,* Norton.

5 | COMPLIANCE AND THE THERAPIST'S DILEMMA: Problems of Coordination in Counseling and Psychotherapy

Donald A. Hansen / University of California, Berkeley

When the Count gave way to the confusing protestations of Amy,[1] he evidenced the commonness of one of the most troublesome problems in counseling and psychotherapy: How to minimize the chances that the client will simply comply with the psychotherapist's suggestions rather than actively participate in the therapy. This problem, in turn, is related to the problem of finding the proper "balance" between social distance and rapport — a problem apparently so inescapable, it has been labeled the "therapist's dilemma" (*Kadushin, 1962*).

In this essay, I will consider these problems, using the constructs developed in Chapter 4. Both sets of problems, I will argue, are properly seen as conditions of coordination, and as such, are found to be closely interlinked with one another.

The Therapist's Dilemma: A Problem of Coordination

Most psychotherapies require that clients not only recognize, but also actively participate in coordination; that is, that clients openly and effectively communicate their ideas, intents and concerns to the psychotherapist, in such ways that they actively help determine the nature of the psychotherapeutic process. That is, though the psychotherapist must actively work for coordination, if the psychotherapy is to be pertinent to

For comments on earlier versions of this essay the author is indebted to Walter Buckley, Aaron Cicourel, Peter M. Hall, and Thomas J. Scheff.

1 This, I confess, is a rather artless suggestion that the present essay might better be understood after reading Chapter 4. On page 128 in that chapter is excerpted a brief exchange between the Count and Amy, from the play, *Kean* (*Sartre, 1960*).

the client's needs, the client, too, must exercise some modes of influence in the coordinated relationship. Further, psychotherapeutic relationships must endure, for psychotherapy is at best slow. Assuring durability is perhaps even more difficult than assuring openness of communication and influence, for the rewards expected by the patient are likely to be gained only in some vague future. Further, the processes of psychotherapy, and even of decision-making in counseling, are often psychically painful, and do not in themselves offer immediate satisfactions. Substitute pleasures must be offered clients. To meet the needs for open communication and for durability, psychotherapists often encourage some special sort of affective relationship of client to counselor: a quality of personal closeness, a *rapport* which provides the security necessary to open communication, and the satisfaction required for durability.

Theoretically, and often in real life, the two conditions of rapport and sanction are not only compatible but even mutually supportive. In the psychotherapeutic relationship, however, they readily become mutually destructive. For the exercise of power, however subtle, is often contradictory to the nurturance of rapport and, perhaps even more dramatically, rapport can be highly destructive of authority and objectivity.

Thus, the deeper-leveled his goals (see pages 155–156), the more likely will the psychotherapist or counselor find himself in a dilemma. To opt simply for social distance in order to maximize objectivity and effectiveness is to risk coercing the client into compliance. Though this may be useful if only constrained behavior changes are desired, in deeper-leveled psychotherapies the result may be confusion and ineffective therapy. Deceptively, such compliance and confusion may be masked by the fact that actions and communications are highly coordinated at a superficial level. On the other horn of the dilemma, to opt for rapport is to risk the loss of objectivity, to forego sanctioning powers and, again, to encourage ineffective psychotherapy. In such cases, too, the defects may go unnoticed, for communications may be uninhibitedly open and the relationship, though not therapeutic, may be intensely satisfying to both psychotherapist and client.

It has been observed that such a stark option is not always required. Though this kind of dilemma has undoubtedly been posed for many counselors and psychotherapists, often there are other social and psychological mechanisms at work which reduce the destructive consequences of opting for one or the other alternative. That is, even when the "Therapist's Dilemma" is more real than imagined, influences outside the counselor-psychotherapy relationship may render either option less stark than it might appear to the participants. Of these influences, those which might be termed *institutionalized expectancies* appear to be among the most pervasive. Implicit in Gallimore and Turner's discussion (in Chapter 3 of this book) of the importance of expectancy in psychotherapeutic processes, for instance, is the proposition that expectancies which enjoy the support of the community or group or "significant others" of the client can profoundly influence the success or failure of the relationship.[2]

More explicitly, Kadushin (*1962*) has suggested that although psychotherapists maintain a fair degree of social distance from their clients, their profession has led to the development of special community mechanisms which help the client and psychotherapist establish a relationship which is both satisfying to the client and yet allows the psychotherapist to preserve social distance. This device consists of an interstitial "community" to which both patients and psychotherapists belong, but in which they need not interact directly. This "community":

> . . . is formed by the union of the "friends and supporters of psychotherapy and psychoanalysis." Knowing others who have had psychiatric treatment, being told by one's friends to go to a psychiatrist, having one's problems noticed by others, and reading works on psychoanalysis are all indicative of belonging to such a community of lay believers and followers of psychotherapy. . . . (*Kadushin, 1962*)

That is, an institutionalized expectancy may be helpful in establishing necessary coordination, and in affording the client the satisfactions necessary for continued involvement with the psychotherapist who maintains social distance. This argument is reasonable, and may be related to the observation that middle-class clients are more successful in psychotherapy than are lower-class clients. It is highly probable that the "interstitial community" described by Kadushin is class related, and that those in certain social categories such as the middle-class are more likely to find membership than are those in other categories such as the lower-class.

Preliminary evidence suggests that such a relationship between expectancies and social categories does, indeed, exist. Comparing users with nonusers of a university psychiatric clinic, Scheff (*1966*) found that some categories were "obviously" overrepresented:

> Their fathers are educated, have high prestige occupation, and are Jewish, not-affiliated or belong to a minority religion. Their place of birth is large and located in the Northeastern part of the United States. In terms of their current activities, members of this group major in the humanities, social or behavioral science, engage in few extra-curricular activities, have somewhat fewer close friends than other students, and participate slightly or not at all in religious activities (pp. 2–3).

The overrepresentation is not explained by the presence of more "illness" in the strata, for the social characteristics of those who reported

2 See also Friedson's (1960) discussion of the "lay referral system."

only a few personal problems were more highly correlated with clinic use than were the characteristics of those who reported a large number of problems:

> These findings are interpreted to mean that persons who come to the clinic with few problems tend to be members of a psychiatric public, whose exposure to the mass media and other members of the psychiatric public lead them to define these problems psychiatrically. This exposure also causes and sustains the motivation and information about psychiatric services which leads them to take these problems to the clinic (p. 8).

This "psychiatric public" differs somewhat from the "interstitial community," or the "lay referral system," both of which involve direct contact of the client with supportive individuals and groups. The "psychiatric public" is even more general, referring to a collective attitude, which may require no personal contact for membership. (The implications of this concept in light of the discussion of "language codes" in Chapter 2 deserves consideration — a task which I must sidestep in this essay.)

Many essential relationships in counseling and psychotherapy, however, involve clients who are in no real sense members of any such interstitial community, or indeed of any functionally equivalent group such as is reported in the psychiatric wards described by Perrucci (Chapter 9 of this book). In the study cited above, Scheff also suggested that a considerable number of the total applicants for the university psychiatric clinic belong to neither the direct-contact groups represented by the terms "lay referral system" and the "interstitial community," nor to the more general psychiatric public. Though they are under-represented (at least, as Scheff's data suggests, among clients with minor problems, though perhaps not among clients with serious problems), because they come from such sizeable populations, in raw numbers they may constitute a sizeable portion, if not the majority, of the psychotherapist's clientele. It is possible, of course, that such individuals will eventually find membership in an interstitial community of supporters of theory, or will tend to leave psychotherapy. Nonetheless, pending further data and argument it seems reasonable to assume that some of these relationships which do not enjoy the support of institutionalized expectancies are successful. This assumption suggests that considerably more inquiry could be expended on the relationship of community expectancies and other social-psychological influences which might mitigate the therapist's dilemma. Such a line of inquiry, however, is not only needed — it is also inadequate by itself.

A second observation develops from the theory of coordination sketched in the preceding chapter, suggesting that the stark option apparent in the therapist's dilemma may be unnecessary: although mechanisms may develop to bridge the gap between rapport and distance, it is also possible that *at least in some cases the gap need not be bridged for the simple reason that it does not exist.* Indeed, the therapist's dilemma may be less general in current counseling and psychotherapy relationships than is realized either by those who study potential contradictions in roles, or by counselors and psychotherapists themselves. For one major example, the concept of a dilemma (or of contradictory expectations) may apply less well to psychotherapy relationships involving lower-class persons, or other categories currently under-represented in psychotherapy. That is, the very existence of the "therapist's dilemma" may be relative to the client's conditions and capabilities; while the contradictions in the psychotherapist's role demands may be very real and problematic with some patients, they may be a pseudo-problem with others, in that they are only imagined by the therapist. In such cases the psychotherapist may act in ways that hinder the development of effective psychotherapy, as he attempts to resolve a dilemma which does not have any basis in fact.

These possibilities rest on the argument that there exists a popular, though not universal, misconception of therapeutic rapport, and of the constraining powers of the structures within which psychotherapy takes place. These misconceptions might be corrected through attention to the general requirements for effective coordination. First, however, I will identify a second set of the problems related to coordination. On examination, it will be seen that the two sets of problems — the therapist's dilemma, and problems of compliance — are themselves closely related to one another.

Compliance: Problems of Coordination

By compliance, I refer to the activities of an individual which correspond to his perception of the expectations of his alter: If a client does what he thinks the psychotherapist wants, he is complying. This simple definition, unfortunately, is not so simple, as will be suggested below.[3] That some sort of compliance occurs in counseling and psychotherapy can hardly be questioned: Indeed, without compliance, the psychotherapeutic relationship could not endure. For one thing, it is likely that some convivial compliance is necessary to the process, just as it is functional in maintaining tension levels and expressive outlets in most relationships. Further, without some continuing compliance on the part of each of the participants, coordination would be virtually impossible. Only in the most fanciful speculations might there be co-

3 In addition to the modifications in definition suggested herein, the complexity should be recognized also in the fact that the definition relates to rather complicated sociological theory of the relation of perceptions, expectations and activity. This relation need not be identified here as it has been pursued in Chapters 1 and 4.

ordination when each person continually acts contrary to what he thinks the other expects. I am not referring, that is, to the simple incidence of compliance as problematic, but rather to certain qualities and frequency of the compliance.

Before entering that discussion, however, it will be useful to further specify the simple definition of compliance offered in the first sentence of this section. That definition indicates that certain types of activities are included as compliance, and others are excluded. Perhaps the most critical aspect of compliance is the relationship of perception to activity; if a client attempts to do what he perceives to be expected, even if his activities violate the psychotherapist's expectations, he is, in some way, complying. This suggests that one variable quality of compliance relates to accuracy of perception. Though "accuracy" is relative, for this discussion it will suffice to refer to a simply dichotomy: *"accurate compliance"* as contrasted with *"inaccurate compliance."* Though either type can pose problems in counseling and psychotherapy, and each deserves attention, my focus will be primarily on accurate compliance, hereafter referred to as simply "compliance."

The above distinction refers to a variant in client activity; others can readily be identified, but for the present discussion this will suffice. Similarly, variants in the psychotherapist's activity might be recognized. Two are most basic to the following discussion. The first is the distinction between the compliance that the psychotherapist intends to occur (*"intended compliance"*) and that which he does not intend (*"unintended compliance"*). The second is the distinction between the compliance which the psychotherapist recognizes, and that which he fails to recognize; thus I will refer to *"recognized compliance"* and *"unrecognized compliance."*

Other qualities of compliance will also be mentioned: "reciprocating compliance" (each person encourages and supports the other in complying; if the participants are to some degree aware of this process, it might be termed "collusion"); "dependency compliance" (in which the client complies in an effort to continue or increase the psychotherapist's supportiveness or good-will) and "constrained compliance" (in which the client is virtually forced to comply, regardless of his own desires). As these terms are relatively self-defining in the context of discussion, I will not dwell on them here.

It is apparent that to attempt to focus on even these few variates would be difficult in an exploratory essay. Though the sensitizing dichotomies could be logically interrelated into an impressive array of combinations (such as: "accurate, recognized, unintended habitual compliance"), it is more profitable to focus on those types of compliance situations which are likely to be destructive to effective psychotherapy. For example, habitual compliance which is unintended and unrecognized is more likely to interfere with the psychotherapist's goals than is compliance which is intended and recognized. Hence, the task is manageable.[4]

Most importantly, on the following pages, rather than speaking of all compliance as problematic, I will refer to "habitual compliance": compliance which occurs frequently enough to potentially thwart psychotherapeutic effectiveness. This suggests a number of questions. How often does compliance occur so habitually that effective counseling or psychotherapy is impossible? Is habitual compliance more likely with certain types of psychotherapy? Does its probability of occurrence correlate with sociological or social psychological categories such as age groupings or socio-economic backgrounds of clients? Is it related to the personality mixes of the psychotherapist and client, or to the situational contexts in which counseling or psychotherapy occur? Or, as is implied in the discussion of the other chapters in this volume, might it be related to the values, institutions and organizations of a society, or, more elementally, to motivational or language capacities and deficiencies? The list of questions could continue, but these few are adequate to suggest that to consider compliance is to consider a wide range of subjects approached and ignored today in behavioral inquiry. The tentativeness of the present discussion, then, should be apparent.

Habitual compliance is not necessarily undesirable in psychotherapy. As Gallimore and Turner (Chapter 3 of this volume) and Goldstein, *et al.* (*1966*), have argued, with some clients, the only practical hope for psychotherapy is to encourage compliance, and even to manipulate the client into unrecognized compliance. Further, even with some clients who might eventually respond to less coercive or manipulative relationships, in early phases habitual compliance might be useful.

At a most general level of analysis, then, problems of habitual compliance can be seen to be related to the outcome goals of the psychotherapist. Simply (as this aspect of my discussion is but a vehicle for more central concerns) I will speak of the therapist's goals as being

4 Other distinctions relevant to compliance could also be drawn. Most importantly, if compliance refers to activities which correspond to *perceived* expectations, then client activity which simply corresponds to expectations is not, by definition, compliance. Yet the psychotherapist may erroneously define such corresponding activity as compliance. For example, in early meetings the psychotherapist may think he has made it clear that he expects the client to relax and speak freely, and subsequently notes that the client is indeed doing so. The client, however, may have failed to understand the psychotherapist's meaning, and has adopted a pose of relaxation as a defiant gambit, or to test the therapist's tolerance. Though correspondence to the psychotherapist's wishes may be close, it is lacking between the client's action and his own inaccurate perception of the psychotherapist's wishes. For convenience, I will simply identify this sort of correspondence as *"pseudo-compliance."* Though such errors on the part of psychotherapist are relevant to the encouragement of compliance, they shall not be directly considered here. Pseudo-compliance and diverse other phenomena related to compliance will be of importance to this essay, that is, essentially in that they are ignored.

more, or less, "deep-leveled." As conceptions of "depth of intent" are common today, rather than argue for their acceptance, I will simply illustrate them, with the suggestion that goals, or outcome expectancies might be typed according to the kinds of behavioral change sought. Using the constructs presented in Chapter 1, for example, three "levels" of change might be distinguished, with level three the "deepest":

1. *Constrained Adjustment:* The psychotherapist may intend to encourage the development of new patterns of behavior which are appropriate to specific social situations, that is, to establish more functional adjustment of the client to specified social conditions. In this effort, it is necessary that the individual learn to select socially approved goals and move toward them on socially approved channels. Often, the most efficient and effective techniques for such learning are those of conditioning or "constraining," in which behavior is determined by the expectations implicit in the structures (e.g., the authority relationship), or by interpersonal relations the individual has cathected. Rather than seeking to make the individual select his actions himself, the intent is to constrain him to act in more socially appropriate ways.[5]

2. *Independence:* In this sort of outcome goal, what is intended is a cognitive and evaluative independence, a development of the capacity to operate at least somewhat free from the constraints imposed by specific situations or other persons. In essence, what is sought is an increased freeing of the individual from binding or constraining psychic and social influences. This means that some change might be required in those cognitive, expressive and evaluative arrangements which are problematic.

3. *Autonomy:* In this sort of outcome goal, the psychotherapist seeks not only cognitive and evaluative independence. That is, he not only attempts to so reorder the cognitive, evaluative and affective arrangements that the individual is less bound or constrained, but also to stimulate the development of cognitive and evaluative capacities such that the individual is not only free to choose, but also *capable* of choosing. Not simply independence, but "adequate independence" is sought, requiring especially the effective elaboration (not simply reordering) of cognitive and, even more importantly in most cases, of evaluative capacities.

Whether this illustrative schema of levels of outcome goals is adequate

[5] Given the state of knowledge and technique today, such outcome expectancies appear appropriate to a fair range of personal problems, and may be supported with the arguments that (1) however coercive or manipulative the techniques, they are all that is available to alleviate the suffering of many mentally and socially ill persons today; (2) such simple changes in behavioral patterns may lead to more deep-leveled psychological changes — that is, cognitive, evaluative and affective changes follow even the most simple of changes in behavior. Whatever the supporting arguments, such a level of outcome expectancies may be characterized as oriented toward constrained adjustment.

is of little importance, as it is generally agreed that the conception of varied depth in psychotherapeutic goals is valid. It can then be argued that *problems of compliance differ in various types of psychotherapy.* To the psychotherapist interested in establishing new regularities in constrained behavior, for example, habitual compliance is problematic essentially in that it poses a danger that the constrained behavior might be *too overly specific* to particular situations or interpersonal relations. That is, compliance may be used as an effective tool in the psychotherapist's efforts to establish desired behavioral changes. The greater the compliance, the easier the change. But with ready and extensive compliance, the possibility emerges that changes in behavior may be of short duration, or so closely specific to certain circumstances that the client will not be able to long maintain the established behavior patterns outside the psychotherapist's office. For psychotherapists interested in such changes, then, it is important that the nature of compliance be understood, and that those processes and conditions which are likely to encourage its development be recognized and, when possible, controlled.

It is all the more necessary for counselors and psychotherapists who seek deeper changes to recognize compliance and its correlates and determinants. Though at times compliance can be used as an effective tool, most often it is an indication that the client is overly dependent or submissive, not working effectively, being defensive or otherwise "playing games." Though even in the most effective of psychotherapies, it may be desirable to encourage compliance at times, at some point continuing and extensive compliance becomes disruptive. As a preliminary hypothesis it can be proposed: *The deeper leveled the psychotherapist's goals, the more does habitual compliance interfere with success.* This proposition is hardly innovative; indeed, casual observation or even common sense suggests its validity. But to predict is one thing, to understand is another, requiring that the phenomenon be placed in more comprehensive perspective than that afforded by common sense. At least a partial perspective — suggesting why it is that habitual compliance is more incompatible with deeper-leveled intent — is suggested by the discussions of Chapters 1 and 4.

Terming the last goal identified above as the "deepest," and following the motivational theory identified in Chapter 1, it may be proposed that:

> *The deeper-leveled the psychotherapist's goals, the greater the affective, cognitive and evaluative involvement required of the client for success.*

This involvement tends to result in a continuing stream of exigencies leading to articulation and falsification, which may bring about a reordering of cognitive and evaluative horizons. Involvement also leads to goal-directed activity (i.e., "motivated action") or other efforts to achieve gratification or satisfaction. Hence, still following Chapter 1, it can be posited that:

> *The greater the amount of motivated or goal-seeking behavior ("action"), the greater the affective, cognitive and evaluative involvement of the individual.*

It follows that:

> *The deeper-leveled the psychotherapist's goals, the more necessary is client "action" for success. That is, the more action is required of the client, the more necessary is symmetry and extensiveness at all levels of consensus and, hence, the deeper leveled the psychotherapist's goals, the more necessary is symmetry and extensiveness at all levels of consensus.*

To restate this less formally, if the psychotherapist's goal is to encourage certain patterns of constrained behavior, extensive and symmetrical consensus may not be necessary and may even stimulate undesired problems. Conversely, if the psychotherapist's goal is to stimulate independence or autonomy, extensive and symmetrical consensus may be not only useful, but essential.

It is now possible to place in this theoretical construct the commonsense proposition introduced above: "The deeper-leveled the psychotherapist's goals, the more does habitual compliance interfere with success." From the argument just presented, the proposition can be restated: *The more necessary is extensive and symmetrical consensus at all levels, the more does habitual compliance interfere with success.* With the proposition in this form, the supporting argument is fairly simple: Whether it is motivated or not, if habitual compliance is unintended it will tend to be contrary to the psychotherapist's goals, whereas habitual compliance which *is* intended by the psychotherapist tends to be contrary to the client's goal or role orientations, or both. It follows that compliance — whether or not it represents "action" or goal-seeking activity, whether or not the psychotherapist intends it — tends to reduce symmetry at the level of goals, at the level of roles, or both.

The Therapist's Dilemma, Compliance and Coordination

It is now possible to identify more clearly the relation of the therapist's dilemma to problems of compliance. It may be emphasized, by way of a summary to this point, that the two sets of problems are joined in large part through their mutual relationship the complexities of coordination. For counseling and psychotherapy relationships do require complex coordination, and the deeper-leveled the psychotherapist's intent, the more complex the required coordination. But other requirements must be met as well; hence, the counselor or psychotherapist may experience a dilemma: whether to exercise his legitimated power in order to maximize objectivity and the influence necessary to effectively attain the complexity of coordination he desires, or to reduce social distance in order to aid in the development of rapport, which may encourage expressive and open communication and offer immediate satisfactions to the client, thereby encouraging durability. The relationship of problems of habitual compliance to the complexity of coordination is suggested by the therapist's dilemma. If there is, indeed, a dilemma, there may be problems of compliance in psychotherapy no matter which alternative is chosen. In the first option, among other problems, there is danger of establishing a "reciprocating" compliance between psychotherapist and client; "reciprocating" in the sense that, as each to some degree shies from potentially disruptive communication, he thereby supports the other in his tendencies to sidestep. In most cases, then, reciprocating compliance will be unintended, and may even be unrecognized by both parties.

The choice suggested in the dilemma is not always as stark as it may appear, however. Institutionalized expectancies may offer the client certain temporary satisfactions necessary to the durability of the relationship, thereby allowing the psychotherapist to maintain the distance he feels necessary. Such a solution is problematic, however. Though reliance on institutionalized expectancies may help resolve the therapist's dilemma, it does not resolve the danger of encouraging habitual and unrecognized compliance, and may offer further pressures toward unintended compliance by adding community sanctions to those already wielded by the psychotherapist. That is, institutionalized expectancies can be two-edged. Though they may afford some counterforce to the intentional or unintentional efforts of the psychotherapist which pressure the client into compliance, they can as readily have the opposite effect.

Two points must be emphasized. First, the seriousness of problems of compliance may be related, for one thing, to the depth of the psychotherapist's goals and for another, to the very nature of the relationship proposed in most psychotherapies. Second, however pertinent to some psychotherapy relationships, the "therapist's dilemma" may not in actuality occur in others; hence, reliance on institutionalized expectancies to counterbalance the effects of the psychotherapist's distance may not be always necessary. This point rests on the argument that the nature of rapport, and its relation to authority and other forms of influence are often misunderstood, partly because of an inadequate conception of modes of psychotherapeutic influence.

Implicit in discussions of the dilemma is a conception of some sort of lineal relationship between "social distance" on the one hand and "rapport" on the other: to increase distance is to reduce rapport, to increase rapport is to reduce distance. The counselor or psychotherapist, then, is

159

seen to face the task of establishing some sort of balance appropriate to each individual client somewhere between the two poles. The task, in this perspective, is troublesome, for to attempt to increase rapport is to risk the loss of objectivity and power to sanction. Thus is encouraged the idea that the therapist's dilemma is all but inevitable: to increase personal influence is to decrease positional; to increase rapport is to reduce distance.

I have argued in Chapters 2 and 4, however, that such a "lineal conception" is an unnecessary distortion of what occurs in human life — that, principally through analogic communication, interacting individuals tend to develop *both* personal and positional relationships, and that the development of one may be somewhat independent of the development of the other. Four ideal types of dyad relations were generated by the intersection of personal relations with positional: Type A, those strong in both modes; Type B, those strong in personal but weak in positional; Type C, those weak in personal but strong in positional; Type D, those weak in both. Some characteristics of these types, and of personal and positional relationships have been discussed in those chapters. The remaining task, here, is to identify the relation of the first three types to problems of compliance. (Type D is taken to be generally inappropriate to voluntary counseling or psychotherapy.)

In *Type C relationships* (weak personal, strong positional influence), compliance may be particularly troublesome. The most immediately apparent difficulty would be seen in the client who seeks refuge in the "security" of the authority relationship. Such an individual might spend the greater part of his energy and time in identifying, from perhaps exceptionally subtle cues, what it is that the psychotherapist desires, and in attempting to respond to these perceptions in order to maintain the relationship. Psychotherapists, however, are traditionally sensitive to such tendencies, and particularly adept at identifying them. Similarly, it is relatively easy to identify the undesired compliance which may result from the application of a theory of psychotherapy which is, by design, directive or authoritarian. Nonetheless, it can be tentatively posited that: *unintended, constrained compliance is more likely the more positional influence is emphasized to the neglect of personal.* As it has already been argued above that habitual compliance is more destructive to psychotherapy the deeper leveled the outcome expectancy it can now be posited that: *the deeper leveled the outcome expectancy, and the more positional influence is emphasized to the neglect of personal, the less likely is success.*

If Type C is recognized as one "horn" of the therapist's dilemma, the *Type B relationship* (strong personal, weak positional influence) might be recognized as the other. Some problems of compliance are shared with Type C, but most generally it can be posited that *reciprocating compli-*

ance is more likely the more personal influence is emphasized to the neglect of positional. Once again, as it has already been posited that habitual compliance is more destructive to psychotherapy the deeper leveled the outcome expectancy it can now be posited that: *the deeper leveled the outcome expectancy, the less likely is success the more personal influence is emphasized to the neglect of positional.*

These propositions should not be taken to mean that there is no problem of compliance, or other problematic qualities inherent in *Type A relationships* (strong in both modes of influence). If the probability of reciprocating compliance is maximized in Type B, and the probability of constrained compliance is maximized in Type C, Type A is vulnerable to both kinds of compliance, and all three types, A, B, and C, are vulnerable to what I have termed "dependency compliance" (see page 154). Because of the openness and expressiveness of communication, however, in Type A, compliance is more likely to be recognized than in Type C, and because of the established positional modes of influence, the compliance is less likely to continue to the point of thwarting psychotherapeutic success than in Type B. In short, it might be posited that *the more effectively both personal and positional modes of influence are established, the less likely is the development of habitual, unrecognized compliance.*

In short, although dependency compliance might be encouraged or allowed by any of the three types of relations, other kinds of habitual compliance are less constant. Constrained compliance is more likely to occur in Type C than in Type A and Type B. Reciprocating compliance, however, is more probable in Type B than in the other types. Further, in Type A relations, the openness and expressiveness of message transmission tends to maximize available cues to the psychotherapist, allowing him to recognize the compliance. In addition, in Type A, the capacity to actively and continuously employ both cohesive and coercive sanctions maximizes the probability of success in attempting to overcome the tendencies toward compliance.

Though discussion has grown somewhat complex to this point, it is possible to combine in simple and efficient form the propositions relating influence modes and compliance (pages 160–161) with those relating consensus and compliance (pages 157–158). Focusing only on relationships involving relatively deep-leveled outcome goals, and taking "deeper leveled success" to refer to attainment of the psychotherapist's goals, where other than constrained behavioral change is intended, it can be proposed:[6]

[6] I have intentionally stated these propositions negatively, in the hope that they will be less likely to be misleading. Though they are no more logically sound that positive propositions (e.g., "The *greater* the symmetry, and extent at all levels of consensus, the more likely is deeper-leveled success"), they are less likely to fall

1. *The less the symmetry and/or extent at any level of consensus, the less likely is deeper-leveled success.*

2. *The greater the habitual compliance, the less likely is symmetry and/or extent at all levels of consensus.*

3. *The less operable either personal or positional influence modes, the greater the habitual compliance.*

These three simple propositions, then, summarize my essential argument. They can be combined, suggesting the potentials of viewing consensus and influence modes as interacting variables. Though not logically necessary, it is a reasonable implication that:

4. *The less operable are personal and/or positional influence modes, the less likely is symmetry and extensiveness at any level of consensus, and the less likely is deeper-leveled success.*

Even in such efficient form, it should be clear that the four propositions are heavy with implications for counseling and psychotherapy. Most pertinent, in the fourth statement is reflected the resolution of the therapist's dilemma. For the proposition suggests that, at least in some cases, the psychotherapist need not opt for either the sanctioning influences necessary to maintain productive coordination, or for the personal warmth which can so effectively encourage symmetrical and extensive coorientation. Indeed, not only is it theoretically possible that in the psychotherapeutic relationship can be attained *both* "rapport" and status sanction; it also appears that to attain both is to facilitate consensus, to reduce the probabilities of habitual compliance and to improve chances of attaining deeper-leveled outcome goals.

Some Concluding Speculations

Clearly, the problems of coordination go far beyond those attended in these essays. Consider, for example, the situation in which the individual client fails to recognize the cues, or even the overt suggestions which the psychotherapist gives for the development of the relationship. If the cues are not received, if they are, for example, beyond the range of daily activities in which the client participates, they may serve to so organize the relationship that the client increasingly engages in those behaviors which he feels correspond to the psychotherapist's expectations. In this

---

victim to the tendency to assign causal significances. When certain variates are seen to be related to an outcome (e.g., "The less the compliance, the more likely is success"), there is a tendency to accept the idea that the variate is a cause of the outcome. Indeed, there *may* be causal relation — but there need not be (e.g., though compliance can discourage success, lack of compliance does little to encourage success).

way, the personal relationship between the psychotherapist and client develops inadequately, and the positional remains dominate, however subtly so, and by its very nature encourages further compliance. Rather than offering guides for the development of a strong psychotherapeutic relationship, the cues which are offered the client only further the problems he confronts, and may insure against effective psychotherapy.

Even in cases in which both personal and positional influence modes are effectively developed, the psychotherapist and client may continually fail to coordinate, fail to share expectations or goals and fail to recognize the orientations and meanings of the other person. For the establishment of effective consensus is, in part, a matter of assuming common background understandings which allow both to recognize the positional and personal cues given one another. The inability to do so may be a matter of individual capacities, some of which are closely related to societal and cultural contexts — as was illustrated in the discussion of language codes in Chapter 2. Or, such incapacities may rest on the particular "mix" of the personalities or background experiences, knowledges and understandings of the participants, which may also be related to differing ways of life, as might be found in different spheres of the socio-economic structures. If people do not understand the lives of one another, it is difficult for them to co-orient, no matter how effectively they have established modes of inter-personal influence. Further, this kind of problem can arise even between persons who have the requisite capacities, and do in fact share common understandings.

Though I did not do so in the present essay, a most penetrating set of distinctions might be derived from a distinction offered in Chapter 1, or from the suggestive works of Garfinkle (*1960; 1964*), and of Schutz (*1943*). The distinction is between unmotivated or responsive behavior and motivated or goal-directed "action." Hence, we might refer to "motivated compliance" and "unmotivated compliance." A related set of distinctions has to do with the psychotherapist's recognition that the compliance is, in fact, motivated or not. Hence, we might refer to "understood compliance" and "misunderstood compliance."

Each of the logical types that might be derived from these sets suggests problems for psychotherapy, but perhaps one is not so obvious as the rest: "motivated misunderstood compliance" can lead to profound disruptions of the psychotherapeutic process, as the psychotherapist mistakenly reacts to the client as if he were a "judgmental dope" (as Garfinkle, *1964,* nicely puts it). Often neglected is the possibility that the common understandings which are shared contain biases that blind and prejudice both participants, rendering them incapable of perceiving the realities of the other person's actions. That is, to offer but one specific and compelling speculation, it is possible that even if effective and strong influence modes are well established between the psychotherapist and client, the psychotherapist may tend to define any recognized compliance on the part of the client as being unmotivated. It may well be argued that there is a common tendency to impute a lack of goal-directed activity to behavior which is compliant, a tendency which may be endemic to Western, industrial societies in which relationships are highly rationalized.

Similarly, Laing, Phillipson and Lee suggest that a "whirling phantasy circle" can develop. Their example is of attributed projection, but illustrates as well a process whereby "motivated misunderstood compliance" might result:

> Sometimes, what appears to be projection is really a complicated mismatching of expectations, i.e., the interpretation that p gives o's not fulfilling his expectation. . . . This commonly happens in analytical psychotherapy when the analyst (Paul) assumes that a detached mirror-like attitude is the most helpful stance he can adopt towards the patient (Peter). However, the patient may feel that only an open self-disclosing person could be of help, and if he goes on to interpret the analyst's stance as not only unhelpful in effect but unhelpful in intention, then the analyst may in turn counter-attribute "projection" to the patient. A vicious circle of mismatched interpretations, expectancies, experiences, attributions and counter-attributions is now in play.
>
> It starts to whirl something like this:

Peter:	Paul:
1. I am upset.	1. Peter is upset.
2. Paul is acting very calm and dispassionate.	2. I'll try to help him by remaining calm and just listening.
3. If Paul cared about me and wanted to help he would get involved and show some emotion.	3. He is getting even more upset. I must be even more calm.
4. Paul knows that this upsets me.	4. He is accusing me of hurting him.
5. If Paul knows that his behavior upsets me, he must be intending to hurt me.	5. I'm really trying to help.
6. He must be cruel, sadistic. Maybe he gets pleasure out of it, etc.	6. He must be projecting.

> Attributions of this kind, based on a virtually inextricable mix of mismatched expectations and phantasy and perception, are the very stuff of interhuman reality (*1966*, pp. 21–22).

These speculations but hint at the possibilities which must be considered if the problems of compliance and effectiveness in counseling and psychotherapy are to be recognized and resolved. They argue, as do the other essays in this collection, that the counselor and psychotherapist might profit from increased attention to the societal and cultural realities within which their theories and psychotherapies have developed and are being practiced.

References

Friedson, Eliot (1960). "Client Control and Medical Practice," *American Journal of Sociology,* 65 (January), 374–382.

Garfinkle, Harold (1960). "The Rational Properties of Scientific and Common Sense Activities," *Behavioral Science,* 5 (January), 72–83.

———— (1964). "Studies of the Routine Grounds of Everyday Activities," *Social Problems,* II (Winter), 225–250.

Goldstein, A. P., K. Heller and L. Sechrest (1966). *Psychotherapy and the Psychology of Behavior Change,* Wiley.

Kadushin, Charles (1962). "Social Distance Between Client and Professional," *American Journal of Sociology,* 67 (March), 517–531.

Laing, R. D., H. Phillipson and A. R. Lee (1966). *Interpersonal Perception: A Theory and a Method of Research,* Tavistock.

Sartre, J. P. (1960). *The Devil and the Good Lord,* Vintage.

Scheff, Thomas J. (1966). "Users and Non-users of a Student Psychiatric Clinic," *Journal of Health and Human Behavior,* 7 (Summer), 1–8.

Schutz, Alfred (1943). "The Problem of Rationality in the Social World," *Economics,* 10 (May), 130–149.

6 | SOCIAL PROCESSES
IN PSYCHIATRIC DECISIONS

Robert Perrucci / Purdue University

The ward is a factory for the Combine. It's for fixing up mistakes made in the neighborhoods and in the schools and in the churches, the hospital is. When a completed product goes back out into society, all fixed up good as new, *better* than new sometimes, it brings joy to the Big Nurse's heart; something that came in all twisted different is now a functioning, adjusted component, a credit to the whole outfit and a marvel to behold. Watch him sliding across the land with a welded grin, fitting into some nice little neighborhood where they're just now digging trenches along the street to lay pipes for city water. He's happy with it. He's adjusted to surroundings finally. . . .
(From Ken Kesey, *One Flew Over the Cuckoo's Nest*, 1962.)

The concept of career, when applied to the world of work, implies the existence of an orderly and patterned sequence of occupational stages, where each stage is interrelated with other stages on performance prerequisites. This concept has most often been used in connection with high status professional occupations where educational sequences are most apparent, but there is no reason why it should be limited to such occupations. In this paper the concept of career will be applied to the life cycle of the mental patient which begins with the identification and classification of a person into the social role of mentally ill, and ends with a reclassification of the person into a category ranging from well to ex-patient. Each stage in the patient's career affects movement to the next stage by generating its own special constraints upon patients.

The main objective of this paper will be to briefly examine the career sequence of the mental patient and to focus primarily upon the final stage: the psychiatric decision process for releasing patients from a mental hospital. It is felt that the release process for psychiatric patients cannot be understood apart from the earlier stages of the patient's career. For in many ways, the final stage bears the burden of the inadequacies, errors, and myths committed and constructed in the earlier stages. The general hypothesis put forth is that decisions for releasing patients have little to do with the state of "wellness" of the patient, and that under certain conditions, it is the "unwell" patient and not the "well" patient who is more likely to be released.

Mental Illness as Social Deviance

The early involvement of sociologists in the study of mental illness was concerned mainly with finding those characteristics of the social environment that were associated with functional disorders. Special attention was given to those social conditions which provided a good fit with psychological theories of mental illness, with the result that sick personalities were found to abound in areas of social disorganization. Thus high rates of illness were found in the central areas of the city characterized by rooming house dwellings, transients, and fleeting social relationships (*Faris and Dunham, 1939*). The mentally ill as compared to the "normal" were more often found to be social isolates, less involved in the mainstream of social life (*Kohn and Clausen, 1955; Jaco, 1954*).

Much of the early work was built upon an idealized view of the sacred, pre-urban society with stable social relationships that bind men to their fellow men and to a cultural tradition of shared beliefs. The contrasting image of the urban society is one of anonymity, alienation from self and others, and self interest as a main principle of social life (*Shils, 1957*). These assumptions about life in the pre-industrial society and mental illness were challenged by the work of Goldhammer and Marshall (*1953*) and Eaton and Weil (*1955*). The former study was an examination of admission rates for state hospitals in Massachusetts, comparing rates from 1840 to 1860 and for the United States as a whole in 1940. Their analysis revealed no significant increase in psychosis over time, thereby failing to give general support for the hypothesis that the greater complexity of modern living gives rise to higher rates of mental illness. The Eaton and Weil study also represents, in a sense, an analysis of the relation between social and cultural complexity and mental illness. They present a picture of the Hutterite community as one of a consistent, well integrated culture, having few internal contradictions and characterized by homogeneity of values. There is virtually no differentiation of class, income, or standard of living, as they are organized on a communal basis. In this setting, where the relative absence of mental disorders might be expected, the authors do not find the Hutterites to be immune from mental disorders, although their rates are considerably lower than those for the U.S. population as a whole.

Sociologists turned their attention from the search for etiological factors in the development of functional mental disorders to an examination of the social institution of insanity (*Cumming and Cumming, 1957*). They

167

detached themselves, so to speak, from actual participation in the cultural pattern itself, standing outside the process and observing its operation. Rather than seeking to develop sociological theories which provide supportive evidence for psychological theories of schizophrenia and psychoneurosis, sociologists become more concerned with the manner in which such illness designations were assigned to persons and how such designations influenced the future course of the illness. Major concern now shifted to how the mentally ill were identified as ill, how they did or did not find their way to becoming patients, how life in the closed communities of patients affected their disorder, how patients move from a state of illness to wellness, and how, having returned to the larger community, ex-patients are able to shed the stigma of their former life.

In 1951 Lemert *(1951)* presented an approach to understanding mental disorders which emphasized the importance of interpersonal relationships in the family and community in defining deviant behavior as mental illness. As Lemert put it:

> It would probably be the consensus of most trained observers of mental disorders that psychotic deviation as described in formal psychiatric categories is not in itself the reason for collective action to bring mentally disturbed persons under restraint. Rather it is the highly visible deviations of the psychotic person from the norms of his group, placing strain upon other persons, which excite his family or the community and cause them to take formal, legal action against him (p. 404).

Thus, collective action by the family or community to commit a disturbed person will be the product of the stressful nature of the deviance and the tolerance of the group for such deviance. A similar view was expressed by Clausen and Yarrow *(1955)* in a paper dealing with the ways in which patients find their way to the mental hospital. They sought to identify those persons and agencies that play decisive roles in defining a patient's difficulties and who aid (or hinder) effective action in getting persons to the hospital.

The relevance of a deviancy perspective for understanding how persons become identified as mentally ill is emphasized by recent surveys which have attempted to measure the prevalence rates of mental illness in the general population. These surveys have obtained very high estimates of the extent of emotional impairment among non-hospitalized persons *(Srole et al., 1962)*. Such findings raise the question of precisely what factors distinguish an emotionally impaired hospitalized person from an emotionally impaired non-hospitalized person. The answer to this question can perhaps be best pursued by looking at the social processes involved in the identification and classification of a person into the *socially defined role* of mentally ill.

The pre-hospital career of the mental patient can be divided into three discernible stages. The stages are interdependent to the extent of the order of their occurrence, but not with respect to the absolute necessity that all three stages take place in the pre-hospital career.[1] Let us examine each stage in terms of how it might increase the probability of becoming identified as mentally ill.

The Reactions to "Unusual" Behavior Which Result in a Definition of Deviancy. Persons find themselves in deviant social roles when other persons respond to their "peculiar" or "unusual" behavior as inappropriate to a situation or not in keeping with a shared standard of conduct, or failure to meet the expectations of some social role. It is the response of the group therefore that places someone in a deviant role. It should also be clear, however, that such a view of deviancy also makes it possible for the originally "peculiar" behavior of persons to be transformed into familiar, expected, and accepted behavior, thereby avoiding definitions of deviancy. Cumming and Cumming (*1957*) in their study of community reaction to mental illness describe the response to deviance in terms of denial, isolation, and insulation. Interviews with wives of mental patients reveal a process of continuous "groping" for definitions of the behavior of their husbands which will help them to interpret and explain the behavior (*Schwartz, 1957*). A similar analysis using hospital documents rather than interviewing family members indicated that families tend to react to a totality of "unusual" behaviors rather than a specific type of behavior, and that the family's tolerance for deviance decreases with close familial relationships (*Linn, 1961*). Such indications of the great ambiguity in defining "unusual" behavior points to the importance that having a vocabulary of explanations may have for defining deviance. Such vocabularies may be part of the idea systems of a family or they may be provided by other persons or agencies in the community.

The Constraints upon the Deviant to Take on a Deviant Role. The existence of a vocabulary for defining certain types of behavior can be seen as a factor which influences a person to take on a deviant role. The deviant individuals themselves may possess such vocabularies which they use to define their behavior, or they may be found among persons of certain educational and occupational characteristics, or they may be found in the existence of mental health agencies and facilities in the community. A recent study reported how differential use of a psychiatric out-patient clinic serving children is related *not* to the incidence or prevalence of mental illness in the child population, but to the extent to which the mental health innovation had been communicated throughout the community and had received a favorable reaction (*Raphael, 1964*).

1 Other stages and sequences of events are of course also possible. We are here attempting to present one possible sequence.

An additional element constraining deviants to take on a deviant role is what Scheff (*1963*) has called the special vulnerability of deviants to the suggestions and influence of others. He has offered the hypothesis that since the "primary deviant may be profoundly confused, anxious, and ashamed" he will be suggestible to the cues and reactions of others to him. These cues may be part of the traditional stereotype of insanity which may also be a part of the deviant's vocabulary for explaining his own behavior. Scheff suggests that "once a person has been placed in a deviant status there are rewards for conforming to the deviant role, and punishment for not conforming to the deviant role" (p. 450).

The Manner in Which the Deviant Role Itself Shapes the Subsequent Behaviors of the Deviant. Once the deviant role is occupied, the deviant is often cut off from "normal" role relationships, from "normal" responses to social situations, and from the supportive relationships of the group in time of stress. In a study of deviance in four cultural groups, Mizruchi and Perrucci suggested that deviants in cultural groups organized around normative systems characterized as proscriptive, inflexible, and unintegrated, are more likely to exhibit extreme reactions to deviance (i.e. problem drinking and alcoholism) than members of cultural groups organized around prescriptive, flexible, and integrative normative systems. This bears a striking resemblance to our earlier discussion of families with a low tolerance for deviance, and suggests that deviants may not be able to shed a deviant role because they are outside of the group and because the group's normative system does not tolerate "gray" areas of behavior. The findings of Glass (*1953*) on combat neurosis (as reported in Scheff, *1963*) suggest a similar pattern on the function of the group context in allowing for deviants to shift from deviant to non-deviant roles. Combat neuroses among soldiers are often self-terminating if the soldier is kept with the unit, but those who are removed from their unit to a hospital often go on to become more seriously impaired.

Thus, the pre-hospital career of the mental patient is shaped by the social context in which deviance occurs, is identified, and in which the response to it takes place. The deviant role itself continues to influence the response of others to the deviant throughout the remainder of his deviant career. Psychiatric decisions concerning commitment, which are often made under conditions of uncertainty, are more likely to err on the side of judging a well person sick than a sick person well (*Scheff, 1965*). Operating with such conservative decision rules ("When in doubt, commit") will undoubtedly generate some anxiety among decision-makers and for the institutions of decision-making. Under such conditions of anxiety and doubt, attempts at justification or rationalizing the decisions are undertaken. Such justification processes can be seen at work in

Goffman's *(1961)* description of how the support of closest kin is sought in order to legitimize the commitment decision. In addition to seeking support for the decision process, once a patient is committed there are elaborate organizational norms and rules which serve to discredit the patient and raise questions concerning the credibility of anything he may say. The patient folder often becomes an extensive dossier of events testifying to the illness of the patient rather than balanced reports representing a sampling of behavior. In a psychiatric hospital studied by the author, "behavior notes" on the patient were only recorded on fights, sleepless nights, inappropriate content in speech, and the like. With the passage of time, idle observations, hypotheses and allegations injected into a patient's folder become transformed into "factual" material when read by physicians trying to make decisions concerning patients.

After commitment, the course and treatment of a patient's illness becomes so intertwined with the social and cultural patterns in the hospital itself that it becomes increasingly difficult to separate out role behavior from that which is a function of an illness. The literature on the mental hospital is rich with descriptions of how the organization impinges upon and shapes the behavior of both patients and staff, and how the social structure on the ward influences staff attitudes and behavior toward patients, as well as patients' own conceptions of their illness.[2]

In the remainder of this paper I would like to close the circle on the career of the mental patient by describing the decision process concerning release from the mental hospital. Going to staff, as it is called, is a special experience for staff as well as patients. Decisions made at staffing are intimately bound up with all the other decisions and folder entries and psychiatric tests and behavioral notes and personal contacts with a patient that have taken place in the course of hospitalization. It is difficult to say whether a patient is better or worse than when he or she was admitted, for who or what a patient was is often lost in a thicket of poorly kept folders and bad memories. How are decisions made concerning release from a mental hospital, and what are the criteria for making such judgments?

Going to Staff: A Search for Release Criteria[3]

The operation of a mental hospital depends, in large part, upon its effectiveness in four areas. The hospital must (1) develop a set of stand-

[2] See, e.g., Stanton and Schwartz *(1954)*, Caudill *(1958)*, Pearlin and Rosenberg *(1962)*. Perrucci *(1963, 1966)*, Brown *(1965)*.

[3] The data reported in this paper were collected during a one-year field study of a state mental hospital located in the Midwest. The hospital had approximately 2,500 full-time patients, 9 physicians, 6 psychologists, and 28 nurses. One phase of the field work was devoted to systematic observation and verbatim recording of disposition staff meetings. The observer attended disposition staff for intermediate

171

ards to determine who shall enter the hospital and who shall not; (2) maintain a program of treatment designed to aid a patient toward recovery; (3) provide for patient needs in accordance with a certain level of living; and (4) develop a set of standards to determine who shall leave the hospital and who shall remain. Theoretically, these four areas are interrelated, in that one area "grows" out of the preceding area, and weaknesses in one area affect all other areas. These four areas strongly suggest the analogy of an industrial organization, where a certain raw material must be transformed into a marketable product. In fact the fourth area — standards regarding release from the hospital — is quite similar to the industrial function of "quality control." That is, the screening of defective products from reaching the public.

However, the problem of "quality control" in the mental hospital is not a simple one. The fund of knowledge available for making specific decisions concerning discharge is relatively scarce and elusive. For example, in the industrial setting, standards for evaluating the organization's product are rather clear and precise. This is undoubtedly due to the intimate link between the processes utilized to transform a raw material into a finished product, and the standards used to check the quality of the finished product. Similarly, in the prison the problem of "quality control" is less difficult since the raw material does not have to be transformed in order to be released, but merely remain a full-time member of the organization. The main criterion is relatively objective, in that the passage of time remains the invariant standard for release.[4] The mental hospital, on the other hand, is not fortunate enough to have clearly objective standards for evaluating their product. Even the actual behavior of the patient, the most objective of the possible standards, cannot be held separate from the different subjective evaluations that can be made of the same behavior.

Thus, we are confronted with the problem of standards for "quality control" in the mental hospital. How does the hospital judge the relative "wellness" of a patient seeking a release? Are the standards used relevant to the patient in the hospital setting, or in the larger society as well? That is, is the patient who "gets on" well according to hospital standards the patient who will "fall apart" in the outside world; or is the patient who develops a bit of an "institutional neurosis" the one who "makes it"

---

treatment patients which took place during a period of two months. Full details on the total study are reported in the author's dissertation entitled *Social Status, Goals and Rewards: A Study of the Social Organization of a Psychiatric Ward*, Purdue University, 1962, and in the two articles by the author cited in footnote 2.

4 Other criteria for release from the prison clearly are not so objective. The system of merits and demerits certainly affects the amount of time spent in the prison, and such a system is bound to the context of interpersonal relations between inmates and staff. Nonetheless, there is a fixed maximum limit to the time one is required to remain in the system, which gives a greater predictability for release to the prison inmate.

in the larger society? These are clearly very important questions with which the persons involved with denying or granting leaves or discharges must be concerned. Whether precise and specific knowledge is or is not available for making these decisions, certain "ground rules" must be established to allow hospital staff to operate in this context. We shall be concerned with these "ground rules," i.e., the question of standards in "quality control." Specifically, we will describe the functions of disposition staff, and the process and meaning of "going to staff." In addition, we will discuss the problem of legitimation in the decision-making process, and examine a number of cases which reveal the various ways in which the actions taken by disposition staff become legitimized.

Disposition Staff. Disposition staff is composed of all physicians having ward responsibilities within a particular treatment service in the hospital. At the time of this study, there were six physicians, including the director of disposition staff, who were generally in attendance at the weekly meetings. In addition, staff is attended by a psychologist, a social worker, and on occasion, an interested nurse or hospital priest or minister. While there may be participation from the non-medical staff, it is the medical staff who participates in the final decision-making process.

The function of disposition staff with which we are concerned, is their responsibility in granting or denying patient requests for leaves of absence, convalescent leaves, work placements, and discharges.[5] The first three of these requests will be considered as "leaves," while the last will be called "discharge." Each of these two occasions for going to staff differs with respect to who requests the leave or discharge. For example, the idea of seeking a leave generally comes from three possible sources: the patient, the social worker, or the family.[6] However, no matter who initiates the idea concerning a leave, the formal request almost always comes from the family. If a patient initiates the idea, she will write to her family (or tell them during a visit) and ask them to write the doctor requesting a leave of some specified type and duration. If a social worker initiates the idea, she will also write the family and ask them to request a leave for the patient in question. Thus, the formal request is used

---

[5] The functions of disposition staff are actually much broader. They also concern themselves with decisions regarding a patient's commitment status. For example, shall a patient be granted an extension of a temporary commitment, or shall he be transferred to a regular commitment. In addition, disposition staff is available "for any purpose for which the ward physician may seek consultation." For the purposes of this paper, however, we will only be concerned with disposition staff functions regarding release from the hospital.

[6] What we are here calling the family includes friends, legal guardians and what the staff likes to call "adoptions," e.g., a volunteer worker who comes to the hospital once a week may become particularly attached to a patient and begin to take the role of a substitute family. The use of the term "adoption" is also interesting in terms of the many overlapping elements between the "patient role" and the "child role."

primarily to indicate that the family does want the patient home, and they are interested in caring for the patient at home.

With a discharge request, we find that staffing proceedings are generally initiated by the patient or ward doctor, and only on occasion by the ward nurse (attendants also initiate the idea by "planting it" with the doctor, but they do not openly pursue the staffing of a patient for discharge). A patient who is continually "on the doctor's back" in expressing a readiness for staff, will eventually be met with the doctor's exasperated comment: "Alright, if you want to go to staff, we'll send you to staff. Then you can see for yourself if you're ready to leave the hospital." In this situation, the patient will go to staff requesting a discharge without the support of her ward physician.

Once a patient has been scheduled for staffing, the preparation phase begins. This preparation involves the patient's attempt to present her best "self" to staff. Thus, a beauty shop appointment is made for a haircut and/or permanent; facial complexions are religiously worked on by the patient in order to present a clean "well-scrubbed look"; a best dress is fixed and cleaned, or if the patient doesn't have a good dress, arrangements are made to borrow one. More important is the preparation made to answer certain expected questions that staff members will ask. Most patients know of approximately a dozen questions that every patient going before staff is asked. This can be seen by looking at the marked similarity of the following six answers given by patients interviewed by the observer, in response to the question: "Can you tell me what kinds of questions patients are asked at staff?"

A. They ask you your name, your age, why you're here. If you think this place has helped you. If you're insane. If you think you should be let out. If they release you, will you do the same things.

A. They asked me if I thought I was better, and if shock treatments helped me out.

A. They delve into your personal business and life too much. They want to find out how you got sick. You have to watch out for arithmetic questions, like subtracting sevens starting from one hundred.

A. The head of staff asks most of the questions. He asks other members if they have anything to ask. He wanted to know if I heard voices, and he asked questions to see if I was in contact with reality, like what time is it? What's the date? Who's the president?

A. Well, they ask about your illness and your condition when you came in. They question you about current events, what your plans are when you leave. You can always depend on being asked if you think the place has helped you. The attendants will usually give you the answers before you go to staff anyway.

A. They usually ask a variety of questions, like: how long you were here, why you came, your age, what medication you're on, how much;

174

what it does for you. They generally ask if you feel you've been helped in the hospital. If you've been a problem in the hospital, they'll ask you why, or the circumstances of the problem.

The similarity of responses to the above questions is quite an accurate reflection of what takes place at staff. An examination of patient folders containing written accounts of staff indicates that the same questions were asked of patients going before staff as long as twenty years ago. The existence of such long-standing traditional elements in the hospital can be seen in a number of other aspects of hospital life. For example, intake interviews, formats for progress notes and nursing notes, and psychological "workups," have remained essentially the same for a good many years.[7]

As one of the above responses also indicated, patients going for staff are "prepped by ward attendants.[8] They are cautioned to be polite, don't get nervous or excited, and don't criticize anyone on the staff. One of the more interesting pieces of advice given to patients preparing for staff is not to talk too much, but to answer each question as briefly as possible. Thus, patients are instructed to limit the amount (as well as the kind) of information they inject into the staff situation. In a sense, what this piece of advice suggests is that the more you talk, the more likely you'll say something wrong. However the attendants may view this piece of advice, we shall try to show later the importance of this aspect of limited information.

Proceedings at Staff. Staffing takes place in a rectangular-shaped room of approximately 20 feet wide by 40 feet long. At the head of the room behind a large plain desk sits the director of staff. Along one side of the desk is a straightback chair for the patient. On the other side, a movable blackboard. On the desk are several stacks of master record folders for each patient scheduled to appear before staff that day. The remainder of the room is filled with rows of chairs split by an aisle down the center of the room. Staff physicians and the staff psychologist sit in the rows closest to the front of the room, while social workers, nurses, and clergy sit behind them. Regular attenders at staff can be found to occupy the same seats week in and week out. Outside in the hall the patients waiting to go to staff are accompanied by one or two attendants. There is generally very little conversation among the patients or between the patients and attendants. Since all the patients on the staff list for that

---

[7] This aspect of the state mental hospital has also been pointed out in Dunham and Weinberg (*1960*, pp. 30–36).

[8] The attendant's interest in insuring a "good performance" on the part of the patient should be seen in the context of certain superordinant-subordinant relationships which are accompanied by an "education" function. For example, in the teacher-student or parent-child relationship (as well as the attendant-patient relationship), the behavior of the subordinant can always be interpreted as a reflection on the training effectiveness of the superordinant.

day assemble at 1:00 p.m., some will have to wait outside as long as two or three hours before going in. After being staffed, the patient returns to his or her ward and awaits information from the ward doctor concerning staff's decision.

We will now present below a description of staff proceedings in three cases of leave requests which were granted.

· CASE 511

DR. HAND: The next one is ———.

DR. STONE: Oh, she'll be here. She's a live one, "hellzapoppin" with her.

DR. HAND: [*Reads briefly from patient's folder, indicating age, sex, race, date of admission, diagnosis, previous hospitalizations, previous leaves, current treatment program. The progress note written by the ward attendant specially for staff is also read. This note usually indicates patient's relationships with others in the ward, and her general cooperativeness or non-cooperativeness with ward staff. Dr. Stone recommends an L.A., leave of absence.*]

DR. HAND: Will you call her in, Dr. Craig, and question her? I have to step out for a minute.

[*Patient enters and sits down.*]

DR. CRAIG:

Q. How long have you been here?

A. About two years.

Q. Have you got a family?

A. No.

Q. You sure you won't have any kids now if you leave?

A. No, I had one of those operations.

Q. Are you going to be an out-patient here?

A. I don't know.

[*Dr. Hand returns at this point, and Dr. Craig turns patient over to him.*]

DR. HAND:

Q. Have you ever been on an open ward?

A. No.

Q. You taking any medicine now?

A. Yes.

Q. What's your official plans?

A. I want to go home to my husband.

Q. Are you anxious to go home?

A. Yes.

Q. Does anything bother you?

A. No.

Q. Do you think you need to be here?

A. That's for the doctors to decide.

176

Q. What happens when you have your nervous breakdowns?
A. I just get all upset, and sometimes I hear voices.
Q. How's the world treating you?
A. O.K.
  DR. HAND: Do you want to ask questions, Dr. Miller?
  DR. MILLER:
Q. Is your husband working?
A. No, he gets social security checks.
Q. How much does he get?
A. I don't know.
[*Dr. Miller indicates he is done.*]
  DR. KIRK (staff psychologist):
Q. You say you heard voices, tell us about them.
A. Oh, most of the time they're not too clear.
  DR. HAND: When did you hear them last?
  PATIENT: Couple of months ago.
  DR. KIRK:
Q. Do the voices make you angry?
A. No.
Q. Are there any other signs of mental illness that you have?
A. Sometimes I think my periods may be some of it. I bleed an awful
  lot, and just feel terrible that time.
Q. Do people talk about you?
A. No.
  DR. HAND: Dr. Stone, you want to ask anything?
  DR. STONE: No, that's all right.
  DR. HAND: O.K., you can leave now, Mrs. ———. Thank you for
coming.
[*Patient leaves.*]
  DR. HAND: She takes Thorazine now, 150.
  DR. CRAIG: [*to Dr. Stone*] Do you think she needs 150?
  DR. STONE: She just cooled down. She was high as a kite before.
  DR. KIRK: Do you think there's anything significant about her comments
on menstrual flow and her illness? Freud said something about it. . . .
  DR. STONE: [*cutting off Dr. Kirk*] Sure he did. I'll give you a lecture
on Freud; he was as crazy as a bedbug.
  DR. HAND: Well, what shall we do?
  DR. STONE: Can't we get social service to check on the home before
giving her an L.A.? They want her, but I didn't think the home situa-
tion was so good.
  DR. CRAIG: Let her go home before she gets sicker. She's alright now.
  DR. HAND: Let's put her on three months L.A. instead of six months.
That alright with everyone?
[*Everyone gives general support to the director's suggestion.*]

· CASE 371

DR. HAND: Let's take ——— next. Dr. Powell has to leave early, so we'll get her now. What about this girl, Dr. Powell?

DR. POWELL: Mr. Holmes [*social worker*] knows this case.

MR. HOLMES: Well, ——— has been here for quite a while. She was out on work placement before, and got along pretty well. Now her sister wants her home.

DR. HAND: Have you got the letter requesting her by her sister?

MR. HOLMES: Yes.

DR. HAND: O.K. Bring her in.

[*Patient enters and sits down.*]

DR. HAND: Dr. Powell is going to talk to you, Miss ———

DR. POWELL:

Q. How long have you been in this institution, [*first name*]?

A. I don't know exactly; it's been a good while.

Q. Yes, it has; it's been 18 years. You've had lots of visits home, but never stayed home.

A. [*No response from patient.*]

Q. What brought you here in the first place?

A. I don't know.

Q. You mean you never have figured out why you're in the hospital?

A. No, I've been here so long.

Q. Did you like your work last time you were out?

A. Yes.

Q. What caused you to come back?

A. I had a lot of arguments with my sister.

Q. What were you arguing about with your sister?

A. It was always over my medicine. She was always taking me to Dr. [*family doctor*] for medicine.

Q. Will you go see Dr. ——— when you're home this time?

A. Yes. But this time I'm going to work. I'm not going to stay home all the time.

Q. Do you think it's best for you to work?

A. Yes.

Q. How much will you get paid?

A. Oh, I don't know.

Q. What kind of work will you do?

A. Office work.[9]

---

[9] Note in this context, that most patients who are making plans to leave the hospital almost invariably indicate their desire for a clerical type of position. This is true in spite of the fact that the great bulk of these patients are from lower income, lower educational levels. Those patients who have worked prior to, or in between hospitalizations, have generally held unskilled labor positions, e.g., dishwasher, domestic. This focus on white-collar employment is probably a good reflection of the "middle-classizing" function of hospital resocialization.

Q. How's your spelling and typing and shorthand?

A. I'll have to brush up on them.

[*Dr. Powell indicates he is finished.*]

DR. HAND: Dr. Miller.

DR. MILLER: Do you prefer office work to housework?

PATIENT: Yes.

[*Dr. Miller indicates "that's all."*]

DR. HAND: Question, Dr. Stone?

DR. STONE: No questions.

DR. HAND:

Q. What have you been doing at the hospital?

A. I'm a ward worker.

Q. Will you get along with your sister this time?

A. Yes, I think so.

Q. Do you have any other sisters?

A. No.

Q. What have we done for you in 18 years?

A. You've done me lots of good.

Q. Have voices been bothering you?

A. No.

Q. How about dreams?

A. No.

Q. Will you take your medicine if you leave?

A. Yes.

[*Dr. Hand nods to Mr. Holmes.*]

MR. HOLMES: You know, [*first name*], your sister insists that you cooperate with her this time, if you go to her.

PATIENT: Oh, I will.

DR. HAND: O.K., Miss ———. Thanks for coming.

[*Patient exits.*]

DR. HAND: What do you think, Dr. Powell?

DR. POWELL: I think she functions pretty well on the ward.

DR. HAND: The only thing is that she's been here so long. [*There is a short pause of silence while Dr. Hand leafs through the patient's folder.*] Well, six months, O.K.

DR. POWELL: I don't think she'll last the six months, personally.

DR. HAND: I agree. She'll be back. Six months then; any other comments?

· CASE 471

DR. HAND: Let's take ——— next. She's up for an L.A., and we have to see what to do with her.

DR. POWELL: I think there's a family feud going on there. One person wants her and the other doesn't.

DR. HAND: Is she pretty institutionalized?

DR. POWELL: Yes, she is. I think she'll be alright if someone will take her.

DR. HAND: [*Reads standard information from patient's folder.*]

DR. POWELL: Isn't there a note there from the social worker about the home situation? [*He goes up and looks through folder and finds no note.*]

DR. HAND: Let's bring her in. Will you start the questioning, Dr. Powell? [*Patient enters.*]

DR. POWELL:

Q. When did you come to the hospital?

A. About 12 years ago.

Q. Were you here before?

A. No.

[*Dr. Hand checks folder and indicates that she did have a previous hospitalization there.*]

Q. What brought you to the hospital?

A. My nerves.

Q. Do you think you're ready to go home?

A. Yes, I want to get back home to my family.

Q. Have you talked to your husband about this?

A. No, I don't see him much.

Q. Has he been here to visit?

A. No.

Q. Any other reason besides nerves that brought you to the hospital?

A. No, I don't think so.

Q. Did you do or say anything?

A. No.

[*Patient was committed for attacking husband. This fact was indicated by Dr. Hand when the patient was introduced.*]

Q. If you couldn't go home with your husband, could you go elsewhere?

A. Maybe someone else in the family, but I got my own home and husband.

[*Dr. Powell indicates he is finished.*]

DR. HAND:

Q. How do you get along with your husband?

A. O.K.

Q. Did you ever hit him?

A. I don't know; I don't think so.

Q. Do you recall what you did in the past?

A. Some things I do.

Q. How do you get along with people?

A. O.K.

Q. Why did you come here?

A. It was my nerves; they got away from me.

Q. How did they get away from you?
A. Oh, I don't know. I had a nervous breakdown.
Q. How is the world treating you?
A. O.K.
Q. Is everybody your friend?
A. I get along alright.
Q. Anybody control your mind?
A. No.
Q. Can you read others' minds?
A. No.
Q. Do people talk behind your back?
A. No.
Q. You hear voices?
A. No.
Q. Do you talk to the Lord?
A. No.
Q. Do you have any future plans?
A. What do you mean?
Q. What can we do for you?
A. Let me go home to my husband.
Q. Have you talked to him about going home?
A. No.
Q. How do you know he wants you?
A. I know he does. He's my husband.
Q. When did you hear from him last?
A. I don't know. He doesn't write.
   DR. POWELL: Do you write him?
   PATIENT: No.
   DR. HAND: Do you think it's normal not to write and see your husband?
   PATIENT: [*No response.*]
   DR. HAND: Do you need to be here?
   PATIENT: I don't think so.
   DR. HAND: Any questions, Dr. Miller?
   DR. MILLER: No.
   DR. HAND: Dr. Stone?
   DR. STONE: No.
   DR. HAND: O.K. You can go now, Mrs. ———.
[*Patient leaves.*]
   DR. HAND: To me, she's a chronic case. She shows no insight. Of
course, she was alright here, no acting out.
   DR. POWELL: What can we do if her husband doesn't want her?
   DR. HAND: Family care placement.
   DR. POWELL: There's no hope of her ever being rehabilitated as I can
see. I'd like to move her off the ward. She's only taking up a bed and

not getting anything. Maybe a county home; she'd be paranoid, probably curse the superintendent, but she's under control.

DR. HAND: We can recommend that she's as stabilized as ever, and is ready for placement, in general, of any kind. That way if they can't get her back to her family, they can try somewhere else. Everybody agree? [*There is general agreement expressed through nods and "yeas."*]

We have presented these three cases concerning leave requests to illustrate the general manner in which disposition staff handles such requests. To the non-psychiatric observer in the situation, *explicit* standards or criteria for the decision process were almost non-existent. The elements which the three cases did seem to have in common appeared to be unrelated to questions concerning the patient's present psychic condition, the patient's ward behavior, or the expected success regarding the patient's post-hospital performance. In fact, one of the striking aspects of the three cases, is the relative ease with which the leaves were granted despite the staff's pessimism concerning post-hospital performance. How can we explain this apparent willingness to release a patient who is not considered well enough to remain out of the hospital?

The main reason for this phenomenon seems to lie in the staff's definition of the seriousness of the staff decision in the situation. That is, the decision to grant a leave is not felt to be so serious as to give the staff members considerable cause for concern. It would seem that the granting of a leave, in light of the pessimistic post-hospital prognosis, would be considered very serious since each error in judgment would put staffing decisions in a questionable light. Would not these errors also raise questions concerning the legitimacy of staff's "quality control" function? Curiously enough, instead of the legitimacy of staff decisions being questioned, their decisions are defined as quite correct, appropriate and unaffected by errors, i.e., patients who do not "make it" on leave. This seems to take place for several reasons. For one thing, the decision to grant a leave does not indicate the success of the hospital in "producing a finished product." They are not indicating that the patient is well, recovered or ready to resume their life in the larger society. Thus, they are not evaluating the effectiveness of the hospital's treatment function by putting the stamp of "approval" on the patient's psychological condition. Second, the leave is granted with the understanding that responsible persons will be substituting for the hospital in providing supervision and continuing the patient on her prescribed medication.[10] This

[10] All patients going out on short leaves are provided with their regular supply of medication. While there are formal hospital procedures concerning the supply of medication to be provided a patient going on leave, there is considerable variation. The formally prescribed amount is sent from the hospital pharmacy to the person responsible for the patient while on leave. When the period of leave exceeds the amount of provided medication, the day attendant will usually make up the difference

feature of the leave also shifts the locus of "blame" for patients who may have some kind of extreme reaction while on leave. That is, while the patient was "intact" on leaving the hospital, the particular conditions in the home environment are viewed as the cause of the patient's failure to stay on leave. The demanding mother, the protective father, or the drinking husband can each shoulder the blame for a patient's failure on leave. A third, and by no means unimportant aspect of the leave, is that the request is coming from outside the system. Thus, in a sense, no particular staff member is "laying himself on the line" by pushing for a patient's leave. In addition, an interested relative, of whom there are few in number in a large state hospital, can become either a happy relative, by having the leave granted, or an unhappy source of pressure, by taking her request to the superintendent.

Turning to the *discharge* request, we find that the seriousness of the staff decision is much more pronounced. A staff decision granting a discharge does put an official stamp on both the patient's condition, and the effectiveness of the hospital treatment program. In a real sense, the staff decision to discharge is a guarantee to the public that a particular patient is ready to "fit in" again. As one physician stated, "It's no joke to discharge a patient. If they're not ready, and we turn them loose, we're really responsible for anything they may do." In addition, any judgment by staff on a discharge request inevitably provokes disagreement among staff members. Not only among staff physicians themselves, but among every level of staff having knowledge of the patient in question, there will be divergences of opinion concerning the patient's readiness for discharge. Therefore, no matter whether a discharge request is granted or denied, there will be a residue of disagreement among various staff persons. Thus errors in judgment in this context, i.e., patients who "blow up" after discharge, can come back to "haunt" the physician who supported the discharge. Staff members who did not support a discharge request for a patient who nevertheless received the discharge and subsequently returned as an "error," will often remind the supporting staff member of his mistaken judgment. This usually comes up in the context of a patient who is seeking a discharge, where one staff member will say: "This case is very similar to Mary Jones' case. You remember how convinced you were that she was ready, and I didn't think so. She got her discharge, and she was back here in three months. This girl will do the same thing if we let her go."

What we find, then, is a rather pronounced "conservatism" among staff physicians regarding the granting of a discharge request, as com-

---

from the ward supply of medications (the attendant will do this only if she feels the family cannot afford to buy the additional medication). Another way around the rule is for a family member to return to the hospital for an additional supply which she will get through the ward doctor or ward attendant.

pared to a leave request. That is, it is easier to get a leave than a discharge. As a result, it appears that despite the fact that a patient does not closely approach some ideal condition of "wellness," thereby giving her a poor post-hospital performance prognosis, he or she is more likely to *leave* the hospital than a patient who more closely approaches some ideal condition of "wellness," but who is requesting a discharge. This appears to be the case because the latter patient is faced with a set of standards which have been re-defined to fit the perceived serious-ness of the situation.

The Need for Structure in Staff Decisions. Staff definitions regarding leave requests and discharge requests can be viewed as providing a set of implicit standards for making decisions. These standards, however, appear to be somewhat extraneous to the question that is presumably at the heart of the function of staff, namely, "Is this patient well enough to leave the hospital?" This question reflects the *ideal* "quality control" function of staff. But, as we have already suggested, the knowledge nec-essary to answer this question is not readily available for use in a highly rational, calculable and predictable manner. How then do staff physicians govern their own decisions? Obviously, they must operate within some framework of standards which provides *structure* for the decision-making process. It is this structure which provides the stamp of *legitimacy* to the staff decision. Again, staff decisions cannot be made without standards of criteria, nor can the standards be "pulled out of a hat," so to speak. The standards must have some credibility, be it relevant knowledge, or "masking" beliefs.

The different staff definitions of seriousness regarding leave and dis-charge requests are examples of the manner in which *structure* is pro-vided for the decision process. Additional sources from which structure emerges can be found in (1) the potential complexity of the decision, i.e., how much additional work or problems will the decision generate, and (2) the strength of the resistance to, or support for, the request by an individual or group in the hospital. Each of these sources of structure are also extraneous to the essential and basic question: "Is this patient well enough to leave the hospital?" Below, are examples of the intrusion of these extraneous considerations into the decision proc-ess. The text of the entire staff discussion is *not* reported as in the earlier cases in this paper; what we report here is the discussion which crystalized the final decision (all reported discussion took place after each patient was questioned and left the staffing room).

· CASE 411

DR. HAND: Well, what shall we do? Dr. Hill and Social Service want her discharged.

DR. CRAIG: I'm not sure about a discharge. Why don't we just give her six months L.A.?

DR. HAND: If we give her an L.A., she won't get the additional social security money she's got coming. If she doesn't get the money, she can't very well take care of herself.

DR. CRAIG: Well, maybe we ought to discharge her and keep our fingers crossed.

DR. HAND: The main problem is that she gets more money after her discharge. If she runs off to California again we'll just have to go get her. What do you think, Dr. Craig?

DR. CRAIG: They [*Social Service*] have it all set up.

DR. STONE: They expect it, so while they're in the mood, let's do it. I'll go along with them any day.

DR. HAND: If there are no objections then, we'll discharge.

·CASE 1141

DR. HAND: She's been a good patient here, but I'd be more inclined to give her six months L.A. instead of a discharge. What do you think, Dr. Powell?

DR. POWELL: I'd just discharge her and let her go to Detroit.

DR. HAND: Why not just give her an L.A. and let her go to her daughter in Detroit?

DR. POWELL: An L.A., out of state!

DR. HAND: Oh, yes. There's a lot of red tape going out of state. It would be a lot easier for us to give a discharge. [*Brief pause.*] O.K. We'll discharge her. Any objection?

·CASE 75

DR. CRAIG: He's not psychotic. He doesn't belong here. A nursing home would be fine, but I think he should be home and his wife should take care of him.

DR. HAND: What do you want to do? He's your patient.

DR. CRAIG: I want to send him home. Discharge him!

DR. HAND: What do you think, Dr. Stone?

DR. STONE: He's just a confused old man. He's strong-minded and gives you a hard time on the ward.

DR. CRAIG: He's a pain in the neck on the ward.

DR. HAND: His wife doesn't want him. How are we going to discharge him?

DR. CRAIG: She's got to take him. It's her responsibility.

DR. HAND: I think it's going to be tough. Not that I don't agree with you [Dr. Craig], but he's been here a long time. It's tough. What do you think, Dr. Powell?

DR. POWELL: [*No response.*]

DR. CRAIG: She's just getting rid of him for forty dollars a month. Let's get him home on L.A. for six months.

DR. STONE: Yes. L.A. for six months, twice a year. [*Everybody laughs.*]

DR. HAND: O.K. Let's get him home for L.A., six months.

· CASE 271

DR. HAND: Well, what shall we do? He's up for discharge. His brother wants him to go to [*name of state*], but he'd rather stay in [*name of another state*]. What do you think, Dr. Stone?

DR. STONE: I think he can go; let's discharge him.

DR. HAND: How can we discharge if he doesn't want to go to his brother? If he'd go to [*out of state*], it's no problem. It's out of state and no work for us. But he wants to go to [*in state*]. That means we have to get a sponsor and give him an L.A.

DR. STONE: Let's forget the discharge then. Give him an L.A. for six months.

DR. HAND: O.K. L.A. for six months. Everyone agree?

These, then, are examples of factors external to the situation which provided the necessary structure that led to a crystallization of the staff decision. In each case, the decision was shaped in terms of its conformability to external conditions, and not to the behavior or psychic condition of the patient. This does not mean that the behavior or psychic condition of a patient does not enter the staff decision as major criteria. Clearly, in many of the staffing decisions, psychiatric knowledge applied to the patient's performance at staff becomes the dominant criterion. In fact, the major premise underlying the function of staff is that the "unwell" patient will reveal herself or be revealed. Thus the "unwell" will not be discharged, while the "well" patient will be discharged. However, we would like to suggest an alternative hypothesis, namely, that under certain limited conditions, the relatively "unwell" patient (as measured by performance at staff) will be more likely to get a discharge than the relatively "well" patient. The suggested explanation for this organizational paradox follows.

Discharge: An Organizational Paradox. "Going to staff" is recognized by most patients and staff as a situation which produces a great deal of anxiety for the patients. Patients are expected to perform in a manner which will ensure a favorable decision by the staff. Often, the sheer anticipation of going to staff is enough to raise a patient's anxiety so as to make her incapable of giving an adequate performance. What is often overlooked, however, is the fact that going to staff also produces a great deal of anxiety for the attending physicians at staff. In exercising their "quality control" function, the physicians are expected to make decisions of considerable importance to patients, the hospital, and the community. However, it is not the decision situation itself which produces the anxiety for staff, but the fact that the decision must be made according to criteria which provides legitimacy for the physician's behavior at staff. The staff physician must provide himself, and, by extension, others, with information that attests to the correctness of his decision.

In this situation, the physician is provided with two sources from which he may legitimize his decision. First, is the *external* structure of which we have spoken above. Here we find the decision being made in terms of such factors as the amount of staff support there is for a certain decision, the legal complications of the decision, the extent of the family pressure for a decision, and the like. In the absence of any external structure to legitimize the decision, the staff physician is essentially thrown back on his own resources. That is, he must, with the tools of his trade such as knowledge of the dynamics of pathology, make the decision to grant or deny a discharge. Thus, the staff physicians depend upon their available fund of questions which are designed to elicit that information from the patient which is necessary to make the correct decision. The curious aspect of this second source of legitimization, is that basically the staff, through their questioning, depend upon the patients to tell them whether they are well enough to receive a discharge. The staff physicians are expected to base their decisions upon an analysis of the patient's responses. All the physician has to work with, then, are his own questions, and the responses of the patient.

In this setting — where there is a relative absence of external legitimation and the physician must depend upon his own resources — we would apply our hypotheses that the relatively "unwell" patient is more likely to get a discharge than the relatively "well" patient. The rationale here, is that the "unwell" patient provides *structure* for the situation with her responses, while the "well" patient only increases the already present anxieties of the staff by requiring them to be able to apply additional knowledge to the situation which they do not possess. The situation for these cases would be something like the following.

At staff, the relatively "unwell" patient is confronted with the standard questions of the physicians. During the questioning, the "unwell" patient will provide what we might call a little "pathological content" in some of her answers. That is, she will give some inappropriate answers to questions of orientation, or provide answers that may be psychiatrically interpreted as recognizable symptoms of a certain diagnosed condition. It is significant that this "pathological content" comes to light very early in the questioning process, for the staff's fund of available questions is never really exhausted.

Once the "pathological content" is given by the patient, the staff members are provided with a "foothold" which allows them to exercise their own psychiatric knowledge. Extended discussions take place concerning whether a "manic in remission is really in remission, or only in a modified depressive phase," or "what is the basic difference between some ideal state of mental health and simply manageable symptoms." Thus, the "pathological content" injected by the patient allows the staff to actually *fulfill their "quality control" function in a legitimized manner.* The anxiety which is built into the staffing situation is relieved by the fact that the physicians are actually activating their psychiatric roles, and utilizing their specialized knowledge in the decision making process. In this process of fulfilling their own psychiatric roles and their "quality control" task, the patient is, in a sense, "forgotten." That is, the existence of the patient at staff becomes secondary to the resolution of questions and the exchange of ideas which "grew out" of the "pathological content" introduced by the patient. As a result, the relatively "unwell" patient has created a situation which will predispose the staff to view her discharge request in a "more favorable" light.[11]

The relatively "well" patient at staff is also confronted with the same set of standard questions used by the physicians. However, in response to these questions the "well" patient does not provide that little "pathological content" that the "unwell" patient does. That is, she is not "helping" the staff by providing any structure to the situation. Thus, while it may seem that the patient who "breezes through" the staff questioning, by giving appropriate answers to all questions, will get a quick and easy decision granting a discharge, it does not appear to work this way. For one thing, the fund of questions used by staff are not the actual criteria for the final decision, but the means by which responses may be elicited and evaluated. The patient who gives appropriate answers to all the questions, then, is depriving the staff of the opportunity to exercise their particular staffing function. Since the staff does not receive any structure from the patient, a legitimized final decision cannot be made.

In response to this situation, there is little that staff can do but continue to ask questions in search of structure. As more and more questions are asked, the familiar questions are soon exhausted; to be followed by a "groping" for questions which range from the repetitious to the irrelevant. In addition, as each subsequent question is asked and answered appropriately, the already existing level of anxiety is rapidly

[11] It should be kept in mind that we are not speaking of the markedly disturbed or psychotic patient who also provides the "pathological content" which integrates the staff by allowing them to fulfill their psychiatric roles. Our "unwell" patient is one who is quite "intact," and who gets on well in the hospital. We are not making an independent judgment as to the "sickness" or "wellness" of the patients in question. For our purposes, the "unwell" definition simply applies to these patients who inject "pathological content" into the staffing situation. It should also be clear, however, that we would extend our discussion here to what takes place at staff for patients of psychiatrically determined degrees of "wellness."

magnified. What will generally happen in this situation then, is that as additional questions are asked, the likelihood that the patient will give an inappropriate answer is greatly increased. More important, is the fact that when the inappropriate answer is finally forthcoming — an answer which might be overlooked under other conditions — the staff reaction to the answer is quite extreme. That is, the staff reaction is markedly different from usual staff behavior during the decision-making process. What is indicated by the staff behavior in this situation is a sort of "tension release" effect whereby anxieties of staff members become redirected toward the patient in a highly emotionalized manner.

We will present below a case which illustrates the hypothesis we have suggested. This case involves a discharge request in which the patient provided no structure for the situation, and the nature of staff reaction to the problem.

• CASE 63

Dr. Hand: The next one is ———, a discharge request. She says she can get a lab job in ——— hospital. Would you tell us something about her, Mrs. Rand [*the patient's ward nurse*]?

Mrs. Rand: Well, ——— has been after a discharge for a while now. I asked Dr. Powell if we shouldn't try, and he said maybe we should, I think it's a shame to keep her here. She's a very bright girl, and she's really learned her lab work. Lately, she has refused to take her medicine. She says it doesn't help her; and besides, she says she doesn't need us to take her medicine.

Dr. Hand: I have a note here from her work supervisor indicating that she works well in the lab and has picked up a great deal.

Dr. Miller: Shouldn't we wait for Dr. Powell before we handle her case?

Dr. Hand: No, he won't be able to make it today, so we'll have to go on without him. Will you show her in, Dr. Craig?

[*Patient enters.*]

Dr. Hand:

Q. I see where you want to get a job at ——— hospital.

A. Yes, I talked with their lab director last time I was in ———, and he was interested.

Q. Do you think you would like lab work as a permanent job?

A. Oh, yes, I enjoy my work here very much.

Q. It's really not easy work running all those tests. Are you bothered by the blood tests?

A. No, I don't mind them.

Q. Do you know who the governor of ——— is?

A. [*Appropriately answered.*]

Q. Who is the President of the United States now?

A. [*Appropriately answered.*]

Q. Do you remember when you first came to [*hospital name*]?

A. [*Appropriately answered.*]

DR. CRAIG:

Q. How do you know you'll get a job at ——— if you're discharged?

A. I told you I talked to the lab director, and he was interested.

Q. Suppose he's not as interested as he appeared to you. Where will you work if you can't get in at ——— hospital?

A. I think I know my lab work well enough to get a lab technician's job somewhere.

Q. Well, let's see how much lab work you really know.

[*Dr. Craig asked the patient more questions pertaining to various lab procedures and lab tests. After the last response, Dr. Craig indicates that the patient does know her lab work.*]

DR. HAND:

Q. How do you get along with the other patients?

A. Not very well. I have a few close friends, but I don't socialize with the other patients.

Q. What bothers you about the other patients?

A. Oh, I don't know. I just don't like living in the hospital.

Q. Do you think we've helped you while you've been here?

A. No, I don't.

Q. What kind of treatment have you had here?

A. Lobotomy and shock.

Q. Do you think it's helped you or tortured you?

A. I think it's tortured me.

[*This response brings a stir from others present at staff.*]

Q. You mean that we did these things just to torture you?

A. Oh, no. I'm sure that when they give shock they mean to help. But I don't think they have.

DR. STONE:

Q. Besides not liking it here, why do you want to go to work?

A. For one thing, I want to start earning my own money, and make my own way.

Q. If you want to make money, we can probably find plenty of opportunities for you to make money right here.

A. You mean like washing cars. I'm already doing that.

Q. [*in an annoyed tone*] No, I don't mean washing cars. You could probably work full-time in the lab right here on a work placement.

A. I already asked Dr. Galt about an opening in histology, and he said there wasn't any. Anyway, I'd do much better if the hospital would free me.

DR. HAND:

Q. What do you mean, "free you"?

A. Well, it would be just like the other work placements I've had You're never really free.

[*It was at this point in the staffing session that the observer noted the beginnings of the change in staff behavior. The patient's response about "never really being free," was followed by the exchange of glances among the physicians. These glances indicated that they had, so to speak, "picked up the scent." Staff participation at this point no longer followed the orderly procedure of the staff director asking individual members if they had any questions. The physicians spoke whenever they wished, sometimes cutting in on each other, and sometimes several speaking at the same time. The normal speaking tone vanished as pronouncements and accusations were directed at the patient.*]

Q. But if you stayed here on a work placement you'd be free to come and go on your own time. It would be just like a job.

A. No. You would still be controlling me if I stayed here.

DR. CRAIG: [*cutting in*]

Q. Do you mean we control your mind here?

A. You may not control my mind, but I really don't have a mind of my own.

Q. How about if we gave you a work placement in ————; would you be free then? That's far away from here.

A. Any place I went it would be the same setup as it is here. You're never really free; you're still a patient, and everyone you work with knows it. It's tough to get away from the hospital's control.

DR. STONE: [*cutting in*] That's the most paranoid statement I ever heard.

MRS. RAND: How can you say that, [*first name*]? That doesn't make any sense. [*The nurse is standing at this point.*] It's just plain crazy to say we can control your mind.

[*Nurse Rand turns to Dr. Stone who is looking at her.*]

MRS. RAND: [*still standing*] I had no idea she was that sick. She sure had me fooled. [*Turning to the patient again*] You're just not well enough for a discharge, [*first name*], and you had better realize that.

DR. STONE: She's obviously paranoid.

[*Immediately following Dr. Stone's remark, Dr. Craig stood up, followed by social worker Holmes. Dr. Stone himself then stood up to join the others, including Nurse Rand who had been standing for some time. It should be noted that this took place without any indication from Dr. Hand, the staff director, that the interview was completed. He then turned to the patient and dismissed her. After the patient left, the standing staff members engaged themselves in highly animated discussion. Nurse Rand was involved in making general apologies for having indicated support for the patient's discharge request at the beginning of the staff meeting. Drs. Stone and Craig were engaged in monologues inter-*]

preting and re-interpreting the patient's statements. Amid the confusion, Dr. Hand managed to comment, "I guess there's no need to vote on her; it's quite clear."][12]

After leaving staff, the observer returned to the ward to speak with the patient in question. She was very disappointed and bitter. Among her remarks was her accusation that Dr. Powell had never really wanted her to get a discharge, for if he did, he would have been at staff to support her request. However, the patient did appear to show some insight into what had taken place at staff. She made the following remark: "I did learn something from that staff, though. If I ever get a chance to go again, I'll keep my big mouth shut, and I'll lie like hell. This time I said what I really felt, and look what happened."

The decision processes described in these case documents indicate the varied criteria that influence staffing decisions. In the cases presented, decision criteria were identified which were related to such matters as the source of, and support for, the release request, the locus of responsibility for "errors" in staff decisions, the degree of legal and organizational complications engendered by the decision, the extent of family pressure for a decision, and in the final case, the degree of anxiety generated by staff's inability to find criteria within the staffing situation itself. In each case, the criteria are not centrally relevant to the degree of illness of the patient, but are related to a number of social conditions which indicate that psychiatric decisions are made within a social system context.

These findings show important similarities to those reported earlier on the pre-hospital career of the patient. In the commitment process, the family member was a central figure whose request for commitment greatly increased the likelihood of commitment. Linn (*1961*) reported that the spouse and parents were more likely to commit than any other relative or non-family agent. Goffman (*1961, pp. 136–145*) also pointed to the part played by the family member in moving the person from a civil to patient status, which he has called the betrayal cycle. The greater the involvement of the family member in the commitment process, the easier the task of hospital psychiatric agents in that there will be greater legitimation of the commitment decision. This same pattern is clearly at work in our data on the release process. Under conditions where a family member is eager to have a patient released, and is pressing for such a release, staff decisions are likely to meet the family requests. This

---

12 While it may appear that the picture of confusion presented here is quite overdrawn, the observer could not help but respond to the very marked aspects of this staff meeting as compared to any other staff meeting he attended. If the descriptive account takes on the aspects of a caricature, it is primarily because of the observed departures from the expected.

occurs precisely because the family shoulders the responsibility for the patient and thereby relieves the hospital of responsibility.

The total career of the psychiatric patient, from identification through commitment through discharge, is clouded by an atmosphere of uncertainty in critical decision situations. Such uncertainty apparently sets in motion patterns of response which serve to justify decisions rather than to make them. The data presented in this paper, as well as the growing literature on the social context of mental illness, would suggest the importance of studying mental illness from a perspective of social deviance. Such a perspective would focus less upon "abnormal" behavior and more on the process of identifying "unusual" behaviors, and the manner in which the response to such behaviors influences the future course of the deviant's career.

References

Brown, Julia S. (1965). "Sociometric Choices of Patients in a Therapeutic Community," *Human Relations,* 18, 241–251.

Caudill, William (1958). *The Psychiatric Hospital as a Small Society,* Harvard University Press.

Clausen, John A., and Marion R. Yarrow (1955). "Paths to the Mental Hospital," *The Journal of Social Issues,* XI (December), 25–33.

Cumming, Elaine and John Cumming (1957). *Closed Ranks,* Harvard University Press.

Dunham, H. Warren and S. Kirson Weinberg (1960). *The Culture of the State Mental Hospital,* Wayne State University Press.

Eaton, Joseph W. and Robert J. Weil (1955). *Culture and Mental Disorders,* Free Press.

Faris, Robert E. L. and H. Warren Dunham (1939). *Mental Disorders in Urban Areas,* University of Chicago Press.

Glass, Albert J. (1953). "Psychotherapy in the Combat Zone," in *Symposium on Stress,* Army Medical Service Graduate School.

Goffman, Erving (1961). *Asylums,* Doubleday–Anchor.

Goldhammer, Herbert and Herbert Marshall (1953). *Psychosis and Civilization,* Free Press.

Jaco, E. Gartley (1954). "The Social Isolation Hypothesis and Schizophrenia," *American Sociological Review,* 19 (October), 567–577.

Kesey, Ken (1962). *One Flew Over The Cuckoo's Nest,* Viking.

Kohn, Melvin and John Clausen (1955). "Social Isolation and Schizophrenia," *American Sociological Review,* 20 (June), 265–273.

Lemert, Edwin M. (1951). *Social Pathology,* McGraw–Hill.

Linn, Erwin L. (1961). "Agents, Timing, and Events Leading to Mental Hospitalization," *Human Organization,* 20 (Summer), 92–98.

Pearlin, Leonard I., and Morris Rosenberg (1962). "Nurse-Patient Social Distance and the Structural Context of a Mental Hospital," *American Sociological Review,* 27 (February), 56–65.

Perrucci, Robert (1963). "Social Distance Strategies and Intra-Organizational Stratification: A Study of the Status System on a Psychiatric Ward," *American Sociological Review,* 28 (December), 951–963.

———— (1966). "Social Distance, Bargaining Power and Compliance with Rules on a Hospital Ward," *Psychiatry,* 29 (February), 42–55.

Raphael, Edna E. (1964). "Community Structure and Acceptance of Psychiatric Aid," *American Journal of Sociology,* LXIX (January), 340–359.

Scheff, Thomas J. (1963). "The Role of the Mentally Ill and the Dynamics of Mental Disorder: A Research Framework," *Sociometry,* XXVI (December), 436–453.

———— (1965). "Decision Rules, Types of Error, and Their Consequences in Medical Diagnosis," in Fred Massarik and Philburn Ratoosh, *Mathematical Explorations in Behavioral Science,* Homewood.

Schwartz, Charlotte G. (1957). "Perspectives on Deviance — Wives' Definitions of Their Husbands' Mental Illness," *Psychiatry,* XX (August), 257–291.

Shils, Edward (1957). "Daydreams and Nightmares: Reflections on the Criticism of Mass Culture," *Sewanee Review,* (Autumn).

Srole, Leo, *et. al.* (1962). *Mental Health in the Metropolis: The Midtown Manhattan Study,* McGraw–Hill.

Stanton, Alfred H., and Morris S. Schwartz (1954). *The Mental Hospital,* Basic Books.

PART THREE

Bureaucratization, Work and Collective Disturbance:

Some Perspectives on Organizational Contexts

In the preceding sections may be recognized an important point about the potential of contemporary sociology for counseling and psychotherapy: sociological inquiry need not be limited to any specific topic, but rather is appropriate to a broad range of substantive interests associated with the human arts. The essence of sociology, that is, is not to be found in its accumulated findings, generalizations, or even in its theories. These are indeed important to the discipline; more than anything else, they are its justification and provide important tools for further inquiry and the development of generalizations and theories. To the counselor and psychotherapist, these findings, generalizations and theories may be useful, arguing for continuing efforts to identify the practical implications of sociological inquiry. Useful though they be, these findings and their implications do not represent the essential sociological potential: they, in fact, are themselves a product of that essential.

The essence of sociology is a perspective — or more accurately, perspectives of somewhat similar type, ways of looking at things such that certain hidden qualities become apparent, such that linkages between seemingly distant occurrences are identified, such that form, repetition, and regularity are recognizable, allowing closer insight not only into uniformities and stabilities, but also into diversities, deviances, and change. "Things are not what they seem," Peter Berger (*1963*) suggests. Beneath surface appearances may be another level of reality, less apparent, less measurable, less appropriate to traditional Western modes of inquiry which emphasize chronological sequence and logical relation to the neglect of atemporal clusterings, and interpenetrant realities.

Sociological perspectives, as they are experienced today, are far from perfect. The pictures they allow are often cloudy and distorted, and in the effort to identify form, data and generalization may be unfairly forced into molds which are inappropriate to the subject. Nor is the perspective complete: as suggested in the preface to this book, sociologists miss essentials allowed only by the "view from within."

Sociologists are aware of these problems, and persist in efforts to overcome them. Just as Pragmatism was in part a response to the awareness of uncertainty and errors in observations, so more contemporary modes of analyses — many of which are variations of pragmatic methods — evidence response to the awareness that "abstracted empiricism" and "grand theory" (as Mills, *1959*, labeled them) are methodologically inadequate, encouraging distorted versions of knowledge, the one so busy gathering data that a fragmented picture emerges, the other so busy processing minimal data that the resultant theories, however intricate, systematic and comprehensive, bear but little relation to the subject they are intended to describe.

The three chapters in this section might be seen as illustrative of some of the directions sociologists are moving today, in efforts to offer more adequate perspective. Chapter 7, by Corwin and Clarke, is perhaps the most familiar in type of the three, deviating from the rigorous methodology of the dominant stream of sociology simply by persistently focusing on a subject matter; for these authors, sociological theory and other methodologies are subservient to the substantive analysis. Yet, as the subject they have chosen is expansive, and as the available data are limited, their discussion necessarily relies on implications and speculative suspicions, rather than the deductive and inductive procedures which would be more desirable in such analysis. It is in the character of current modes of inquiry that, faced with expansive subjects, certainty can be represented only by cogency; cogency, when frustrated by limited data, requires "aware speculation" and the astute exercise of implication. This mode of analysis is represented in this book also in the discussions of Gerstl and Bernard (introductory chapter and Chapters 12 and 13), and in other substantive areas by the work of Lipset or of Wilensky.

Analyses such as Corwin and Clarke's, then, must be evaluated not simply on the basis of supportive evidence but, more importantly, for their general adequacy to the subject. This suggests, for one thing, that imperfections in particular arguments need not invalidate the general argument. As a corollary, general adequacy of the argument cannot be taken as evidence that every particular of the analysis is valid.

In a nearly polar position to Corwin and Clarke's perspective is Zimmerman's discussion of the practical bases of work in a welfare agency. In this research, he seeks to describe the social caseworkers' common-sense understandings of their practical work situations and how these understandings enter into the organization of modes of dealing with clients. Rather than starting with a conception of what these personnel ought to be doing according to the formal plan of the organization, the author seeks to identify the considerations entertained by personnel in deciding the meanings of policy and procedure. He makes no attempt to impose the frameworks of existing theories of organizational behavior and decision-making. In downplaying traditional theoretical notions, he avoids some of the troublesome distortions of data that plague most sociological inquiry. By attending to such matters as common-sense understandings and everyday routines and decisions, he increases the sensitivity and completeness of the sociological perspective, thereby offering the reader an increased sensitivity to the intimate knowledge of the participants, and to the ways this knowledge relates to their ways of dealing with clients.

Perrucci's chapter illustrates a mode of inquiry similar in some ways to each of the other two. Like Corwin and Clarke, Perrucci focuses consistently on his subject matter, employing sociological constructs, concepts and theories only in analyses of those data to which they appear appropriate. Perrucci's focus is more restricted, however; where Corwin and Clarke must turn to secondary sources and depend heavily on gross interpretations, Perrucci, as does Zimmerman, relies on firsthand observation. His *focus* differs from that of Zimmerman, however: he attends closely the interplay of participants in a specific situation, giving less attention to the routine behavior in order to more incisively analyze the process of decision making. He identifies the context of the decisions, but the context is one in which only those aspects which he deems to be most immediate and salient in the decision-making of the psychiatrists are attended. Those who endorse the methods of Zimmerman, then, might question certain basic assumptions which Perrucci allows; those assumptions — for example, of a commonality among psychiatrists of understanding about everyday routines — might themselves be the subject of an ethnomethodological study, and the study might reveal surprising faults in the assumptions commonly made about everyday life and routine. Yet Perrucci's mode of analysis — in which salient features are emphasized to the necessary neglect of others — has, in its

197

longer history, yielded findings more powerful in theory and in practical activities than are evidenced to date in published ethnographic reports. Once again, the contemporary researcher working with limited resources and in a nascent discipline is forced to choose between minimizing the distortions of his analysis and maximizing its significance.

Each of the three essays in this section, then, illustrates perspectives with which sociologists demonstrate that "things are not what they seem." Each may be recognized as contrasts to the brands of empiricism that have in recent decades dominated sociology, but they do not represent the full range of emerging perspectives in sociology; indeed, others are apparent in this book, and the increasing concern with systems theory, which also holds great promise, is not here represented. The three perspectives differ markedly from one another, and each, it must be stressed, has its own strengths, weaknesses and potentials; each, at least in current form in today's society, appears more appropriate to some subjects than are the others; none need be accepted as unconditionally preferable to the others.

The value of this section is not limited to a demonstration of various perspectives or methodologies, however. For the essays in this section, each in a different way, address one of the most pervasive and problematic developments in contemporary society: the large-scale organization of human experience. It is not only economic and political activities which today are organized on a large-scale; to be sure, these are the most highly structured, but in almost every facet of human experience, including leisure and recreation, creative art, and even, to a lesser but noticeable degree, sexual expression — can be seen the benefits, restrictions, and demands that attend large-scale organization. Increasingly, to work is to be a part of a company or corporation, to learn is to participate in a large school system or university; to worship, or to relax and play — to bowl, to ski, to watch T.V., to read the newspaper, to play Scrabble or wander through Disneyland — is to utilize the offerings of large organizations and usually to utilize them in ways prescribed. Even to die, unless one does it quickly and without warning, is to participate in a variety of organizations peculiar to contemporary times.

With justification, the consequences and dangers of accelerating large-scale organization in contemporary society have been actively decried as antithetical to human life and autonomy; as actively they have been defended as necessary to the solution of contemporary problems, and as productive of unparalleled development. The experience of physical or mental illness, for example, is today less horrendous for most sufferers because of the contemporary organization of treatment; yet, as is suggested by Perrucci's observations, in Chapters 6 and 9, the organization is not unflawed.

Perrucci's essays, however, should not be read simply as arrays of evidence for on-going debates about the desirability of large-scale organizations in contemporary and future society. Rather, as do those of Zimmerman and Corwin and Clarke, they represent efforts to come to grips with the actuality of organization, to discover what it means to organize human life in these ways, to specify not only the requirements and constraints of formal organization, but also its limits and inapplicabilities, to identify the informal arrangements that develop, continue, and change, even as appearances of rigid formality are maintained.

Because they deal with service organizations, the essays in this section are heavy with implications not only for the person who works within the organizations, but also for those individuals who are served by the organizations. To the attentive reader the implications may prove appropriate to far greater ranges of organized activity than those addressed in these essays.

7 | ORGANIZATIONAL
CONTEXTS AND CONSTRAINTS:
Reflections on the Counseling Movement

Ronald G. Corwin and Alfred C. Clarke / The Ohio State University

Today most counselors work in bureaucratic organizations. The fact that the practices of such organizations tend to reinforce many of the ideologies to be described in Chapter 10 would be sufficient reason for examining the bureaucratic setting of counseling with some care. But the historical role of bureaucracy goes beyond simple reinforcement of ideology, for several of the events that steered the counseling movement along its particular course were the direct *results* of bureaucratic practices. This chapter attempts to capture some of the drama that has unfolded as counseling practices have become adjusted to centralized, standardized, and specialized organizations and to suggest some further modifications that may be waiting offstage as a result of professionalization. It will be shown that in bargaining for a place in the administrative system, counselors have in some respects contributed to displacements of goals, while in other respects they have not yet gained the full advantage of their professional status.

Since counseling cannot be fully comprehended apart from this organizational context, it seems advisable to review briefly the general character of organizations. Bureaucratic organizations are, in a sense, the regulating agencies responsible for translating the demands made upon occupations into daily routines. To cope with the stubborn realities of social power, change and cooperation, every organization employs regulatory procedures as part of its normal machinery. These procedures

For their thoughtful comments on an earlier version of this chapter, we are grateful to Russell Dynes, John Cuber, Herman Peters, James Pedersen and Francis Robinson. Chapters 7 and 10 were originally written as a single essay. Readers especially interested in the counseling movement may be well advised to read Chapter 10 prior to this essay.

both permit and require compromises between occupation, organization and outside forces. The very basis of complex organization is therefore a series of compromises between coalitions of sub-parts having varying degrees of autonomy and responsibility for separate but interdependent functions. In the public schools these sub-parts include the English department, athletic department, counseling staff, administration, office force, and janitors. Each part is further segmented by differences of opinion among the members about their rights and obligations, and in particular by differences about the importance of their cosmopolitan-professional obligations relative to their more localistic employee loyalties.

To the extent that the functions of sub-parts are interdependent, attempts will be made to reintegrate them by means of a hierarchy of supervisors and sanctioned rules. But within the limits imposed by these rules and by supervision, *bargains* between the segments occur routinely; the resources of one part are exchanged for the cooperation of another. A major resource, which is available even to a group without independent sources of income and power, is the capacity to perform services in demand. A unit can increase or *capitalize* its bargaining power by taking on additional responsibilities and members and by increasing its scope of control over present members. However, the price of capitalization often is paid in the form of additional commitments which bind the organization to a course of action not otherwise dictated by the goals themselves.

The ironic chain of events, then, is that in order to achieve the goals some of the energy that otherwise might have been applied directly to attaining them is used to increase the organization's power. Although this may be a necessary step toward attaining the degree of control necessary to achieve the goals effectively, the hazard is that in the process of bargaining for strength the goals may become displaced in favor of increased power. For example, as schools have assumed responsibility for extracurricular activities, an increasing amount of the time and energy of teachers and students has been sapped from curricular programs. The extracurricular programs have helped to improve public relations, to hold students' interest in school and to improve their performance, to the extent that eligibility to participate in them is used as an incentive and leverage; but there are cases where the extracurricular program has completely dominated the curricular program in the process.

In a parallel development, vocational guidance counselors have increased their bargaining positions by assuming responsibility for the prestigious function of counseling for college admission, which is supported actively by influential middle-class citizens. But as a result, they have become employed disproportionately in the middle-class suburbs which are willing to pay for their services, while the city schools, pressed by problems of drop-outs, discrimination and high unemployment rates among graduates, are far less adequately staffed.

Both federal support and the formation of professional organizations improve an occupation's bargaining advantage in some respects, but such alliances also entail compromises. Professional status, for example, may be achieved at the expense of client welfare when it leads to the practice of setting standards of education so high that the number of practitioners available to serve clients is arbitrarily limited.

In the course of bargaining, one adversary may gain an advantage which, if large enough, can be used to coopt the other. Cooptation refers to a tactical arrangement wherein a weaker party is invited to join his stronger adversary in an attractive but subordinate status where he can be more effectively watched and controlled. A sufficient number of counselors have been coopted by school administrators — as a result of exchanging their loyalty to administrative objectives for administrative positions — to have altered the professed goals of the movement. Cooptation, however, is a precarious relationship, for the co-opted party can use his position as a stepping stone to more power and reverse the balance.

Summarily, to strengthen their positions and to cope with constraints, subgroups in organizations make commitments not directly related to their official objectives. An organization can obtain support from a wider range of groups by increasing the scope of its services, but the goals themselves, or the resources otherwise available for goal achievement, can be bargained away in exchange for support (cf. *Blau, 1964; Gouldner, 1959*). The organization's operating goals, then, evolve out of its bargains for support. The dilemma of organization is that while some degree of support is needed for it to accomplish its goals, that support often is purchased precisely at their expense.

Part of this dilemma is captured in the concepts of "adaptation" and "lag," which comprise the organizing concepts of this chapter: As the counseling movement has adapted to its bureaucratic surroundings, its basic goals and character have become transformed; but the adaptation is not yet sufficiently complete for bureaucracy to be used as an instrument to serve the purposes of counselors. This thesis is more fully described and further illustrated in Chapter 10, which the reader should read in conjunction with this chapter.

Before proceeding, the reader is cautioned that the purpose of this chapter, as of Chapter 10, is to illustrate how a *sociological* perspective might help to illuminate the *problems* of the counseling professions. To dramatize this objective and to make our task more manageable, we have chosen to limit our discussion in two fundamental ways. First, we have deliberately confined ourselves to an exclusively sociological view of counseling; there has been no attempt either to represent probably equally compelling views of counselors, who may or may not agree with us, or to summarize the counseling literature which we have purveyed. We trust that counselors can adequately and more appropriately present their own views. Secondly, we have chosen to concentrate on the problems of counseling. In so limiting ourselves, we obviously have not been able to present a total, or "balanced," picture of the vocation. The advantage of focusing on the pathological aspects, however, is that it allows us to concentrate on those facets of the occupation which are under the most pressure to change, and hence which are of most relevance to the future course of counseling; again, we suppose that the more positive side has been presented adequately enough by counselors. However, the reader will find our discussion more appropriately qualified in Chapter 10 (pages 294–328), which should be read in conjunction with this chapter.

Bureaucratization of Counseling

As one of the fundamental developments of this century, bureaucratization in the Western world needs no documentation here. By and large, within the past half-century, the public schools and allied organizations, where counseling takes place, have developed bureaucratic forms. Among the counselors affected by bureaucratization, besides those in the schools are some industrial psychologists, hospital psychologists, advisors to domestic courts, counselors employed in government agencies, and those in large private counseling "agencies," universities, businesses, and the military. So extensive is the counseling movement bureaucratized that someone said, perhaps unfairly, that whereas at first counseling was nothing but unorganized good intentions, it has now become organized technique without clear intentions. Though exaggerated, this characterization calls attention to the direction of change that has occurred. It also suggests additional problems.

Adaptation

Counselors have adjusted so well to complex organizations that they typically achieve administration positions. In a recent study of 28 selected high schools by one of the authors (*Corwin, 1967*) a majority of the 900 teachers interviewed agreed that counselors "usually line up with the administration" in case of any friction involving teachers or students. In bargaining for administrative positions, counselors sometimes have accepted perfunctory duties not entirely in accord with their professed goals. One teacher observed:

> I think they (counselors) line up very well and do what the administration wants them to do. But I'm not sure that I wholeheartedly agree with the objectives of counseling here in this school inasmuch as they seem to devote

203

most of their time to handling administrative functions such as scheduling (*Corwin, 1967*).

Some of the forms of marriage between counseling and administration will be considered in this chapter, along with a more complete inventory of the consequences of the latter on the status and functions of the former. In more bureaucratic organizations, counseling programs themselves can be characterized in terms of three primary components of bureaucratic administration: standardization, centralization of control, and specialization of responsibility.

Standardization. In adjusting to their bureaucratic roles, counselors have developed uniform standards and have adopted standardized practices of working with clients. From the bureaucratic perspective, potential clients sometimes appear as logical categories to be assigned and treated on the basis of the organization's interests rather than those of clients. One school counselor, for example, complained, "Some (boys) are going into biology and sciences that have no business in there; some have good manual dexterity and should be going into vocational instead."

Now on the threshold of an era, counseling is experimenting with new developments in bureaucratized techniques. Part of what the future holds may be forecast in Magoon's (*1964*) proposal to expose potential clients to audio-visual presentations of counseling situations as a means of "vicarious counseling" for clients unable to contact a counselor in person. The vicarious experience, he believes, has the added advantage of reducing the number of cases seeking treatment, as well as reducing the length of personal treatment required of those who seek it.

Specialization. At one time some groups vigorously resisted attempts merely to separate counseling from the rest of the teaching process. But now it not only is considered to be an autonomous function, but the function itself has fragmented into a network of distinct tasks carried out by specialists. Some counselors are testers, some psychotherapeuticians, others are curriculum counselors or in charge of student conduct, and still others specialize in vocational education. As programs continue to expand and the boundaries of the movement become somewhat more delineated, it seems likely that an even more complete division of labor will develop. The specialties that evolve may prove to have more of a fundamental influence on the aims of counseling than standardization.

As diversified services have been absorbed by educational counseling programs, new positions have been created to perform them. This proliferation of specialized roles undoubtedly increases the overall skill level of counseling, just as the elaboration of counseling services increases the total benefits available to clients. But specialization also upsets the balance among sub-parts and increases internal conflicts.

Whenever specialists monopolize information and resources needed by other specialists, conflicts arise, and when there are only minor differences in authority between positions, these conflicts can result in stalemates. Clients are one of the primary resources for which professionals compete. Members of schools, including counselors, compete among themselves for final authority over students. The type of students assigned to teachers influences the methods they can use, the nature of the material they can present and the rate at which it can be taught, the problems they face with discipline, and ultimately, their very prestige. Because counselors frequently are in charge of scheduling and in a position to influence students' choices about the curriculum, they often become involved in the competition among teachers for students. It is noteworthy, however, that the same conflicts which can arise when a counselor attempts to expand his jurisdiction also can curb the excessive authority of other groups and serve to compromise competing interests. The outcomes of such competition often depend on the skill of counselors relative to teachers in manipulating organizational procedures, such as to use roles to their advantage or to violate the chain of command if necessary. Their skill in these matters is indicative of the extent to which counselors have adapted to their organizational environment.

The complexities that surround specialization are compounded by differences among counselors in their own definitions of appropriate objectives and methods. Some of the differences are reflected in this typical disagreement among counselors at one school:

> M— believes that if you let individuals alone, they will solve their own problems. If there is a complaint from a teacher, *we* believe in going in and taking a definite stand and trying to find out what the problem is and finding a solution. M—'s answer would be that they are strong, let them work out their own problems (*Corwin, 1967*).

One type of counselor (roughly speaking, the *school counselor*) limits his role to providing services and information and to helping clients with routine decisions. The *psychotherapist,* on the other hand, sees his role more clinically and helps individuals to accomplish some degree of personal insight or personality reorganization. Both guidance counselors and psychotherapists can be distinguished further on the basis of whether they use *directive* or *non-directive* techniques and whether the counseling is being done with or without the *client's consent* (see Table 1). While the typology in Table 1 is an oversimplification of the available approaches and possible combinations among them, its purpose is to suggest gross contrasts. There is an element of "coercion" in directive guidance used to treat clients who do not welcome it (types a and e). This contrasts with more "participative" situations where nondirective techniques are used at the client's own request (types d and h). To the extent that psychotherapy has a more lasting and pervasive impact than guidance, types a and h can be considered polar opposites, respectively representing *control* and *influence*. The technique used in types c and g, where non-directive techniques are used with unmotivated clients, might be characterized as *manipulation,* whereas the situation in which the client fully cooperates with directive counseling (types b and f) loosely speaking might be called *"authoritarian."*

Table 1
A Typology of Counseling Relationships Based on the Objectives and Methods of the Counselor

Objectives	*Methods*			
	Directive Techniques		*Nondirective Techniques*	
	Client does not seek counseling	Client seeks counseling	Client does not seek counseling	Client seeks counseling
Personality Reorganiza-tion (therapy)	a	b	c	d
Services Information (guidance)	e	f	g	h

Directive techniques are probably most effective in controlling behavior, and especially so when they are combined with psychotherapeutic objectives, since some degree of personality change seems necessary for lasting behavioral change. Nondirective psychotherapy on the other hand, although it may be accompanied by behavioral change, is more appropriate for *self-understanding.* A degree of understanding that leads to a crisis requiring either self-acceptance or basic personality reorganization seems more probable in type d than in type c.

Because the appropriateness of each objective and method presumably depends upon the type of problem being treated, counselors having different skills have attempted to specialize in different problem areas. But the division of labor has been ambiguous. The major obstacle stems from difficulties in diagnosing problems with sufficient accuracy to distinguish between at least these five types: (1) problems of deviance — e.g., theft, assault, and other illegal behavior, sexual deviation or perversions; (2) life cycle problems — e.g., marital problems, maladjustment to puberty and old age; (3) age-status delinquencies — e.g., young people smoking, staying out late, or old men chasing young women; (4) circumstantial problems — e.g., lack of money, unemployment, discrimination, or physical handicaps; (5) problems involving minor nonconformities — e.g. growing a beard, inappropriate dress, use of foul language, premarital intercourse, or interracial marriage.

Some of these problems reflect deep-seated psychological difficulties, but others are largely cultural or circumstantial. Partly to justify their use of psychotherapy, psychologically-trained counselors in schools and universities have attempted to specialize in problems that lie somewhere between the deep-seated personality disturbances normally treated by psychiatrists and the types of problems that school social workers handle; as social work has moved toward psychiatry, even this distinction has become difficult to maintain in practice. The paradox that seems to have resulted is this: school counselors seem to be concentrating on those problems which are essentially *sociological* in character — i.e., problems involving the social roles of individuals in relationship to one another and to their society — but the problem is that most counselors are probably better trained to diagnose and treat *psychologically*-rooted problems. Therefore, although serious personality disorders are supposed to be referred to psychotherapists, marginal problems are easily mis-diagnosed and in all probability in favor of psychological biases; they would be treated accordingly — i.e., inappropriately. Basically circumstantial problems, such as lack of money, for example, have been diagnosed as "deviance" and treated coercively. Dropping out of school illegally to obtain work is frequently looked upon as a deviance problem; inappropriate dress and improper use of language sometimes are regarded as indicative of basic personality problems rather than as minor nonconformities; and the smoking and drinking which adolescents do to gain adult status are easily seen and treated as deviance problems. One consequence can be that clients seeking someone to give them practical assistance with what they consider to be circumstantial or conformity problems find themselves being treated psychotherapeutically or coercively.

In schools, the rapport between counselors and clients is undermined by the fact that neither party to the counseling relationship is completely free to terminate it. Many students attend school because they are legally compelled to do so or because there are few available alternatives. Many of these very same students are the ones with problems, but they will be reluctant to seek assistance if counselors are identified with the system responsible for the problems in the first place. Added to this is the fact that, to many students, counselors are simply anonymous officials. One of the 600 high school teachers interviewed in a study of 28 schools in the Midwest by one of the authors describes the situation at his school:

> It is a matter of the school being so large, the system being so complex, that of all the people who might be involved in a decision-making situation, no one knows the whole picture. I am sure that to an outsider or to an administrator outside the building, it looks like it works very well. On the records counselors see a great many students and seem to do what they are supposed to be doing. To the student, however, it does not look that way (*Corwin, 1967*).

As part of the administration, school counselors are expected to enforce the regulations. Faced with the discipline problems of uncooperative students and knowing them only impersonally, the school counselor probably employs coercive measures disproportionately more often than psychotherapists in private practice. Even so, it is not feasible to use open coercion too frequently where there are large numbers of unmotivated clients. Rather, *manipulation* probably is relied upon more in organizations which cannot select or expel their clientele than in those which have more control over admission practices. School counselors, for example, have been accused of promoting an illusion of democratic student government which in fact they have coopted in order to manipulate. They also are known to subtly "cool out" unwanted students from academic courses and steer them into vocational programs, the arts and extra-curricular activities, all of which have served at one time or another as "dumping grounds" for recalcitrant students (*Clark, 1960*). One vocational teacher expresses this suspicion, "I think that some of the better students are not given a choice. In other words, counselors are strictly saying 'you should do this.' So they are not presented all the facts."

Centralization. The distinct functions of counseling are reintegrated by means of a centralized administration. This hierarchy bears on counseling in two ways. First, of course, counselors in settings like schools and universities themselves occupy administrative positions in the hierarchy. These positions give them official authority, but their actual influence with classroom teachers and students is restricted by the fact that their interests are more closely identified with those of administrators.

Secondly, counselors themselves are stratified. Downtown counseling supervisors in the largest urban systems and supervisors of state bureaus and community service agencies are examples of high-level officials with potential control over a testing program, classifications of occupational information and counseling policies. Centralized administration of counseling activities releases more of a school counselor's time for counseling, but more importantly it strategically links him to the superintendent's office. Representation in the central administration can buffer a counselor from the pressures of laymen and from some of the pressures emanating from higher levels of the system and can even provide some leverage over his own principal. At the same time, this arrangement can operate in reverse, because the presence of counselors in the central office makes it easier for the superintendent to coopt counseling activities throughout the entire system. The influence of central office administrators means that the persons most removed from daily contact with clients are disproportionately responsible for the policies by which their problems are defined and treated.

Lags

Despite gains in bureaucratization, counseling programs do not as yet have a well defined place within the bureaucratic scheme of things. The problem of clarifying the authority and functions of counselors remains. In a sense, the movement has experienced many of the problems of bureaucracy without yet having realized all of its advantages. The marginal status of counseling in the official organizational structure is a major obstacle to the full realization of counselor's potential. Despite their administrative status, their authority, and indeed, their very utility is widely questioned. Some of the perceptions that a faculty commonly holds about *college* counselors reported by Darley include these:

In essence counselors are administrators and the nicest thing you can say about administrators is that they are a necessary evil which may be tolerated but better yet eradicated.

Counselors provide ancillary services and therefore are expendable.

Counselors' pseudo-Freudian, pseudo-psychometric jargon is the purest nonsense.

His pretense of confidentiality is merely a shield to hide behind when the welfare of the institution is involved or his activities challenged (*Darley, 1956*).

A similarly tenuous position of counseling programs in high schools is reflected in this comment:

Sometimes I think we do more guidance in our classrooms than they do in guidance. And when they step in, sometimes I don't feel that it is necessary. I feel that classroom teachers know more about their students and what their trouble is than anyone else.

A counselor reported this situation at one school:

I would say that counselors as a whole have a dispute with the board of education. About a year or so ago, when they cut the increment off, they came up with the idea that the counselors should be put on the substitute list. They were going to do away with the guidance department because of financial difficulties (but) it stated in our contracts that we were hired specifically as counselors. We argued over this, and one board member stated after we left that if we ever came back, he would make it rough for us. We stayed on, and we checked into it. They found that they would lose many thousand dollars a year doing this, according to the state (*Corwin, 1967*).

This account also provides a clue that the authority of counselors is supported by federal and state legislation. To that extent, their programs can become more autonomous from the control of local officials. But in a sense, counselors have bargained for more independence from the local system at the possible price of more state and federal controls.

A lack of administrative backing for counselors is reported in a study of Hoedt and Rothney who found that between eleven and twenty-six percent of the principals interviewed about guidance programs for superior students said that they saw little value in counselors' suggestions pertaining to the program, and that they would not strongly support the implementation of suggested services (*Hoedt and Rothney, 1963*).

Teachers do not always support them either, as already indicated. One reason is that teachers are skeptical about their competence. Their suspicion is reflected in the following teacher's statement:

> If you take A- and B- (two specified teachers), they had a discipline problem but they wouldn't take it to certain counselors here because they knew that they were rated as the worst teachers we had in the building. . . . Their viewpoint would be that these people got kicked upstairs to eliminate their problems in their classrooms (*Corwin, 1967*).

The problems of building rapport with the faculty and of creating sufficient confidence in students to encourage them to frankly discuss their problems are not helped when counselors are defined by administrators as assistants, by teachers as poor-teachers-turned-administrators, and by students as disciplinarians.

Boundary Maintenance. Their tenuous status is undermined further by intruding third parties, particularly parents. They frequently complain about parents trying to persuade them to have their children's grades changed, or to get their sons on the athletic team. One mother threatened to commit suicide unless her daughter's grade was changed; another was so persistent that she went "right down the line and tried to call each one of her daughter's teachers."

These minor incidents sometimes explode into full scale community splits. Between 1961 and 1963, well over a dozen major school systems were attacked for their testing practices and guidance programs. Schwirian reports vehement resistance in one community to the use of a certain psychological test which some groups considered to be "subversive." The charge was that questions which require the child to give information about personal family matters hurt the children's "father image" and that the use of such tests constitute invasions of privacy of the home and family. One protester asked, "Who authorized this school administration to tamper with the minds of our children and violate their God-given rights of conscience by exposure to the subliminal suggestions of these pseudo-scientific instruments?" (*Schwirian, 1963.*)

Displacement of Goals

Counseling functions, then, have not been completely integrated into the administrative framework. But, looking at the other side of the coin, insofar as some degree of bureaucratization *has* been achieved, other problems have arisen.

Centralization. Because of their positions of authority, school counselors are subject to certain role conflicts. They are, for example, responsible to different hierarchies of authority, represented by the counseling supervisors in the downtown office building and by the building principal. Their authority is easily compromised in this dual system of authority. For example, the downtown office might request counselors to administer additional tests, but building principals might resist because of the intrusion on the rest of the school program which testing often involves. Then, too, the obligations of counselors to their administrative superiors do not always correspond with their professional roles. They are sometimes requested to violate professional ethics, such as revealing confidential information; for in contrast to the downward flow of most communication in organizations, counselors are strategically positioned to relay upward information about the personal activities of students. In such situations, the counselor's choice is between compliance and insubordination in the interest of clients. The fact that administrators control salaries and promotion weakens the counselor's position, although perhaps he can rely on some protection from his colleagues.

The authority of counselors also is compromised by the fact that, often near the bottom of the administrative hierarchy, they are delegated residual duties (the "dirty work") and, in particular, the clerical chores of administration, handling discipline, and routine scheduling. Each of these duties will be considered in turn.

The weight of clerical responsibilities assigned to counselors is a burden. Much of the typical school counselor's time is not spent in counseling students but analyzing test results, indexing occupational information, maintaining cumulative records on students, checking attendance, filing, programming courses, administering audio-visual programs and handling transfer students. In 1951, between one-fifth and one-third of elementary school counselors in one California study alone claimed to have attendance responsibilities (*Martinson, 1951*). A decade later, the majority of administrators queried in another study said that less than half of their counselors' time is allocated to counseling duties (*Knapp & Denny, 1961*). Evidence that most of them do a large amount of routine clerical work is reported in the same study, which shows between forty and eighty percent of their time involving clerical work.

At least some counselors have accepted their clerical roles, as the comments of this counselor seem to indicate:

I tried a year ago to eliminate some clerical functions and a couple of these same counselors (whom I feel are poor) are the people who fought against it. I'll give you an example. I think it is a waste of time for counselors to accept attendance notes from home. I think that this can be done by a secretary. Now, when I brought this up I was in a meeting. Some of the counselors said that this is how we get to know students, when they bring their notes back from absence. So as a result I was chopped down instead of getting support. Now don't get me wrong, this is not all of them. But there are enough who seem to take delight in climbing back into clerical work (*Corwin, 1967*).

Performing such a wide variety of miscellaneous duties probably has gained counselors the support of administrators and several other groups benefiting from their assistance, but such a wide scope of commitments does not favor the development of a distinct competence. Administrators expect the counselor to be active in certain administrative and instructional areas such as curriculum planning, pupil attendance, schedule making, discipline, substitute teaching and the like. The situation and some of its consequences have been described by these writers:

Administrators usually base their request for counselors on the argument that they are needed to provide individual counseling relationships for students. However, once hired, the counselor is too often used as a jack-of-all-trades operating in quasi-administrative areas. This places crippling limitations on the performance of appropriate counselor duties. If an administrator hires a counselor to do one thing, loads him down with a second and a third and a fourth set of tasks, he is unable, or at least unlikely, to perform his proper assignment. Counselors must share the blame with administrators for this situation . . .

The counselor who is required to function as an administrative assistant, or who permits himself to be used in this way, will inevitably be seen by students and parents as no more than this. In most cases, students do not bring problems to an administrator; to the degree that a counselor functions as an administrator, he is rendered impotent as a counselor (*Shertzer & Stone, 1963*).

The traditional homeroom teacher, for all his lack of formal training in counseling probably was in closer daily contact and rapport with school children than the better trained counselor of today.

It is probably inevitable that an advisory relationship in combination with administrative authority produces a disciplinarian role. The problems of coupling disciplinary roles with the authority to evaluate students (i.e., job employment references) and with therapeutic counseling roles are well publicized (cf. *Friedenberg, 1959*).

Though a "confidant," the counselor is not expected to return the confidence — i.e., he must not confide his own problems to his client. This illusion of a "one-way trust" is, at best, difficult to manage successfully, and when combined with disciplinary responsibilities it becomes quite improbable. Nevertheless, by handling discipline, counselors perform an important function: they relieve teachers of the tension-ridden aspects of teaching which jeopardize student-teacher relationships in the classroom. Counselors, together with the courts and the police, are part of the system for removing from the close quarters of the classroom the coercive measures that jeopardize student-teacher rapport.

Among the administrative duties which school counselors have assumed are the advising of students about their programs and scheduling them into classes in the most efficient way. These responsibilities put them in a position to influence the curriculum indirectly through their recommendations of courses to students. That efficiency in scheduling at times takes precedence over responsibility for students is reflected in the comments of a physical education teacher who remarked, "Kids will come to us before they will go to guidance. Really all that guidance is interested in is curriculum."

Because of their scheduling responsibilities, counselors frequently find themselves under cross-pressures from the teachers, who do not want the slow learners, and the students who do not want the difficult teachers. The comment of this counselor is typical:

> Quite often the teacher comes to me and convinces me that this youngster is a total failure in his class; he is a poor reader, he has low ability. I think maybe he belongs in a basic class, and I will agree with the teachers (*Corwin, 1967*).

Other teachers, however, especially those who teach the "basic" classes, complain along with this teacher that the real problem is that:

> they have too many disciplinary kids . . . that are being placed there because teachers want to get rid of them, or because they think the counselors are gullible enough to buy the problem. . . . In other words, to use the local language, we are "unloading" them on these poor people who have the basic classes.

Some teachers, like this one, display remarkable resistance when discipline cases are assigned to their classes at the request of other teachers who wish to get rid of them:

> I wanted to know the reason why this boy was put there, and he gave me the "reason" that the boy wasn't doing anything; just sitting in the class and getting suspended. And why was he put in the slow learners class? He said, "Maybe it would help him." I got rid of him. I went and told the counselor I didn't want him (*Corwin, 1967*).

However, not all teachers are that successful:

> The administration does not like for the teacher to feel that he determines who comes into his class. The administration likes to keep the authority to

213

place a youngster in a teacher's class whether he likes it or not (*Corwin, 1967*).

The problems of allocating disciplinary cases and slow learners have been institutionalized to a certain extent, then by the fact that some areas of the curriculum have been defined as "dumping grounds." Despite objections from teachers in the industrial arts and home economics, these courses often serve this function. But dumping grounds are not confined to vocational programs. A teacher of art in a large high school complained that counselors regard her course as a place to put students who do not do well in an academic class, saying that, "they want to put him in here to get this credit. Well, this is one way to help him graduate. . . . It's a matter of getting these counselors to realize that we need students in there who have the ability. I just don't think that they fully realize what kind of student should go into art."

Similar problems have arisen concerning assignments to basic and advanced math and English courses, and in one school, counselors were accused of deliberately counseling girls out of physics. In many of these cases, faced with the problem of unwanted students for whom little provision has been made, and in the interest of expediency, the primary consideration of counselors appears to be the preservation of harmony and of the teachers' status system. The students' problems remain unsolved:

> One of the things that counselors are supposed to try to resolve or help kids to resolve is some of their problems in their (academic) classes. I don't think the answer to a discipline problem is to throw them into an "adjusted curriculum" class — which is a way they "solve" these problems, a lot of them (*Corwin, 1967*).

Counselors are hired only in part to solve the slow learner's problems, for what is expected from them primarily is protection of the school. As one counselor expressed it, "When you expel someone, my question is, what happens to the whole school? I answer my own question by saying it improves the school." However, the same man also described the other horn of the dilemma, "When you expel kids, what happens to them? You dump them out into the cold." Some counselors have attempted to resolve this problem by "unloading" delinquent cases onto schools for the disturbed.

Just as they have taken responsibility for "cooling out" unwanted students, counselors have been perhaps equally conscientious about capitalizing on whatever prestige a school can gain from talented students. The way students perform on standardized tests, their participation in extracurricular activities, the proportion going to college, and the prestige of the college they attend all contribute to a school's reputation. Although it is often difficult to know what is best for the welfare of a *student,* the bases of a *school's* prestige are clearer, and hence can intrude as a factor in the counselor's perceptions and advice. The fact that an individual's prestige is likely to benefit from gains in the prestige of his organization makes the latter all the more salient. Probably some of these prestige elements help to explain the way one counselor reputedly treats students:

> I had the experience several years back of a boy who wanted to take the commercial course, and his counselors refused to put him in the commercial course because they said he was too bright. And as a result, the boy was leaving here and going into college in a commercial course for which he had no background. I feel this is going past the authority of a counselor. Then you are a dictator, not a counselor (*Corwin, 1967*).

This teacher's comments are revealing, too, "One of the counselors was trying to make this boy go to college. He didn't want to go. He said that he would be just another pin on his (the counselor's) map showing where all the various students were." Though they are presumably hired to assist students in making curriculum decisions, counselors, in short, have become such an integral part of the system that one of their important functions is to preserve the schools' status system by disciplining, purging, or segregating unwanted students and by capitalizing on the prestige value of talented students. The risk is that in identifying with the administration, they will become alienated from the student clientele they are attempting to assist.

Standardization. Although system standards and regulations are designed to improve a school's effectiveness, too much regulation can jeopardize it as well. The paper work and administrative responsibilities required by central offices can be time-consuming and achieving external standards, such as a given level of education, is sometimes permitted to substitute for an evaluation of how well the original objective is being accomplished.

One of the glaring dysfunctions of standards has appeared in some vocational education programs which, in an effort to improve their quality, have set admission standards so high that the very students most likely to benefit from them have been excluded. The very uniformity of standards compromises the diversity of problems and situations confronting counselors. The standards appropriate for a college counselor in a middle-class suburb may be liabilities for those who work with children in the slums of the central cities.

Advanced levels of education can become a liability if educational background is allowed to become a social barrier between the counselor and his client. Students in nine central New York City high schools indicated that they wanted help from *non*school people to the extent that the problem they faced was unrelated to educational planning (*Grant,*

1954). Only four percent of the students noted that they would approach the counselor first with their more personalized behavior problems. Nonschool people were preferred 36 percent of the time even in educational planning, 46 percent of the time in vocational planning, and in 75 percent of the time in personal-emotional problem areas. At least some of these aversions that students have to counselors probably can be attributed to status differentials reflected in educational background. For, the same reasons which are responsible for a man's entering a counseling program also probably tend to encourage him to aspire for middle-class surroundings and values. As a corollary, perhaps the potentially most effective counselors for slum schools will be found among the untrained laymen living in slum areas, or among those now participating in programs such as VISTA or the Peace Corps who are already dedicated to assisting underprivileged people with their own problems on their terms.

Whatever efforts that have been made to evaluate the individual performances of counselors have been handicapped by the lack of consensus in the field about what results counseling is supposed to achieve. In lieu of the other standards, the number of students processed each year can become a convenient criterion of effectiveness. Seeking to see all students, some counselors have instituted mandatory "call in" procedures, thereby initiating the counseling relationship themselves. Nevertheless, the practice of soliciting clients undoubtedly uncovers some emotional problems that otherwise might have remained undetected.

The success of counseling is sometimes associated with the stability of decisions made by those who have been counseled and their long-range satisfaction with the choices they made under the influence of counseling. One study, for example, shows that fewer counseled students changed out of college preparation programs and that they expressed more satisfaction with the choices they made under the influence of counseling than those who had not received counseling (*Rothney and Roens, 1952*). When, on the other hand, a client and counselor work out a solution which the client later reverses or which leads to his dissatisfaction, laymen sometimes interpret this as evidence of the counselor's inadequacy.

The idea that mature middle-class people should be without tension and should be *certain* about what they want to do while lower class people should "strive" to change their values seems to be anchored in pre-industrial notions which are not always helpful in an urban society. But to the extent counselors subscribe to them, counseling advice will become more specific and decisions will become stabilized earlier. As the counseling process extends down into the elementary years and people are encouraged to accept commitments at an earlier age, curiosity about the alternatives which may become available in later years could be deterred.

216

The *tension-reducing* quest of middle-class people for security and the planned career, in other words, contrasts with the *tension-producing* challenge and uncertainty which comes from exploring alternatives that can lead to radical shifts in values and new experiences after adulthood. In the past counselors seem to have sought to reduce the tensions of middle-class people and increase the anxiety of lower-class people by encouraging upward mobility. Ultimately, counselors may have to decide between assisting large numbers of students through successive steps that lead to relatively tranquil and standardized life goals," and counseling a few persons who seek help in reaching unique, unclearly defined, nonstandardized goals that may be anxiety provoking and difficult to achieve. Under bureaucratic constraints the measure of counseling achievement so far seems to favor the first of these alternatives.

Specialization. The pattern of specialization in counseling is modeled after other professions. Some lawyers, for example, handle divorce cases, while others specialize in water-rights problems for a different group of clients. However, the division of labor has not been without problems in these professions. Currently, for example, medical authorities are asking whether there is anyone in the modern hospital who is responsible for the "whole" patient, i.e., who sees the patient in terms other than the "appendectomy in Ward 3?" The nurses, who once fulfilled this psychotherapeutic role, have themselves become so specialized in time-consuming administrative and technical duties that perhaps the only personnel in the hospital who have time or opportunity to chat informally with the patient are the lower echelon aides and orderlies.

The problem is equally relevant to counseling. Although the expansion of counseling services has been encouraged by the "whole person" philosophy, there still is really no one in a bureaucratic society responsible for helping individuals deal with those personal problems that lie outside of a few institutionally defined categories. The division of counseling programs into distinct specialties and the resulting "referral" system by which the individual is referred from one specialist to another within the profession or within a university or large school system, seems to violate the intent of the "whole person" philosophy. A division of services for administrative convenience does not necessarily correspond with the way clients classify their own problems. The basic question is whether or not division-of-labor principles can be effectively applied to a person's problems.

The existence of separate career routes into counseling, signified by a trend toward full-time counselors who may or may not have had teaching experience, and the departmentalization of counseling will increase the separation between teachers and counselors. As separate departmental statuses have developed, jurisdictional disputes also have arisen with classroom teachers, administrators, homeroom teachers, school social workers, attendance officers, and the like. As a way of clarifying responsibilities, in-service training is provided in many schools to educate teachers about their role in the counseling program, which some advocate should include maintaining cumulative records and performing other functions of use to counselors. A few counselors even seem to think of counseling as equivalent to the educational process itself, which of course, implies that theirs is a central rather than an auxiliary status in the educational system.

Although classroom teachers have welcomed the opportunity to refer the more difficult cases to counselors and, although counseling has grown within the schools partly because teachers had insufficient time and opportunity to work with students as "whole" individuals, more than one teacher has resented their encroachment. For the presence of counselors has tended to reduce further the opportunity of teachers to work with students as individuals and sometimes has interfered with teachers' relationships with students. One teacher reported that because he was late for class a few times, students complained to a counselor, who in turn spoke to the teacher about the situation. The teacher explained, "Well, as a result, it was a touchy situation in that the student would not come in to me first with the complaint and went to the counselor; and then the counselor actually had no capacity to tell me what to do in my classroom."

Teachers also resent the fact that counselors sometimes have more access than teachers to certain information necessary for assisting students, as this comment suggests:

> For instance, some child has some kind of a handicap, perhaps a mental handicap, "psychological" is what I mean to say — caused maybe — by poor home conditions or something. Sometimes a teacher can help that child. But if we are never told about it, we never know a thing. We are never told anything. It seems to be a policy. It has always been that way (*Corwin, 1967*).

Hierarchies of prestige and authority over students develop between teachers and counselors as each vies with the other to extend his scope of activities, to slough off unwanted functions, and to influence potential clients. The backing which college counselors have from middle-class communities and the support of disciplinary counseling from teachers, gives those functions disproportionate influence in schools in comparison to the less sympathetic *assistance* that is given to the lower-class students. Some of the other consequences of this competition will be considered further in connection with professionalization.

In sum, counseling shows signs of succumbing to some of the very forces that contributed to its emergence. Standardized, specialized and centralized counseling systems seem to be developing in precisely the largest communities and most complex organizations where the individual's sense of personal worth is most threatened. The professional relations between counselors and clients often are undermined because of counselors' obligations to the employing organizations and because some client goals have been bartered in exchange for administrative authority.

But, however much administrative status may interfere with the immediate counseling functions, administrative status may have been a necessary initial step toward obtaining more authority. Administrative posts have given counselors the potential power to cope with faculty resistance and to exert more direction over a school's program. With the weight of administrative authority, counselors eventually may be able to achieve a more central position for counseling itself. But before such a development can take place counselors probably will have to become more professionalized.

Professionalization of Counseling

As the economy has shifted its base from agriculture to technology, the intuitive approach to counseling has yielded to technicism and science. Increasingly, those in the movement were to encounter unexpected problems in reconciling their conventional modes of operation with the efficiency-conscious society that had developed around them. Their dilemma was that, if the conventional techniques were maintained, the movement would be out-of-step and powerless in a technological society; but the very process of adapting to a technological orientation threatened to alter their activities, and subsequently, their objectives.

Changes

The growth of technology and science over the past 40 years has permitted self-conscious increases in the social prestige and influence of occupations. Professional organizations have been formed to protect their monopolies over fields of knowledge, codes of ethics have been evolved to control members, sophisticated political pressure-tactics have been used, selective admission standards have been set, and occupational titles have been changed. Some of these themes have been evident in the counseling movement.

Adaptation to a Professional Society. The evolution of professional technical norms in counseling was delayed during an early period of reluctance. From the beginning, counselors were practical, busy men attempting to provide a well-intentioned, useful service in a society that watched its tax dollars closely. Chiefly concerned, at first, with training students for specific skilled and semi-skilled lines of work, they were not closely tied with the academic traditions from which science and tech-

219

nology had developed. In gaining independent status within schools, their functions became further removed from the academic program; and until recently, most colleges of education have been more oriented to the public responsible for hiring teachers than to the academic traditions of universities. Each of these developments, in effect, helped to insulate the movement from the intellectual tradition.

With little time or inclination to develop a body of theory, counselors did not readily adopt a scientific orientation. In fact, some have continued to deny the possibility of putting counseling on a scientific basis and few of them seem to be vitally concerned with the task. A few years ago, Hobbs analyzed 10 textbooks on guidance and found one-half the pages were devoted to the program of guidance and its organization and one-third of them to guidance techniques (*Hobbs, 1958*). Very little attention was given to the social foundations of guidance and even less to a coherent philosophy. The requirement of teaching experience, rather than ability to do research, does not encourage the development of a scientific basis for the field either.

Marriage and family counselors also found themselves burdened with increasing numbers of clients and with little time for basic research. The movement as a whole, then, continues to reflect a theoretical basis inadequate to support its ambitions and, in some cases, its claims.

The movement was attempting to deal with the fundamental problems of a scientific technological society without itself having an adequate theory or technology for doing so. (This shortcoming, however, may have been functional to the extent that the practical orientation helped keep the movement in touch with lower-class clientele having values less compatible with scientific forms of counseling.) But in a society where science has assumed many of the characteristics of a religious movement, the absence of a theoretical body of knowledge eventually proved an embarrassment. For an emerging profession to be without scientific theory and techniques was to be almost without justification or influence. In this connection, school counselors, like other professionals were attempting to differentiate themselves from lay counselors and charlatans. School counselors had to contend with the clergy, vocational agencies, testing bureaus, social workers and clinical psychologists and psychiatrists in private practice. Psychiatrists and psychologists in independent practice were licensed to counsel, and more important, to use therapy. The medical status of psychiatry puts that profession, in particular, in a position to review the decisions of school psychologists who are accorded one of the lowest statuses among the licensed counselors. According to at least two studies, the high school counselor ranks second from the bottom of the prestige hierarchy of twenty psychological occupations as rated by advanced students and by a random sample. Professors of psychology in large universities, general experimental psychologists, clinical psychologists and social psychologists all are ranked relatively high by both the random sample and a sample of advanced students. Counseling psychologists are ranked lower by the random sample (rank 7.7) than by advanced students (4.9). Personnel psychologists, rehabilitation psychologists, psychometrists and employment interviewers, all rank low *(Porter and Cook, 1964)*.

In view of competition from so many types of counselors, some counselors are resorting to the monopolistic strategies used so successfully by other occupations. Several groups seek (1) to expand their sphere of influence, (2) to develop a technology of their own and (3) to strengthen their professional organizations. Each of these strategies will be considered in turn.

Empire Building. Blocked from expanding their psychotherapeutic functions by psychiatry to which the more difficult "problem" cases usually are referred, school counselors have sought to expand their functions over more "normal" individuals. In the areas of marriage and occupations some have found a large adult market for their services; a market promoted by increased divorce rates and technological changes which make adult re-training necessary. Other counselors have sought to expand their influence over younger persons; a trend which is reflected in the elementary school counseling movement. It is based on a "developmental" conception of human behavior in which decision-making and the need for counseling are viewed as part of a long series of decisions leading to progressively refined self-conceptions.

Probably of greater significance than the expansion of influence over different age groups, has been the elaboration of counseling services for individuals within each group. As Mayer has noted in another connection, the "whole person" philosophy, and the progressive education on which it is based, has had the effect of decentralizing control over students; for if the individual student develops uniquely, then only persons who "know" him can make the decisions important to his progress *(Mayer, 1963)*.

In the whole person philosophy, vocational and marriage choices are viewed as vehicles for discovering a more general identity. Hence, counselors become vitally concerned with all of a client's decisions bearing directly or indirectly upon these crucial choices. The concern of modern counselors is with the total life of individuals, insofar as it bears on a specific problem area. These ambitions extend to even those individuals who have not yet recognized that they have problems and need to be counseled. Personality tests and interest inventories administered to all students, and mandatory "call in" counseling sessions scheduled for every individual in a school, facilitate this expanding sphere of influence over the life pattern of clients.

Forced to justify themselves in terms other than good intentions, counselors have evolved a technology of tests to supplement fragmentary theories. Thirty million tests were given to school students during 1960 (*Goslin, 1963*). Goslin reports that somewhere between 75 and 90 percent of all public elementary and secondary school systems in the United States make use of standardized tests at least once between kindergarten and grade 12.

Professionalization. Though not yet fully organized, further professionalization of counseling occupations seems to be a likely development. A little less than a third of the school counselors belong to the American School Counseling Association, but several such associations act as pressure groups in state and national governments. The guidance and counseling labels have been replaced by such terms as "psychological counseling" and "psychotherapy." A code of ethics has begun to emerge which, for example, obligates counselors to keep information about students confidential. A technical language has been invented which includes such impressive terms as "over achiever," "permissive atmosphere," "undefined interest," "emotional block," "occupational fantasy" and "nondirective counseling." Finally, educational standards have been increased and efforts are being made to enforce licensing restrictions. Each of these characteristics has had the effect of setting apart each counseling profession from its companion occupations.

Lags

Despite their bid for professional status, however, counselors still have a distance to go. One of their major handicaps lies in the system of professional recruitment, especially in the relaxed licensing standards which permit administrators to promote inside teachers to counseling positions as a reward for loyalty. Part of the problem can be traced to constraints imposed on colleges of education by school boards wanting to hire compliant and tractable employees; colleges in turn screen out candidates whose personalities make them a poor placement risk. Part of the problem also stems from the character of the training programs, themselves. A lack of confidence in counselors is revealed in this teacher's comments:

> They run about 550 students to a counselor. I guess he can't know them too well. But as far as I am concerned, I think that any teacher who has gone to college and has common sense can do counseling as to what you need to take in college. We have one example in the school now, a boy who is a senior, and he has always wanted to go to medical school. . . . It is impossible now because when he was in the ninth grade, the counselor told him he didn't need any mathematics, medical doctors didn't use it (*Corwin, 1967*).

Regardless of the situation in which they are likely to find themselves, counselors typically are trained in relatively uniform programs saturated with educational and psychology courses. The primary assumption behind these programs appears to be that because problems are *experienced* by individuals, the *source* of their problems is personal. It is therefore the counselor's job to help the person cope emotionally with the situation — to adapt or to strive harder.

His psychological training must be contrasted with the fact that the counselor deals with problems which develop from sociological situations. The paradox is that *psychologically trained counselors are actually assisting clients with sociological problems*. When attention is shifted away from emotional adjustment to the situations responsible for client problems, the counseling role assumes larger proportions. The client is more likely to be seen as a victim of his circumstances; the counselor must have knowledge about the social sources of the problem; he needs to be skilled in calculating the relative risks and rewards of alternative courses of action to a client in terms of his (the client's) values.

An Emergent View of Counseling. To speculate, this latter view of counseling seems to involve at least three steps: (1) helping the client to clarify his objectives and arrange them in a hierarchy from least to most valued; (2) helping him to calculate the relative risks and advantages associated with as many courses of action as are relevant to the problem; (3) giving him practical assistance in achieving the alternative that he has chosen. There are signs that the field has been moving in these directions. Many counselors already accept at least the first of these tenets, and some are willing to advocate all three; probably fewer actually practice all three.

Implementing these tenets in public organizations is a formidable task, and in some cases, an overwhelming task. The doctrine not only requires a counselor to accept the client's definition of a problem (after he has considered alternatives), but obligates him to assist with accomplishing his client's objective even for example, to drop out of school, to marry against his parents' consent, or to seek an abortion from a competent physician. Many counselors who otherwise accept some of these tenets would draw the line at cases of illegal conduct; others would feel that it is irresponsible to ignore the problems of people who do engage in such widespread hazardous practices.

The question of illegal behavior aside, counselors could assist with many situational problems, such as finding inexpensive public entertainment for slum school children or places for them to study, locating jobs for dropouts, or babysitters and jobs for the parents of potential dropouts, finding housing for citizens displaced by slum renewal, helping students obtain loans, promoting special education programs, working for VISTA or the civil rights' movement, supporting a guaranteed wage for laborers, helping to raise minimum wage laws and working to improve out-patient medical care. These, and similar problems, being primarily sociological rather than psychological in nature require knowledge of the job market and the latest developments in civil rights, community institutions, and demand skill in using influential "contacts" and a general knowledge of the community power structure.

Many counselors undoubtedly do have ambitions for counseling to become something more than a one-to-one relationship with clients, and certainly, something more than an elaborate technology. But what that "something" else becomes will depend primarily on the role that counselors develop within bureaucratic organizations. This role, in turn, will depend partly on their ability to accurately perceive the significance of modes of organization. Having usually confined their concerns to the individual level, counselors do not yet appear to be fully cognizent of the connection between their own objectives and the organizational constraints on teachers and students — of standardized practices and curriculum offerings in slum schools, of pressures on teachers to "cover" material in large classes, of the disregard shown for problems of poorly motivated and belligerent students — just as they seem not to have been completely aware of the toll that unfair employment, discriminatory housing practices and lack of political power has taken on minority group children. And yet it is plausible that the bureaucratic elements of school and society are *as responsible* for the academic, behavioral, and emotional problems of youngsters as their own physics or life cycles.

If the humanitarian vision which originally inspired the movement regains prominence and if the signs of restless professional ambitions are at all indicative, a new role soon may begin to emerge for counselors in large-scale organizations as they become fully aware of the implications — that of *agent-of-organizational-change.*

Probably with some pangs of conscience, counselors customarily have concentrated on changing individuals, whereas the current pressures for change are on organizations themselves. Some of these changes could have drastic implications for the welfare of students (e.g., open districting and the demands of students for more participation in governing schools). Counselors are likely to be called upon to play more active leadership roles in some of these internal reorganizations.

Changes in the counseling role of such proportions are likely to occur only gradually however, although the general ferment and climate of experimentation which is becoming more characteristic of schools is favorable. Once under way, so basic a transformation undoubtedly would eventually prompt still other changes. For example, counselors would play an active role in revising the system of justice now found in most bureaucratic organizations toward the end of guaranteeing their clients the same right to a hearing and defense that they would have in a court of law. In schools, counselors might act on behalf of students as bargaining agents, presenting their cases before the administration and working to remedy those organizational practices which do not now seem to be in their best interests.

This comment of one counselor suggests that a few already are assuming such a role:

> I think a definite line is drawn there — that his function is as a counselor. He has the student's interest in mind and if it comes to a point of defending one or the other, it will usually be the student (*Corwin, 1967*).

Another reported that:

> One afternoon the teacher came to me after school and said that I should take this boy out of his class. I went through a long discussion on the boy and his situation and problems, etc. He quite readily agreed that he should be in his class and he accepted it (*Corwin, 1967*).

Counselors, then, potentially are capable of representing the students' interests to the faculty and administration. As agents of change and as bargaining agents, they essentially would become "institutionalized mavericks." By comparison, administrators and often teachers as well, are in inopportune positions for defending students or for scrutinizing the organization for changes on their behalf. Administrators are not only under constant pressure to keep the system coordinated in the interest of system requirements, but they also are removed from the daily problems of students. Teachers, though closer to students, are under similar pressure to maintain order in large classes and to cover material, and more important, are without sufficient power to assume this role. Even with more power, changes on behalf of the student are often threatening to teachers and their objectivity toward students is easily blurred in their competition with one another for students.

Clearly, the administrative status of counselors is not sufficient to support a role of the magnitude visualized. Other, more powerful, professional organizations will provide some defense and it is likely that counselors will become more active politically using pressure group tactics more effectively. But, there also are more immediate possibilities. One is that counselors' salaries will be paid entirely from state or federal funds, making them representatives of the state education department rather than being regarded exclusively as employees of the local system. At the college level, it seems possible that student organizations might directly engage their own counselors, paying them from dues. Only with such defenses could counselors develop sufficient autonomy to resist administrative intimidation, to persuade accrediting associations to relax standards when deemed advisable, or to modify irrelevant evaluation standards — in short, to create an organizational environment favorable to learning and to the personal interests of students.

While such developments do not appear to be completely realizable in the immediate future, some signs of restlessness are beginning to appear which could move the profession along the lines indicated. In an article significantly entitled, "The Militant Counselor," Stone and Shertzer maintain that a counselor's willingness to show deference toward authority is inversely associated with his counseling effectiveness (*Shertzer and Stone, 1963*). They conclude that the counselor must know "who he is" and where he is going, and then set out to fight for the professional role he wants. There are similar implications in the following quotation by Farwell:

> The counselor who assumes some form of leadership in each aspect of the school guidance program will be serving the guidance movement in two ways: he can develop his own conception of his role — a conception that is consonant with the guidance theory and philosophy that he has adopted. Also, he can clarify the aims and functions of the guidance program for teachers and administrators and help them to understand their roles in guidance (*Farwell, 1963*).

Yet, some of the roles which counselors are attempting to carve out for themselves are not coincidental with the traditional expectations that school administrators and teachers have of them. Farwell continues, "The conflicts between the counselor who adopts the client-centered approach to counseling and the administrator who emphasizes the mechanistic aspects of the services approach are obvious" (*Farwell, 1963*).

Loyalties and Militancies. Some indications of school counselors' loyalties and sense of militancy were found in a study of staff conflicts in 28 public high schools.[1] Questionnaires measuring conceptions of employees and professional teaching roles were answered by 64 counselors in schools of varying degrees of bureaucratization. The employee orientation scale consists of 28 statements inquiring about the degree of loyalty to the administration and to the organization that is appropriate for teachers, the relation of teaching experience to a teacher's competence, the appropriateness of standardization and of treating personnel interchangeably, the amount of emphasis on rules and procedures that is desirable, and the expected degree of loyalty to the public. Professional orientations were defined by 4 types of statements, 16 in all: dedication to students, orientation to the profession and professional colleagues, the belief that a teacher's competence is based on knowledge, and the belief that teachers should have decision-making authority. An example of each type of item will be found in the appendix on page 235.

Alternatives for each statement range from "strongly agree" to "strongly disagree." They were weighted from five to one in such a way

[1] The research reported here is supported through the Cooperative Research Program of the Office of Education, U.S. Department of Health, Education, and Welfare, Contract No. 2637 (*Corwin, 1967*). The instruments and procedures used will be described more fully in that report. See also *Corwin, 1965, Chapter 8*.

that the magnitude of scores on the professional scale increases with intensity of professional orientation, while scores on the employee scale are inversely related to intensity of the employee orientation. Since both of these scales pertain to *teaching* roles, rather than to counseling roles *per se,* the interpretation of counselors' responses to them must be made with some caution, for it is possible that counselors who hold low professional expectations for teachers subscribe to correspondingly higher expectations for themselves. However, a recently completed study, which reanalyzed their data using measures specifically adapted to the counseling situation, supports some of the interpretations presented here (*Swisher, 1967*).

Militancy was estimated from the total number of disagreements that each counselor reported having with each other member of the faculty. Several indices also were developed in the study to measure several bureaucratic characteristics of schools. Centralization was estimated from teachers' reports on the level at which a series of major policy decisions (such as hiring and curriculum planning) are normally made in their schools; standardization was measured with a Guttman-type quasi-scale based on statements about the amount of discretion permitted teachers in using lesson plans and curriculum guides and their role in preparing them, their options in the choice of textbooks, and policies governing the use of tests. Close supervision was measured by another Guttman-type scale inquiring about the number of classroom observations administrators normally make and the nature of follow-up and consultation afterwards, whether or not permission must be obtained to discuss controversial issues, the amount of supervision by the central office (including frequency of superintendent's visits to the school and number of reports required), and teachers' judgments of the fairness and accuracy of their administrators' evaluations of them.

In general, it was found that counselors are *less* committed *both* to the employee and to the professional roles than either teachers or principals in the sample (Table 2).[2] They are not as dedicated as teachers to the interests of students,[3] but they do show more sympathy to them than principals and other administrators which, together with their lower

[2] As these data are considered to be only suggestive and illustrative, tests of statistical significance have not been computed. It is not known whether the specific differences reported here are statistically significant. The primary concern is with the general patterns implicit in the data.

[3] Orientation to students is based on a sub-scale of the professional scale consisting of the following statements: it should be permissible for the teacher to violate a rule if he is sure that the best interests of the students will be served in doing so; the teacher should not do whatever he is told unless he is satisfied that it is best for the students; a good teacher should not do anything that he believes may jeopardize the interests of his students regardless of who tells him to or what the rules state. Like the other scales, there were five possible responses to each statement; a higher score indicates a higher orientation to student welfare.

Table 2
Professional and Employee Orientations
and the Militancy of Counselors in
More and Less Bureaucratic Schools

Type of Orientation

Counselors in:	Employee Orientation*		Professional Orientation		Client Orientation (Sub Scale)		Militancy (Rate of Disagreement)**	
	Full-time Counselors	Part-time Counselors	Full-time Counselors	Part-time Counselors	Full-time Counselors	Part-time Counselors	Full-time Counselors	Part-time Counselors
Large Schools (N = 54)	79.61	81.21	54.11	59.26	8.89	9.32	3.48	5.06
Small Schools (N = 10)	78.10	—	58.20	—	9.10	—	8.13	—
Highly Centralized Schools (N = 27)	86.93	80.33	51.40	57.92	8.87	9.33	5.70	1.55
Less Centralized Schools (N = 37)	78.96	—	57.73	—	9.03	—	6.04	—
Closely Supervised Schools (N = 40)	79.46	79.07	53.42	59.00	8.50	8.93	1.11	6.85
Less Supervised Schools (N = 24)	84.04	—	60.30	—	10.13	—	7.18	—
Highly Standardized Schools (N = 38)	80.28	78.42	54.08	60.17	8.68	9.17	2.11	7.36
Less Standardized Schools (N = 25)	82.96	—	58.50	—	9.64	—	5.75	—
All Counselors								
Combined (N = 64)	81.09		56.28		9.05		6.88	
Total Faculty (N = 148)	77.69		58.15		9.44		2.35	
Principals (N = 22)	77.09		57.82		8.45		5.35	

* For this scale only, higher scores indicate *less* loyalty to the orientation. Since the scores have not been standardized, the means of separate scales are not comparable.

** Number of disagreements involving counselors reported per counselor.

employee orientation, probably means that they are more inclined than other members of the *administration* to defend students against organizational constraints. Finally, the fact that they report higher rates of disagreement than either teachers or principals is evidence of the militancy inherent in their positions. Only further analysis will confirm the extent to which this militancy is in behalf of students, but the fact that within each type of setting considered in Table 2, counselors with higher militancy rates uniformly are more client-oriented, tends to support the interpretation that the more client-oriented a counselor is the more prepared he must be for institutionalized conflict.

Considering only the *full-time* counselors, those in larger more centralized schools appear to be slightly *less* employee oriented, while those in closely supervised, standardized schools are perhaps slightly *more* dedicated to the employee role in comparison to counselors in less bureaucratized settings. It appears that some elements of bureaucracy are more likely than others to attract and produce counselors loyal to the administration. The tendency in more bureaucratized schools for counselors' professional orientations and more specifically their cient orientations to be uniformly *lower* than those in less bureaucratized settings, together with the corresponding fact that their militancy seems to be lower too, suggests that bureaucracy does take a toll on professional militancy. The least militant full-time counselors are found in closely supervised and standardized schools where employee orientations also are relatively high and professional and client orientations relatively low. Also, the fact that their client orientation is uniformly lower in more bureaucratized schools is a clue to the possibly deteriorating effects that bureaucratization is having on the client-counselor relationship.

However, there are differences between full-time and part-time counselors in these respects. The role conceptions of part-time counselors in bureaucratized schools are uniformly *more professional* and more client centered than those of their full-time counterparts and, with the exception of those in centralized schools, part-time counselors are also *more militant*. Part-time positions would seem to provide all of the advantages of administrative authority without undermining the ability of counselors to identify with their clients. Part-time positions seem to insulate them from some of the bureaucratic constraints that seem to alienate their full-time counterparts from clients and (except in centralized schools) make them inert.

Of course it would be premature to draw firm conclusions from these data, which represent only a small and select group of school counselors, and which have not been tested for statistical significance. However, they do serve to suggest important patterns which raise questions

229

worthy of further analysis. This has been the intention of the preceding discussion.

Displacement of Goals

To the extent that it is successful, professionalization will create problems of another order. In this connection, for example, Darley believes that, due to inherent status struggles and communication problems, premature specialization will retard the development of sound faculty-counselor relationships (*Darley, 1956*). There is little doubt, too, that professionals sometimes act as vested interest groups concerned primarily with their own welfare. They engage in status races in accord with middle-class ideologies. The quest of the professions for respectability sometimes has hampered their ability to implement professional principles because of their preference for middle-class standards and middle-class incomes. The whole-person philosophy behind empire building has been used to justify violating the individual's right to privacy and to personal taste; the humanitarian notion that everyone is a distinctive individual is difficult to reconcile with the practice of assigning all persons, some of whom have not requested it, to a standardized counseling program; the philosophy, moreover, has been translated into inclusive programs which permit a counselor to use his official authority to influence many facets of personal life, including a person's private sex practices, modes of dress, his length of hair, dance steps, and language.

As a drive for status, professionalization increases the social distance between a counselor and his client. The communication problem is aggravated by the fact that bureaucratic employees are typically more interested in communicating with their superiors than with their subordinates, which is a situation that can make communication with students less gratifying. When positions are as marginal and *insecure* as many counseling positions, communicating with subordinates can be threatening; for in such cases social distance and official authority are likely to be emphasized as ways of clarifying and guaranteeing their status prerogatives and obedience. However, at the same time it should be noted that this social distance also can help to *protect* clients against the probings of counselors.

Besides accentuating the status gap, professional standards also tend to discourage flexibility in evaluating lower-class clients. These standards emphasize the "objective" performance of these students, which makes it inappropriate to take into consideration either their environmental handicaps or their own social and moral expectations.

The testing technology, too, is challenging a number of traditional assumptions behind the client-counselor relationship. Undoubtedly, tests often are effective tools. They simplify the work by providing standardized simple answers to some basic questions and serve as valuable diagnostic tools when used in conjunction with other evidence. But once under way, the testing program tends to become more than simply a tool; it easily can become an independent influence on the counseling program. The status-enhancing functions of tests *per se* among laymen, who appreciate their technological basis, encourages their indiscriminate use. In some communities nationwide standardized achievement tests are used to evaluate their school's social prestige, and they have played an instrumental role in the nationwide talent hunt. The number of tests given is sometimes used as a basis for judging the quality of a school's program. (*Cambell and Bunnell, 1963*). They buttress the counselor's status in relation to his client, too, since they are so constructed that clients typically do not know entirely what their responses are actually conveying to testers, whose interpretations take precedence over those of clients.

In the absence of validated theoretical knowledge, extensive reliance on tests easily could transform counselors into technologists valued primarily for their testing skills, and, more important, testing effects that could have long range effects on relationships between educators and students. Test scores can simply harden teachers' attitudes toward the child's abilities or they can stabilize his performance at the present level by confirming his present self-conception. Some teachers grade children with high tested ability more strictly than those with lower ability, using high test scores as a penalty against the better students. Goslin notes, too, that because the teacher's reputation is at stake, he will tend to concentrate on helping his students do well on a test.

The influence of testing on an individual's relationship to his group, also, is virtually unknown. What is the effect of defining an individual in terms of his IQ score? What is the relationship between testing and the adolescent status system? How do an individual's test scores affect his relationship with his parents or the expectations of his teacher's? How does knowledge of test scores affect a person's eventual achievement and the level of motivation?

In final analysis, testing provides only probabilistic knowledge about group norms. All interpretations about individuals based on statistical inferences are subject to the usual statistical errors. If counseling arose partially to combat the impersonality of a bureaucratized and specialized society, then it is ironic that the movement has become so enamored with standardized statistics that are reliable only when applied to group norms. Yet, it is possible at the same time that testing itself is at times only a facade used to justify and implement knowledge and values derived from other sources — that inconclusive statistical tests are used to justify conclusions reached on a nonstatistical basis.

The role that testing has assumed in the organized counseling movement is a classic example of the kind of separation between stated goals and operational procedures which tends to develop in organizations. Unanticipated pressures from outside groups, a precarious occupational status and the immediate pressures connected with daily work schedules all are forces which converge in the form of a testing program and divert the movement from its original aims.

Implications

Increasing professional militancy potentially could reconcile many of the dilemmas discussed in this chapter. Although professionalization will create other problems (e.g. self interest, status struggles and social distance from clients), militant professionalism offers counselors the prospect of increased power to combat some of the most fatal of the effects that bureaucracy has had on counseling objectives. Perhaps professional status will at least help counselors to shape aspects of the educational and social system in closer accord with humanitarian objectives and provide a means of defending the individual's interests over those of the organization and local community. It also offers the prospect that a more theoretically sound approach will be developed for use with diverse types of clients. If counseling theory becomes more sociological, it could prepare counselors to be more critically aware of the anomalies they must learn to cope with and the values that are likely to be violated with any particular line of action.

The fate of counseling, in any event, will depend upon the direction which professional militancy takes, and this in turn depends upon the relative strength of counselors' professional and employee loyalties. The unknown element is whether the original humanistic vision which inspired the movement will become sufficiently revitalized to provide a new thrust against the forces that have so persistently threatened to displace it.

Conclusion

The underlying problems of counseling are not due entirely to the personal shortcomings of counselors, nor are they merely the by-products of transitions from a pre-industrial to an urban-industrial society. Many of them reflect the relative powerlessness of individual counselors to resist outside pressures. Often the only alternatives available have been either to risk being completely ineffective in order to maintain the purity of objectives or to bargain them away in exchange for outside support. One of the major contributing factors to the above problems has been the tendency of counselors to view clients' difficulties as individual maladjustments to the dominant social order, rather than as products of that

order. For example, the common view of the dropout problem emphasizes the individual's academic problems and personality characteristics
rather than attributing its cause primarily to the school itself — the
standardized, age-graded, college-oriented traditional curriculum. The
growing demand for professional counselors itself must be attributed
partly to the fact that the present institutional arrangements generally
have been taken for granted and are considered to be unamenable to
modification. It is safe to say that for all but a select minority, the
counselor's function has been to defend existing social structures by
adjusting individuals to them.

It is not surprising, therefore, that counselors also have blamed their
problems on their own personal ineffectiveness — lack of knowledge,
ineffective techniques, and inadequate education — when, in fact, their
own problems, like those of their clients, are caused by a fundamental
condition of the social order itself. Counselors are doomed to treat symptoms rather than causes. Perhaps some counselors do, in fact, have the
knowledge and could use it to develop a few techniques to alleviate at
least some educational, personal or marital problems. But they do not
have the social license to "operate" on the cause — the existing social
arrangements. They do not have the power necessary to adapt the
schools to potential dropouts; they are forbidden (even if they were inclined) to strongly advocate modifications in marriage and family arrangements that would tailor them to personal idiosyncrasies. Thus far,
they have been unable to alter the bureaucratic structure even sufficiently
to solve their own problems of professional status.

As a marginal occupation in many cases, counseling has been delegated
inappropriate functions and has been exploited by local institutions.
Counselors, at the same time, have willingly accepted many diverting
irrelevant obligations in order to justify themselves and expand their
influence. Their bargaining position has been weakened by a segmental-
ized leadership, indifference on the part of some members toward professionalization and by boundary disputes between professional counseling
groups.

In lieu of an acknowledged professional status, a segment of counselors have relied on their technological skills for justification and authority. Many have expediently bargained for support from influential
outsiders who have sought to use counseling to advance their own special
causes. The government has supported the movement for nationalistic,
militaristic and patriotic purposes, and in many communities, counselors
have permitted themselves to be defined as public servants or employees
responsible for handling discipline problems and for creating a favorable
"image" for the organization.

But even within the present system, with the support of other school officials and community leaders, they are likely to become more effective than they already are. Until now counselors often have been employed by administrators to perform chores irrelevant to counseling, and they have been expected to safeguard the values of particular schools and communities and of certain interest groups more frequently than to defend their clients' interests. Now counselors have begun to recognize that conflict is inherent in their positions within large organizations. As they become better organized, their militancy may be concentrated on clarifying their distinct functions and increasing their authority.

The fundamental issue is whether it is possible to implement a humanitarian conception of counseling within the severe limits imposed by the organization, values and techniques which have dominated the counseling movement to date. Many of the problems — lack of power and legitimacy, segmentalization, premature institutionalization, and bureaucratization — are characteristic of the professionalization of most modern occupations. But in the case of counseling, a question can be raised as to whether the goal displacements and the inadequate theories and techniques do not represent a more fundamental problem. Can counselors, enmeshed in bureaucracy, effectively assist clients with their distinctive problems? Or have the very conditions which stimulated the movement in the first place — mass, organized society, specialization and centralized power — rendered permanently ineffective the traditional humanitarian philosophy behind the movement? That philosophy assumed that effective counseling was dependent on a continuous and intimate personal relationship between the counselor and his client. The powerlessness, alienation, and neuroses characteristic of modern life perhaps have created an unprecedented need among some individuals for these intimate personal relationships, but it is these relationships which increasingly are being threatened by forces now shaping the counseling movement. In attempting to exert guidance of a morally-charged nature in a society whose moral standards are fluctuating, the counselor has been prepared to invade privacy, to extoll adjustment to middle-class standards, to enforce discipline, and at the same time, he has attempted to demonstrate how all of this contributes to self-realization, creative self-expression, and the individuality of those in his charge. If counselors fail to reconcile the dilemma, they may themselves contribute further to the problems of alienation and inauthenticity.

Perhaps in an urban society the frantic efforts on the part of some counselors to preserve the personal relationship no longer represent the most feasible way out of the dilemma that has arisen. Rather, if the fundamental problems confronting counselors are derivative of the social structure, then learning to cope with the sociological problems is perhaps their most crucial challenge, their primary potential contribution. For, as professionals who are themselves constrained by the demands of their bureaucratic and social positions, counselors are perhaps as likely as any group to become fully cognizant of the fundamental principle of amelioration in a mass, bureaucratic society: That helping others does not require controlling *them* so much as it demands helping them to control their environments.

APPENDIX

Examples of Items Comprising the
Bureaucratic and Professional
Status-Orientation Scales

Bureaucratic-Employee Status-Orientation (28 items total): *

1. *Loyalty to the Administration* — Personnel who openly criticize the administration should be encouraged to go elsewhere.
2. *Loyalty to the Organization* — What is best for the school is best for education.
3. *Experience Orientation* — Pay should be in relation to experience.
4. *Interchangeability Orientation* — The work of a course should be so well planned that every child taking the same course throughout the state will eventually cover the same material.
5. *Rules Orientation* — Rules stating when teachers should arrive and depart from the building should be strictly enforced.
6. *Loyalty to the Public* — Teachers should take into account the opinions of their community in guiding what they say in class and in their choice of teaching materials.

Professional Status-Orientation (16 items total): **

1. *Client Orientation* — It should be permissible for a teacher to violate a rule if he or she is sure that the best interests of the students will be served in doing so.
2. *Colleague Orientation* — Teachers should try to live up to the standards of their profession even if the administration or the community does not seem to respect them.
3. *Monopoly of Knowledge* — Teachers should be evaluated primarily on the basis of their knowledge of the subject matter that is taught and their ability to communicate it.
4. *Decision-Making Authority* — Small matters should not have to be referred to someone higher up for a final answer.

* The split-half reliability of this scale is $r=.74$, or $r_n=.84$ when corrected with the Spearman-Brown Prophecy formula.
** The split-half reliability of this scale is $r=.48$ or $r_n=.64$ when corrected.
Each scale also discriminates between select groups of respondents in the sample who approximate high and low professional and employee norms.

References

Bereiter, Carl, and Mervin B. Freedman (1962). "Fields of Study and People in Them," in *The American College* (ed.) Nevitt Sanford, Wiley, p. 565.

Blau, Peter M. (1964). *Exchange and Power in Social Life,* Wiley.

Campbell, Roald F., and Robert A. Bunnell (1963). *Nationalizing Influences on Secondary Education,* Midwest Administration Center, The University of Chicago.

Corwin, Ronald G. (1967). *Staff Conflicts in the Public Schools, Phase II,* Cooperative Research Program of the Office of Education, U. S. Department of Health, Education, and Welfare, Contract No. 2637. (To be published by Appleton-Century-Crofts, 1969.)

―――― (1965). *A Sociology of Education,* Appleton-Century-Crofts.

Clark, Burton R. (1960). "The 'Cooling-Out' Function in Higher Education," *American Journal of Sociology,* 65 (May), 569–576.

Darley, John G. (1956). "The Faculty Is Human Too," *Personnel and Guidance Journal,* 35, 225–230.

Farwell, G. F. (1963). "Counselors' Role and Function: Conceptions and Conflicts," *Theory into Practice,* 2 (February).

Friedenberg, Edgar Z. (1959). *The Vanishing Adolescent,* Dell.

Goslin, David (1963). *The Search for Ability,* Russell Sage Foundation.

Gouldner, Alvin W. (1959). "Reciprocity and Autonomy in Functional Theory," in *Symposium on Sociological Theory,* Llewellyn Gross (ed.), Row, Peterson.

Grant, C. W. (1956). "How Students Perceive the Counselor's Role," *Personnel and Guidance Journal* (March), 386–388.

Hobbs, N. (1958). "The Compleat Counselor," *Personnel and Guidance Journal,* 36, 594–602.

Hoedt, K. C. and J. W. M. Rothney (1963). "Guidance for Superior Students: Some Problems," *Vocational Guidance Quarterly,* 11 (Spring), 199–201.

Knapp, Dale L. and Earl W. Denny (1961). "The Counselor's Responsibility in Role Definition," *Personnel and Guidance Journal* (September), 48.

Magoon, Thomas (1964). "Innovations in Counseling," *Journal of Counseling Psychology,* II (Winter).

Martinson, Ruth A. (1951). "Duties of Elementary School Counselors," *Occupations,* 30 (December), 167–170.

Mayer, Martin (1963). *The Schools,* Doubleday and Company, Inc.

Porter, Thomas L., and Thomas E. Cook (1964). "A Comparison of Student and Professional Ranking of Jobs in Psychology," *Journal of Counseling Psychology,* II.

Rothney, J. W. M., and L. A. Roens (1952). *Guidance of American Youth,* Harvard University Press.

Schwirian, Kent P. (1963). "Testing at Issue: A Case Study of School and Community Conflict," *Theory into Practice* (October), 232.

Shertzer, B., and S. C. Stone (1963). "Administrative Deterrents to Guidance Program Development," *Theory into Practice,* 2 (February), 24–32.

Swisher, John (1967). *Professional School Counselors and Staff Conflicts.* Doctoral dissertation, The Ohio State University.

8 | TASKS AND TROUBLES:

The Practical Bases
of Work Activities in a
Public Assistance Organization

Don H. Zimmerman / University of California, Santa Barbara

This paper reports one aspect of a larger research project[1] directed to the investigation of how caseworkers and other personnel in a public assistance agency conducted their everyday, practical affairs. It was primarily concerned to describe the ways in which members' management of their "practical circumstances"[2] bore upon *their* determination of the operational meaning and intent of organizational rules and procedures in concrete, exigent work situations, and intimately related to this judg-

This study was inspired by and is heavily indebted to the work and teaching of Harold Garfinkel. This study has had the benefit of discussion and criticism in a number of seminars conducted by Professor Garfinkel, and has employed many specific suggestions provided by him and by members of the seminar. The author also wishes to express his gratitude for the permission to quote from Professor Garfinkel's unpublished materials. The author alone is responsible for the use of these resources in the present document. The author would also like to acknowledge the many helpful suggestions concerning the organization of the present paper given him by Aaron V. Cicourel.

1 Zimmerman (*1966*). The author was supported during the project by a National Science Foundation Cooperative Graduate Fellowship which also provided a small research grant which facilitated the completion of the project. Further financial assistance was furnished by the project on "Decision-Making in Common-Sense Situations of Choice" being carried on by Drs. Harold Garfinkel, Lindsey Churchill and Harvey Sachs, sponsored by the Air Force Office of Scientific Research, Office of Aerospace Research, United States Air Force, under A.F.O.S.R. grant number 757-65. Other research funds contributing to this work were provided by the Committee on Research, University of California, Santa Barbara. The author also wishes to express his deep gratitude to personnel at all levels of the Metropolitan County Bureau of Public Assistance, and in particular to those with whom he worked in the Lakeside office. Without their cooperation, this study would not have been possible.

2 See Garfinkel (*1959, 1962, 1967a*) and Garfinkel and Churchill (*1964*). See also footnote 6, below.

mental work, their selection from among alternative "approaches" to the management of their tasks. The observational materials presented below will attempt to depict the pressure of the intake caseworker's practical circumstances on her choice between the alternative ways of addressing her task, and how that choice relates to the determination of what policies and regulations "really" intend.

The alternatives were formulated by the investigator in order to organize a range of field observations which suggested that there were apparently two different patterned ways of operating upon the task environment practiced by personnel in the setting. These alternatives will be designated the "caseload-oriented" and the "applicant-oriented" approaches, respectively. In general terms, the caseload-oriented approach may be characterized as a set of related practices permitting the worker to manage the pressing practical exigencies of work in the setting, thereby satisfying the prevailing standards of competent work. The applicant-oriented approach consisted of a contrasting set of practices defining the task as primarily one of providing "help" with and "understanding" of the applicant's self-formulated problems, placing a secondary emphasis on the management of the practical features of work in the setting.

The choice of one or the other of these alternative ways of proceeding, and the consequences following from that choice, were observed to be matters of pressing practical concern for personnel faced with the responsibility of turning in an acceptable day's work. It will be proposed that only the caseload-oriented approach was sanctionable in the setting as an adequate-for-all-practical-purposes way of routinely managing the task in a fashion recognizably in accord with the rules, policies, procedures and goals of the organization. This proposal may be taken as equivalent to saying that the socially organized practices to which the term caseload-oriented approach refers provide for the situated determinations of what the rules, procedures, policies and goals of the organization actionably consisted in. These practices furnished the means for adequately demonstrating by implicit and explicit reference to the practical features of action in the setting that particular actions undertaken in satisfaction of the task were in accord with what the rules, procedures, etc., really, or "reasonably," could be taken to intend. The implications of this proposal will be elaborated in the following section.

Perspective

Numerous studies of formal organizations have found worthy of remark that some portion of the observed activities of bureaucrats are often not easily reconciled with the investigators' understanding of what the formally instituted rules and regulations dictate.[3] For example, it has been observed that formal rules and organizational arrangements have a variety of situated uses presumedly not envisioned by the rule makers.[4] Bureaucrats, in conducting their everyday affairs in organizations, have been found in study after study to honor a range of presumedly "non-rational" considerations in making decisions and concerting actions. The asserted contrasts between "theory" and "practice" reported by organizational studies are so commonplace that documentation seems hardly necessary.

It is important to note how such contrasts are obtained.[5] They are typically produced by the investigator's use of his own common-sense understanding of what behavioral dispositions are called for by the rules, or by consulting the accounts given by various personnel in the organization (usually those in positions of authority) of what activities are properly to be considered in "compliance" with the rule. The empirical issue of what such rules mean to, and how they are used by, personnel on *actual occasions* of bureaucratic work is set aside in favor of a definition of proper rule use empirically unlocated in any on-going course of activity in the organization in question. Rather, the implicit assumption is usually made that rules have, in principle, a stable, determinant meaning invariant to the exigencies of actual situations of use and distinct from the practical interests of the rule user.

Research studies of formal organizations have had no difficulty enumerating a variety of conditions under which observed actual behavior fails to accord with the sociologist's definition of what the rules provide. These studies consistently document the fact that bureaucrats, employing rules and procedures designed to effect "rational" goal accomplishment, are keenly attuned to what here would be called the features of their practical circumstances[6] as these are grasped by them as constraints or

[3] See for example: Anonymous (*1946*, pp. 365–370); Bensman and Gerver (*1963*, pp. 588–598); Blau (*1963*); Cohen (*1962*); Dalton (*1959*); Page (*1946*, pp. 88–94); Roy (*1954*, pp. 255–266); Scheff (*1962*, pp. 208–217); Turner (*1947*, pp. 342–348); and Zawecki (*1963*).

[4] See for example: Dalton (*1959*, pp. 31–57); Blau (*1963*, pp. 100 *ff.*, and pp. 217–219); Gouldner (*1955*, pp. 157–176).

[5] The discussion that follows has profited from the author's reading of Bittner (*1965*, pp. 239–255). Bittner's article is concerned with a specification of the relevance of Garfinkel's work for the study of formal organizations. The remarks made in this section of the present paper closely parallel Bittner's argument in the work cited above.

[6] The term "practical circumstances" is employed here to refer to the properties of common-sense situations of choice delineated by Harold Garfinkel. In brief, these properties encompass a set of related, pressing concerns which practical decision makers appear to honor in deciding between alternatives of fact, sense and action in socially organized settings. These concerns are for the temporal coordination of action, the management of the risk of unfavorable outcomes, the persistent fact that performances are subject to evaluation, the practical problem of "what to do next," the

facilities, justifications or contraindications, resources or troubles in the course of pursuing bureaucratic work. Indeed, these practical circumstances often seem to be critical elements in determining the bureaucrat's use of the rules and resources of the organization. In light of this, such features of the bureaucrat's circumstances are variously treated as "problems" or "obstacles" to be overcome if the organization is to rationally, effectively, and efficiently achieve its goals, evidence that the system of rules, or their enforcement, is defective in one respect or another, grounds for arguing the "dynamic" character of organization in adjusting to its changing environment or for identifying "pathological" elements in organizational interaction, and so on. Whatever the perspective taken on such findings, investigators typically find it necessary to invoke such features of the bureaucrats' circumstances, and their situationally enforced interests in dealing with them in order to account for the supposed discrepancy between the formally ordained and observedly actual state of organizational affairs.

In rendering such an account, the discovery of "deviations" (accomplished by the use of the procedure described above) is typically treated as evidence that the persons involved were complying with yet another set of rules which remain to be formulated by the investigator. If formally constituted rules are found to be violated "systematically" then these violations are to be accounted for by the bureaucrats' compliance with alternative "informal rules" which have arisen in the course of interaction over time in the organization.

This line of reasoning would propose that whatsoever patterned conduct is observed, it is formulable as conduct in accord with some rule. If there is prior reason to suppose that some set of rules should control this behavior, and they are found inadequate, other rules must be sought. This way of proceeding leaves out of account any question of *what it takes* to employ a rule in concrete situations, and ignores the need to investigate the situated judgmental processes by which rules are brought to bear on relevant occasions.[7]

---

constraint that the decider give evidence by his choice of his competent grasp of "What Anyone Knows" about the operation of setting in which the choice is made, the problem of determining the socially adequate and effective determination of rules and procedures in dealing with actual concrete situations — given that such rational constructions are merely advisory to action, and the confrontation of these circumstances and the alternatives of choice and action undertaken selected by reference to them as together the part and parcel of a serious, realistic domain of action. See Garfinkel and Churchill (*1964*). See also Garfinkel (*1959; 1962*), and in particular Garfinkel (*1967a*). A more extended discussion of these features in relation to the topic under investigation here may be found in Zimmerman (*1966*, Chapter I) and Zimmerman (forthcoming).

7 Bureaucrats are thereby cast in the role of "judgmental dopes" who "produce the stable features of the [organization] by acting in compliance with preestablished and legitimate [or, as the case may be, illegitimate] alternatives of action that [the formal or informal organization] provides." See Garfinkel (*1964*, p. 224).

How rules may be used to deal with the matters to which they pertain, and the sanctioned courses of everyday judgment which are required to interpret, recognize, or instruct others as to the operational intent and implications of such rules is rendered empirically unproblematic. The very features of the bureaucrats' circumstances which are often identified as factors leading to the modification or violation of formal rules and occasioning the emergence of alternative "informal rules" may in fact be features *which bureaucrats consult in order to decide what the formal rules might reasonably mean and what it would take to employ them in the first instance.*[8] It is proposed here that some illumination of bureaucratic practices, and "rule-governed" conduct in general, may be obtained by addressing the problem: how is it that members of an organized setting go about finding the sense, import, and actionable features of rules and other rational constructions within, with respect to, and by their artful management of, the actual contingent situations of their use?[9]

This problem is addressed in the present study in the following fashion. It will attempt to describe, from the perspective of the worker, what is entailed for her in *doing* her task in the setting *as it is organized.* Work must proceed apace with demands exerted, deadlines are to be met, activities must be coordinated, work is subject to evaluation, troubles occur which must be managed — what are the consequences of these persistent, often urgent features of the setting for the daily decisions that must be made by personnel committed to work in such a place, given that this work is to be done in accordance with rules? In short, the study will attempt to identify the intake caseworker's "practical circumstances," and examine the varied practices undertaken in response to them. The study will view these practices as providing, by their "artful management of the actual contingent situations" of work, situated determinations of operational meaning of organizational rules and policies.[10]

The chapter is organized as follows. A brief discussion of the setting of the study will be undertaken in which attention will be focused on the features of the intake caseworker's task, with particular emphasis on the temporal contingencies of her task activities. Following that, the methods of research will be outlined. The research procedures involved

[8] This argument is not to be construed to mean that rule violations do not occur, or that bureaucrats might not respect alternative "informal rules" in conducting their affairs. The point is that the issue of how rules and other rational contructions are used by actors within concrete occasions of work must be treated as empirically problematic.

[9] A statement of the theoretical considerations upon which this view is based may be found in Garfinkel (*1967b*) and Bittner (*1965*).

[10] As will become clear, this paper deals with the determinations of the intent and meaning of "rules and policies" on a rather general level. Such a general treatment must be counted as a shortcoming of the research. An attempt to deal with instances of rule use in concrete situations is made in Zimmerman (forthcoming).

will be seen to be ethnographic in character. In the body of the paper, the descriptive materials relevant to the examination of the problem posed above will be presented and discussed.

The Setting of the Study

The study from which the materials reported here were drawn was conducted on one district office of a metropolitan county public assistance operation in a large western state. Within the Lakeside Office, as it will be called here, the research was focused upon the day-to-day processing by the intake function of applications for assistance.[11] Of Lakeside's eight intake work units, typically composed of five intake workers and a supervisor, three were studied in detail.

The Lakeside Office was located in a three-story building of moderate size which housed the two hundred and sixty-three administrators, supervisors, social caseworkers and clerks of the office staff. The first floor was given over to the seventy-five personnel responsible for intake, reception and related functions. Located on the second floor were the one hundred and nineteen personnel charged with the management of approved caseloads. Housed on the third floor were sixty-nine clerical personnel.

For the purposes of the discussion to follow, it is necessary to briefly characterize several of the different functions performed by the staff of the Lakeside Office. The duties of the intake division will be discussed in more detail shortly; accounts of the "approved" and reception functions follow below.

The "Approved" Function

Caseworkers handling "approved" caseloads deal with cases for which eligibility to assistance has been previously certified by intake. Approved workers deal with a case on a continuing basis. A prominent task of approved work is the performance of an annual or semi-annual affirmation (depending on the category of assistance involved) which is a formal re-consideration of the client's "eligibility" and "need." In addition to the affirmation procedure, the approved worker also deals with emergency situations that develop in a case, makes adjustments in the budget (the document controlling the amount of aid received by the client) according to changes in the client's income or need, and oversees the client's compliance with the conditions of assistance, e.g., seeking employment, if judged able to do so.

11 Lakeside processed applications for the following Federal categories of assistance: Aid to Families with Dependent Children (AFDC) and Aid to Families with Dependent Children, Parent Unemployment (AFDC-U), Old Age Assistance (OAA), Aid to the Totally Disabled (ATD), Medical Aid to the Aged (MAA), and the county-financed and county-controlled General Relief (GR).

The "Reception" Function

As the approved worker's caseload is assembled by virtue of the prior performance of the intake worker in certifying eligibility, so the intake worker's investigation is preceded by the work of receptionists in pre-processing new applications for public assistance. The transaction between applicant and agency which occurs within the jurisdiction of reception personnel marks the starting point of a series of subsequent activities which may be organized under the notion of "processing a case." Reception duties include the screening of persons presenting themselves at the reception counter, assigning those with the announced or elicited intention of requesting assistance to the appropriate category of aid, collecting preliminary information concerning their present circumstances, checking for the existence of previous contact with the agency, and at the terminus of these activities, assigning the applicant to an intake worker who then pursues the investigation of the claim.

The Intake Caseworker's Task

The caseworker in the intake division is responsible for the establishment of the entitlement and need of applicants to receive public assistance. Entitlement is based on the applicant's current status with regard to a variety of factors which include age, marital status, property holdings, income, dependents and employability.[12] It is the caseworker's task to ascertain the factual character of the applicant's claims regarding these factors, and having done so, to decide whether the applicant falls within the legislatively given parameters defining a "needy" and "eligible" person.[13]

The warranted character of such decisions is based upon the assembly, generation, and interpretation of documents which attest to the factuality of the applicant's statements. The flow of paper in the intake process is largely concerned with the generation of a case record consisting of an assemblage of documents, statements by the applicant, and a case narrative dictated by the worker which interprets the significance of the above and details the steps taken in the procurement of such information. The case, subject to the scrutiny and approval by a supervisor, is then presumed able to withstand review as evidence of an objectively and impersonally executed consideration of the applicant's claim for assistance. It suffices here to note that documentation — its assembly and production

[12] The criterial "factors" are given by statute and are specific to the particular category of assistance involved. Space limitations preclude their discussion here. See Zimmerman (*1966*, Chapter 2).

[13] In the language of public assistance, the worker is responsible for the execution of a "means test."

— is a crucial element in deciding a case, and of a case "decided properly."[14]

Not only must the intake worker's investigation of a claim for assistance withstand supervisory review as to its adequacy, the decision on the case must be completed within the thirty-day period specified by statute. Failure to do so may unfavorably affect the reimbursement of the Federal-State portion of assistance payments to the County.[15] A case filed subsequent to this period is termed "delinquent," and administrative controls operate to monitor the progress of an application in these terms. The deadline attached to each case is multiplied in its significance for the worker by virtue of the fact that she deals not with one case at a time but with a caseload.

Caseload size is utilized as a standard of performance itself. The device for controlling caseload size consists in a monthly "activity report" compiled by intake supervisors and submitted to the Assistant Director in charge of intake. The report details by work unit and by worker the balance of cases undecided at the beginning of the month, the number of new cases added in that month, the disposition of cases decided that month (approved, denied, cancelled, transferred to another worker) and the balance of cases left in the worker's file (and in the unit as a whole) at the end of the month. The report is used by the Assistant Director as an indicator of how well workers are managing the job. A caseload consistently in excess of thirty was typically taken as a sign of trouble. Since workers seldom received more than twenty new cases in any one month, a caseload of thirty or more indicated holdovers from subsequent months, and as a corollary, delinquent filings.

Caseload, as computed in this monthly report, and the "due date" given by the statutory deadline for filing taken together constitute two major concerns in the processing of a caseload. The intake caseworker's task may be characterized as the management of a series of occasions in which she must deal first with this case, and then another (and back to the first again) within a context of varied contingencies and yet somehow make the caseload "come out right" at the end of the month. These two concerns, as typically enforceable standards of "good work" in the setting, provide for the significance of both the occasional and endemic troubles bearing upon the prompt disposal of applications encountered in pur-

---

14 How an accomplished case is adjudged to have been "decided properly" would have to be referred to an examination of the situated methods employed by supervisors and other administrative personnel upon actual occasions of review. In agency practice, a "properly decided case" is a contingent and revisable judgment. See Zimmerman (*1966*, Chapters 5 and 6).

15 The formula governing reimbursements according to the relationship between date of application and date of filing need not concern this discussion. See Zimmerman (*1966*, Chapter 2).

suing the task. The relationship between these standards, work-day contingencies, and the grounds for selection among alternative strategies of caseload processing is the concern of the balance of the chapter.[16]

The Intake Process: Temporal Features

The set of tasks involved in the processing of a caseload is repeated over a more or less regular and continuing cycle of activities. This cycle may be roughly described as consisting in, with considerable overlap, the addition of new cases, the "processing" of previously introduced cases which are at various stages of completion, and the disposal of cases on which decisions have been made. From a perspective on this process "in motion," there is no unambiguous "beginning" or "end" point, save perhaps for that point at which individual caseworkers first assume a caseload, or lay it down. As a way of sectioning this process for the purpose of describing it, the intake day will be examined.

The Intake Day: Coordination of Intake with Reception

The paramount relevancy of reception is the "efficient" (i.e. orderly and appropriately paced) processing of applicants-in-the-office. A crucial feature of this flow is the availability of intake workers who move the applicant into the interview booth and out of the office.[17] This is controlled by a list in a determinate order of workers assigned to intake for that day. When her name appears on this list, the routine procedures of the reception function "assume control" over the intake worker as a prime resource. It is on the worker's intake day that she becomes a resource for reception and is subject to a measure of control by the reception process.

The worker "up" that day looks to such control as her guide to her movements that day, and to the process as the harbinger of her "fate" — that is, the additions to her caseload that she will have to carry through most probably beyond her next intake day the following week when her lot is again under the control of the reception routine.

The occurrence of an intake is independent of and takes precedence over other tasks that might be pending. The processing of each new application occasions the initiation of a set of procedures which are also independent of the previous or concurrent demands of the worker's file,

16 By way of qualification, it must be noted that these two standards are by no means the only ones employed to judge a worker's competence, nor is their employment "absolute" or invariant to the contingencies of actual occasions of review of performance. They are "typically," "usually," or "normally" employed, which is to say, they are realistic *considerations* for workers when deciding or assessing strategies of work.

17 For a more detailed account of the reception function, see Zimmerman (*1966*, Chapters 3 and 4).

e.g., the requirement to make a home-call,[18] the necessity of doing an "initial" dictation (a preliminary formulation of the issues of the case and the procedures initiated to resolve them), and perhaps, the chore of dealing with an emergency confronting a new applicant.[19] The major point to be made is that the addition of new cases (and hence, further work to be done) continues with predictable regularity without reference to the status of previously added cases and the work that remained to be done on them. The implications of this feature of the organization of work, which are of considerable importance to personnel in the setting, will be drawn below.

Scheduling Contingencies

The very organizational arrangements providing for the coordination of the reception and intake functions contribute to the scheduling contingencies encountered by intake workers in pursuing their task on a day-to-day basis. This may be seen in the following considerations.

The intake worker's caseload is typically uneven with respect to the stage of the investigation of the constituent cases — there may be cases simply awaiting the return of some form, new cases which will require the initiation of forms, problematic cases which will require conferences with the supervisor as to "what to do next," problem cases which exert many demands, or are marked by difficulties in the relationship between applicant and worker, complicated cases demanding special consideration; and favored cases, where the worker has "identified" with the client and is extending "extra effort."

Further, the "demands" exerted by the caseload are varied and unpredictable. Requests and complaints are directed to the worker by the applicant through phone calls and office visits at all hours of the day; landlords may telephone about the overdue rent of an applicant; relatives may inquire into the reasons why decision on an applicant's case has been delayed (particularly in OAA cases); forms initiated earlier may be returned which fail to establish points of eligibility that the worker anticipated would be proved by them (or may not be returned at all); cases may become ready for approval or denial (requiring final dictation); the supervisor may be asking questions and demanding answers about a case that will soon become delinquent; another applicant may be appealing a previous decision, necessitating a session with the Assistant Director who will critically review the handling of the case in terms of her task of answering on behalf of the agency to the issue of the appeal, and so on.

[18] The "home-call" typically takes place the next working day following the intake interview; the applicant is visited in her home by the worker.

[19] "Emergencies" typically involved a lack of food, an impending eviction, or a shutoff of utilities.

Workers have commented on this feature of their work day and its implications for the performance of their task in a number of ways. One worker remarked, for example, "Here is the only place where the day of the week matters. You have something to do every day of the week, and a holiday means getting behind." She went on:

> Not only do you have this application to process, you're getting forms back on old applications which will refer (further investigations) elsewhere. You'll have problems coming up because, you know, they're people. New ones all the time. You have to do this. You've also got to file, you know, the cases that are ready for filing. Some of these cases have been ready for filing for three weeks. And every time I get to dictate, well, I've got initials [the preliminary dictation done after the home call] I've got to dictate. I have this I have to do, I have that I have to do, and I simply don't file it.

Another worker commented: "Each new case cuts into you. It takes hours out of your life." He termed the press of work demands a "billiard ball effect," referring to the ways in which claims on the worker's time were presented by telephone, by the supervisor, by the applicant in the office, by the intake day, and so on, irrespective of the worker's current situation.[20] It appears to be a persistent and significant "fact of life" for the worker that whatsoever her problems may be with her present caseload, she may count on the fact that they very likely will be further complicated by the regular addition of from one to six new cases of unknown complexity.[21]

Research Strategies and the Research Plan

The aims of this study dictated that an attempt be made to observe and record on-going activities in the setting, in their natural sequence, as they were paced according to the relevancies guiding the timely accomplishment of tasks, and as they were phased in terms of the organizational conditions for coordinating such activities. These activities were conceived to be undertaken with respect to the contingencies of task accomplishment in the setting, guided by the concern for the fact that their adequacy was subject to review in terms of prevailing standards of performance, and managed with an eye to the possibility that unfavor-

20 In response to this "billiard ball effect," several workers expressed the wish to take cases home (a forbidden practice) and work on them in a relaxed manner, without phones ringing and applicants in the office demanding attention, this "even without claiming overtime."

21 The "uncertainty" of the new additions is a function both of the variations possible for types of cases within a given category of aid and by the fact that the assignment procedure is typically out of the worker's hands. The features of her future caseload are, as a rule, not predictable in advance. The same number of cases from two different intakes may entail radically different proportions of effort. This feature of work accounts, in part perhaps, for the practical concern for the rapid disposal of individual cases in the context of caseload and processing time maximums.

247

able outcomes would occur. Personnel were viewed as persons who, as a condition of their competent membership in the organization, employed their understanding of the setting's organized ways in order to find the relevance and appropriate use of rules, procedures and policies to effect acceptable outcomes of their activities.

Nothing short of an attempt to observe these activities "in motion" would suffice for the concerns of this study. To approach this goal, a research plan was formulated which called for the "integration" of the investigator into the work organization of the setting, specifically, that segment of it dealing with the processing of cases. The observer wished access to the normal round of activities connected with the accomplishment of the operational goal of the organization: the provision of public assistance to qualified applicants.

It was decided to employ the casework unit as the basic context of the field research. It was planned that the observer would "join" several such units as an overt participant observer. He would attempt to integrate his research activities into the natural rhythm of activities in the unit by "shadowing" each worker in the unit in turn, literally following each of them through several work days. He would accompany them to intake interviews, on home-calls, sit at or near their desks to observe their work, and as the occasion permitted, he would interrogate them concerning activities and events observed in the course of the day's work. When the workers consulted with the supervisor, or engaged in "shop talk," the investigator would endeavor to be present. Assuming sufficient rapport, he would attempt to gain access to all the usual interactions taking place in conjunction with the pursuit of the task. The same strategy would be employed with respect to the supervisor's activity, and for any other function observed in the setting.[22] In this fashion, the primary control over what was observed would presumably be exercised by the normal work routines in the setting. The field of observation would consist, then, in any and all activities and events encountered in the course of tracking personnel following this routine.[23]

To conclude this brief discussion of the procedures employed in the study, it must be made clear that no claim is advanced that the descriptions offered below in any sense "demonstrate" the validity of the proposals set forth in this chapter. Viewed as illustrations, however, they

[22] Data recording techniques consisted of the use of field notes and a portable tape recorder. Whenever possible, the tape recorder was used, both for interviews and more crucially for recording on-going work transactions. For an evaluation of these techniques, see Zimmerman (*1966*, Appendix on Method).

[23] This statement, as a potential description of how the investigator actually attended to events in the setting as eligible observables, must be viewed as a mere gloss to the issue of how in fact the data were collected. The investigator cannot provide a principled account of how he selected, among a range of possible observations, those focused upon here.

do recommend these proposals on plausible grounds and suggest the importance of further investigation of "practical activities."[24]

The Management of Caseload Processing

The scheduling contingencies of caseload processing, taken together with the enforced emphasis on caseload size and processing time limitations render highly salient the caseworker's management of her caseload.

Given the emphasis on caseload and delinquency reduction, the features alluded to above must be managed in some fashion if the worker is to "come out" at the end of the month with a respectable showing on the activity report. If she is to preserve her status as a competent worker and make her work day tolerable, she must deal with such features as a matter of course. The problem is particularly acute in the case of new workers who must learn what is important in the processing of a case, e.g., how to "manage" the applicant rather than having the applicant manage them, and how to dispose of the cases that they can "get out of" in order to have the time to work the cases that they cannot "get out of."

The import of these concerns must first be assessed relative to the stress on the conduct of an investigation of eligibility. The requirement that each case be "fully documented," given the variety of situations of differing complexity, and the ability (or willingness) of the applicant to cooperate (an essential for speedy processing), operates "normally" to extend the course of investigation in many cases.

Second, as enforceable criteria of performance in the setting, the dual caseload-delinquency standards tend to structure how far one may sanctionably go with any given case in order to determine its eligibility. That is, the "pressure" of these concerns tend to provide a situated definition of that point at which, for example, there is "insufficient information" to establish eligibility, or that the applicant "has failed to cooperate in providing essential information."[25] Put another way, these circumstances provide a setting-relevant definition of what "efficient" case processing would consist in, and, as will be seen, a set of guides to the strategies of "efficient" case processing.

---

24 For a discussion of the methodological problems of developing "adequate evidence" in the investigation of social action see Cicourel (*1964*) and Cicourel (*1968,* particularly Chapter 1).

25 Defining a situation in these terms provides a warranted means for disposing of an application prior to a decision on the issue of eligibility. The worker, however, must "make a case" for the insufficiency of information or the inadequacy of the applicant's cooperation. The basis for supporting such contentions typically consists in a detailed documentation of the steps taken by the worker to secure information and of the instructions issued to the applicant. The case is made by then proposing that these steps failed to produce the necessary information and/or that the applicant repeatedly failed to follow instructions.

It would seem, on the basis of the discussion thus far, that reduced to its simplest terms, the intake caseworker is confronted with the practical necessity to reduce her caseload, minimize the delinquencies, and conduct an investigation of eligibility that will satisfy her superior. The organization of work, its contingencies, and the prevailing concerns of persons in authority in the setting combine to provide "penalties" for the worker who by deliberate election, or by ignorance, conducts her affairs in disregard of these "necessities." By the same token, the worker who is keenly attuned to such "caseload considerations" and manages her activities accordingly is "rewarded."[26] It might seem to follow that caseworkers are *obliged* to approach their task in a fashion adequate to manage the contingencies, risks, and demands placed upon them by these circumstances.

Workers in the intake division at Lakeside cannot, however, be characterized as uniformly attuned to features and implications of their work circumstances, nor uniformly committed in each and every instance to act in accordance with the "interests" generated by these circumstances. This appears to be the case for the following reasons.

First, some proportion of Bureau personnel at any given time are novices. They are, at least initially, strangers to the ways of the setting. However much they may be instructed or cajoled to respect the "facts of life" and "limitations" of action in the office, it appears that they must come to an appreciation of these concerns over a course of dealing with actual occasions of task activity. It will be suggested below that the process of becoming socialized to the ways of the office proceeds by way of a confrontation with the troubles generated by ignorance of, or inattention to, the practical features of the task and the enforced standards of performance in the setting.

Second, workers may entertain a conception of the task and its objectives which motivates an approach to case processing incongruent with the practical concerns discussed above. The conjunction of organizational naïveté and a *structurally unlocated*[27] conception of the task produce a variety of troubles for the workers concerned, and a problem of control for those in authority.

26 The "penalties" referred to follow from the assorted troubles and stresses that accompany a high caseload. These difficulties are related, first, to the sheer volume of work associated with a high caseload, and second, to the administrative sanctions that follow from the fact of a high caseload and delinquency rate. "Rewards" have to do with the avoidance of such troubles by keeping the caseload, and hence the workload, to a minimum, and to the administrative approval, i.e., non-intervention which typically parallels continuing accomplishment of such "good work."

27 By "structurally unlocated" is meant a conception of the task (with concomitant explicit and implicit strategies and assignment of priorities) lacking adequate reference to the practical contingencies and enforced emphases of a concrete scene of organized action from the point of view of competent members of the setting.

The following section deals with the relationship between the case-worker's practical circumstances and the processing of a caseload. Specifically, concern will be with how such circumstances come to be recognized as a basis for action, and how they serve as "reasonable" grounds for choice between alternative approaches to the task.[28]

Alternative Approaches to the Task

As an approximation, two general alternative approaches may be identified and described. The "caseload-oriented" approach is, as the label implies, one which accords first priority to the practical problem of managing a caseload given the features discussed above. The "applicant-oriented" approach accords first priority to dealing with what is conceived to be the applicant's problem, with a secondary emphasis accorded to caseload considerations. The consequences of following these two approaches will be examined in order to see more clearly the import of the caseworker's practical circumstances as a guide to decision and action in the setting.

A preliminary question that must be addressed is the source of these alternative approaches. It may be said that the caseload-oriented approach is "native" to the setting. It is a *received* alternative, structurally locatable within the organization of the setting and routinely sanctionable, i.e., institutionalized as a method of dealing with the task. What is the origin of the other alternative, given the assertion above that it is structurally unlocated? The following section attempts an answer to this question.

The Source of the Applicant-Oriented Approach

While the task of documenting a case, and the time and paperwork it entails, constitutes a major element of the worker's activities, some workers, and particularly (but not exclusively) new workers consider such work to be an obstacle standing in the way of doing "social work." An ironic contrast is often made between the (usually vaguely defined) activity of "social work" and the perceivedly routine clerical duties of the actual task. This kind of contrast is found in the following comments by one worker:

> I found — I am not doing this much anymore — I found myself doing approved work [intake workers equate the tasks of the approved worker with "social work"] with these people which isn't — it's just not a function of intake. Its more interesting, though, than property investigations. You have

[28] The construction of "alternative approaches" to caseload management to be reported below is based upon the investigator's observation of everyday work practices in the setting, and upon interviews with personnel. While these constructions intend a reference to an environment of objects and events known and assessed from the perspective of personnel in the setting, this reference must be viewed as a hopeful assertion rather than a demonstrated fact.

to spend too much time — it makes you feel like a real estate assessor instead of a social worker.

Another worker, discussing a complicated case on which she was working remarked:

> This woman, she just doesn't know anything about property, or how to handle what she had. It just all went. But there again, it is not enough for her to just say that it is gone and then we can just take it like that and approve it. This is not social work, what I am doing, you know. Really, I don't think you could call that social work — figuring out the financial situations — could you?

These remarks suggest that some workers find the enforced features of their task incongruous with their conception of what it should consist of. The concern here is with the source of this incongruity.

While the concern to do "social work" may be based upon a conception in the general culture of the social work occupational role, it has a specifiable source within the Bureau. What is here termed the "social work" approach is strongly emphasized by the personnel of the Training Division in the one-month training course required of all new workers entering the Bureau. These personnel, largely professionally trained social workers (i.e., holders of the M.S.W. degree) envision a change in the character of public assistance in line with their professional interests in providing supportive "therapy" to distressed and underprivileged persons. They emphasize the sympathetic understanding of the problems of such persons, encourage an "accepting" attitude toward them, and attempt to develop a concern on the part of new workers to search out actively the possibilities for extending services and assistance to these persons.

Lectures[29] emphasized a "non-judgmental" approach to the applicant, the importance of providing emotional support in interviews, the "individualized" treatment of the applicant, and an "empathic" understanding of her problem. For example, one lecturer suggested that when confronted by a difficult, hostile or aggressive applicant, workers keep in mind the "horrendous life experiences" of such persons. They were urged to consider how the applicant's problems might be aggravated by financial difficulties, and it was stressed that the "good worker" should attempt to preserve the applicant's sense of dignity and self-worth.

Along with the attempt to orient the new worker to such an approach, the training program provides a course of instruction in the "mechanics" of the job, i.e., the regulations, policies, procedures and forms with which she must become familiar and skilled in using. However, the conditions under which the case worker's task is displayed in the training division

---

[29] The author was enrolled in the one-month training course and participated in all scheduled training sessions and lectures.

differs markedly from the conditions found in the operational setting. For example, in training, the novice deals with one case at a time, and is free to devote considerable time and effort to the details entailed in its processing under sympathetic supervision.[30]

Personnel of the Training Division were aware of the contrast between the training situation and the operational setting. Trainees were warned of the "reality shock" they would inevitably experience. It is interesting to note, in this connection, that in terms of the Training Division's criteria, those trainees who had spent less time in their respective district offices prior to reporting for training are considered to have performed best, i.e., proved to be more receptive to this favored orientation. This may indicate that those more experienced workers, and hence, those presumably more attuned to the "realities" of the task find the applicant-oriented approach less relevant to what they will be expected to accomplish on the job than instruction in the technical details of eligibility investigation and certification which is emphasized in the operational setting.

For example, one training supervisor spoke of four of her four "best trainees," i.e., trainees she believed to be talented, and committed to this orientation. Of the four, three had quit their jobs due to the difficulties encountered in pursuing this approach and the fourth, while still employed, was reported to be "despairing." Nonetheless, there was a marked concern among training personnel to indoctrinate new personnel in this "New Look" in public assistance (as it was sometimes called), presumably in the hope that some of them would be able to put it into practice.

There also appeared to be some degree of tension between district line personnel and the training staff. One supervisor at Lakeside exemplified this tension by defining the "New Look" (i.e., the approach of the Training Division) as "not following agency rules." Training supervisors, on the other hand, sometimes characterized line supervisors as "punitive," rule-bound types who took personal delight in denying an applicant's claim for public assistance.

The newer caseworker, who is most likely to adopt this approach by virtue of her recent attendance at the Training Division, is typically frustrated by the collision of her "uninformed" expectations with the enforced demands of her daily work. The first response to this frustration is typically to criticize the regulations and policies of the agency as constraints on providing the services seen to be needed by applicants.

30 New workers in the Lakeside Office commented on several occasions concerning the contrast between training and the actual task situation. One remarked that when she was in training she had time to make three home calls on each case, as opposed to only one in the operational setting. She regretted this, for she had enjoyed working with AFDC mothers and their problems. She added: "Why can't we give service? The sun goes up, the sun goes down, and you have another intake!"

Significantly, after the caseworker has acquired some experience in the agency, she begins to talk in "knowing ways" about the contest between her initial approach and what she has learned about the task (and applicants) subsequently. It appears to be the case that the applicant-oriented approach is not rountinely sustainable, which is to say, it cannot be adopted as a matter of course way of approaching the task.[31]

The Alternatives in Context

The contrast between the applicant-oriented and caseload-oriented approaches may be most clearly seen when viewed with respect to certain key aspects of case processing. They are "key aspects" in that they are points at which the approach taken is consequential for the outcome of case processing. These aspects are the control of information elicited (particularly in the intake interview), the stance taken with respect to the applicant's statements concerning her circumstances, and the management of applicant cooperation.[32]

1. The Control of Information. When the caseworker picks up her intake assignment at the reception counter, she assumes responsibility for an investigation which is to provide the organizationally warranted grounds for a decision on the case. The first step in this investigation is the intake interview. In many cases, this is the first contact between the worker and the applicant, and the way in which this first contact is managed is often consequential for the subsequent course of the investigation.

It is in this initial interview that the character of the applicant's problem is elicited, important information obtained, and necessary instructions given.[33] The intake interview may serve as a further screening as it sometimes occurs that information obtained in the interview permits a

[31] What is meant here is that adopting this stance requires "special effort." In order to pursue this approach, the worker must have a skilled grasp of procedure such that she can simultaneously satisfy the enforceable standards in the setting and honor her concerns to provide "service." This is a difficult task. One worker who practiced this approach had considerable experience in the Bureau, and hence was able to maintain acceptable standing on caseload and delinquency indices. Even she encountered difficulty, for her supervisor knew of her interests and regularly challenged her for getting "involved" with applicants and keeping her cases "longer than necessary."

[32] The construction of alternative approaches was guided by the question: What was involved in successful as against unsuccessful management of the caseload? The "criteria" of success were those observed to operate in the setting, e.g., supervisory approval, low delinquency and low caseload standings.

[33] "Necessary instructions" are those which direct the applicant to secure certain documentation, or take steps to produce required documents. For example, applicants may be instructed to contact the Social Security Administration for a statement of their monthly grant from that source, make application for Unemployment Insurance, or secure evidence that their benefits under that program have been exhausted. These are important steps in the process, since they will typically be required in most instances, and the case will not be disposed of until they are accomplished.

quick disposition of the case (e.g., the applicant may be found to be "obviously ineligible"). In any event, the character of the information obtained at this point — its adequacy and decisiveness with respect to the criteria of eligibility[34] — partially determines the dispatch with which the case may be decided. This is so if for no other reason than that failure to secure adequate information in the intake interview (or, at latest, in the subsequent homecall) and to issue the appropriate instructions to the applicant defining her role in securing information, entails further contact with the applicant at a later time and increases the risk of generating "difficulties" in the relationship between the applicant and the worker, and between the worker and supervisor.[35]

For the worker concerned with managing her caseload (the caseload-oriented approach) this entails assigning highest priority to the collection of information pertinent to eligibility, and controlling the interview accordingly. In terms of caseload priorities, control of the interview entails directing the applicant's remarks to matters pertaining to eligibility, and avoiding any extended discussion of the applicant's self-defined problem if it is deemed irrelevant to these issues.

The applicant-oriented approach, on the other hand, accords first priority to the issue of the applicant's problem as such, which then emerges as the controlling concern in processing the case. That is, the control over the information elicited — with respect to content, sequence, and elapsed time — is given over to the presenting problem. This typically represents an allocation of time and effort to matters not directly germane to the collection of information deemed pertinent by supervisors to the establishment of eligibility. This is one of the points of tension in the setting between the two alternative approaches, and it is recognized by workers. For example, one worker commented:

> I always try to avoid [placing a strong emphasis on eligibility] unless somebody really begins to give me a hard time. You have to point out to

34 A complexity insufficiently developed in this paper is the fact that the "adequacy" of an investigation with respect to the issue of eligibility consists of a judgment rendered upon some concrete occasion of review, and hence is a contingent and often revisable determination. See footnote 14.

35 The three main parties to this process, the applicant, the worker, and the worker's supervisor, may be said to have an interest in the speedy disposition of the application. The applicant's interest is given in her financial needs, for which she seeks assistance. The supervisor's interest also lies with a speedy disposition, but conditional to this is the establishment of eligibility. Should the worker's investigation be faulty in the eyes of the supervisor, she will typically issue a set of instructions for further investigation which the worker is obligated to follow. This often means further contact with the applicant and re-tracing the ground of previous interviews in a more detailed fashion. This, in turn, may lead to resentment and overt hostility on the part of the applicant who perceives this further investigation as sheer "red tape" or excessive suspiciousness on the part of the agency. The applicant's hostility may in turn generate resentment on the part of the worker, who is under pressure from the supervisor to decide the case.

them that we have so much time to work on this, this is what must be done, but I never throw it at them the first time. I know persons in this office who have a very small caseload because they are so cold and abrupt to people that they make them withdraw. . . . In the first interview, I have the feeling that this seems awfully cold and abrupt, just to get names and addresses and information and never listen to the real reason they have come in. I have heard workers on the phone. . . say, "Now, Mrs. Smith, just a minute, you listen to me. I want you to get this, one, two, three," and this is no exaggeration of their tone of voice. [She had affected a sharp, severe tone of voice.] To me, that isn't the way to treat people, but it is more efficient.

Another worker had a different view:

. . . if someone wants to go into "My mother comes over and we fight, and my husband, I think, is going out with this person and I think my child had this problem in school," they are not really pertinent to intake. They are in approved but not in intake and many workers will sit two and a half, three hours in an intake [interview] and just listen to this crap!

Accordingly, the prominent operational feature of the applicant-oriented approach may be formulated as the worker's practice of permitting the applicant's concern with her problem to control the course of the interaction. One consequence of this practice is the risk of failing early in the investigative process to secure necessary information, requiring subsequent contact with the applicant at a later time.

2. Stance. Directly related to the character of control exercised over the intake interview is the concern for documentation, and its consequences for the subsequent course of the investigation. The investigative emphasis[36] appears to require, at minimum, a *suspension of belief* in the truth or accuracy of the applicant's statements taken at face value and the commitment to the use of available procedures as the organizationally sanctionable means of resolving the issue of eligibility. It appears that, at least from the supervisory perspective, the investigative stance is more centrally one of the *presumption of ineligibility,* i.e., a readiness to see in the applicant's (unverified) statements and actions a motivated project to "manipulate" the agency for illegitimate ends.

The caseload-oriented approach, then, with respect to this aspect of case processing, accords primary emphasis to scrutiny of the applicant's statements for inconsistency or contradiction and a readiness to entertain the doubt that the situation is as it is presented. Commitment of belief and action is withheld prior to the establishment of documented proof of the "facts of the case." It appears to be the case that this willingness to doubt, and hence to raise a variety of issues for investigation in a given

---

[36] The "investigative emphasis" is discussed in detail in Zimmerman (*1966,* Chapter 5).

case, provides a way in which a case is made "investigatable." One worker, in discussing the GR application of a single man, unemployed for a considerable length of time, spoke of her doubts concerning his statements:

> I find it very questionable [that he could not relocate in a job, in a year and a half], particularly since he is in good health. A man who is trained in a trade, which he is, . . . that he might not find a job this week or last week all right, but . . . I don't accept that he could not find a job in that length of time. Some kind of a job. When I say I don't accept it, I don't mean I disbelieve him. I find it, ah, worthy of more closer scrutiny . . . I wanted to find out more information and clear up more of the story. I wanted to talk to [A.B., her supervisor] before I offered anything I might be sorry for, you know?[37]

The applicant-oriented approach, as suggested above, appears to involve a suspension of doubt, or, alternatively, a willingness to accept at face value the applicant's statements concerning her situation. From the supervisor's point of view, according first priority to the applicant's problem and the willingness to accept her statements as correct are seen as related in a particular fashion. One supervisor spoke of what she felt was a tendency for the workers in her unit to be "manipulated" by applicants. Manipulation was seen by her to involve the applicant's inducement of guilt in the worker over her plight, and for the worker to identify with the applicant rather than the agency (i.e., assigning first priority to the applicant's problem). As a consequence, applicants were seen as able to "sell" the worker on their stories, who try in turn to "sell" the supervisor, "contrary to the testimony of the case record." In the supervisor's words, workers "try to sell me a story that the client only wants temporary aid when there is a fat record on the desk." It may be inferred from the nature of the supervisor's comments that such an approach to a case is negatively sanctioned, and furthermore, is named as a particular type of trouble that a worker might get herself into (i.e., being "manipulated").

3. Applicant Cooperation. Related to the issue of the determination of eligibility is the concern that the applicant's cooperation in the processing of the case be effectively managed. As indicated elsewhere, the applicant is assigned a crucial role in the establishment of her own eligibility, i.e., she is required to cooperate in providing information essential

---

[37] The concern to "clear up more of the story" and to check with the supervisor illustrates the withholding of the commitment of belief and action in the absence of verification. This practice anticipates a kind of trouble the alternative approach — which does commit belief and action early in the process — is open to: promising the applicant certain assistance which may be delayed or withheld altogether due to the worker's failure to address promptly the issues of eligibility (e.g., "diligent" search for employment) for which the supervisor will hold her accountable.

257

to the documentation of her case, and, as the situation may dictate, take the steps necessary to generate further documentation.[38]

"Effective management" of the applicant's cooperation appears to involve the explicit structuring of the course of investigation to be undertaken and the role in it of the applicant. She is to be instructed in clear terms what her "responsibilities" are, and informed of the fact that the approval of the case is contingent upon her fulfilling these responsibilities.[39]

This "management" of the applicant is seen by supervisors to be an essential part of expeditious case processing. As a caseload oriented strategy, enforcement of this cooperation provides a resource for disposing of the case, both by reason of the fact that the applicant may thus be "motivated" to cooperate in anticipation of the consequences of not doing so, and if she is not so motivated, the case may be denied (and thus disposed of) on these grounds.

In contrast, the applicant-oriented approach is characterized by a more permissive management of the applicant's cooperation in the process of establishing eligibility. This permissiveness appears to be motivated by the view that the applicant is a troubled person, perhaps incompetent in matters others could deal with as a matter of course. Hence, there is the disposition to "excuse" the applicant if she is hostile, uncooperative, or repeatedly fails to follow through on the instructed courses of action relevant to documenting the case. The consequence of this permissiveness is, often, to extend the length of time the worker must deal with the case.

Emphasis on applicant responsibility, on the other hand, appeared to be related to the view that the applicant's conduct, whatever its character, is primarily motivated by the interest in securing assistance whether entitled to it or not. Of course, particular cases would often be recognized as technically difficult without specific reference to the applicant's conduct. The favored view, however, is that encountered difficulties are motivated ones, to be managed by imposing strict requirements for cooperation on the part of the applicant.

The Practical Bases for Choice Among Alternative Approaches

In terms of the preceding discussion, the worker who adopts the applicant-oriented approach to her caseload encounters both troubles and

---

[38] For example, if her capacity to maintain gainful employment is at issue, she must go to the "Work Test Clinic" established by the County for an examination by a physician to determine if this is the case. She may be required to apply for Unemployment Insurance benefits in some instances, or to contact certain third parties whose testimony is deemed relevant, and so on.

[39] There is considerable concern that such structuring be a part of the case record. If the applicant's cooperation is deemed to be inadequate, and the case denied on these grounds, such a record would stand as the warrant for that action.

sanctions as a consequence. She runs the considerable risk of accumulating a caseload as well as incurring the displeasure of her supervisor. These two facts alone would seem to render this approach a difficult basis for guiding action in the setting as constituted. But perhaps even more persuasive is the progressive "disillusionment,"[40] with the applicant that often comes about.

It is necessary to examine the role of the applicant in the process and the character of her practical interests in its outcome from the point of view of "experienced" members of the organization. Applicants are thought to have a vital interest in securing assistance. For a variety of reasons, it is assumed that they find it in their interest to omit certain details concerning their circumstances, falsify or misrepresent information, and so on.[41]

A typical complaint voiced by supervisors is that new workers (i.e., those workers most likely to hold to the applicant-oriented approach) fail to properly appreciate this "fact," and moreover, fail to grasp the point that organizationally warranted procedures are available whereby the "facts of the case" may be decided in a fashion presumptively independent of the applicant's interest in its outcome. Hence, the supervisor typically attempts to get the worker to realize this by forcing her to follow through a course of investigation which has as a possible outcome the discrediting of the applicant's claim, and often, of the applicant herself.

As the possibility of applicant duplicity comes to be appreciated by the worker, the character of the applicant's problem as she presents it often becomes subject to a different and organizationally persuasive interpretation. Since it may, from this altered perspective, be suspected that the applicant is attempting to "manage" the course of the interaction in the interest of securing assistance, her "problem" in its detail and declared urgency may emerge for the worker as a facility for the applicant in such a project. That is, the worker may come to *see* the applicant's asserted "problem" as potentially employable by her as an instrumental means to control the investigation in accordance with her interests. Further, the worker may see in retrospect that in disregard of caseload considerations, she had committed action and belief in the past in particular cases where now it was clear that after all and all along such commitment was mistaken. The interpretation is available to her that

40 See Blau (*1960*, pp. 347–351).

41 It should be made clear here that these remarks do not imply anything about what is "really the case" with the applicant. What is "really the case" cannot be viewed apart from the particular, sanctioned methods whereby "what is really the case" is determined. That the applicant is highly motivated to secure assistance, even to the point of falsification of her statements, and that investigation can reveal discrepancies in her story are "facts" about applicants generated from the perspective of the caseload-oriented approach.

had she but relied upon the very procedures and investigative concerns which she had previously relegated to secondary importance, such mistaken commitment (and its consequences) could have been avoided.

To continue to make the assumption of applicant "honesty" is to run the risk of being shown (in some number of cases) as one who was duped. To accept this risk incurs the possibility of being seen to be a "fool," i.e., as one who disregards a "fact of life" known by any competent person in the setting, namely, that applicants sometimes lie, and most particularly, that procedures exist whereby it is possible to "determine" this. Even more critically, to continue to ignore this "fact," and thereby to invest time in cases that might otherwise be resolved expeditiously, brings a variety of troubles which also might be avoided, and which are desirable to avoid.

Reliance upon the investigative procedures of the agency, as was seen above, renders specifically relevant the character of the applicant's cooperation in the process. Should the applicant's conduct pose problems for the collection of information, dealing with that conduct becomes a salient issue. It was noted that the applicant-oriented approach is characterized by permissiveness in this regard. If, however, in the process of disillusionment, such "obstructive" conduct comes to be seen, as is likely, to be a project to obfuscate the issues addressed by the investigation, or in some cases, as blind, purposeless hostility, such permissiveness may be less automatically granted.

This process of disillusionment must be understood in terms of the practical considerations generated by the fact of a caseload and the character of performance standards in the setting. It has already been indicated that a number of difficulties follow upon the accumulation of a caseload, and that the applicant-oriented approach is characterized by practices which entail the risk of such accumulation. Furthermore, in terms of the prevailing concerns relevant to performance in the setting, great emphasis is placed upon the investigation of eligibility, the reduction of caseloads, and the minimization of delinquency. Disillusionment is generated by these features of the setting in the following ways.

First, the applicant-oriented approach, while according a secondary emphasis caseload considerations, cannot put them aside altogether — in order to file the case, for example, the worker must satisfy her supervisor that the applicant is eligible. One consequence of this approach is to defer that definitive resolution longer, resulting in an accumulating caseload. The fact remains, however, that for some portion of cases, retaining them in the file for any period of time will not in the end change the outcome. In those cases in which it subsequently becomes evident that the applicant was duplicitous, concealing or distorting information that had it been known would have clearly made her ineligible, the worker's commitment of time and energy, and the consequences following from that commitment, may come to be seen by her as a costly investment, the more so since the applicants turned out not to be deserving of it "all along."

Second, in terms of caseload considerations taken by themselves, as the press of work demands and the application of sanctions are felt, workers appear to be less and less patient with applicants who, by their conduct, display apparent disregard for the worker's problems in processing the case. As the worker comes to recognize the "costs" of alternative ways of allocating priorities and effort, she appears to become resentful if the applicant does not "appreciate" what she is doing for her, and show this appreciation by cooperating more fully.

Furthermore, the worker's election not to accord first priority to caseload considerations in processing a case (or simply her failure to do so) renders organizationally ambiguous the assignment of responsibility for any difficulty encountered in the working of the case. If the worker has not explicitly structured the processing of the case in these terms, and if this structuring is not a matter of record, this alternative is not readily available. Hence, should the investigation of a case become prolonged due to the worker's permissiveness toward a difficult applicant (e.g., one who is hostile, aggressive, and has not cooperated in providing information), the supervisor is likely to seek an accounting of the source of the "troubles."

If the troubles seem to be generated by the applicant's conduct, supervisors typically read such difficulties as consequent to the applicant's attempt to "work" the agency, particularly if the applicant is invoking the desperate character of her situation as a higher priority consideration than her legal entitlement to assistance. The supervisor's specific response to the difficulty at hand is in part a function of the supervisor's perception of the role of the worker in the encountered difficulty. Insofar as the worker appears unduly sympathetic with the applicant, or has indicated a willingness to "go along" with her or honor the desperate character of her situation as a prior consideration to the demands of the eligibility investigation, she may be seen to be undergoing "manipulation" by the applicant, or to be "personally involved."[42] This constitutes a defect in the caseworker's management of the case from the supervisor's perspective, and her response to this is usually the specification of further steps in the investigation. She typically sets forth a set of issues to be resolved by some form of documentation, and instructs the worker to inform the ap-

---

[42] Evidence of "impersonality" in the processing of cases is provided by the worker's manifest assignment of priority to the issue of eligibility invariant to other possible considerations.

plicant in a firm manner that these issues must be resolved, and that she must cooperate in their resolution, or the case will be denied.

The supervisor's assignment of such a stance to the worker (i.e., "being involved") results in what may be called "close supervision." This close supervision is called forth by the supervisor's concern that the worker's employment at such a tactic will typically result in excessive caseloads, delinquencies, improperly worked cases, and as a consequence, delay in the provision of financial assistance to those applicants eligible to it.

Summary and Conclusions

It has been seen that the organization of the caseworker's task, as it unfolds in day-to-day operations, is such that the addition of new cases, and hence, further work to be done, proceeds with predictable regularity without reference to the status of cases previously added and the work that remains to be done on them. A persistent feature of the worker's circumstance, one she can count on, is the regular influx of new work invariant to the demands of her current caseload.

While the occurrence of the intake day, and the work entailed by it, is relatively routinized, the occasions of "work to be done" of various sorts on previously added cases is neither rigidly scheduled nor temporally predictable. Furthermore, the worker's caseload is typically uneven, both with respect to the stage of the investigative process for a given case and in terms of the amount of work required to resolve the issue of eligibility. The cases in the worker's file may present themselves to her under a number of different aspects at different times and with different degrees of urgency. Such features, in conjunction with others to be reviewed below, confer upon the work day a somewhat "hectic," even "chaotic" character from the point of view of personnel.

Such a work situation may be conceived as posing problems of temporal coordination and allocation for the worker. Part of this problem is given by the fact that many occasions in which she will be required to gear her activities to others are out of her manipulative control. The intake day is one such occasion. With respect to the occurrence of "emergencies" in her caseload, these too may require her immediate attention, and involve contacts with the applicant, with her supervisor, and concerned third parties. The supervisor may require a review of one or more of her cases; a previously denied case may be appealed, requiring a session with the assistant director, and so on. She must deal with the requirement of scheduling initial and final dictations, which entails gearing to the dictation needs of others in her unit since dictating machines are allocated on the basis of one per unit.

Scheduling her activities is a problem inasmuch as she has work to be done in a certain way and in a certain time, and the scheduling of her effort is consequential for the outcome of this work. She is subject to the prevailing standards of adequate performance in the setting, which as sanctioned evaluations of the adequacy of her work define the character of both favorable and unfavorable outcomes.

Considerable concern is focused on the documentation of eligibility. The supervisor typically requires of her worker that the details of the applicant's circumstances be documented, and that it be established that the applicant is legally entitled to assistance. This requires attention to the formulation of the cases as an investigable matter, and to the timely initiation of the documentary processes which will satisfy the questions posed by this formulation.

Making a case investigable entails the appreciation, first of all, that the applicant might be motivated to misrepresent her circumstances, and, in the particular case, the appreciation of what features of the applicant's circumstances must be investigated to affirm or disconfirm this doubt. This may be a relatively simple matter, or it may involve an extended and complex investigation.

The problem of temporal coordination and allocation, taken together with the enforced requirement for detailed documentation of the applicant's circumstances, focuses practical concern on those elements of the task which are within the worker's manipulative control. Within the context of the scheduled intake interview, it was suggested that a crucial concern for the worker attuned to her practical circumstances and committed to act in accordance with the interests generated by them was the control of information elicited in the interview. This provides one way to manage, or bring under control, the temporal development of the case, for to address herself to the collection of information requisite to the documentary process early in the history of the case provides for the likelihood that a decision may be reached earlier. The disposition of the case at the earliest possible moment (i.e., reducing the caseload) provides a way to reduce the aggregate demand on her time and hence alleviate her scheduling problems. Failure to accord priority to this element of the task increases, as was seen, the risk of an unfavorable outcome, i.e., an extended course of investigation which may have consequences for the size of the caseworker's aggregate caseload and occasion supervisory intervention in the case.

A further step in the worker's control of the caseload is the assumption of an investigatory stance toward the information elicited. That is, the information collected as a representation of the applicant's circumstances must be treated as a matter to be investigated, rather than to be accepted on its face. Not only will this be required of the worker by her supervisor, but the adoption of such a stance may result in an early disposition of a case which otherwise might have remained in the caseload for a longer time (given that an investigation will at some point be insisted on).

Correlative to the above is the management of applicant cooperation. It was seen that the applicant's role in the documentation of a case is viewed as crucial to the timely resolution of the issue of eligibility. In the first instance, the applicant must tell her story. She must then provide the documents necessary to verify the story, or lacking them, provide the information required to secure them. The readiness with which this cooperation is forthcoming is a factor in the speed with which the case may be decided. Should the applicant be reticent, hostile, or uncooperative, this will typically result in a delay of the disposition of the case unless steps are taken to enforce cooperation. Such steps are typically the instruction to the applicant that such and such must be accomplished within a specified time, or the case will be denied. The practical advantage of managing the applicant in this fashion is not only the expediting of the case, but the specification of a clear priority of the investigation and its outcome over the matter of dealing with the applicant's need. That is, effective treatment of the applicant's need is made contingent upon the adequate resolution of her entitlement for assistance. This permits the worker to control yet another kind of demand on her time while serving her practical interest in reducing her caseload and minimizing her delinquent filings.

These considerations suggest that the intent and operational meaning of rules, policies, procedures, and the like, are provided by members' practices dealing with the practicalities of action in the setting. It was noted that different "interpretations" of the task and its constituent procedural rules were available for choice in the office. The sanctionability of the choice was seen to be related to its consequences for the adequate management of the practical circumstances circumscribing the task. It was intimated that such matters as applicant motivation, the priority to be assigned to the applicant's presenting problem, the length of time an investigation would be pursued, the latitude of permissible applicant conduct, and the like were operational decisions closely related to the management of the practical features of the task.

In short, the selection of one as against the other "alternative" appeared to result in a different organization of the task as an ensemble of related operations, and in a different perception of the applicant as an ensemble of related motivational characteristics. Election of the caseload-oriented approach, for example, operationally consisted in the assignment of a different set of priorities to the elements of the task, and following from that assignment, a different "interpretation" of the rules governing the task, than was the case with the election of the other alternative. Similarly, the election of one or the other alternative provided for differing "interpretations" of applicant conduct as it related to the pursuit of the task.[43]

The choice elected by caseworkers was observed to be a matter of serious consequence. It was not in the nature of an option available to personnel as a matter of mere personal preference. The recognition by other personnel of the alternative chosen by a given worker, accomplished on the basis of daily interactions in the setting in which the worker's conduct of the task was displayed, bore upon the assessment of the worker's grasp of the commonly known and taken for granted "facts of life" in the setting available as a sanctioned scheme of interpretation for deciding the "necessary" perspective on the character of the task and the "real" motives of applicants encountered under its auspices.

To follow out the implications of this observation (and move at the same time somewhat beyond the data presented here) it may be suggested that the choice displayed by the chooser's pursuit of the task was crucial upon occasions of supervisory review when it was necessary to decide that the investigation conducted was "objective" in its execution, that "factually" warranted grounds could be asserted for the decision reached, that the worker's "personal interests" in the outcome of the case were demonstrably independent of its actual outcome, and that throughout the course of work the worker conducted her activities in such a fashion as to indicate an abiding concern for the constraints of available organizational resources and the adequate for all practical purposes allocation of efforts within these constraints, i.e., "efficiency." In brief, it appeared that the production and recognition of organizational activities displaying the features of "administrative rationality" were intimately related to this "choice."[44]

References

Anonymous (1946). "Informal Social Organization in the Army," *American Journal of Sociology*, LI (March).

Bensman, Joseph, and Israel Gerver (1963). "Crime and Punishment in the Factory: The Function of Deviance in Maintaining the Social System," *American Sociological Review*, 28 (August).

Bittner, Egon (1965). "The Concept of Organization," *Social Research*, 32 (August).

43 The term "interpretation" has been placed in quotes to alert the reader to the fact that it is being employed as a gloss for the practices members use to decide that particular environmental displays are to be counted as appearances of this or that social object, accountable to this or that rule, etc.

44 It should be explicitly stated that the features of "administrative rationality" referred to here are those recognized as such by competent members of the organization through their engagement in the socially organized practices whereby such features are detected and demonstrated. See Garfinkel (*1965*) and also Garfinkel (*1960*, pp. 72–81) for a general discussion of the concept of "rational action."

Blau, Peter M. (1960). "Orientations Toward Clients in a Public Welfare Agency," *Administrative Science Quarterly*, 5 (December).

―――― (1963). *The Dynamics of Bureaucracy*, University of Chicago Press.

Cicourel, Aaron V. (1964). *Method and Measurement in Sociology*, Free Press.

―――― (1968). *The Social Organization of Juvenile Justice*, Wiley.

Cohen, Harry (1962). *The Demonics of Bureaucracy: A Study of a Government Employment Agency*, unpublished Ph.D dissertation, University of Illinois.

Dalton, Melville (1959). *Men Who Manage*, Wiley.

Garfinkel, Harold (1959). "Aspects of the Problem of Common-Sense Knowledge of Social Structures," *Transactions of the Fourth World Congress of Sociology*, IV, Milan and Stressa.

―――― (1960). "The Rational Properties of Scientific and Common Sense Activities," *Behavioral Science*, 5 (January).

―――― (1962). "Common Sense Knowledge of Social Structure: The Documentary Method of Interpretation" in *Theories of the Mind*, Jordan M. Scher (ed.), Free Press.

―――― (1964). "Studies of the Routine Grounds of Everyday Activities," *Social Problems*, 2 (Winter).

―――― (1965). "Remarks on Ethnomethodology," unpublished paper distributed to the members of the Methodology Section, American Sociological Annual Meeting (August 30).

―――― 1967a). "Practical Sociological Reasoning: Some Features in the Work of the Los Angeles Suicide Prevention Center" in *Essays in Self Destruction*, Edwin S. Schneidman (ed.), Ronald Press.

―――― (1967b). *Studies in Ethnomethodology*, Prentice-Hall.

Garfinkel, Harold, and Lindsey Churchill (1964). "Some Features of Decision Making in Common-Sense Situations of Choice," unpublished research proposal, Department of Sociology, University of California, Los Angeles.

Gouldner, Alvin W. (1955). *Patterns of Industrial Bureaucracy*, Routledge and Kegan Paul.

Page, Charles H. (1946). "Bureaucracy's Other Face," *Social Forces*, 25 (October).

Roy, Donald F. (1954). "Efficiency and 'The Fix,' Informal Intergroup Relations in a Piecework Machine Shop," *American Journal of Sociology*, LX (November).

Scheff, Thomas J. (1962). "Differential Displacement of Treatment Goals in a Mental Hospital," *Administrative Science Quarterly*, 7 (September).

Turner, Ralph H. (1947). "The Navy Disbursing Officer as a Bureaucrat," *American Sociological Review*, 12 (June).

Zawecki, John Stanley (1963). *The System of Unofficial Rules of a Bureaucracy: A Study of Hospitals*, unpublished Ph.D. dissertation, University of Pittsburgh.

Zimmerman, Don H. (1966). *Paper Work and People Work: A Study of a Public Assistance Agency*, unpublished Ph.D. dissertation, University of California, Los Angeles.

―――― (forthcoming). "The Practicalities of Rule-Use," in *Contributions to Ethnomethodology*, Harold Garfinkel and Harvey Sacks (eds.), Indiana University Press.

9 | HEROES AND HOPELESSNESS IN A TOTAL INSTITUTION:
Anomie Theory Applied to a Collective Disturbance on a Psychiatric Ward

Robert Perrucci / Purdue University

Large-scale organizations such as universities, hospitals, prisons, and the like, embrace such a large segment of the lives of their participants that they have been referred to as total institutions. Members of these organizations include those such as students, patients, and inmates who come voluntarily and involuntarily because of some common characteristic and those such as teachers, physicians, and staff who handle the "machinery" of the organization that is designed to deal with that common characteristic. A portion of the energies of such organizations is devoted to the goal of educating, healing, or rehabilitating. It is intriguing, however, how such organizations, quite independent of the intentions of those running the organization, often continue to encourage that which they are designed to eliminate. Students become disillusioned with education and leave; patients get worse rather than better; and prisoners become more dedicated to their unorthodox careers. It is difficult to know when organizations are contributing to such unwilled ends because it is difficult to separate the attributes of individuals from influence of the organizations: Do students drop out of school because they cannot do the work or because the environment is sterile and stifling; do patients deteriorate because of physiological processes or social-psychological processes; do inmates return to prison because they are "hardened" criminals or because other alternatives have not been made available.

There is, however, one situation which has the potential for revealing when an organization is not operating in the manner in which it was intended. Collective disturbances such as student unrest or prison riots are revealing for what they tell us about the organization, rather than the characteritsics of its members. Internal disorders and the breakdown of social control in institutional settings have long provided excellent opportunities for analysis of the sources of strain and stability in a social system. Studies maintaining this focus have been concerned with what they have called a "collective disturbance" or a "riot." These terms indicate that the phenomenon is not an individual disturbance or an aggregate of individual disturbances, but a disturbance which has a contagious element that is transmitted in an interpersonal context. As Stanton and Schwartz (*1954*, p. 382) describe it, "the collective disturbance involves the participation of a number of people in such a way that *the disturbance of one patient is integrated with the disturbance of many other patients.*"

In seeking to locate the elements involved in a collective disturbance on a psychiatric ward, Stanton and Schwartz (*1954*, Chapter 17) focus primarily upon covert staff disagreements and disruptions of normal communication channels. The consequences of these internal disruptions were increased disturbances of many patients, the magnifying of staff problems such as errors in technique, distorted messages, increased absenteeism, and the partial withdrawal of staff members from normal participation on the ward. Similarly, Caudill (*1958*) focuses attention on the strains created by an imbalance between affective and cognitive communication among staff members. This, in turn, led to staff disagreements which were still, for the most part, covert and unexpressed. That is, the disagreements tended to "attach themselves" to discussions of plans for individual patients, who then became the vehicles through which the disagreements were expressed. A later stage in the disturbance was characterized by the mutual withdrawal of staff groups which cut the channels of communication between patients and staff, and within staff groups. The still covert nature of the disagreements led to the formation of various support-seeking coalitions, which Caudill labels as "paired role group responses." The final "restitution" phase, or the return to equilibrium, occurred when the "real" disagreements between staff members were openly discussed.

Looking at prison riots, Bates (*1953*) suggests that one of the direct causes of the tensions which contribute to riot and disorder is the enforced idleness of the inmates. His hypothesis suggests that a certain amount of free-floating tension will, from time to time, manifest itself in various types of disturbances.

Lacking in these discussions of collective disturbances is any explicit analysis of the disturbances in light of the sociological concept of anomie. That is, there is relatively little discussion of the disturbance in terms of the state of the system as it operates as a mechanism of social control. For example, the Stanton and Schwartz definition of a collective disturbance could very well include the case of an individually disturbed patient who upsets other patients by her presence and behavior. Thus, the contagious aspect of the disturbance might develop only because other patients get upset by the simple presence of a patient in their midst who is extremely disturbed, hostile, or critical of others. This possibility is strongly suggested in both the Stanton and Schwartz and Caudill studies, in that each of them presents the situation of an especially disturbed or obnoxious patient or patients as key figures in the overall collective disturbance.

We shall offer in this paper an explanation of the collective disturbance as a condition of a social system. That is, we focus upon a *chronic* condition of a system in which various aspects of its social and cultural structure are likely to produce a breakdown of social control — a condition in which the system is so arranged that it continually contains the "seeds" of its own disequilibrium. In this analysis, emphasis will be on an aspect of Durkheim's concept of anomie which has received relatively little attention from sociologists as well as clinicians.

Means, Ends and Anomie

When the normative systems of a society fail to influence and direct the behavior of its members we may say there is an absence of social control. Individual behavior is no longer a response to collective definitions of the "appropriate," but is, rather, a case of individual determination of behavior. Perhaps the single most important study dealing with the breakdown of normative control is Durkheim's *Suicide* (1951). Durkheim was primarily concerned with analyzing the situation in which the means and ends of individual behavior no longer correspond to the normative definitions of means and ends. When the ends of individual action are no longer subject to normative definitions, that is, when a state of *de-regulation* of behavior exists, society is said to be in a state of anomie.

Durkheim identified two general conditions in the means-ends system of behavior that give rise to a state of de-regulation. The first refers to a condition where, due to acute changes in society, e.g., economic crises, the means and ends of a system of action that existed *prior* to the crises no longer work. That is, the links between means and ends are inappropriate in a new social context; behavior which once "paid off," i.e., yielded a desirable end, is no longer applicable to the new situation. With economic crises, both booms and depressions, Durkheim suggests that "something like a declassification occurs":

> Then, truly, as the conditions of life are changed, the standard according to which most needs are regulated can no longer remain the same. . . . The scale is upset; but a new scale cannot be immediately improvised. Time is

required for the public conscience to reclassify men and things. So long as the social forces thus freed have not regained equilibrium, their respective values are unknown and so all regulation is lacking for a time. The limits are unknown between the possible and the impossible, what is just and what is unjust, legitimate claims and the hopes of those who are immoderate. Consequently, there is no restraint upon aspirations (pp. 252–253).

The second condition discussed by Durkheim refers only to the ends or goals of action. Here we find a description of goals which can never be attained; a condition of unattainability of goals because the goals are by definition unattainable. Referring to this point, he wrote:

Appetites, not being controlled by public opinion become disoriented, no longer recognize the limits proper to them. . . . But then their very demands make fulfillment impossible. Overweening ambition always exceeds the results obtained, great as they may be, since there is no warning to pause here. Nothing gives satisfaction and all this agitation is uninterruptedly maintained without appeasement. Above all, since this race for an unattainable goal can give no other pleasure but that of the race itself, if it is one, once it is interrupted the participants are left empty-handed. At the same time the struggle grows more violent and painful, both from being less controlled and because competition is greater (p. 253).

That is, it is not a case where the means and ends of action are out of joint and must be readjusted, it is a case where the goals could not be attained by any goal-directed means.

Durkheim's analysis of anomie received its fullest elaboration in the now well known essay by Merton (*1957*) entitled, "Social Structure and Anomie." In addressing himself to the social and cultural sources of deviant behavior, Merton has focused upon the first condition of anomie raised by Durkheim: that the means and ends of action are distributed in society in such a way as to make certain sought-after ends unattainable. As Merton states:

Anomie . . . is a breakdown in the cultural structure, occurring particularly when there is an acute disjunction between the cultural norms and goals and the socially structured capacities of members of the group to act in accord with them. In this conception, cultural values may help to produce the behavior which is at odds with the mandates of the values themselves (p. 162).

The emphasis by Merton is on the pressure for deviant behavior which is the result of the selection of normatively *proscribed* means for the attainment of cultural goals. This outcome of anomie results in a disruption of the normative system in its effectiveness in ensuring "conforming" behavior. However, it should be noted that the pressures for deviant behavior produce the deviant adaptations primarily within the lower classes. Thus, it is possible that the existence of deviant adaptations may in fact *reinforce* the legitimacy of the normative system for the larger society precisely because compliance with *prescribed* means does result in the attainment of desired goals. Put differently, we are suggesting that the existence of deviant adaptations which are the result of the way the system is organized, does not necessarily question the legitimacy or moral fiber of the system. Clearly, the deviant has not utilized the appropriate means for attaining his ends, and as long as the system contains examples that appropriate means are available and *do work,* the action of the deviant can only deserve the moral disapproval of the society. For example, even though it may be recognized that the lower strata are economically disadvantaged and have fewer chances to attain higher education, there is a sufficient masking overlay from the open class ideology and from examples of the rags to riches success story.[1]

The question we are raising here, in a roundabout way, is this: under what conditions is the legitimacy of the normative system questioned? When will the actors in the system no longer comply with the normative definitions of acceptable means and ends governing behavior? This involves a broader type of normative disruption than concerns Merton. We are thinking here of the kind of moral sickness or *malaise* described by Durkheim. Individual reactions to such a condition are best described by terms like demoralization or disenchantment. Under such conditions, the legitimacy of norms is discredited, and the usefulness of the existing institutionalized system is questioned.[2]

We suggest that the system will be blamed, so to speak, for failures to attain cultural goals primarily under conditions where *prescribed and culturally appropriate means have been utilized and the expected ends are still not forthcoming.* It is under these conditions that the normative system is put to the test and found to be lacking while in the Merton paradigm, the normative system is not *necessarily* shaken. Here is where we see the second condition of anomie discussed by Durkheim; namely, where the goals are unattainable because of the *nature of the goal,* and

---

[1] It is also possible that those who do follow the deviant adaptation are also unable to blame the system for their personal difficulties. Since they have probably had some exposure to examples of "those who have made it" via appropriate means, they can turn to such adaptations as self-blame, withdrawal, transferring aspirations to children, stressing luck, chance and fatalistic ideologies, and out-group hostility. Each of these adaptations functions to blame everything but the existing institutional structure.

[2] It should be noted, that the discussion here is very close to Merton's *(1957)* "Rebellion" mode of adaptation. He states: "When the institutional system is regarded as a barrier to the satisfaction of legitimized goals, the stage is set for rebellion as an adaptive response" (p. 156). The precise question we are asking is: *When is the institutional system regarded as a barrier?* We suggested earlier, that under Merton's means-ends paradigm the legitimacy of the existing system need not be questioned. Merton implies that the prerequisite for rebellion is a stage of "awareness" or "consciousness" of faults of the system. In this sense, then, our question resembles the Marxian concern of looking for the specific social conditions which are necessary for the proletariat to "see" the factors influencing his class situation.

271

irrespective of the means of attainment utilized. However, we are primarily concerned here with the situation where the means used and the goal pursued are *both* culturally approved, yet they do not work when they become part of an individual's behavioral system. Several sources of evidence in existing sociological literature may illustrate more clearly the idea we are concerned with here; some are explicitly developed, while others are only suggestions of evidence which seem to fit our framework.

The analysis of inspirational religious literature by Schneider and Dornbusch (*1958*) focuses in large part upon the process of "de-religionization." Aside from the fact that the authors identify a strong secular bent in popular religion, they also describe a "de-religionizing" process which they link to what they call a "spiritual technology." This process involves the conscious pursuit of certain goals as expected results or benefits of religious activity. As the authors put it:

> These desired ends [health, wealth, happiness and "peace of mind"], however, time after time have come to realization in the form of *latent* functions of religion, that is, in the form of not-deliberately-sought consequences of religious activity undertaken, again, for reasons having little or nothing to do with the consequences themselves or with any foresight thereof (p. 67).

Thus, we find the pursuit of goals which are by definition unattainable put within the framework of instrumental means. The implication of this process is that to turn religious activity into an expectation of certain ends, through an explicit means-ends system of action, is to "eat away" at the very foundations of religious commitment when these ends are not forthcoming:

> It is an intriguing speculation that, when faith lapses, the things it may ordinarily achieve for us without any particular thought or effort on our part become objects of technologically oriented behavior. The speculation is of interest both within and outside of religion. It has been suggested that preoccupation with the technology of sexual intercourse is likely to occur when love has become a problematic and dubious matter, as well as that technologies of child-rearing appear to flourish when "natural" love for children is no longer an easy and spontaneous thing. Similar considerations may apply in the field of religion. If this speculation has any merit, then the emergence of a technological orientation in certain fields of human concern may be interpreted as in some sense a sign of "degeneration." Unfortunately, our knowledge on these matters is exceedingly meager (p. 70).

Additional suggestive evidence can be found in Mizruchi's (*1964*, pp. 92ff) study dealing with a test of the Merton hypothesis on social structure and anomie. In one part of the study, Mizruchi explored the relationship between scores on Srole's anomie scale and income (above or below $5,000) with education held constant. For grade school graduates there is no association between anomie and income, and for high school graduates a moderate association. However, for the college graduates the strongest pattern of association is found. This suggests that for those persons who utilize appropriate institutionalized means (education) *without* attaining the expected cultural rewards (increased income) the consequence of disenchantment with the system (i.e., high anomie scores) is more likely. For those who have not used the appropriate institutionalized means (grade school and high school graduates) there is less expectation of certain ends, and hence less disenchantment when rewards are not forthcoming.

Similarly, research done on the relationship between social class origins and intra-occupational mobility of professional engineers suggests that non-attainment of goals after the utilization of appropriate means is associated with the social origins of the engineers (*Perrucci, 1961*). Engineers of lower class origins are more likely to experience limitations on the extent to which they can "move up" in their own profession. A social structure which imposes what Drake and Cayton (*1945*) have called "the job ceiling" on occupational opportunities for persons who *have not* used the appropriate means for "moving up" may be legitimized; but a social structure which imposes such restraints on certain groups of persons (e.g., the engineers of lower class origin) who *have* utilized the appropriate means, would seem less likely to provide support for the inequities.

What we have suggested then, is that the Merton paradigm for anomie focuses upon structural constraints which lead to *deviation* from normative patterns of behavior. When, as Merton (*1957*, p. 135) states, "the technically most effective procedure for the attainment of culture goals, whether culturally legitimate or not, becomes typically preferred to institutionally prescribed conduct," a state of anomie or normlessness will result. However, while these socio-cultural conditions may lead to deviant adaptations, it is not necessarily true that it will result in a general rejection of the "moral rightness" of acting in accord with the normative system, i.e., the legitimacy of the system. For as Merton himself has indicated, these deviant adaptations tend to become *localized* to various segments of the social structure; a feature which may, in turn, serve to further reinforce the existing normative system.

Thus, we would offer the hypothesis that *conformity* to a culturally legitimized and approved set of institutionalized means and culture goals, *when the goals are not realized,* will be more likely to result in disenchantment with and/or rejection of the institutionalized system than will *deviation* from the normative prescriptions as evidenced in the selection of the most effective means, whether culturally legitimate or not. We shall try to illustrate the relevance of this hypothesis in examining the events leading to a collective disturbance on a psychiatric ward.[3]

Some Preconditions for the Disturbance

A good many of the patients on a psychiatric ward have been through the "treatment mill." During present and previous hospitalizations, they have been exposed to one or another of the physical, chemical, mechanical, or analytic psychotherapies available in psychiatric practice. It is by no means unusual to find patients who have had insulin shock, electro-shock, lobotomy, group psychotherapy, individual psychotherapy, drugs, and assorted occupational and recreational psychotherapies. Given the considerable amount of existing treatment that has already been received by most patients, what can one expect of the ward physician who has the responsibility of trying to provide some therapeutic program for these patients? It is not unusual for a ward physician to adopt the pose of the surgeon who has just completed a difficult operation saying, "I've done all I can, it's out of my hands now." The responsibility for getting "well" again somehow winds up in the hands of the patients themselves. As one physician put it, in speaking of the patients: "A lot of them here are somewhere between the hospital and the community, but they won't get off the seat of their pants. If they don't make a move, there's nothing we can do for them." Similarly, the ward physician, in response to the numerous questions such as, "When can I go home," or "Am I getting any better," or "Do you think I'm ready to go to staff," will generally respond, "I can't tell you that, Mary; you've got to tell me when you're ready to go home."

In many respects, then, the patient is thrown back on her own resources to get estimates of just how well she is or isn't doing. Patients thus become overly sensitive to the little nuances of staff behavior that they take to be signs full of various meanings. For example, in an attempt to cheer up a patient who had been very depressed for several days, the ward attendant called her into the office and offered her a relatively new winter coat that a volunteer worker had donated (it was late July at the time). While the patient tried on the coat, the ward nurse and attendant both commented on how well the coat fitted her and how nice she looked in it. After listening to them for a few moments, the patient turned to them and said, "In other words, I'll be here this winter."

Thus, in this setting, we find a fertile ground for the emergence of various belief systems dealing with the problem of obtaining various

[3] The data reported in this paper were collected by the author during a one-year field study of a psychiatric hospital. For a report on the procedures of the study and additional findings see Perrucci, *1963* and *1966*.

indications of one's therapeutic position on the ward. If we may be permitted the analogy, the patients are similar to Durkheim's Protestants, who must, through their own resources and free inquiry, come to terms with their maker (*1951*, pp. 157–159). In response to this situation, what we find is the emergence of what we will call a "release ideology," or a collection of beliefs referring to available means for obtaining a release from the hospital.

The Construction of a Release Ideology

Every socio-cultural system which persists long enough to develop a "history" generally creates "culture heroes." These figures, either real or fictitious, are thought to reflect the most highly valued qualities of the culture; and as such they often become, in a vague sort of way, a potential source of culturally approved aspirations for group members. In this respect, the mental hospital also creates its culture heroes. On the study ward in particular, these heroes tend to be patients who "have made it," who have been released from the hospital. Thus, these culture figures may be viewed as reflecting the most highly valued patient aspiration, namely, getting out of the hospital.

The creation of culture heroes, however, does not occur only among the patients. Ward staff are also quite instrumental in influencing the patient's concern with exemplary heroes. For example, ward attendants are repeatedly telling and retelling the success stories of patients who went from incontinents on a back ward to rehabilitated members of society. It is a clear counterpart to the Horatio Alger myth, only in a psychiatric setting. The main reason why attendants seem to retell these success stories is primarily due to the paucity of cases in which the attendants can illustrate how they helped patients to recover. Thus, in the success stories, the attendants can indicate the role they themselves played in the rehabilitation process.

With this impetus from Ward staff toward a focus on patients who have made successful recoveries, the patients themselves also tend to focus upon these ex-patients. For one thing, the patients probably hope they can enjoy some of the praise which attendants heap upon the heroes for real or alleged behavioral or personality characteristics. For another, it becomes a tangible piece of evidence from which they may judge their own stage of progress in the hospital; a piece of evidence which, as we indicated earlier, is not easily obtained from the ward physician.

In the actual "putting together" of the ideology, the patients tend to focus upon the most prominent features of the culture hero's life in the hospital; especially in the period of time just prior to discharge. These prominent features of exemplary heroes that patients seemed to isolate most often were:

1. *Working with Companion Service.* This involves a patient-organized and patient-run service to the hospital (with staff supervision) whereby the participating patients provide an escort service to all wards of the hospital. They escort single patients or groups of patients to and from activities, appointments, and the like, thereby releasing considerable time for the regular hospital staff to turn to more important work. This program has received much publicity both within and outside the hospital, and is considered a very desirable position by most patients.

2. *Coming off medication.* As this implies, it simply means a ward physician's decision to take a patient off any mood-elevating or tranquilizing drug program.

3. *Becoming a patient leader.* What we generally find here is the recognition of the formal patient leader, in terms of the elected ward president or vice-president. Thus, the leadership role would exclude informal leaders, since they would not have the recognition and approval of the hospital staff members.

4. *Getting along well with ward staff.* This is the loosest or vaguest characteristic of the culture heroes which the patients recognize. It generally means that a patient "talks well" with staff members; that they engage in extended conversations on topics which transcend the patient-staff role relationships. For example, the freedom to walk in the nurse's office and sit down and chat with the attendants, or more important, to be taken into the confidence of a ward staff member.

These are the four main factors that the patients tend to isolate in reflecting upon the pre-release behavior of the culture heroes. In most cases, these four factors quite accurately characterize the pre-release behavior of discharged patients. We would suggest that the reason these four characteristics are manifested by the culture heroes, is that they are the *results* or consequences of a poorly understood process of "getting better." That is, the patient who is making good progress "putting himself together again," will be very likely to go on to Companion Service, to come off medication, to become a patient leader, and to get on well with ward staff. However, in the creation of the release ideology, these four characteristics are viewed as *things to be done in order to get better.* The patients on the ward take the behavioral manifestations of the "getting better" process and make them the causes of the process. In the language of Schneider and Dornbusch (*1958*, pp. 58–77) the patients have taken certain "latent" functions of the recovery process and made them "manifest" by pursuing them as goals. What had previously been realized as a by-product is now "instrumentalized" as a means for attaining mental health.

The Concretization of the Ideology

The release ideology described above allows the patient to maintain the belief that there is a clear-cut way to get better and get out of the hospital. The actual reality of the belief system is never an issue, since it has been created out of rather reliable evidence (i.e., discharged patients), and also since it has never been shown not to be true. That is, the only patients who have ever embodied these four ideological characteristics have been the culture heroes. Aside from them, several patients may have one or two of the characteristics, e.g., work on companion service, and get on well with ward staff, but never all four characteristics.

In this part of the process of the collective disturbance, we will describe the case of the patient who did embody all four characteristics, i.e., the "concretization" of the ideology. That is the case of Marie I., a patient who represented the unfolding of the ward's "Horatio Alger" myth.

Marie I. came on Ward X during the last week in May. She came to the ward with what might be considered "poor credentials." That is, she was not the most desirable type of patient for an open ward. The ward attendant upon hearing of Marie I.'s transfer made the following comment: "Well, we're getting two new girls. Dr. Powell said we're getting one good one and one of the other kind. The good one is Connie Green; the other girl is Marie I. She's coming from a back ward, a real fighter. I don't know how they expect us to help her on this ward."

On the ward two days later, the day attendant pointed out Marie I. to the observer.

That's Marie. She came over from the disturbed ward. You better watch out for her; when she blows, she really blows. I feel sorry for the night attendant. She can sure have trouble sometimes, especially with girls like Marie.

The first two weeks on the ward for Marie I. were rather uneventful. She was immediately assigned to a job doing housework in one of the hospital buildings, which she did without difficulty. Her medication program included two depressants (Thorazine and Equanil) which she took without incident. Aside from a few minor evening complaints of inability to sleep, and several physical complaints requiring absence from work, Marie was a good patient. She was good in the sense of being unobtrusive, keeping to herself, and causing no difficulties for other patients or ward staff.

On June 20, Marie had her first extended contact with the ward physician during office hours. The interview was a pleasant one, with the doctor indicating his interest in Marie's condition, and the importance, to Marie, of this move to an open ward. The doctor stressed the fact that this was probably an important turning point in her illness. Marie was clearly pleased with the doctor, and repeatedly stated how much she liked the ward, the staff, and the other patients.

At this point, Marie was observed to have become much more outgoing. She established a close friendship with Mary G., one of the very well-liked patients on the ward. The ward staff also became sensitive to the fact that Marie was "coming out of her shell." On June 29, Mrs. Talbot, the day attendant, made the following reply to Dr. Powell's inquiry concerning Marie. "She's getting along real fine. She fits in well, and most of the girls really like her. Just the other morning she went by the office door and said, Hi, Tommy (nickname). Well, my head just shot up. She came back and apologized because she thought I was mad. Well, I wasn't; it was just a surprise to hear her say that. A lot of the old timers call me that, but a new girl usually won't."

On July 1, the ward president received a six-month leave of absence. A special election was held, and Marie I. was elected the new president. The ward staff, and by extension, the patients made quite a bit of "noise" about it. At attendant lunches or coffee breaks, Marie became a living testimonial to the therapeutic atmosphere of the ward. "A little over a month ago she was fighting and scratching on a back ward, and now she's president at the ward council," was the comment of the day attendant.

On July 12, the evening shift attendant wrote the following unsolicited progress note on Marie:

> This patient has shown a wonderful improvement on my time since she first came on this ward. She is no longer a sleeping problem. She sleeps all night. She gets up very bright and cheerful at 5:30 A.M.

During this time, Marie made a definite effort to convince the ward attendants and ward physician that she no longer needed her medication. Each time the ward physician came for office hours, Marie managed to see him and repeat her request. On July 20, the following note appeared in Marie's chart:

> Patient asked doctor to have her medication discontinued again. Discontinue Thorazine and Dulclox. Reduce Equanil to 200 mg.

At this point in Marie I.'s stay on the ward, she had managed to exhibit the four most highly valued factors which made up the release ideology. She was an escort for Companion Service; she was ward president; she was off medication; and she got along very well with ward staff. Regardless of the "workability" of the ideology in actually yielding the desired result of a release from the hospital, a patient who exhibited these four characteristics should carry a rather favorable prognosis. For Marie I., however, we find a very rapid process of deterioration setting in; a transition even more marked than her meteoric rise from a back ward to a ward hero. We will now turn to Marie's individual "breakdown," and the manner in which it affected the other patients on the ward.

The Ideology Put to the Test

The rapid decline of Marie I. made its first appearance with the news that two patients on the ward were in the planning stage for a release from the hospital. While plans were apparently in progress for some time through the Social Service Department, it now became public ward information that Carla W. was being considered for a six-month leave of absence and Lizzie S. was under consideration for a work placement. Neither of these two patients was very popular on the ward. In fact, Lizzie S. was one of the patients receiving the highest number of negative sociometric choices on the ward (*Perrucci, 1963*). In addition, the news of these plans was not met with the wholehearted approval of the ward attendant. As Mrs. Talbot put it:

> I can't understand it. Neither Carla nor Lizzie is ready to leave here; they're both very disturbed. Not that I'm not glad to get rid of them, but they'll never make it. They shouldn't even be considered for leaves.

This news became public on July 26. On July 27, Lizzie S. was put *on* additional medication (Reserpine). On July 28 and 29, the following notes were written in Marie I.'s chart.

> Patient came to office with a thin blouse on and a pair of jeans. Told her to get a brassiere and slip on because you could see through the blouse. Said she was alright, no one couldn't see through her. Just stood and stared at me. After a while she finally put on a dress. Said she didn't like to be told about her clothes. Patient seems very nervous. First complaining of constipation and was given laxative. This patient stated bowels acted some. Stayed on ward this P.M. saying didn't feel well. Is trying hard to get upset. Is disturbed at times. Is very irritable and very unreasonable. Patient came to office saying she might as well go back to work for she had to listen to Celine's radio. Tried to talk with patient but she became very sullen and held her mouth open running her tongue around the inside of her mouth and stared into space. Patient went to room to rest up.

On July 31, the following note was written on Carla W.

> Patient given medication for upset stomach. Patient restless, found her crying. Stated she was having bad dreams. Was very unhappy all evening.

The following three notes were written on Lizzie S. for July 30, 31, and August 1, respectively.

> This patient has been getting up for the last week complaining of pains in stomach. States she has a lot of diarrhea.
> Patient has been very talkative several times during night. Very restless.
> Patient put on Equanil to relieve anxiety.

On August 3, the following note was written on Marie I.

> Patient is very strong against Elsa P. sleeping next to her. She is continually calling her names to this attendant. States Elsa watches her all the time.

On August 6, both Carla W. and Lizzie S. were released from the hospital on a leave of absence and a work placement, respectively. The departure of these two patients was discussed by the ward attendant and ward nurse in the following manner.

> Attendant: Well, Carla went out, but was she high. She went around demanding that things be done for her. She said to me, "I demand that you call [*social worker*] about me going home." I don't know how they let her go. Just two days ago the doctor gave orders to seclude her or send her to [*closed ward*] if she acted up, and today they let her out.
> Nurse: Lizzie was just as disturbed. Monday she told me that Beth L. was threatening to kill her, and she started crying. Anyway, I'm glad to see her go.

With the release of these two patients we find a move into the acute stage of the disturbance. For up to this point (July 29 to August 6), what we found was primarily the individual upset of Marie I. The rest of the patients on the ward were apparently affected only to the extent that there appeared to be a marked increase in complaints about physical ailments.[4] Thus, the acute phase of the disturbance involved the "complete breakdown" of Marie I. (by staff definitions, this involves a psychotic episode and return to a closed ward), as well as a number of extreme upsets of other patients that were presumably related to Marie's disturbance. We will relate each incident by the day of occurrence and the patient involved.

August 7: Marie I., nursing note, day shift.

> Patient has burning sensation when she urinates.
> Patient said she felt stuffy, and needed a bowel movement.

August 8: Marie I., day shift, observations on the ward.

---

[4] It is interesting to note in this context that the one and only case of incontinence on the ward (during the field study) occurred during the disturbance phase. On August 3 and 4, Joan B. became incontinent. At this time she was "specialed" by the evening and night attendants. That is, she was awakened periodically during the night and taken to the bathroom. She was generally awakened at 11 P.M. and 3 A.M. This solved the bed wetting problem, but then Joan became a "problem sleeper," i.e., it was very difficult getting her up in the morning.

Marie: Could I have a soda mint or bicarb?

Nurse: Why?

Marie: So I can belch.

Nurse: Are you under tension at work, Marie?

Marie: [*laughs*] Who isn't under tension here. Can I have a soda mint?

Nurse: Well, Marie, you know what we are trying to do here is to get you people off medications. You can't always be running for a soda mint or a bicarb when you get out.

Marie: Well, I'm sure I can get a bicarb if I need it.

[*Marie walked away from the office into the day room and out to the loggie. She spoke of the incident to a group of patients who were smoking on the loggie.*]

Marie: She told me, "We don't want you to get used to the medication" [*in a mimicking voice*]. I'll get my own stuff to burp. I can spend a dime on a Coca Cola so she won't have to chart a soda mint. They don't worry about shock treatments becoming habit forming, but they worry about soda mint.

August 9: Marie I., nursing note, evening shift.

Patient very disturbed. Was restless and fault-finding all evening. Attendant talked with her at 7 p.m. She quieted down for a while. Later came in office while supervisor was here. She walked up to a medicine cabinet and tried to open it. She was very angry to find it locked. Threatened the supervisor. Attendant talked with her again. She threatened her life; also stated she would run away if doctor did not transfer her to ward _____. Was very insulting to some of the other patients. Seemed to think she was as well or even better than two of the patients that had been sent out on work placement. Patient was watched very close.

August 10: Marie I., day shift, observations on the ward.

Marie went to work on Companion Service at 8:30 a.m. At 10:15 a.m. Marie was brought back to the ward by the attendant in charge of the service. The patient was very upset and crying. Mrs. Talbot, the ward attendant, asked Marie what was the matter. Marie stated, "If we'd get rid of Beth L. and Betty L. [two other patients on the ward] things would go a lot better on this ward." Mrs. Talbot helped Marie to her room to lie down. Dr. Powell was called and he came right over. Marie was asked to come to the nurses' office and talk with him.

Dr. Powell: I understand you've been a little upset, Marie. You want to tell me about it.

Marie: It's this whole goddamn place. You ask for a soda mint and they make a big deal out of it. I tried to get some powder from the medicine cabinet and the attendant and the supervisor jump on me. They told me that the office was for the nurses and attendants and that I should stay out.

Dr. Powell: You have to understand that there are some rules around here, Marie. Don't you think you have to abide by the rules?

281

Marie: Yes, I know there are rules, I've been following them for weeks. I was the good Marie, the sweet Marie. I worked hard to go on Companion Service and to get along without my medicine, and what did it get me? [*Patient starts crying at this point.*] You let Carla and Lizzie go out, and I was better than either of them. Lizzie even went on medicine before she went out.

Dr. Powell: Well, what do you want me to do, Marie? You think I should let you go home?

Marie: I want to go to Ward O [*closed ward*]. At least over there I can cry and no one looks at you as if something's wrong.

Dr. Powell: I'll tell you what. Why don't you go lie down and rest for a while. I'll give you something to help you rest and we can talk again later.

Marie: I don't give a shit for your medicine or your hospital.

[*Marie gets up and walks out of the office. Mrs. Talbot goes after her and gets her to lie down in her room. Mrs. Talbot returns to the office.*]

Mrs. Talbot: You think we should send her over to O [*closed ward*]? She's going to blow any minute.

Dr. Powell: Let's hold her here for now. She's made such great strides these past months; I'd hate to set her back without a good try. Keep her in her room and keep an eye on her once in a while. I'll talk to her again tomorrow.

That noon at lunch time, Marie did not go to lunch with the ward but remained in her room. The ward attendant escorted the patients from the study ward and the upstairs ward to the dining room. The attendant from the upper ward was to keep an eye on the patients who do not go to regular lunch. When the attendant and the observer returned to the ward, the following incident was reported by the upstairs attendant:

> I was upstairs in the office when all of a sudden I heard a big racket coming from below. There was some yelling and screaming. I ran downstairs and there at the end of the hall were Marie I. and Beth L. rolling around and fighting on the floor. It was a job getting them apart, but I finally got them in their own rooms. I couldn't get anything out of Marie because she'd been crying all this time. Beth told me that she was in her room minding her own business when Marie walked in and called her a "goddamn whore" and started hitting her and pulling her hair. Marie picked on the wrong one this time, because Beth was really giving it to her when I got down here.

Mrs. Talbot called Dr. Powell and reported the incident. Marie was immediately sent over to a closed ward. Later that evening, and through the night, a number of additional incidents occurred.

It becomes most difficult to establish anything like a causal link between Marie I.'s disturbance and the subsequent upsets of several other patients. At this point, we will only relate the incidents and then attempt to establish their relationship to Marie's disturbance. Reported below is the statement made by the day attendant to the observer on August 11, the day after Marie I. was sent to a closed ward.

Last night it was really a madhouse here. You knew that Marie "blew" yesterday, didn't you. Well, that's not the all of it. About 8:00 last night, Mary G. went psychotic. She was running up and down the hall yelling and singing hymns. Then she started talking to God, saying how sorry she was and all that. Minton (evening attendant) said it was a real mess. They sent her over with Marie I. on O [*closed ward*]. Then to top it off, Elizabeth K. tried to choke Julia T. in the middle of the night. Julia started yelling and practically woke up the whole ward. They moved Elizabeth to the empty room at the end of the hall, and they're going to keep her door locked at night.

Aside from these remarks by the day attendant, the observer also noted some additional incidents which may or may not be relevant to the disturbance. However, their occurrence at this particular time, i.e., the acute stage of the disturbance, makes them potentially relevant. The incidents simply involve three patients who did not go to work on August 11. Wanda R., Bertha G., and Betty L. all claimed that they were not feeling well, for one reason or another, and wished to be excused from work.

As stated above, the causal connection between Marie I.'s disturbance and the subsequent upsets of other patients is difficult to establish. The one common element in all these events is their occurrence in a certain time sequence. Aside from this, we would be hard put to explain the connections among *all* these events. Nevertheless, the following explanation is offered.

The psychotic episode of Mary G., which followed very closely the disturbance of Marie I., is most interesting in view of the fact that Mary G. and Marie I. were very close friends on the ward. On the sociometric questionnaire, they were among the few pairs of mutual friendship choices made by patients. There does, then, seem to be some likelihood that the two disturbances were connected. The other significant feature of all of the disturbances which followed Marie I.'s is the fact that they occurred among relatively active patients holding significant status positions within the patient group. For example, of the six patients involved in these upsets, five were patients who were either very popular or very unpopular according to our sociometric questionnaire. Mary G., Elizabeth K., and Wanda R. were all among the patients most frequently chosen for potential roommates; Julia T. was one of the two ward leaders; and Betty L. and Lizzie S. were two of the four most frequently negatively selected patients on the ward. Thus, it is quite possible that due to the fact that they were all active patients, they were perhaps more sensitive to the symbolic meaning of the breakdown of Marie I. — that her disturbance represented a breakdown of the release ideology. It is with respect to the release ideology that we would expect the active patients to be concerned, since they would be more likely to be cognizant of the presumed utility of the ideology in attaining a release from the hospital.

Unattainable Goals and the Collective Disturbance

The collective disturbance described in this paper was seen to be the result of a release ideology which provided a framework of instrumental means for the attainment of a hospital release. The ideology, however, was badly constructed, in that the specific means isolated by the patients were not necessarily related to the indicators used by staff to establish a patient's release prognosis.[5]

The existence of the strong ideological factors found among the patients raises some questions concerning the persistence of magic within the rationalized framework of the hospital. The combination of uncertainty in treatment technology, and anxiety concerning one's personal prognosis leads to a dependence upon a belief system that makes institutional life bearable. Since patients are "kept in the dark" as to expectations regarding treatment effectiveness and release prognosis, the patients build an explanatory system which provides this information and allows them to accept the constraints imposed upon them by legitimizing the authority of those above them in the hospital hierarchy. The functions of magic in a social system are examined by Parsons (*1949*, pp. 203–204) in discussing Malinowski's work on magic:

> Malinowski, however, went beyond this in attempting to understand the functional necessity for such mechanisms as magic. In this connection, he laid stress on the importance of the emotional interests involved in the successful outcome of such enterprises. *The combination of a strong emotional interest with important factors of uncertainty, which on the given technical level are inherent in the situation, produces a state of tension and exposes the actor to frustration.* This, it should be noted, exists not only in cases where uncontrollable factors, such as bad weather or insect pests in gardening results in 'undeserved' failure, *but also in cases where success is out of proportion to reasonable expectations of the results of intelligence and effort.* Unless there were mechanisms which had the psychological function of mitigating the sense of frustration, the consequences would be unfavorable to maintaining a high level of confidence or effort, and it is in this connection that magic

[5] The previous chapter by the author on "Social Processes in Psychiatric Decisions" indicates that the criteria for releasing patients developed by the psychiatric staff are often vague and unrelated to estimates of "wellness" and patient's behavior in the hospital. Such a situation encourages the emergence of belief systems which have little relationship to reality.

may be seen to perform important positive functions . . . . It would follow that wherever such uncertain elements enter into the pursuit of emotionally important goals, if not magic, at least functionally equivalent phenomena could be expected to appear [emphasis added].[6]

Thus, while both Parsons and Malinowski point out the functional significance of magic in coping with uncertainty, it is quite clear that the magical beliefs *coexist* with the rational knowledge rather than serving to *replace* the rational knowledge in a system of goal directed activity. As Parsons points out:

Side by side with the system of rational knowledge and technique, however, and specifically not confused with it, was a system of magical beliefs and practices. . . . *Correspondingly, the practices were not rational techniques* but rituals involving specific orientation to this world of supernatural forces and entities (p. 202).

It appears in this interpretation that the contribution, i.e., functional significance, which the magical system makes to maintaining order in the system, comes primarily from the fact that the belief system stands *outside* any expectation of results in goal directed behavior. This is also quite similar to Durkheim's distinction between the sacred and profane in religious activity, where one of the major sources of strength for the religious system is that it exists apart from the utilitarian orientation of rational techniques (*Durkheim, 1947; Parsons, 1937,* pp. 411–429).

The psychiatric setting seems to generate pressure for converting magical beliefs into rational, technical means designed to achieve certain goals. This pressure can be traced to the absence of intermediate goals which patients may pursue in their own right, and which may be related to a hospital release as a consequence of involvement with such intermediate goals.[7] In the absence of limited and more readily attainable goals, *that are defined by staff as indicators of progress,* patients will continue to erect belief systems which help them to cope with their situation. Since such belief systems tend to be "private," i.e. not shared by staff personnel, they can easily be viewed by staff as evidence of "disoriented thinking." The consequences of such a situation for psychotherapy and patient progress is that it tends to encourage further withdrawal of patients from staff and from the psychotherapeutic potential of the hospital in general. Unworkable ideologies may either lead to a kind of despair that encourages an otherwise promising patient to "give up," or to construct and embrace beliefs that serve to further remove them from the world about them.

---

[6] It should be noted that in a footnote to the quoted statement, Parsons explicitly refers to the importance of these ideas on magic in the field of health and medicine.

[7] For a discussion of such mechanisms as "gain by indirection" and "attractiveness of intermediates," see Schneider (*1962*).

References

Bates, Sanford (1953). *A Statement Concerning Causes, Preventive Measures, and Methods of Controlling Prison Riots and Disturbances,* American Prison Association.

Caudill, Wililam (1958). *The Psychiatric Hospital as a Small Society,* Harvard University Press.

Drake, St. Clair, and Horace R. Cayton (1945). *Black Metropolis,* Harcourt, Brace.

Durkheim, Emile (1947). *The Elementary Forms of the Religious Life,* Free Press.

―――― (1951). *Suicide,* translated by John A. Spaulding and George Simpson, Free Press.

Merton, Robert K. (1957). "Social Structure and Anomie," in his *Social Theory and Social Structure,* Free Press.

Mizruchi, Ephraim H. (1964). *Success and Opportunity.* Free Press.

Parsons, Talcott (1937). *Structure of Social Action,* Free Press.

―――― (1949). "The Theoretical Development of the Sociology of Religion," in *Essays in Sociological Theory,* Free Press.

Perrucci, Robert (1961). "The Significance of Intra-Occupational Mobility: Some Methodological and Theoretical Notes, Together With a Case Study of Engineers," *American Sociological Review,* 26 (December), 874–883.

―――― (1966). "Social Distance, Bargaining Power, and Compliance With Rules on a Hospital Ward," *Psychiatry,* 29 (February), 42–55.

―――― (1963). "Social Distance Strategies and Intra-Organizational Stratification: A Study of the Status System on a Psychiatric Ward," *American Sociological Review,* 28 (December), 951–962.

Schneider, Louis (1962). "The Role of the Category of Ignorance in Sociological Theory: An Exploratory Statement," *American Sociological Review,* 27 (August), 492–508.

Schneider, Louis, and Sanford Dornbusch (1958). *Popular Religion,* University of Chicago Press.

Stanton, Alfred H., and Morris S. Schwartz (1954). *The Mental Hospital,* Basic Books.

PART FOUR

Social Functions, Values and Change:

Some Perspectives on Societal and Cultural Contexts

Whereas the previous section represented various forms of sociological perspectives, the four essays in this section are similar to one another, and to the type represented in Chapter 7 by Corwin and Clarke. As was argued in the introduction to the third section, inquiries of this type are best evaluated not simply for their supportive evidence, but more importantly for general adequacy to their subject. In these four discussions, that subject — counseling and psychotherapy in societal and cultural contexts — is revealed as diffuse and complex.

Inquiry and Latent Effects

Corwin and Clarke move toward a breadth of perspective and of focus adequate to that diffuseness in Chapter 10, in which they discuss the interplay of ideology and practice in the development of the counseling movement. Their discussion takes even broader form, however, if read in conjunction with Chapter 7, for together the two chapters present a picture of continuous adjustment and compromise between ideology and incompatible institutional pressures and organizational constraints, as related to five themes dominant in American society:

humanistic ameliorism, social adjustment to middle-class standards, federal influence, and the bureaucratization and professionalization of work.

Opler's discussion, in Chapter 12, is more limited in focus, but evidences a similarly broad perspective on the relation of values, beliefs, and myths to the emergence of social psychiatry. In the final two chapters of this section, Bernard considers the functions and limitations of counseling and psychotherapy, and their relation to social problems, all within the context of professional and societal values. Her discussion ranges widely, and is richly laden with suggestive insights, speculative interpretations, and tentative generalizations.

Analyses of such diffuse and fluid phenomena must necessarily proceed with methods which must appear rather rough and ready to the exact scientist, the laboratory psychologist, or the strictly empirical sociologist. As was suggested in the introduction to section three, such analysis must often rest on implication, interpretation, speculation and suspicion rather than on procedures involving the careful application of analysis, synthesis and logic. The pitfalls of these interpretive social analysis, then, are many, as is strikingly evidenced by the conclusions drawn from the same body of data by Opler in Chapter 11 and by Bernard in Chapter 12. These authors note the evidence on the incidence of mental disturbance from various surveys, such as the Midtown Manhattan Mental Health Study which indicates that less than one-fifth of the urban subjects could be rated "well" (see Opler, pages 338–339, and Bernard, pages 353–354). The two authors use these data in arguments that fairly contradict one another. For Opler, such data suggest that mental health is a "myth"; for Bernard such an argument is "a *Reductio ad Absurdum.*" This example alone suggests the importance of a basic sociological caveat: Let the reader of social criticism beware.

Whatever the difficulties and defects of such critiques, however, they are overshadowed by the importance of the discussions for practical affairs and for the development of sociological perspectives. Those who see in analyses such as these no more than journalistic excursions miss an important point: The inquiries are guided by more-or-less coherent structures of analytic concept, so related to one another that the probabilities of penetrating analyses are significantly increased; in such discussions it is possible to identify levels of reality beyond the scope of the laboratory researcher or the strict empiricist. This level of discussion, then, serves importantly in the development of the unifying and synthesizing capacities of sociology and in the discovery of functional and structural relationships and processes to which more precise methodologies are insensitive.

On the practical level — the level at which the counselor and the psychotherapist ultimately works — inquiry of such scope is also important, especially in an increasingly organized and interdependent society. Totally without such scope, men are but "cats looking at kings"; given only unsystematic discussions of such scope, they may approximate the baboons in Huxley's *Ape and Essence,* whose armies keep Einsteins as mascots. In the fantasy, the armies destroy one another. The Einsteins, as they lay dying, ask how such a thing could happen. The answer is delivered clearly:

> Surely it's obvious.
> Every schoolboy knows it.
> *Ends* are ape chosen.
> Only the *means* are man's.
> (Huxley, 1948)

Whatever the strengths and limitations of the four essays in this section, they should serve to illustrate what is perhaps the most important contribution sociology can today make to counseling and psychotherapy. Traditionally, in those practical fields, attention is focused on immediate, as contrasted with latent or long-term effects of their practices and their profession in general; this attention, further, is focused on the individual rather than on the societal effects. Discussion of latent societal effects is not common, and almost without exception tends to be glib, and highly emotive. Dispassionate analyses and sweeping perspectives are needed, but only cheap bromides are offered — and accepted. Questions about the latent effects of practices and professions such as those of counseling and psychotherapy clearly demand comprehensive perspective of greater breadth and depth than they have yet enjoyed.

A Speculative Illustration

Discussions about the effects of counseling, for example, clearly must go beyond consideration of what goes on within the counselor's office and its subsequent effects on the development of the client. The activities and competencies of the counselor, for one thing, are related not only to his own efforts, but are also a function of the efforts of the associations which support his professional roles, of the universities which support his education, and of the organization within which he works. In the context of societal expectations and values, the conflict and accommodation of individual, association and organization closely influence the limits of counseling effectiveness.

But the resources and activities or associations and organizations are, in turn, related to other influences — for example, to federal welfare programs. Since Sputnik, federal programs have exerted marked influence on the counseling profession, both stimulating its development, and presenting serious challenges and demands. In recent years, these demands have been exceptional, as is suggested by the 1963 *Manpower*

Report, which called for 32,000 additional full-time counselors by mid-1967 — more than a 50 percent increase over the total number of full-time counselors in 1964 (Wrenn, 1965). This recent relation of government to the counseling profession does not appear to be unique, however, I suspect that close investigation would support my casual impression that counseling has come to its present state through surging rhythms of development, stimulated in great part by federal programs. Although original emphases for counseling appeared in private community organizations, major phases in the development of the profession during the past half-century appear to have been influenced by federal programs, which either catalyzed or directed the surges of growth.

The first phase in each surge appears to have begun with a widely recognized crisis on the national level, most notably World War I, the Great Depression, World War II and its demobilization, and the post-Sputnik drive for national potence and social justice. In response to these national concerns, executive and legislative programs established projects which quickly demanded facilitation: draftees and applicants had to be screened, individuals had to be placed in organizations, morale and interpersonal relations had to be controlled if programs were to be effective.

In each case, a second phase quickly followed the beginning of these programs, as it became apparent that the existing supplies of counselors and other program facilitators were inadequate. Federally endorsed and supported programs were then developed to stimulate recruitment, employment and training in guidance and counseling.

Following the periodic rash of program innovation the federal government appears to have developed some degree of unconcern, which afforded professions and organizations a period of calm in which the sudden growth of ranks and organization could be rationalized. These periods of rationalization are interesting, as they reveal two distinct strains of response to the occupational expansion.

The first strain is to make the newly created or expanded *organizations* efficient. Rules and routines (which developed rapidly to meet the crisis) are examined for their contribtuion to organizational goals. The second strain is to establish or reestablish *professional* control and autonomy of the counselor from organizational constraints, primarily through an examination of the processes of interpersonal counseling, with the goal of increasing the client's interpersonal effectiveness. The profession, that is, in these periods of calm tends to polarize, until a new crisis again leads to new federal programs which once more bring the two disparate efforts into mutual concern.

It would be unwarranted to present this as a sociological or even historical generalization. All that can be said is that casual acquaintance with the development of counseling suggests that over the past half century a more or less sequenced rhythm appears to have emerged from the interrelations of governmental, professional and organizational influences. Most simply, the rhythm appears to be one in which recognized crisis leads to federal and state legislation, leading to programs of occupational expansion; after some time, a polarization appears to take place within the profession. On the one pole, efforts dominate to establish counseling as an organizationally effective practice; on the other pole, efforts dominate to establish counseling as a method of increasing the client's interpersonal effectiveness. This rhythmic sequence — again, if casual acquaintance is accurate — has been repeated on a large scale at least four times in the past 50 years.

This polarization of professional effort in large part is a reflection of an enduring confusion of counseling images — whatever the stimulation provided by the government, the profession itself has never clearly resolved the question of what its roles are in American society. Since the days of Frank Parsons, two images of counseling have struggled for recognition, at times seeming to fuse, but at others emerging as distinct, revealing contradictions among their compatibilities. As suggested above, in most simple statement the images are, on the one hand, to further the collective good (for instance, aiding in manpower utilization) and, on the other hand, to further the individual good (for instance, adding in development of autonomy). The first image in essence presents the question: Given a particular, specific social structure, where will the individual fit best? To answer the question requires not only a breadth and depth of knowledge about society but also about the individual — but if a choice must be made the image prescribes commitment to the "collective good." The second image presents the question: How might the capacities and resources of the individual be developed most fully? How might he be helped to develop his capacities for, say, autonomous responsibility? To answer this question, also, the counselor must consider both community contexts as well as the essential qualities of the individual; but always, in a choice situation, the image requires the counselor to opt in favor of the individual.

Counseling literature today reflects a general awareness of these images, and many counselors are articulate in their defense of one or the other. Represented as simple alternatives, however, the images are unnecessarily confusing. A dominant theme of this symposium has been that the individual and society are not in opposition, but are interpenetrant: one cannot be understood without understanding the other, neither can change unless the other changes in some way. The question, then, of whether counseling serves national programs or serves individual growth invites attack: it is obvious that it can, and does, serve both — even that any action of a single counselor can serve both at the same time.

From this argument, it is a journey of only a few steps to the idea that there need be no real tension between the individual and society and, hence, that the distinction between the two images is artificial. Unfortunately, the short journey must be made over a dizzying chasm, for which no secure bridges are available. For, although collective and individual needs may often be compatible, they remain far from identical; however effectively the two *can*, ideally, coexist, they must by nature coexist in some tension. It is a demonstrable fact that individual needs do clash with collective needs, at times overtly, more often subtly, the conflict imperceptible, unarticulated, yet profound. It may also be argued that neither the demands of the individual nor society can or should always be honored, and that the conflicting demands of both often *must* be.

In this perspective, the two images of counseling which have struggled for dominance may be seen as less polar. On the one hand, *there exist today marked strains to improve the abilities of counseling to maximize effectiveness of societal programs* (for example, the programs of the Office of Economic Opportunity, the Department of Labor, the Department of Health, Education, and Welfare), *in such a way that restraints on individual autonomy and development are minimized.*

On the other hand, there exist *strains to improve abilities to maximize individual development, in such a way that impositions on society are minimized.* Counseling is one of the few professions today which is so situated that it might contribute in both ways; but to date, perhaps at least in part because of governmental programs, most effort has gone to the first.

Each of the two images, thus clarified, involves some sort of "balancing" of potential service against potential disservice. A fundamental tension, then, exists in the counseling profession. Ideally that tension — just as the tension between the political liberalism and conservatism — not only protects both the individual and society from dysfunctional demands of the other, but also allows and even stimulates development of both. It is important to note that one image does not necessarily challenge the legitimacy of the other (as they appear to when in polar form): as in the relation of Republicans and Democrats, neither questions the right of the other to compete for favor, so long as the competition does not destroy the social arrangements that make the competition possible. Theoretically, the proponents of each image might accept the other as legitimate, though of different perspective; each might recognize that the two can contribute to the effectiveness of both. If there were this kind of basic agreement in the profession, the tension between the two images could be turned to productive expression, as it was expressed in a competition of ideas and programs. A necessary prerequisite to such a working agreement would be a careful differentiation of organizations which operate with one image or the other.

Today, however, only few counseling organizations appear to be so clearly structured, and even most educational counselors must work in ambiguous situations. However clearly the images might be identified in academic discussion, in practical settings the competition of images is not waged between organizations or between groups of practicing professionals — rather, it takes the form of tensions maintained within the individual counselor. If he is sensitive to the potential conflicts of the images, the result may be role conflict, perplexity and vacillation; in dealing with a difficult case, he may succeed in serving neither the individual nor the social program.

It is important to recognize that counselors, as other professionals, are increasingly employed in organizations which approximate the bureaucratic modes of large-scale business. Experience in such organizations suggests that when the tension between service images is maintained within the individual, it is probable that his effectiveness will be impaired, unless he successfully ignores one image or compartmentalizes the two — but to ignore, compartmentalize, or rationalize is to lose the productive potentials in the competitive interchanges of the two.

These are but casual speculations, of course. Even as speculations, however, they may argue for a practical effort within the counseling profession — an effort to develop a clear image of its various roles in society, and to identify the personal, educational, and organizational requirements for the effective attainment of each.

As speculations, however, they require considerable thought and systematic inquiry if they are to be accepted in a careful argument. To so argue has not been the purpose here — rather the speculations have been offered to illustrate the potentials of applying broad social perspectives to even such apparently "private" activities as those of counseling and psychotherapy. The illustration is more effectively and systematically furthered in the following four chapters.

References

Huxley, Aldous (1948). *Ape and Essence,* Harper.
Wrenn, C. Gilbert (1965). "A Second Look," in *Counseling, A Growing Profession* (J. W. Loughary, ed.), American Personnel and Guidance Association.

10 | SOCIAL CHANGE

AND SOCIAL VALUES:

Further Reflections on the Counseling Movement

Ronald G. Corwin and Alfred C. Clarke / The Ohio State University

Counseling as a *field of knowledge* is diffuse, running a gamut from guidance activities concerned with information-giving and assistance with routine decisions, to therapeutic attempts to help other persons reorganize their personalities on the basis of self-insight. Counseling as *an activity* is both a favorite pastime of amateurs and central to several fledgling professions. And as *an occupation,* counseling takes place in settings so diverse as high schools, universities, and government and private agencies. All of these situations are further complicated by inconsistencies in practice and by an endemic hiatus between theory and practice. Obviously, short of platitudes and tautologies, few observations can do equal justice to so many groups and activities found in so many contexts.

Nevertheless, the more or less unified movement behind these specific hybrid forms *does* provide some basis for generalization. For, regardless of the setting, the diverse components are parallel parts of broader institutional developments: all are to some degree subject to the humanitarianism, middle class, political, bureaucratic and professional forces that have shaped counseling functions in this country. Consequently, differences existing between the various groups and orientations are likely to be fewer than the broader similarity that underlies all of them. Although this discussion necessarily will be selective of examples drawn from specific areas of counseling practice not always representative of the entire

For their thoughtful comments on an earlier version of this chapter, we are grateful to Russell Dynes, John Cuber, Herman Peters, James Pedersen and Francis Robinson. Chapters 7 and 10 were originally written as a single essay. Readers especially interested in the counseling movement may be well advised to read Chapter 7 immediately after this chapter.

294

movement, then, the issues raised are nevertheless generic to the counseling *role* and are likely to be experienced in one form or another by a substantial number of counselors.

Our task can be made more manageable by limiting ourselves to the identification of the *existence* of potential dilemmas and dysfunctions which seem inherent to the field; the frequency of occurrence of these problems and their variable relevance to particular situations remains an open question.[1] This obviously unbalanced treatment will permit us to focus more intently on pathologies within the field. Just as the study of disease in medicine has advanced knowledge of the healthy organism, much can be learned about the field of counseling by examining its problem areas. Admittedly, of course, many counselors with greater facility than others have been able to avoid or overcome some of the problems discussed in this chapter. What follows must be regarded as tentative formulations of the broad social developments that have challenged the movement.

The Frame of Reference

Counseling can be viewed as a social movement subject to the same fate as other movements. In the rapidly changing United States some movements, at the expense of reduced effectiveness and drastic alterations in structure, have successfully maintained the original objectives which inspired them. For example, the temperance movement seems to have managed to maintain its original objectives by shifting attention to a new audience, changing the composition of its membership, and modifying its strategy (*Gusfield, 1955*). Perhaps more typically, however, the members of social movements become so committed to established procedures that they are reluctant to disband the organization or even to make the adjustments necessary to preserve the original objectives. Organizational commitments take precedence over accomplishing given objectives, and the objectives themselves are transformed in order to preserve and enhance the organization's position and the positions of its members. The YMCA is such an organization. Organized to "improve the spiritual condition" of young men engaged in certain occupations, its goals have been transformed for the sake of self-preservation in the face of fundamental changes in the social environment (*Sills, 1957*). The adult education movement illustrates the disparity that can arise between the objectives that inspire a movement and objectives and practices subsequently formed. In this case the drift occurred because competition in the "enrollment economy" has forced adult programs to resort to

---

[1] At the end of the chapter, a preliminary scheme is introduced for adjusting the generalizations being proposed more appropriately to specific contexts.

craft and hobby courses as a way of attracting enough popular support to provide their own economic support (*Clark, 1956*).

The objectives of the counseling movement have shown similar vulnerability to social pressures. The original humanistic ideology usually identified with the movement is not always apparent in its theoretical concerns and especially in its current practices. Institutional forces and organizational constraints have left their mark. And yet, if the movement has not defended its original objectives with the obstinacy of a WCTU, neither has it completely lost sight of them. Much of the initial ideology remains, often only as an echo, but available nevertheless and capable of resuming a more viable influence on the movement's direction if opportunity permits.

Unfortunately some discussions of counseling, preoccupied with its public statements and logical functions, have missed the drama of the movement, the repeated adjustment and compromise continuously occurring between its ideology and incompatible institutional pressures and organizational constraints. These incompatibilities between ideology and practice occur along three dimensions of the American social system:

Strain between the dominant cultural values and the individualistic-humanistic form of amelioration which originally inspired counseling;

Strain between individualistic-humanism in counseling and the impersonal character of industrial society;

Strain between counseling objectives and the actual positions of counselors in a bureaucratic society.

It is useful to consider the contributions to these strains of the five themes dominating American society: humanistic ameliorism, social adjustment to middle-class standards, federal influence, and the bureaucratization and professionalization of work. The first three themes, which are largely ideological, will be considered in this chapter. Bureaucratization and professionalization, which are more concretely embedded in the organization of public agencies and educational systems and which form the organizational structure of the movement, have been treated in Chapter 7. Chapters 10 and 7, then, might be read as a single essay, affording an overview of one counseling movement in sociological perspective.

Thesis

At the risk[2] of over-emphasizing the dysfunctional problems, this dilemma can be posed: *as American society has moved from a pre-indus-*

---

[2] This is the same risk counselors take. We start with the assumption that social process and change are more discernible at those points in a social system which are experiencing greatest tension. Most counselors also routinely place emphasis on the problem cases of individuals.

trial era to a post-industrial setting, the counseling movement has not fully adapted to changing conditions in several important respects; but when it has adapted, its basic goals and character have become transformed in the process. To the extent that practitioners do attempt to adapt counseling values and techniques to a changing society, they must face the prospect that the original goals of the movement might become *displaced* by attention to procedure and *re*placed by emergent goals. On the other hand, to the extent that counseling fails to adapt to changed social conditions, its objectives and techniques are likely to become outmoded and ineffective; in this case, the counseling movement will lag behind the current demands of the society. The major themes of this chapter, then, will revolve around *goal displacements* and *social lags* which have characterized the counseling movement as it has accommodated to some of the major institutional developments of our times: namely, humanistic ameliorism, growth of the middle class and nationalism.

Humanistic Themes in Counseling

There is a strong element of humanism in counseling. The movement once had as its objective the amelioration of personal problems of underprivileged groups and of youngsters unable to solve their own problems. Originally, counseling seems to have been *largely* a response to growing national concern about problems being faced by these groups, the underprivileged and the young, problems such as divorce, increasing unemployment, the complexities of occupational choice, sub-standard living conditions, and delinquency. Of this early epoch in counseling history, Schwebel has remarked:

> Was it not the same new population of students and out-of-school youth that stirred the interest of Frank Parsons in Boston and Eli Weaver in Brooklyn, and countless others? A multitude of forces had combined to make this the moment in history when taxes would come from the pockets of the rich, and money from the coffers of the community to provide the higher education for which Americans had been clamoring for a century or so; the loudest voices were those of the trade unions, workers and immigrants. These new breeds of students needed to be understood, respected, tutored and guided, and their needs struck a respondent chord in men and women who were humanists not technicians and who sought to encourage the hopes and aspirations of young people whose parents could offer them little in the way of educational and vocational guidance. Parsons was many things, but among them he was a muckraker immersed in the great issues of the day, fighting for social change. This was no culturally encapsulated counselor out of touch with the realities that molded men's lives (*Schwebel, 1964*).

In attempting to cope with such problems, counselors were seeking to implement a humanitarian conception of man. It was a personalized humanism with roots deep in agrarian traditions. In attempting to help people bridge the transformation from pre-industrial society to an urban way of life, counselors were naturally using a perhaps outdated individualistic and personalized model of the "good society" based on conditions which were rapidly disappearing. The counselor seems to have unwittingly used a less complex model of society — one characterized by stable, voluntary, cooperative, personal relationships, sustained by widely shared internalized values, where work roles served as both an integrating force and a major source of personal identity — for interpreting an industrialized society characterized by bureaucracy, expediency, superficial conformity, and manipulation in personal relations. Ironically, the concepts behind the humanitarian conception of the counseling movement were better adapted to the society that had been and had already passed them to the society that actually was emerging.

As it became increasingly difficult to implement pre-industrial humanitarian conceptions *in toto* in the emerging society, the original objectives behind the movement were modified to fit new realities. These issues will be elaborated further in the course of this chapter. First, however, it will be useful to review some of the major economic and social changes responsible for altering the course of the counseling movement.

Changes

Since the initial impetus for counseling stemmed from a growing humanitarian consciousness of the problems that accompanied social and economic changes following in the wake of the Industrial Revolution; since this was an era of reform — against poverty, slums, family disorganization, housing and long working hours; since, moreover, the social sciences offered a hope of implementing humanitarian motives, it is not surprising that many of the early counseling leaders, of the guidance segment of the movement in particular, were social workers, critical of existing child labor practices, and attempting to assist adolescents adjust to their adult roles in an increasingly complex world of work.

Changes in economic and family institutions provided especial incentives for the growth of counseling. Transfer of work to places outside of the home had altered family structure. In the urban family, the father began to spend most of his time away from his children, who themselves were away at factories and later in school. Accordingly, the male lost much influence wihin the family, and control was assumed largely by the mother, who had become separated from the rest of the labor force (or, in the case of the working woman, spent much of her time away from her family also). As a result of such developments, adults reluctantly relinquished much of their traditional influence over their young. Elders, particularly in immigrant families, no longer were regarded as the source of wisdom, and instead became "squares" in their own lifetimes.

With these changes, the society became progressively child-oriented. As children have assumed more importance for the modern family's very existence, they also have acquired more authority over decisions about their careers and their marriage plans and other questions that were once within their parents' prerogative. The delegation to children of these vital decisions, an ultimate expression of the philosophy of the worth and dignity of the individual, created a new freedom of children over their own lives which proved to be an awesome responsibility in this secular age. With the diffusion of vocational programs and separate educational tracks in the public schools students were required to take distinctly separate training programs for college and the vocations. Vocational decisions were faced at an earlier age; aspects of the troublesome period of adolescence thus extended into the elementary years. At the same time, traditional standards of morality were being challenged in urban ghettoes, and splintering religious groups, scientific relativism, wars and depressions combined with world-wide change to make adult-based moral systems less relevant. Adolescent societies developed their own confused and faddish standards of behavior and their own semi-adult idols. Many now have adopted a "cool" indifference, while at the same time others continue to search for forms of moral involvement in causes opposed to adult actions and standards. In either case, the moral spine of youth has remained pliable as adolescents have attempted to adapt themselves to an adult world radically altered from the one their parents and grandparents knew. Without the benefit of traditional standards to guide their decisions, adolescents have been thrown on their own inadequate resources. Ironically, many have sought to escape the responsibilities of freedom by anxiously conforming to their peers and to the faintest wishes of those adults whom they respected.

During the first half of this century each adolescent emerged on the labor market as part of a work force that was doubling each decade. Work was monotonous, and automation had removed the mass of people from the products of their own efforts. They became progressively less identified with the jobs they performed. Alienation from work was, and remains, especially a problem of the lower occupational groups, but with automation a growing number of white collar workers can expect to experience similar problems. The diffusion of mass culture, automation and population growth and mobility, mass layoffs in industry, computerized planning, the wholesale destruction of life in wars, are all developments during the century which have served to progressively diminish the significance of the individual. Not the least of these developments has been the growth and bureaucratization of school systems, standardization of curriculums, the proliferation of required courses, increased specialization of teachers, and a growing number of specialized courses of study. These developments have merely augmented earlier trends and increased the basic problem — the encroachment of societal changes on the worth of the individual.

In short, at precisely the time when society has become more individualistically oriented and adolescents have been able to experience greater freedom within the family, they have been rendered less significant and less adequate by the facts of an increasingly complex and standardized society that has emerged.

Industrialization, which displaced the apprenticeship system as a means of selecting and socializing replacements for the labor force, was responsible for some problems. Several factors compounded the problems of decision-making that were confronting adolescents no longer able to follow in their fathers' vocational footsteps. Among them were the proliferation of new forms of specialization (e.g., machinists and tool and die makers), and the rapid disappearances of outmoded occupations (e.g., harness makers and homestead farmers), the increasing number of women entering the labor force, and the complexity of the division of labor. These changes were already so profuse by the turn of the century that parents, many of whom had only recently migrated into the growing cities, were confused and uncertain of their own judgments. The masses of immigrants who had entered the nation before the turn of the century were even less able to cope realistically with the complexities that had developed during their own lifetimes; their problems involved the entire realm of social transition into a new culture. The nation's industries were not only demanding new skills but also were providing new opportunities for the sons of displaced farmers and second generation immigrants. If the vocational aspirations of these new generations were merely consonant with those of their parents, the problems surrounding their vocational choice would have been fewer.

Adaptation

Vocational guidance was a response to these conditions. In early phases of urban industrial society, characterized by breakdowns in traditional norms and increases in available alternatives, a person's vocational role, more than any other single factor, determined his life chances. Because of the specialized skills demanded in such a society, education becomes a paramount means for achieving the more rewarding social positions. It is not surprising, then, that the problems associated with vocational education were an early incentive to counselors. The origins of the vocationally oriented segment of the counseling movement, i.e., "vocational guidance," can be traced to 1908, when the Boston Vocational Bureau was established under the leadership of Frank Parsons

(Miller, 1961).[3] The Bureau's responsibility was to select students to attend the already overcrowded vocational schools in the area. While the stimulus to which men like Parsons were responding was primarily economic, the objectives they were pursuing were essentially humanitarian. They sought not merely to meet the demands of industry, but to help young individuals find their "rightful place" in the changing society.

It is significant that guidance and counseling developed in the schools as part of a progressive movement, which held that educational practice should be guided by the interests of the individual. Guidance workers maintained a broad conception of vocational choice, which was viewed as a vital part of the young person's discovery of identity. Parson's early interest in vocational guidance stemmed from his dedication to the principle of achieving economic equality for all social classes. Early textbooks on the subject of vocational education paid considerable attention to moral and religious instruction *(Miller, 1961)*.

Thus, the primary initial aim of the vocational guidance wing of the counseling movement (and probably of other segments of the movement as well) was to preserve the humanistic conception of "man the individual" in an industrial society built on the image of "man the worker."[4] Moreover, many leaders of the movement embraced a democratic philosophy which also had matured during this century. In this sense, the movement reflected an underlying faith in the inherent worth of the individual. In its most ambitious earlier forms, counseling promised to defend the individual against the increasing bureaucratization of life. It was an attempt to keep the "whole person" in perspective as he became specialized within the machinery of industry, commerce and standardized school systems. Barry and Wolf contend that even now, the counselor is the last stronghold of the individual in the modern bureaucratic school *(Barry and Wolf, 1962)*.

Lags

Despite its success in adapting to new demands, the counseling movement has been encumbered by handicaps. For the most part, it was an ambitious undertaking pursued at first as a part-time effort by practical, busy men. It is understandable that, working with overcrowded schedules and facing many practical demands, the pioneers of the movement were

[3] By way of comparison with another counseling area, the first marriage education course was not offered in a major university until 1925, although the folk origins of the family movement can be traced much further back.

[4] There is a parallel development in the marriage counseling movement in the sense that eventually counselors began to emphasize the individual rights and personal happiness of marriage partners instead of saving marriage exclusively. A primary objective of family counselors has been to prevent personal dissatisfaction which might otherwise arise from "poor marriage risks." Also, psychoanalysts sometimes have stressed the priority of the client's mental health over conventional codes of behavior.

not inclined to develop a systematic philosophy of counseling specifically *applicable to the problems faced by the urbanite.* Rather, they were obliged to rely on largely outmoded pre-industrial ideals — distrust of formal organization and the idealization of close interpersonal relationships and stability. The early leaders had not (and have not yet), for example, developed a philosophy that would help men face the realities of living in automated factory systems and standardized business offices where they were defined as interchangeable units. Counselors have not yet developed an alternative of society to the "big family" industry and group-oriented community model which has been idealized by American writers from Thoreau to Frank Lloyd Wright, and they have perpetuated the expecations of previous generations, e.g., that one's personal satisfactions, his sense of success, and his friendships should be derived from his job, and that personal happiness should be sacrificed for the sake of family stability.

Nor have counselors developed effective procedures for implementing their ideas. Even when the initial humanitarian vision prevailed, its complete fulfillment lagged due to the ill adapted means being employed in practice. The ineffectiveness of some of its strategies is one reason why counseling has not yet fulfilled its promise, despite the many good intentions of its practitioners. For example, in the formative years few aptitude tests had been devised, and an effective classification of occupational information still had not been developed. Finally, until recently little interest has been demonstrated in designing research which would yield more realistic information about workers' problems and which would develop better procedures for implementing counselors' ideals and for testing their theories. Lags in these respects still have not been adequately compensated for.

Displacement of Goals

However, as procedures became adapted to an urban industrial setting, other problems developed due to neglect of the original objectives. Under pressure of daily practice and in search for effective procedures to solve immediate, often administrative, problems the humanistic objective of helping individuals with their own problems was easily obscured and partly replaced by other objectives. The balance between "help" and "direction" was delicate in theory, and in practice the line between alleviating the young person's sense of alienation in an overwhelming environment and violating his sense of individual worth was blurred at best. (These points will be developed throughout the chapter.) Therefore, although the ideology of individual worth is so well ingrained in the movement that there can be little doubt of the sincerity of those who express it; and while the effective contribution that individual counselors have made to the development of many persons is not to be challenged, the point noted in the discussion which follows is that the tools with which counselors work, their own preconceptions, aspirations, and work environment, and the pressures of the adult middle-class community, each are forces which have distorted and partially replaced the original counseling objectives.

Counselors are handicapped by lack of scientific knowledge and must rely on partial information, impressions, personal experience and their own values and interpretations. Even the validity of the extensively used intelligence tests is disputed, and Darley once reported little correspondence among different methods of identifying "problem cases" (*Darley, 1937*). The possibility must be entertained, therefore, that the counselor's judgments reflect personalized middle-class biases that can obscure the individual interests of clients, and that *the tools he uses are employed to justify a priori judgments based on his position in society rather than on the client's own interests and objectives.* Attention now is turned to this consideration.

Middle-Class Themes in Counseling

Most counselors, themselves of middle-class origins, probably have embraced the middle-class value system, a perspective that unavoidably colors perceptions of client problems and interests. The counseling movement, like the reform movement generally, was not requested by those who were the objects of its services, but was conceived by middle-class teachers, professionals and politicians and implemented in school systems and other agencies whose middle-class character and control is too well known to require documentation. Counselors have been able to maximize public support by upholding middle-class objectives, and yet the same values often have required subtle compromises in some of the principles underlying the notion of humanitarianism.

In order to appreciate the role that the middle-class value system has played in the development of counseling and psychotherapy, it is useful to recall some of its characteristic themes. A very simple model of stratification necessarily has been adopted for this purpose. A fuller treatment would require a more complex model that takes into consideration several dimensions of stratification and the degree of consistency among them, and which accounts for recent trends, including recently noted differences between bureaucratic and entrepreneurial families. This discussion, too, necessarily must be limited to typical cases. But contrary to Kagan's assertions, literature on variability within classes *does* exist which necessarily would be included in a more complete account (*Kagan, 1964*). It should not be necessary to point out also that class position is only one of many sociological variables influencing behavior and does not "explain everything"; no one advocates that counselors should stereotype their clients solely in terms of their socio-economic character-istics. But social class position is a vital part of a large configuration of sociological variables that help to explain much about the behavior of individuals.

DuBois *(1955)* and Kluckhohn *(1953)* have identified what are termed American "focal values," most of which are typically those of the middle classes in the United States. The value of *man as master* of a materialis-tically conceived universe is pervasive in American culture, and closely tied to a faith that if a man is industrious and thrifty he can be success-ful. Work is regarded as inherently good; it represents a major source of a man's identity and a principal means through which he can "express himself."

A closely related belief is that *man is perfectable.* One way of perfect-ing himself is through his occupation, by leaving evidence of his accom-plishments. Thus, a truly successful man "proves" himself through his social mobility in competition with others *(Rosen, 1956)*. However, a man's relationship to other men is believed to be one of equality — even though this value can be inconsistent with the fact of successful mobility. The belief in equality restrains the successful man from competing too much, and requires him to respect the inherent value of others, avoiding the depreciation of those who are less fortunate than he. Finally, the belief in self-improvement and social progress reinforces *optimism about the future (Schneider and Lysgaard, 1953)*. This future orientation is re-flected in a faith in planning. Even parenthood and child spacing are subject to planning by groups advocating distinctly middle-class defini-tions of sexual intercourse. The concept of work as a lifelong career, too — i.e., an orderly progression of jobs — is an expression of this faith in the future and a firm expression of the middle-class person's faith in personal progress.

Adaptation

It seems safe to assume that on most criteria of social stratification, counselors are middle-class and they can usually be expected to embrace middle-class values. Counseling owes its very existence to the belief that man is perfectable and can control his own future by long-range plan-ning. There is not only evidence that the most promising students se-lected for training for counseling (as judged by their professors) have longer time perspectives than less promising students *(Sattler, 1964)*, but also that vocational counseling *enhances* their future — more than their past — orientations *(Matulef, Warman and Brock, 1964)*.

The social prestige of most counselors seems to exceed both their in-come and their social power. If so, this is a type of disparity which could affect their sense of status security and lead to defensiveness *(Seeman, 1960)*. The role of a counselor's personal values is an important consideration, in any event. For counseling seems to be more effective when the counselor is able to transfer his own values to the client. One study shows that college students in psychotherapy improved when they began to adopt the psychotherapist's values, provided that they were able to translate them into their own peculiar framework and language (*Landfield and Nawas, 1964*). Hence, it is possible that one outcome of psychotherapy is to help the client to passively accept rather than to challenge the underlying assumptions of the culture. The hazard is that from the middle-class perspective it is natural for the student to appear as a member of the labor force, a potential dropout, a divorce statistic. Counselors are expected to manage an awkward balance between community-acquired perspectives and those ingrained in their professional ideology. It would be surprising if the community perspective did not prevail at least some of the time.

If *both* person and work are valued, then job satisfaction, the optional unification of self and work, becomes not only a moral right of the individual but a basis for justifying the emphasis on work so necessary for the advancement of industrial societies. For the man who takes his status seriously, choice of curriculum, job, and spouse are grim obligations; indifference to planning for career and evidence of disinterest in work assume the proportions of sin.

The importance which the 20th-century middle-class American attaches to his work is not typical of all societies. In pre-industrial society, work was regarded almost solely as a condition of survival, and whatever identification with work that did develop was due primarily to tradition and necessity. As the economy advanced the survival motive was replaced by a success motive, and the acquisition of material objects became evidence of that success. Hence, children who once were told that if they did not work hard they and their neighbors would not eat, later were warned that they would not become successful unless they did work hard.

Presumably, vocational success would create personal satisfaction as well as an unbeatable combination which would not only provide incentive for a career but moral justification for working hard. However, it was also clear that the vast majority of laboring people were *not* successful in the materialistic sense of the term and their morale was compromised by the degrading or boring quality of the majority of industrial jobs, and by the confusing array of alternatives available. With widespread dissatisfaction, with work threatening many of the assumptions behind the industrial society, counselors adopted two basic strategies which were utilized to increase levels of job satisfaction. First, as it seemed entirely possible that some persons were better adapted to poor work conditions than were others, low expectations were held of certain segments of the population, notably the lower-class slum children; they commonly have been the main source of enrollments in job-training programs in high schools. The other hope was that certain individuals might be trained and otherwise encouraged to escape the more degrading and unsatisfying jobs, so a few were encouraged to take precollege courses. These developments were, of course, occurring in a stratified and segregated urban society where the plight of minority groups was becoming increasingly apparent; clearly, it was they who most needed help up the socio-economic ladder.

So well adapted were counselors to the premises of the existing social order, however, that few of them were prepared to work for the elimination of the low-paying insecure jobs themselves and other underlying conditions responsible for the lower class condition. Ironically, the humanistic-individualistic bias of the counseling perspective in effect has served to reinforce this conservativism. In concentrating on the purely personal, private lives of individuals, the public realms of social structure could be ignored. If social problems are in reality problems experienced by individuals, then their solution depends upon increasing personal adjustment and satisfaction. The solution to employment discrimination against a Negro in one's office is, for example, a phone call to an employer known to be tolerant. The leap between the counselor's immediate concern for one man's problem and any long-range responsibility that he might have for leadership in the civil rights movement apparently has been too large for most counselors attempting to assist specific individuals with their immediate problems.

Lags

Some of the lags and goal displacements implicit in the foregoing general comments deserve additional treatment. Even with the humanitarian vision clearly before them, it was often difficult for counselors to implement it in practice. With increasing automation and mechanization it has become progressively difficult to combine vocational success with a high degree of intrinsic job satisfaction. Workers, especially those engaged in routine assembly-line work, have found it difficult to identify with their jobs because work patterns are set largely by machines, with little opportunity remaining for spontaneous activity for individual creativity. The lack of incentive for workers to identify with their work or their work place is reflected in a study of three Midwestern plants, where Dubin found "that only about 10 percent of the industrial workers perceived their important primary social relationships as taking place at work. The other 90 percent preferred primary interactions with fellow-men elsewhere than on the job" (*Dubin, 1956*). There is also reason to believe that alienation from work may be moving upward into executive and professional levels as they become automated. Thus, while work retains its crucial role in forming the worker's conception of himself, the unstable and frustrating conditions under which much of it is performed makes the job a source of insecurity and personal anxiety.

Nevertheless, counselors have found few alternatives and persist in their use of job satisfaction and career commitment as criteria of the ideal coincidence between a man and his job. Insistence on these traditional criteria may have deterred some counselors from helping their clients to make a full adjustment to the realities of work which have developed.

The typical counselor, laboring under traditional concepts of the work force, encourages young people to arrive at "clear and certain" decisions. However, the ability to live with *indecision* in areas such as vocational and marriage choices may be an increasingly useful skill in a society where there is often little connection between what one wants to do and the opportunities available at a given moment. One-half of the jobs currently available to a high school graduate probably did not exist when he was in the eighth grade, and the typical individual can expect to have several careers and more than one spouse in a lifetime. Under these circumstances, the underlying assumption that everyone must "know" what he wants to "do" or to "be" early in life is not entirely reasonable. The fact is that in a mobile, industrial society characterized by short working hours and early retirement, it is becoming less true that an individual's material success and prestige hinges on his identification with a specific career line. Rather, the less attached a person is to a particular line of work and to a specific work place, the freer he is to take advantage of new opportunities that arise elsewhere. Thus, to the extent that counselors continue to suggest to young people the virtues of company loyalty and dedication to a career, they may inadvertently innocently perform a more helpful service to employers than to their clients, whatever their sympathies. Many counselors probably have not yet fully taken into account the function that emotional *de*tachment, or the ability to remain *un*committed, plays in a changing society.

It is ironic that members of the lower class, the very group which from a middle-class viewpoint appears to have the most problems, may be better adapted emotionally to the type of society that is emerging than are members of the middle class. For example, lower-class peoples seem better conditioned to the fact that much work is routine and boring, their expectations focusing on requests for shorter hours and a stable salary. With less of his self-image determined by the work setting, the lower-class person is less likely to experience personal defeat when he obtains a low-status position or loses his job temporarily. It also probably is true that the lower-class child whose father has found it necessary to move frequently from job to job is better able to cope with the problem of technological unemployment than is the middle-class child who has a fixed idea of what he wants to do and has prepared himself for a limited range of vocational alternatives. Even the best intentioned counselor may do disservice to his clients unless such considerations are taken into account.

Moreover, there is a danger that counselors will underestimate the contributions that the lower-class images of the "good life" can make to the emerging society. For, typically having adjusted their conceptions of the "good society" so thoroughly to the middle-class industrial order, only the most sensitive of counselors will be able to entirely anticipate the full implications of a shorter work week with increased emphasis on leisure time that it involves. Though many continue to act as though efficiency, commitment to work, personal industriousness and other notions inherited from the age of scarcity still are important, these traditional concepts are inadequate for the younger generation now facing problems of leisure and of abundance. Ironically, lower-class students may have fewer problems in adjusting to leisure than do counselors themselves.

Displacement of Goals

Counselors can be trapped in any event. For if they maintain outmoded conceptions of the good society, they might act unrealistically and ineffectively due to failure to anticipate changing circumstances. But, if they accommodate to these new circumstances, they run the risk of compromising some of their objectives. For example, counselors seem to have compromised their belief in man's superiority over his environment to the extent that they have advised Negroes and other minority group members realistically not to expect too much. Yet, recent militancy has opened up opportunity for educated Negroes who have not prepared themselves for it.

Caught up with the status system, much of the advice which counselors give to adolescents tends to reaffirm social stratification rather than the value of individual needs and interests. For example, the advice to persons to marry others who are like themselves is in fact advice to marry their status peers. Also, counselors are more disposed to emphasize the advantages of college than to point out to students that the bulk of jobs do not require a high school education. To the extent that lower-class children are likely to be guided into what is termed the Vocational Program, their present status is reinforced, while middle-class children are encouraged to enroll in an academic program leading to college. The counselor is apt to shift his perspectives on such points when counseling lower-class and middle-class children. For example, Hollingshead reported that when teachers counseled middle-class parents, they stressed pupils' academic performance; but when they counseled lower-class parents, they emphasized discipline problems (*Hollingshead, 1949*).

Even the humanistic vision of the early leaders in vocational guidance was interpreted from the perspective of middle-class beliefs about the importance of work and careers as central life interests. The importance of careers now has made college counseling a central theme of the movement. Many counselors, like their students, have come to regard education as a means to the end of vocational preparation. Knowledge skills applicable for professional and other types of careers have crowded out less utilitarian subjects from the curriculum. Because science is instrumental for engineering and for the cold war, science courses have received preference to less immediately usable though more individualizing expressive subjects, such as art and music. In this regard teachers of art and music occasionally complain that counselors tend to encourage able students to take science courses while discouraging them from art and music. The following type of statement typifies this concern:

> I know of one counselor here who has told two students not to take art. It's too easy for them. I felt, that's really great! No wonder my classes are so low, if they're getting this kind of counseling.

It is noteworthy too that, contrary to counseling theory, in practice counselors typically find themselves responsible for dealing with discipline problems, which disproportionately involve lower-class students. While these disciplinarian functions probably are growing less important, they continue to limit the attainment of empathy and rapport necessary for a successful counseling relationship and alienate the very group which is in some ways in most need of sympathetic assistance.

In adopting the practices and demeanor of successful professions, counselors run the risk of subordinating their humanitarian concerns to other considerations. The white shirt and tie, symbols of the counselor's middle-class status, serve to remind the lower-class child of the social distance between them. The detached and impersonal professional relationship preferred by many counselors to some extent also seems incompatible with the person-oriented egalitarian relationships to which lower-class clients are more accustomed.

The same perspective which has, in effect, resulted in the kind of ineffective counseling with some lower-class groups already alluded to also contributes to the preferential treatment of middle-class groups. Hollingshead and Redlich sampled mental patients from five social classes in New Haven: Class I (upper class), Class II (upper-middle), Class III (middle-middle), Class IV (lower-middle and upper-lower), and Class V (lower). They report that Class I-II patients received psychotherapy, which is regarded as the preferred therapy, more frequently for every type of disorder than did patients in Class V. The opposite, custodial care, was given most often to lower-class patients and least frequently to upper- and upper-middle class cases. The use of organic therapy, of which electro-shock is the most common, varied among the classes, but was more frequently applied to persons from the lower socio-economic levels. Financial expenditures varied by class even more in the same direction.

The data in this study also revealed that the attitudes of psychiatrists toward their patients is related to the patients' social class standing:

> The class I through III patients were the ones who were "liked" and the class IV and V patients were "disliked." Some of the "dislikes" were due to the frustration of pseudo-therapists who had to work with "bad" cases, patients whose desperate environmental conditions and personality characteristics made their work difficult. Practically all the psychotherapists interviewed disapproved of the dominant behavior patterns in the class V patients. They were repelled by their crude, vulgar language, their outbursts of violence, at times by their passivity and apathy, or by their acceptance of such behavior as a husband beating his wife and the wife taking the beating for granted, and their endurance of poverty and economic insecurity. The psychotherapists were puzzled and upset over the sexual mores of their class V patients. As a group, the psychiatrists were irritated by the patients' inability to think in their terms. They complained about the dullness and stupidity of these patients and particularly of their apathetic dependency. The following remarks are illustrations of such attitudes: "Seeing him every morning was a chore; I had to put him on my back and carry him for an hour." "The patient was not interesting or attractive; I had to repeat, repeat, repeat." "She was a poor, unhappy, miserable woman — we were worlds apart" (*Hollingshead and Redlich, 1958*).

Becker, too, has observed that middle-class teachers are more likely to be successful with middle-class children, and hence prefer teaching in middle-class schools (*Becker, 1953*). It can be hypothesized that counselors prefer to work with middle-class children for similar reasons.

Other approaches to psychotherapy, when carefully examined, are caught up with middle-class biases, if in more subtle ways. Non-directive counseling, or client-centered therapy as it is sometimes termed, represents a school of psychotherapy associated with Carl Rogers which starts with the assumption that each individual has within himself the necessary resources to participate in his own psychological guidance. As the client talks about his problem in the presence of a sympathetic counselor he supposedly discovers effective solutions to his problems. The counselor assumes a role of subtle influence in the counseling process or limits himself almost entirely to listening. In critiquing this approach to psychotherapy in 1948, Green makes the following comments, based on an analysis of Rogers' "successful" cases as he practiced psychotherapy at that time:

> In the first place, however disguised and denied, the members of this school are in fact propagating social values . . . Rogers claims that the psychotherapist must possess no moralistic or judgemental attitudes whatso-

ever. Yet, it is interesting that in every single case he describes as successful the client always attaches himself to goals, or accepts roles, that would meet the hearty approval of any Methodist minister: Mrs. Land sees what harm she has been doing to her child, and decides to become a "better, more mature mother"; Barbara, with pronounced masculine trends, puts an end to her "intellectual" endeavors in favor of bobbing her hair, using make-up, going out with boys, and learning how to cook; Sally, who hated school, adopts a "more constructive attitude." (*Green, 1946,* pp. 211–212.)

The very idea of one person "helping" another, which is implicit in the concept of counseling, can subtly convey a sense of superiority and righteousness to be in a position to help others *is* to be in a superior position in that relationship. In helping others, to what extent is the counselor demonstrating his own moral superiority? To what extent is he defending the superiority of his own moral system and his position in life?

The Federal Interest in Counseling

To fulfill their objectives and increase their influence, counselors also have bargained for political support. In view of the magnitude of Federal support for programs in counseling, vocational education, and related areas, they appear to have been successful. Often, however, the objectives of the movement themselves have been compromised in the process. In exchange for the government's backing, at times, counselors have permitted themselves to be co-opted by the government and used in several respects. As a result, the original aim of helping individuals to obtain their own goals has gradually become transformed into one of implementing national goals.

Changes

The emergence of counseling as a special role represents more than simply another case of specialization in which the family has delegated its functions to one or more outside groups. One social function of counselors is to defend against the gradual relinquishment of *adult control* over the younger generation. Decisions involving vocational and marital choices are so vital to the culture, and to the economy in particular, and adolescents are so unprepared to cope with them in a specialized economy, that it is unlikely that such decisions would be left entirely to the whims of youth. The emergence of guidance as a special position can be interpreted partially in these terms. The counselor represents the adults' interests and serves as an intermediary between the adult and non-adult worlds. Although he represents the interests of adolescents in a complex world as a representative of the adult society, the counselor also is obliged to take into consideration the national interests.

Adaptation

Federal interest in the guidance of young people was early demonstrated in the National Youth Administration and the Civil Conservation Corporation. The government was becoming so actively engaged in guidance work, in fact, that the Educational Policies Commission, fearing dual control, recommended in 1941 that these governmental functions be transferred to the U.S. Office of Education (*Miller, 1961*). The role of government in shaping the movement, Miller points out, is evident in widespread use of testing during World Wars I and II for selective and for assignment of personnel and in the role of the U.S. Census Bureau in classifying occupational information. More direct influence has been exerted through the publications of the U.S. Office of Education and its advice on the use of the Barden Act funds. The National Manpower Council has emphasized the national interest in its search for gifted students. Each state has exercised other vital influences over the direction of the movement through its control of certification and training requirements for school guidance personnel.

It is understandable that under this degree of political influence, leaders of the movement have absorbed some features of the Federal perspective. Several years ago, upon discovering that only two-thirds of the ablest high school students planned to attend college, Berdie interpreted the situation as a "waste" of the nation's talent (*Berdie, 1954*). In the same tradition, Wolfle sought to identify "America's resources" of specialized talent (*Wolfle, 1954*). Currently, Flanagan and his associates are following a similar theme in a nationwide study termed "Project Talent" (*Flanagan, 1963*). Counselors seem to have taken seriously their obligations to promote the national interests.

Lags

At the outset, it should be noted that some counselors have thought through this problem and have resisted nationalistic pressures. However, it is difficult to ignore the demands of the economy, and when counselors do attempt to resist government pressure, their assumptions get out of step with the social order. To the extent that counselors help students to realize their unique and unusual interests, independently of national demands, in effect they may be encouraging them to accept a marginal way of life — that of the artist, actor, inventor — and all that this implies, such as lower income and prestige, and alienation and their own resulting resentment and hostility toward people who hold more conventional views. In short, the counselor who attempts to maintain the individualistic goals of counseling in a society that rewards activities in keeping with national needs is, in effect, preparing his client for a deviant status, which also possibly aggravates maladjustments within the family of orientation.

Regardless of the way this question is resolved, the present preoccupation of counselors with the role that nationalistic interests does and should play in counseling may contribute to still another social lag. Concern about the immediate pressing demands of the economy for more scientists and engineers could easily obscure the implications for a far-reaching development — the problem of mass leisure. Central to the entire issue of nationalism is the premise that the nation's welfare is dependent on certain types of *work*. However, while this has been true traditionally, the appearance of automation and a shorter work week is likely to require a new integrating principle, a leisure orientation, which counselors as yet probably have not fully translated into their day-to-day counseling perspectives. Widespread leisure is already a part of the American scene; "in fact," says Riesman, "so great is the sheer quantity of our available leisure resources, that I do not think we can find very helpful models in other countries."

With automation and more efficient production methods, the work week has dropped from sixty hours to forty or less. In some industries the twenty-four hour week appears imminent. The accomplishment of more leisure involves a curious irony, for it has been attained through a Puritanical devotion to work for work's sake — an ethic which gives little explicit attention to leisure. Now that the dream of leisure time is about to be realized by many, because of the absence of a tradition for leisure few are prepared to enjoy it. It can be expected that eventually counselors will be called upon to help individuals adapt to a more leisure-oriented economy, and nationalistic perspectives can easily blind them to these trends. To the extent that the premise is accepted that the welfare of the nation depends on the kind of work that a man does, with personal talent being conceived solely in terms of vocational resources, there is a danger of overlooking the kinds of problems that the nation may be facing twenty years hence when the current generation of adolescents is attemping to perform its adult roles.

The significance that some long-range developments will have for the counseling of youth can be illustrated by considering the current problems that the aged are facing. For example, one study compared the adjustment of retired persons on the job before retirement to their adjustment to retirement. Unexpectedly, the evidence indicated that those who had been satisfied with their occupations made relatively poor adaptation to retirement, while those who were largely dissatisfied with their jobs made a very satisfactory shift (*Michelon, 1954*). What does this imply about the relative importance of the counselor's obligations to youth and to society in counseling young people about middle-class

313

occupations where identification with the job traditionally has been high? Under these conditions, is a national "search for talent" necessarily in accordance with the best interests of talented individuals?

The problems of mass leisure stem from a conflict between attitudes and conceptions of those born in an economy of abundance as against those born in the work-centered pre-1920 society — as were many counselors who are now in practice. Younger persons entering the labor market today will probably have the dubious fortune to experience a time when the traditional work norm no longer predominates, and where the work that man does is no longer as crucial as before to the welfare economy, where even a Cold War may be fought on other bases. This implies that the counselor will somehow have to come to terms with a different kind of economy, one in which work as an integrating factor in life has been largely replaced by a new integrating principle based on the realities of leisure.

Displacement of Goals

The influence that the nation's need for trained manpower is having on counseling objectives is forcefully illustrated in Ralph Berdie's report, *After High School — What?* On the opening page of his study, he asserts:

> Thus manpower is this country's most valuable natural resource. Classifying men as a resource to be used has unpleasant connotations for some people, but such a concept is not necessarily degrading since manpower, along with timber, or metallic ores, or animal products, is used for man's own betterment.
>
> Just as other natural resources have to be processed and subjected to various degrees of refinement, so does manpower . . . . The degree of refinement of petroleum depends upon the purposes for which the final product is to be used. Manpower also must be refined progressively as more exacting demands are placed upon the final product. (*Berdie, 1954,* pp. 3–4.)

In the above statement there remains little of the original vision. Degrading or not, the classification of men as natural resources with ore and timber is hardly recogntiion of their individual problems and interests. The net effect of the talent hunt smacks, as Miller puts it, of Jefferson's notion of "a natural aristocracy": ". . . Although deference is paid in most discussions to the maximum development of each individual as a goal of guidance, it is abundantly clear that this is not really the dominant drive" (*Miller, 1961*). There has been a relative disregard for the *un*talented. Also, the fact eventually must be faced that there actually are more talented lower-class youths than there are positions open to them. The implicit conception of students that emerges is not that they are primarily "individuals" but that they are primarily "workers" needed in the labor force; in effect, their interests are considered only to the extent that fulfilling them will satisfy the immediate demands of the larger society.[5]

The foregoing discussion is not meant to imply that there is a necessary contradiction between the needs of the economy and the self-realization of individuals in it. However, the two are not identical. One of the major objectives of the counseling movement was to combat some of the overwhelming and degrading effects that the economy was having on the individual. Much recent legislation does not reflect this broader concept of counseling, as many counselors themselves have objected. It is obvious, for example, that the Barden Act emphasized vocational guidance primarily in the interest of the national economy. Also, the intent of the National Defense Education Act of 1958 was to provide for trained manpower for the nation, in contrast to what counselors say they are attempting to do for individuals. For a state to qualify for Title Five funds of that act, for example, it must have a program for testing, and it must pledge to encourage outstanding students to enroll in programs that will enable them to go on to higher education. Indeed, the recent expansion of mathematics and science programs in high schools, and the growth of counseling itself in the past six years, as counselors well know, has not represented a response of local schools to local needs so much as it has reflected the Federal Government's concern about national interests.

Similarly, Conant's prescription of courses for talented persons is hardly based on the philosophy of individual differences. He asserts, "All who can benefit from learning should be enrolled in professional schools or universities . . ." (*Conant, 1961*). It is not clear whether this implies that all who can benefit also wish to, or whether college would be to their benefit regardless of their wishes. To the extent that talented persons have little inclination to capitalize on their talent, a national policy which utilizes talent as a basis for guiding persons into jobs is as arbitrary in its way as was the ascription of jobs at birth formerly.

The way in which governmental interests have blended with, and in some cases, predominated over the interests of individuals is reflected at certain points in a report of a panel of consultants on vocational education, which was commissioned by the Federal Government in 1963 to review and evaluate the National Vocational Education Act. On the one hand, they accepted with approval the criticism from Barry and Wolf that counselors seem to find security in information-giving-and-receiving. The panel professes to believe that counselors should deal with the "whole person," not merely with the vocational segment of his needs.

[5] Admittedly, the influence of political goals is not equally evident in all areas of counseling. However, there is a parallel among family counselors in the emphasis on "democratic" family relationships. The effectiveness of applying democratic political principles to the family has not been completely demonstrated, despite the emphasis. In fact, democratic expectations have tended to undermine the clear and stable authority system characteristic of most European cultures.

On the other hand, it also cites with apparent enthusiasm, the following statement of the National Manpower Council:

> The newer emphasis on dealing with the pupil's adjustment problems may compete with vocational guidance for the available resources . . . It seems likely that the increasingly broad goals of guidance may work against more effective vocational guidance. . . . The effectiveness of vocational guidance may be endangered by the increasingly ambitious goals of the guidance movement. *What can be done to encourage school officials to use their guidance and counseling staff primarily for vocational guidance purposes? (National Manpower Council, 1964,* p. 278; emphasis supplied.)

It is not clear, then, whether this panel views counseling primarily as a means to help the individual regardless of his problems, or whether it views counseling as a vehicle by which to steer him into areas of the economy which have a high demand for certain skills. The same anomaly reoccurs at a later point in the report. On the one hand, the authors cite with approval the statement taken from the President's Commission on National Goals:

> The status of the individual must remain our primary concern. All our institutions — political, social, and economic — must further enhance the dignity of the citizen, promote the maximum development of his capabilities, stimulate their responsible exercise, and widen the range and the effectiveness of opportunities for individual choice. (*Goals for Americans, 1960,* p. 3.)

On the other hand, in the same context, the authors state that:

> . . . the productive skills and the creativity of the American people have been major factors in the great economic achievements of the United States. The ability to produce has been closely allied with the system of education. Preparation of the individual for occupational competency through vocational education can be of unique assistance to *the national economy* during this period of technological, economic, and social change. . . . Manpower supply and laobr market demands are often in imbalance [emphasis supplied].

There is a possibility that, in the quest for talent, the dedication and creativity of the nation's most important workers will be sacrificed. Ironically, the very practice of encouraging people to work where their talent can be utilized most efficiently could jeopardize what is potentially their greatest contribution, creative effort. Yet, although educators have long been interested in the problem of creativity, in few areas is standardization so apparent than in training programs. Courses are rigidly prescribed, and creativity is compartmentalized by encouraging children to be imaginative in areas that "don't matter anyway" — art and music — while ideological conformity is expected of them when thinking about the family, religion, international relations, politics, and economics.

Under the threat of a Cold War, the strategy has been to capitalize on talent in a program of peacetime vocational conscription. This issue is as strategic as it is moral. Even if the nation's needs are taken as the primary consideration, encouraging people to follow their own inclinations to realize creative potential may actually facilitate the nation's ability to adapt to an unforeseen future.

Questions concerning what will happen if this nation goes to war have been raised frequently. But as significant is the question: What will happen if the nation does not go to war? What is the Cold War doing to us? What will twenty years of directive guidance, standardization of work and a search for talent do to the nation's creativity and vocational commitments? (*Corwin, 1965.*)

Conservative Themes in Counseling — A Recapitulation

A convergence of these forces behind the growth and direction of counseling has always threatened to transform the movement into an institutionalized means of defending the existing social order. This tendency, though an implicit theme of preceding discussions, will be treated here more systematically.

Changes

Counseling has been shaped by many of the same social forces which prompted progressive education, a philosophy which arose from the efforts of educators to preserve individualistic conceptions of the educational process in urban settings. In cities was growth. The needs of industry for specialized skills were creating unprecedented demands on existing public school facilities, and urban schools were accommodating the diverse interests of lower-class children who were swelling the cities and classrooms. The schools were forced to adjust their curriculums and procedures to this new clientele. However, it was not only *schools* that had to adjust, for it was apparent that the students too would have to learn to reconcile themselves to the new society. Eventually, in fact, social adjustment became the guiding principle, and the progressivism which had promised to redirect the spirit of education in the interests of the socially deprived turned into an adaptive philosophy in defense of the *status quo.*

They advocated some changes in educational practices, but the progressives were not anxious to challenge the existing social structure. The "progression" was clearly in step with the society which existed at the turn of the century. And here was the dilemma of progressivism, as it has been the dilemma of counseling: the desire for change was tempered by the fear of alienating the groups in power. Change was not encouraged either by the traditional respect for the virtues of small-town life with its consensus on middle-class values and its emphasis on primary group relations and stability. Progressive education literature has reflected a persistent concern about maintaining close school-community relations and a longing for the ideal "community school." In the midst of racial, social-class, and rural-urban upheavals, progressive schools concentrated on building a cohesive nation from immigrants and fractionalized regional groups. Democratic values, a common heritage and language, procedures for arriving at accepted standards and good citizenship were all emphasized as ways of adjusting Americans to the established order. The philosophy provided educators with a rationale for their custom of submitting to local interest groups.

The emphasis on social adjustment in the progressive movement was part of a broader trend toward conformism in American society which critics have variously referred to as the trend from "individualism to conformity," from "moralistic puritanism to social-ability," or from "the inner-directed to the other-directed man." Implied in these developments is the superiority of group cooperation over unbridled competition. In progressivism, the principle that one should voluntarily adjust to the wishes of others, was expressed in terms of the premium placed on cooperative, egalitarian relations among the students and their teachers. One underlying assumption is that the ends of both self-realization and the society's best interests are identical. This assumption is more appropriate in an agrarian society than in a complex urban one.

Adaptation

Literature on counseling often equates the goals of professional counseling with those of the school and the larger society. The assumption that there is no conflict between counseling and other facets of society, it should be noted, represents a departure from the conception of those who pioneered the field, for they advocated progressive modifications of economic conditions, and objected to certain "unhealthy" developments in the schools.[6]

In view of the concern expressed by the pioneers of the movement with the problems of unionism, fair wages, and child labor laws, it is significant that these problems have been largely ignored by the present generation of counselors. Even more significant, as some critics have noted, is the absence of discussions in recent literature of the fundamental issues of capitalism, concentration of wealth, growth of the Federal Government, and of governmental regulation, unequal incomes and poverty. There is also little evidence that counselors have engaged in concerted efforts to combat even the problems of job discriminations in race, sex, and age. To the extent these problems have been recognized, the entire focus has been to help selected *individuals* escape the worst

[6] Among the goals of the original guidance movement as expressed by the committee on Vocational Guidance in 1918 were the progressive modification of school practices, and progressive modification of economic conditions.

prospects of those conditions rather than to improve the bargaining power of workers. This limited view that counselors have adopted toward their responsibilities is a natural development of specialization. In concentrating on the personal, they have left more difficult public problems for the other occupations. But the other occupations have not yet clearly assumed the mandate which counselors abdicated.

Although invited to testify before Congress, counselors have developed little political power. They hardly have been in a strong position to criticize the establishment, especially now that they are an object of Federal concern; they remain relatively small, unorganized independent groups. But they also are middle-class by persuasion, and this perspective often simply has blinded the profession to imminent problems. It is noteworthy, for example, that VISTA and other attempts by laymen and college students to improve slum schools and living conditions which have developed in connection with war on poverty programs, were not organized by counselors; nor in most cases, have colleges of education, oriented to the interests of middle-class school boards, exerted prominent leadership in such programs. Counselor training programs do not yet officially encourage students to obtain experience living and working in slum areas, nor do they even officially recognize the relevance of such experience for counselor training.

Along with other professionals, counselors probably would like to enhance their own social status. The fact that middle-class teachers and parents have needed help with large numbers of children in school against their will has created an important market for their services; similarly, in exchange for administrative authority they have been assigned to work with the discipline cases. Counseling has become known as a profession which "helps people adjust."

Lags

It is ironic that even though conforming so well in some ways, those in the movement have advocated certain viewpoints which ultimately have been disruptive in an urban society. In the process of adapting to some of the newer features of urban society, progressives attempted to achieve a rather uneasy compromise with the pre-industrial agrarian virtues they were so anxious to retain by advocating creative spontaneity and close interpersonal relations in the classroom, and by de-emphasizing formal organizational structure. But, could these pre-industrial concepts be applied to an urban setting in other than a limited or superficial way? Significantly enough, the persons who objected to progressive methods may have shown more adjustment to urbanism than the educators who sought progressive reform but lagged in their willingness to fully accept the new society.

Compatability and "togetherness" perhaps counteract the fact that a depersonalized, standardized society has developed, but at most, the primary relationships are *illusions* and often not conducive to learning about another's more fundamental problems and needs. Although friendly, personal relations of mutual trust and personal respect are central components of the customary image of an effective client-counselor equation. The fact that the modern counselor is responsible for as many as 100 or 1000 clients, unavoidably, makes the counseling relationship a fleeting, superficial one — one in which it is difficult to even understand the clients' basic problems. This is as true of the marriage counselor or the clinical psychologist in private practice. Indeed, the professional relationships that members of these groups establish with their clients are based on a contractual agreement which involves the payment of a fee. These are pseudoprimary relationships at best, and some critics might question the effectiveness of a psychotherapeutic situation based on the "puchase of friendship."[7]

The paradox of the impersonal-personal counseling relationship is complete when it is recognized that the very clients who are able to accept depersonalized counseling are already better adjusted to the existing society than are those who seek from counselors more deep-seated interpersonal relationships. In stressing the deeply personal in their own relationships with clients, counselors seem to be advocating a set of expectations that are perhaps wanted but that are increasingly inaccessible to the present society and which they seldom can achieve in practice. Rather than helping people adjust to depersonalization counselors seem to have perpetuated the belief that depersonalization is bad while themselves employing depersonalized counseling techniques. This incongruity probably has aggravated rather than alleviated the problem of personal alienation.

Displacement of Goals

In the conservative context in which the movement was spawned, it appears that it has not yet been either anxious or able to implement many of the reform ideals of the pioneers. The movement veered from the idea of helping people by helping to improve social conditions to that of assisting selected individuals adjust to the better and the worse aspects of the existing society. In the process of this shift, two ideologies have played important roles. One comes from the mental health movement. Mental problems were defined broadly in terms of personal adjustment, and more conformity was prescribed for their solution. The pain of discrimination, poverty, inequality and unfavorable working conditions was to be eased by helping those who did not qualify for better positions to modify their expectations. For ex-

---

[7] However, there is reason to expect that the payment of a fee encourages some clients to maximize the benefits of the counseling relationship.

ample, despite the fact there is little reason to believe that many people inherently enjoy performing routine factory work, much effort has been devoted to matching personal characteristics to job requirements and to counseling those individuals who do not accept their assignments, those who are not steady and loyal employees. Whatever reform that is necessary is the responsibility of worker, not of the society.

The other and companion ideology is realism, or the repudiation of visionary idealism in favor of things as they are. The consequence of helping youngsters make realistic decisions about their work and marriage is to reduce the likelihood of their failure. Noting the emphasis on realism in the guidance literature, Barry and Wolf suggest that this fear of failure is characteristic of a security-conscious segment of the middle class *(Barry and Wolf, 1963)*. The advice, ironically, cannot be entirely realistic since it is normally based on a still unverified set of assumed standardized needs (and reactions to them) as much as it is based on knowledge about the parties involved. The effect may be to destroy much of the imagination, individual choice and hope of many youngsters who seek to become actors, artists and spacemen.

What is convenient about the principles of both mental health and realism is that they have usually reinforced traditional morality. For example, when counselors advise against early marriage or advocate matched pairing of persons on objective criteria, and the like, they can enjoy the luxury of being both conventional and realistic about marriage success. Seldom is unconventional advice offered. This is, of course, true when an unconventional solution would violate the principles of realism and mental health. For example, probably few counselors would encourage clients, especially women, to give serious consideration to the advantages of unmarried life as a valid alternative to marriage. But it seems equally true that conventional morality takes precedence even over the principles of realism and mental health. Evidence is accumulating, for example, to suggest that the incidence of premarital sexual relations is not so closely associated with postmarital success as spokesmen for conventional morality have asserted. In some cases, sexual promiscuity may be positively correlated with mental health. Parallel situations exist in the work realm, as symbolized by the "happy hobo." In such cases, is the counselor more likely to follow his principles of realism and mental health and inform his client of the research evidence which challenges conventional beliefs, or is he more likely to ignore the evidence in deference to conventional morality?

The theologian who engages in counseling as part of his professional role emphasizes a *special* hybrid of realism and idealism. Pastoral counseling, almost by definition, must be oriented within the framework of a given religious doctrine. Here, the value premises of conforming are explicit, and usually little deviation from them in the interest of client viewpoint is permitted. Other counselors, perhaps a majority, start with the assumption that democratic principles offer the most satisfactory approach for resolving most marriage and family problems, and perhaps unwittingly impose a political doctrine on family behavior in advance of verified empirical knowledge.

Perhaps emphasis on realism ultimately discourages innovation and risk-taking in a changing society that in many ways is better able to afford risk taking than ever before. Ironically too, from the standpoint of the larger society, which we are suggesting many counselors are serving, realism eventually reduces competition for the higher status positions, and perhaps selectively reduces the competence of those who attain them. In that respect, realism is no more advantageous to the broader society than to the individual.

Conclusion

The functions of counselors in American society have been shaped by competing principles of equality and of stratification. The ideal of equality was reflected in the motivation for the movement which originated with a distinctively lower-class focus in defense of the value of the individual. The appearance of counselors in schools promised that lower-class students would be represented in the adult middle-class school system. Yet, in practice, counseling efforts have had distinctively middle-class meanings, either social mobility or social adjustment. In neither case has the force of the movement challenged the social order itself. Much of the impetus behind the movement actually came from its promise of assisting individuals to fulfill the American Dream that anyone can be more successful than he is. A basic aim, at least in the vocational guidance segment of the movement, is quite clear — to help youngsters get ahead, or in lieu of that, to help them to adjust to the situation. This aim has almost completely overshadowed the early reform objectives.

The discrepancy between the dedication of early counselors to humanitarianism and their actual activities and sources of support seems to have grown. In order to impress middle-class influentials, it has been necessary to compromise the humanitarian drive to help those in need; the ambition of assisting everyone regardless of whether they have self-acknowledged problems or not has taken its place. In their quest for status, counselors have focused on the search for talent and discovery of the more readily soluable problems of "normal" individuals in the middle-class suburbs which leave more impressive records of accomplishment. The perplexing social problems of dropouts, delinquency, divorces, and unemployment have been relatively overlooked.

Then, *whose* problems are counselors attempting to solve? If the counselor is free to accept or reject his client's objectives, then surely the "need" for counseling is not solely that of the client. Would the typical counselor assist a group of rebellious Negroes attempting to organize for civil disobedience in protest of *de facto* segregation, unfair housing practices, or alleged discrimination in the school? Are counselors obliged to endorse the dominant cultural values, and if so, what will become of their positions as these change? The question remains: whose responsibility is it to assist and defend the social outcasts with their unacclaimed problems and objectives?

Theoretical Implications

Whenever one ventures to analyze colleagues in another discipline, it is certain that more is involved than a dispassionate exchange of ideas. Inevitably at stake are the statuses of the disciplines involved. For the invitation to analyze another discipline is an invitation to speak "objectively," and hence irreverently, about hallowed traditions; to question and reinterpret basic assumptions from another bias; and to speak of heroes without appropriate awe. Hence, opinions ventured by outsiders may be viewed suspiciously, even defensively. As outsiders, their opinions will be easily dismissed as naive, misinformed, and one-sided, and they may be regarded with a jaundice as rank amateur journalists. For outsiders are not well informed of the day-to-day practices of the profession in its diverse settings; they are neither familiar with the latest unpublished paper of the field's most distinguished spokesman, nor of all of the emergent power struggles and scars from previous struggles.

However, perhaps the perspective of outsiders can be of some utility precisely because they *are* outsiders — hence without visions beclouded by sacred cows and by skeletons in the closet. Outsiders, of course, will bring their own biases and experiences with them. They will not be neutral and will be blinded in many ways, but their blind spots may not be the blind spots of those whom they analyze. Therefore, in this and in our other chapters in this volume, a *sociological interpretation* of some of the dominant themes of counseling has been presented unabashed and with full recognition that no single analysis of such a broad topic can satisfy the diverse exceptions and the varying practices. The analysis is further limited by its focus on dilemmas and by an intentional exclusion of contrary viewpoints which are found in the counseling literature and elsewhere. The objective has been to sketch only in the broadest outline the types of *problems* that a sociological analysis of the counseling movement must take into consideration.

Having done this, however, we feel compelled to at least mention some of the factors which qualify the general observations, i.e., the sources of variability *within* the movement. Perhaps the most important sources of variation among counselors stem from their liberal and conservative attitudes toward people, attitudes that periodically have alternated with the course of the movement itself. Individualistic "liberalism" in counseling, by which is meant a dedication to the personal values and interests of clients, has been tempered simultaneously by middle-class values and nationalism, by bureaucracy, and finally by professionalism of the movement itself. Of these forces, professionalization probably represents the most liberal course of action, at least to the extent that a professional license implies a mandate to protect clients' interests. Granted that professionalism does not always work this way in practice, it is possible that some of the experiences and qualities contributing to a counselor's professional attitudes also influence his point of view toward his clients. Therefore, some consideration now will be given to some of the variables that contribute to the strength of professional norms in counseling and to others which effect the autonomy necessary to implement professional values.[8]

Professional Norms

As a monopoly of knowledge, a profession's character is largely determined by the amount and type of education of its typical members. A crude positive relationship can be expected to exist, therefore, between the amount of education of different types of counselors and (a) their self-awareness of their own ethnocentrism — e.g., middle-class bias — and (b) their tolerance and acceptance of unconventional attitudes and modes of life other than their own, or roughly their "liberalism." Perhaps it can be said, then, that most of the statements made in the preceding discussion, are more applicable to counselors practicing with a B.A. or with an M.A. degree than to those who have achieved more advanced education.

This simple statement, however, is obviously inadequate, since it fails to account for extensive variability in the capacity of persons with equivalent *levels* of education to define problems from the perspectives of others. This variability is partly a function of the *type* of education. There is some evidence to suggest that, in comparison to college students in the liberal arts, students in colleges which emphasize applied vocational education (such as education, engineering, agriculture, and veterinary medicine) are relatively conservative, at least politically (*Bereiter and Freedman, 1962*).

Conservatism toward unconventional values and behavior can be partly attributed to the type of students attracted to various programs, and, it undoubtedly, also, is related to at least two characteristics of the occupations they will enter: Emphasis upon narrow specialization and lay control. Specialization is likely to accentuate rather than offset a conservative

[8] For evidence that *political* liberalism increases with level of education, see Hagstrom and Selvin (*1960*) and Miller (*1958*).

bias. It can be expected that at every level of education, by comparison with counselors who have had extensive training in the humanities and liberal arts, those whose training has been confined to education, counseling and clinical psychology and other applied disciplines will show less tolerance of unconventional behavior and solutions for their clients. Some of these conjectures have vital implications for the way professional training programs have been organized.

Autonomy

Lay control can have an equally important influence on an occupation's values to the extent that counselors are hired to perform a predetermined service for an employer. They are under compelling pressures to "justify" themselves by producing desired results, their very careers being dependent upon their ability to please laymen. In the case of counseling, these "results" often depend as much on their ability to persuade their clients to go to college, stay in school, or out of marriage as on their ability to sympathetically support them in their own objectives.

The public's demand for practical results is probably so integral to the modern economy itself that no occupation escapes it. However, professions such as counseling, where the professionals usually are employed by the public, are especially subject to the scrutiny and control of laymen. It is hypothesized that, in comparison to counselors with equivalent levels of education in independent practice, those employed in tax supported institutions are more conservative and less tolerant of idiosyncratic attitudes toward the nation, the middle-class standards and alternative ways of coping with problems. This simple dichotomy could be refined further in terms of the institution's size, number of financial sources, type of community and other relevant distinctions.

Although the status of an occupation can be elevated by increasing the minimum level of education, there are several other relevant bases of status. In particular, the applied and creative sciences and the arts seem to produce different behavior at equivalent levels of educational status. Much of this difference can be explained by the amount of *autonomy* — or the power of an occupation to control its own work. Autonomy is sometimes derivative of status but hardly equivalent to it; and in the last analysis it is autonomy and not status which is the lifeblood of a profession, for it gives it the means to protect its clients' interests.

By hiring out their services to special interests such as government and business, counselors often have purchased status at the price of autonomy; they have achieved prestige and other rewards by permitting others to set their objectives and evaluate their practices. Hence, it is hypothesized that at a given level of professionalization, the efforts of counselors to protect the individual interests of their clients varies with the number of outside clients to whom they are obligated, such as government, business, and voluntary associations. At the same time, some counselors situated in independently wealthy universities, where they are likely to be under less pressure to show immediate results, can take relatively more sympathetic and tolerant views of clients. Even they, however, are constrained by the attitudes of the administrators who hire their graduates.

In this context, it might be asked, What effects do federal financing of counseling programs have on counselor-training programs? Which universities are selected to receive federal financing? And why? Are the counseling programs in privately financed non-sectarian universities more client-centered than their public-supported counterparts? Just as counselors have achieved their positions of authority by becoming associated with administration, just as they have purchased increased status by sacrificing their autonomy to laymen, so federal influence may be the price of becoming more autonomous from local control.

Bureaucratization also threatens a profession's autonomy. Counselors have been tempted to compensate for inadequacies of theory by relying on the authority of their official positions. But in schools, these positions often depend more upon their ability to maintain discipline than upon their effectiveness in helping students to solve their idiosyncratic problems, especially when solutions to them would require unconventional behavior. It can be expected that the ability of counselors to protect their clients' interests is lower in more bureaucratic organizations. But within a given bureaucracy that ability probably is irregularly (curvilinearly) related to their position: the lowest positions are powerless and the power of higher positions is so dependent upon the evaluation of high level administrators that counselors in them are not likely to use their influence in support of clients. It is those counselors with positions at the administrative level, but without normal administrative responsibilities, who are expected to develop the most autonomy in interests of their clients. Still relatively unexplored are the organizational mechanisms, such as part-time employment by which they are insulated from administrative and outside pressures.

The liberal, individualistic bias of professionals, then, is compromised not only by il-liberal education and outside constraints but also by a conservative organizational bias which defines people in aggregate form. Perhaps, in settings where profession meets bureaucracy, the long-run solutions will not be to return to the past or to re-emphasize the individuality of clients at all. Perhaps the solution will be more social action on the part of counselors themselves, action designed to alleviate some of the *conditions* which threaten underprivileged groups and anxious individuals in a mass urban society.

References

Barry, Ruth, and Beverly Wolf (1963). *Modern Issues in Guidance,* Teachers Press, Teachers College, Columbia University.

―――― (1962). *Epitaph for Vocational Guidance: Myths, Actualities, Implications,* Teachers Press, Teachers College, Columbia University.

Becker, Howard S. (1953). "The Teacher in the Authority System of the Public Schools," *Journal of Educational Sociology,* 27 (November), 128–144.

Berdie, Ralph (1954). *After High School — What?,* University of Minnesota Press.

Clark, Burton (1956). *Adult Education in Transition,* University of California Press.

Conant, James R. (1961). *Slums and Suburbs,* McGraw-Hill, 88–89.

Corwin, Ronald G. (1965). *A Sociology of Education: Emerging Patterns of Class, Status and Power in the Public Schools,* Appleton-Century-Crofts.

Darley, John G. (1937). "Tested Maladjustment Related to Clinically Diagnosed Maladjustment," *Journal of Applied Psychology,* 21 (December), 632–642.

Dubin, Robert (1956). "Industrial Workers' Worlds," *Social Problems,* 3 (January).

Dubois, Cora (1955). "The Dominant Value Profile of American Culture," *American Authropologist* (December), 232–239.

Flanagan, John C. (1963). "The Effective Use of Manpower Resources," *Personnel and Guidance Journal* (October), 115.

Green, Arnold W. (1946). "Social Values and Psychotherapy," *Journal of Personality,* Karl Zener (ed.), Duke University Press, 199–228.

Gusfield, Joseph R. (1955). "Social Structure and Moral Reform: A Study of the Women's Christian Temperance Union," *American Journal of Sociology,* 61, 221–232.

Hagstrom, Warren, and Hanan C. Selvin (1960). "Determinants of Support for Civil Liberties," *British Journal of Sociology,* XI (March).

Hollingshead, August B. (1949). *Elmtown's Youth,* Wiley, 9.

Hollingshead, August B., and Frederick C. Redlich (1958). *Social Class and Mental Illness: A Community Study,* Wiley.

Kagen, Norman (1964). "Culture, Counselors and Clients: Three Dimensions of Counselor Encapsulation," *Journal of Counseling Psychology,* 1 (Winter), 361–365.

Kluckhohn, Florence (1953). "Dominant and Variant Value Orientations," in *Personality in Nature, Society and Culture,* Clyde Kluckhohn, *et al.* (eds.), Knopf, 342–360.

Landfield, A. W., and M. M. Nawas (1964). "Psychotherapeutic Improvement as a Function of Communication and Adoption of Therapists' Values," *Journal of Counseling Psychology,* 11 (Winter), 336–341.

Matulef, Norman J., Roy E. Warman and Timothy C. Brock (1964). "Effects of Brief Vocational Counseling on Temporal Orientation," *Journal of Counseling Psychology,* 11 (Winter), 352-356.

Michelon, L. C. (1964). "The New Leisure Class," *American Journal of Sociology,* LIX (January), 377.

Miller, Carrol (1961). *Foundation of Guidance,* Harper & Row.

327

Miller, Norman (1958). *Social Class Differences Among American College Students,* unpublished Ph.D. Dissertation, Columbia University.

Rosen, Bernard C. (1956). "The Achievement Syndrome: A Psychocultural Dimension of Social Stratification," *American Sociological Review,* 21 (April), 203–211.

Sattler, Jerome M. (1964). "Counselor Competence, Interest and Time Perspective," 11, 357–360.

Schneider, Louis, and Sverre Lysgaard (1953). "The Deferred Gratification Pattern: A Preliminary Study," *American Sociological Review,* 18 (April), 142, 149.

Schwebel, Milton (1964). "Ideology and Counselor Encapsulation, *Journal of Counseling Psychology,* 11 (Winter), 366–369.

Seeman, Melvin (1960). *Social Status and Leadership: The Case of the School Superintendent,* Bureau of Educational Research, Ohio State University.

Sills, David L. (1957). *The Volunteers,* Free Press.

Wolfle, Dael (1954). *America's Resources of Specialized Talent,* Harper & Row, 259.

11 | CULTURAL MYTHS
AND SOME FUNCTIONS OF
SOCIAL PSYCHIATRY

Marvin K. Opler / State University of New York at Buffalo

Mental illnesses vary from intensely severe disturbances which totally incapacitate an individual to mild and often fleeting symptoms which perhaps trouble the sufferer more than others in his environment. A basic tenet of Freudian thinking, much too often forgotten by those inwardly anxious about their own mental status, is that mild and moderate impairments are extremely widespread in modern societies. In fact, the former mild disabilities were conceived by Freud himself to be so prevalent that he insisted that practitioners of psychoanalysis, or those physicians who encountered mental disorders generally, be themselves psychoanalyzed as a prelude to helping others. This doctrine of "Physician, heal thyself" has now spread into clinical and counseling psychology and even into social science sectors concerned primarily with human behavior. Nor is this trend in psychoanalysis a new growth or sudden fad. The author, as a social scientist interested in human behavior and its vicissitudes, subjected himself to such training as a lecturer for the Institute of Psychoanalysis of Los Angeles over two decades ago. Today, the number of psychoanalytically trained behavioral scientists is legion, and the fields of clinical psychology, anthropology, and sociology, as well as psychiatry, abound with them. Similarly, a much later development, rapidly accelerating today in social psychiatry, is the training of mental health personnel in the social and cultural variations of mental illness and therapy, and in the new directions toward community mental health.

The latter interests stem from the establishment in 1948 of the National Institute of Mental Health, now part of the U.S. Department of Health, Education, and Welfare, and from certain studies in the last decade, namely the New Haven Study (*Hollingshead and Redlich, 1958*) of the prevalence of those in treatment in a New England town, the Midtown Manhattan Study (*Srole et al., 1962*) of mental health among ethnic and class groups in a large segment of New York City, and the Stirling County Study (*Leighton et al., 1963*) conducted in a rural and small town area of Nova Scotia. While the New Haven Study limited itself to persons undergoing treatment, the Midtown Manhattan Study indicated that about 45 percent of a total population of adults, twenty to fifty-nine years of age, could be classed as being at least moderately impaired. Similarly, the Stirling County Study revealed that 37 percent of those examined at random in a small town area needed treatment. In their study of emotional disturbance among surgical patients, Zwerling, Titchener, Gottschalk, Levine, Culbertson, Cohen and Silver (*Cowen et al., 1963*) reported that nearly 55 percent of their sample could be classified as neurotic or psychotic.

Despite differences in the design of these surveys, the prevalence figures for mental disturbances disclosed are roughly similar. The variations in prevalence are less between communities studied, be they urban or semi-rural, than among the class and subcultural groups within a community. Cross-cultural epidemiological studies, where the cultural variations and contrasts are greater, enormously expand such differences in prevalence. Since mental illnesses, both in type or form and in extent or amount, may vary with cultural and class conditions or backgrounds, it is no longer thought sufficient for counselors or psychotherapists merely to undergo a self-evaluatory or self-explanatory training, but instead to supplement such sensitizing procedures with rigorous training in the multidisciplinary aspects of social psychiatry. We shall return to the significance of epidemiology at a later point.

Why are cultural contexts crucial in counseling and psychotherapy? In the first place, all cultures, and the various societies of mankind that contain human cultures exist as instruments of human adaptation. We are merely at this point mentioning the obvious. We are not implying that such instruments of human adaptation are perfect — far from it. The student of mental health epidemiology is typically aware that some cultures contain stress systems for large enough enclaves or groups within the system to be called, in part, maladaptive. Nor do we imply that by some mysterious Darwinian fashion, the best cultures survive. Again, the evidence is mounting that technologically modern and populous societies have not only better ways of recording mental health impairments, but the facts emerge simultaneously as we study so-called primitive cultures in the field and compare them with "modern" ones, that Western European culture as a type has not only greater amounts of mental illness epidemiologically, but more serious ills less open, as it were, to simple and spontaneous remissions.

What we mean by adaptation is that the anthropologist or sociologist studying cultures — either societies as whole systems of adaptation, or the groups within a society as adaptive or functional groups — tends to regard the system as such as having greater force or effect in the patterning of behavior than the private idiosyncrasies and unique qualities of individuals acting within social and cultural contexts. For example, failure to seek therapy or outright avoidance of it may stem more from attitudes about illness and concepts of sin and guilt which are common in the culture than from a lack of personal awareness of the problem. The social scientist is aware, perhaps more than most other behavioral scientists, of the pervasive influence of these larger contexts on individual action and conflict. In short, he studies the system as such because it is influential or even wholly determinative of outlines, significances and demarcations in conduct.

To a large extent, other students of human behavior — the psychologist, the philosopher concerned with ethics, or the psychiatrist — benefit from these insights, each in some particular way. The social psychologist will frame most questions in terms of ego-involvements of the individual in group functioning. Similarly, a philosopher will see ethical judgments as deriving in large part from social necessities, social processes, and social perceptions. Most recently among these professions, psychiatrists with the aid of behavioral scientists have developed perhaps their most active sub-field, social psychiatry. The practitioner in counseling or psychotherapy has of course been influenced by these trends in behavioral sciences leading to social psychiatry, in part because he requires the most detailed kinds of information about those who come seeking help from various backgrounds, kinds of communities, and differing cultural contexts.

The Myth of Individual Autonomy

All of the cultures of mankind, and the various societies and groups of people living in social systems also exist in time or in a stream of history. No matter how irrelevant this passage of time or course of history appears to the unsophisticated individual, his particular cares or problems, triumphs or strivings, ambitions or failures occur in this context. If an individual is blocked in growth or regresses to more immature levels, or even if he appears never to have outgrown certain infantile characteristics, we call such problems "impairments in life functioning" as well as failures in emotional maturation in the individual life cycle. In this way, we are thinking simultaneously of the context of development as well as of the process of personality evolution from relative immaturity to relatively unimpaired functioning.

From the standpoint of social psychiatry, this concept of impairments in life functioning in given social and cultural contexts is the key concept. Without it an evolutionary notion of adaptation or adjustment begs the question, Adjustment or adaptation to what? The idea of impairments in life functioning was devised in the course of the Midtown Manhattan Mental Health Research Study, (*Srole et al., 1962*) as giving due weight to environmental contexts and as freeing one from the sterile abstraction that adjustment or adaptation is a process apart from environment, a thing *sui generis*. It therefore referred to a continuum from "well" or relatively symptom-free and well integrating (well-balanced) personality in known social and cultural contexts down to degrees of impairment in such contexts. Obviously, the conditions under which a person lives include the basic biological factors such as age, physical condition and sex. But there are other conditions of existence, often modulating the organic substrata. Such factors are a person's social class, his culture or subculture, his economic placement, education and the like, factors which often define a way of life in special aspects which orchestrate organic functioning or modify it and produce a wider, more relative notion of impairment in life functioning. Such broadened perspective is more related to cultural contexts, of course, but is also more related to the individual's total adjustment or adaptation. Consequently, it is more realistic.

In his theory and practice, the psychotherapist or counselor is, after all, confronted with individuals first and foremost. Yet we do not invite him into the trap of the false conception that he will be dealing, when dealing with individuals, with a single paradigm of human development, a single evolution of personality, or in short, Man in the singular. The social sciences have matured too fundamentally in theory and in data aggregation to condense the pluralistic world of social and cultural differences into a frozen, monolithic unity. We therefore remind the practitioner at the outset that the relationship of the individual to his society and culture is an essential part of the definition of individuality. As John Donne said, no man is an island. Neither is human growth and development an insulated process.

While we begin with an evolutionary continuum, in the sense of stages from infantile to more mature and productive behavior, the stages themselves may be seen to have a variety of social and cultural contexts which modify them profoundly. Not only is the course of development modified in each person by his own relationships, but in a much wider context by the social relationships of those whom George Herbert Mead called "significant others" (*Strauss, 1956*). We refer to Mead to call into question who these significant others may be. In study of the individual, clinical psychiatry has usually employed an essentially biographic method, focussing attention on a series of events that begin with the antecedent family history, the circumstances surrounding the individual's birth, his early infancy, childhood and the temporal extent of his life span or life cycle to the present time. In certain restricted theories in psychiatry, primary attention is given to the infant and child, or at best to the adjustments of the adolescent period, as these set or exemplify the dominant patterns of a person's responses, feelings, attitudes and ways of interpersonal functioning.

Yet again, the average psychiatrist, unless recently trained in rudiments of social psychiatry, is often blissfully ignorant of concomitant patterns affecting personality structure and functioning that go back to forms of family structure and function, to child rearing practices in each and every type of infant discipline (including not only feeding, weaning, toilet training and genital awareness, but bodily contact, handling, responses to dependency, regression, independence, aggressiveness, anger, withdrawal, and what not), and to a whole gamut of relationships to own and opposite sex, to age, and to authority. The latter ranges of social relationships are the common coin of anthropological studies, and of late they have included more data from the whole area of emotional communication. In contrast, the blind faith that the practitioner can relate to any other type of individual, following self-exploration, while remaining ignorant of such outlines, significances and demarcations in human cultural behavior is a myth which has been criticized and demolished in studies of therapeutic effectiveness.

The Social and Cultural Roots of Mental Illness

In the first myth of counseling and psychotherapy is the myth of individual autonomy, the second is the belief that psychopathological syndromes are neatly classifiable as disease entities, unchanging in time and immutable in space. Besides the necessity of moving from the study of the individual as isolated from the environing conditions of his cultural milieu, one must study his problems as responses to the same environmental circumstances. The opposite position, stressing single disease entities, prevailed for decades in Western European psychiatry, assuming that there was one kind of "normality" and one kind of "well" individual — something which anthropologists now find patently untrue. In reaction against this assumption, sociologists have devoted considerable skill to study of the sick role in various kinds of social systems, be these families, occupational statuses, hospitals or wards. In accord with our notion of impairments in life functioning, we propose to proceed on the basis that sick individuals are, indeed, ill, but that role-playing is also not an elective process, but an inevitable one. One does not choose to enact a role as a voluntary action; but in terms of contexts of class and culture, or conditions of existence, all of these systems of belief, of activity, of values, and of emotional selectivity become the actual responses which are developed in individuals. One must therefore assess the social

333

and cultural conditions of existence from which individual conduct, whether normal or aberrant, is inseparable.

The fact that social psychiatry is now looking to the broad spectrum of behavioral sciences for knowledge of the etiology and dynamics of mental illnesses is an extension from the biographical method of inquiry about patients, in earlier psychiatry, to a more scientific concern for the role of psychiatry in medicine, in social science, and in preventive efforts. When perspective is limited to the question of how a given patient became ill, one abandons hard-headed quantitative thinking, generalizing formulations, and preventive considerations. It is true that profound Freudian insights were based originally on less than a dozen cases, chiefly from limited strata of Western European society in Freud's time. Yet it is equally true that early psychonoanalytic writers combed the then-limited literature of both primitive and classical cultures to broaden their formulations.

Actually, the two fields of psychoanalysis and anthropology were always in close relationship in subject matter and method. Psychoanalytic theory, when first developed by Freud, was in close agreement with the anthropology of those times. Anthropology alluded to primitive societies, in Spencerian terms, as the childhood of man, whereas early psychoanalytic writers spoke of the neurotic as regressed to primitive stages of thought. In one of the psychoanalytic variations on this theme, the child was seen as recapitulating the past of his "race" by virtue of a racial unconscious, or mass psyche. Jung, who devised this extravaganza of theory in human growth and development, agree with other psychoanalytic doctrines of the time that the child could be compared with both the neurotic and with primitive man. In the *Question of Lay Analysis,* Freud (*1950a*) himself argued that in the mental life of children today, one can still "detect the same archaic factors" once generally prevailing in "primeval days of human civilization" while his most orthodox follower, Flügel, 1961, developed the empty analogy between savage and child in "conflicting beliefs and actions" or "taboos based on repression" for which there was little conscious, or indeed "civilized" control. Freud's biographer, Ernest Jones, addressing the Royal Anthropological Institute in 1924, made the same comparisons of a "more archaic layer of mind" represented in neurotics and in the folklore and mythology of primitives "of the present time" concluding that both equally represent a primitive "stage of mental development."

Nor did early Freudians limit themselves to this general analogy. Karl Abraham (*1927*) waxed eloquent over the response of language to the Oedipal problem, claiming that sex gender was a "principle of language classification." While anthropologists in North America piled up linguistic evidence that widespread language families like Algonquin, Athabaskan and dozens of others did not employ sex gender at all, but used other classifiers, stalwarts of the Freudian position like Geza Roheim turned to myth and folklore for still other strained exemplifications of their view.

In general, however, a more psychosocial position developed in psychiatry, and while it made use of Freudian insights chiefly in the area of defense mechanisms, it nevertheless came to stress variations in development (as did anthropology!) rather than the single, unitary theory of developmental process. The adherents of the psychosocial position were impressed with the impact of culture and social environment upon the growth of personalities. They were consequently interested in the incidence and the prevalence *and* the variations in psychopathologic states. Again, in both anthropology and in psychiatry, a major emphasis was on the effect of particular cultural settings upon different individuals. It is in this setting that the individual grows and develops.

By social and cultural environment we refer to the gamut of patterned social and family influences which are transmitted and acquired by the individual through symbols (language, culturally stylized values and activities, commonly shared meanings). To these may be added the patterns of child rearing. To paraphrase Clyde Kluckhohn, these are forged into a way of life by being affirmed and reaffirmed in the common currency of custom and by having significant values and discernible connotations for the individual. Culture is, then, a transmissible body of facts, artifacts and historically derived ideas which regulate patterns of behavior, ethics, child-rearing practices, taboos, and even attitudes toward health and illness. Such elements are incorporated into personal functioning and into social controls of behavior so that each person lives his life span in a constant relationship with this sometimes "invisible" but always implicit background. While we readily concede that individuals possess their unique qualities, a social perspective insists that families vary in form and function, as do class and occupational strata, ethnic subcultures and other large segments of a typical modern culture. To study man at specific intervals in his life biography while failing to view him in historic time and in social dimensions is a fallacy of taking the part for the whole. Psychiatrists have worked pragmatically with just such kinds of limited data in the orderly accumulation of case records, but the task of formulating larger principles of human behavior has lagged behind the social sciences. To stimulate wider generalizations, consistent with a psychosocial position, social psychiatry has developed in the last few decades.

The question may be raised whether counseling and psychotherapy have also grown as a result of certain changes in ideology and values, for example, the weakening of the Protestant Ethic. Certainly, the proliferation of helping personnel, particularly in the United States, is a part of a picture of recent social change familiar to all of us. Such ideas appear cogent, since one hundred years ago, the typical American family was a unit of different size, activity and outlook from what it is today. From a fairsized unit, whose members labored together in rural districts, it has shifted in size, location, mobility and functions from a relatively stable unit, self-sufficient and self-contained. There is, in the first place, the transfer of basic economic activities to outside agencies, with more complete dependence on factory-made goods and urban services. There are extra-familial agencies of recreation and education. There are multiple family dwellings, apartment houses, residential hotels, tenements and blighted areas. There is segregation of ethnic and national minorities, and diversity of occupational level and income, all within the new settings of city and suburbia. When we group these factors together, we begin the analysis of these changes with the increased import of large scale industries, services and automation, the resulting concentration and growth of cities, and the separation, as a second process, of suburban districts. The consequences of all this for older family structure, and the transformations in social organization that have occurred, convince some that counseling and psychotherapy are basically the results of family functions drifting away to outside agencies.

Since social changes affect ideologies, the direction of social psychiatry is more probably influenced by changes in social organization itself. Spinoza wrote long before Freud that intellectual knowledge becomes effective or leads to innovation only if it is also emotional knowledge. In this sense, the seismograph of recordings of psychotherapeutic innovations, the rapid growth of counseling and community psychiatric services have been less a product of mere novel ideas than a mark of widespread familial dislocations and resulting social and psychological problems.

In 1955, when a small group of us founded and launched *The International Journal of Social Psychiatry*, we hoped to add to various innovations (like group psychotherapy, counseling centers in schools, and day hospitals) a rather long list of major changes in the organization and direction of psychiatry and clinical psychology. This list included both day and night hospitals, milieu psychotherapy, psychotherapeutic patient clubs and self-government, home treatment services, the walk-in clinic, "open hospital," and psychiatry in general hospitals. More important, the journal added greater recognition of social and cultural backgrounds of patients and awareness on the part of psychotherapists themselves of the importance of such backgrounds for doctor-patient relationships. This emphasis was corrective of classical unitary views in psychoanalysis, which were considered reductionist; but they were, as a series of innovations, considered to be a major extension of Freud's central psychoanalytic doctrines of transference and countertransference.

The Day Hospital, which extends services to patients on a daytime basis, had two experimental innovations, one in London through Dr.

Joshua Bierer and one in Montreal through Dr. D. Ewen Cameron. South of the Canadian border, Day Hospitals were pratically unknown and certainly nonexistent in 1955. Today, in one decade, both Day and Night hospitals are commonplace throughout the United States, and along with these, home treatment, milieu psychotherapy, patient government, walk-in clinics, "open hospitals" and psychiatric beds in general hospitals are more the rule than the exception. These developments took place less for intellectual reasons alone than because of social and cultural necessities.

With widespread emotional ills recognized in modern society, the attitudes towards illness, especially psychiatric illness likewise changed. Psychiatry and psychoanalysis were required to focus not only on how the individual patient got that way, but more and more on the typical problems of patients' lives, what was going on about them, and what could actually be done to change both the patient and his environment. One heard more of interactional models, of roles in hospitals, of symbolic communications. The latter focused not simply on consciously intended verbal communications, but also on silence; it emphasized habitual behavior patterns, facial expressions, or more subtle postures in addition to the sweating, tics and tremors of earlier history-taking and clinical pigeon-holing. The seemingly bizarre behavior and utterances of the schizophrenic came to be regarded by a Frieda Fromm-Reichmann (*1950*) as remarkably condensed and symbolized communications. To a psychotherapist and theoretician like Fromm (*1962b*), new definitions of individuality and freedom seemed to be required, demanding that one view the bonds of illusion chaining patients, as being the same bonds familiar to the run-of-the-mill neurotic personalities of our time.

Psychiatry without realistic moorings in the changing scene of society can only propose the narrowest analytic and conceptual model, limited to a single class and culture of a Western European type. It is interesting to note that the Joint Commission on Mental Illness and Health of the U.S., publishing some ten volumes largely in the 1950's, arrived at similar conclusions after social psychiatry was well-established in this country. In the same period, the author of this chapter published a volume, *Culture, Psychiatry and Human Values* (*Opler, 1956*) which defined human behavior as cultural behavior and mental illnesses as resulting from cultural stresses. Following this approach, it was shown that human cultural evolution was marked by behavioral changes in all aspects of personality from earliest times to the present. However, not only did normative behavior change, but mental illnesses had also changed in form or structure and also quantitatively in epidemiology. Sections of epidemiology and etiology documented these variations in historic times, and for anthropological aspects, continent by continent. The attitudes towards illness, especially psychiatric illness had likewise

337

changed. So, finally, had modes of psychotherapy. Before the close of that decade, it was possible to edit a second volume, *Culture and Mental Health (Opler, 1959)*, in which psychiatrists, social scientists, psychologists and public health experts applied these principles of sociocultural variation and change to current studies of mental health and illness, again on every continent.

The Myth of Mental Health

We may now consider the Midtown Manhattan Mental Health Study of the 1950's for which the volume, *Mental Health in the Metropolis*, Volume I *(Srole et al., 1962)* was a partial and initial statement. A crucial tabulation in the Midtown Study is found in Table 3 (page 138) which lists those rated "Well" as only 18.5 percent, compared with 36.3 percent showing "Mild Symptom Formation," 21.8 percent showing "Moderate Symptom Formation," and 23.4 percent showing varying degrees of Marked, Severe or Incapacitating impairments. This last figure is more than double previous estimates, which used less exacting methods of sampling and personality assessment. Earlier, in urban Boston and Baltimore surveys which yielded the familiar "one out of ten" of government mental health literature, no random samples were attempted. Whereas the mental health literature had continually referred to one out of ten Americans as someday requiring psychiatric care, current studies from Midtown Manhattan and from Nova Scotia more than tripled this figure. In the severely or markedly disturbed group of 23.4 percent, impairments varied from a 13.2 percent showing marked symptom formation, to 7.5 percent exhibiting severe symptom development, down to 2.7 percent who were virtually incapacitated. In the total study, only part of which is described in Volume I, lower social class and specific ethnic group membership were found to be pathogenic, as conditions of existence within a certain style of life functioning sometimes can be. Neither class nor ethnic group membership act singly to define such pathogenic conditions of existence. Rather, the cultural or ethnic group and class position combine to form a total aspect of subcultural conditions.

Commenting on the immediate reaction of the nation's press, particularly in New York City, we can note that some newspapers chose to emphasize, as we did, that one out of five Midtown New Yorkers could be designated as "mentally well" or comparatively symptom-free. Other publications seized upon the 80 percent as being an unrefined rate (actually 81.5 percent had definable symptom formations) of "mental illness." Of course, the 81.5 percent produces a congealed figure for the percentages given above of Mild, Moderate, and Marked, Severe or Incapacitating impairments; the virtue of such a congealed figure is that it represents in a continuum of increasing disability or disturbance the total problem of an ideally preventive psychiatry. If one similarly congealed all of the organic impairments of an adult population in an American city, total organic, dental and orthopedic disabilities might well reach such a figure of 80 percent without stirring the slightest publicity. It is because mental ills are unconsciously regarded as governing total performance or effectiveness that the congealed figure seemed shocking. Ideally, it is, as is such a hypothesized figure for all organic ailments going from mild disturbances to those definitely "Impaired." In our study, impairments referred to life functioning and adequacy in social and cultural contexts, certainly as serious a dimension as one could consider. Whether one focuses on the 23.4 percent of serious disabilities, or the 81.5 percent which contains those seriously impaired and extends to Mild and Moderate disturbance, depends really upon what is meant by preventive and social psychiatry. An earlier paper by the author (*Opler, 1958*) on methods and scope of the Midtown Study, stresses that *total* epidemiology is important in assessing the range of our mental health problem — not just those totally incapacitated or markedly and severely impaired. If one wished to indicate the greatly impaired in a community, treated and untreated, one could use the 24 percent. But if one wished to face up to the total preventive and social tasks of psychiatry, no doubt the 80 percent would be a more honest and less shame-faced assessment.

Obviously, as even Freud (*1950a*) noted, there are not enough psychoanalytic couches to go around, and the variety of services we have designated under social psychiatry labels is designed to meet the problem more fully in the community. Of equal importance to the development of community and educational services is the expansion of counseling and psychiatric science to more adequate behavioral science levels. The traditional systems of individual diagnosis and nosology in psychiatry, based on a single analytic and conceptual model of Man, are archaic, outmoded and misleading. It is not a "disease entity" in the sense of a discrete and invariable "illness" which brings the patient to the psychotherapist, but a derivation from conditions of existence, impairments in life functioning, and actual situations in which the patient is living or has lived. In like fashion, reliance upon remote and putative causes of mental illness, like heredity and constitution, have limited usefulness only in certain recognized organic syndromes. A recent Finnish study of an entire population of twins (all twins born in Finland between 1920 and 1930) has revealed that not one case of concordance for schizophrenia was found among identical twins (*Rosenthal, 1964*). American studies which have not used total twin populations, as did the Finnish study, are now viewed as worthless epidemiologically and misleading in that they have erroneously posed as epidemiology, or been quoted as representing twin studies.

The practitioner in counseling or psychotherapy has of course been influenced by these trends and directions in behavioral science. Yet he requires the most detailed kinds of information for individual applications, and for the most part he receives only generalized analytic and conceptual models concerning Man which avoid the specific social and cultural perspectives. Genetic models of inherited psychopathology, or psychogenic models applying to Man in general both fail to background the client properly, or to lead to a contextual consideration of an individual's problems. Notions of psychopathology as disease entities encourage a process of labeling patients and clients and thereby promote neglect of specific backgrounds and interpersonal transactions which give psychopathological maladjustments, as traits, real meaning and function. Thus, the realistic conditions and contexts of psychopathology may become totally lost from view.

In contrast to these stilted and overformalized abstractions, impairment in life functioning becomes the safest criterion for epidemiology of mental disorders. This is why the concept of impairment points to larger psychotherapy needs than have hitherto been estimated for modern society, and why it raises the sights for greater preventive efforts. Much of the work in transcultural or cross-cultural studies of mental health and illness, carried on by the writer *(Opler, 1959; 1963; 1965)* and colleagues, notes not only changes in the types of mental disorder as one goes from nonliterate to modern cultures, but more seriously it has pointed to an increase in both the extent and the depth of the disorders. As modern data indicate, nonliterate tribes, especially those without class segmentation (the hunting and gathering peoples of a fast-vanishing age), have mainly hysteriform illnesses, often simple conversion hysterias. If personality disintegration further occurs, as in primitive forms of schizophrenias (with simple echolalias, echopraxias or negativisms prominent), we find that they are primarily schizo-affective disorders in which shamanism and community supports can work wonders, or in which, often, spontaneous recoveries occur. The simple echolalias, echopraxias, and what we have earlier called "confusional anxiety states" with outbursts that the classicists might call "catatonic" turn out to be less serious than the dominating paranoid schizophrenias, so recalcitrant to treatment and so tightly constructed as defenses "in depth", of persons in modern cultures *(Opler, 1967)*. It is true that the primitive forms are probably best called schizophrenias, and are not as Linton *(1945)* earlier assumed, other mere repressive forms of neurotic conflict, or hysterias. Yet when nonliterate cultures are swept into the mainstream of modern times and experience modern forms of competitiveness, exploitation and disorganization (or in fact, change toward our type in acculturative processes), then their rates of mental disturbance also change to our type (including paranoid schizophrenias) so that the rates increase, as have ours, and the disorders themselves approach or merge with the kinds of illnesses in depth that we know. Linton rightly identified the conversion hysteria model as the chief illness form of the simplest nonliterate cultures; he erred in assumptions that echolalias, echopraxias, and confusional states were also mere hysterias. It is widely noted, however, that new and serious forms of psychosis have emerged in so-called modern times. In addition, there is evidence that neuroses have shifted from simple conversion forms, and that higher rates of psychosomatic ills have eventuated. All indications are that if the number of psychoanalytic couches are in short supply now, they will be still more inadequate to the problem as these trends continue, and as deeper conflicts or problems in culture become further mirrored in personality.

We presume therefore that counseling and psychotherapy will have still larger tasks in the future. We predict that the public, sensing the sickness in society, will require and demand more services related to their needs and types of problem. The community clinic, the multi-disciplinary team, the educational counseling program will all be more greatly necessitated. When this occurs widely, social psychiatry will have come of age. At present, it is growing in that direction.

The Values of Preventive Psychotherapy

Besides cross-cultural, and urban and rural studies, pointing to large-scale psychotherapy needs in modern society, perhaps the most shocking disclosure of the enormity of the problem has come from a study of third-grade school children in Rochester, New York.

> Several aspects of these findings with the "Red-Tag" group (children who evidence a need for psychotherapy M. K. O.) warrant further consideration. First of course, the absolute incidence figures are, in and of themselves, striking. Given a more than usually close psychological scrutiny which was made possible by the concentration of psychological services during the primary grades, 37 per cent of a class of third grade youngsters were identified, sometimes between the ages of six to nine, as having emotional problems ranging from moderate to severe. It is instructive to compare data with those from other incidence studies. For example, Bower reviewed several studies which had been done in school settings and reported in one case that 42 per cent of the school children in Columbus, Ohio evidenced at least a moderate degree of poor adjustment. He reported also that in Santa Barbara County, California, schools it was found that from five to 35 per cent of the children, depending on the school district, were moderately or severely handicapped emotionally. (*Cowen et al., 1963*, pp. 348–349.)

The authors compare these figures with the 37 percent needing treatment in Stirling County, Nova Scotia, and with the 45 percent prevalence figure emanating from the Midtown Manhattan Study, concluding that preventive efforts require early recognition and identification of disturbances. Indeed, the study of Bower is further cited as demonstrating that even teachers' ratings and certain standardized test scores could differentiate the emotionally handicapped and the "normal" youngsters above the fourth grade. As a matter of fact, present findings indicate this can be done still earlier.

Obviously, from figures given for childhood disturbance, as well as from adult studies, one can infer that the problems and scope of counseling and psychotherapy are enormous, as judged in independent studies, all from the United States and Canada. Furthermore, these studies are both urban and rural, adult and child, east coast, midwest and west coast. We believe these data on childhood incidence and adult prevalence are strictly comparable, or more exactly, it is to be expected that the 37 percent rate for children in Rochester might increase to a 45 percent rate in Midtown Manhattan for adults, particularly since Midtown rates were found to increase with age. Today, the task of the clinical counselor may seem to extend from child adjustment through general psychotherapy, including educational, vocational and marital counseling, and extending to personnel counseling in industry, institutional work on criminal psychopathology, pastoral counseling and the like. Social work and rehabilitation counseling can be added. All of these modalities exist because of the size and extent of the basic problems.

Just as mental illnesses themselves exist in a continuum or series, from mild cases to severe ones, so the counseling task applies to childhood and youth guidance and to educational services with special force to prevent serious illnesses from developing. School systems today provide services ranging from simple informational or vocational guidance, perhaps some of this having to do with sparking motivation on to cases where the child or youth is deeply troubled or severely disturbed. One can allude to this continuum of conditions for counseling because the counseling function itself needs support from such facts of epidemiology so that it can be planned for effectively. Too often in the new service, the school counselor is saddled with extraneous functions of running student clubs and activities, or drawn into the public relations functions of a modern school. Professionalism demands that the counseling function be protected from such incursions. The task is large, urban or rural, east or west, third grade or adult. To combat waste of limited counseling or psychotherapeutic resources, the typical dangers still obtaining in school systems are enumerated below.

The first danger is inadequate professional organization in the face of the enormous tasks of counseling or psychotherapy. The school counselor too often becomes a mere non-professional appendage of administration. For example, administrative pressures may exist to transform psychotherapeutic functions to disciplinarian ones. Once such administrative tasks are assumed, both counseling and research become impossible. No doubt, schools vary in class composition as do neighborhoods, so that the lower-class school disciplinary functions are matched, in middle and upper-class schools, by the now excruciating tasks of placing students in "prestige" colleges. Parents and school administrations can develop almost hysterical movements to achieve these goals. The "law and order" functions of lower class schools are replaced by the "status seeking" of upper class ones and in either case, professional standards of a guidance and counseling program may suffer irreparably. The middle- and upper-class schools, which are future or prestige oriented, may just as easily forget the problems of the child "here and now." Conversely, the lower-class school, busy picking up the pieces in the present tense, can end up far too little interested in what the child potentially might become or even, in cases of severe disturbance, insensitive to the actual realistic background of a present disturbance. In either case, the losses to preventive psychiatry are severe. One might call both types of error a danger of ignoring the child "here and now," since in one instance this occurs for reasons of fulfilling other prestige functions, and in the other because of a blind adherence to false ideals of maintaining a middle-class façade in the lower-class school.

A second danger stems from the first. If the school counselor is heavily saddled with administrative tasks, be they punitive and disciplinary or on the college placement and public relations level, his psychological evaluatory functions and distinct professionalism suffer further setbacks. The students, for one thing, see him as a disciplinarian or administrator, so that he is the last person they would approach with any sense of personal and confidential concern about themselves and their problems. Teachers also tend to feel a "discipline problem" or a scholastic and vocational "record" is open to administrative scrutiny. Rather than lean on well-known facts of disturbance etiology, they hope to prevent the blot from appearing on their escutcheon to keep the appearance that neither the disturbed child nor the behavioral problem could occur in their well-oiled classroom machinery. A school principal can also become confused to the extent of interpreting referrals as a negative danger sign; to some, an inactive psychological service is a most euphoric sign of well-being. However, the facts of epidemiology show that an inactive counseling service is unwarranted. The same facts indicate that adequate referral services are necessary if school psychologists are not to be overwhelmed. At any rate, teacher and counselor must understand their complementary and differing functions, and come to respect the limits and boundaries of each. Perhaps the best name for this specific danger is "the light touch" of school psychology, when it does not undertake to dispel existing problems. Teacher and counselor can grow apart or so lose contact that real problems fall by the wayside.

A third danger occurs when professionalism is so watered down, when referrals become so infrequent that the problem best caught on grade school levels is left to fester to the college scene or even into further adult life. The question is, how many counselors are encouraged to make psychiatric referrals when necessary, or what extra-curricular agencies exist to buttress their case-finding functions? One may suspect, from the number of hitherto untreated cases on the college level that not enough research has occurred of the sort of the Rochester study to impede in an earlier stage the seriousness and extent of college-level breakdowns. This is the danger of "too little and too late" and its chief implication is the need for further research elucidation of the extent of the problem and the modalities for intervention. A stronger professionalism, tied in with community mental health resources, including paid psychiatrists and clinical psychologists, plus increasing numbers of social psychiatry services (short-term, ambulatory and preventive) would cost more only in the short run. In the long run, the benefits of prevention and real care in the sense of the counselor's professional connections between school and community could be most productive.

One can think of other dangers, even that of an isolated overdevelopment of professionalism which is neither research minded, community connected, nor practically oriented. The counselor can easily become so precious a diagnostician, and devoted a specialist that he does not make referrals of the most serious cases or communicate his essentially private art to the better trained or most capable and more receptive teachers, administrators or parents. This is the type of operation which requires more alertness to vocational problems, awareness of the class distances between middle-class teachers and lower-class students, or between middle-class schools, on the one hand, and deprived homes or problematic parents on the other. Perhaps in larger systems, the vocational, college placement and administrative tasks could be separated out from the far more subtle psychological functions. Yet referrals must always be made between these wings of counseling functioning, and in general social psychiatry emphasizes the team functions rather than the separate roles.

The fact that social psychiatry demonstrates a connection between social and community influences on the one hand, and the resultant behavior of children and youth on the other has meant that the counselor and psychotherapist must become not merely psychologically-oriented behavioral scientists, but to some extent also interested in social science as well. If he is professional in his outlook and protected in his functioning from the diverting and probably lesser tasks of administration, he will be freed accordingly to look upon research, team functions, referrals and community roles as more vital elements in his own functioning. A school psychologist, for example, should have access to panels of psychiatrists and practicing clinical psychologists, and at the same time know the social agencies, welfare workers and community resources outside the ivory towers or brick walls of academic buildings. He may be encouraged in such arrangements by knowledge that a major hospital in New York City (Montefiore Hospital) decided recently that social psychiatry meant inclusion of information from its district on welfare services, unemployment statistics, delinquency and youth problems known to local agencies, etc., as a way of adequately backgrounding health necessities. As a matter of fact, the entire "open hospital" movement in English and American social psychiatry has been premised on the knowledge that once the community relationships are secure, the hospital doors will open as a consequence.

Social scientists have known for some time that tensions in society become mirrored in the very conditions with which the psychotherapist struggles, whether these be rising rates of youth suicidal attempts, a greater prevalence of childhood schizophrenias, or more obvious delinquency and youth sociopathy. On the side of research, lack of communication between social and psychotherapeutic sciences can only deprive the former of important areas for testing hypotheses, and the latter of information useful in developing preventive interventions and organizational strategy.

The uniqueness of diverse cultural backgrounds is a matter easily recognized in studies of the ethnic and subcultural groups in any modern community; they configure also in the range of differences that exist within or between generation levels, religious sects, geographical migrants, or occupational strata. Such variations in the course of life create for modern city dwellers the definable differences in value systems, roles, aspirations and socially determined stresses, all of which they see enacted constantly in urban centers. The social scientist, particularly, has familiarized himself with techniques for describing and contrasting such varying textures in families, ethnic groups, social classes and the like. Such metaphors as L. K. Frank's that "society is the patient" or Henry Sigerist's famous dictum that "medicine is a social science" are insightful statements meaning, in essence, that individual and family functioning become distorted, maladaptive or "sick" under certain social and cultural conditions. Such processes, however, begin in the family or individual only when relating in certain particular or peculiar ways with others; and the parts of social systems which apply functionally for some may prove to be dysfunctional for others. To derive or determine these points of stress requires interdisciplinary cooperation between behavioral scientists, both from the side of psychotherapy or dysfunctional study concerned with psychopathology, and from the side of social analysis which alone can describe the backgrounds of epidemiologically significant cultural stress systems.

Finally, epidemiological data such as we have adduced from total cultural settings become more useful to the psychotherapist as they are localized, pinpointed, or developed for the discrete subcultural groups within the total scene. On such bases it is possible to erect a scaffold from which to build more careful etiological studies of specific community groups. The playback or feedback technique developed between psychiatric or psychological knowledge of patterns of behavior, and knowledge of particular stress points in a culture or subculture allows one to replace a crude and unreasoned distributive system of causes ranging from organic to social by a more properly weighted analysis of what social effects and psychodynamic happenings are inducing pathology. Because social events are so frequently reiterated and social functions reduplicated, it is there that cultural contexts become overwhelmingly important in individual psychopathology. The psychotherapist or counselor who enters into this domain of sociocultural patterns and values as preexisting phenomena, antecedent to and yet important in his individualized cases, will discover quantitatively large and qualitatively potent aids in the ordinary course of his everyday work. Without this, the painstaking elucidation of seemingly personal psychodynamics will fall easily into empty formulae, or if it is not grist for oversimplified psychogenic mills, will simply lead to pictures of persons which are distorted and unreal. While a person's portrait of his own background may depart from realities of his setting as these actually exist and function, only social perspectives and cultural contexts can correct the patient's illusion and the psychotherapist's inadvertent limitations.

Turning from psychiatry and the particular value-orientations of particular groups, psychiatry and social science meet on common ground only when we speak of a more general, but realistic and encompassable unity based on a multidisciplinary science of human behavior. Beyond the varied texture of modern urban society, beyond the differences in culture and variations in pathology, one discerns a shrinking of technological space and a slow progress towards what might be referred to as processes of greater cultural unification. Basic human values, which belong to the realm of ethics, developed from the actual lives of people and communities, are seen generically across cultural boundaries. Like the differences, the similarities too have been built up over generations. It is, however, a unity amid cultural diversities at present, and only scientific unification, as in social and behavioral sciences, can assess the tempo of its development. It has been suggested here that the diversities in studies of cultural contexts and their human consequences are one proving ground for behavioral science. Only knowledge of diverse values, contexts and attitudes in different environmental settings and cultures with such inevitable human effects can give us empirically the kinds of data required in final evaluations. At this moment in time, one thing is certain. The cooperative efforts of social scientists and psychotherapists have begun and will of necessity increase.

References

Abraham, K. (1927). *Selected Papers,* International Universities Press.

Cowen, Emory C., L. D. Izzo, H. Miles, E. Telschow, M. Trost and M. Zax (1963). "A Preventive Mental Health Program in the School Setting: Description and Evaluation," published as separate, and in *The Journal of Psychology,* 56, 307–356.

Flugel, J. C. (1950). "Freudian Mechanisms as Factors in Moral Development," reprinted in J. C. Flugel (1961), *Man, Morals and Society,* Viking.

Freud, S. (1950). *The Question of Lay Analysis,* Norton.

Fromm, Erich (1962). *Beyond the Chains of Illusion,* Simon and Schuster.

Fromm-Reichmann, Frieda (1950). *Principles of Intensive Psychotherapy,* University of Chicago Press.

Hollingshead, A. B., and F. C. Redlich (1958). *Social Class and Mental Illness,* Wiley.

Leighton, Dorthea C., J. S. Harding, D. B. Mackin, A. M. Macmillan, and A. H. Leighton (1963). *The Character of Danger,* Basic Books.

Linton, Ralph (1945). *The Cultural Background of Personality,* Appleton-Century-Crofts.

Opler, Marvin K. (1956). *Culture, Psychiatry and Human Values,* Charles C Thomas.

——— (1959). *Culture and Mental Health: Cross-Cultural Studies,* Macmillan.

——— (1958). "Epidemiological Studies of Mental Illness: Methods and Scope of the Midtown Study in New York," in *Symposium on Preventive and Social Psychiatry,* Walter Reed Army Institute of Research, U.S. Government Printing Office.

——— (1963). "Cultural Definitions of Illness," in: *Man's Image in Medicine and Anthropology,* I, International Universities Press.

——— (1965). "Cultural Determinants of Mental Disorders," in *Handbook of Clinical Psychology,* B. B. Wolman, McGraw-Hill.

——— (1967). *Culture and Social Psychiatry,* Atherton Press.

Rosenthal, D. (1964). "Discussion of Dr. Kallmann's Paper: "The Norway and Especially the Finland Studies of Concordance Rates," in *Recent Research on Schizophrenia,* P. Solomon and B. C. Glueck (eds.), Psychiatric Research Reports, number 19.

Strauss, A. (1956). *The Social Psychology of George Herbert Mead,* University of Chicago Press.

Srole, L., T. Langner, S. Michael, M. K. Opler and T. A. C. Rennie (1962). *Mental Health in the Metropolis,* McGraw-Hill.

12 | FUNCTIONS AND LIMITATIONS
IN COUNSELING AND PSYCHOTHERAPY

Jessie Bernard / Pennsylvania State University

Counseling and psychotherapy belong in the category of approaches which emphasize changing individuals rather than, like the social reform or social psychiatric approach, changing institutions. They belong further in a category of approaches to changing individuals which emphasizes a certain way of changing them, a way which differs from, let us say, a missionary's or a warden's or a salesman's. A traditional man of the cloth may think nothing of praying with a sinner, hours if necessary, to bring the good news to him, until the pall of misery has lifted and the sinner knows that he is saved. A salesman, analogously, may think nothing of playing golf with a prospect for hours, entertaining him lavishly, "working" on him, to produce the change he aims at.

Counseling and Psychotherapy: Identical Instruments

The counseling-psychotherapy way is different. It is a way of changing individuals which may vary among different schools, but which nevertheless has uniquely characterizing qualities which distinguish it from all other ways of changing individuals. Ford and Urban (*1963*) have summarized these distinguishing characteristics as follows:

> Individual verbal psychotherapy appears to have four major elements. First, it involves two people in interaction (which is confidential, intimate, highly private, unobserved, very personal). . . .
> Second, the mode of interaction is usually limited to the verbal realm. . . . They do not go to movies together; they do not live together; they do not caress one another. They think, talk, and share their ideas. In so doing, they are likely to arouse emotional reactions in each other, but the mode through which this is accomplished is primarily verbal.
> Third, the interaction is relatively prolonged. A friendly conversation with a bartender or a confidant has something in common with a psycho-

348

therapy interview, but is not likely to produce marked, permanent behavioral changes of the same order. A single conversation may temporarily relieve anxieties, make one feel less lonely, or give one a feeling of well-being. However, fairly extensive and permanent behavioral change ordinarily takes time.[1]

Fourth, this relationship has as its definite and agreed purposes changes in the behavior of one of the participants . . . The focus on only one of the two participants is one of the important ways in which the psychotherapy relationship differs from most other close relationships . . . The patient must agree . . . to devote most of his energies to attempting to change himself (pp. 16–17).

On the basis of these characteristics, they view individual verbal psychotherapy as "a procedure wherein two persons engage in a prolonged series of emotion-arousing interactions, mediated primarily by verbal exchanges, the purpose of which is to produce changes in the behaviors of one of the pair" (p. 17).

Ford and Urban are talking about psychotherapy. Counseling evidences some of the same characteristics, that is, it involves a face-to-face confrontation in which talking is an important if not a crucial element and the goal is to change one of the members of the pair. It is also true, as Carl Rogers points out, that successful counseling is therapeutic or healing; and it may be necessary to heal a patient before he can be counseled.[2] Still whatever similarities psychotherapy and counseling may share, they differ in the functions they perform in the social system.

Counseling and Psychotherapy: Different Functions

Sociologists are accustomed to the idea not only that the same function may be performed by different tools (a tree, for example, may be felled with either a hatchet or a saw or, for that matter, an axe) but also to the idea that the same instrument or tool may be used for quite different functions (a gun may be used for hunting animals for food or for prosecuting a war). And they are more likely to be interested in the functions performed than in the instrument used.

For the purposes of the present discussion a distinction will be made between psychotherapy and counseling: not on the basis of the processes involved, which may, indeed, as Rogers maintains, be the same, but on the basis of the functions performed. Psychotherapy, therefore, will here imply a situation in which a pathology of some kind, serious or mild, is present. One member of the dyad is judged to be ill, suffering from some disturbance. The change sought is a curative one. In counseling,

---

[1] Note the different point of view of Rogers (*1951*) and of Robinson (*1950*).

[2] Sundberg and Tyler (*1962*, pp. 305–306) note a certain ambiguity in the term "counseling." They think of counseling as "the kind of therapy . . . where the emphasis is put on assets rather than liabilities."

on the other hand, the relationship is here conceived to be between a client — not a patient — no sicker than the man-on-the-street, nor even sicker than the counselor himself, and a counselor whose service may be therapeutic or healing, to be sure, but is not addressed primarily to healing a pathology. The difference is in goals and means, not in health. Perry distinguishes between the change sought by the two processes as "intrapsychic" in the case of psychotherapy and "role clarification" in the case of counseling. Counseling is not, in any event, a relationship between a well and a sick person but one between two well persons.[3]

The difference need not be conceived of as categorical. We may think in terms of a continuum. At one extreme, psychotherapy is a form of treatment which may even depend on chemotherapy to make the patient available for treatment; at the other extreme, counseling may be viewed as not too different from teaching, as the lawyer or investment counselor "teaches" his client the law, the market, or what-have-you.[4] The tool or instrument may be the same but the functions being performed are not.

Because not all illnesses are fatal and because so many of them show spontaneous remission of symptoms, societies can survive without specific institutional provision for the performance of the healing function. It cannot, therefore, be said to constitute a universal societal requisite. It is possible to conceive of a society with no such institutional provision for healing the sick. In our society, however, as in all modern industrial societies, healing has been assumed to be a basic and purposive societal function. Thus the social or interpersonal function of psychotherapy as here conceived is fairly clear-cut: it is to heal the sick individual so that he and others in his role networks do not suffer. The societal function is similarly clear-cut: it is to minimize disruptive non-conformity resulting from illness and restore functional social relationships.

Since there is little controversy about the importance of healing the sick no matter what one's political, economic, religious, or other ideology may be, the major point at which issues arise is in the area of defining who are sick. Once this issue is settled, other issues become technical and scientific, such as, what form of healing is most likely to succeed? But defining the sick is itself not a scientific question, as we shall note presently.

The counseling functions are somewhat more complex. Counseling shares with psychotherapy indeterminacy with respect to who needs counseling. But it is involved in other issues also. Critics might accuse it of serving as a polite form of change by coercion, as a handmaiden of

[3] Many clients would be offended if they were defined as patients, as needing psychotherapy.

[4] Tolbert (*1959*, pp. 3–4) emphasizes the learning aspect of counseling; he thinks of it as a learning situation in which a normal person learns about himself and his situation so that he can use them in satisfying and satisfactory ways.

the status quo. Whether or not such criticism is justified, it can be said that in a society which permits a wide variety of choices on the part of individuals and which expects some sort of order to result from such individual choices, help of one kind or another in making choices must be forthcoming. One function of counseling may be viewed as precisely that of helping the individual make the best — most rational — decisions, both for himself and for the social order as a whole. This is, in effect, a positive or preventive function.

Another function of counseling, however, is that of "cooling the mark out," that is, of reconciling failures to their lot, of "adjusting" people to their fate. This process protects the social system from the aggressions of the unsuccessful, of the aggrieved, of its victims.

Stated baldly, and hence inaccurately, psychotherapy is here viewed as a technique for performing the function of helping individuals overcome an illness; counseling will be viewed as a technique for performing the functions of helping individuals make rational decisions and also of reconciling individuals to failure or defeat.

Psychotherapy and counseling, it should be emphasized, are not the only ways of performing these functions. The same functions may be performed in other ways. Therapy, for example, may take the form of chemotherapy or surgery. Optimum decisions may be achieved by administrative orders, advice, persuasion, brainwashing. "Cooling" may be achieved by catharsis, religion, protest. The emphasis on counseling and psychotherapy in our discussion here is not intended to denigrate other ways of achieving the same goals.

Psychotherapy

Illness as a Social and Societal Problem

Little discussion is required to establish the fact that all but the mildest illnesses are social problems in the sense that they interfere with interpersonal relations or with role performance. They are societal problems also in the sense that the whole society is affected by them.[5] Illnesses susceptible to psychotherapy involve sociological problems also with respect to definition, as already indicated in our discussion above.

Social and societal problems arising from physical illnesses — infec-

5 Contagious illnesses have been viewed as societal problems for some time. Sanitary engineering and public health movements were the answer. Nutritional illnesses took somewhat longer to achieve recognition as societal problems; they were less dramatic in onset and their effects took longer to show. It is harder to diagnose them; it is easier to judge a man lazy and shiftless than as suffering from vitamin deficiency. The degenerative diseases have only been recognized as societal problems as the size of the older population has increased and research began to show that control, if not cure, was often possible. Stress illnesses are the most recent to achieve recognition as societal problems.

tious, nutritional, or degenerative, or even stress — create few issues with respect to definition and the assigned function of therapy is clear and unequivocal, if not always successfully implemented. It is to restore the patient to good physical health and hence to the capacity to resume his normal interpersonal relations and role obligations.[6]

If the reason why people cannot behave according to role expectations lies in some physical pathology, the relevance of therapy is clear-cut and indisputable.[7] The therapy may be long, involved, and include an extensive program of rehabilitation. But the theory is straightforward. There are consensually accepted standards for organic functions and measures of deviation from them. The blood pressure is abnormally high, the red cell count is abnormally low, the visual acuity is abnormally low. There is little if any disagreement about the pathology or the need for therapy.[8] Even in the case of the psychosomatic illnesses, the malfunctioning can be diagnosed as an illness, whatever etiology is ascribed to it. Even if the symptoms lie in the area of mental or emotional behavior, as in the case of paresis or senile dementias or other organic disorders, there is agreement that these people are ill. The illness may be serious or mild and the prognosis may be favorable or unfavorable. Plans of treatment may vary. But the diagnosis is demonstrably correct.

It is when we move from the organic psychoses to the functional ones, and especially to the neuroses, that problems begin to multiple. If, for example, there is no infection, no nutritional deficiency, no degenerative disease, no psychosis present, consensus is harder to achieve. Is Johnny a sick boy or just a mean one? Is the alcoholic only weak or is he sick? When is any condition an illness? When a character defect? The line of demarcation between the sick and the well is not always clearcut and unequivocal. And when we come to emotional or mental illness or health there is a wide margin of indeterminacy.

---

[6] Ford and Urban (*1963*, p. 640) summarize the expectations typical of Western culture as follows: "In these cultures, people are expected to be highly mobile so that they can enter most types of situations in case job demands change. They are expected to resolve the vast majority of day-to-day problems on their own. They are expected not only to be able to provide for themselves economically but also to be able to shoulder the economic support of a family. They must be able to fight under some conditions and not under others, since they must be both a reservist in time of war and a civilian in time of peace. The list of behaviors expected could be indefinitely extended and some could be demonstrated to be quite contradictory. But this is sufficient to indicate what an extensive net of behavior is necessary."

[7] Even if the patient does not want to be cured because of religious scruples against the use of medical techniques, courts have ruled that therapy must be applied. Thus members of a religious sect which does not permit blood transfusions have been forced by the courts to accept such transfusions to save their lives and, in one case, the life of an unborn child.

[8] The name of the illness may vary as well as the therapy, as in the case of Christian Scientists.

How Many Are Sick? A Reductio ad Absurdum. For reasons sketched above, among others, the concept of mental illness has been enormously extended in our day, as already noted. As a result, surveys of mental health show all but a small proportion of the population suffering from minor or major mental or emotional pathologies.

In the Manhattan survey, for example, more than four-fifths of the subjects were judged to be suffering from some degree of mental health impairment. Hartung cites one commentator — Edgar Z. Friedenberg — who argues that if middle-class anxieties about the stock market, bad schools, or civil liberties had also been included, the proportion with some degree of mental health impairment would easily have reached nine-tenths (*Hartung, 1963*, p. 262). "On this matter," Hartung (p. 263) notes, "he is in the best of company, namely, the Joint Commission on Mental Illness and Health which . . . held that people who worry about their marriage, parenthood, and work are 'persons with various psychiatric or psychological illnesses or maladjustments.' "

Even nine-tenths is too conservative for some writers, Hartung continues. In 1948, for example, L. K. Frank was writing about *Society as the Patient*. Ruth Benedict in *Patterns of Culture* in 1934, he comments, had concluded that " 'ordinarily the most bizarre of the psychopathic types of the period' are those who most faithfully conform to the norms of their society." He also quotes Theodore Roszak to the effect that "Freud . . . became progressively aware that 'normalcy' may actually be the socially acceptable form of psychic sickness. Man, Freud concluded, is the neurotic animal; the disease is of his nature. . . . What historians may really be studying, not occasionally but at all times, is diseased matter. Human history becomes a *case* history of the greatest of all neuroses: that of civilized man" (p. 263). Harry Stack Sullivan conceives of mental illness "as being disturbed or inadequate self-other relationships." Mental illness, in his conception, "ranges from forgetting the name of a person whom one is about to introduce — or, from whom one is about to request a favor — to the person who is chronically psychotic" (pp. 265–266). Hollingshead and Redlich define mental illness as what psychiatrists treat or are expected to treat, which may include anything a bored matron wants to bring them (p. 266).

If it is indeed true that almost everyone is more or less ill, such illness can scarcely be viewed as either a social or as a societal problem. It is probably then the condition of the human species, an adaptation to the world it lives in.

When Freud was able to show in himself, in his friends, and in the more grossly disturbed, phenomena that he claimed were identical or highly similar, he destroyed the wall between the normal and the abnormal. Psychiatrists who followed his thinking, Redlich comments, abandoned the island of psychiatric disease "and thus were engulfed in the boundless sea of human troubles" rather than in problems of diagnosis and treatment only (p. 262).

An assessment of pathology which embraces everyone is not very useful for our purposes here. Nor do all serious and responsible theorists accept it.[9]

But a too-narrow definition of illness may have harmful consequences also. Thus the president of the American Psychiatric Association has noted that people — like Lee Harvey Oswald, for example — who have "tenuous control" over their aggressions may threaten or even attack public figures. They tend "to associate themselves with extreme causes of a patriotic or revolutionary nature. . . . Many express their feelings in vulgar, defamatory or threatening letters. Many take authoritarian positions regarding public issues. . . ." But psychiatric examination sometimes reveals that these people are not "mentally ill." Because they are not schizophrenic or manic-depressive or paranoid, they are simply labeled as kooks, or odd-balls or cranks. Actually "in a social sense they are more deviant than many an ambulatory schizophrenic." He concluded that it was irresponsible for psychiatrists to ignore these people on the basis that they were not mentally ill (*Ewalt, 1964*). And if one were forced to make a mistake, it may be better to err on the side of overstating the incidence of mental illness than on the side of understating it. Still there are hazards both ways.

The Age of Anxiety. Having rejected the point of view which sees everyone as mentally ill we return to find the kernel of truth in the allegation. It is true that mental illness is a major social and societal problem at the present time. Our age has, in fact, been characterized as an age of anxiety. Every age is. For it is, indeed, true, as Roszak was quoted above as implying, that civilization is purchased at the expense of anxiety. The socialization process inevitably inculcates at least a modicum of anxiety. Many spontaneous human impulses — "good," "bad," or indifferent — do have to be inhibited or repressed. A certain amount of anxiety is therefore the lot of civilized man. Even the peasant suffers it.[10] Absence of such anxiety is itself a form of pathology as in the case of the psychopathic or sociopathic personality.

[9] The escape from the difficulty used by some writers on mental health is to speak of people not as "ill" but as behaving in a learned maladaptive manner. Still, if the behavior of a very large proportion of people is interpreted in this way, not much is gained.

[10] Photographs of the faces of preliterate peoples all over the world—with the notable exception of the Polynesians — show similar traces of anxiety. Even the urbanized Polynesians are beginning to show signs of anxiety, Lewis' (*1964*, p. xxxv) accounts of those who live in the "culture of poverty" evidence no absence of anxiety. The mother of Pedro Martinez was beset by "anxieties about food and shelter and the threat of being beaten, jailed or abandoned by her husband." And Pedro himself lived a life in which anxieties were never far away.

The sources of anxiety vary from time to time and place to place. Two archetypes may be distinguished: (1) survival anxiety, like those of pre-literate peoples or Lewis' peasants or urban slum dwellers and (2) status anxiety, like that of peoples in more affluent societies (*Bernard, 1957*).

It has been suggested that although anxiety or stress may accompany socialization in any society, in some societies and at some times there are more agencies instituted to reduce anxiety. Religion in the past was a stress-creating but also a stress-relaxing institution. In a world where religion mattered, everyone know that God *cared*. One might not be able to live up to His demands; one might spend a good deal of time fighting Him. But one belonged to Him. God was always there. Frowning or smiling, He was there. One could talk to Him. One could explain to Him. One could hear oneself tell Him. And in the process come to understand oneself. Without that constant presence, an important function was left unperformed. Part of the function may be taken over by the psychotherapist. He may be called upon to help supply the enormous needs of a modern population for personal caring, attention, significant others, even — it is embarrassing in this day to use the term in a scientific statement — love and affection.

What Is "Sick"? Definitions and Criteria of Sick Behavior. Psychologists have certainly not been unaware of the difficulties involved in delineating health and illness. Ford and Urban candidly admit that the definition of what is sick or pathological — "disordered," to use their terminology — is by no means easy.

They conclude from their examination in systematic detail of ten of the outstanding systems of psychotherapy that all are, in effect, culture-bound:

> It is impressive that all of these theorists represent West European and American culture and are primarily of Anglo-Saxon background. None arise from the culture of Asia, Scandinavia, Africa, the Near East, or South America. In the most general sense, therefore, all the systems have much in common, since they may reflect a view of man and an approach to the study of his behavior strongly influenced by the general themes of the Greco-Judaeo-Christian tradition. Therapy systems deriving from another tradition, such as that of the Asian culture, might emerge with very different theories about human behavior and its treatment. This similarity in the personal background of the theorists suggests that the theories and the data upon which they are built may be somewhat culture-bound (*Ford and Urban, 1963,* p. 594).

Behavior, in brief, which might be viewed as disordered in our culture may not be so viewed in another culture; and, conversely, behavior which might seem wholly appropriate to us, might seem disordered in another culture.

But even in our own culture, the definition of what is disordered is by no means easy.[11] In their survey, Ford and Urban found some theorists (Dollard and Miller) who concluded that disordered behavior differed from normal behavior only in degree. The problem, as was argued by Hart as early as 1912, was one of determining at what point it exceeded the bounds of normality. Other theorists (Horney, for example) believed that disordered behavior differed from the normal in kind. Ford and Urban (p. 638) themselves find that "although distinction of degree and kind are necessary, they are apparently not sufficient criteria for the definition of disorder."

Their own preference is for a conceptualization of disorder in terms of the appropriateness or inappropriateness of behavior. ". . . the disordered person can be characterized as one in whom inappropriate situation-response and response-response relationships have become established" (p. 639).

They do not blink at the fact that there is always a human judgment of the appropriateness or inappropriateness of behavior.

> Every judgment of this kind is based on some assumptions, implicit or explicit, about what is considered desirable. Is an inability to think in logical sequence, as in schizophrenia, a set of inappropriate or disordered interconnections? Only if one assumes it is bad to be unable to do so. But if such an inability seriously interferes with the effective performance of life tasks, is that not inappropriate? Only if one assumes that the effective performance of life tasks is good. But if life tasks are ineffectively performed, the individual cannot survive; is that not inappropriate? Only if one assumes that survival is good (p. 650).

If one accepts this set of values, then anything that implements them is appropriate or healthy and anything that prevents their implementation is inappropriate or sick.

> If one wishes a person to survive, remain healthy, be productive in some kind of work, have intimate warm relationships with people, form a close love attachment to a member of the opposite sex, be a responsible provider, then a series of things follow. He cannot be paralyzed into inactivity by conflicting and incompatible responses; he must not be so frightened of situations that he begins to avoid large collections of them; he must be able to perceive events accurately, think through problems logically, love under appropriate conditions, fight under others, or engage in sex with the "right partners" (p. 640).

With these objectives, behaviors which are disordered can be specified.

> . . . In the light of the Western tradition and its cultures . . . it is not surprising to see certain common features appear as to the unwanted conse-

[11] Sociologists have made as much of class differences in definition of appropriate behavior as the psychologists have made of cultural differences. They find behavior appropriate in a lower-class situation that would not be so in a higher-class one and vice versa.

quences which are characterized as disordered: the occurrence of negative affects, such as hate and fear instead of affection and love; avoidance of situations, interpersonal and otherwise; inability to respond because of conflicting response sequences; or inaccuracies of conception as to what is occurring in the external world or within one's behavioral repertoire (p. 641).

In keeping with the current emphasis on culture as related to personality, Ford and Urban reiterate the cultural bias in their criteria of disordered behavior:

> . . . other cultures may value other things . . . [such] as suspiciousness, acts of deception and trickery, and revenge. . . .
> It should be apparent that such characterizations of what is good and bad are man-made and culture-bound; the psychotherapist must be intimately concerned with what they are and how he can assist a particular person in relation to them. He should not, however, slip into the error of defining what is appropriate for a particular culture and then conclude that what is ideal for that set of conditions is an absolute ideal for man at large (such as Rogers' fully functioning person) (p. 641).

Whatever the limitations of the Ford-Urban conceptualization of disordered behavior may be, it has the virtue of reasonable restrictions, so that it does not imply that everyone is sick, as well as reasonable extent, so that it includes people even if they are not patently psychotic. It does not wholly satisfy the sociologist, however, because it does not give adequate recognition to the class bias in definition of what is appropriate.

Ford and Urban do muse on the fact that despite their emphasis on the culture-bound nature of their values and criteria, few theorists accord similar recognition to their class biases.

> . . . few of the theorists pointed to conditions other than interpersonal interactions as the antecedents to disorder, for instance, protracted states of physiological deprivation such as intense hunger or economic deprivation, such as poverty. One wonders whether this results from the fact that they worked within reasonably affluent segments of Western cultures, or whether there lies within their observations a very useful conclusion, namely, that learned disorders (neuroses, psychoses) are a product of the way people interact with one another. If a person is deprived of food, he becomes hungry; if he is mistreated by others he can become neurotic (pp. 650–651).

So far so good, say Ford and Urban. But, they add: "It is also possible that hungry and poor families can indirectly produce neurotic children, if those conditions cause them to hate, to neglect, and to punish each other unduly." Then, disregarding the substantial literature on the impact of class, if not physical hunger, on mental illness, they suggest casually in passing that "this would appear to be a fruitful area for investigation by sociologists and social psychologists" (p. 651).

357

What Is Appropriate? "*The Pathology of Moderation.*" Quite aside from the documentable incidence of mental impairment by class, which shows the lower socioeconomic classes to be especially vulnerable, there has been some comment on the definition of what is appropriate.

If behavior really is inappropriate, if it really is self-defeating, then of course we may agree that a pathology is present and psychotherapy is called for. But appropriateness is not always rational in the survival sense. Stuart Chase, for example, once commented on the fact that during the great depression of the 1930's, people passively starved while warehouses stood full of food. The man from Mars, archetype of rational objectivity, might well question the appropriateness of accepting hunger in the face of food. And Schorr (*1964*) has raised the question whether or not the often-complained-of apathy of the poor may not be appropriate for them, a form of emotional conservation.

Riessman and Miller (*1964*) even speak of the "pathology of moderation." How patient should people be with injustice? How tolerant should they be of discrimination? How long should they wait for their rights? Outsiders viewing a foreign society often note the startling contrast between rich and poor and ask why do the poor stand for such inequality? How appropriate is such acceptance of an unjust status quo? The rebel-without-a-cause for rebellion may, indeed, be sick. But how about the non-rebel with a cause for rebellion?

Whatever definition of illness is accepted, whatever limitations or extensions may be imposed, there are very serious restrictions on psychotherapy as related to social problems.

Some Limitations on Psychotherapy as Related to Social Problems

The scientific evidence for the success of psychotherapy is not unequivocally convincing. But if we suppose for the sake of argument that it was uniformly successful, the question then arises how and to what extent would it modify the current situation with respect to social and/or societal problems?

Those who were reached by psychotherapy would tend to be happier people, more independent, freer from anxieties, hostilities, aggressions, and fears. Their families might — or might not — also be happier. If they were now better parents because of their psychotherapy, their children would be socialized under more favorable circumstances. They might be better workers, more cooperative and productive; their employers would be satisfied with them. More alcoholics would have control of their illness. A great many psychosomatic illnesses would be healed. There would be fewer cranks, kooks, and odd-balls.[12]

[12] There might also be fewer creative people perhaps? Goertzel and Goertzel (*1962*) report that three-fourths of the 400 eminent people they studied were born into broken

But despite these individual successes, the total impact would not be great. For the proportion of people known to need psychotherapy who actually received it would still be small; and those who needed it most would probably be the least likely to get it, or would get it too late, or be unreachable because of defective theory. And, finally, the conditions specified by theorists as required for success in psychotherapy are not very widespread.

Who Receives Treatment and When?. It has long since been recognized that there are not now enough psychiatrists or clinicians to give everyone who could profit by psychotherapy the long, costly hours of individual attention which it involves. Nor are there likely to be enough in the foreseeable future. The scarce supply of psychotherapy is a great restriction on its usefulness. The characteristic American reply to any scarcity is to create more; if there is not enough of anything, get more. The expansion of therapeutic services and their availability to those who need them come themselves to constitute a societal problem, and how to do it, a sociological one. Psychotherapy cannot tell us how to recruit and train the corps of psychotherapists required to treat all those who might profit from its ministrations. One of the programs in the war on poverty was designed to help in this connection; it will be noted presently.

It has also become clear that there is a great class bias in the availability of what little psychotherapy there is; those in the lower classes — who are most likely to need it — are far less likely to receive it (*Hollingshead and Redlich, 1958*). And if or when they do, it often comes too late.

The complaint is sometimes made that the victims of our social system come to our attention when it is already too late to do anything for them. We do not catch the alcoholic until he is past healing; we do not catch the emotionally disturbed until they are past saving; etc.

The question may well be asked, of course, at what point does help come too late? At what point is personality so fixed that therapy can no longer heal? The extreme genetic determinist might argue that personality is fixed at the point of conception. After that all is settled so far as personality is concerned. Some might argue that the critical point is birth; personality, they would maintain, is then fixed. Psychoanalysts, laying great emphasis on early family relations, would allow more fluidity until, let us say, about the Oedipal period, around the age of six. And so on. Sociologists find that personality may be changed at almost any age, admittedly with greater difficulty as behavior sets become hardened. But cases of "rebirth," of conversion, of "salvation," of reform may be

---

or poverty-stricken homes and had unhappy childhoods. Since the list included Hitler, Mussolini, and Mao Tse-tung, however, as well as Adlai Stevenson, the eminence might not have resulted from positive creativity.

cited for all ages. Saul of Tarsus has a blinding vision and becomes a changed man. Augustine mends his sinful ways. The alcoholic gives up drinking. The earlier psychotherapy can be administered, of course, other things being equal, the better; but it can be useful at almost any age.

It may, of course, be a matter of definition as to whether or not a change has actually taken place. But change at a behavioral level — with or without therapy — does occur, whether or not change at a deeper level occurs as well. Still it must be recognized as a limitation on psychotherapy, when related to social problems, that it often does come at a time when healing is difficult, if possible at all.

Nor can we exonerate psychotherapy. We let the Lee Harvey Oswalds slip through our hands even after we have diagnosed them as very sick boys. We cannot excuse ourselves by saying we didn't catch them early enough. Thus a follow-up study of 227 patients some 30 years after they had been "carefully evaluated" in the St. Louis Municipal Psychiatric Clinic, 1924 through 1929, showed far greater incidence of psychoses, alcoholism, sociopathic personalities, and marital failure than did a control group (*O'Neal et al., 1960,* pp. 99–117).[13] They had been brought to our attention as children, but they were "seldom treated." The delay in treatment, which is such a convenient face-saving excuse, is not necessarily the patient's doing.

Related to delay in treatment is the indeterminacy about psychotherapy. Just how curable is the patient, whenever we get him, young or old? Even granting that some change is possible, how much can psychotherapy help him? Is the investment of time and energy in psychotherapy going to be worthwhile? Or, at any rate, as worthwhile as the same investment in some other more promising case?

Defective Theory. It now appears that psychotherapy by middle-class psychotherapists dealing with lower-class patients — by far the largest segment of the population that needs help — is not the same as psychotherapy with middle- and upper-class patients. It must be admitted that little of the current practice of psychotherapy is based on adequate theory for dealing with lower-class patients.[14] The psychotherapist just

[13] The story is no different, however, from that of physical defects in school children routinely reported year after year which remain untreated until Selective Service gets them and finds them unfit for military service.

[14] Ford and Urban (*1963*, p. 595) recognize the deficiencies in theory, although they do not emphasize their enormity. They point out that the theorists they analyzed "studied adults as opposed to children; disordered rather than healthy persons; neurotics rather than psychotics, criminals, or addicts; ambulatory rather than hospitalized patients; and probably persons drawn from the higher educational and socioeconomic strata. Such restrictions limit the value of their observational data and hence probably produce a biased view of human nature. Thereby placing limitations on the general applicability of the resultant theory."

360

does not know what to do or how to do it. For many years social case workers rejected people who were "unworthy" or "uncooperative." Psychotherapists give up on patients who cannot fulfill the specifications for the psychotherapeutic relation as listed below. These are admissions of failure. The best thing that could happen would be for theorists to go to work to re-think, re-conceptualize, and re-create their principles so that psychotherapy could be made available to all who needed it, not only to a privileged few.

This is precisely what some of them are beginning to do. And they are finding problems of sheer communication enormous, even in some instances, prohibitive. The Ford-Urban definition of psychotherapy in terms of a verbal relationship — often referred to as "the talking cure" — means that it depends largely on verbal communication. Not only between the therapist and the patient but also within the patient himself. He has to be able to tell himself — in the process of telling the therapist — what is "bugging" him. Without minimum verbal skills, the whole process breaks down. There is no way for the therapist to make his healing skills available to the patient or for the patient to receive benefit from them. It is as though treatment for blindness were dependent on vision in the patient. The most skillful ministrations would fail.

Bernstein (*1964*) has suggested that members of the lower working-class who are limited to a particular speech system are likely to find the requirements of therapy difficult to meet. The lower working-class patient will have difficulty in verbalizing his personal experience and in receiving communications which refer to the sources of his motivations. These difficulties, Bernstein argues, originate in the speech system the child learns in his culture, a speech system which patterns the child's psychological reality. What the psychotherapy relationship requires to be made relevant is almost the antithesis of what *is* made relevant by the speech system the individual normally uses in his class environment. The therapy relationship is ambiguous to him, tends to cause a loss of feeling of identity on his part, forces an unsupporting conception of his personal identity upon him. The net result is great passivity and dependence. The instrument — psychotherapy — is obviously completely incapable of performing the function — therapy. (For elaboration, see Hansen, Chapter 2 of this volume.)

Bernstein does not conclude that psychotherapy with such patients cannot be successful; but he does emphasize that it calls for great insight, sensitivity, and willingness to adapt techniques to patient's needs. Not only, then, does the quantity of psychotherapy have to be extended to include a far larger segment of the population, but also the quality or kind has to be modified and improved if it is to have any significant impact on social or societal problems.

Conditions Necessary for Successful Psychotherapy as Major Limitations

But perhaps the greatest limitation on psychotherapy as a way of dealing with social problems lies in the difficult conditions necessary for its success.[15] These have been summarized by Ford and Urban and highlight the very restricted contribution psychotherapy can currently be expected to make.

> Some theorists seem to believe that no selection of patients is required, since their procedures are applicable to anyone (Adler, Rogers). Others were far more cautious and believed certain patient responses were desirable or necessary for therapy to begin (Freud, Sullivan).
>
> As a group, the theorists seem to be in agreement about certain points. The patient needs to be suffering, miserable, subject to anxiety, or unhappy and dissatisfied with at least some of his behavior. Apparently there is consensus that what the patient is thinking, feeling, and doing must terminate in a negative or dissatisfying state of affairs or he will not be interested in changing his habits. This implies that if his habitual sequences lead to "pleasure" or "satisfaction," the therapist will have a very difficult time even though what the patient is doing may be judged by others as abnormal or inappropriate. The patient must consent to the rules of therapy and believe some benefits or improvement will follow therefrom. The behavior changes must be subject to learning. The patient must be able to talk. It is not clear whether these conditions should be present at the beginning of therapy or whether the early interviews should focus on the development of such responses. We interpret them to mean that the therapist should try explicitly to elicit some of these responses if they are not already present.
>
> Several other response characteristics are mentioned by a few theorists. The patient should have some minimal degree of intellectual ability. He must be able to observe and report in a reasonably accurate fashion. It is better if he is living in a real-life situation, rather than in a hospital, where his reactions occur to "meaningful" surroundings, and where real-life satisfactions are readily available as therapy progresses. It is preferable for him to be relatively free to change his way of life if he wishes to, than to have to defer to the decisions of others, such as parents (*Ford and Urban, 1963*, pp. 672–673).

This is a formidable array of restrictions on any attack on a social problem. If the person is not suffering, miserable, subject to anxiety, or unhappy and dissatisfied with at least some of his behavior, he is

---

[15] The therapist himself and his system are not here discussed as conditions for success. It appears that regardless of the theory or technique used in psychotherapy the degree of success seems to be about the same. The therapist rather than his technique seems to be crucial. As in the case of the physician, some therapists appear to be more successful than others with some patients rather than with others. It is well known that patients will shop around for doctors who can help them, ignoring the fact that the treatment for most physical pathologies is fairly standard. The person who offers the treatment may be more important than the treatment.

apparently not a promising candidate for psychotherapy.[16] This leaves out the psychopathic or sociopathic personality. It leaves out a good many hostile, aggressive, prejudiced, destructive people who enjoy their hostilities, aggressions, prejudices, and destructiveness. It leaves out — as emphasized above — the inarticulate, the lower class. It leaves out those who do not understand the rules of therapy and those of little faith. It also leaves out the wordless, the unobservant, the institutionalized. . . . In fact, it leaves out almost all the disturbed people. It is like a tiny little beebee gun aimed at an elephant.

This is a formidable array of restrictions or limitations of psychotherapy as related to social problems. Attempts to overcome them are now being experimented with. Of special interest are those sponsored by federal legislation in the areas of mental health and poverty.

For example, in October, 1965, eight high-school drop-outs, 17 to 21 years of age, completed their training to become mental health aides in Washington, D.C. Each was assigned ten youngsters with adjustment problems, whom they were to help (*Raspberry, 1965*). In New York City, Lincoln Hospital has organized a mental health program which begins at the bottom with "first-aid" stations or neighborhood service centers, staffed with local people as aides (*Pines, 1955*). These experiments reflect a response to the criticisms of psychotherapy as now organized which have been made by social scientists, referred to above. They attempt at one and the same time to increase the supply of psychotherapy available to the poor and to offer it in the form in which they can use it. Although it is too early to evaluate them, they will be watched with the greatest interest.

Counseling

Salvaging the Rational

Along with the enormous emphasis on the psychiatric world view, with all its consequences, there has been another trend, this time in the opposite direction, that is, an emphasis on rationality. Modern industry is, to use Max Weber's terminology, rationalized. There has developed a whole science of rational decision-making. Industry and government have recruited the best brains to show them how to make decisions on more rational bases.

Economic man was always presumed by definition to be highly rational, making his decisions on the basis of a calculated analysis of rewards. Political man was also viewed as essentially a rational decision-maker; issues were debated and, in the "market place of ideas," the best were expected

---

[16] Not all counselors feel that counseling must be voluntary. Williamson (*1955*, p. 29), for example, challenges this "dogma."

to win out. There is still a large segment in both economics and political science devoted to the study of non-rational aspects of economic and political behavior. But recent thinking, especially in the field of game theory, has revived interest in rational behavior, in the concept of rationality, in behavior which best implements the attainment of goals. (In some cases, to be sure, what looks like non-rational behavior from the observer's standpoint is rational in the sense that it looks better to the decision-maker than any other.) There has been almost as great a brouhaha against this revival of rationality as there has been against the psychiatric world view. And there has been almost as great difficulty arriving at a suitable definition of rationality as at a suitable definition of illness. But the rationalistic approach has given us some extraordinary insights to ponder and it certainly cannot be ignored in any sociological discussion of counseling.

For if psychotherapy is viewed as reflecting the psychiatric world view, counseling may be said to be viewed here as reflecting a rational point of view. It presupposes that psychotherapy, if needed, has healed or is in process of healing the need for, or the compulsion toward, inappropriate behavior. It is assumed to be dealing with clients, not patients; with people, that is, who are no more ill than the counselor himself; with people who do not need psychotherapy; with people who are as normal as the man-on-the-street.

The concept of rationality is hardly less ambiguous than the concept of illness. And current theorists in the area of decision-theory or game-theory — areas most concerned with rationality — have almost as hard a time coming to terms with it as do those dealing with the concept of illness. It would not be difficult to make an argument to the effect that the Ford-Urban definition of disordered or sick behavior as inappropriate behavior is merely the converse of rational behavior. That is, one might merely identify or define rational behavior as appropriate behavior. Actually, as we shall presently note, rational behavior in some situations — as, for example, in the so-called Prisoner's Dilemma — may be quite inappropriate. Rather than digress to find a suitable definition of rationality, it will be assumed that counseling is dealing with clients capable of adapting means to ends when given the opportunity.

Two Basic Functions of Counseling

In the first section of this chapter two basic functions of counseling were referred to briefly. One was that of helping individuals make optimum decisions and that of secondly, "cooling the mark out," a term introduced by Erving Goffman to refer to a very special kind of decision situation — that of a confidence man's victim — but which has many more uses.

A modern society is so inordinately complex that without an extensive background of sheer factual information, rational decisions become extremely difficult. On the basis of this need the "research industry" rests. There are certain strategic points in such a society where erroneous or incorrect decisions by individuals can lead to social and/or societal problems. The decision to stay in school or to drop out, to go into one occupation or another, to keep or surrender an out-of-wedlock child, to seek a divorce or not to, may add up to both social and societal problems. Sometimes people make erroneous decisions because they are emotionally incapable of making correct ones. They may need psychotherapy. But sometimes they make incorrect decisions because they do not have enough knowledge or information — about themselves as well as about the world — to make correct ones. There may, of course, be many other emotional factors involved in their decisions but they are not — by definition for purposes of this discussion — insuperable or determinative. The function of counseling here is to supply the information — about self as well as about the outside world — and intellectual know-how needed to make the best decision. For the individual making life decisions the counselor may be thought of as a guide through the complexities that assail him on all sides, inside as well as outside. What can I do? What should I do? By definition we are excluding the compulsive, the irrational, the sick, and all who need psychotherapy before they can use counseling.

A competitive society has also to cope with the problem of what to do with failures, with injustice, with victims (*Bernard, 1962*, pp. 72–74). The rebel-without-a-cause we can refer to the psychotherapist. But what about the rebel, or worse still, the non-rebel-with-a-cause? This is where the cooling function is called for, to be discussed at greater length below.

Counseling theory holds that although there may be many fields of counseling, specialized on the basis of the subjects being counseled — students, workers, married persons, and the like — still the processes themselves are basically the same. There are generic principles and processes valid for all. One of the persons is trying to change the other and there are certain ways that are more likely than others to succeed.

Sociologically speaking, however, although the instrument may be the same in all kinds of counseling, it is not always performing the same function. If one is concerned with the processes and techniques to produce change in people, then the role and status and problem of the counseled person is a matter of indifference. But if one wishes to view counseling as related to social — and in this case to societal — problems, then the role, status, and problem of the counseled person make a difference. The emphasis is not on the instrument used to produce the change but on the function of the changes sought.

Functionally, counseling is not the same in all situations. The same tool, as noted also in connection with psychotherapy, may be used for different functions. Although the vocational counselor and the potential dropout in the school, the family physician and the bride in his office, the social worker and the applicant for a divorce in the court, the clinician and the delinquent at the detention center, the personnel officer and the worker at the factory, the counselor and the unmarried mother at the Florence Crittenden Home may all be involved in an identical process as counseling theory maintains, still they are not all in the same situation from a functional point of view. It may be that in all cases one person is trying to change the other. All the specifications for a counseling situation may be present. Even so they are not necessarily the same from a functional point of view. In some cases the function the counselor is performing may be that of helping the client to arrive at an optimum decision; in others, it may be that of cooling the mark out. In some cases, cooling may be the best way to arrive at an optimum decision.

Optimising Decision Making

The counselor performing this function may be viewed as a matrix formulator in a game-theoretic situation. He is, in such types of situation, in effect applying game theory to a situation, as a lawyer or investment counselor might do (*Bernard, 1959,* pp. 264–274). The client is in a game against either a human opponent or, more likely, against Nature (or Society or the System or Them). He has to make a decision in the presence of risk or uncertainty.

There are several critical points in the process of decision-making at which the counselor can be of substantial assistance: (1) helping the client determine what he wants; (2) supplying help with strategies or alternatives — both the client's and his opponent's; (3) determining probabilities; (4) predicting outcomes; and (5) evaluating payoffs.[17]

Determining What the Client Wants. Sometimes the client is in such a state of conflict that he doesn't even know what he wants. If counseling is viewed as ranging from the rational relationship between, let us say, a lawyer and his client at one extreme and the almost psychotherapeutic relationship between a marriage counselor and a distraught wife at the other, the complexity of this function becomes apparent. At one extreme it is assumed that the client knows what he wants; the counselor knows the best way to achieve it. The client sets the goal; the counselor then advises on optimum strategies. At the other extreme, the client scarcely knows what he wants; he is confused, conflicted. The counselor has to help him determine what he wants. Sometimes it is simply a matter of the client not even knowing what there is available to want.

---

[17] Sometimes optimum decisions constitute the best way to prevent failure and hence the necessity for cooling later.

Supplying Strategies or Alternatives. It is a commonplace that an outsider — almost any outsider — may see more alternatives in a situation than the involved person himself sees.[18] In addition, the counselor is trained to know more about alternatives. He "knows the ropes," has a wider perspective on the problem, is more knowledgeable about means to ends. He knows not only the vocational aptitudes and interests of the client but also the place to train them and the market to sell them in; not only the feelings of the wife, but also the domestic law of the community; not only the abilities of the student, but also the college's policies; not only the client's difficulties, but also the law's specifications for assistance; not only the drop-out's discouragement, but also the trends in automation. He is therefore better able to suggest strategies. He knows a good deal more about alternatives available not only to the client but also to his opponent, Nature, Society, or what-have-you. The counselor may have a hard time demonstrating that there are alternatives, but this is part of his job.

Determining Probabilities. If the probabilities of one's opponent's strategies are known, the decision is said to be made under conditions of risk; if they are not, of uncertainty. Uncertainty is likely to prevail more often than risk. All the counselor can offer here is the research results obtained in the past, his own experience, his judgment, his assessment of the situation. And it is here, as we shall note presently, that his values are likely to show through.

Predicting Outcomes. The next step is to clarify the outcomes of each set of paired strategies or alternatives. If Ego (client) does this and Alter (Nature, Society, or what-have-you) does this, the outcome will be X; if Ego does that and Alter does that, the outcome will be Y. If both Ego and Alter have two alternatives, there will be four outcomes — X, Y, Z, and W.

Evaluating Payoffs. Each outcome has a certain payoff for the client. He prefers some more than others. The value of each outcome, or payoff, depends on both the intrinsic desirability of the outcome and also on its probability. No matter how desirable any given outcome may be, if it is extremely improbable, it will not have a high expected payoff for the client.

At all of these critical points, the counselor's values are likely to show.

[18] A great industrialist was once quoted as saying of the first Henry Cabot Lodge that he was the greatest lawyer the corporation had ever had. Other lawyers told Boards of Directors what they could not do: Henry Cabot Lodge told them what they could. Legal counseling presupposes that the counseled party knows what he wants and the counselor knows the best way to get it. Similarly with investment counseling. It is taken for granted that the client can tell the counselor what he wants — growth, security, tax advantage, or what-have-you. The counselor is paid for telling him how best to achieve his goal. But not all counseling is of this straightforward nature.

They show especially and significantly in both of the parameters involved in determining payoffs, namely evaluating outcomes and determining probabilities.

The professor in a branch college of a state university once sent out an SOS to a colleague at the main campus. A young man with a fabulous IQ — about 180 — was dropping out of school. The colleague rushed to the local campus to talk to the boy. "If you complete your education we can practically guarantee you a well-paying job when you graduate." The boy agreed; he listened patiently to all the arguments and replied, "I know; but I'd rather shoot pool." It turned out that in his home — his father was an unskilled worker — there had never been a book; no one read even comics. Not only was there no encouragement to read, there was positive discouragement. Readers were queer people who sat staring at printed pages. On the other hand, everyone applauded his genius at the pool table. In his matrix the three punishing years of college far outweighed the promised success in industry as compared with success in industry as compared with success in the pool hall. Information did not help. (Nor, for that matter, did counseling.)

The counselor's values show also in the assessment of probabilities of the several strategies of Nature or Society. The Negro boy contemplating dropping out of school may accept the counselor's alternatives as valid. he may even agree with the counselor that a secure, well-paying job is a much-to-be desired outcome of remaining in school for more training. But if he considers the probabilities of such an outcome minuscule, this outcome will not have a high expected payoff value for him. Here the counselor's biases show. He may support the Negro boy's assessment of the probabilities. He may accept the fact that discrimination exists and agree that although the sure well-paying job is very desirable, in his case it is not probable and hence has a low payoff.[19]

[19] Counselors have been criticized for accepting limitations in the job market based on discrimination and steering minority-group children into relatively low-level jobs, despite their potential. Here, for example, is a Negro child with a high — "unrealistically high" says the counselor — aspirations. He wants to be an engineer. He has the ability to complete engineering school. But the counselor knows he will encounter discrimination and that he may be stranded at the lower levels of the profession. In working out the matrix, therefore, he assigns low probability to success for the strategy "going to engineering college" and high probability to success for the strategy "going to trade school." The payoff for strategy "go to engineering school" combined with Nature's or Society's strategy "success" is very small and the boy chooses the trade school. The counselor may justify this as aimed at preventing failure and hence necessity for later cooling. William Kolb once raised an analogous question with respect to intermarriage. Why is our research so commonly oriented to showing up its hazards rather than to showing how to meet these hazards? The counselor presumably knows the research findings. He is aware that uniformly they show intermarriage to have greater probability of instability than other marriages. Is the logical policy therefore to emphasize this fact with the client? Or should he concentrate on showing under what circumstances such marriages succeed? In some cases, of course, the information and emphases offered by the counselor are slanted in more optimistic directions. In any case it may change the client's assessment of probabilities and

This decision-making function of counseling is preventive and constructive. It helps to make available to the client as much as possible of what he needs to know — about himself, we repeat, as well as about the outside world — in order to make an optimum decision. Optimum decisions are important both for the client himself and for his role network; they are also important for the whole social system.[20]

The function of counseling as help in rational decision-making is, then, to make sure that critical decisions are made under optimum circumstances. The counselor does not coerce his client, does not force the choice of one alternative — however much more beneficial he might consider it for society — over another. He can, however, supply the knowledge and the information which could change the client's preferences. And if he is dealing with a non-compulsive client, he might even change his values. He is preventing choices that might lead to failure and hence he is forestalling the necessity for later cooling. If this function of counseling were uniformly successful, there would be fewer square pegs in round holes, fewer divorces perhaps, fewer school drop-outs, fewer college failures.[21]

Cooling the Mark Out

If psychotherapy deals with ill people and counseling in its decision-making function with people trying to be rational, counseling in its cooling function may be said to fall somewhere between. It deals with people for whom the optimum decision is to accept less than they feel entitled to or, even in some cases, failure.

What to do about failures is a problem for any society, but more especially for a competitive one like ours. A competitive society requires that there be failures. The very process of selecting winners must, ipso facto, select losers also (*Bernard, 1949,* pp. 98–99). For despite all that can be done to minimize or prevent failure, it does inevitably occur. Counseling as cooling has to do with reconciling people to their fate, with "adjusting" them to failure and defeat. Or, as the counselor himself might prefer to phrase it, with helping the clients maintain their self-respect in the face of self-disparaging experience. If they have become

---

hence of payoffs. The counselor, in brief, is himself a chip which the client tosses on one side or the other of the balance when weighing alternatives, assessing probabilities, and arriving at payoffs for outcomes.

[20] As related to guidance, this function is viewed as so important that specific provision is made for training counselors in the National Defense Education Act of 1958 amended 1963. Title 5 authorizes a considerable amount of money for training institutes "to improve the qualifications of personnel engaged in counseling and guidance of students in secondary schools . . ." (Section 511, Title 5, Part B). In Domestic Relations courts in some jurisdictions, counseling is also prescribed for couples seeking divorce. Unfortunately such counseling often comes too late.

[21] The counseling program inaugurated by Robert Bernreuter at the Pennsylvania State University, for example, has been especially successful in achieving such a goal.

demoralized and disorganized, as noted above, they become the charge of the psychotherapist. But we are here dealing only with those who retain a normal degree of organization.

We are indebted to Goffman for his insightful analysis of the process involved in cooling the mark out, a term applied to the archetypical behavior of confidence men or operators. With them it is a process of dissuading a victim from retaliation. It is the function of the cooler to deal with

> . . . persons who have been caught out on a limb — persons whose expectations and self-conceptions have been built up and then shattered. The mark is a person who has compromised himself, in his own eyes if not in the eyes of others. . . . An expectation may finally prove false, even though it has been possible to sustain it for a long time and even though the operators acted in good faith. So, too, the disappointment of reasonable expectations, as well as misguided ones, creates a need for consolation. Persons who participate in what is recognized as a confidence game are found in only a few social settings, but persons who have to be cooled out are found in many. Cooling the mark is one theme in a very basic social story (*Goffman, 1962,* pp. 485–486).

Cooling applies to any situation in which a person with a genuine grievance is led to accept the situation rather than make something of it. In the archetypical case it may be a matter of convincing the mark that the payoff for notifying the police is far less than the payoff for swallowing his pride or his anger and dropping the whole thing. Since the mark is not wholly innocent himself — he lent himself to the operator's dishonest scheme in the first place — the operator has better cards.

Counseling as Cooling. But, as Goffman notes, the underlying process of cooling is not necessarily limited to the relationship between con men and marks. The concept of mark may apply to any person, says Goffman, who has been involuntarily deprived of his position and returned to a lesser one. If the deprivation does not reflect on him as a person — as in bereavement or retirement — he may still require someone to pacify and resign him to his loss; but insult has not been added to injury. If the deprivation does reflect unfavorably on him as a person, it is "ultimate proof of an incapacity" and there is loss of face, humiliation. Cooling occurs whenever a person with a genuine grievance is reconciled or adjusted or in any other way pacified so that he decides to accept a bad situation rather than rebel against it.

> [The process of cooling itself is one] of adjustment to an impossible situation — a situation arising from having defined himself in a way which the social facts come to contradict. The mark must therefore be supplied with a new set of apologies for himself, a new framework in which to see himself and judge himself. A process of redefining the self along defensible lines must be instigated and carried along; since the mark himself is frequently in

too weakened a condition to do this, the cooler must initially do it for him (*Goffman, 1962,* p. 493).

Goffman's analysis is based largely on the loss of face that results when the mark — whoever or wherever he is — finds he is not as good as he thought he was, when he has to lower his own estimate of himself, when he has to recognize that he is not as good as the opposition, when he is deprived of self-respect. Unless he makes an adaptation to this loss, he may become disorganized or, as Goffman vividly puts it, "die" socially.[22] It is therefore important both for those in his role network and for society as a whole that such social "deaths" be avoided.[23] This function, as contrasted with the preventive function of counseling as help in rational decision making, is a kind of holding action. It prevents things from getting worse, but it does not do much more.

Cooling may also be viewed as a charge on the conscience of the successful. If we begin with the Freudian hypothesis that civilization is purchased at the expense of instinctual satisfactions, then a basic function of counseling might well be viewed as, in effect, a way of making amends for the demands we make on people who cannot meet them. The successful ones, those who gain most by civilization, have to make amends to the unsuccessful ones, those who pay most. It is not at all necessary to assume that successful people are deliberately cooling the mark out. The best way to test the fact that they are, however, is to imagine their choice if offered these alternatives: either (1) change our institutions in such a way as to make, let us say, poverty or war or crime impossible or (2) leave institutions unchanged and mitigate the punishment for failure.

There are many points in the structure of social life at which cooling is called for. In a competitive society, for example, those who are downwardly mobile may obviously need it. But so also may the near-wins. They have pictured themselves as potential winners; it is demoralizing to have to face the fact that they are not. There are situations

[22] "Attention may be directed to the things we become after we have died in one of the many social senses and capacities in which death can come to us. As one might expect, a process of sifting and sorting occurs by which the socially dead come to be effectively hidden from us. This movement of ex-persons throughout the social structure proceeds in more than one direction. There is, first of all, the dramatic process by which persons who have died in important ways come gradually to be brought together into a common graveyard that is separated ecologically from the living community. For this is at once a punishment and a defense. Jails and mental institutions are, perhaps, the most familiar examples, but other important ones exist . . . . old-folks homes and rooming-house areas . . . Skid Rows . . . . hobo jungles . . ." (*Goffman, 1962,* p. 504).

[23] ". . . no matter how insignificantly or unimportant he may seem to be, no one may be unnecessarily deprived, frustrated, humiliated or otherwise neglected and mistreated because those who are so ill-used will be unable to participate in a free society and incapable of developing the kind of human relations required for a democratic social order" (*Frank, 1961,* pp. 47–48).

in which the self-image or illusion is denied by the world. A student does not make the college of his choice; he is not invited to join the fraternity he prefers; he cannot make the grade in college; he does not get the job he applies for, or the promotion he feels entitled to, or the girl he wants; he cannot gain admittance to the Jones' social set . . . .

Personnel work in industry has been defined by critics as performing primarily a cooling function. With industrialization came the so-called rationalism of bureaucracy. Machines do not tolerate human rhythms. They accept regulation, they will go slow or fast; but they have to operate mechanically. They will not accommodate to fatigue or boredom. For a long time, in fact, there were observers who could not decide whether the machine was the slave of man or man the slave of the machine. In any event, the war between the two has never been wholly settled. There is an accommodation for varying periods of time. The machine takes over more and more of the work; men submit to the discipline imposed by the machine. Industry is, as noted above, rationalized.

But a real loss to the worker, it is alleged, results. It is not the dramatic kind of loss Goffman describes so perceptively. But it is a loss nevertheless. The work shop becomes, therefore, a stage for the conflict between both the rational and the non-rational behavior of human beings. In the early exuberance of rationalization, men were viewed as part of the machine. Time and motion studies showed how the muscles of men could be used to best advantage vis-a-vis the machine. Great industrial plants were designed with complacent men in mind, assuming that men could be used efficiently by engineering logic. Perverse men rebelled.

What's on the worker's mind? What does he want? These were among the questions that industrial leaders found themselves facing when confronted with these resistant — or, to use Goffman's term, "sour" — workers. Issues like wages and hours industrialists could understand if not concede. They fit into a rational system. Of course men were greedy and lazy. But why was it that they remained recalcitrant even when the conditions of work were good? Why were they never satisfied?

Mayo (*1945*) thought he could answer the social problems of an industrial civilization. What was needed was recognition of the *social* relations of workers. At the mercy of machines and bureaucracy, they had lost part of themselves, they were robbed of autonomy, they were "pushed around." Mayo defined the situation in terms of social factors. Personnel departments were installed designed to deal with workers' dissatisfactions on a counseling basis.

Union leaders had other ideas. They decried this movement precisely on the grounds that it was a way of cooling the mark out, of reconciling the worker to his lot, dissuading him from doing anything to improve his situation. They preferred other alternatives. They did not want workers to be cooled. For, as Goffman notes, "associations dedicated to the rights and the honor of minority groups may sometimes encourage a mark to register a formal squawk; politically it may be more advantageous to provide a test case than to allow the mark to be cooled out" *(Goffman, 1962, p. 497).* If a worker had a grievance the union often wanted to make something of it. It was not to the union's advantage to have the worker cooled by a counselor. And if for any reason it did seem to be a good idea to have a worker cooled they preferred that the cathartic function be performed by a grievance committee of the union than by a management counselor.

Similarly, when social case work during the 1920's changed from an attempt to improve the client's housing, to get jobs for him, to see that children were taken to the clinics, and the like, to an attempt to explain inadequacies in terms of childhood trauma and to use the worker-client relationship "therapeutically," it was also accused of settling for merely cooling the mark out.

The techniques for cooling, according to Goffman, include turning the job over to someone several echelons higher in the organization — on the theory that consolation and redirection will be more effective coming from high places; or to a friend and peer, or to doctors or priests, specialized in certain areas which require cooling. Or, we might add, turning the job over to a counselor or — in extreme cases — to a psychotherapist.[24] Another technique is to substitute some alternative status which saves face. Or to give the mark another chance, or an opportunity for catharsis by exploding. Or by stalling. Or by a tacit agreement between mark and operator to keep the whole matter secret so that only the mark himself but no one else knows of his loss of face. Or, finally, bribery.

If the mark refuses to be cooled out, he may become completely disorganized. "Sustained personal disorganization is one way in which a mark can refuse to cool out." Or he can raise a squawk, protest, write

[24] If a person cannot compensate for loss in one role by recourse to another, if the loss to his ego is so great that he cannot act like a "good scout," he may become completely shattered and require psychotherapy.

On these occasions the shattering experience in one area of social life may spread out to all the sectors of his activity. He may define away the barriers between his several social roles and become a source of difficulty in all of them. In such cases the play is the mark's entire social life, and the operators, really, are the society. In an increasing number of these cases, the mark is given psychological guidance by professionals of some kind. The psychotherapist is, in this sense, the society's cooler. His job is to pacify and re-orient the disorganized person; his job is to send the patient back to an old world or a new one, and to send him back in a condition in which he can no longer cause trouble to others or can no longer make a fuss. In short, if one takes the society, and not the person, as the unit, the psychotherapist has the basic task of cooling the mark out. . . . Psychotherapists . . . are willing to take responsibility for the mark because it is their business to offer a relationship to those who have failed in a relationship to others *(Goffman, 1962, pp. 495, 501).*

letters to the editor, report to the manager, make a fuss. He may accept his loss outwardly but turn "sour," withdrawing "all enthusiasm, good will, and vitality from whatever role he is allowed to maintain" (*Goffman, 1962,* pp. 496–497). He may try to set up a new situation in which he retains his old status but in a new context.

Because of the social and societal hazards of failure in cooling, it is expedient to prevent the necessity. Goffman suggests that weeding out unsuitable applicants for any position is one way to minimize occasions for cooling. Carrying the load of incompetents is another; and "here, perhaps, is the most important source of private charity in our society" (p. 499).

Because cooling is required in so many critical points in the social structure and because non-counseling techniques for performing the cooling function are either so painful and disagreeable that most people shrink from it or so ineffective, a major part of the load may be turned over to the counselors. They are trained professionally to perform this function without becoming personally involved.

If the cooling function of counseling were successfully performed there would be more reconciled people, more who like Margaret Fuller "accepted the universe," more people who knew their place. It is precisely on this score that some argue against counseling. It is too accepting of things-as-they are. "Accepting the inevitable" may be a rational decision for individuals; it may add up to non-rationality for the society as a whole. The "pathology of moderation" may be an accurate expression, not a figure of speech.

Protest Versus Counseling as Methods of Cooling

With respect to some societal, if not social, problems there has been a traditional cleavage between those who advocated social action so-called or organized protest and those who advocated some kind of individual social work, including case work, counseling, or psychotherapy. The arguments have been numerous and convincing on both sides. "You only pick up the pieces after the harm has been done; you return your individual to the destructive conditions that broke him in the first place; you move the family from their hovel but another family moves in; you don't reach the conditions that make for the problem in the first place; etc." "General laws don't touch the individual; you can't expect impersonal forces to help all the individuals that need help; you can't apply a law indiscriminately; you have to tailor services to the individual; rehabilitation can only be done case by case; etc."

Actually both protest and counseling are forms of cooling. In both forms, however, more than mere cooling may be involved. Both protest and counseling may be — though they need not necessarily be — rehabilitative processes. The protest movement of the Negroes in the 1950's and early 1960's, for example, served as a powerful rehabilitating force for many of them. Even in communities where it did not wring concessions and might therefore be judged objectively as unsuccessful, it did serve to develop identity among participants. Negroes learned that they need not sit supinely by and accept exploitations. They learned that they need not succumb to apathy. They achieved some of the goals that a good counselor might have wanted working individually with them, one by one. The counselor has a limited repertoire of techniques available to him in a dyadic relationship. The protest movement or social action has group and collective processes available as resources for rehabilitation also. The old settlement houses, without benefit of psychological or social-science theory, used both counseling and protest with remarkable success.

The rebel without a cause almost certaintly belongs to the psychotherapist. No matter what the rules are he remains an angry young (old) man (woman). He dissents. He protests. He votes nay. He rejects the world he never made. He is probably ill. But very often rebels do have a cause. They are, indeed, victims of injustice or hatred or what-have-you. Sometimes the injustice is blatant; but more often, perhaps, it is not. It is built into the social system so that it is simply taken for granted by most people, even the victims, until they are roused. Many Negroes and poor people belong in this category.

> For many generations, with only a few dissents or protests usually ignored or suppressed, many have been sacrificed, exploited, humiliated and sometimes destroyed by the operation of our established laws, institutions and relations. We have explained and justified these practices by a variety of social, economic, legal, political and theological beliefs and sanctions. These beliefs have been accepted, with little or no protest, by those who have been thus misused and exploited, until recently. Now those who formerly accepted their unhappy lot in life as inevitable, are becoming restless, sometimes resentful and increasingly are protesting against their inferior status and mistreatment. But this protest comes, may I say, as they begin to develop a new image of themselves, a sense of their own worth and dignity, a belief in themselves as personalities who should not be so mistreated. This new aspiration of people who have long accepted inferiority and offered submissive obedience to those who dominated them is of immense significance for our democratic aspiration toward a free social order . . . (*Frank, 1961,* p. 47).

Protest is more effective than counseling for achieving this "new image of themselves." Could it be that counseling theorists might benefit from a study of "protest psychology"? And could it be that social action carries unrecognized capacities for rehabilitation and even fundamental therapy?

That such questions appear novel evidences once again that we have yet much to learn about the functions and potentials of counseling and therapy.

References

Bernard, Jessie (1949). *American Community Behavior*, Dryden.

———— (1957). *Social Problems at Midcentury*.

———— (1959). "Counseling Techniques for Arriving at Optimum Compromises: Game and Decision Theory," *Marriage and Family Living*, 21 (August).

———— (1962). *American Community Behavior*, Holt, Rinehart, and Winston.

Bernstein, Basil (1964). "Social Class, Speech Systems and Psychotherapy," *British Journal of Sociology*, 15 (March).

Ewalt, Jack R. (1964). Quoted in the *New York Times* (June 30).

Ford, Donald H., and Hugh B. Urban (1963). *Systems of Psychotherapy, a Comparative Study*, Wiley.

Frank, Lawrence K. (1961). *The Planning of Change*, Bennis, Benne and Chin (eds.), Holt, Rinehart and Winston.

Goertzel, Victor, and Mildred Goertzel (1962). *Cradles of Eminence*, Little, Brown.

Goffman, Erving (1962). "On Cooling the Mark Out," in *Human Behavior and Social Processes*, Arnold Rose (ed.), Houghton Mifflin.

Hart, Bernard (1912). *The Psychology of Insanity*, Cambridge University Press.

Hartung, Frank (1963). "Manhatten Madness: The Social Movement of Mental Illness," *Sociological Quarterly*, 11 (Fall), 261–272.

Hollingshead, A. B., and F. C. Redlich (1958). *Social Class and Mental Illness*, Wiley.

Lewis, Oscar (1964). *Pedro Martinez, a Mexican Peasant and His Family*, Random House.

Mayo, Elton (1945). *Social Problems of an Industrial Civilization*, Harvard University Press.

O'Neal, Patricia, John Bergman, Jeanette Schofer, and Lee N. Rabins (1960). "The Relation of Childhood Behavior Problems to Adult Psychiatric Status: A 30-year Follow-Up Study of 262 Subjects," *Scientific Papers and Discussions* (February).

Pines, May A. (1965). "The Coming Upheaval in Psychiatry," *Harper's Magazine* (October).

Raspberry, William J. (1965). "Youths from Slums Learn to Aid Others," *Washington Post* (October 17).

Riessman, Frank, and S. M. Miller (1964). "Social Change Versus the Psychiatric World View," *American Journal of Orthopsychiatry*, 34 (January).

Robinson, F. P. (1950). *Principles and Procedures in Student Counseling*, Harper.

Rogers, C. R. (1951). *Client-centered Therapy*, Houghton Mifflin.

Schorr, Alvin L. (1964). "The Nonculture of Poverty," in a paper presented at the American Ortho-Psychiatric Association (March 19).

376

Sundberg, Norman D., and Leona E. Tyler (1962). *Clinical Psychology,* Appleton-Century.

Tolbert, E. L. (1959). *Introduction to Counseling,* McGraw-Hill.

Williamson, E. G. (1955). "Counseling from the Perspective of a Dean of Students," in *New Perspectives in Counseling,* Vivian H. Hewer (ed.), Minnesota Studies in Personnel Work.

13 | COUNSELING,
PSYCHOTHERAPY AND SOCIAL PROBLEMS
IN VALUE CONTEXTS

Jessie Bernard / Pennsylvania State University

All three subjects in the major title of this chapter are heavily value-laden. The concept of "social problems" implies a judgment that something should be done about a social situation. "Therapy" of all kinds, including psychotherapy, implies a judgment that some kind of illness is present and that therefore healing is called for. "Counseling" implies a judgment that there are better ways of doing things and that more rational decisions are needed. These value-orientations are freely granted by both psychologists and sociologists. The juxtaposition of the three terms assumes that counseling and psychotherapy — rational decisions and healing — have relevance for dealing with social problems.

Three terms are missing. The term "individual problems" is, understandably, not included; most of the literature on counseling and psychotherapy deals with them in relation to individual problems and further discussion is not called for here. The term "societal problems" is also missing; the absence of this term implies that the functions of psychotherapy and counseling with respect to the total society are not to be dealt with. The term "social reform," finally, does not appear in the title either; this omission suggests that our concern is not to be the relative effectiveness of an individual, as contrasted with an institutional approach to social problems, but only with the nature of two, among several, individual approaches to dealing with social problems, namely, counseling and psychotherapy.

Some Distinctions

Before we can proceed with our discussion, the foregoing statement, delimiting the concerns of this chapter must be fleshed out, with a brief elaboration of two sets of distinctions: (1) between social and societal problems and (2) between sociological and psychological problems.

Social and Societal Problems[1]

Sociologists have long insisted that "individual" and "society" were merely different ways of looking at the same thing. The distinction between them is justified on practical rather than on theoretical grounds. It reflects a division of labor among the several disciplines. In a very real sense, therefore, every individual problem is also a social problem.

It is, of course, granted that every concrete, specific illness, every concrete, specific failure, every concrete, specific trauma is an individual and even a unique problem. And if such illness, failure, or trauma affected only one individual, so that no one else became involved — a most improbable assumption — we might then speak of it as an individual problem. But such a situation is not likely to occur. For almost everyone except the completely isolated or alienated, is part of a role network, interacting with others as son, daughter, mother, father, employer, employee, husband, wife, what-have-you, so that the stresses — illness, failure, or trauma — of any one inevitably affect others to some extent or other. Human beings are, to use a term no longer fashionable, *socii*, that is, persons in association with one another, so that what happens to one affects what happens to others.[2]

Even if it were possible to keep one's problems to oneself there would still be no really individual problems in the sense that no one else had them, for despite the uniqueness and individuality of every human being, anything that can happen to one person can and does happen to many persons. There is nothing unique about the incidence of illness, failure, trauma, or suffering. No matter how unique we feel our own private stresses to be, there is nothing more certain than the fact that there are hundreds or thousands or even millions with similar ones. We need place no statistical boundary line about any problem. And the conditions which produce large numbers of isolated, alienated, lonely individuals — even in the improbable case that they are not socii or members of role networks — constitute a problem for the social system or society as a whole, if not for their role networks. They would be, that is, societal, even if they were not social, problems.

Even individual problems, then, are likely to be either social or societal, or both, not only in their incidence, but also in their cause and in

1 For a detailed analysis of the concepts "social problems" and "societal problem" and a history of their use, see Bernard (*1957*).

2 It is interesting, if not significant, that the poem of Donne has become so widely quoted in this day: No man is an island, the bell tolls for all of us if it tolls for any of us; if one of us is diminished, we are all diminished. And Frost's lines echo through many minds, reminding us that there is something in us that does not like a wall.

their effect. For no other reason than expedience, we shall use the term "social problems" when we are looking at *socii* and the term "societal problems" when we are looking at society as a whole. Thus we shall view poor people as social problems, but poverty as a societal one; criminals as social problems, crime as a societal one; disgruntled, unhappy, alienated workers as social problems, labor relations as a societal one.

Social problems arise when the socius does not — cannot or will not — interact according to role expectations. His behavior may be better or worse than the expected behavior. Still he prevents others from performing their part of the role relationships. The problem for others may be minor and trivial if the non-performance is insignificant. But it may be major and even traumatic if the distance from expectations is great, as in the case of the psychotic. The stresses associated with social problems have long been recognized; those related to societal problems are of relatively recent recognition.

> . . . the concept of "social" problems, that is, the problems of interpersonal relationships or of relationships within face-to-face groups, is quite old, for "social" problems in this interpersonal sense are not difficult to formulate. Anyone can see that the widowed woman with dependent children will suffer unless someone takes care of her; anyone can see that the sick man must have help. In this personal sense, then, the concept of "social" problems is not new, but quite old.
>
> The concept that is new is that of "societal" problems. It is by no means easy . . . to perceive human suffering or misery as a societal problem, that is, as something that concerns others than those immediately involved (*Bernard, 1957,* p. 90).

The two concepts are not mutually exclusive. Some societal problems, like those mentioned above, may also be social problems. But some are not. Air pollution, for example, is a serious problem for our society as, indeed, are traffic problems, water shortages, stream pollution, weather control. They may be related to social problems and, in fact, may create them, as when air or water pollution causes illness in the population. But in the sense we have defined social problems, they are not themselves social problems, that is, problems of the socius, of the interacting individual in role relations. Counseling and psychotherapy have only minor relevance for societal problems that are not also social problems. Neither counselors nor psychotherapists (except as case workers)[3] make any claims with respect to dealing with societal problems.[4] They are concerned with

---

[3] Social case work, according to Robinson (*1934,* p. xiv) has "the responsibility of helping to maintain and to improve the social order."

[4] Hartung (*1963,* p. 261) speaks of interest in mental illness as a social movement, and he cites Kingsley Davis as showing "that it possesses a characteristic essential to any social movement. Its proponents conceive it to be a panacea."

the individuals they deal with and how best to help them even, if necessary at times, at the expense of others. That their work does have implications for societal problems is of secondary concern to them.[5] Since, however, so many social problems are also societal problems, both must be included in our discussion.

Sociological and Psychological Problems

It is useful to distinguish psychological from sociological problems. Both deal with how to think about things, how to conceptualize them. How to define individual, social, and societal problems is itself a sociological problem. How to evaluate psychotherapy and counseling as institutional phenomena is a sociological problem; how to evaluate them as technical phenomena is a psychological problem. Sociological and psychological problems, in brief, are theoretical, conceptual, even technical.

Such theoretical, conceptual, and technical problems are usually characterized on the basis of which discipline is most suitable for dealing with them. This greater suitability is by no means always obvious or even apparent. Is poverty, for example, a sociological, a psychological, an economic, or a political problem? Or crime? Or race relations? Which is the most suitable way of looking at any of them? Each discipline sees something different or interprets what it sees differently.

The distinction between psychological and sociological problems is relevant in determining the proper limits of our discussion. It would not be appropriate for a sociologist *qua* sociologist to evaluate the research and theory on, let us say, the physiological aspects of learning or the relative merits of tranquilizers in psychotherapy. These are primarily psychological questions. On the other hand, fashions — trends which sweep through a population, even a scientific one — and collective beliefs in any — even, again, a scientific — population are sociological phenomena and invite sociological attention, as do also the functions performed by institutions.

Two sets of phenomena relevant for our discussion are presented at this point: one has to do with the nature of human nature, which is both a psychological and a sociological problem and one has to do with a contemporary "fashion" in the approach to social problems.

---

[5] That sometimes helping an individual which implies acceptance of nonconforming behavior can put the counselor or psychotherapist in a difficult spot is clearly recognized by Robinson (*1934,* p. xiv). Social case work, she says "is threatened from without by the change and uncertainty in established institutions, in moral standards and social norms. Furthermore, an even more serious inner source of insecurity arises in the conflict between these norms and the new personality values in relation to which social case work in the evolution of its own self-conscious practice in human relationships is essentially creative."

The Nature of Human Nature:
Psychological or Sociological Problems?

Ford and Urban point out that all systems of psychotherapy depend on some theory of human nature.

> A theorist's generalized image of man significantly influences the theories he develops. It determines what he considers important to study and therefore the kinds of behavior he will seek to observe; the conditions he arranges and the procedures he selects for making his observations; and finally the concepts and propositions he develops from those observations (*Ford and Urban, 1963*, p. 595).

Despite the basic Christian ideology of Western culture, scientists as scientists are antiseptically non-committal or uncommitted on the moral or ethical goodness or badness of "human nature." It is their professed objective to understand and explain human behavior, not to judge it. They do not, in fact, think in terms of a generalized "human nature," but rather in terms of specific forms of "human behavior." Still specific behavior does not occur at random.

Because the theorists are dealing with value-laden behavior the problem of judgment cannot be ignored. It arises inevitably. Among psychotherapists, for example, Ford and Urban found that two *conceptions* or *images* or *assumptions* about man have been accepted. One is the image of man as pilot, as exercising control, as choosing his course and hence responsible; the other is the image of man as a robot, which follows the currents of life, powerless to control them and hence not responsible. If the pilot conception prevails, then the deviant person has only himself to blame for any misfortune that befalls him. If he chose certain courses of action, he is, in the old discarded terminology, if not the new, "bad." If, on the other hand, the robot conception prevails, he is a victim, not to blame, and, in the old terminology, not "bad."

Actually neither of these images was found in pure form in any of the systems of psychotherapy analyzed by Ford and Urban (1963, p. 599). All accepted both, although there were differences in emphasis. Ford and Urban conclude that overemphasis on either one may lead to theoretical weaknesses:

> Excessive emphasis on the "pilot" image omits reference to and incorporation of the many facts established about physiological, motoric, and glandular responses, and their more complex organization into emotional patterns — something of immediate and direct relevance to psychotherapy .... Exclusive emphasis upon the "robot" features of man leads to corresponding deficiencies. It can lead to a restriction of attention to those behaviors easily observed and manipulated, in which automaticity is typical . . . . We believe more rapid progress will follow from assuming that behavior is both automatic and consciously determined . . . .

Closely related to the pilot-robot contrast is the conception of innate characteristics and their influence on behavior. If innate patterns govern behavior, the tendency would be in the direction of the robot image, of man at the mercy not only of the "currents in the sea of life" but also of the behavior patterns that had been "programmed" into him by genetics.

Ford and Urban (p. 602) report that psychotherapists differ in the explicitness of their assumptions in this area. Some, like Karen Horney, ignore innate behavior patterns "because 'they can't be changed anyhow' "; others, like Sullivan and the Existentialists, have considered "specifications of the 'nature of man' essential." Ford and Urban (p. 614) feel that psychotherapy theorists have given too little explicit attention to this problem, and what attention they have given to it is connected with a too-restricted sample, namely of adult patients:

> Too often the error appears to have been made by observing complex patterns of adult behavior and imputing some innate tendency of human behavior as the cause. Careful distinctions between what is innate and how this influences future learning will help produce a more effective psychotherapy theory.

Equally significant is the conception of the nature of innate tendencies of human behavior. How are they viewed? Freud (*1958*, pp. 61–62), it will be recalled, re-discovered the Christian idea of original sin:

> . . . this tendency to aggression . . . is the factor that disturbs our relations with our neighbors and makes it necessary for culture to institute its high demands. Civilized society is perpetually menaced with disintegration through this primary hostility of men towards one another. . . . Culture has to call up every possible reinforcement in order to erect barriers against the aggressive instincts of men and hold their manifestations in check.

From quite a different approach, a sociologist, Durkheim (*1951*), arrived at essentially the same conclusion. He viewed man as equipped with infinite, insatiable wants, so that in order to achieve social life at all, "the passions must first be limited . . . by some force exterior to him" (p. 248). True, he emphasized the socially induced rather than the inherited needs of man, but the end result was similar:

> At the very moment when traditional rules have lost their authority, the richer prize offered these appetites stimulates them and makes them more exigent and impatient of control. The state of deregulation or anomie is thus further heightened by passions being less disciplined precisely when they need more disciplining (p. 253).

Implicit in the theories of both Freud and Durkheim is a conception of human nature strongly reminiscent of the Christian conception:

The Christian fathers, Freud, and Durkheim are strange bedfellows. But they do have in common a conceptualization of normative breakdown which specifies an ongoing battle between human depravity, human instincts or libido, or acquired social drives on one side and restraining forces however conceived, the Church in the case of the Christian fathers, civilization in the case of Freud, and societal norms in the case of Durkheim, on the other (*Bernard, 1962*, pp. 374–375).

Everything that human beings do is natural. It is natural for them to kill, destroy, hate, envy; it is also natural for them to create, love, be generous. The non-violence of the Negro protest movement in the South was as natural as the violence of the Negro protest movement in the North. There is an enormous potential for both destruction and construction in the genes of the human species. Which of these potentials is realized and which not realized depends to a large extent on the way the individual infant or child is socialized.[6] In our society, many kinds of parent-child and sibling relationships may go wrong — inevitably do, according to some theorists — resulting in aggressions, anxieties, and fears of one kind or another. A modicum of distress is inherent in the socialization process.

Implicit in the current theories of personality on which psychotherapy and counseling are based is the assumption that the socializing process will be successful, that institutions will succeed in internalizing societal norms, that whatever the raw material they begin with, the end result will be conforming or "good" people.

Ford and Urban (1963) find a high degree of consensus among psychotherapy theorists with respect to the importance assigned to the processes of normal development which produce this result. Still they report that the theorists do not pay too much attention to it.

> Without exception they all regard it as the crucial antecedent to the adult behavior with which their theories were concerned, even though this was not always reflected in the extent to which they tried to account for the way it comes about (p. 614).[7]

[6] Ruth Benedict, Abram Kardiner, and Cora Dubois have documented the differing kind of personalities produced under differing cultural institutions. It is interesting to note how much more influence recognition of these cultural differences has had on psychotherapy theory than has recognition of the equally striking class differences within any one culture. Once it became known that forms of behavior which we labelled pathological were highly prized in some cultures (epileptic seizures, for example), or that hysterias waxed and waned according to the cultural context, we became much less sure of ourselves vis-à-vis the sick. Perhaps they only *seemed* sick because of our own cultural biases. . . . It took a long time for the psychoanalysts to recognize that much of their theory, therapy rested on research, and experience with a type of "human nature" which was the peculiar product of nineteenth century Vienna culture. Recognition that class culture may be as crucial as any other kind is only slowly finding its way into psychotherapy, a point to be commented on in more detail below.

[7] Ford and Urban note that few theorists — Dollard and Miller are among the

Disordered behavior is viewed as the result of inappropriate conditions of training:

> One generalization can be made at the outset. The theorists seem agreed that inappropriate learnings are attributable directly to inappropriate conditions of training; this, in turn, is the consequence of the significant teachers who unwittingly or mistakenly train the growing person in undesirable, inappropriate, ineffective patterns of behavior (p. 614).

The implication is that if the conditions of socialization — training and teachers — were normal, then undesirable, inappropriate, or ineffective behavior would not occur. Normal behavior can be taken for granted; it is "natural" in the sense that it is the normal result of the developmental process; it is the undesirable, inappropriate, ineffective patterns of behavior however defined that have to be explained. They cannot be taken for granted as "normal" or "natural."[8]

Human behavior — whatever "human nature" might be like — would be "good" if the developmental conditions were normal. The blame — although, of course, the scientist never thinks in these terms — is therefore assessable to the socializing forces, not to evil "human nature." "Bad" human behavior is not something we take for granted, to be expected, as the "natural" or "normal" thing as it was among old theologians. If it weren't for such-and-so, the behavior would have been "good" or at least not "bad."[9]

---

exceptions — concern themselves with the way disordered behavior is learned. It is the derangement of development which attracts them.

[8] ". . . When an individual, whether he is in psychotherapy or not, expresses a need to develop himself, or a democratic impulse, or any of the attributes of the new hero, the motives underlying these feelings are not typically sought for or uncovered. Their acceptability is usually considered self-evident. Motivational reductions are less apt to be made than, if, by contrast, an individual were to express a revolutionary wish, or authoritarian tendency, a deep belief in religion, or, for that matter, any highly conservative, well-established middle-class value. . . . If democratic, co-operative, warm feelings . . . are seen as an individual's true motives they are not inspected further, whereas authoritarian. revolutionary and traditional beliefs would not be accepted as genuine motives" (*Riessman and Miller, 1964*, p. 33).

[9] After a generation-long detour, there seems to be a return among at least some theorists to emphasis on constitutional or biological factors in relation to at least some social problems, not at the earlier naive hereditarian level, but at a more sophisticated level. Thus Kiell (*1964*), in contradiction to the old Margaret Mead orthodoxy, finds that adolescence is, indeed, a time of stress and strain in many cultures and not, as once argued, entirely a result of cultural pressures. The success of tranquilizing drugs has also had some influences on current thinking. There is now increased search for biochemical "flukes" or errors as the basis for disturbed behavior (*Fleming, 1964*, p. 75). Biological anomalies in sex are also receiving research attention (*Staller, 1968; Money, 1967*). The implications of the constitutional and biological emphasis are not in the direction of minimizing the importance of psychotherapy. They may, in fact, point in the direction of underscoring it. Therapy may be of greater importance in dealing with constitutional or biological problems than with so-called functional ones, for once a biological base is found it may be treated, thus removing one of the barriers to successful psychotherapy.

Psychotherapy theorists are, of course, certainly far from naive. They have plenty of evidence of "evil" human nature. They face "original sin" and all of the mortal sins every day of their professional lives. Aggression, hostility, vengefulness, sloth are surely not something they can ignore. But even if, like Freud, they begin with aggressive human nature, they take it for granted that institutions will normally socialize it. They are not likely to take a fatalistic point of view. Their profession is built on faith. They think something can be done about aggression and hostility and sloth and vengefulness. They do not, of course, think in terms of any behavior as good or bad; still one could classify them with those who think of it as at least potentially good.

Neither are sociologists naive. They observe that "human nature" allows genocide, lynching, violent crime. But they, too, tend to view the social constraints as normally successful in controlling it.

So far so good. Both psychologists and sociologists as scientists are noncommittal about the moral or ethical nature of human behavior, while interested only in understanding and explaining it. Both seem to feel it is problem rather than non-problem behavior that needs explanation; if the conditions of socialization were appropriate, it would not occur. Both, that is, show the same bias judging that it is deviant or non-conforming behavior which cannot be taken for granted, which needs explanation. Both tend to go back to early socialization patterns.

But at this point they tend to diverge. For the psychologist will tend to find going back to the early stages of socialization far enough. If he finds trauma, rejection, complexes, neglect, or what-have-you, he is satisfied. And the psychotherapist would feel he knew enough at least to diagnose the difficulty and perhaps even enough to heal it.

But the sociologist wants to know more. He wants to carry the analysis back — or forward — another step. Granted that Freud's family drama is played out in the theater of every home (and, of course, not even all psychologists do grant that it is), he is curious that the damage done is so much more serious in some homes than in others. He wants to know why there is so much more mental and emotional illness in some classes than in others, in some neighborhoods than in others, in some ethnic and racial groups than in others. Why, he asks, does the socializing process "go wrong" in some times more than in others, in some areas more than in others, in some groups more than in others, in some classes more than in others. Is there, perhaps, some "law" involved here? Is it inevitable that defects or failures in socialization occur? Are they somehow or other built into the social system? Are they perhaps the price we pay for success in other areas? Are the conditions which give rise to them performing some intrinsic "latent function" in our society? And is it perhaps a societal function of psychotherapy and counseling to preserve this system, which to its victims is so costly?

These are, of course, subversive questions. They lead perilously close to an orthodox Christian conclusion: while some people have grace, some people are damned, that is, condemned to failure, misery, fears, anxieties, or what-have-you. The sociologist would say it was because they were born into a certain part of the social system. He might even conclude that such damning parts of the social system were inevitable, an intrinsic part of it. He might "blame" institutions for the mishaps in socialization that beset mankind; but he might conclude that any particular institutional status quo was the outcome of conflicting forces, with a payoff intrinsically unfavorable to some and favorable to others. His view would not necessarily require him to accept it. He could reconcile action to change the status quo in the direction of minimizing its costs or of spreading them more evenly over the class spectrum. But it would be a view which did not grant much beyond a holding or stop-gap or remedial function to psychotherapy.

To summarize the above contrast between the psychological and the sociological point of view on the nature of human nature, we may say that by and large psychologists and psychiatrists, who have supplied most of the theory on which psychotherapy and counseling rest, have implied both (1) a human nature which required socialization and (2) institutional failure, in order to account for social problems. People are deviant because something has gone wrong in the socialization process which normally processes them, a failure which leaves them hostile, aggressive, apathetic, depressed, or in some way or other incapable of dealing appropriately with their problems. Psychologists and psychiatrists are not likely to ask why the socializing institutions fail with such patterned regularity. If they do, they tend to find the answer within the family.

The work of the sociologist, who until the present volume, has contributed little if anything to the theory on which psychotherapy and counseling rest, agrees with that of the psychologist and the psychiatrist in supporting the idea that something has gone wrong with the socialization process of the deviant. He can accept the research that finds family failure the basis of much social failure. But he finds that these failures show such patterned regularity — class, ethnic, racial — that he is loath to invoke intra-psychic or even intra-family relationships as the ultimate target. He looks to the total society and to its structure, and to the latent function which the failure producing conditions perform in the social system. Some — like the old laissez-faire or like some, not all, of the structure-function school — may draw fatalistic conclusions: poverty or crime or prejudice or what-have-you are the price a society has to pay for a system which pays off very handsomely for most people; reforms which would reduce them might cost more than the gains obtained. Most, however, draw more optimistic conclusions: any societal function being performed by poverty or crime or prejudice or what-have-you can be better performed in other ways with less cost. We know enough about how societies operate, they believe, to repair the institutions which make the creation of deviancy inevitable for so many people.

Frank *(1961)* bemoans the fact that the several social sciences approach their problems with so unstandardized a set of conceptual tools.

> . . . We must try to develop a common conception of human nature which all the disciplines and professions can use to replace the variety of beliefs and assumptions held by economists, political scientists, sociologists, lawyers, anthropologists, biologists, psychologists, psychiatrists, etc. Surely we must some time agree upon an acceptable theory or common assumption about human conduct and how it is produced . . . This does not imply that the various disciplines are to give up their chosen fields and problems, but rather that they construct some acceptable conceptual framework and some shared assumptions which each can use on whatever problems it may study in its field or profession (p. 46).

Whether such a common conceptual tool kit is desirable could be mooted. Even in physics it has been noted that some conceptualizations — of the nature of light, for example — are more efficient than others for certain problems while different conceptualization of the same phenomena work better in other problems. It is probably just as well that we have a variety of conceptions of human nature, one of which leads the psychologist to examine the delinquent's emotions and another of which leads the sociologist to examine the boy's peer culture; one of which leads to the recommendation of more services to boys and their families, and another of which leads to the recommendation that other ways be found to pay the costs of our social system.

Trend Toward the Psychiatric World View

A second enormously important sociological phenomenon has to do with a currently pervasive "fashion" in the intellectual world, namely a belief in the psychiatric approach to all kinds of social problems. For conceptualizations, scientific or other, do seem to follow fashions. Sometimes the emphasis is on one theory or paradigm, sometimes on another. And sometimes different theories or paradigms compete concurrently for acceptance by the scientific world. In the field of psychology, for example, there are times when the rational forms of behavior are popular areas of study; there are other times when the irrational forms are. In the first part of the nineteenth century, economics and political science built their systems on a model of man as rational. Markets and constitutions reflected men who knew what they wanted and how to get it. Toward the end of the century, the non-rational and even the irrational aspects of human behavior came to command more attention; collective behavior — crowds, mass hysterias, manias, fads, crazes — and instincts were examined with more care.

In recent years emphasis on the non-rational has tended to prevail, despite efforts to salvage the rational, referred to below. There is, in the present, an interesting and characteristic slant on the non-rational which distinguishes it from others. It differs from past emphases on the non-rational in that it tends also in the direction of defining more and more kinds of behavior not only as non-rational but also as evidence of illness. There has come almost a mania for explaining behavior in psychiatric terms. This is new. In the past, non-rational — for example, instinctive — behavior was not viewed as in any sense pathological. Today there is no clear line drawn between the normal and the sick (*Fleming, 1964,* pp. 72–76).

Hartung (*1963*) reviewing the Manhattan survey of mental health, calls this tendency to label almost anything as an illness "Manhattan madness," and other sociologists have followed suit.

There are, they recognize, a myriad of reasons for this trend. Only one is presented here, namely Rein's (*1964*) explanation in terms of professional status-striving. He points out that there are several competing conceptualizations involved in the serving professions. Thus the recipients of services, for example, may be viewed: as customers who purchase services; as clients or patients whom a therapist helps to achieve self-understanding and self-realization; as victims of circumstances or of society, deprived, helpless, who need aid in winning access to resources and rights; or as deviants, "who have broken moral and legal rules and whom the service network must bring into line." Some of these helping relationships are accorded higher prestige than others.

Addressing himself to social workers, but illustrating points of view relevant to the present discussion, Rein states that "those who serve 'clients' and provide 'psychotherapy' enjoy the highest professional prestige" and that those who take care of " 'victims' have the lowest prestige." As a result:

> . . . each dispenser tries to improve his social status by calling what he does "psychotherapy," and by trying to reclassify his recipients as "clients" — or at least by excluding those who stand little chance of becoming clients. There is always a tendency for deviants, victims, or customers to be transformed into "patients" and for their problems to be treated as "sickness." . . . Delinquency and dependency come increasingly to be considered malfunctions or flaws of personality — with less and less emphasis on changing the conditions in which they occur (p. 4).

This explanation by no means exhausts the possible explanations for the current fashion of labeling so much behavior as pathological. A complete explanation would involve greater attention than we can devote to it. Rein's is most relevant to the discussion here. We shall have more to say about the implications of this trend presently.

Conceptualizations Count: Some Consequences of the Psychiatric World View

The modern trend toward emphasis on the psychiatric viewpoint might be of only academic interest if it did not have serious consequences, scientific, administrative, and political. Since it does have such consequences it is of far wider significance.

Scientific Consequences

Some of the dysfunctional consequences of the trend in the direction of defining all kinds of social problems as psychiatric in nature have been presented by Riessman and Miller as follows:

> [Since] all kinds of problems — social, medical, educational, political — were interpreted through the new psychiatric world view, problems were not searchingly examined to determine their variable causes or whether and how psychological causes might play a role. Rather, presumed psychological diagnoses were readily given and typically went unquestioned. This world view was costly in at least two ways: it deflected analysis and action away from nonpsychodynamic (for example, social) approaches and it often contaminated the original problem by introducing inappropriate modes of attack *(Riessman and Miller, 1964,* p. 31).[10]

Administrative Consequences

The psychiatric world view has administrative as well as scientific consequences. Rein points out that it makes a great deal of difference not only in research but also in the administration of social services which conceptualization is being applied, illustrating the point in the case of illegitimacy:

> How, for instance, should an illegitimate birth be defined? To many professionals it is a symptom, an outcome of internal emotional stresses — the mother must therefore be treated as a client or patient. But morally she may be a deviant — and there are frequent movements to abolish, or severely limit, welfare payments to mothers who continue to have illegitimate children — the hope being that this may also limit immorality. But socially and economically the illegitimate mother may be a victim. Many studies have established a strong relationship between illegitimacy and inequality. . . .

---

[10] The use of the term "inappropriate" is interesting in view of its use by Ford and Urban in their definition of pathological behavior, discussed below.

From this view effective help is a matter of reducing inequality and expanding opportunity. In short, how we define "illegitimate birth" determines the fate of mother and child — and, in practice, the fates of many mothers and children.

To wrongly label a victim a client can have the unintended effect of "cooling the mark out"[11] — that is, disposing of the case without disposing of the cause, and keeping the victim from seeking further help (or demanding it) by impressing on him that the fault lies only within himself rather than in outside circumstances *(Rein, 1964,* p. 4).

An allied practical, if not entirely administrative, consequence is that not the behavior itself but its explanation tends to become the focus of concern. On one side, if we can explain the criminal's behavior as the result of an unresolved Oedipus complex, this fact somehow or other makes a difference in our interpretation of what he does. His crime is not, seemingly, so serious; it is less of a problem. Conversely, and more subversive perhaps, if we can explain the agitation of a reformer as the result of an unresolved Oedipus complex (for, of course, the same "cause" is sometimes invoked to explain widely different kinds of behavior), this fact somehow or other cancels out the evils he was trying to get rid of. If we could reach the criminal or the reformer and heal his emotional wounds, he would no longer have to commit crimes — or agitate for reforms.[12]

Political Consequences

There are, according to Rein, political repercussions also. For policy often hinges on the way one defines a situation. Should public relief, for example, be defined as "a form of public subsidy for low wages in an economy which cannot keep all its labor force working" or should it be viewed as handouts to "personal failures with low intelligence, low motivation, and high pathology — that is, the poor have only themselves to blame for their poverty?" *(Rein, 1964,* p. 5). The definition determines the policy.

The New Hero

Another consequence of the psychiatric world view is the model of normal or healthy personality which it propagates. It spreads "middle-class values and ethics under the guise of science. It presents the . . . [archetype] of the middle-class or upper-class person as being in all important respects equivalent to that of the mentally healthy person" and

---

[11] See Chapter 12 for discussion of the process of "cooling."

[12] A conference on Negro youth had a session on participants in sit-ins and other forms of direct action. Almost the entire time was spent analyzing their anxieties, their hostilities, their aggressions, and the like, as though they were pathological phenomena instead of normally resentful victims of injustice.

deviations from that archetype as ill," says Hartung *(1963).* No wonder, he continues,

> that when psychiatrists and other clinicians (who are professional and upper-class) interview and otherwise "examine" lower class children, especially delinquent boys, they find that the boys are "emotionally disturbed" or "mentally ill" in some form and to some degree (p. 261).[13]

Essentially the same point is made by Riessman and Miller *(1964)* who describe the "new hero" implicit in the current psychiatric world view.

> A new hero emerged in the age of psychiatry. He had a number of interesting attributes. He was expressive and calm, free and well-balanced, self actualized and moderate, autonomous and cooperative. He was neither intense nor overemotional; a good team man, he was a productive being. He evidenced his ability to work, love, and relate to people. Through it all, he was an individualist — not a conformist.
>
> The new hero was thoughtful, knew and accepted himself, and possessed just the right amount of extroversion and introversion. He cared about people and society. He was democratic, antiauthoritarian and antibureaucratic. He had a mild interest in politics, and strongly rejected the masses and mass culture — one of his few strong feelings. He was not too overly competitive, disliked conspicuous consumption, and favored sex equality. He preferred relatively permissive — although currently more balanced — child rearing and education.
>
> Our new hero did not get burningly angry, nor was he known for his passionate conviction or intense ardor. He was, in sum, the new well-adjusted middle-class man.
>
> Contemporary psychiatry in the United States typically questions extreme, intense behavior. This questioning arises, in part, out of psychiatry's fundamental concern with pathological self-damaging behavior, which is often extreme. On the other hand, many healthy urges of the patient are underdeveloped and therefore unlikely to manifest themselves in intense form. Thus, unwittingly, psychiatry has come to look with suspicion on very strongly held beliefs and urges, often characterizing them as resistances or reaction formations (pp. 31–32).

This consequence of the new psychiatric world view is considered to be dysfunctional, for it discourages creative differences, passionate commitments, deep concern about anything; it exalts what they call the "pathology of moderation," and hence, by default, the status quo with all its defects.

> Twentieth century psychiatry . . . has not sufficiently developed a high order of creative people. More often it has produced "balanced" people, who have rid themselves of their earlier neurotic intensities, but have not replaced them by new constructive zeal. Too often the implicit advice is to avoid soaring for "unrealistic" heights. Better never to have tried and lost

[13] The resulting reductio ad absurdum is discussed in Chapter 12.

than to have tried at all, seems frequently to be the implicit motto (pp. 31–32).[14]

Admittedly it is difficult to tread one's way between the dedicated zeal of a Hitlerian *Jugend* and the alleged apathy of pre-civil-rights agitating American youth; this is, according to Riessman and Miller, what modern psychiatry attempts to teach us to do. They deplore this lesson.

Moral Consequences

Only one more consequence of the new trend toward a psychiatric world view need concern us here. It has to do with absolving people of blame for their behavior. Hartung (1963, p. 261) criticizes the downgrading of rational and responsible behavior which accompanies the modern psychiatric world view and the substitution for them of "concepts of irresponsibility and exculpation." This tendency, he tells us:

> . . . accords to irrationalism a constantly increasing respectability. An enormous increase in the kinds of conduct classified as irrational has resulted in the past few decades from the work of some of the most highly educated and intellectual students of human behavior. One corollary is a decrease in the kinds of behavior classified as rational. This has been accompanied by a violent attack upon the concepts of reason and individual responsibility, and by attempts to substitute the concepts of irresponsibility and exculpation. These attempts have been successful to a great degree. . . .

True to the psychiatric world view, whatever the specific technique used today by psychotherapist and/or counselor, it is consensually agreed that he does not censor or blame the patient or client. He accepts whatever is told him without shock or condemnation. And, of course, the same is true of the researcher.

This viewpoint, so functional in the psychotherapy or counseling session, has tended to ramify, as Hartung notes; a large segment of the public has also learned not to blame or condemn — themselves no more than others. This trend raises some interesting problems. If violation of the mores, alcoholism, for example, is accepted without invoking sanctions, how can they be enforced? Is the accepting stance subversive? How can the psychotherapist or counselor who is paid by social work agencies or even the school counselor, justify his acceptance — even defense — of behavior which would be disapproved of by his supporters? Even more to the point is the fact that sometimes it looks to the observer that "disapproved of" behavior is not only accepted but actually rewarded by the psychotherapist and/or counselor, for reasons demanded by the psychotherapeutic process. We shall have more to say on this topic in

---

14 True to the psychiatric world view, the impassioned followers of Barry Goldwater were at first referred to as "kooks."

our discussion of social case work. It is raised here only to suggest some of the moral consequences of the new psychiatric world view.

Psychotherapy, Counseling and Some Selected Social Problems

As noted in Chapter 12, psychotherapists and counselors make no claims with respect to "solving" societal problems.[15] Their perspective is close, focused on the individual. It is doubtless true that if all disturbed people had to be treated or counseled before they were permitted to drive, we could reduce traffic accidents; but neither psychotherapy nor counseling can contribute much to the solution of urban traffic problems, nor of air pollution, nor of water shortages. It is therefore unfair to imply that they ought to solve them or that we should berate them for not doing so.

Even in the case of societal problems which overlap more broadly with social problems — crime, race relations, poverty — should we expect help from psychotherapy and counseling? It might be argued that if Adolf Hitler had received treatment in his youth, or if Stalin had been treated for paranoia, or if any other disturbed great leader had been cured of his irrational disturbance, some of the most heinous crimes might have been avoided. But it is not at all clear how psychotherapy or counseling could change the structural factors in any society which produce the conditions auspicious for crime, bad race relations, or poverty.[16] Their practitioners make no such claims. We have no right to demand that they should.

Psychotherapy and counseling do, however, hope for success in dealing with individuals and hence it is legitimate to discuss their contributions to social problems. So far as one of our major social problems — mental illness — is concerned, the discussion above, truncated as it is, will have to suffice. Only three kinds of social problems, namely criminals and delinquents, prejudiced people and their victims, and poor people are discussed here. These are areas in which research concern is shared by psychologists and sociologists (whose cognate problems are crime and delinquency, race relations, and poverty).

Criminals and Delinquents

Most of what we know about criminals in any detailed or scientific way is based on prison populations which constitute very biased samples. For we know that only a minuscule, if indeterminate, proportion of all

---

15 Still Dr. F. C. Redlich is quoted as saying "When I go to professional meetings nowadays, I hear more about poverty, segregation, and racial strife than about schizophrenia and neuroses" (*Pines, 1965,* p. 60).

16 In our discussion of the psychiatric world view above, there was the clear implication in the work of some of the writers cited that psychotherapy and counseling, so far from helping in the attack on societal problems might even be dysfunctional on the community or societal level. See pages 388–394 above.

violators of the law are ever caught, or, if caught, reported, or, if reported, prosecuted, or, if prosecuted, found guilty, or, if found guilty, sentenced, or, if sentenced, incarcerated. "In fact, one study found that, as a result of all the sieves through which violators are screened, only about 3 percent of all crimes known to the police — itself an indeterminate percent of all crimes committed — led to commitment to a penal institution" (*Bernard, 1957,* p. 516). One does not need to accept the Lombroso theory — that criminals are atavisms, primitives in a modern world, with inborn stigmata — to recognize that prison inmates do not represent a random sample of the criminal, let alone of the total population. By far the largest proportion of law violators — the white collar criminals, for example, guilty of fraud, embezzlement, violation of trust, monopolistic practices, unfair labor practices, tax evasion, or members of the criminal syndicates — are not even caught.

The white collar criminals who are caught show no stigmata beyond those of the normal man-on-the-street. They are not compulsive; they are not sex perverts; they are not psychopathic, or sociopathic, personalities. They are ordinary business men and think of themselves as such. Their behavior seems eminently appropriate to them. They do not appear to be promising subjects for either psychotherapy or counseling. They are, technically, criminals in the sense that they have violated the law. To those who wish to reserve the term "criminal" for traditional types of offenders, Sutherland makes a point-for-point analysis showing that white-collar criminals satisfy all — except one — of the criteria of criminality that apply to, let us say, a professional thief. Their criminality is persistent and more extensive than shown by records; like the professional thief, they feel contempt for law-enforcement agencies. The only important difference — the one exception noted above — is that the professional thief thinks of himself as a criminal, the white-collar criminal does not (*Sutherland, 1949,* pp. 219–220).

Even if, as some researchers prefer, we reserve the term criminal for those who are in some manner or other marked deviants from the normal — the compulsives, the sex perverts, the addicts, the psychopathic, or sociopathic, personalities — the contribution of psychotherapy is not impressive. Usually they do not come under the legal specifications for insanity. Thus, despite some spectacular cases of rehabilitation of criminals, the proportion of all criminals amenable to such rehabilitation is not great. If we assumed that every criminal sooner or later passed through prison gates, even the current rate of recidivism, high as it is, might offer encouragement, since *some* criminals do not return to crime. But not a great many.

No branch of criminology has attracted more attention than that dealing with the criminally insane, or the insane criminal. The compulsive killer or thief is a fascinating subject. And forensic medicine, or medical jurisprudence, has attracted some of the best professional minds. In some cases the criminal acts are themselves symptoms of a disorder. There is consensus and the perpetrator is judged insane and dealt with accordingly, although not usually psychotherapeutically. In some cases, however, there is some logic, an apparent or assumable "motive" in the behavior and consensus is not easily reached with respect to its pathology. Is or is not this criminal mentally or emotionally ill? The legal and the medical criteria do not always coincide. He may be ill by medical criteria but not legal. The availability of psychotherapy may hinge on whether medical or legal criteria are applied.

But even if medical opinion prevails, there is no guarantee that hospitalization rather than imprisonment will rehabilitate the criminal, that hospitalization will even mean that he will receive psychotherapy.[17] We must, of course, continue to do all we can to heal by whatever means — psychotherapy or other forms of therapy — the illness that evidences itself in criminal behavior. But it would be an optimistic observer who predicted that even complete success in every case would make much of a dent in the overall picture of even traditional crime in our country.

Delinquencies are often defined as character or behavior disorders lying between that of the psychopathic, or sociopathic, personality and genuine criminal behavior and they are more characteristic of young than of older persons. Thus the problem is usually thought of in terms of juvenile delinquents, so-called.[18] For some, like gang members, delinquency may be a phase of development; they outgrow it as they reach adulthood, marry, and end gang affiliation. The newly established profession of the street worker has been found to perform a useful service in such cases, often on a counseling level. The boys are for the most part as normal as others and what counseling is required may be done as part of the day's work. Although the street worker does not eliminate juvenile delinquency, he greatly moderates it (*Bernard, 1957*, pp. 435–438). Group psychotherapy has been reported as successful in treating juvenile delinquents in an institutional setting.[19] And promising also is the psychiatrically oriented clinical work and the open-door homes for probationers.

The record of success in individual counseling with delinquents is not, however, encouraging. The most famous study is the so-called Somerville project begun in 1935. A sample of 325 boys who had been referred to the project was selected as the Treatment group and 325 as the Con-

---

[17] Szasz (*1963; 1964*, pp. 50–53) is of the opinion that hospitalization is not a more lenient disposal of such cases than incarceration in prison, despite popular opinion to this effect. The accused themselves often prefer imprisonment to hospitalization; a prison sentence has a determinable end, hospitalization may not.

[18] Juveniles who commit adult crimes are often dealt with as delinquents. Theoretically, however, there is a distinction between delinquencies and crimes.

[19] See, for example, the report on Highfields (*Weeks, 1958*). The work of Bruno Bettelheim and Fritz Redl should also be noted.

trol group. A specially selected staff supervised a program to help the Treatment group; the Control group was observed at the same time. The results of surveys made to evaluate results during treatment were by no means unequivocal. Although 40 percent of the subjects who entered the agency were shown to profit from counseling, there was no proof that the counseling was effective in reducing delinquency.

Nor was a 9-year study of 179 Washington school children any more encouraging. This study showed that it was quite possible, using present prediction devices, to predict which children were likely to become delinquent. But case work did not seem to be able to prevent them from becoming delinquents. Four years after the program of maximum benefits was terminated in 1958, a follow-up showed that 69 percent of the 72 children who had received intensive treatment had become delinquents, while only 63 percent of the 34 untreated youngsters had (*Hodges, 1963*).

The follow-up study of children seen at the Child Guidance Clinic in St. Louis in the 1920's, referred to above, was not much more encouraging.

It is quite possible, of course, that the current trends (noted in passing, above) — homes in a neighborhood in which an open door is offered to juvenile probationers, more sociologically sophisticated techniques, for example — and the powerful new insights offered by the work of such men as Bruno Bettelheim, Fritz Redl, and Erik Erickson will vastly improve the batting average of therapy and counseling case work.

> [Still] social case work has serious limitations for delinquency prevention. While such treatment may be of value to some potential delinquents the evidence seems compelling that it will fail in many others, at least the way it is conventionally offered in the United States today (Hodges, 1963).[20]

In some cases, improvement does occur, and we take credit for the change; it was our treatment that produced it. But the scientific evidence is not flattering to these claims.

One has only to read the account of a young Negro who made a career of delinquency and crime — Henry Williamson's *Hustler!* (*1965*) — to realize how terribly wide of the mark most of our conceptions of treatment are.

Prejudiced People and Their Victims[21]

A distinction is made by sociologists between discrimination and prejudice. Discrimination can be dealt with by legislation; prejudice

[20] Nina Trevvett, Executive Director of the Commissioners' Youth Council, which sponsored the project, was quoted as saying that "the weakness in the present case work approach is that it is not able to change the home" (*Hodges, 1963*). Williamson (*1965*) makes clear that the weakness is far more extensive than this.

[21] We are not here discussing race relations in their entirety. Even the over-

cannot.[22] The actual administration of the legislation may well involve a great deal of counseling under the guise of conciliation in the form, perhaps, of cooling. The conciliator may, that is, have to serve the cooling function to bring about observance of a hated law. In this role, counseling-via-conciliation is of the utmost importance in dealing with social and societal problems. Its contribution can not be over-estimated.

Otherwise there is probably no social problem in which psychotherapy or counseling has less to offer than in that of prejudice, nor is there one in which the objectives of counseling — a change in the "hearts of men"[23] — are more appealed to as a solution. The prejudiced person will continue to discriminate no matter what the law; and in extreme cases will violently defy it. The educational function of the law which sociologists emphasize cannot serve here. For we are dealing with hostile, if not sadistic, people who desperately need their prejudices.

We are indebted to a series of studies of prejudice — by victims of racism themselves — for deeper understanding of the nature of prejudiced people. All the studies did not agree in all their specific findings, but they did find certain underlying characteristics which tended to be associated with prejudice. In addition, an extensive literature on race prejudice by psychiatrists and social psychologists has extended our knowledge of the prejudiced personality. The details may change from time to time, from study to study, but prejudice is still viewed, especially by psychoanalytically oriented researchers, as "mainly the consequence of defensive efforts of the ego or superego" (*Bettelheim and Janowitz, 1964,* p. 50).

Bettelheim and Janowitz have summarized the psychiatric interpretations of prejudice, including the psychoanalytic, the ego-psychology, and the identity approaches. Whatever the theory used, the conclusion seems to be that prejudice serves an important function in the emotional economy of the prejudiced person. This does not necessarily mean that it is beyond the reach of change; but the change may have to come from "society and social organization" which reduces the need for prejudice rather than from individual psychotherapy. For "drives which previously were conceived of as unchanging are now seen as subject to the impact of the environment" (p. 51). The consequences of this change in orientation are far-reaching.

---

coming of prejudice would not solve the problems of race relations. There are unprejudiced people who, on other than racial grounds, object to, let us say, sending their children to school with Negro children.

22 If we consider our goal to be desegregation, the elimination of barriers, we are concerned mainly with social controls and institutional arrangements. If we are to have integration as our goal, then the effectiveness of personal controls and the content of attitudes become more important (Bettelheim and Janowitz, 1964, p. 80).

23 "I don't think we can go as far as their present civil rights bill tries to go and say you have to like me and I have to like you" (Goldwater, 1964).

Psychoanalysis. But few psychoanalytically oriented students have probed them as yet.

> The implications of these developments in psychoanalytic thinking have not yet been applied to social problems. Hence . . . ethnic prejudice is still viewed by psychoanalysts as mainly the consequence of defensive efforts of the ego or superego. Contrary to such older formulations, the newer theory postulates that what happens in society can and does influence both the drives (in this case hostility) and the manner in which the ego deals with them. According to the older theory, society and social organization could at best inhibit hostility, redirect it, or lead to the exchange of one defensive mechanism (for example, in the case of prejudice, that of protection) for another. The new theoretical position assumes that society and social organization may reduce hostility and make the use of projection unnecessary or unacceptable; or conversely, social events may increase hostility (*Bettelheim and Janowitz, 1964,* p. 51).

This newer orientation, the authors tell us, is still not widely accepted by psychoanalysts. "The traditional psychoanalytic outlook remains one of seeking causes inside the individual only, with little respect to his social situation and the stresses within his society" (p. 52). As applied to prejudice, this viewpoint would tend to emphasize individual psychotherapy and to preclude social action to affect institutions. But it has the effect, actually of precluding the extirpation of the prejudice by psychotherapy.

> The few who have been analyzed but nevertheless remain prejudiced (and there are quite a few of those) as well as the large number of prejudiced people who have not been analyzed, can hardly derive any benefit from such type of understanding of unconscious causes (p. 53).

Ego Psychology. While giving more emphasis to the social setting, ego psychology is not much more encouraging with respect to prejudice. It sees prejudice as helping the individual perform, but only if he is supported by related societal norms.

> . . . prejudice permits the prejudiced person to function better in society than he might without being prejudiced. This is possible if society accepts or condones such prejudices; otherwise to be prejudiced would lead to further aggravation of difficulties. Thus, prejudice strengthens or weakens a person within himself, depending on the prevailing social norm toward his particular prejudice (p. 53).

The concept introduced by Hartmann and Kris of —

> . . . regression in the service of the ego when applied to prejudice suggests that in certain critical phases of the inner life of the individual, projection (or simple discharge of tension through ethnic hostility) is such regression in the service of the ego, permitting a re-establishment of the threatened ego control over the rest of the instinctual forces (p. 54).

Whatever hope might be introduced by recognition of the part played by the social order, or institutions, in prejudice is thus dispersed by recognition that prejudice performs an important function. And, further, not only for the individual but for the group as well:

> Ethnic hostility and prejudice are part of a particularistic way of life which protects the continued existence of social units by binding them even more closely together, and by inuring them against universalistic tendencies. The dangers of particularism, at a time when economic, technological, and social developments make increased universalism an essential aspect of solution of the pressing problems, led us [originally, in our book *Dynamics of Prejudice* in 1950], to deplore ethnic hostility. Because of our concern with social reform, we might not have been equally sensitive to how great are the desires of many to hold on to the comforts particularistic group life can offer, and how prejudice seems to offer them protection against losing their feeling of selfhood (p. 54).

Identity Psychology. The school of thought introduced by Erik H. Erikson lays great emphasis on the "search for identity," the attempt to find out who we are, to find our individuality. This, too, can be used to understand prejudice, for

> . . . as a person develops his need for securing his identity, this need may feed ethnic hostility and prejudice. The search for identity, and with it the search for ego strength and personal control, might very well involve as a detour the desire to find one's identity, or to strengthen it, through prejudice (pp. 56–57).

In addition to serving as a buttress for a weak sense of identity, prejudice may, in effect, cool the mark out. It can protect the ego against diffusion, or loss, of identity.

> No social psychological study of ethnic hostility and of prejudice can afford to overlook the contribution that fear of identity diffusion makes to intolerance. . . . Whoever has not yet reached a secure personal identity of his own is threatened by feelings of self-doubt, by confusion about who he is, a nagging anxiety that he may be a "nobody." This fear he tries to silence by telling himself, "at least I am not a Negro, or a Jew; and this makes me at least something more than a nobody" (p. 58).

This might seem precisely the kind of situation in which psychotherapy would be most promising. The psychotherapist might aim to strengthen ego identity and preclude ego diffusion or loss. If we were dealing with isolated individuals, this conclusion might be warranted. But we are dealing with individuals in groups, with socii, and not with individuals in isolation.

> Efforts at racial integration threaten not only the social status and economic security of a prejudiced group but actually the inner sense of

identity of its members. Steps toward integration mean criticism of their prejudices — a criticism that increases certain guilt feelings they may be unable to admit even to themselves. As a result they may feel psychologically trapped, because now both criticism and guilt threatens their sense of identity. At a loss in seeking to protect their identity, such prejudiced persons may try to further buttress it by maintaining their prejudice (p. 60).

Whether or not prejudice can be labeled a pathology in all cases, whether or not it performs an important function in the psychic economy of individuals, whether or not it performs a similarly important function in group preservation, it is doubtful whether either individual psychotherapy or counseling can be of much help. The prejudiced personality is not likely to seek either psychotherapy or counseling in the area of his prejudices. And if the prejudice does serve a function for the individual and his group, he might be worse off without it. If, as the newer trend in psychoanalytic thinking suggested by Bettelheim and Janowitz is valid, it might conceivably be possible to extirpate prejudice by extirpating the conditions which give rise to the need for it. But such an operation would be far from the area of psychotherapy and counseling.

Victims of Prejudice. It is only recently that we have come to plumb the depths of the effects of discrimination and prejudice on Negroes. The "mark of oppression," as Kardiner calls it, is so pervasive, so all-encompassing, so inescapable that the wonder is that any Negro even approaches the normal. It may be impossible for a Negro to have a normal personality in the circumstances under which he lives. If the dictum "everyone is emotionally ill" has validity for any population, it would have for the Negro population. It is doubtful if psychotherapy can do anything more than cool the mark out, if even that.

Abram Kardiner carried on intensive interviews with 25 Negroes and analyzed the Rorschach protocols. Although himself a psychotherapist he had to conclude that psychotherapy could not do much for these patients. They *were* up against a hostile world; the pathologies were functional, even adaptive. Thus, for example, adaptation to low self-esteem may take the form of apathy, hedonism, living for the moment, or criminality. Adaptation to aggression may take the form of hate or rage, fear, submission or compliance, flippancy, masochism, psychosomatic illness, or depression.

> In the center of the . . . adaptational scheme [of the Negro] stand the low self-esteem (the self-referential part) and the aggression (the reactive part). The rest are maneuvers with these main constellations, to prevent their manifestation, to deny them and the sources from which they come, to make things look different from what they are, to replace aggressive activity which would be socially disastrous with more acceptable ingratiation and passivity. Keeping this system going means, however, being constantly ill at ease, mistrustful, and lacking in confidence. The entire system prevents the

affectivity of the individual that might otherwise be available from asserting itself (*Kardiner and Ovesey, 1962*, pp. 303–304).

The result is a necessarily unhappy, even sick, person and a less effective society;

> We can summarize the total picture of the 25 personalities that follow in a few sentences. The Negro, in contrast to the white, is a more unhappy person; he has a harder environment to live in, and the internal stress is greater. By 'unhappy' we mean he enjoys less, he suffers more. There is not one personality trait of the Negro [as represented in our sample] the source of which cannot be traced to his difficult living conditions. . . . The final result is a wretched internal life. This does not mean he is a worse citizen. It merely means that he must be more careful and vigilant, and must exercise controls of which the white man is free. This fact in itself, the necessity to exercise control, is distractive and destructive of spontaneity and ease. Moreover, it diminishes the total social effectiveness of the personality, and it is especially in this regard that the society as a whole suffers from the internal stresses under which the Negro lives (p. 81).

We have already noted the perplexities a counselor faces in dealing with minority group members. If, despite everything, the Negro or Mexican-American or Puerto Rican child wants to become an engineer or an accountant, should he define this as an "unrealistic" ambition because discrimination will make success improbable? If so, then counseling will be, in effect, a process of cooling the mark out. The counselor will try to change the boy's ambition, to lower his sights. He will try to reconcile the boy to becoming, let us say, a postal clerk or a porter instead of an engineer.

Suppose he is dealing with a very bright boy, a boy bright enough to know that discrimination will work against his advancement in any job. He has "realistic" goals. What is the counselor's obligation in such a case? Should he attempt to improve the morale of the boy so that he is willing to fight the unequal battle and take his chance on winning, on achieving the higher goal despite the odds against him?

All the resources for societal and social change at our disposal — individual or institutional — will be called for in the next generation of relations between Negro and white. So far, says Frank (*1961*, p. 48) we have not been very successful.

> . . . thus far we have not been able to invent a technique of social change which will enable us to relinquish our now anachronistic beliefs and replace them with new assumptions and patterns consonant with our responsibilities, our new awareness of the meaning of human dignity so long ignored or ruthlessly denied by those who could dominate and exploit others. The great conflict facing the world today is between those who believe change must be imposed by force and coercion — the authoritarian program — and those who believe that a free social order can change through education and persuasion,

exhibiting the capacity for self-repair and self-regulation which is the basic conviction of a democratic society.

The job of change may be easier, hard as it will doubtless be, in the case of the prejudiced person than in the case of his victim. Among the techniques needed will surely be those of the counselor. It is not going to be easy for individual Negroes of the transitional generation to make the hard decisions called for by new legislation. Hard as integration may be for the white population, it is going to be even harder for the Negro. The counselor will have to be trained to know when cooling is the only thing he can do; but he will also have to be trained to know when to weigh probabilities in a favorable way for hard decisions.

Poor People

There are technical difficulties in defining the status of poverty which need not distract us here. Whatever the criteria for defining it, at any one time the population in this status is diverse, heterogeneous, and variegated in composition. For there are many kinds of poor people, or rather, of people living in the status of poverty defined in terms of low income. Some, like college students living on stipends or allowances are in the status of poverty only because they are young. We may dismiss them. They will soon leave the "poverty" status. Some have low incomes only because they are sick; as soon as they get well their earning power and income will pull them back out. Some are in poverty only because they are newcomers, "greenhorns;" as soon as they learn the ropes they, too, will climb out. In brief, some people are only temporarily in the status of poverty. All they need is time. If, in addition, they can also get counseling, that helps. They are, in fact, the best prospects for counseling.

Some people are in the status of poverty only because they are old; all they need is more income to raise them from the poverty level. (Almost a third of those in the status of poverty are old.) Counseling can do little for them except cool. Raising their pensions or social security payments or assistance grants would be more help.

Vocational Guidance and Counseling. Some people are in the status of poverty because, through no fault of their own but as a result of technological or industrial change, they are unemployed. Here counseling is useful. It may involve helping a man decide to move away from the town his family has lived in all their lives and take their chances in some other community. It may involve helping a man decide to undertake a difficult training or re-training program. It may involve helping a man decide to do any one of a number of difficult things required to adjust the supply of workers to the demands of the labor market. If they are unemployed because they are young, old, unskilled, illiterate, it is

403

possible that counseling may perform important services in preparing them for employment. If they are unemployed because of some remediable or compensatable defect, counseling and psychotherapy may even perform spectacular and phenomenal prodigies of rehabilitation.[24]

All this counseling success presupposes that there are jobs available for prepared workers. This is, of course, not necessarily the case. If there are no jobs to move into or to train for, all that counseling can probably do is cool.

Whether or not unemployment is to grow, enormous importance is currently attached to counseling and guidance to help people take advantage of what opportunities there are. The National Education Defense Act, as noted above, includes the training of counselors as a "defense" effort and, indeed, it is. Counseling is part of our defense if not against an external enemy, certainly against an internal one, unemployment resulting from unmotivated or untrained people.

Social Case Work.[25] The form which psychotherapy and counseling have taken in dealing with poor people as such has traditionally been that of social case work. Indeed, long before counseling and psychotherapy had achieved their current professional and scientific status, social workers were wrestling with the problems of poor families by way of individual case work. In the 19th century, to be sure, "counseling" and "psychotherapy" constituted only one aspect of case work, and usually only a minor one. For in addition, case work included getting medical treatment, finding jobs, working out family budgets, finding suitable living quarters, returning fleeing husbands, and the like. But giving counsel, inspiring self-respect and self-reliance as well as giving advice, persuading, and exhorting were all part of the job.

An all-but-complete preemption of social case work by psychotherapy did not occur until the second decade of the 20th century. The time may almost be pinpointed as about 1918–1919. But there was a long history before that time of the recognition of the relationship between client and worker as itself the essential treatment ingredient. As early as 1879, a report of the first Charity Organization Society in the United States, in Buffalo, expressed hope that the poor might be bettered simply by their contacts with the worker in her own home. Mary Richmond, patron saint of the profession of social case work, as early as 1899 recognized "the case work relationship . . . [as] the most fundamental and important factor in treatment." Still the first decade of the 20th century did not make much headway in understanding the psychotherapeutic

[24] Miller (*1964*, p. 210) lists the unemployed as: workers in depressed areas, rural workers displaced by automation on the farm, Negroes and other minority group workers, older workers, younger workers, particularly school dropouts, unskilled workers, and displaced skilled and semiskilled workers who need retraining.

[25] The first four paragraphs in this section follow Robinson (*1934*).

possibilities of the worker-client relationship, partly because the psychological basis was not adequate and partly because social work itself was in an environment-emphasizing, preventive, and reforming phase of its development.

But the groundwork for the burgeoning of psychotherapy in case work was being laid in the work of G. Stanley Hall on children, in the increasing recognition of the importance of sex, and in the elaboration of mental testing techniques which highlighted individual differences. Of special relevance, says Virginia Robinson, was the work of William Healy, who "described the method of unearthing . . . conflict to be based first on an attitude on the part of the observer which never condemns or judges, whose approach is sympathetic and patient and gives the impression that the inquiry 'is born of the desire to help.' " But as the trend to the psychiatric world view accelerated, it was to be psychiatry, not psychology, which molded social case work from 1910 on.

The sudden appearance during World War I of clients who were not in the status of poverty forced a re-assessment of old patterns. The new schools of social work — Smith, New York, and Pennsylvania — were powerfully influenced by the new psychiatry. The 1919 National Conference of Social Work centered on psychiatric social work. "The swing of opinion . . . seemed to be in favor of accepting the psychiatric point of view as the basis of all social case work." Such emphasis was feasible because other agencies had taken over some of the functions formerly assigned to case work. So now the worker-client relationship which had been only one aspect of treatment in the past not only became central but also monopolistic. This relationship *was* treatment; this was it. The worker might not be sure of what she was doing, or the results she was achieving, or even of the value of these results; but she was sure something was happening.[26]

From the very beginning there were critics and opponents of this psychiatric orientation of case work. But it was not until the great depression of the 1930's that it faced a major test. Then it became clear that however valuable the treatment involved in the client-worker relationship might be, it was not the treatment required for the new kind of client. In the 1920's the middle-class client who came to the case worker may have needed some kind of treatment and not relief or assistance. Not so in the 1930's. The college-trained engineer who had lost his job and exhausted his savings and his credit was not likely to take kindly to a treatment that satisfied the social worker but left his family unfed. The private agencies, in which the relational treatment

[26] In view of the ignorance of the worker of what she was doing, and how, it is surprising how god-like she felt in deciding whom to bestow her services on. If she really knows her job, she will "be able to refuse to give to the client, simply, without accusation, apology, or protest" (*Robinson, 1934*, p. 187).

had developed, frankly recognized the new facts of life. Administration of the New Deal Programs was not for them. But the existence of these programs, which took over the giving or assistance function, left them free for the treatment function. Little by little they re-oriented themselves until they were serving a clientele that did not necessarily need assistance at all; many could even pay for their services.

The trend was, therefore, in the direction of social case work, emphasizing family counseling or psychotherapy, for middle-class clients and selected lower-class clients on one side and simple relief or assistance for those in the status of poverty on the other. In effect, social case work had come full circle. By administering public welfare laws, it was back where it started from. It was alms-giving or dole-dispensing, and definitely not charity or philanthropy, for there was little love in it. It was investigating eligibility, not to make a diagnosis but to determine which category, if any, the applicant fell into.

Dissatisfaction with the bifurcating drift was not long in arriving. Even before relief was split off from case work, criticisms of the psychotherapeutic emphasis were manifold. One, especially, was difficult to deal with. It had to do with the charge that psychotherapy was basically subversive. The taxpayers and contributors to voluntary social work agencies who supported social case work were, in all likelihood, sober and responsible upholders of the status quo, believers in the Protestant Ethic, accepters of the mores of the community. Still, again in all likelihood, it was precisely these norms to which the client did not conform. If the case worker demanded conformity (read "worthiness") as the price for her help, the chances were great that she would lose him and any chance of ever helping him become rehabilitated. Still, if she were permissive, accepted him, assessed no blame — as psychotherapy if not always counseling demanded — she betrayed the people who paid her. She was subverting the mores; in effect, she was rewarding nonconformity. The hardworking, self-supporting families on the block might well raise a hue and cry that the family on relief was better off than they were.[27]

So, too, with the criminal. Most people feel that justice is a basic value. The man who does wrong must "pay for his crime." If he kills another, justice demands that he be punished. He must suffer as did his victim. Just what constitutes adequate payment or justice may vary from place to place and from time to time. But whatever form the payment takes, the public derives catharsis from making the punishment fit the crime.

All would be well if this were the way things always worked out. But it is not. It is one of the most frustrating lessons taught by experience, if not by doctrine, that however fair or just or deserved any particular

---

[27] Robinson (*1934*, pp. 184–186) analyzed the social worker's quandary in candid detail. She herself opted for therapy, whatever the consequences.

punishment may be, it may prove to have harmful results. It may bring about effects worse than those of the original deed. The punishment which is so cathartic to the public may leave the criminal a more dangerous man than he was in the first place. For justice is not always the best way to achieve our goals. The social worker knows that if she wants to rehabilitate her client she must do a great deal for him. But to his neighbors it looks as though she is rewarding him for his failures and this is not fair.[28]

The psychiatric social worker, who is accepting, understanding, non-critical, non-punitive, seems to the unsophisticated observer to be on the bad person's side. For this reason among others she, like other psycho-therapists, is viewed by them with hostility and suspicion.[29]

In a certain sense the social case worker was more successful than she anticipated. Her clients came to use her own vocabulary against her. Nothing highlights this situation more effectively than the famous song in *West Side Story* in which the young men parrot the case worker's gobbledy-gook back to him.[30]

Technical as well as community-resentment factors operated to denigrate the social case work function as related to poor people. An extensive research and theoretical literature developed documenting the inability of accepted and standard techniques to apply in psychotherapy or counseling if there was a large class barrier between therapist and client or patient, as noted above in the work of Bernstein.

By the 1960's distrust and in some cases even annoyance with the old case-work approach reached a high mark. Critics spoke of a crisis in the social services. Neither routinely administered public welfare legislation for the poor nor psychotherapy was adequate to the job. There was a call for change.

Miller and Rein (*1964*), listed several "models for change" called for in the field of the social services and specified among them that case work be separated from other areas of social work so that it would no

---

28 On the other hand, of course, people often feel sorry for the bad man. True, justice must be done; but it must be tempered with mercy. The punishment should not be too harsh. There is a genuine ambivalence. We are dealing here with a vastly complicated set of phenomena. The successful operation of a social system may be said by analogy with small task-oriented groups to depend on having both the instrumental and the emotional-expressive functions adequately performed. Human beings must be disciplined; they must also be cherished. Justice and mercy, to use the archaic form of this paradox, are both basic.

29 The unsophisticated view psychotherapy with hostility and suspicion for reasons of fear also, as well as of resentment. In the 1940's and 1950's for example, the fear of manipulation by psychiatry was evidenced by popular themes in moving pictures. Many still think of psychotherapy as a fearsome tool for turning a strapping young bull into a placid steer.

30 Community center workers found themselves in an analogous trap. Despite all their proffered understanding and good will, they found their windows broken, their equipment destroyed, their athletic gear vandalized.

longer dominate the profession. Whatever contribution psychotherapy and counseling could make was so limited in scope and restricted in effect that its total impact was negligible in face of the problems of the times. They called for greater use by social workers of protest and social action as a cooling technique as well as a way of bringing about change. They urged social action to change conditions as well as people, that is, to develop

> . . . self-reliant people, even if poor . . . by helping the poor to do something about their own lives through neighborhood organizations strongly pressuring for change and improvement. . . . The major gain is frequently not the concrete reforms that are won but the development of people in the struggle to achieve change, and the expansion of involvement to prevent alienation and to reduce disengagement (p. 28).

Not the precious, uncertain, isolated, interpersonal dyadic relationship of individual case work "treatment" but the robust outward-looking group and communal forces generated and used in social action were to be utilized in rehabilitating people.

Miller and Rein also called for a revival of what they called the *intercessor* function, a function which had been so spectacularly performed by the old settlement houses. This function consisted of seeing to it that individuals were not left unserved because of agency defects and spotlighted deficiencies in the service picture. They called also for resumption of another old settlement function, that of educating elites — businessmen, legislators, politicians — to be able to respond to pressing issues. And, again an old settlement function, expansion of political activities pushing for certain programs, serving as "politicians of the poor" were called for.

They called, finally, for more social criticism, that is, "a unique research-action activity serving to assess and point up the directions of society and their impact upon individuals" (*ibid.*, p. 32). All this would involve enlarging appropriate work settings for social workers so that they would be less restricted in their service opportunities and introducing new technologies and tactics into social work, requiring new kinds of personnel in addition to those concentrating on the dyadic "treatment" process.

For some warriors against poverty a major strategy lay in increasing the volume and quality of services provided for poor people. Massive service programs should saturate slums and depressed areas until all needs were taken care of. Among these, of course, would be individual social case work or "treatment." At the other extreme were those who advocated a strategy of leadership development, "politicalizing," instruction in the uses of power. The idea was that services that were granted to people did not do much for them; services which they wrested from others, did.

It was recognized by the advocates of the power approach that counselors and psychotherapists could not advocate rocking the boat, attacking the status quo, "politicalizing." Usually the money that supported their programs came from some government- or community-supported agency. Still they felt that the net effect of their counseling should be to develop leadership that could demand services rather than passive reception of service. They should not merely cool the mark out; they should prepare him for protest.

Different functions attract different kinds of people. Those who are attracted to individualized social case work with its relationship-as-treatment approach are not likely to be attracted to such strategies as social action and protest. They probably feel much more at home with the hushed, isolated, protected dyadic relationship of traditional social case work. They are likely to be attracted to work with middle-class clients where success is most likely. And no one can deny that there is tremendous need for these services, so useful, necessary, and even increasingly valuable. But it would be something of an exaggeration to argue that they have much to contribute in the massive onslaught necessary in the war on poverty.

Counseling Slum Dwellers. The withdrawal of social case work from those in the status of poverty was accompanied by a physical retreat from the slum. In the 19th century there was a strong feeling that those performing services for the poor should be near to them physically as well as emotionally. The Charity Organization Society of Buffalo in 1879 may have been somewhat excessive in their ideal that counseling be done in the social worker's own home:

> Now the first thing we did was to lay it down as a rule that the District Office should be near the center of the district, in order to be easy of access to the poor, and that, if practicable, it should be in the dwelling house of the paid Agent who was to have charge of the district, so that there should be no tint of officialism about our work, but that the poor might come to a real home, with home surroundings, and thus be, perhaps unconsciously, bettered by the contact (*Robinson, 1934,* p. 6).

The idea was analogous to the current idea of the sidewalk clinic. When people need help they need it right now. If they have to dress, take the bus, wait in line for an appointment or interview, they are less likely to get help; their inability to undertake such a simple, but organized, operation is, in fact, part of their difficulty.

Many of the old settlement house ideas seem still to have validity, as the models for change suggested by Miller and Rein referred to above suggest. The residents of the old settlement house did not leave the neighborhood at night; they were not visitors. They identified with their neighbors. They supplied not only counsel but also leadership until the residents could supply their own. They did counseling as one part of their manifold activities. "All those acts and devices which express kindly relation from man to man, from charitable effort to the most specialized social intercourse, are constantly tried" (*Addams, 1899*, p. 36).

Modern housing projects as part of urban renewal programs have been criticized on many scores, including the charge that they have built into the program an acceleration of the natural attrition of local leadership.[31] The successful are ejected as soon as they make the grade. Plans to keep residential areas multi-class in composition run up against the sociological tendency for areas to segregate themselves by use, including different class residential use. Multi-class neighborhoods as an idea have an appeal for many persons; but they are not necessarily the answer to the problems of leadership.

What seems to be needed is a modern analogue to the old settlement house. Slavish imitation would not do, because the slum dweller today is not the same as the slum dweller of the 19th century. But somehow or other channels could be hewed out by which the best aspects of the culture of the outside world could be made available to those in slums, along with counseling when needed. Much of it might be by way of the all-day nursery school, with generous doses of counseling and psychotherapy where needed.

In one large midwestern city in the 1930's two privately financed housing projects were built, one for white and one for Negro families. Deterioration was confidently predicted for both. Within a few years the white project did indeed validate the prediction. But not the Negro one.

The supervisor of the Negro project was a former minister. He ran his establishment with an iron hand. He used threats and actual ejection with few if any qualms. He kept very close watch over all his families. Even if their maintenance and housekeeping standards met his demands he did not hesitate to threaten eviction if their moral behavior did not. When a white social worker who admired his results but deplored his methods protested, he made this justification. The people he was dealing with had absolutely no preparation for living in a modern industrial city. They came for the most part from plantations and backwoods of the South. They were accustomed to throwing garbage into the yard; the pigs would scavenge. They had never seen modern plumbing and

---

[31] Addams (*1899*, p. 55) commented on this process a long time ago. "When a given neighborhood becomes shabby, or filled with foreigners . . . the best people . . . move out, taking with them their initiative and natural leadership . . . A settlement deliberately selects such a neighborhood, and moves into it, but must not lay too much stress upon that fact in and of itself."

if it broke down they did not feel distressed. None of the sanitary precautions against insects struck home with them; if the screens became torn, so what? Of if food lay around to attract rodents, so what? Drunkenness, similarly, was an old family custom. He did not blame them; he did not condemn them; he understood them. But he did not overlook their mistakes either. He defined his role as a teacher, as a person responsible for the acculturation of these neglected people. He was not a martinet; he was not unsympathetic; he was not sadistic. He did not enjoy threatening or punishing people. But neither was he a psychotherapist or counselor. If they could not profit by living in the project there were others who could and he preferred that the facilities be available to those who could.

This man was performing an important, one of the most important, functions in our society today. The way he was doing it did not conform to the principles of counseling. He was changing people by techniques even frowned upon by theorists of counseling. He had at his disposal rewards, punishments, threats and he used them. But it is possible that the same function could be performed with counseling techniques instead. Octavia Hill had the idea of the rental manager who might well perform such social work functions. The idea had also been suggested for public housing projects.

Contraception Counseling. One area of counseling which has relevance in conection not only with the poor but also with the societal problem of the so-called population explosion should be given at least passing recognition here, namely that of contraception. For in no social- or societal-problem area does the contribution of counseling seem to be of greater potential value. This statement is not intended to denigrate the importance of the necessary preliminary work that has to be done to change laws, mores, creeds, and the like. But even when such changes have been effected, there will still remain the vast task of implementing the changes, of bringing about the conditions necessary to make contraception not only wanted but also successful, couple by couple in many areas.

For the problem is only in part one of education. Even when all the underlying technical, legal, political, moral, and other barriers are overcome, there still remains the problem of how to present contraception to users and render it effective. Even medical doctors in private practice are not always competent here.[32] And even those who are, reach

[32] In a study of 514 North Carolina physicians, 403 did frequent premarital examinations. Of these, "37 percent reported that they offer contraceptive advice on their own initiative during such examinations, and an additional 28 percent reported that they provide such advice if requested to do so by the patient. . . . Contraceptive advice is routinely offered more often by younger physicians and by obstetricians" (*Herndon and Nash, 1962*, p. 398). This study was made before oral contraceptives were generally available. But most of the physicians — 62 percent —

only a limited clientele. There is going to be an expanded demand for such counseling as the possibility of control becomes more widely known and services requested.

Maternal health clinics so-called have learned that the mere transmission of information is far from enough. The effective use of contraception is a complex process; in some cases it requires a change as drastic as any sought in other areas of counseling. When, in addition, there is the inertia of culture to contend with, counseling becomes even more complex. No wonder that studies of the effectiveness of different forms of contraception report that effectiveness is as much a function of the personalities involved as of the technique used. Almost any technique is successful with some people; almost no technique is successful with others.

The questions then arise, what is the best method for this particular couple? What is the best way to motivate people to care in using contraception? How can fears and anxieties be allayed? A host of special problems have to be answered for each individual couple. It is not only the accommodation of method to religious scruples that raises problems, but also a host of intrapsychic difficulties, not easily reached by a scientific or rational approach. But they are not insuperable. Indeed, compared to many other social and societal problems, these are relatively simple. But this does not mean that solutions are necessarily easy or automatic.

Somewhat more difficult is the problem of motivating couples to use contraception in the first place. The above discussion implied that the couple wished to limit family size. But many poor families, despite inability to provide for them, want many children. *Miller (1964, pp. 79–80)* cites such a case:

> . . . . Despite their poverty and uncertain future, both parents [age 25 and 20] were very anxious to have more children. The social worker reported that when the inadvisability of increasing their family was mentioned Maria replied, "Whether you can afford children or not, you sometimes just decide to have them."

Both were in poor health, both physical and emotional; the husband was uneducated and unskilled, and "could hardly expect ever to move out of the ranks of the poor." Conceivably counseling might make no difference. But it would at least assure that whatever decisions were made with respect to children were made with as full and complete information as possible. The time may not be far off when contraceptive counseling may take its place in the list of counseling specialties along with vocational, personnel, and other specialized areas.

---

refused to fit diaphragms premaritally. Among the reasons were: embarrassment to the girl, difficulty, necessity to re-fit later.

In closing this brief discussion of selected problem areas, one over-riding conclusion is inevitable: despite a proliferation of research and increasing knowledge of the dynamics of psychotherapy, the actual contribution which that field can make to the resolution of social problems is extremely limited by the many and special conditions required for its successful application and by the many forces operating to nullify its effectiveness. So, too, with counseling. It is probably as true today, as it was in the 1950's, that counseling (and, more so, therapy) is paced by social change rather than itself a pace setter, that it "reflects but slowly and participates but little in social change" and even in some ways fails seriously to keep pace *(Habein, 1954, pp. 68, 70).*

References

Addams, Jane (1899). "A Function of the Social Settlement," *Annals of American Academics Political and Social Sciences,* 13 (May).

Bernard, Jessie (1962). *American Community Behavior,* Holt, Rinehart and Winston.

———— (1957). *Social Problems at Midcentury,* Dryden.

Bettelheim, Bruno, and Morris Janowitz (1964). *Social Change and Prejudice,* Free Press.

Durkheim, Emile (1951). *Suicide,* translated by George Simpson and J. A. Spaulding, Free Press.

Fleming, Donald (1964). "The Meaning of Mental Illness," *Atlantic Monthly,* (July).

Frank, Lawrence K. (1961). "Fragmentation in the Helping Professions," in *The Planning of Change,* W. G. Bennis, K. D. Benne and Robert Chin (ed.), Holt, Rinehart and Winston.

Ford, Donald H. and Hugh B. Urban (1963). *Systems of Psychotherapy, a Comparative Study,* Wiley.

Freud, Sigmund (1958). *Civilization and Its Discontents,* Doubleday.

Goldwater, Barry (1964). Speech at New England College, Henniker, New Hampshire, December. Reported in the *New York Times* (July 18).

Habein, Margaret (1954). "Counseling — Reflecting and Participating in Social Change," *Journal of the National Association of Deans of Women,* 17 (January).

Hartung, Frank (1963). "Manhattan Madness: The Social Movement of Mental Illness," *Sociological Quarterly,* 11 (Fall), 261–272.

Herndon, C. Nash, and Ethel M. Nash (1962). "Premarriage and Marriage Counseling, A Study of Practices of North Carolina Physicians," *Journal of American Medical Association,* 180 (May).

Hodges, Emory F. (1963). Paper delivered to the Ohio Psychiatric Association, September. Reported in the *Washington Post* (September 30).

Kardiner, Abram and Lionel Ovesey (1962). *The Mark of Oppression, Explorations in the Personality of the American Negro,* Meridian.

413

Kiell, Norman (1964). *The Universal Experience of Adolescence,* International Universities Press.

Miller, Herman (1964). *Rich Man, Poor Man,* Crowell.

Miller, S. M., and Martin Rein (1964). "Change, Ferment and Ideology in the Social Sciences," Paper given at the Council of Social Work Education, Toronto (January).

Money, Jolin (1967). *Errors of the Body,* Johns Hopkins.

Pines, Maya (1965). "The Coming Upheaval in Psychiatry," *Harpers Magazine* (October).

Rein, Martin (1964). "The Social Service Crisis," *Transaction,* 1 (May).

Riessman, Frank, and S. M. Miller (1964). "Social Change Versus the Psychiatric World View," *American Journal of Ortho Psychiatry,* 34 (January).

Robinson, Virginia (1934). *A Changing Psychology in Social Case Work,* University of North Carolina Press.

Staller, Robert J. (1968). *Sex and Gender,* Science House.

Sutherland, E. H. (1949). *White Collar Crime,* Dryden.

Szasz, Thomas (1963). *Law, Liberty, and Psychiatry,* Macmillan.

—— (1964). "What Psychiatry Can and Cannot Do," *Harper* (February), 50–53.

Weeks, Ashley (1958). *Youthful Offenders at Highfields,* University of Michigan Press.

Williamson, Henry (1965). *Hustler!,* Doubleday.

Coda

COUNSELING AND PSYCHOTHERAPY
TOMORROW: Forecasts and Questions

David F. Ricks / Teachers College, Columbia University

The future, like the blank card that confronts us as we near the end of the Thematic Apperception Test, invites almost pure projection. Lacking the memories that guide us through the past and the sensory cues that orient us in the present, we populate a world still in the making with shadowy images of our hopes and fears. Our prophecies take shape in reaches of the mind largely unknown to us. The omens with which we support them require time — always more time than we have — to become facts. Yet we must predict, or at least forecast on the thin ice of partial knowledge, if we are to manage our affairs with any rationality. The only alternative is to improvise from crisis to crisis as "events overtake ignorance" (*Michael, 1965*). While some incorrigibly muddy minds prefer this course, modern societies are increasingly committed to the strategy of trying to study trends, anticipate needs, realize limits, and prepare long term programs to meet and manage the future.

For societies, preparation means education and the design of institutions, both requiring decades of effort. In a world changing at an accelerated rate, it is increasingly necessary to plan educational programs with enough foresight to be reasonably hopeful that their graduates will not be obsolete before they finish their working lives, as many products of current vocational training are. And if our institutions are not to be empty hulks (like many hospital inpatient facilities) before they have paid off the social investment in them, they must be designed around the shapes, however unruly, of still growing needs and possibilities.

Not only is it increasingly necessary to meet the future half way — it is also increasingly feasible. Both the rationalistic optimism of the 18th century and the apocalyptic visions of the 19th have passed their peaks

415

of influence, and current predictive efforts are based more on modest scientific and statistical methods than charismatic individuals or visions.

> What has remained of the utopian traditions, however, and this is the under-
> lying element in our renewed interest in the future, is its eudaemonism —
> the proposition that each person is entitled to happiness and that it is one
> of the functions of government to try and assure him at least the precondi-
> tions of happiness (*Bell, 1965,* p. 120).

What remains of the apocalyptic tradition, of course, is the awareness that a major war qualifies all predictions, including the prediction that there will be any future for most of us.

Among the new elements making prediction more accurate and useful are the exponential growth of knowledge, which has greatly increased understanding of some elements in the natural world and at times made their control possible; increasing commitment to growth and economic planning; econometric forecasting methods; and the spread of the open, self-corrective, speculative scientific approach to operations once thought beyond the domain of science. As more of life comes within the realm of tested theory, believed because predictions made from theory were found to hold up, our lives will become increasingly organized and rationalized (*Michael, 1965*). Society will increasingly operate in ways designed to maximize control, predictability, and flexible adjustment to changing conditions. One consequence for psychotherapists and guidance personnel will be growing demands for early selection and training, since this is more efficient than late in most instances. More crucial will be a growing need to help people deal with the frustrations generated by what will often seem, from a humanistic standpoint, a one-sided emphasis on rationality, a tyranny of ego at the expense of other parts of the whole man. We are already living with some of the early aspects of this in the specialized high schools of the large cities and the track systems of the suburban schools, which select out a pre-elite of students who receive superior or advanced preparation at each level, which in turn prepares them for more advanced, more demanding, and only occasionally more rewarding special education at the next level. As the pressures in the top schools and colleges increase, psychotherapy, through guidance and counseling personnel, will be an increasingly necessary safety valve.

A major corrective to the trend of increasing organizational life will be accelerated growth in the service sector of the economy — hospitals, universities, research institutes, government agencies, and professional groups — in which work can often be on a small enough scale, contain- ing enough human contact and sense of service, to offer varied rewards (*Fuchs, 1966*). In some services, including psychotherapy, a distinction between necessary work and chosen leisure may be as hard to draw as it was for the small farmer or artisan of the last century.

The general outlines of the future, the trends and mass actions, and even the rates of change, can be predicted in some detail — better in those areas of life subjected to the rationality of organized society, less well in the areas reserved for private life. Singular events and individual decisions will remain unpredictable, even with increasing knowledge of man's cognitive processes. The emergence of some new Weber, Freud, James, or Dewey could still change the social sciences in unpredictable ways. We cannot predict when or where such men will appear, but we can be sure that the social sciences are becoming scientific and non-ideological enough to forsake old positions for new truths when they are produced. Those portions of psychological and social science that remain tradition-directed have steadily lost influence for the last decade. Orthodox psychoanalysis is the most striking instance, but other examples, such as dogmatic behaviorism, are not hard to find.

Before turning to the specific tasks and opportunities ahead in the fields of psychotherapy and counseling, one figure remains to be sketched against the broad canvas of society — the ideal man of the future, the implicit standard of health to which the various forms of psycho-pathology and failure are likely to be contrasted and found wanting. An abbreviated picture of what one set of college students hoped to become emerged from one computer like this:

> Stands on his own two feet. Interested in learning and likes to study. Serious, has high standards. Accessible to new ideas. Knows who he is and what he wants out of life. Productive, hard working. Genuine and friendly (*Ricks and McCarley, 1965*).

Keniston has described the same character more eloquently:

> Increasingly, only the most menial jobs are within the competence of the uneducated . . . most desirable positions in our society require advanced and specialized training and, with it, high levels of dispassionateness, ability to remain cool under stress, capacity to concentrate, to maintain long-range goals yet adapt readily to new conditions, to deal with remote and distant situations, to abstract, to coordinate complex operations, to synthesize many recommendations, to plan long-range enterprises, to resist distraction, to persevere despite disappointment, to master complex conceptual assignments, to be impartial, to follow instructions (*Keniston, 1965*, p. 368).

As social complexity and the rate of social change increase, raising the level of competence necessary for even minimal functioning, there will be rivalry for the professional right to deal with those who fall short. For the last decade there has been a trend to define every kind of failure as mental illness. Children once considered the province of the teacher have increasingly been redefined as psychological or psychiatric problems requiring treatments beyond the teacher's competence. A growing literature on "learning blocks," "school phobias," "underachievement," and "delinquency proneness," has often assumed uncritically that deviations from the norm of optimal ego function required specialized medical treatment and understanding. Recently, viewpoints have become more critical *(Szasz, 1964)*. If a "mental health" approach results in further lowering of the teacher's self-confidence, if it foolishly over-generalizes the medical model of illness to problems that are essentially educational, or if it pays attention to the emotional unfolding of children only in the interests of the subordination of emotion and fantasy to cognition, the mental health movement is going to generate more opposition than it can well afford. The little red schoolhouse is not going to give way to the little white clinic without a fight *(White, 1965)*.[1] The strongest statement of opposition to the spread of mental health models comes from Cutler and McNeil *(1962)*.

> The transplanting of the clinical design within the public schools cannot be over-stressed as a factor which has brought us to our present state of despair. . . . Among its consequences have been: 1) a continuing allegiance to what Redl has called "pressure chamber treatment," in which the child is removed from his classroom habitat, subjected to a special kind of laying on of hands (termed "being seen"), and then returned (repaired?) to the classroom for another go at it; 2) the perpetuation of established clinical jargon as a means of describing and understanding children, in a setting where this jargon has little real (or even translatable) meaning; 3) the establishment of empires of influence and hierarchies of power concerned with the issue of who really is responsible for the management of the "whole child"; 4) the cultivation of interprofessional enmity, and the development of various levels of citizenship among professionals dealing with children in the schools; 5) the increased fragmentation of the child and the taking away from the classroom teacher of an additional opportunity for feeling competent to deal with her charges; 6) the domination of mental health in education by mental health professionals, with consequently little attention to the basic educational issues raised by the programs and by dealings with individual children; and 7) a stultification of effort to develop programs and treatment designs which would meet the unique problems of the moderately disturbed child in school (pp. 16–17).

It is clear that on the issue of who defines mental health and mental disorder, as well as that of who treats it, we are not dealing with unitary trends, whose outcome can be predicted clearly at the present, but with rapidly changing standards, programs, and aims.

---

[1] When I first saw the motto, "Help Stamp Out Mental Health," on the wall of a public junior high school, I was not completely sure it was written by an adolescent — at any rate no teacher had taken the trouble to erase it.

Where We Think We Are Going:
A Sampling of Current Programs

Community Mental Health

"The time has come for a bold new approach," Spoken by a bold young president in 1963, these words, coming fourteen years after the founding of the National Institutes of Mental Illness and Health (*1961*) marked the moment when community mental health became a movement, with resources, a program, dedicated workers, and at times a sense of manifest destiny (*Hobbs, 1964*). There is little question that the largest new innovations in mental health work for at least the next decade will come about through experimentation with the varied services the community mental health center can offer. It is likely that those mental disorders which are illnesses in the traditional sense of the word, i.e., are due primarily to biochemical, genetic, or other organic disorders, will be the first to yield to prediction and control, as general paresis already has, and as PKU is now doing. But even disorders that are primarily physical in origin will be managed differently by the community mental health clinic than by the traditional hospital. Disorders that are predominantly transmitted, not through the genes or disorders in body chemistry, but by the family and the community, will be handled in radically new ways, some of which, such as family psychotherapy, promise to yield as much in general knowledge about man and his institutions as they yield in immediate psychotherapeutic gain.

The sheer size of the program is impressive.

Projections made in 1962 — and confirmed by recomputations made in 1964 — show that there will be a need in 1970 for 87,000 members in the four core mental health professions . . . based on the projections we would have by 1970 enough personnel to provide community health centers with 5,100 psychiatrists, 3,800 psychologists, 4,600 social workers, and 8,000 nurses, while still allowing for growth in the supply of professionals working in other than center settings (*Yolles, 1965*).

Albee (*1963*) estimates slightly smaller numbers than these will be needed, but even his more modest estimates would require more than half of the professional membership of the American Psychological Association, the American Psychiatric Association, and the National Association of Social Workers to staff the mental health centers alone, and more would be needed if all centers, including rural ones, were to be staffed at the levels desired. It is, of course, questionable whether so many people will concern themselves with mental health, but if federal programs continue to support mental health training, and if the number of college graduates continue to expand, it seems reasonable to be optimistic. We are rapidly becoming a service economy, in which education and medicine are two of the largest growth industries, and the mental health professions seem likely to grow with both. In an increasingly affluent society young people no longer worry as much about making money, and the mental health fields appeal to the same need to do something valuable, to make one's life mean something, that has proved so appealing to young people in the Peace Corps and civil rights work. President Johnson has continued the interest that Kennedy took in mental health, and he has increasingly coupled it with the attack on poverty. The professional popularity of these programs and their wide base of citizen participation and enthusiasm favors continued federal support. If they demonstrate competence to do the things they are aiming for there is good reason to believe that the community mental health center will be our major mental health resource within a decade.

No existing institution yet does all of the things the community mental health center is designed to accomplish. A recent survey (*Classcote, et al., 1964*) listed the following services that a community mental health center might be expected to offer:

1. inpatient treatment
2. outpatient treatment
3. part-time hospitalization (day, night, or week-end hospital)
4. emergency service
5. consultation service for other community agencies
6. diagnostic and evaluative service
7. transitional and placement services, such as halfway house, vocational placement, foster home and nursing care placement, etc.
8. rehabilitation service — vocational, recreational, resocialization, etc.
9. aftercare program
10. formal community education program

All this, plus training and research, in one agency! Each of the above is, of course, a mere chapter heading for a very detailed set of possibilities. An aftercare program, for instance, can include making someone always available on the telephone for immediate consultation, suicide prevention, and crisis management; a walk-in clinic, to deal with similar problems more intensively; a screening and referral unit to help patients find appropriate community resources; and home visiting teams to help families both with crises and with long term problems (*Carlton, 1965*). As the mental hospitals admit more patients and discharge them more rapidly, so that re-admissions become a major part of their patient population, aftercare programs, precare programs, and rehabilitation work merge functions and case loads. A considerable literature has developed around each of the methods described by Carlton, testifying as much to the enthusiasm these new methods develop as to their psychotherapeutic efficacy. These programs have also generated a new body of knowledge about the paths to hospitalization, the decision makers in the process, and the types of information that enter into decisions to hospitalize or release patients.

The community mental health center did not spring full grown from the mind of Washington — it had a number of predecessors on which to model itself. The most important is the child guidance clinic. Several aims of the community mental health center, in fact, come directly from the achievements of child guidance work: early identification of disturbed children; treatment in the home and in the community, with minimal disruption of family life, schooling, and work; understanding of emotional problems in terms of exogenous as well as endogenous causes; research into etiology; and research monitoring of results. It seems likely that child guidance clinics can make the transition into community mental health centers rather smoothly, and that many guidance clinics will do so. When this is not done, it will be because child guidance personnel are not adequately trained in active community intervention and education, resist family and group psychotherapy in favor of the one-to-one psychotherapy model to which they are accustomed, and feel that the broad range of purposes in the community mental health center might dilute their efforts so much as to make them less effective than they now are. All of these objections seem to be answered by the success of those child guidance clinics that have made the transition, such as the South Shore Guidance Center in Quincy, Massachusetts (*Rosenblum and Ottenstein, 1965*). It is clear, however, that the child guidance clinics and mental health centers will have to improve their community relations — a persistent theme in teacher evaluations of their work is that their waiting lists are too long; they take too much of the teacher's time in getting information and offer little help in return; and they are far too selective in the types of children with whom they work. Most child guidance clinics had their origins in work with the poor, the delinquent, and the patient returning from the hospital. Over the years their imposition of waiting lists on people whose lives made waiting impossible, their greater comfort with middle-class patients who would accept talking psychotherapy, and their unwillingness to work in and through the working class milieu have made their case loads primarily middle class. The community mental health centers will have to be careful if they are not to follow the same route.

The Changing Mental Hospital

Mental hospitals will also move toward becoming community mental health centers. For hospitals located in urban areas the transition has already begun, as the older expectation that the hospital would only care for the mentally ill has begun to give way to the more ambitious aim of curing or at least minimizing the impact of the mental disorder by intervention and treatment. The extent to which new forms of tranquilizing and treating mental disorders can appease the disgruntled, make contented the discontented, and solve the problems of the perplexed is, of course, not known, but a brave effort to test psychotherapeutic limits seems likely to absorb much of our effort for the next few decades. If the now faint indications that psychotherapy can really help become more definite society will ask even more of psychotherapy than it now asks. We can hope that as clinical experience and research increase our knowledge of the limits of new procedures, mental health professionals will be able to educate the public in what not to expect. Failing this, the new methods will be oversold, with each new drug or treatment approach being reported in the news media before it is firmly established through responsible investigation, and the frustrations of hopes unmet will be vented on the mental health movement.

In a careful review of the portent of some current emphases (*Barton, 1962*) the dean of hospital psychiatry has outlined the major trends apparent in the mental hospitals. Partly as a result of innovations in community work, the barriers between the hospital and the community are decreasing and will continue to decrease. The recent decline in the hospital census, reversing a very long term trend, will continue, as admissions increase but are more than compensated by the shortened period of hospital stay. Since the middle of the 1950's, application of early and intensive treatment, increasing use of tranquilizing drugs, and a change in community attitudes that allows more ready acceptance and re-employment of the discharged patient have allowed many patients who would once have remained chronic hospital inmates to reassume life in the community. Since the transition from the protected and undemanding life of the hospital to responsible participation in social life is a difficult one for many patients, hospitals will increasingly offer rehabilitation services, transitional stages such as day wards and day hospitals (*Kramer, 1962*), halfway houses, clinic and home visiting services, and preventive work (*WHO Report, 1957*).

As the mental hospital increasingly treats people intensively for short periods of time, on either an in-and-out or a revolving door basis, the median age of the patient load will shift toward youth. In a few private hospitals the dominant age group will come to be adolescent and very young adult. In such hospitals it may be necessary, and psychotherapeutically useful, to adopt a new model for the institution.

> I suggest that the medical model for the treatment of disease is not entirely appropriate when applied to the management of the emotionally disturbed and mentally ill. We in psychiatry suffer from some ambiguity in our own minds as to what we are doing when we try to help patients inhibited or

422

immobilized by emotional disorders. A supplement to the medical model is necessary.

Instead of thinking of our mental hospitals solely as places to send patients for treatment, and protection of themselves or others in the community, I believe that we might profitably think of them primarily as educational institutions concerned with aspects of living which no other of our agencies or institutions has had the resources or the courage to undertake *(Farnsworth, 1963,* p. 3).

In such an educationally oriented hospital the staff will be concerned with teaching patients how their problems in living started and reached the proportions that led to hospitalization, with education of families and the community so that the lessons the patient learns in the hospital will not be cancelled by unfortunate home visits or rejection after discharge, and above all, with learning from the patients so that further work will become increasingly effective. With increasing efforts to understand background factors in the crises that lead to hospitalization, and to study the process of treatment in order to improve it, research into mental illness will increase, and ties between the mental hospital and other teaching institutions, particularly the medical schools and the universities, will strengthen. With increasing research will come new sources of funding for experimental programs, and new role opportunities and conflicts as the researcher tries to find a place for himself within the constellation of mental health professions. Since both the medical profession and the research scientist are accustomed to control their own spheres, the role conflicts between the two are likely to create problems for the mental hospital. It will be necessary to create institutional channels of communication to prevent medicine and scientific research from carving out autonomous domains.

Like the mental patient, the mental hospital is now rejoining the community. We have many programs for educating and helping the patient. We must also plan how to help the mental hospital, since we know that growth of the currently more exciting community services is not going to take from the mental hospital its traditional role as the work horse that carries the hardest portion of the mental patient load *(Brown, 1964).*

The Social Agency

The third major mental health resource is likely to remain the social agency. With the recent growth of interest in poverty as a social problem, and the growing awareness of the role of ethnic and class factors in the breakdown of personality, the role of the social agency, particularly in early family and child care, is likely to increase. Within the social agency, particularly, new methods of work with naturally occurring groups — families, gangs, neighborhoods, and ethnic societies — are likely to grow.

Coda

Psychological Service Centers

A new light on the horizon, not yet definite enough to make its future predictable, is the psychological service center. Albee, its most ardent proponent, argued in his provocatively titled paper, "A declaration of independence for psychology," that a generation of clinical psychologists had been "trained as guests in houses not our own" (*Albee, 1964*), with the result that they assumed too much validity and generality to the medical model of mental disorder. Albee argues that a social learning model is more appropriate and more useful to clients, who are seen not as patients, not as sick, not as treated, but as people to be helped, often in purely psychological and educational ways. A later generation of psychologists is likely to look back to the 1940's and 1950's with gratitude to psychiatry for sharing its domain so willingly — a characteristic not noted in most fields of medicine. But many in the current generation of psychologists are no longer enthusiastic about the Oedipal triad of father psychiatrist, mother social worker, and fledgling psychologist who make the clinical treatment team. And since it appears that psychology now has the tools, the self-confidence, and the money to set up its own service centers, in which work with disturbed children or adults would be one of several related functions, the psychological service centers are likely to grow rapidly.

It is to be hoped that in this growth psychology will tend to its own gardens and not waste its strength in rivalry with professions to which it owes a great deal. It will help if organized psychiatry takes credit for its generosity in helping psychology apply its learning and does not waste efforts trying to roll back the clock. Try as he might, this particular psychologist cannot bring himself to feel that he is a "spreading cancer in the field of psychiatry" or even a "flagrant offender" (*Levine, 1965*), nor can he see cancerous qualities in Erik Erikson, Anna Freud, and other non-medical therapists.

> In the retreat from reason the position of psychoanalysis is ambiguous. As a psychology it has been applied fruitfully in many fields, being changed in the process. In this sense it participates in the continuing progress of knowledge and exerts an influence counter to the retreat from reason. As a therapeutic science, however, it surrounds itself with barriers and tends to become encapsulated. It still provides some open-minded inquiry, but there are indications that it may harden into dogma. In America it has nestled under the wing of the medical profession, becoming inaccessible to those who are not physicians. From this association it does not enrich itself as a science; it gains only as a guild. It secures for itself the institutional protection and prerogatives of medicine, but loses by the exclusion of those persons whose consistent interest in human nature has led them to the study of subjects more pertinent to this interest than those taught in medical school (*Wheelis, 1958*, pp. 152–153).

Psychotherapists Without Labels

It is clear that persistent interest in human nature is not a monopoly of any particular profession. There is as yet not enough research evidence on the characteristics of good psychotherapists, but the available evidence suggests that psychotherapists who are particularly useful to one group of patients may not help others (*Whitehorn and Betz, 1960, McNair, Callahan and Lorr, 1962*). Until the criteria for help are better understood, and until the characteristics of those able to help have been studied, there is no reason to prevent any person from trying to help others. There are, of course, reasons for preventing untrained people from practicing medicine — but most emotional problems are "illnesses" only by grant of metaphor and analogy. Perhaps the best psychotherapists will turn out to be housewives or other indigenous non-professionals who have had some experience in life and some appropriate training in understanding a helping role (*Pines, 1962; Rioch, 1963*). Those with degree-oriented standards will view these people, and others like them as marginal people with marginal preparation, or as only ancillary to those who do the real work. But if the history of science is any clue, the most rewarding and interesting new ideas are not going to come from those too securely within the establishment, but from outsiders. We can hope that these people will experiment with new models for therapy, using art, music, and other activities in which they are especially trained, and that the result will be a broader range of methods available to any helping person able to use them.

The movement of the mental patient back into community life is also a movement into community concern. Volunteer work with mental hospital patients began many years ago, but only in recent years has it grown into a definite force to consider in mental health work. The varied activities that volunteers can offer patients go far beyond the traditional realms of psychotherapy, occupational therapy, and recreational work. Students at Harvard, Brandeis, Radcliffe, and other colleges in the Boston area have taught psychotic children to swim; helped inhibited schizophrenic boys to loosen up by playing basketball, football, and even fencing; taught young girls modern dance, and older girls ballet; tutored children who had fallen behind in school; and organized social activities and visits away from the hospital for patients as they improved. One group of students has even organized and successfully run a halfway house in which they live with patients as a cooperative community. Students who do this work may aim to go into psychiatry, psychology, social work, or some other helping profession eventually. But vocational aims explain only part of their motivation. For other students, who plan to go into fields as far from mental health work as physics and politics, vocational aims seem to have no role in the choice to spend an afternoon or day each week in a mental hospital. These students, and the adult volunteers who have organized similar programs, appear to work in hospitals because it is interesting, gives them a feeling of worth, and seems a way of asserting their common humanity with people whose humanity has been constricted and tried. The personal growth shown by students doing this work is one of its most impressive aspects. Their youth, the varied interests and skills they bring to their work, and their energy and optimism seem to reach many withdrawn patients and motivate many apathetic "institutionalized" people who can not be reached by the usual hospital personnel. A few volunteer programs have failed, but the success of most programs is a matter of common observation. During the next several years the general trend of this work will be upward, involving more students and adults, more hospitals, and more patients. The apparent success of these untrained amateurs, if it is confirmed by careful research, will raise some interesting problems for a theory of psychotherapy and training for psychotherapy. While amateurs are not able to do the complex work involved in vocational training and placement, and while the deeper reaches of personal psychotherapy may be beyond their reach, professionals will have to consider the possibility that many kinds of psychotherapy may, like loving or befriending a person, be better done by an amateur than by a professional. In a society increasingly oriented around specialized training for expert performance of narrow functions, it is hard to conceive of the broad based, tentative efforts of the amateur having value. But if retreat from human relationships is the prime problem of mental patients, it is not at all obvious that any of our current types of "experts" are more adept at restoring contact than people who approach the disturbed person with less cognitive skills but often offer more spontaneous human warmth.

One important aspect of psychotherapy is an attitude and approach rather than application of a specific set of skills. The spread of psychotherapeutic attitudes into correctional institutions, making guards into correction officers in deed as well as name, has radically changed some prisons. As nurses, aides, and teachers learn to regard problems from a psychotherapeutic standpoint the hospital and the school will also become more understanding, and potentially more helpful.

Psychotherapy Research

It is clear that future forms of psychotherapy will be subjected to much more searching and thorough research than forms of psychotherapy that developed in the past. In the next few years, old forms of psychotherapy will be in for new questioning. As more people become available, offering a larger range of services, in more diverse settings, and increasingly as insurance companies, businesses, unions, and the government rather than individual patients are asked to pay the bill for treatment, there will be increasing pressure on psychotherapists to make their assessment and helping procedures more orderly and demonstrable. As long as bills for psychotherapy are paid by the individual patient, a subjective sense of relief or satisfaction may be enough to support the psychotherapeutic enterprise. When someone else pays he is likely to demand evidence that procedures work, and to scrutinize the evidence presented with some scepticism.

New forms of research likely to be especially useful are study of the sociology of patient care (*Hollingshead and Redlich, 1958; Freeman and Simmons, 1963*), and of the psychology of psychotherapists. Psychotherapists generally come to believe that they are particularly helpful to certain types of people, either classified as to age — children, adolescents, or adults, or classified according to type of disturbance — anxious, depressed, under-achieving, schizophrenic, delinquent, or whatever. They also realize that some colleagues are likely to be non-helpful to certain groups of patients, and if they are insightful they become aware that they also may harm some of the people who come to them for help. Still less frequently, they give attention to optimal timing for intervention (*Waldfogel et al., 1957*). As research accumulates, these clinical impressions will be clarified and assume the status of knowledge — we will know fairly accurately whether a given type of person should attempt to help children or adolescents, depressed people or schizophrenics, under-achievers or over-achievers. And we will know which types of disorder call for early identification and intervention, as contrasted to those, if any exist, that can safely be put on a waiting list.

A growing awareness of the limitations of traditional psychotherapists is likely to lead to increasing study of what Wheelis called the "vocational hazards" of psychoanalysis and of other forms of psychotherapy. Several people have noticed not entirely benign effects of psychotherapeutic work on its practitioners.

As the daughter of an analyst, I have known most of the important European and American analysts since I was a child, observing them over the years, and since working in the field with hundreds of therapists. Quite often I have been struck by the increasing withdrawal of some of them; their narrowing of interest; their loss of a sense of humor and zest; their inability to cope with any situation outside their "protected environment"; and their growing indecision and unrealistic attitude. I have observed in some analysts an atrophy through disuse in areas of mental functioning, in particular of reality testing, decision-making, logical arguing, etc. (*Schmideberg, 1964*, p. 65).[2]

[2] The son of a prominent psychoanalyst recently consulted me about a problem a close friend was having. After talking with him about it, I mentioned that his father

As instances of the way in which long continued psychotherapeutic practice can decrease awareness and sensible living accumulate, it will be important to study how these effects might be overcome.

Other aspects of psychotherapists — their training, attitudes, cognitive and emotional styles, and their preferred modes of operation — will also be extensively studied. Strupp and his colleagues have listed over 200 studies of psychotherapists in a bibliography concentrated on individual psychotherapy with adults (*Strupp et al., 1964*). If studies of group psychotherapists, psychotherapists working primarily with children, or with special groups, such as delinquent adolescents, were included, the list could be made much larger. Psychotherapy research will develop many quasi-therapeutic analogues or experiments reproducing ingredients of psychotherapy. The psychotherapy relationship (Gardner, 1964), including the match in ethnic background, social class, personality styles, and expectations of the persons involved will also be studied. Technical innovations will include more use of computers to handle the problems raised by many variables changing together or in opposition over time, increased use of sound films of psychotherapy, and new scoring systems for describing psychotherapeutic processes and outcomes (*Luborsky and Strupp, 1962*).

The technical innovation likely to have the greatest impact over the next two decades will conceive of psychotherapy as one influence within the context of the whole career of the mental patient, in his trajectory through all of the helping or hindering institutions he encounters. For this purpose it will be necessary to build up and maintain a few research oriented case registers, containing cumulative coded records of each psychotherapeutic contact the patient has made, together with extensive background data. Such registers can best be maintained by using modern high speed computers, and their expense, coupled with the advantage of comprehensive coverage of whole states or regions, make it unlikely that many will be established. The few that are developed, however, will lead to the development of comprehensive longitudinal conceptions of mental disorders that will largely replace the current hospital based diagnostic system. In such long term registers, new research designs organized around longitudinal "person-statistics" will be used more than "event-statistics," e.g., characteristics of children noted in early treatment records can be related to later outcome, leading in time to earlier identification of disorders and more complete pictures of the lifetime course of each type of disorder. The technical problems involved in development of comprehensive case registers are well on the way toward solution,

---

was one of the experts on this issue and suggested that he talk with his father about it. "I called him," he said, "but he can't give me an hour until next Thursday."

primarily through the use of more systematic data collection and reporting in each cooperating agency.

The larger issues raised by systematic data files, such as protection of patient rights to confidentiality, require special action not ordinarily considered by psychotherapists. Maryland and Hawaii have passed special state legislation assuring the confidentiality of case registers and their use for research only, protecting the records against court subpoena and the reporting agencies against suit. In addition, administrative safeguards such as maintainance of records by case code numbers only, with names removed; keeping records in locked files; and training of research personnel in the traditions of clinical confidentiality, are also required. Case registers enormously increase the power the researcher can exercise for good or for evil. It is important that he recognize his power and develop an appropriate sense of responsibility (*Bahn, 1964, 1965a, 1965b*).

The issue of what data to record in comprehensive psychiatric and psychological case registers will depend on gradual accumulation of research information and on the development of theoretical understanding into mentally troubled lines of development. Although current research (*Nameche, Waring, and Ricks, 1964; Waring and Ricks, 1965; Roff, Mink, and Hinricks, 1966*) and the developmental theories of Erikson (*1963*), Anna Freud (*1965*), Cameron (*1963*), and others suggest some of the areas that require study, development of new technology is ahead of conceptual understanding in this area.

The desire to test and to demonstrate results is one of the main distinguishing characteristics of psychotherapy as a field. Counseling and psychotherapy inherited this emphasis from both medicine and education . . . imagine how differently they might view evaluation if they had begun as offshoots of law! Both reviewers with an axe to sharpen (*Eysenck, 1960*) and those with more balanced viewpoints (*Bergin, Murray, Traux, and Shobin, 1963*) have noted that impartial evaluations of psychotherapy usually fail to show unambiguously helping results. The many defects in this research — simple-minded criteria, short term follow up of persons in whom effects of psychotherapy could only be expected to be manifest over a long period, no study of naturally occurring helping contacts in control groups, inadequate investigation of the selection of patients, etc. — are well known. It is tempting to conclude that the better the study the less result it shows. But this is not entirely true — as studies carefully differentiate both the patients and the psychotherapists, and as they make their criteria appropriate, it is possible to show that psychotherapy has effects. Bergin's (*1963*) careful review indicates that psychotherapy both helps and hinders — some patients get better as a result of contact with especially helpful people, while others get worse, probably as a result of deficiencies in the psychotherapist, not in his techniques. As case registers accumulate these results will become more striking. Over the next decade it will be possible to differentiate clinics in terms of the number of children they see who go to jails or mental hospitals in adult life. Within two decades it should be possible to specify the characteristics of psychotherapists who are most competent to prevent adult criminal or psychotic outcomes in children with given backgrounds and childhood symptoms. As this becomes possible, psychotherapy will move toward further differentiation, with professional psychotherapists increasingly specializing in the types of problems they are most competent to handle.

Psychotherapy on the Street

As research develops it will feed back into clinical practice new understanding of deviant life patterns and new suggestions for treatment methods. And as psychotherapy becomes more differentiated and more active people are recruited to active types of psychotherapeutic practice, current outcasts will become accessible to help. More people will come to agree with Laing (*1960, 1962*) that all varieties of human lives are intelligible. Groups once considered untreatable, such as regressed schizophrenics, people with character disorders, and autistic children (a set of already outmoded but still heuristically useful terms) will be sought out by psychotherapists interested in broadening their experience and helping people more interesting than the discontented, over-privileged, and over-treated middle class patients that now make up the bulk of private practitioner's case loads. New methods for educational intervention into the development of children whose lives are warped by poverty, deviant family patterns, and social discrimination are likely to play a large part in future counseling and psychotherapy (*Riessman, 1964*). Work with these groups can widen horizons for the middle-class professions of counseling and psychotherapy. Perhaps, through acquainting counselors with the direct, present oriented, informal, active, spontaneous world of those whose hands labor more than their mouths, it will make psychotherapy less verbal, intricate, and scholastic. Vocationally oriented psychotherapy (*Massimo and Shore, 1963*) will usually be the treatment of choice for boys who have begun to develop delinquent acting out ways of life in response to social and educational rejection. This form of psychotherapy, with its intense involvement in the community, its active intervention in the life of the boy, and its careful avoidance of the traditional office and schedule-oriented schemes of middle-class psychotherapy, will demand especially trained psychotherapists, and perhaps special selection as well. Not every chairbound psychotherapist can rouse himself to this kind of work, but those who can are likely to have the experience, rare for psychotherapists, of helping most of their clients in clearly demonstrable ways (*Ricks, Umbarger, and Mack, 1964*).

Early Identification and Intervention

With increasing knowledge of the conditions that favor development of various forms of mental illness and the characteristics they show in their developmental course, there will be increasing interest in preventive work, both educational and psychotherapeutic. Since many problems of mental disorder come together around the issue of competence, methods that might increase the competence of the child to deal with school demands, social relationships, and later with work will be increasingly studied. One of the most striking paradoxes of mental health work is that the methods of helping children that show the most definite results, and which are most appreciated by the child, such as remedial tutoring, help in reading, and vocational guidance, currently have the lowest pay scales and status within the mental health professions, while psychotherapies with questionable value enjoy high status and provide enormous incomes to their practitioners. As research and evaluation play a larger role in mental health work those fields which can demonstrate results are likely to increase in pay and social respect. While promoting competence is less dramatic than "treating illness," it may in the long run have more lasting effects.

Exiling the Old

The growing influence of existential ideas and the clear evidence all about us that growing old in America is increasingly painful as rapid social change makes the skills and characters of old people obsolete too soon will lead to increased study of ways to understand the experience and ameliorate the problems of the aged (*Kastenbaum, 1964*). The social changes that create their problems are likely to increase generational gaps and decrease the understanding younger people have of their elders much faster than understanding gained by the slower processes of study can be developed. Unless current trends change, the aged will be the outcasts of the future. As the frustrations of the aged increase, in a society geared to promoting work and preventing disengagement, it is not entirely unreasonable to expect future expressions of public concern with geriatric delinquency, use of drugs by the elderly, and other symptoms of unrest. If old people are segregated into special villages or housing units, this unrest may find organized means of expression similar to some of the protests now coming from ethnic ghettos. Other old people, whose protests are less coherent and less socialized, will continue to be relegated to the scrap heap of old age in mental hospitals.

No other group will be comparable to the elderly in the extent to which it will need understanding that will not be there. Criminals, homosexuals, the poor, and other traditional outcasts all have some access to the mainstream of life in America. Special forms of psychotherapy

431

will develop for these groups, in part because they well ask for them, as prison populations often demand and get vocational help, and in part because they will be forced upon them by a society that wants to cure deviants. As the aged increase their protests, they also may hope to get attention and help.

Freud's Hold on Psychotherapy: Terminable or Interminable?

The phenomenal richness of Freud's mind furnished psychotherapy with its main ideas for more than half a century. In a period of rapid change, in which physics, biology, and other sciences have undergone a series of revolutionary advances, this is both a tribute to the man and a commentary on the field. Only in the last two decades has psychoanalysis begun to grow beyond Freud, developing a more systematic theory of ego functions, studying psychoanalytic propositions and finding them modifiable, and opening up the inner sanctum of analytic ideas to the data of early childhood observation and the dream research laboratory. Psychoanalysis is now beginning to realize Freud's hopes for it as a developing science, but it is at the same time becoming less Freudian. As Jones' great eulogy showed, quite unintentionally, Freud is dead.

Those who are critical of the Freudian approaches to psychotherapy characteristically argue against the psychoanalysis of the 1930's. Newer approaches, thoroughly grounded in Freudian theory, but utilizing the research designs and psychotherapeutic methods of the 1960's, would be more appropriate targets (*Newton-Baker Project, 1962; Eiduson et al., 1964*). There is no reason psychoanalytic methods and ideas should not be open to scientific investigation, and as psychoanalytic theories are subjected to test they can be expected to develop at a new pace.

Most other psychotherapists offer little more than variations on Freudian themes. Even Rogers, who is often seen as opposed to Freud, is essentially similar in his approach to psychotherapy. His theories are a stark, schematized, American Protestant translation of thought rooted in a richer and more complex culture. It is unlikely that a cult of client-centered psychotherapists will persist. Rogers' emphasis on individuality and following one's own experience will operate against the perseveration of a dogmatic school. Over the next decade or two his influence will be reflected through systematic research methods in psychotherapy — a trend that shows every indication of growing — and his freeing of many psychotherapists to develop into their own forms of genuineness.

Therapies based on learning theory are another story. In spite of some basic philosophical correspondences to Freudian theory — environmentalism, concern with drives and drive modification, etc. — most learning theory therapists are essentially opposed to Freudian theory and methods.

Although they have old predecessors, their current vogue is too new to allow a balanced evaluation or extrapolation of trends. Their literature currently reads like the early literature of psychoanalysis — case reports of striking successes together with careful description of therapy methods, followed by subjective, short term evaluation of results. But since much of this work is done by men well trained in research methods, it will quickly move on to more adequate research, with before-and-after control group designs and long term follow-up. As psychotherapies based on learning theories develop more adequate research designs, and as they differentiate work based on narrowly conceived models from the more broadly based social learning work, their influence is likely to increase.

Since learning theory therapies are more openly manipulative than Freudian or Rogerian methods, they will raise sharp issues of values and goals in psychotherapy. A Russian Pavlovian has no issue as to who he works for. An American learning theorist, on the other hand, has to ask himself who he is working for, the patient or the society, particularly when he is treating social forms of deviance. These forms of psychotherapy are coming into prominence at the same time as psychotherapy is being extended to many groups previously denied help. Often the bill for psychotherapy is paid by a society that wants to eliminate some delinquent, frightening, or otherwise obnoxious behavior, whether or not the patient wants to change. So long as psychotherapy is ineffective the psychotherapist need not worry about his effect — he has none — but if learning theory methods are as effective as they are currently claimed to be, the psychotherapist must ask himself when he wants to go along with his society, or some segment of the psychotherapeutic establishment, and when he should oppose it. Since some forms of acting out, for instance, may well be developmental stages toward greater maturity in a troubled child, the psychotherapist must sometimes choose between helping the child grow through his symptom or forcing him to give it up, perhaps at the cost of further regression. In long term follow-up of children treated with other forms of psychotherapy it is possible to find one psychotherapist's notes ending with optimistic assurance that some delinquent behavior has been stamped out, only to find in later psychiatric contact that self-depreciation and hate growing out of the first psychotherapy have led to depression or suicidal attempts at some later date. The short term manipulations of learning theory therapists will have to be studied for side effects like this, as well as the more benign effects of long term symptom-free activity.

With a growing realization that differentiated groups will need differentiated types of psychotherapy, offering help to large numbers of people at the lowest possible cost, learning theory therapies will offer a wide range of possibilities currently beyond the reach of traditionally trained psychotherapists. Taking seriously the viewpoint that the symptom is the disorder, and not just an expression of underlying causes, should in time expose both the possible limits in this approach — its inclination to an overly simple ahistorical approach, for instance — and indicate its possibilities for systematic classification of disorders. The viewpoint that many neuroses and psychoses are basically learned patterns of behavior should lead to careful thought as to how they are learned, with attendant growth of interest in the conditions for learning deviant responses in infancy and childhood (*Mednick, 1958*). As it develops a sense of its context, the learning theory approach may seem less laboratory bound, less gimmicky, and more adequate to the solution of real life problems than it now appears to be.

The Psychotherapist as a Social Critic and Moralist: Are Our Directions Right?

In a society of other-directed men, no one is the leader. The little Martian just landed in a field, telling a cow to "Take me to your leader!" expresses the common dilemma in a world that seems often to be without clear authority or direction. And like a pilot who loses his bearings while flying a jet, a technological society can move a long way in a short time, even without knowing where it is going.

In this situation the psychotherapist is often tempted to become a social critic. His work is with the discontented. He hears, often at exasperating length, of all the things that frustrate and hinder them. In time he may overcome his feelings of professional limitation and attempt to take society as his patient. When a psychotherapist does this he moves out of his traditional role, that of a helper in the solution of problems brought to him, and attempts to transmute the lessons of his field into a social philosophy. He ceases to be an expert and to some extent takes on qualities of the ancient roles of teacher and priest. In a society that trains and values experts, he risks becoming ineffectual. But the view from behind the couch does offer some special perspectives (*Wheelis, 1958*) and the view from a playroom through which troop unhappy children may offer insights that suggest ethical decisions (*Erikson, 1964*) transcending the limits of one's profession.

Clinical perspectives may also be involved in research work, and if research evidence points to sore points in a society, the researcher may be moved to speak as much about the society as about the subjects of his research. The object of criticism may be as small as a particular school that seems to constrict its students into occupational or social roles that deny full development, or it may be American society as a whole (*Keniston, 1965*). In either case, a view of man developed through participant observation in the struggle of people to be more wholly human tends to be sharply critical of all the structures in society that force men to appear less (*Fried, 1964*).

The other main element that comes through this work is appreciation for the diversity of human life styles, and a morality that rejects diminishing the other man's life in order to promote one's own. When the clinician says to his patient, "Be yourself," he says it with Freud's vision of man's depths and potentialities behind him. When he envisions the competent, caring society he sees it as one that will offer to all men the chance to grow to the full depth and diversity possible in their nature, and which will appreciate the rich variety of life styles into which people grow. As the society presses toward the monistic ideal of rational efficiency, the psychotherapist will need to keep alive a powerful awareness of humane pluralistic possibilities.

Trends already operating suggest that the future will hold more kinds of psychotherapists, working with more kinds of troubled people, increasingly more often in community settings and with additional community support. There are no areas in which psychotherapeutic care has reached clear limits, though the role, population, and approach of the traditional mental hospital is changing radically and custodial care is no longer a major hospital goal. After a period of rapid growth, the private practice of psychotherapy appears to be leveling off, and it is in the area of community mental health work, especially with children, that the major innovations in thought and practice will come in the next two decades.

It has become clear that overgeneralization of the "mental illness" model to all forms of unhappy or inadequate ways of life will be increasingly corrected by treating educational problems as educational, and vocation problems as vocational, without the excess conceptual baggage of medical analogies. Paradoxically, this will probably lead to closer collaboration between medical and other disciplines, with each working in its area of competence on complex problems such as those presented by brain damaged children with school learning difficulties.

As further psychotherapeutic experience with disturbed people accumulates and is validated by research studies, there will be growing realization that all varieties of emotional and mental dysfunction are intelligible, that they make sense in terms of the life of the suffering individual or family. New forms of understanding will generate new training programs and new professions. Our current diagnostic schemes will gradually be replaced by longitudinal, life history oriented conceptions, eliminating the current artificial distinction between diagnosis and dynamics.

All of this will increasingly happen in an atmosphere permeated by research standards, so that new methods as well as old will have to demonstrate their value. The fields of psychotherapy and counseling have generated a great deal of criticism within themselves, and as social criticism has waned and the practice of the helping professions has won general social acceptance, they have increasingly replaced external criticism with internal conscience. This is likely to increase — Henry Murray has pointed out that as the general social morality grows less powerful in America, special groups, especially those influenced by science, have developed more morality, evident mainly in growing care in evaluating their ideas and their work. As these fields move toward full maturity, not yet doing very well, but knowing how to improve and rapidly improving, psychotherapists are on the way toward doing a better job of solving some personal and social problems than any group — legal, medical, or educational — that has tackled them in the past.

As Senator Eugene McCarthy has said, our task now is to act on what we know, and in so doing, to learn more, to:

> Continue to go out of your offices and homes into the streets — to places, homes, and institutions that frighten you by their darkness, their poverty, and their strangeness — to bring the light of your knowledge and the powers of your skills into these places, in a continuing attack on "fear of fear," which leads to desperation and despair and the ultimate destruction of the human personality and society (*McCarthy, 1965,* p. 8).

References

Albee, George (1964). "A Declaration of Independence for Psychology," *Ohio Psychologist* (June).

Bahn, Anita K. (1964). "A New Psychiatric Epidemiology," *Israel Annals of Psychiatry and Related Disciplines,* 2 (April), 11–18.

—— (1965, a). "An Outline for Community Mental Health Research," *Community Mental Health Journal,* 1 (Spring), 23–28.

—— (1965, b). "Experience and Philosophy with Regard to Case Registers in Health and Welfare," *Community Mental Health Journal,* 1 (Fall), 245–250.

Bell, Daniel (1965). "The Study of the Future," *The Public Interest* (Fall), 119–130.

Barton, Walter E. (1962). "The Portent of Some Current Emphases," Part I of a panel "The Future of the Mental Hospital," *Mental Hospitals* (July 2–3).

Bergin, Allen E., Edward J. Murray, Charles B. Traux, and Edward J. Shoben. "The Empirical Emphasis in Psychotherapy: A Symposium," *Journal of Counseling Psychology,* 10, 244–268.

Brown, Bertram S. (1964). "The Impact of the New Federal Mental Health Legislation on the State Mental Hospital System," Paper presented at the Northeast State Governments Conference, Hartford, Connecticut (October 22).

Cameron, Norman (1963). *Personality Development and Psychopathology,* Houghton Mifflin.

Carlton, M. G. (1965). "The Pre-Admission Period and Pre-care Programs for the Mentally Ill: A Review of the Literature," *Community Mental Health,* 1 (Spring).

Cutler, R. L. and E. B. McNeil (1962). *Mental Health Consultation in the Schools: A Research Analysis,* Michigan Society for Mental Health.

Eiduson, Bernice T., S. H. Brooks, and R. L. Motto (1964). "A Generalized Psychiatric Information Processing System," Paper presented at the meetings of the American Psychiatric Association.

Erikson, Erik H. (1963). *Childhood and Society,* second edition, Norton.

Expert Committee on Mental Health (1957). "The Psychiatric Hospital as a Center for Preventive Work in Mental Health," *World Health Organization Technical Report Series, No. 134,* World Health Organization, Geneva.

Eysenck, H. J. (1960). "The Effects of Psychotherapy." *Handbook of Abnormal Psychology,* in H. J. Eysenck (ed.) Basic Books, 697–725.

Farnsworth, D. (1963). "The New Role of the Mental Hospital," Paper given at the dedication of the new adolescent unit of McLean Hospital (October 18).

Freeman, H. E., and, O. Simmons (1963). *The Mental Patient Comes Home,* Wiley.

Fried, M. (1964). "Social Problems and Psychopathology," in *Urban America and the Planning of Mental Health Services,* V. Group for the Advancement of Psychiatry Reports, New York, 403–446.

Fuchs, V. R. (1966). "The First Service Economy," *The Public Interest* (Winter).

Gardner, G. Gail (1964). "The Psychotherapeutic Relationship," *Psychological Bulletin,* 61, 426–437.

Glasscote, R. M., D. S. Sanders, H. M. Forstenzer, and A. R. Foley (1964). *The Community Mental Health Center: An Analysis of Existing Models,* The Joint Information Service, American Psychiatric Association and the National Association for Mental Health.

Hobbs, N. (1964). "Mental Health's Third Revolution," *The American Journal of Orthopsychiatry,* 34 (October), 822–833.

Hollingshead, A. B., and F. C. Redlich (1958). *Social Class and Mental Illness,* Wiley.

Joint Commission on Mental Illness and Health (1961). *Action for Mental Health,* Basic Books.

Kastenbaum, R. (ed.), (1964) *New Thoughts on Old Age* (Spring).

Keniston, K. (1965). *The Uncommitted: Alienated Youth in American Society,* Harcourt, Brace and World.

Kramer, B. (1962). *Day Hospital: A Study of Partial Hospitalization in Psychiatry,* Grune and Stratton.

Laing, R. D. (1960). *The Divided Self,* Quadrangle Books.

––––––– (1962). *The Self and Others,* Quadrangle Books.

Levine, A. (1965). "The time has come . . ." *The Bulletin,* New York State District Branches, American Psychiatric Association (September).

Luborsky, L. and H. H. Strupp (1962). "Research Problems in Psychotherapy: A Three Year Follow-Up," in *Research in Psychotherapy: Volume II,* American Psychological Association, 308–329.

437

McCarthy, Eugene J. (1965). "Civil Rights and Mental Health," Address to the annual meeting, National Association for Mental Health, New York.

McNair, D. M., D. M. Callahan, and M. Lorr (1962). "Therapist 'Type' and Patient Response to Psychotherapy," *Journal of Consulting Psychology*, 26, 425–429.

Massimo, J., and M. Shore (1963). "The Effectiveness of a Comprehensive Vocationally Oriented Psychotherapy Program for Adolescent Delinquent Boys," *American Journal of Orthopsychiatry*, 33, 634–642.

Mednick, S. A. (1958). "A Learning Theory Approach to Research in Schizophrenia," *Psychological Bulletin*, 55, 316–327.

Michael, D. N. (1965). *The Next Generation: Prospects Ahead for the Youth of Today and Tomorrow*, Vintage Books.

Nameche, G., Mary Waring, and D. F. Ricks (1964). "Early Indicators of Outcome in Schizophrenia," *Journal of Nervous and Mental Disease*, 139, 232–240.

Newton Baker Project (1962). *Juvenile Delinquency Demonstration Project: First Annual Report*, Judge Baker Guidance Center.

Pines, Mays (1962). "Training Housewives as Psychotherapists," *Harper's*, 224 (April).

Ricks, D. F. & R. McCarley (1965). "Identity at Harvard and Harvard's Identity," *The Harvard Review*, III (Winter).

Ricks, D., C. Umbarger, and R. Mack (1964). "A Measure of Increased Temporal Perspective in Successfully Treated Adolescent Delinquent Boys," *Journal of Abnormal and Social Psychology*, 69, 685–689.

Riessman, F. (1964). *New Approaches to Mental Health Treatment for Labor and Low Income Groups*, National Institute of Labor Education, Mental Health Program, Report No. 2.

Rioch, Margaret J., *et al.* (1963). "NIMH Pilot Study in Training Mental Health Counselors," *American Journal of Orthopsychiatry*, 33 (July), 678–689.

Roff, M., W. Mink and Grace B. Hinrichs (1966). *Developmental Abnormal Psychology: A Casebook*, Holt, Rinehart and Winston.

Rosenblum G. & D. Ottenstein (1965). "From Child Guidance to Community Mental Health: Problems in Transition," *Community Mental Health Journal*, 1, 276–283.

Schmideberg, Melitta (1964). "From Progressive Education into Mental Institutions," *Journal of Offender Therapy*, 8, 61–67.

Strupp, H. H., R. W. Balentine, D. Kemp, P. W. Mayfield, and M. Wogan (1964). "A Bibliography of Research in Psychotherapy," Psychotherapy Research Project, University of North Carolina.

Szasz, T. S. (1964). "Psychiatry in Public Schools," *Teachers College Record*, 66 (October), 57–63.

Waldfogel, S. Ellen Tessman, and P. B. Hahn (1957). "Learning Problems: A Program for Early Intervention in School Phobia," *American Journal of Orthopsychiatry*, 27.

Waring, Mary, and D. F. Ricks (1965). "Family Patterns of Children Who Became Adult Schizophrenics," *Journal of Nervous and Mental Disease*, 140, 351–364.

Wheelis, A. (1958). *The Quest for Identity*, Norton.

White, Mary Alice (1965). "Little Red Schoolhouse and Little White Clinic," *Teachers College Record,* 67 (December), 188–200.

Whitehorn, J. C., and B. J. Betz (1960). "Further Studies of the Doctor as a Crucial Variable in the Outcome of Treatment with Schizophrenic Patient," *American Journal of Psychiatry,* 117, 215–223.

Yolles, S. F. (1965). "The National Mental Health Programs: Status and Prospects," Address to the Conference of Division Executive Directors, National Association for Mental Health.

Name Index

Subject Index